C000125847

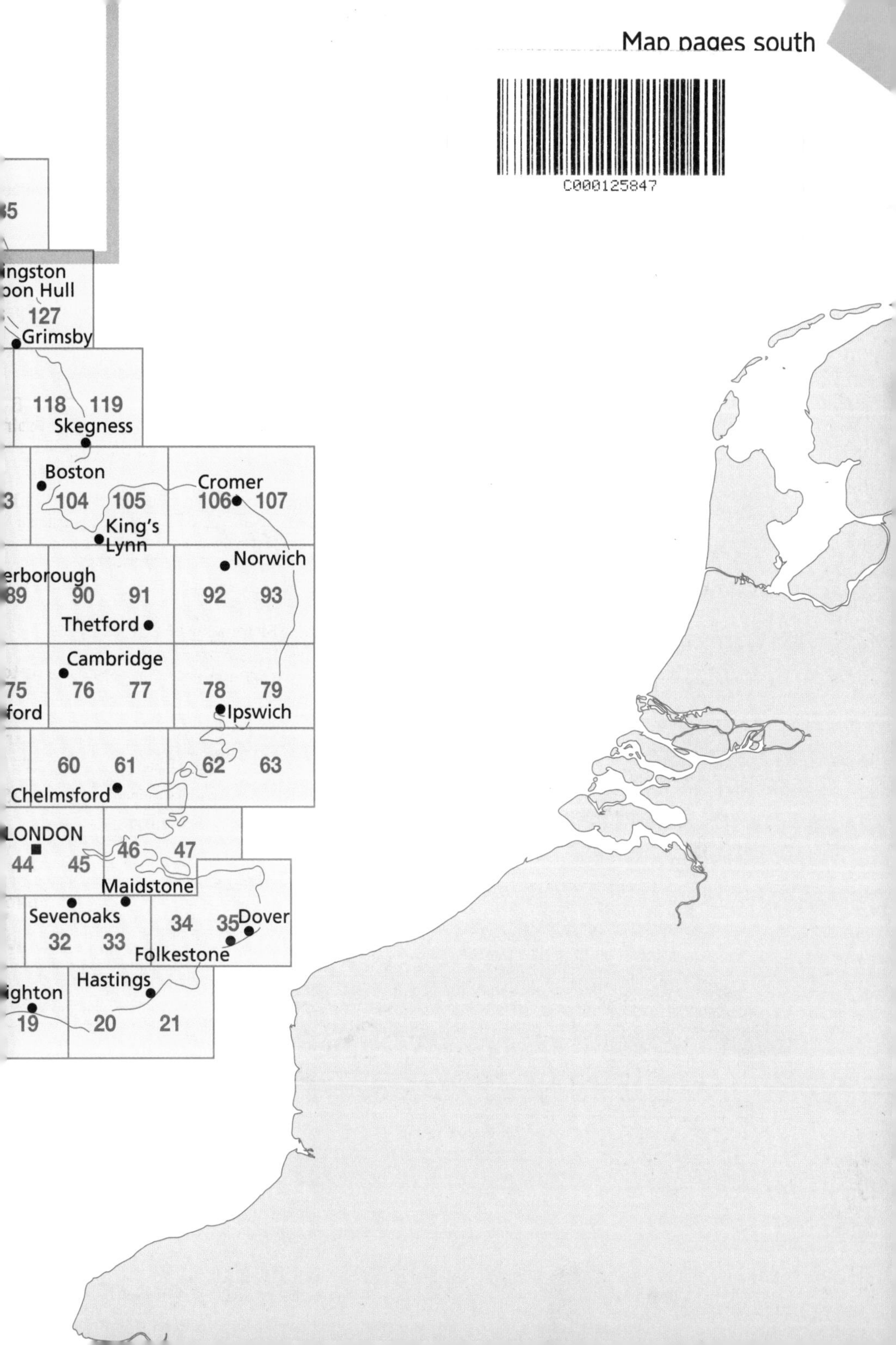

5

ngston
on Hull
127
Grimsby

118 119
Skegness

Boston
104 105
King's
Lynn

Cromer
106 107

3

erborough
89 90 91

Norwich
92 93

Thetford

Cambridge
76 77

78 79
Ipswich

75
ford

60 61

62 63

Chelmsford

LONDON
44 45

46 47

Maidstone

Sevenoaks
32 33

34 35 Dover

Folkestone

ighton
19 20

Hastings
21

Mileage chart

The mileage chart shows distances in miles between two towns along AA-recommended routes. Using motorways and other main roads this is normally the fastest route, though not necessarily the shortest.

The journey times are shown in hours and minutes. These times should be used as a guide only and do not allow for unforeseen traffic delays, rest breaks or fuel stops.

For example, the 376 miles (605 km) journey between Glasgow and Norwich should take approximately 6 hours 45 minutes.

Journey times

Aberdeen
Aberystwyth
Barnstaple
Birmingham
Brighton
Bristol
Cambridge
Cardiff
Carlisle
Carmarthen
Dorchester
Dover
Edinburgh
Exeter
Fort William
Glasgow
Gloucester
Guildford
Hereford
Holyhead
Hull
Inverness
Kendal
Leeds
Lincoln
Liverpool
Maidstone
Manchester
Middlesbrough
Newcastle
Northampton
Norwich
Nottingham
Oxford
Penzance
Perth
Peterborough
Plymouth
Portsmouth
Preston
Salisbury
Sheffield
Shrewsbury
Southampton
Stoke-on-Trent
Stranraer
Taunton
Wick
York
LONDON

Distances in miles (one mile equals 1.6093 km)

DRIVER'S ATLAS
BRITAIN

Contents

Map pages south	inside front cover
Mileage chart and journey times	endpaper
Route planner	*II–VII*
Motorways	*VIII–X*
Restricted junctions	*VIII–IX*
Smart motorways	*X*
Atlas symbols	1
Road maps 1:250,000 scale	2–237
Channel Islands 1:150,000 scale	236
Isle of Man 1:317,000 scale	237
Orkney Islands 1:636,000 scale	234
Shetland Islands 1:636,000 scale	235
Western Isles 1:700,000 scale	232–233
Index to place names	238–318
County, administrative area map	238–239
Place name index	240–318
Ireland	endpaper
Map pages north	inside back cover

18th edition June 2019

© AA Media Limited 2019

Cartography: All cartography in this atlas edited, designed and produced by the Mapping Services Department of AA Publishing (A05691).

This atlas contains Ordnance Survey data © Crown copyright and database right 2019.

Contains public sector information licensed under the Open Government Licence v3.0

Ireland mapping and Mileage chart and journey times contains data available from openstreetmap.org © under the Open Database License found at opendatacommons.org

Publisher's notes: Published by AA Publishing (a trading name of AA Media Limited, whose registered office is Fanum House, Basing View, Basingstoke, Hampshire RG21 4EA, UK. Registered number 06112600).

ISBN: 978 0 7495 8130 5 (flexibound)

A CIP catalogue record for this book is available from The British Library.

Disclaimer: The contents of this atlas are believed to be correct at the time of the latest revision, it will not contain any subsequent amended, new or temporary information including diversions and traffic control or enforcement systems. The publishers cannot be held responsible or liable for any loss or damage occasioned to any person acting or refraining from action as a result of any use or reliance on material in this atlas, nor for any errors, omissions or changes in such material. This does not affect your statutory rights.

The publishers would welcome information to correct any errors or omissions and to keep this atlas up to date. Please write to the Atlas Editor, AA Publishing, The Automobile Association, Fanum House, Basing View, Basingstoke, Hampshire RG21 4EA, UK.
E-mail: *roadatlasfeedback@theaa.com*

Acknowledgements: AA Publishing would like to thank the following for information used in the creation of this atlas: Cadw, English Heritage, Forestry Commission, Historic Scotland, National Trust and National Trust for Scotland, RSPB, The Wildlife Trust, Scottish Natural Heritage, Natural England, The Countryside Council for Wales. Award winning beaches from 'Blue Flag' and 'Keep Scotland Beautiful' (summer 2018 data): for latest information visit *www.blueflag.org* and *www.keepscotlandbeautiful.org*

Ireland mapping: Republic of Ireland census 2016 © Central Statistics Office and Northern Ireland census 2016 © NISRA (population data); Logainm.ie (placenames); Roads Service and Transport Infrastructure Ireland

Printer: Oriental Press, Dubai.

Scale 1:250,000
or 3.95 miles to 1 inch

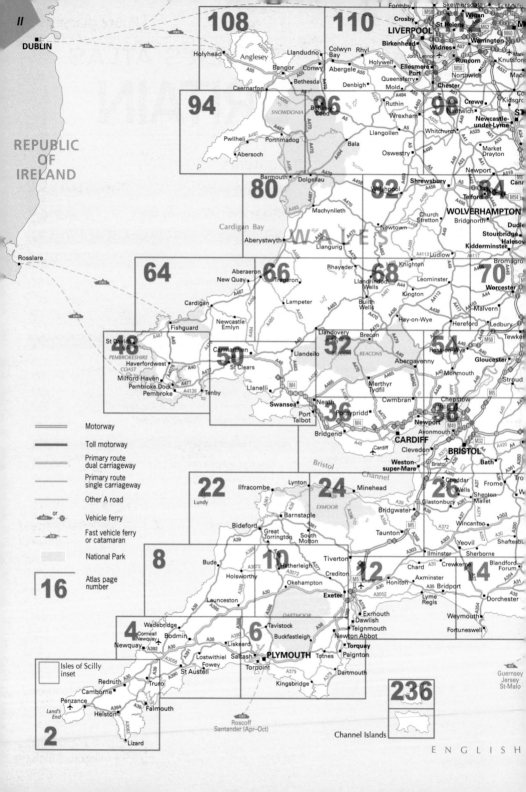

Route planner

ENGLAND

Grid numbers: 114, 116, 118, 100, 102, 104, 106, 86, 88, 90, 92, 72, 74, 76, 78, 58, 60, 62, 40, 42, 44, 46, 28, 30, 32, 34, 16, 18, 26

SHEFFIELD · CHESTER · Doncaster · Rotherham · Barnsley · Brigg · Cleethorpes · Grimsby · Worksop · Retford · Gainsborough · Market Rasen · Louth · Mablethorpe · Buxton · Bakewell · Chesterfield · Lincoln · Horncastle · Skegness · ON-TRENT · Mansfield · Alfreton · Matlock · Ashbourne · Ilkeston · Newark-on-Trent · Sleaford · Boston · The Wash · Sheringham · Cromer · Hunstanton · North Walsham · DERBY · NOTTINGHAM · Grantham · Long Eaton · Loughborough · Spalding · King's Lynn · A148 · Fakenham · Aylsham · Burton upon Trent · Melton Mowbray · Bourne · Dereham · Norwich · Caister-on-Sea · Lichfield · Tamworth · LEICESTER · Oakham · Stamford · Wisbech · Swaffham · Great Yarmouth · Walsall · Wigston · Peterborough · March · Downham Market · Attleborough · Bungay · Beccles · Lowestoft · BIRMINGHAM · Nuneaton · Hinckley · Market Harborough · Corby · Chatteris · Ely · Thetford · Diss · Southwold · COVENTRY · Rugby · Kettering · Huntingdon · Bury St Edmunds · Stowmarket · Aldeburgh · Royal Leamington Spa · Warwick · Northampton · St Neots · Cambridge · Newmarket · Woodbridge · Ipswich · Daventry · Towcester · Bedford · Haverhill · Sudbury · Felixstowe · Stratford-upon-Avon · Evesham · Banbury · Brackley · Milton Keynes · Royston · Baldock · Halstead · Braintree · Colchester · Harwich · Hook of Holland · Chipping Norton · Bicester · Leighton Buzzard · Luton · Stevenage · Stansted · Bishop's Stortford · Witham · Clacton-on-Sea · Cheltenham · Witney · Aylesbury · Dunstable · Hertford · Harlow · Chelmsford · Maldon · Burnham-on-Crouch · Oxford · Thame · St Albans · Hatfield · Brentwood · Southend-on-Sea · Swindon · Wantage · Abingdon-on-Thames · High Wycombe · Beaconsfield · Watford · Basildon · Canvey Island · Faringdon · Maidenhead · LONDON · Dartford · Tilbury · Gravesend · Sheerness · Margate · Reading · Windsor · Slough · Richmond · Swanley · Rochester · Chatham · Ramsgate · Sandwich · Deal · Marlborough · Bracknell · Staines-upon-Thames · Croydon · Sevenoaks · Maidstone · Canterbury · Devizes · Newbury · Woking · Leatherhead · Reigate · Tonbridge · Ashford · Dover · Basingstoke · Farnham · Guildford · Dorking · Redhill · Royal Tunbridge Wells · Channel Tunnel Terminal · Folkestone · Amesbury · Andover · Alton · Crawley · East Grinstead · Crowborough · Tenterden · Hythe · New Romney · Winchester · Petersfield · Billingshurst · Horsham · Uckfield · Heathfield · Rye · Calais · Salisbury · Romsey · Eastleigh · Midhurst · Shoreham-by-Sea · Lewes · Hastings · Bexhill-on-Sea · SOUTHAMPTON · Chichester · Arundel · Worthing · Brighton · Eastbourne · Ringwood · Lymington · Gosport · Portsmouth · Bognor Regis · Newhaven · Bournemouth · Christchurch · Cowes · Ryde · Sandown · Shanklin · Isle of Wight · Swanage

Guernsey · Jersey · St-Malo · Caen (Ouistreham) · Le Havre · Bilbao (Jan–Oct) · Santander (Jan–Oct) · Cherbourg (May–Aug) · Cherbourg · Dieppe · Dunkirk · Calais / Coquelles Terminal · Rotterdam (Europoort) Zeebrugge

CHANNEL · FRANCE

Scale:
0   10   20   30 miles
0 10 20 30 40 kilometres

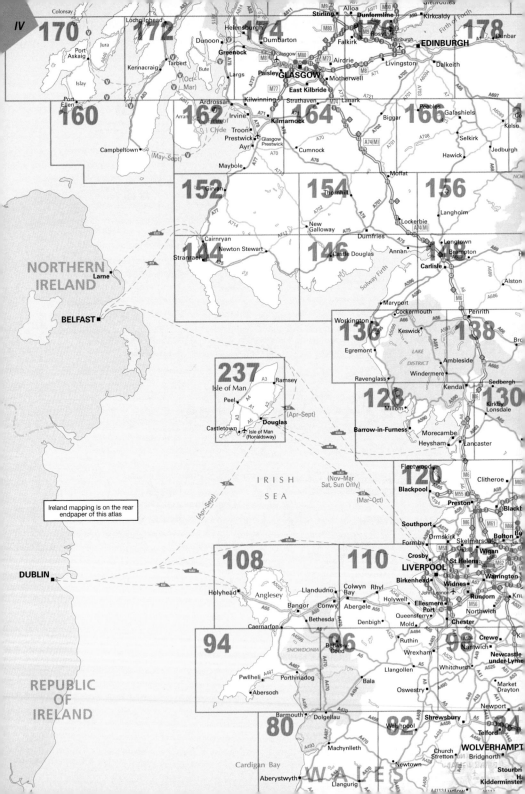

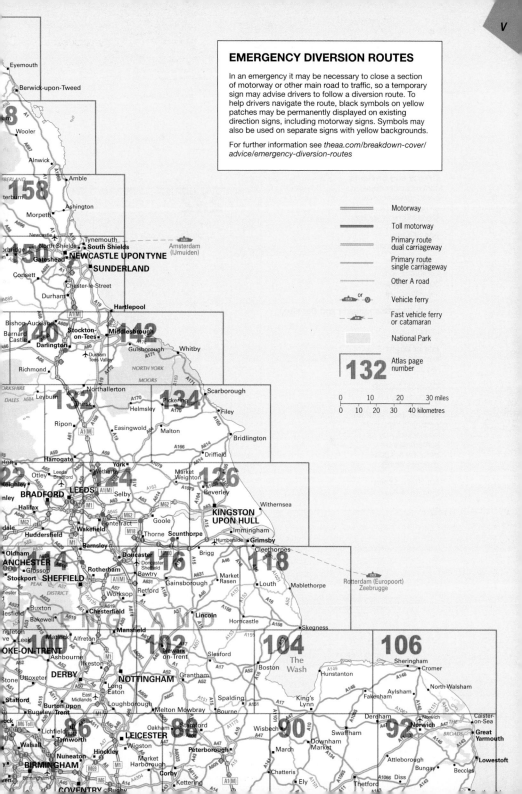

EMERGENCY DIVERSION ROUTES

In an emergency it may be necessary to close a section of motorway or other main road to traffic, so a temporary sign may advise drivers to follow a diversion route. To help drivers navigate the route, black symbols on yellow patches may be permanently displayed on existing direction signs, including motorway signs. Symbols may also be used on separate signs with yellow backgrounds.

For further information see *theaa.com/breakdown-cover/advice/emergency-diversion-routes*

Motorway

Toll motorway

Primary route dual carriageway

Primary route single carriageway

Other A road

Vehicle ferry

Fast vehicle ferry or catamaran

National Park

132 Atlas page number

```
0        10        20       30 miles
0   10   20   30   40 kilometres
```

FERRY OPERATORS

Hebrides and west coast Scotland
calmac.co.uk
skyeferry.co.uk
western-ferries.co.uk

Orkney and Shetland
northlinkferries.co.uk
pentlandferries.co.uk
orkneyferries.co.uk
shetland.gov.uk/ferries

Isle of Man
steam-packet.com

Ireland
irishferries.com
poferries.com
stenaline.co.uk

North Sea (Scandinavia and Benelux)
dfdsseaways.co.uk
poferries.com

Isle of Wight
wightlink.co.uk
redfunnel.co.uk

Channel Islands
condorferries.co.uk

France and Belgium
brittany-ferries.co.uk
condorferries.co.uk
eurotunnel.com
dfdsseaways.co.uk
poferries.com

Northern Spain
brittany-ferries.co.uk

═══	Motorway
▬▬▬	Toll motorway
══	Primary route dual carriageway
──	Primary route single carriageway
····	Other A road
🚢 or Ⓥ	Vehicle ferry
⛴	Fast vehicle ferry or catamaran
▨	National Park
192	Atlas page number

0   10   20   30 miles
0 10 20 30 40 kilometres

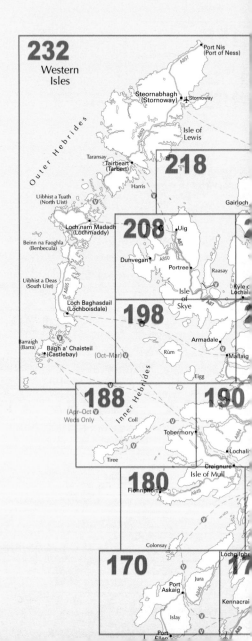

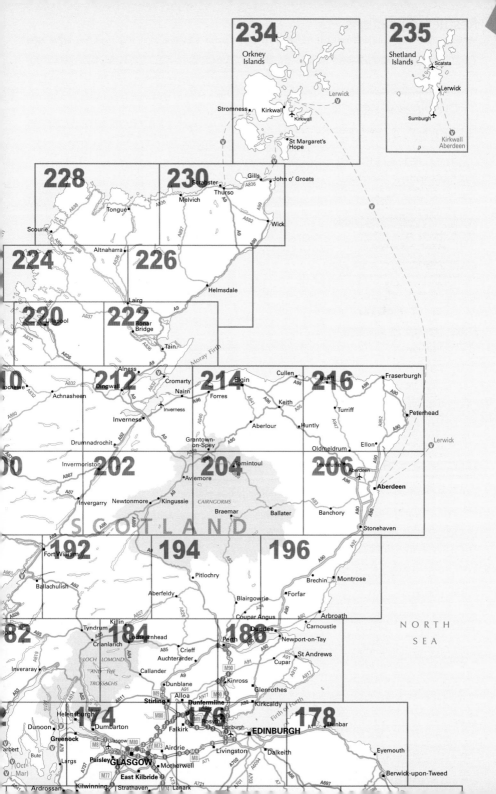

234
Orkney Islands
Stromness • Kirkwall ✈ Kirkwall
Lerwick
St Margaret's Hope

235
Shetland Islands
✈ Scatsta
Lerwick
Sumburgh ✈
Kirkwall
Aberdeen

228
Scourie •
Tongue •
Altnaharra •

230
Scrabster • Gills • John o' Groats
Thurso
Melvich
Wick

224

226
Lairg •
Helmsdale •

220
Ullapool •

222
Bonar Bridge
Tain •

212
Dingwall
Achnasheen •
Inverness
Drumnadrochit •
Cromarty
Nairn
Inverness ✈

214
Alness •
Elgin
Forres
Aberlour
Keith
Grantown-on-Spey

Moray Firth

216
Cullen •
Banff • Fraserburgh •
Turriff •
Peterhead •
Huntly
Oldmeldrum • Ellon •

Lerwick

202
Invermoriston •
Invergarry •
Newtonmore •
Kingussie •

204
Tomintoul •
Aviemore •
CAIRNGORMS
Braemar •
Ballater •

S C O T L A N D

206
Inverurie •
Aberdeen ✈
Aberdeen
Banchory •
Stonehaven •

192
Fort William •
Ballachulish •

194
Pitlochry •
Aberfeldy •
Blairgowrie •
Coupar Angus •
Killin •

196
Brechin • Montrose •
Forfar •
Arbroath •

NORTH SEA

182
Tyndrum •
Cranlarich •
Inveraray •
LOCH LOMOND AND THE TROSSACHS

184
Lochearnhead •
Crieff •
Auchterarder •
Callander •
Dunblane •
Alloa •
Stirling

186
Dundee
Perth
Newport-on-Tay •
St Andrews •
Cupar •
Kinross •
Glenrothes •
Kirkcaldy •
Carnoustie •

Firth of Forth

174
Helensburgh •
Dunoon •
Dumbarton •
Greenock •
Largs •
Bute
Paisley •
GLASGOW
Glasgow ✈
Motherwell •
East Kilbride •
Kilwinning •
Strathaven •
Ardrossan •

176
Falkirk •
Rosyth •
Dunfermline
Airdrie •
Lanark •

178
Dunbar •
EDINBURGH
Livingston •
Dalkeith •
Eyemouth •
Berwick-upon-Tweed •

Restricted junctions

Motorway and primary route junctions which have access or exit restrictions are shown on the map pages thus:

M1 London - Leeds

Junction	Northbound	Southbound
2	Access only from A1 (northbound)	Exit only to A1 (southbound)
4	Access only from A41 (northbound)	Exit only to A41 (southbound)
6A	Access only from M25 (no link from A405)	Exit only to M25 (no link from A405)
7	Access only from A414	Exit only to A414
17	Exit only to M45	Access only from M45
19	Exit only to M6 (northbound)	Exit only to A14 (southbound)
21A	Access only, no exit	Access only, no exit
24A	Access only, no exit	Access only from A50 (eastbound)
35A	Exit only, no access	Access only, no exit
43	Exit only to M621	Access only from M621
48	Exit only to A1(M) (northbound)	Access only from A1(M) (southbound)

M2 Rochester - Faversham

Junction	Westbound	Eastbound
1	No exit to A2 (eastbound)	No access from A2 (westbound)

M3 Sunbury - Southampton

Junction	Northeastbound	Southwestbound
8	Access only from A303, no exit	Exit only to A303, no access
10	Access only, no exit	Access only, no exit
14	Access from M27 only, no exit	No access to M27 (westbound)

M4 London - South Wales

Junction	Westbound	Eastbound
1	Access only from A4 (westbound)	Exit only to A4 (eastbound)
2	Access only from A4 (westbound)	Access only from A4 (eastbound)
21	Exit only to M48	Access only from M48
23	Access only from M48	Exit only to M48
25	Exit only, no access	Access only, no exit
25A	Exit only, no access	Access only, no exit
29	Exit only to A48(M)	Access only from A48(M)
38	Exit only, no access	No restriction
39	Access only, no exit	No access or exit
42	Exit only to A483	Access only from A483

M5 Birmingham - Exeter

Junction	Northeastbound	Southwestbound
10	Access only, no exit	Exit only, no access
11A	Access only from A417 (westbound)	Exit only to A417 (eastbound)
18A	Exit only to M49	Access only from M49
18	Exit only, no access	Access only, no exit

M6 Toll Motorway

Junction	Northwestbound	Southeastbound
T1	Access only, no exit	No access or exit
T2	No access or exit	Access only, no exit
T5	Access only, no exit	Exit only to A5148 (northbound), no access
T7	Exit only, no access	Access only, no exit
T8	Exit only, no access	Access only, no exit

M6 Rugby - Carlisle

Junction	Northbound	Southbound
3A	Exit only to M6 Toll	Access only from M6 Toll
4	Exit only to M42 (southbound) & A446	Exit only to A446
4A	Access only from M42 (southbound)	Exit only to M42
5	Exit only, no access	Access only, no exit
10A	Exit only to M54	Access only from M54
11A	Access only from M6 Toll	Exit only to M6 Toll
with M56 (jct 20A)	No restriction	Access only from M56 (eastbound)
20	Exit only to M56 (westbound)	Access only from M56 (eastbound)
24	Access only, no exit	Exit only, no access
25	Exit only, no access	Access only, no exit
30	Access only from M61	Exit only to M61
31A	Access only, no exit	
45	Exit only, no access	Access only, no exit

M8 Edinburgh - Bishopton

Junction	Westbound	Eastbound
6	Exit only, no access	Access only, no exit
6A	Access only, no exit	Exit only, no access
7	Access only, no exit	Exit only, no access
7A	Exit only, no access	Access only from A725 (northbound), no exit
8	No access from M73 (southbound) or from A8 (eastbound) & A89	No exit to M73 (northbound) or to A8 (westbound) & A89
9	Access only, no exit	Exit only, no access
13	Access only from M80 (southbound)	Exit only to M80 (northbound)
14	Access only, no exit	Exit only, no access
16	Exit only to A804	Access only from A879
17	Exit only to A82	No restriction
18	Access only from A82 (eastbound)	Exit only to A814 (eastbound)
19	No access from A814 (westbound)	Exit only to A814 (westbound)
20	Exit only, no access	Access only, no exit
21	Access only, no exit	Exit only to A8
22	Exit only to M77 (southbound)	Access only from M77 (northbound)
23	Exit only to B768	Access only from B768
25	No access or exit from or to A8	No access or exit from or to A8
25A	Exit only, no access	Access only, no exit
28	Exit only, no access	Access only, no exit
28A	Access only from A737	Exit only to A737
29A	Exit only to A8	Access only, no exit

M9 Edinburgh - Dunblane

Junction	Northwestbound	Southeastbound
2	Access only, no exit	Exit only, no access
3	Exit only, no access	Access only, no exit
6	Access only, no exit	Exit only to A905
8	Exit only to M876 (southwestbound)	Access only from M876 (northeastbound)

M11 London - Cambridge

Junction	Northbound	Southbound
4	Access only from A406 (eastbound)	Exit only to A406
5	Exit only, no access	Access only, no exit
8A	Exit only, no access	No direct access, use jct 8
9	Exit only to A11	Access only from A11
13	Exit only, no access	Access only, no exit
14	Exit only, no access	Access only, no exit

M20 Swanley - Folkestone

Junction	Northwestbound	Southeastbound
2	Staggered junction; follow signs - access only	Staggered junction; follow signs - exit only
3	Exit only to M26 (westbound)	Access only from M26 (eastbound)
5	Access only from A20	For access follow signs - exit only to A20
6	No restriction	For exit follow signs
11A	Access only, no exit	Exit only, no access

M23 Hooley - Crawley

Junction	Northbound	Southbound
7	Exit only to A23 (northbound)	Access only from A23 (southbound)
10A	Access only, no exit	Exit only, no access

M25 London Orbital Motorway

Junction	Clockwise	Anticlockwise
1B	No direct access, use slip road to jct 2. Exit only	Access only, no exit
5	No exit to M26 (eastbound)	No access from M26
19	Exit only, no access	Access only, no exit
21	Access only from M1 (southbound). Exit only to M1 (northbound)	Access only from M1 (southbound). Exit only to M1 (northbound)
31	No exit (use slip road via jct 30), access only	No access (use slip road via jct 30), exit only

M26 Sevenoaks - Wrotham

Junction	Westbound	Eastbound
with M25 (jct 5)	Exit only to clockwise M25 (westbound)	Access only from anticlockwise M25
with M20 (jct 3)	Access only from M20 (northwestbound)	Exit only to M20 (southeastbound)

M27 Cadnam - Portsmouth

Junction	Westbound	Eastbound
4	Staggered junction; follow signs - access only from M3 (southbound). Exit only to M3 (northbound)	Staggered junction; follow signs - access only from M3 (southbound). Exit only to M3 (northbound)
10	Access only, no exit	Access only, no exit
12	Staggered junction; follow signs - exit only to M275 (southbound)	Staggered junction; follow signs - access only from M275 (northbound)

M40 London - Birmingham

Junction	Northwestbound	Southeastbound
3	Exit only, no access	Access only, no exit
7	Exit only, no access	Access only, no exit
8	Exit only to M40/A40	Access only from M40/A40
13	Exit only, no access	Access only, no exit
14	Access only, no exit	Exit only, no access
16	Access only, no exit	Exit only, no access

M42 Bromsgrove - Measham

Junction	Northeastbound	Southwestbound
1	Access only, no exit	Exit only, no access
7	Exit only to M6 (northwestbound)	Access only from M6 (northwestbound)
7A	Exit only to M6 (southeastbound)	No access or exit
8	Access only from M6 (southeastbound)	Exit only to M6 (northwestbound)

M45 Coventry - M1

Junction	Westbound	Eastbound
Dunchurch (unnumbered)	Access only from A45	Exit only, no access
with M1 (jct 17)	Access only from M1 (northbound)	Exit only to M1 (southbound)

M48 Chepstow

Junction	Westbound	Eastbound
21	Access only from M4 (westbound)	Exit only to M4 (eastbound)
23	No exit to M4 (eastbound)	No Access from M4 (westbound)

M53 Mersey Tunnel - Chester

Junction	Northbound	Southbound
11	Access only from M56 (westbound). Exit only to M56 (eastbound)	Access only from M56 (westbound). Exit only to M56 (eastbound)

M54 Telford - Birmingham

Junction	Westbound	Eastbound
with M6 (jct 10A)	Access only from M6 (northbound)	Exit only to M6 (southbound)

M56 Chester - Manchester

Junction	Westbound	Eastbound
1	Access only from M60 (westbound)	Access only from M60 (eastbound) & A34 (northbound)
2	Exit only, no access	Access only, no exit
3	Access only, no exit	Exit only, no access
4	Exit only, no access	Access only, no exit
7	Exit only, no access	No restriction
8	Access only, no exit	No access or exit
9	No exit to M6 (southbound)	No access from M6 (northbound)
15	Exit only to M53	Access only from M53
16	No access or exit	No restriction

M57 Liverpool Outer Ring Road

Junction	Northwestbound	Southeastbound
3	Access only, no exit	Exit only, no access
5	Access only from A580 (westbound)	Exit only, no access

M58 Liverpool - Wigan

Junction	Westbound	Eastbound
1	Exit only, no access	Access only, no exit

M60 Manchester Orbital

Junction	Clockwise	Anticlockwise
2	Access only, no exit	Exit only, no access
3	No access from M56	Access only from A34 (northbound)
4	Access only from A34 (northbound). Exit only to M56	Access only from M56 (eastbound). Exit only to A34 (southbound)
5	Access and exit only from and to A5103 (northbound)	Access and exit only from and to A5103 (southbound)
7	No direct access, use slip road to jct 8. Exit only to A56	Access only from A56. No exit, use jct 8
14	Access from A580 (eastbound)	Exit only to A580 (westbound)
16	Exit only, no access	Exit only, no access
20	Exit only, no access	Access only, no exit
22	No restriction	Exit only, no access
25	Exit only, no access	No restriction
26	No restriction	Exit only, no access
27	Access only, no exit	Exit only, no access

M61 Manchester - Preston

Junction	Northwestbound	Southeastbound
3	No access or exit	Exit only, no access
with M6 (jct 30)	Exit only to M6 (northbound)	Access only from M6 (southbound)

M62 Liverpool - Kingston upon Hull

Junction	Westbound	Eastbound
23	Access only, no exit	Exit only, no access
32A	No access to A1(M) (southbound)	No restriction

M65 Preston - Colne

Junction	Northeastbound	Southwestbound
9	Exit only, no access	Access only, no exit
11	Access only, no exit	Exit only, no access

M66 Bury

Junction	Northbound	Southbound
with A56	Exit only to A56 (northbound)	Access only from A56 (southbound)
1	Exit only, no access	Access only, no exit

M67 Hyde Bypass

Junction	Westbound	Eastbound
1	Access only, no exit	Exit only, no access
2	Access only, no exit	Access only, no exit
3	Exit only, no access	No restriction

M69 Coventry - Leicester

Junction	Northbound	Southbound
2	Access only, no exit	Exit only, no access

M73 East of Glasgow

Junction	Northbound	Southbound
1	No exit to A74 & A721	No exit to A74 & A721
2	No access from or exit to A89. No access from M8 (westbound)	No access from or exit to A89. No exit to M8 (westbound)

M74 and A74(M) Glasgow - Gretna

Junction	Northbound	Southbound
3	Exit only, no access	Access only, no exit
3A	Access only, no exit	Exit only, no access
4	No access from A74 & A721	Access only, no exit to A74 & A721
7	Access only, no exit	Exit only, no access
9	No access or exit	Exit only, no access
10	No restriction	Access only, no exit
11	Access only, no exit	Exit only, no access

M77 Glasgow - Kilmarnock

Junction	Northbound	Southbound
with M8 (jct 22)	No exit to M8 (westbound)	No access from M8 (eastbound)
4	Access only, no exit	Exit only, no access
6	Access only, no exit	Exit only, no access
7	Access only, no exit	No restriction
8	Access only, no exit	Exit only, no access

M80 Glasgow - Stirling

Junction	Northbound	Southbound
4A	Exit only, no access	Access only, no exit
6A	Access only, no exit	Exit only, no access
8	Exit only to M876 (northeastbound)	Access only from M876 (southwestbound)

M90 Edinburgh - Perth

Junction	Northbound	Southbound
1	No access, access only	Exit only to A90 (eastbound)
2A	Exit only to A92 (eastbound)	Access only from A92 (westbound)
7	Access only, no exit	Exit only, no access
8	Access only, no exit	Access only, no exit
10	No access from A912. No exit to A912 (southbound)	No access from A912 (northbound). No exit to A912

M180 Doncaster - Grimsby

Junction	Westbound	Eastbound
1	Access only, no exit	Exit only, no access

M606 Bradford Spur

Junction	Northbound	Southbound
2	Exit only, no access	No restriction

M621 Leeds - M1

Junction	Clockwise	Anticlockwise
2A	Access only, no exit	Exit only, no access
4	No exit or access	No restriction
5	Access only, no exit	Exit only, no access
6	Access only, no exit	Access only, no exit
with M1 (jct 43)	Exit only to M1 (southbound)	Access only from M1 (northbound)

M876 Bonnybridge - Kincardine Bridge

Junction	Northeastbound	Southwestbound
with M80 (jct 5)	Access only from M80 (northeastbound)	Exit only to M80 (southwestbound)
with M9 (jct 8)	Exit only to M9 (eastbound)	Access only from M9 (westbound)

A1(M) South Mimms - Baldock

Junction	Northbound	Southbound
2	Exit only, no access	Access only, no exit
3	No restriction	Exit only, no access
5	Access only, no exit	No access or exit

A1(M) Pontefract - Bedale

Junction	Northbound	Southbound
41	No access to M62 (eastbound)	No restriction
43	Access only from M1 (northbound)	Exit only to M1 (southbound)

A1(M) Scotch Corner - Newcastle upon Tyne

Junction	Northbound	Southbound
57	Exit only to A66(M) (eastbound)	Access only from A66(M) (westbound)
65	No access Exit only to A194(M) & A1 (northbound)	No exit Access only from A194(M) & A1 (southbound)

A3(M) Horndean - Havant

Junction	Northbound	Southbound
1	Access only from A3	Exit only to A3
4	Exit only, no access	Access only, no exit

A38(M) Birmingham, Victoria Road (Park Circus)

Junction	Northbound	Southbound
with B4132	No exit	No access

A48(M) Cardiff Spur

Junction	Westbound	Eastbound
29	Access only from M4 (westbound)	Exit only to M4 (eastbound)
29A	Exit only to A48 (westbound)	Access only from A48 (eastbound)

A57(M) Manchester, Brook Street (A34)

Junction	Westbound	Eastbound
with A34	No exit	No access

A58(M) Leeds, Park Lane and Westgate

Junction	Northbound	Southbound
with A58	No restriction	No access

A64(M) Leeds, Clay Pit Lane (A58)

Junction	Westbound	Eastbound
with A58	No exit (to Clay Pit Lane)	No access (from Clay Pit Lane)

A66(M) Darlington Spur

Junction	Westbound	Eastbound
with A1(M) (jct 57)	Exit only to A1(M) (southbound)	Access only from A1(M) (northbound)

A74(M) Gretna - Abington

Junction	Northbound	Southbound
18	Exit only, no access	No exit

A194(M) Newcastle upon Tyne

Junction	Northbound	Southbound
with A1(M) (jct 65)	Access only from A1(M) (northbound)	Exit only to A1(M) (southbound)

A12 M25 - Ipswich

Junction	Northeastbound	Southwestbound
13	Access only, no exit	No restriction
14	Exit only, no access	Access only, no exit
20A	Access only, no exit	Access only, no exit
20B	Access only, no exit	Exit only, no access
21	No restriction	Access only, no exit
23	Exit only, no access	Access only, no exit
24	Access only, no exit	Exit only, no access
27	Exit only, no access	Access only, no exit
Dedham & Stratford St Mary (unnumbered)	Exit only Access only	

A14 M1 - Felixstowe

Junction	Westbound	Eastbound
with M1/M6 (jct19)	Exit only to M6 and M1 (northbound)	Access only from M6 and M1 (southbound)
4	Exit only, no access	Access only, no exit
31	Exit only to M11 (for London)	Access only, no exit
31A	Exit only to A14 (northbound)	Access only, no exit
34	Access only, no exit	Exit only, no access
36	Exit only to A11, access only from A1303	Access only from A11
38	Access only from A11	Exit only to A11
39	Exit only, no access	Access only, no exit
61	Access only, no exit	Exit only, no access

A55 Holyhead - Chester

Junction	Westbound	Eastbound
8A	Exit only, no access	Access only, no exit
23A	Access only, no exit	Exit only, no access
24A	Access only, no exit	No access or exit
27A	No restriction	No access or exit
33A	Exit only, no access	No access or exit
33B	Access only, no exit	Exit only, no access
36A	Exit only to A5104	Access only from A5104

Since Britain's first motorway (the Preston Bypass) opened in 1958, motorways have changed significantly. A vast increase in car journeys over the last 61 years has meant that motorways quickly filled to capacity. To combat this, the recent development of **smart motorways** uses technology to monitor and actively manage traffic flow and congestion.

Various active traffic management methods are used:

- Traffic flow is monitored using CCTV
- Speed limits are changed to smooth traffic flow and reduce stop-start driving
- Capacity of the motorway can be increased by either temporarily or permanently opening the hard shoulder to traffic
- Warning signs and messages alert drivers to hazards and traffic jams ahead
- Lanes can be closed in the case of an accident or emergency by displaying a red X sign
- Emergency refuge areas are located regularly along the motorway where there is no hard shoulder available

Smart motorways can be classified into three different types as shown below. The table lists smart motorways operating by 2020 and the colour-coded text indicates the type of smart motorway.

CONTROLLED MOTORWAY	Variable speed limits without hard shoulder (the hard shoulder is used in emergencies only)
HARD SHOULDER RUNNING	Variable speed limits with part-time hard shoulder (the hard shoulder is open to traffic at busy times when signs permit)
ALL LANE RUNNING	Variable speed limits with hard shoulder as permanent running lane (there is no hard shoulder); this is standard for all new smart motorway schemes since 2013

SMART MOTORWAY SECTIONS	
M1	J6A–10, J10–13, J16–19, J23A–25, J25–28, J28–31, J31–32, J32–35A, J39–42
M3	J2–4A
M4	J19–20, J24–28
M5	J4A–6, J15–17
M6	J4–10A, J10A–13, J16–19
M9	J1–1A
M20	J4–7
M25	J2–3, J5–6, J6–23, J23–27, J27–30
M42	J3A–7, J7–9
M60	J8–18
M62	J18–20, J25–26, J26–28, J28–29, J29–30
M90	M9 J1A–M90 J3

Quick tips

- Never drive in a lane closed by a red X
- Keep to the speed limit shown on the gantries
- A solid white line indicates the hard shoulder – do not drive in it unless directed
- A broken white line indicates a normal running lane
- Exit the smart motorway where possible if your vehicle is in difficulty. In an emergency, move onto the hard shoulder where there is one, or the nearest emergency refuge area
- Put on your hazard lights if you break down

M4	Motorway with number
Toll T4	Toll motorway with toll station
5	Restricted motorway junctions
S R	Motorway service area, rest area
	Motorway and junction under construction
A3	Primary route single/dual carriageway
1	Primary route junction with and without number
3	Restricted primary route junctions
S	Primary route service area
BATH	Primary route destination
A1123	Other A road single/dual carriageway
B2070	B road single/dual carriageway
	Minor road, more than 4 metres wide, less than 4 metres wide
	Roundabout
	Interchange/junction
	Narrow primary/other A/B road with passing places (Scotland)
	Road under construction
	Road tunnel
Toll	Road toll, steep gradient (arrows point downhill)
5	Distance in miles between symbols
	Railway line, in tunnel
	Railway/tram station, level crossing
	Tourist railway
628 637 Lecht Summit	Height in metres, mountain pass
	Snow gates (on main routes)
or V	Vehicle ferry
	Fast vehicle ferry or catamaran
	Airport (major/minor), heliport
F	International freight terminal

H	24-hour Accident & Emergency hospital
C	Crematorium
P·R	Park and Ride (at least 6 days per week)
	City, town, village or other built-up area
	National boundary, county or administrative boundary
	Scenic route
i i	Tourist Information Centre (all year/seasonal)
V	Visitor or heritage centre
	Caravan site (AA inspected)
	Camping site (AA inspected)
	Caravan & camping site (AA inspected)
	Abbey, cathedral or priory
	Ruined abbey, cathedral or priory
	Castle, historic house or building
	Museum or art gallery
	Industrial interest
	Aqueduct or viaduct
	Garden, arboretum
	Vineyard, brewery or distillery
	Country park, theme park
	Agricultural showground
	Farm or animal centre
	Zoological or wildlife collection
	Bird collection, aquarium
	RSPB site
	National Nature Reserve (England, Scotland, Wales)
	Local nature reserve, Wildlife Trust reserve
	Forest drive
	National trail

	Picnic site
	Waterfall
	Viewpoint
	Hill-fort
	Prehistoric monument, Roman antiquity
1066	Battle site with year
	Steam railway centre
	Cave or cavern
	Windmill, monument
	Beach (award winning)
	Lighthouse
	Golf course
	Football stadium
	County cricket ground
	Rugby Union national stadium
	International athletics stadium
	Horse racing, show jumping
	Air show venue, motor-racing circuit
	Ski slope (natural, artificial)
	National Trust site (England & Wales, Scotland)
	English Heritage site
	Historic Scotland site
	Cadw (Welsh heritage) site
	Major shopping centre, other place of interest
	Attraction within urban area
	World Heritage Site (UNESCO)
	National Park and National Scenic Area (Scotland)
	Forest Park
	Heritage coast

8

A   B   C   D   E   F

1
2
3

Higher Sha

Lower Sha

4

Bud
Bay

5

Dizzard Point
St
Gennys
Crackington Haven   Co
Cambeak
Sweets
Wai
Co

6

15   B3263
Marsh
Witchcraft
& Magic
Pentire Point - Widemouth
Heritage Coast
Boscastle
Trevalga
Tresparrett
Lesnewth

TINTAGEL HEAD
Castle
Tintagel
Bossiney
Old Post Office
Trethevey
B3266
Davidstow
Penhallic Point
Trewarmett
Tremail
Treknow
Arthurian
Centre
B3314

7

South West Coast Path
Delabole
Pengelly
Crowdy
Reservoir
Westdowns
Lanteglos
Camelford
Port Isaac
Bay
Trewalder
Helstone
Varley
Head
Port Gaverne
B3314
Kellan
Head
Port Isaac
St Teath
Rumps
Point
Port Quin
Bay
Port
Quin
Treveighan
Pentire Point
Bee Centre
Long
Cross
Michaelstow
419
BROWN
WILLY
8
Padstow Bay
Hayle Bay
Polzeath
Trelights
Pendoggett
Treveighan
Churchtown
Stepper Point
St Endelli
relill
St Breward
A   B   4   C   D   E   F 3 O

Trevose
Heritage Coast
St Minver
B3314
Jamaica
TREVOSE HEAD
Trequite
St
Tudy
Dinas
Head
St Kew
St Kew
Highway
Constantine
Trevone

0   1   2   3   4 miles
0   1   2   3   4   5 kilometres

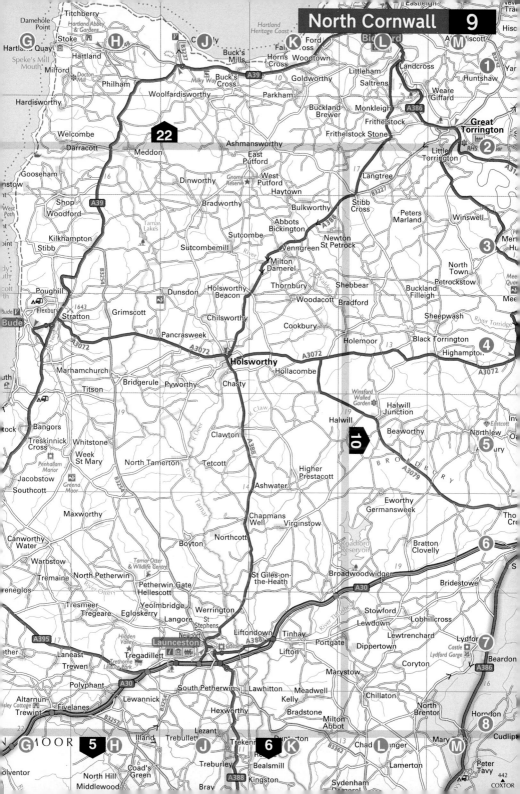

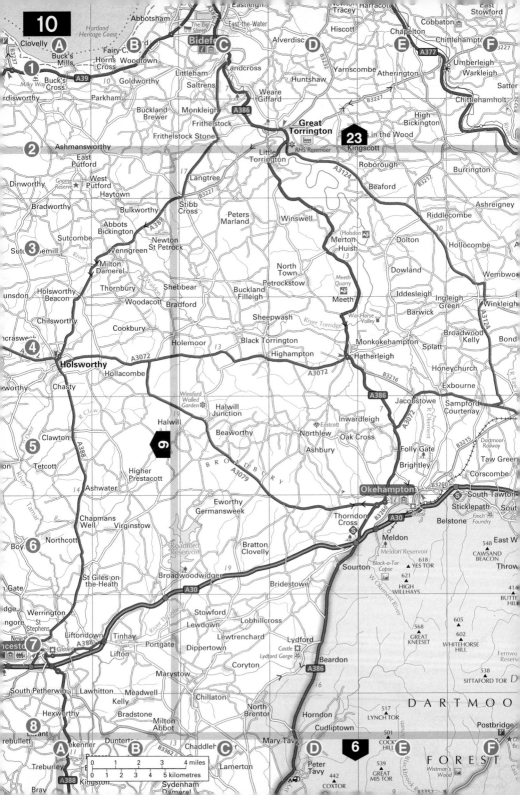

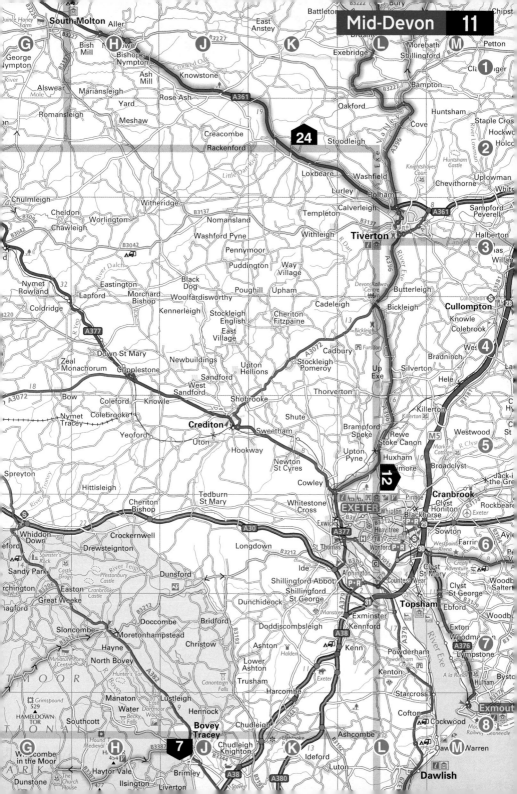

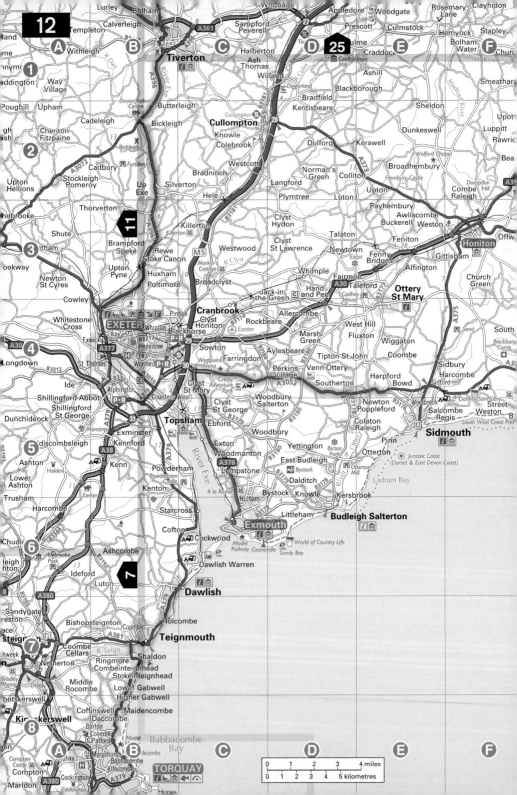

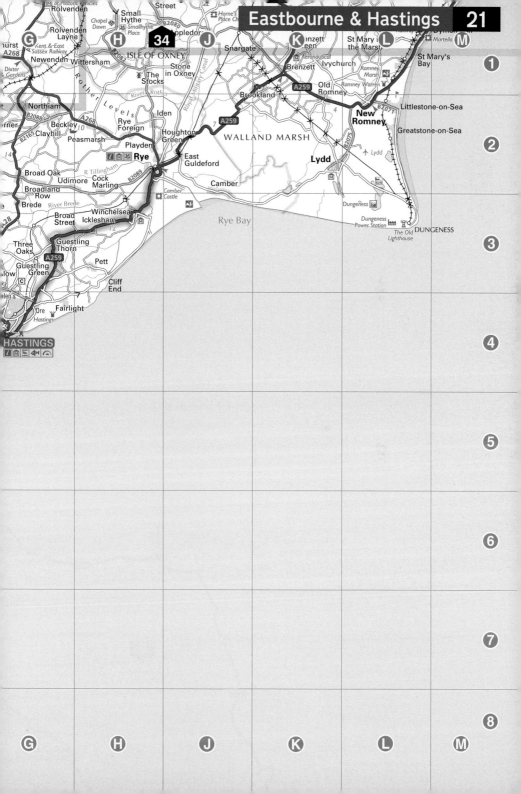

22

A   B   C   D   E   F

1

2

North West
Point

*Lundy
Heritage Coast* LUNDY

3   142

*Marine
Reserve*   *Marisco*

Shutter Point   Surf Point

Bagg
Poir

Croyde

4

B A R N S T A P L E

O R

5   B I D E F O R D B A Y

Westwar

Shipload
Bay

HARTLAND POINT   Titchberry

Damehole
Point   *Hartland Abbey
& Gardens*

Stoke   Clovelly   *Hartland
Heritage Coast*   Abbotsh

6   Hartland Quay   B3248   Buck's
Mills   Fairy Cross   Ford

*Speke's Mill
Mouth*   Hartland   4   Horns
Cross   Woodtown

Milford   *Docton
Mill*   *Milky Way*   Buck's
Cross   A39   10   Goldworthy

Philham   Woolfardisworthy   Parkham

Bucklar
Brew

Hardisworthy   Fri

Welcombe   Ashmansworthy

7   Darracott   Meddon   East
Putford

9

Gooseham   16   Dinworthy   *Gnome
Reserve* ★   West
Putford

Morwenstow   Haytown

Higher Sharpnose Point   Shop   A39   Bradworthy   Bulkworthy

*South West
Coast Path*   Woodford   *Tamar
Lakes*   Abbots
Bickington

8   Lower Sharpnose Point   Sutcombe   Ne
St P

Kilkhampton   Milton
Damerel

Steeple Point   bb   Sutcom ill   *River*   en

A   B   C   D   E   F

0   1   2   3   4 miles
0 1 2 3 4   5 kilometres

*Northcott
Mouth*   Poughill   Dunsdon   Holsworthy
Beacon   Thornbury

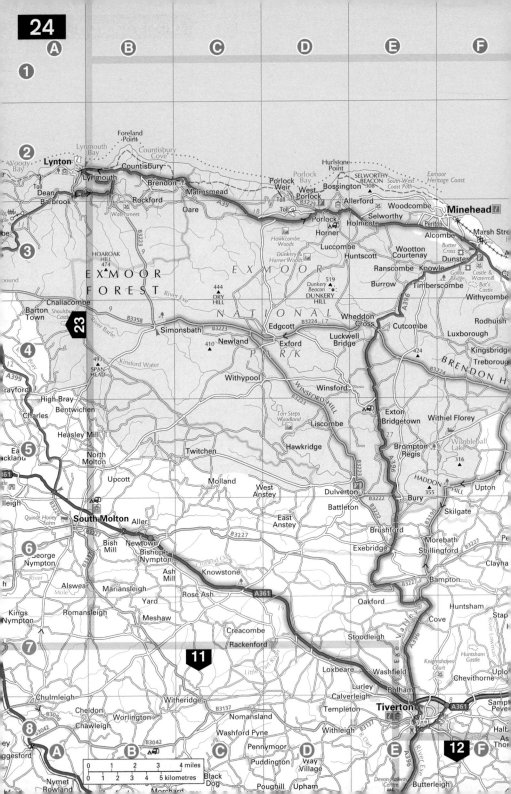

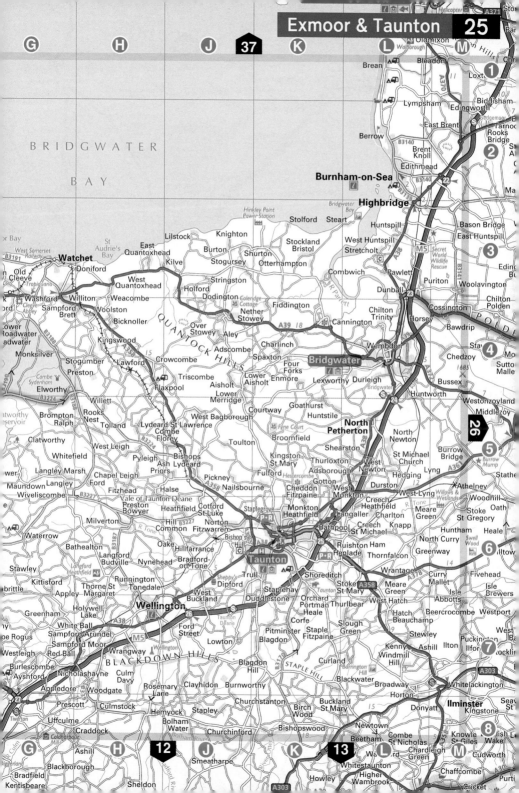

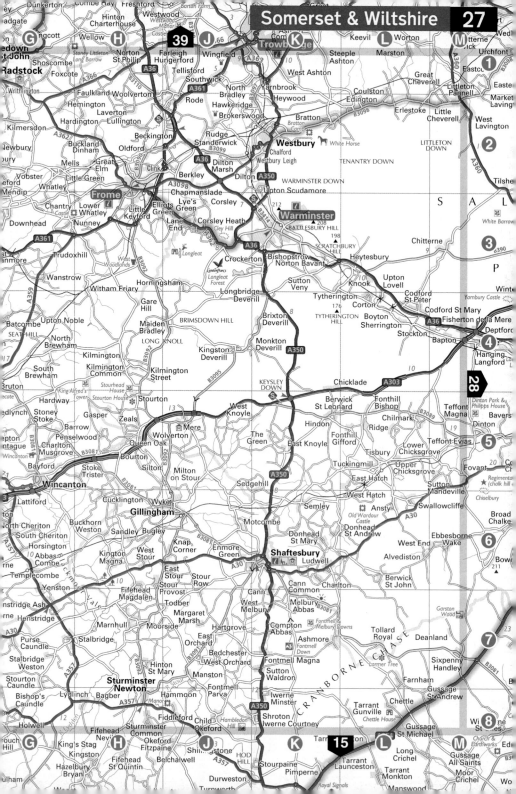

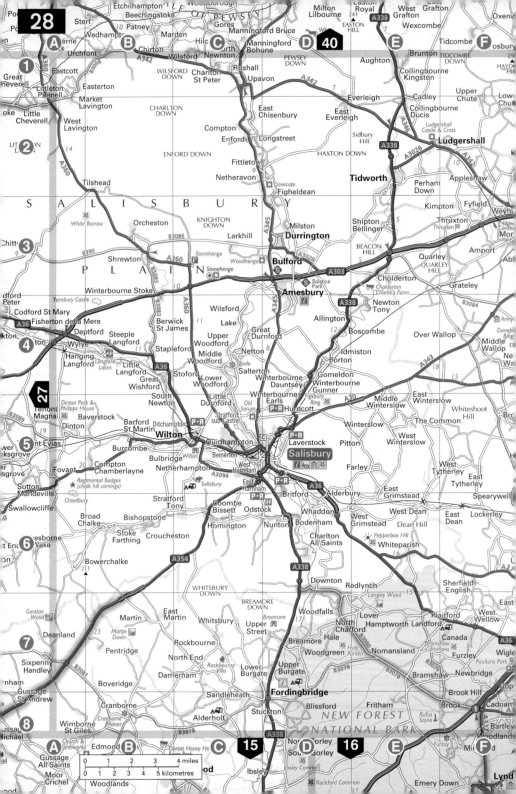

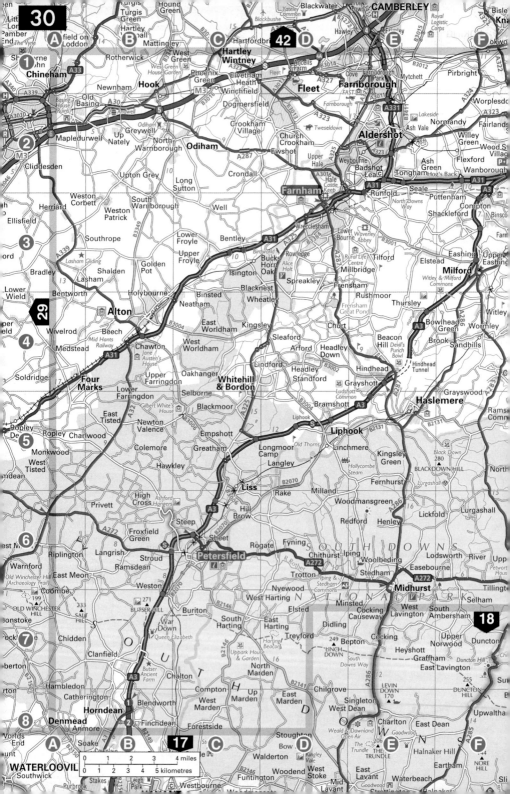

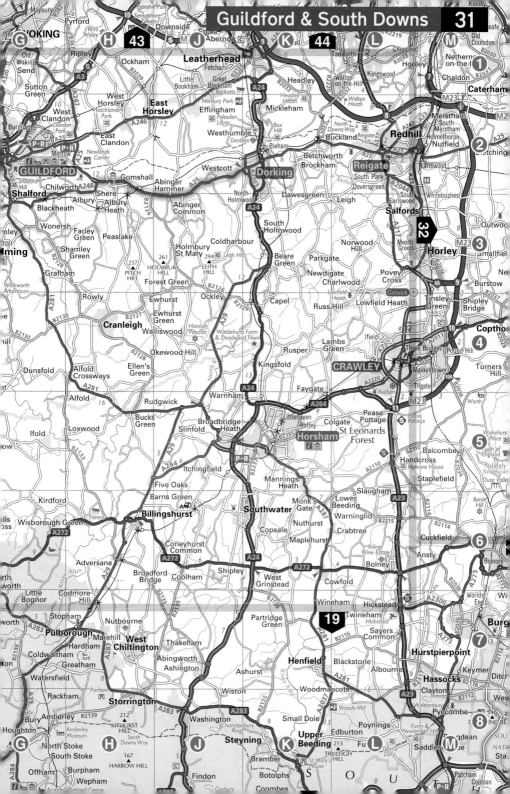

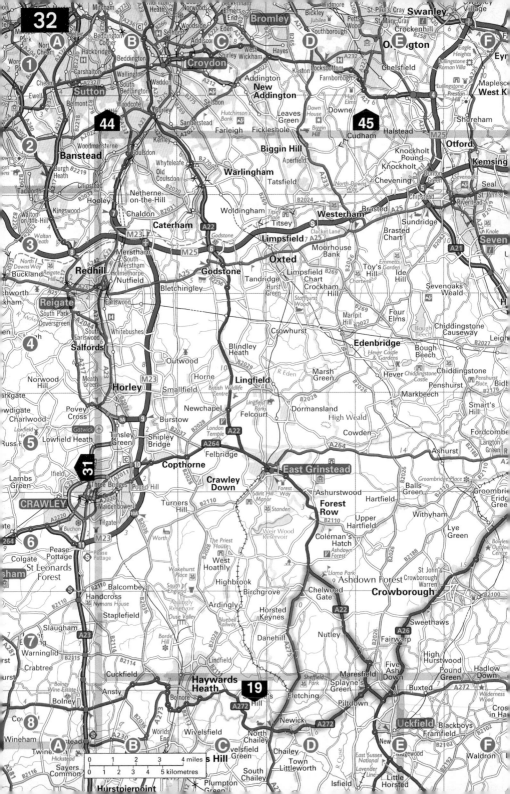

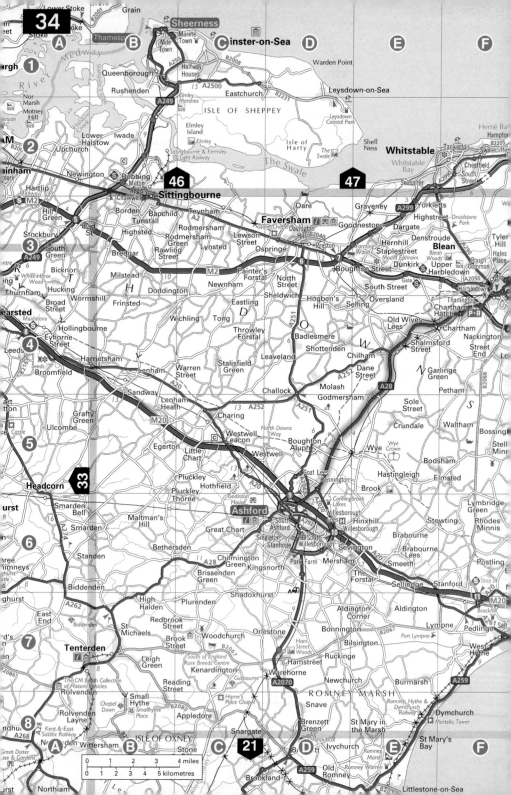

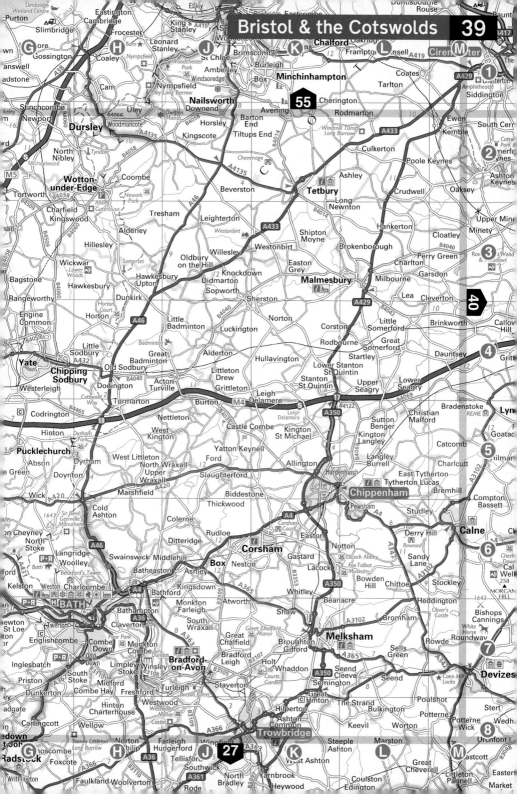

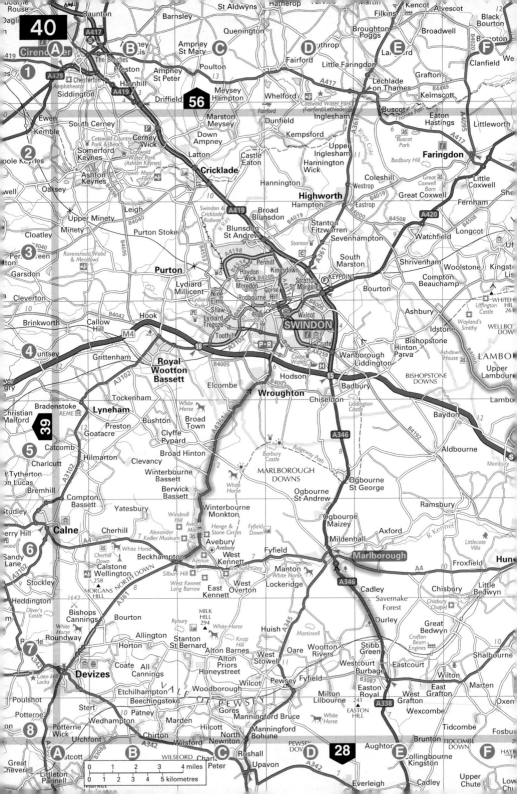

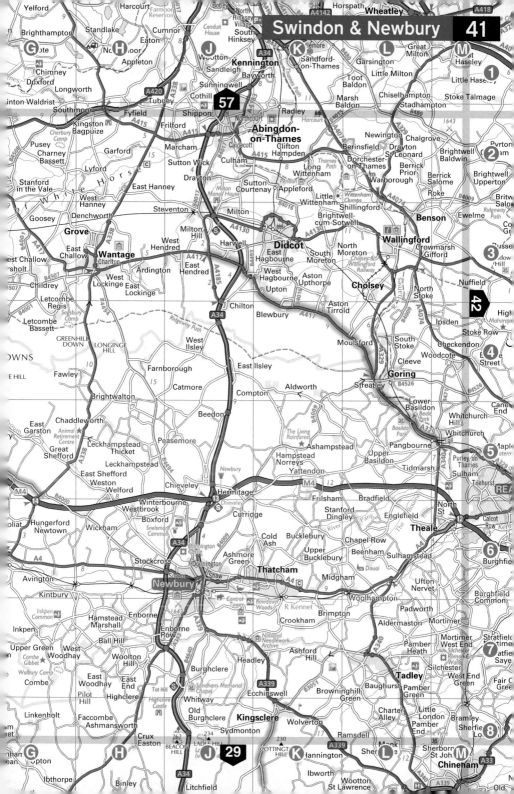

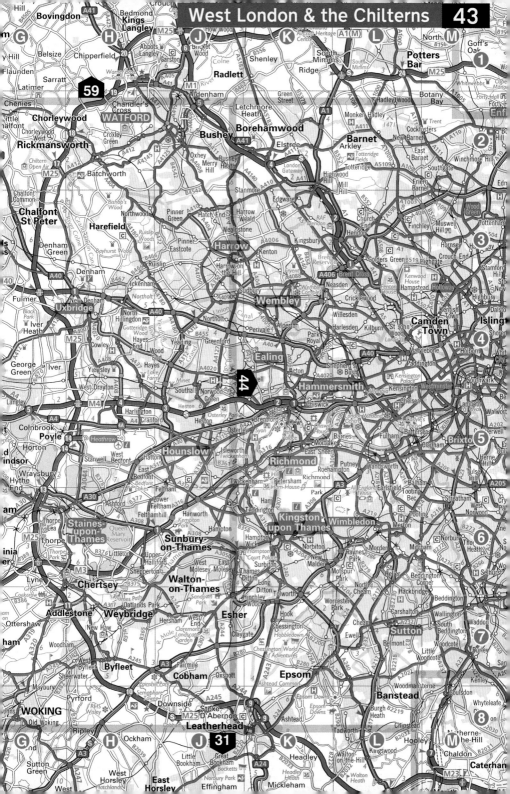

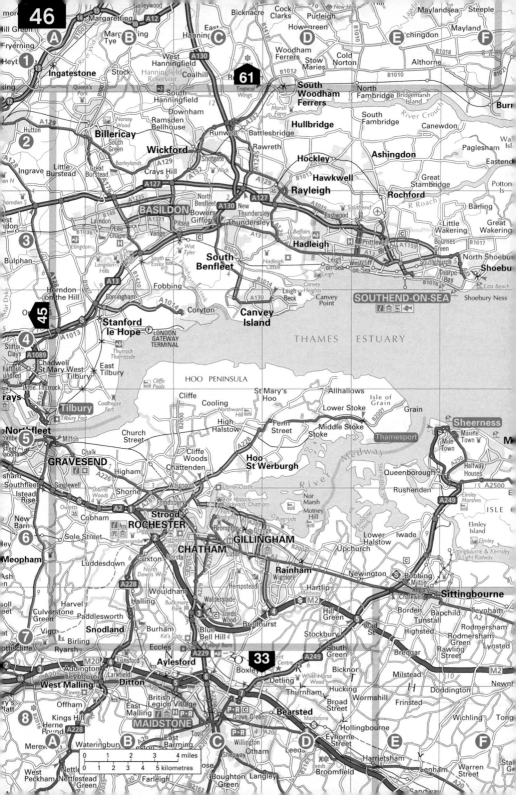

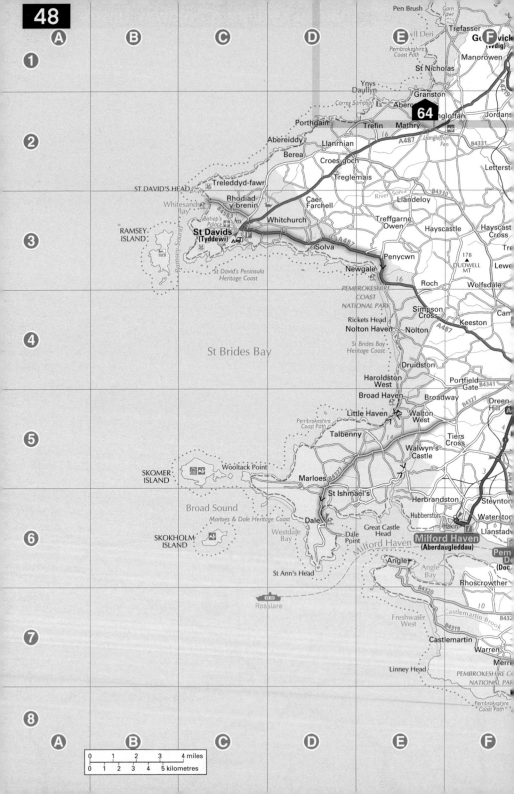

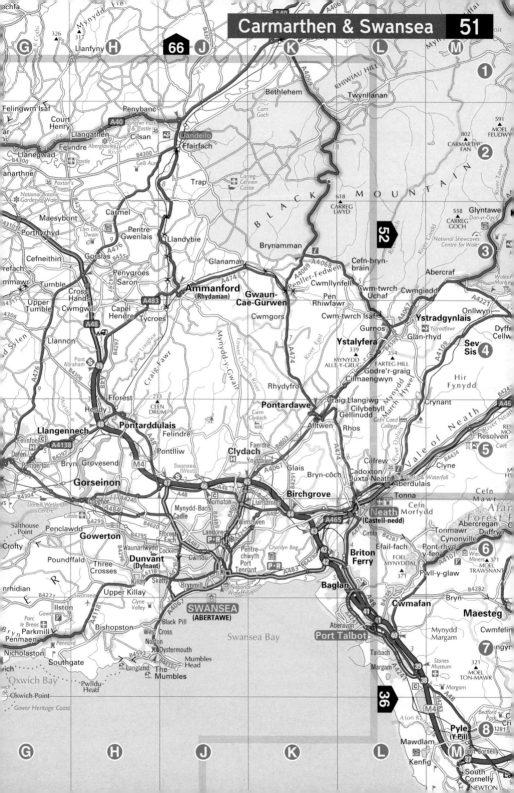

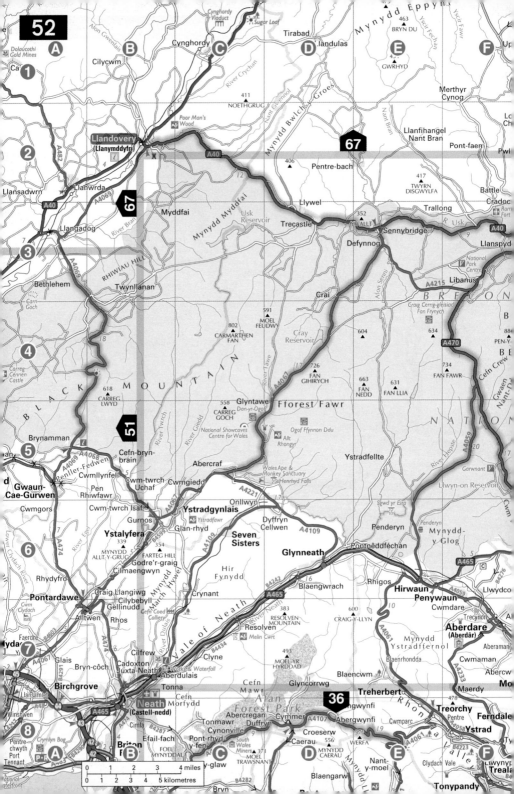

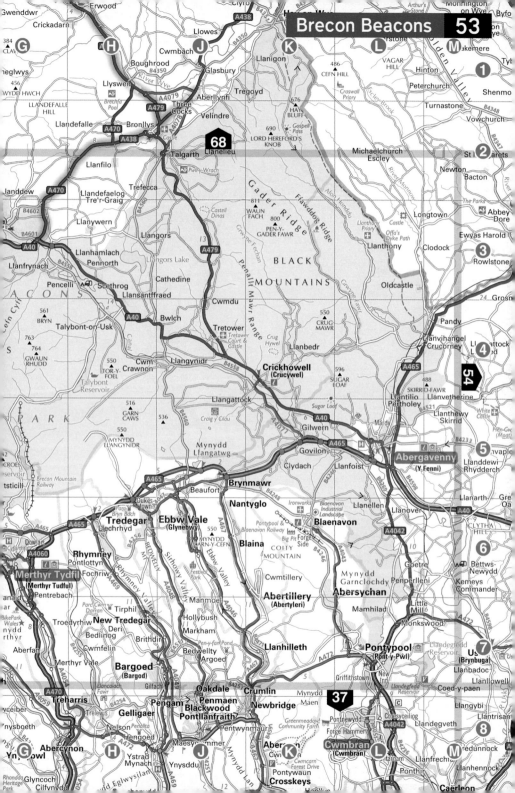

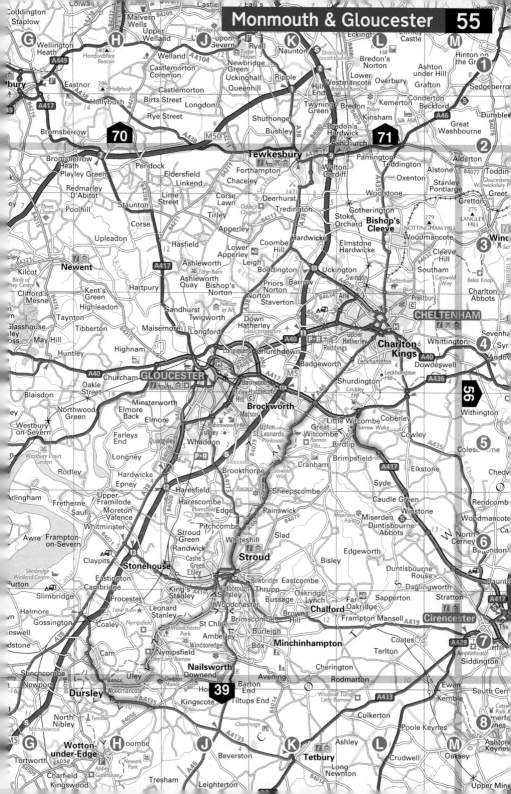

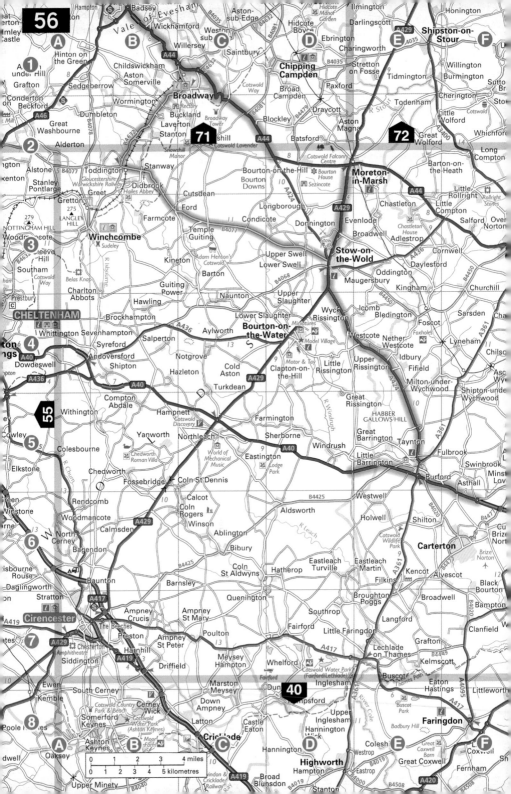

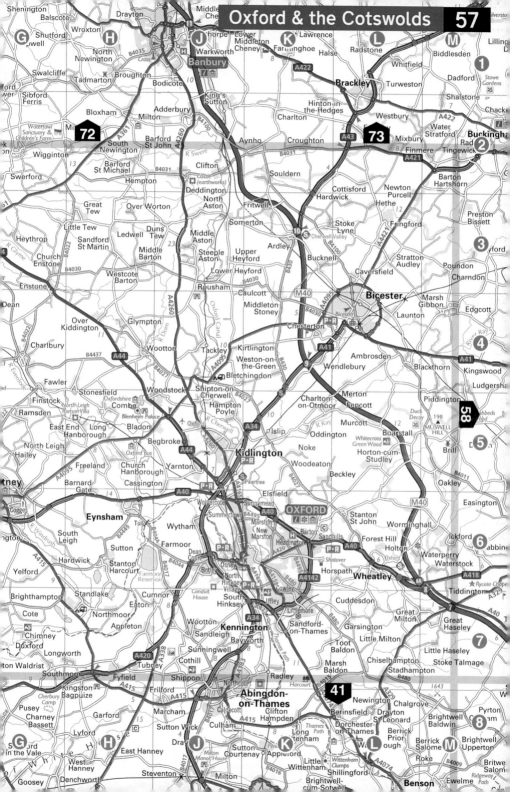

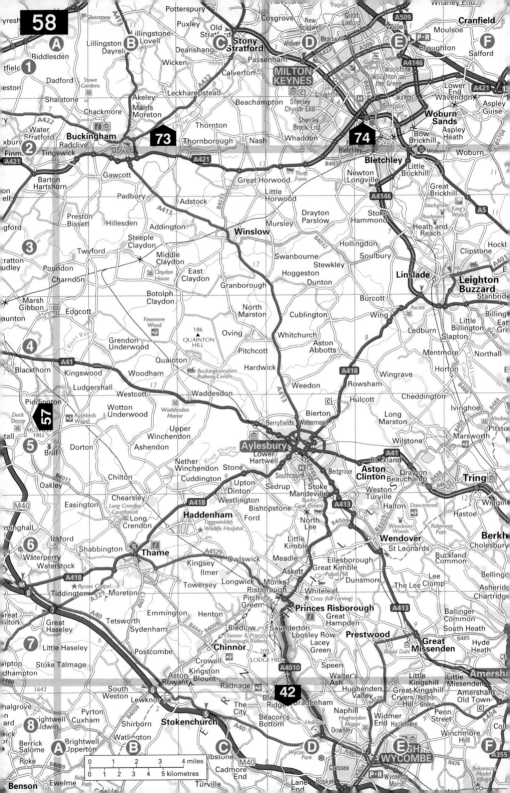

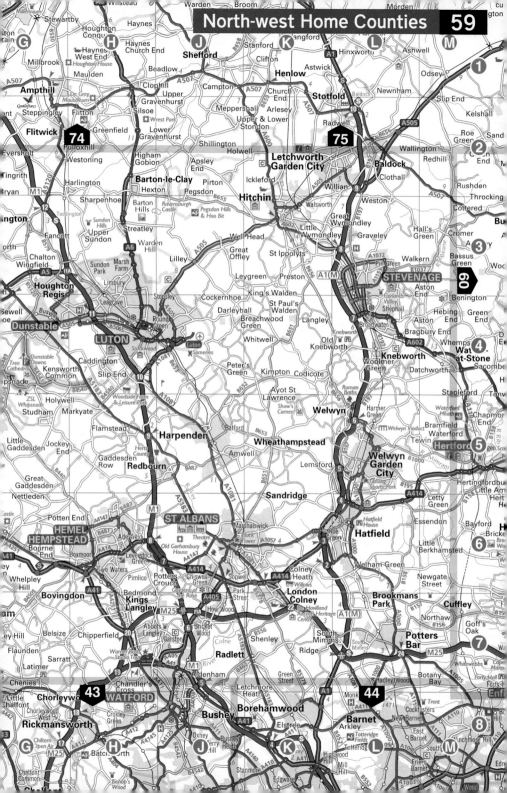

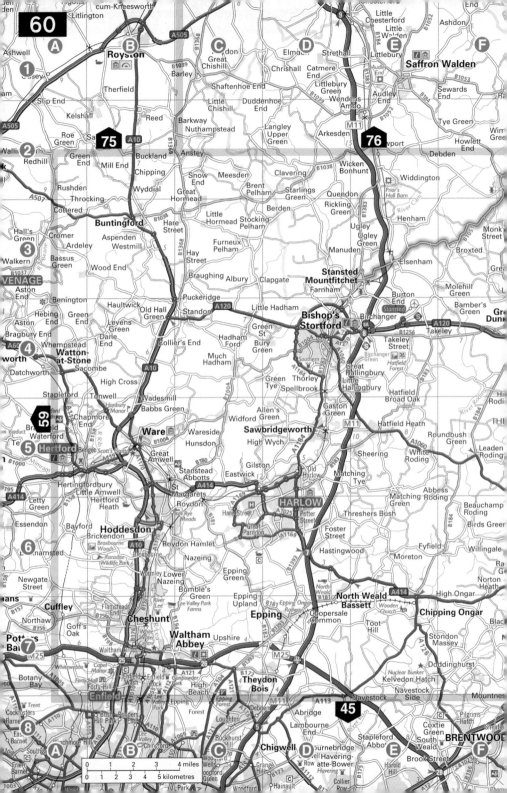

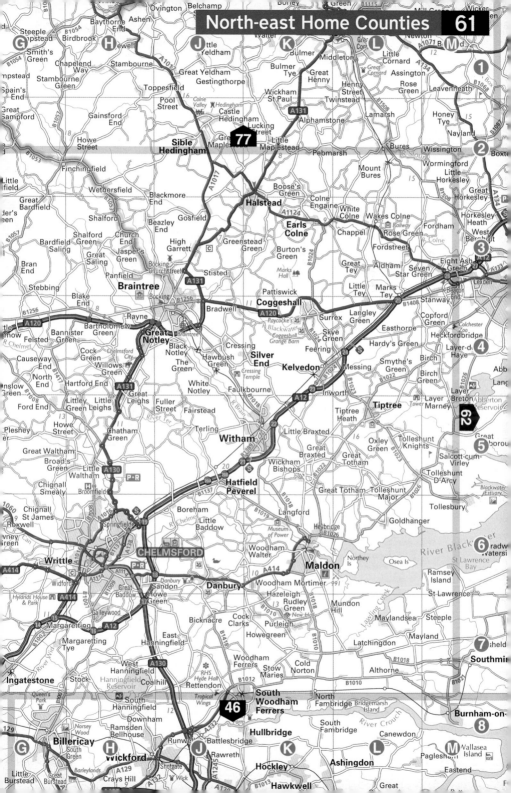

G Alderton H Hollesley Bay J K L M

1

Bawdsey

Falkenham

Old
Felixstowe

Felixstowe **79**

2

ndguard Fort

ndguard
nt

Hook of Holland

3

4

5

6

7

8

G H J K L M

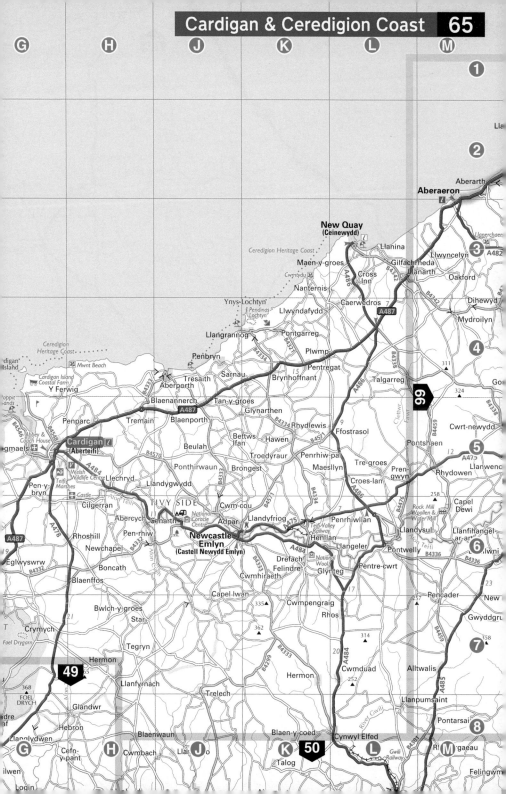

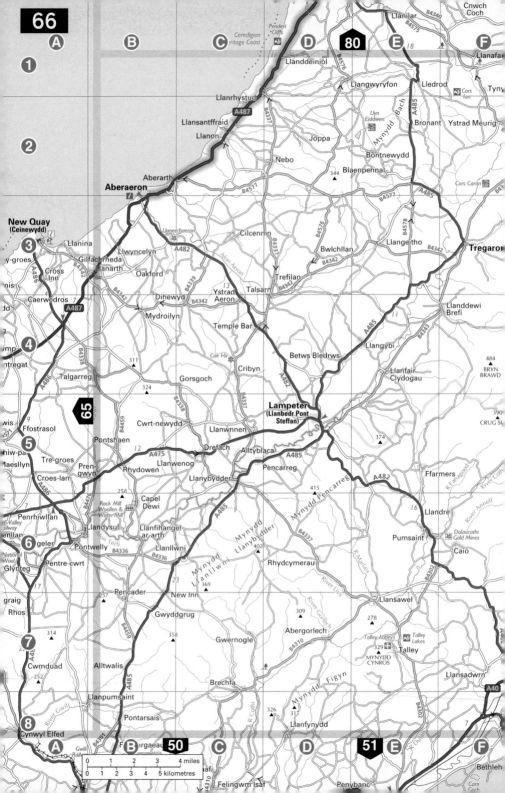

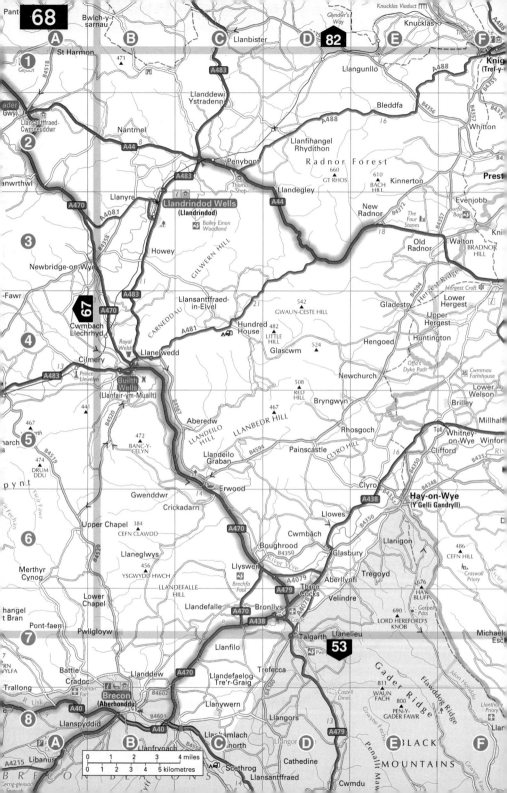

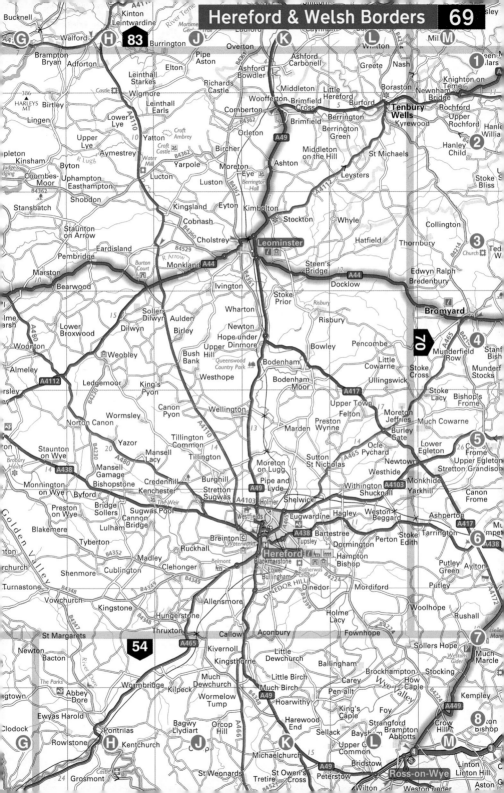

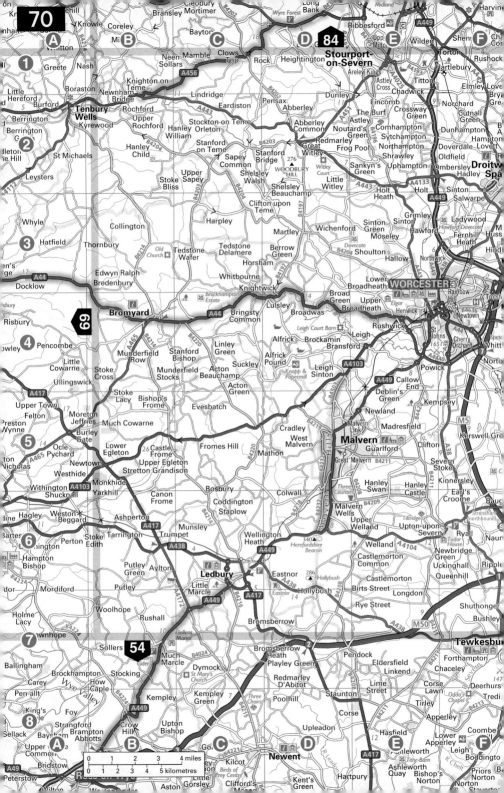

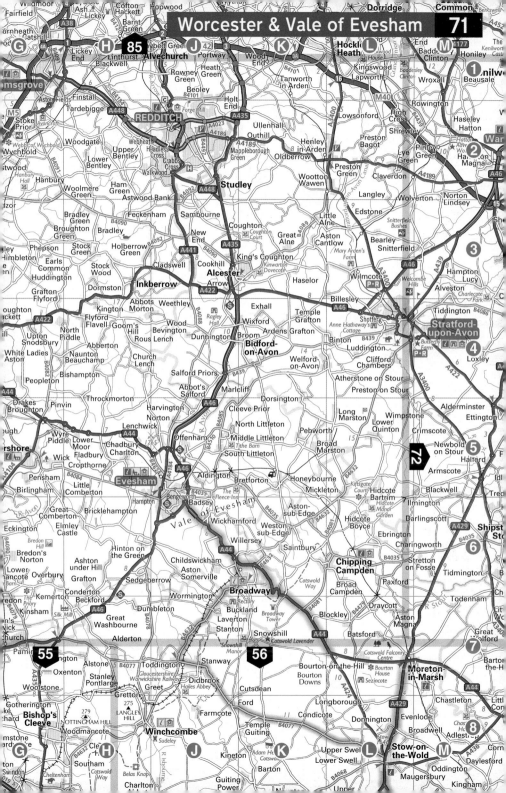

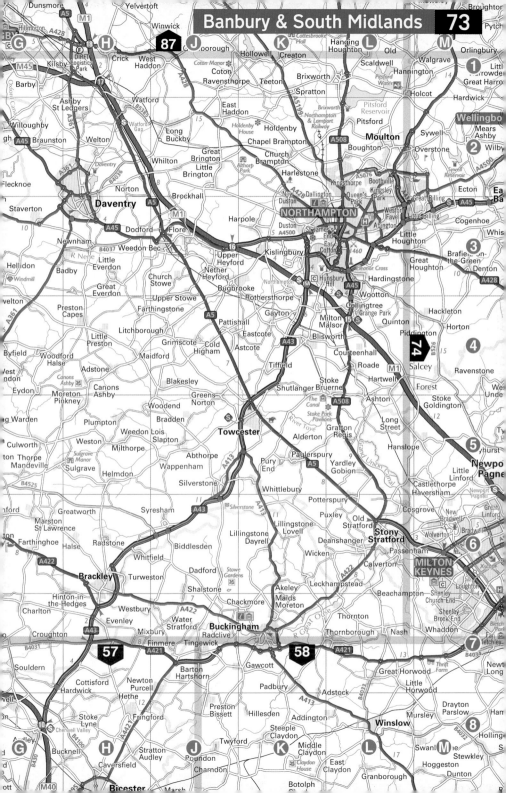

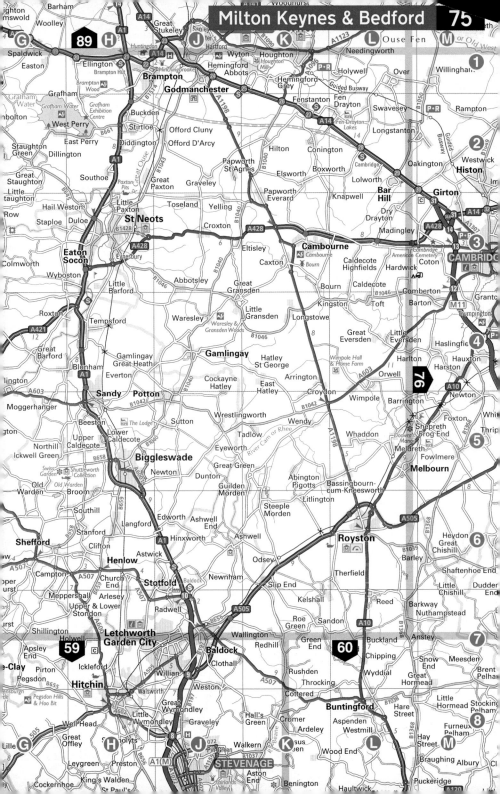

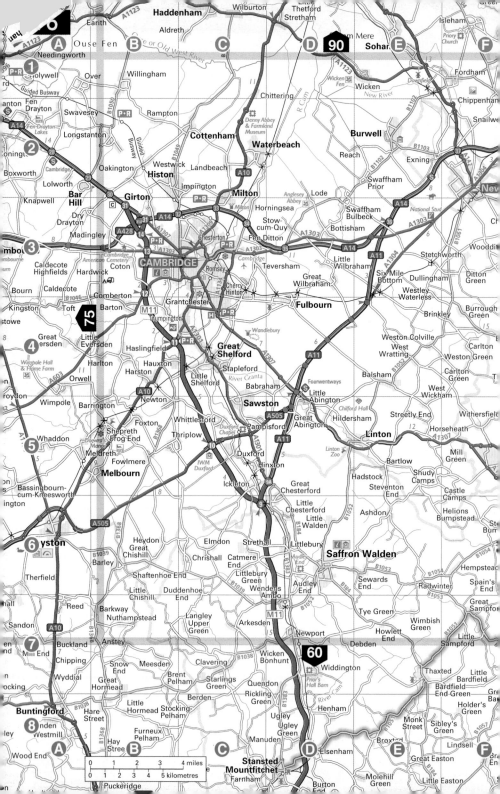

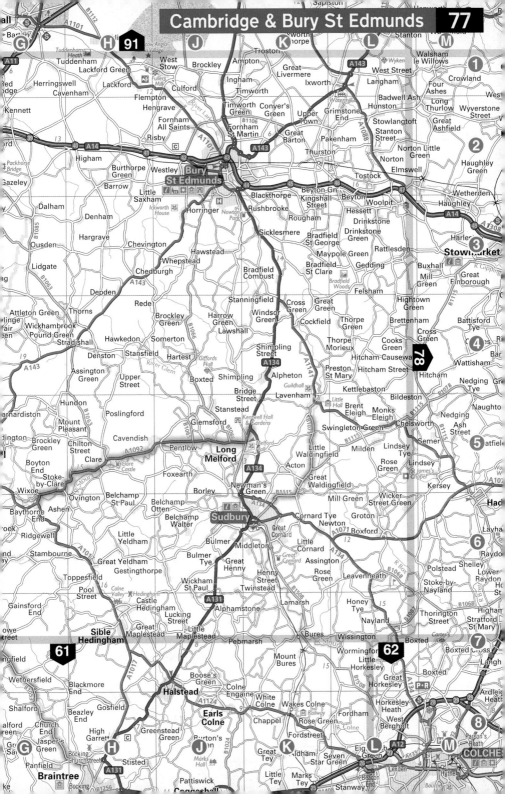

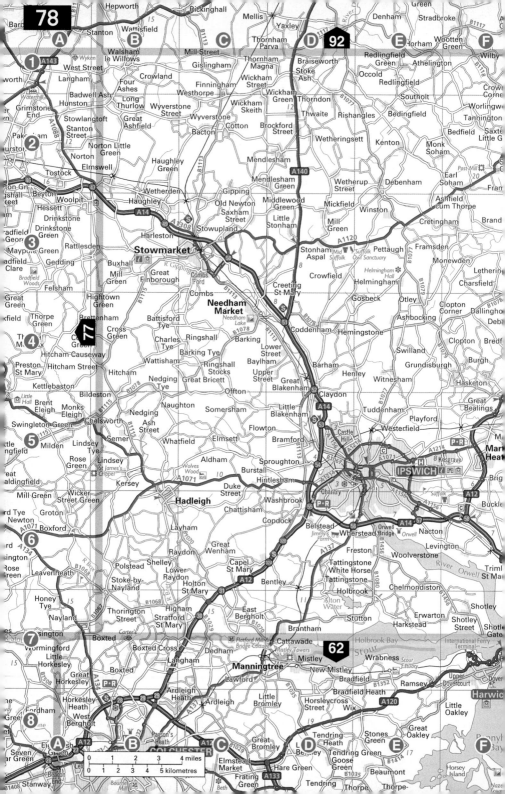

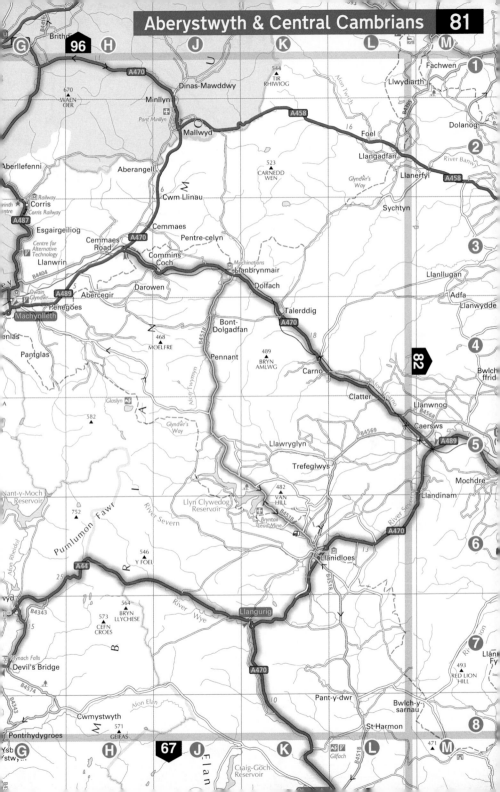

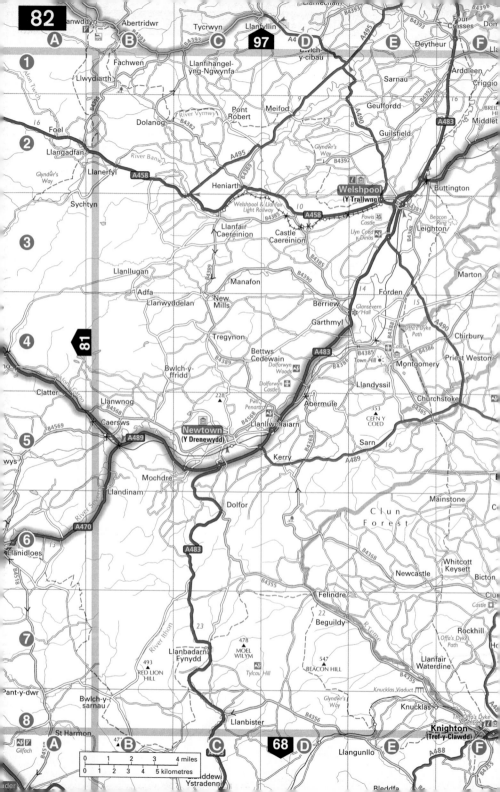

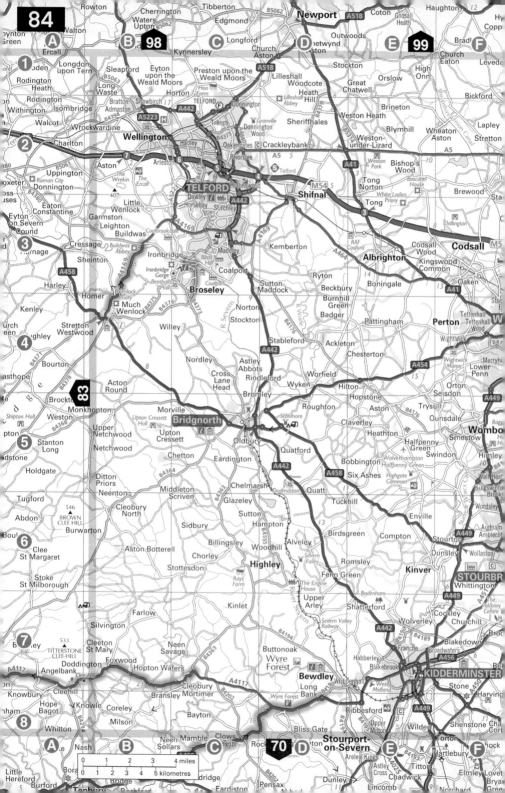

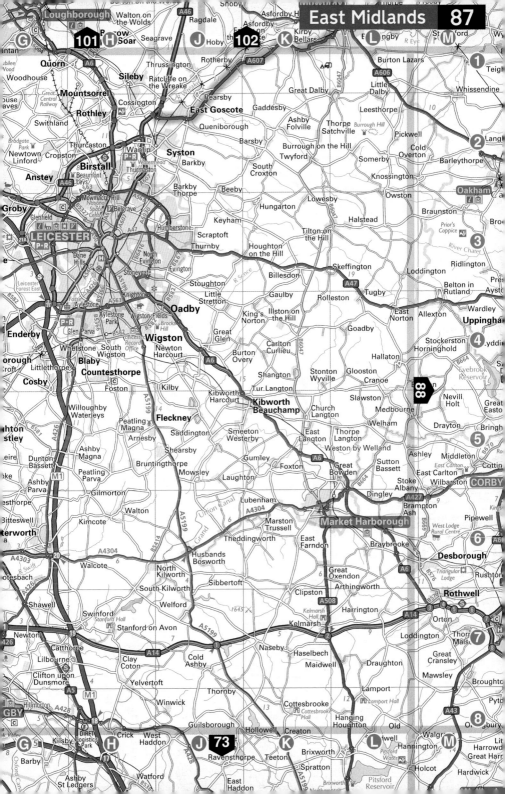

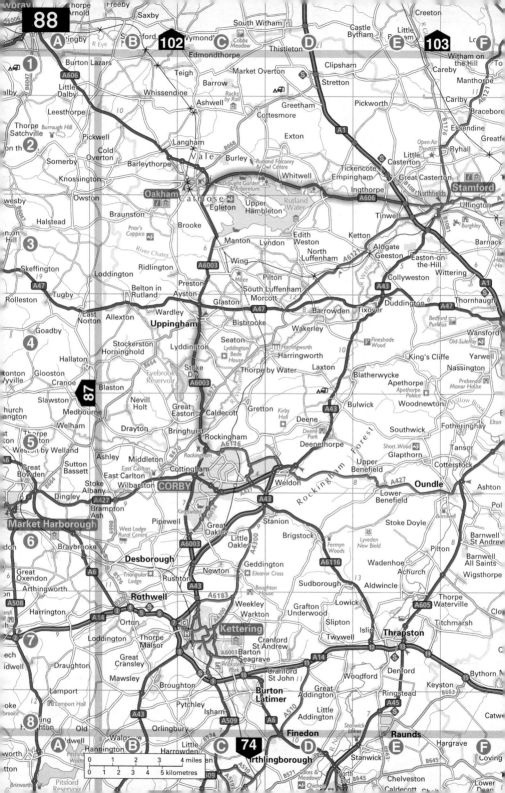

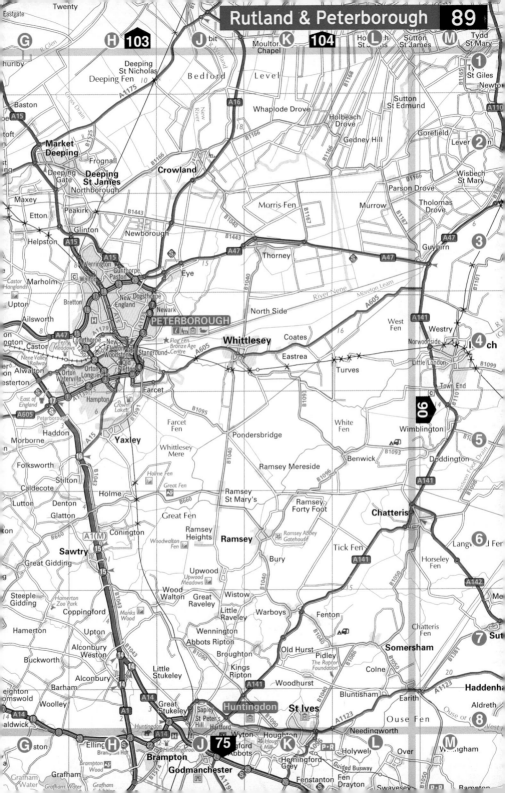

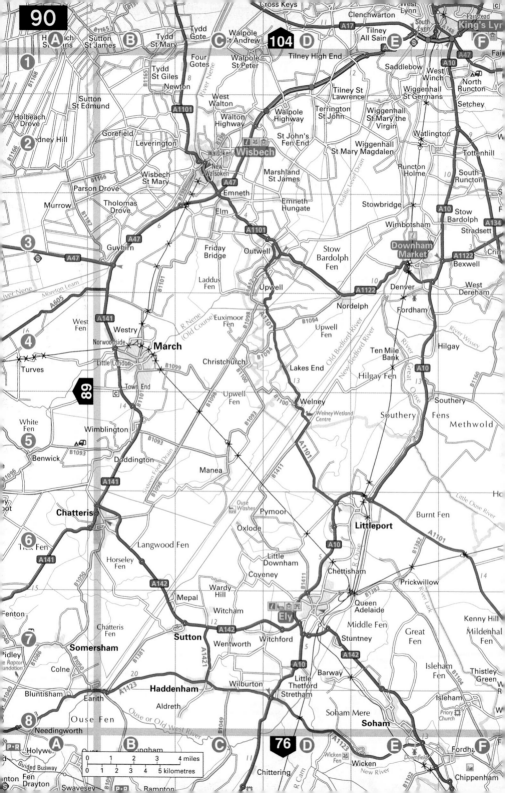

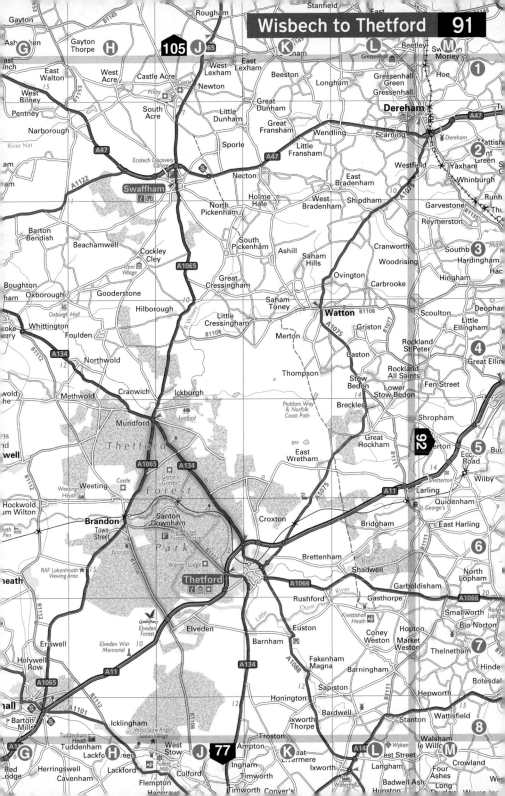

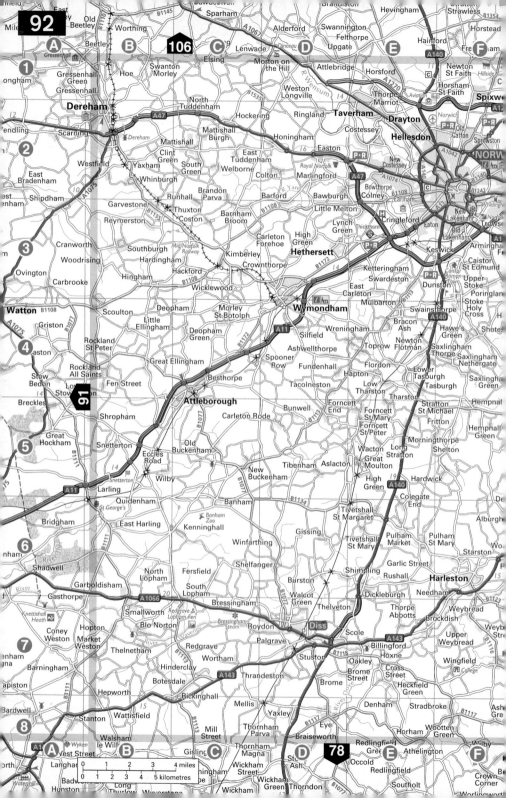

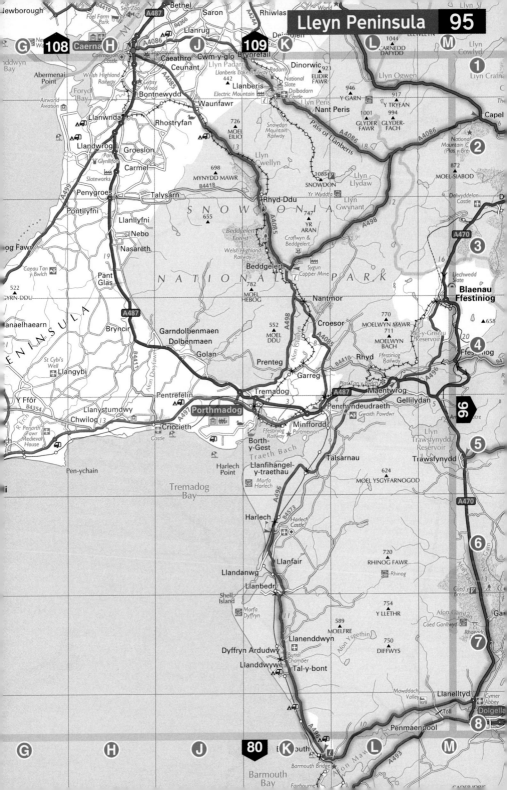

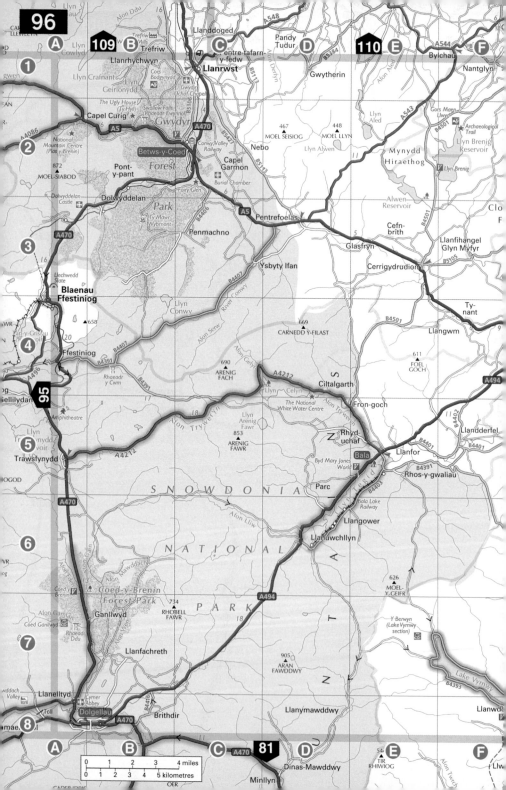

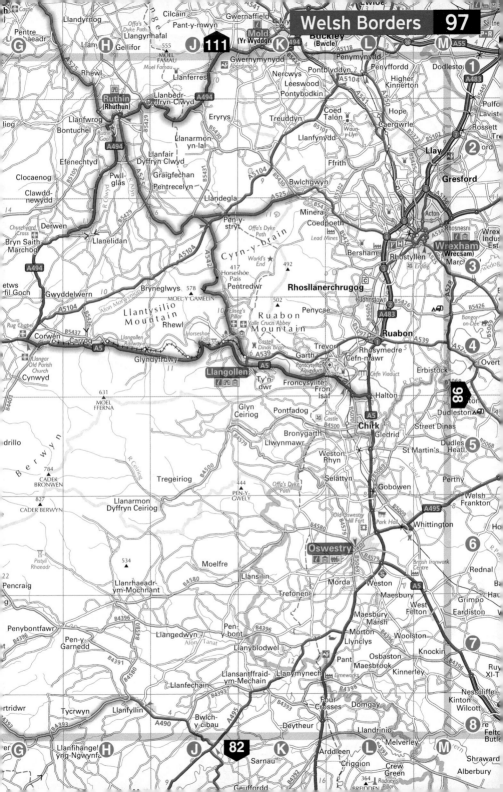

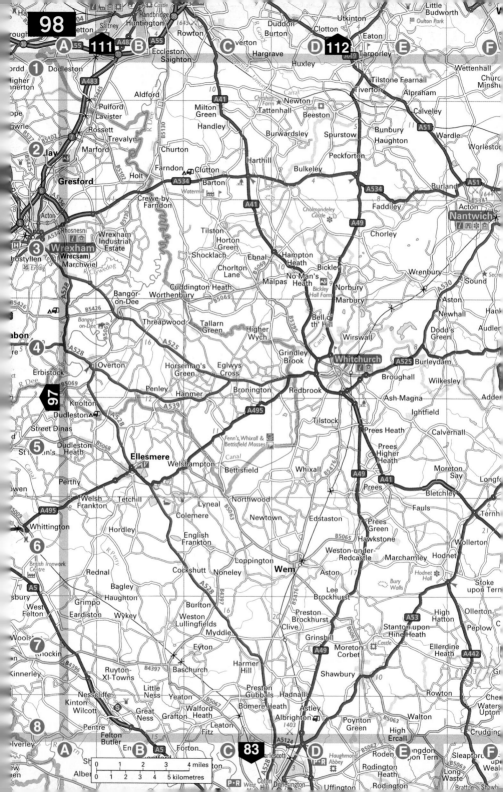

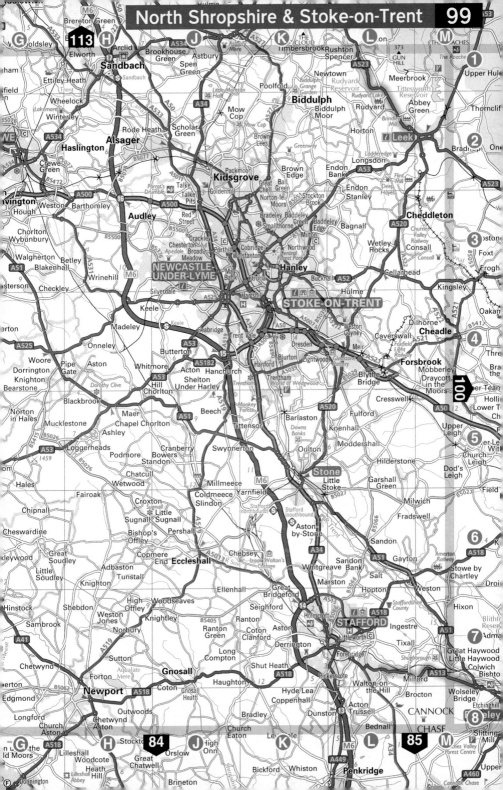

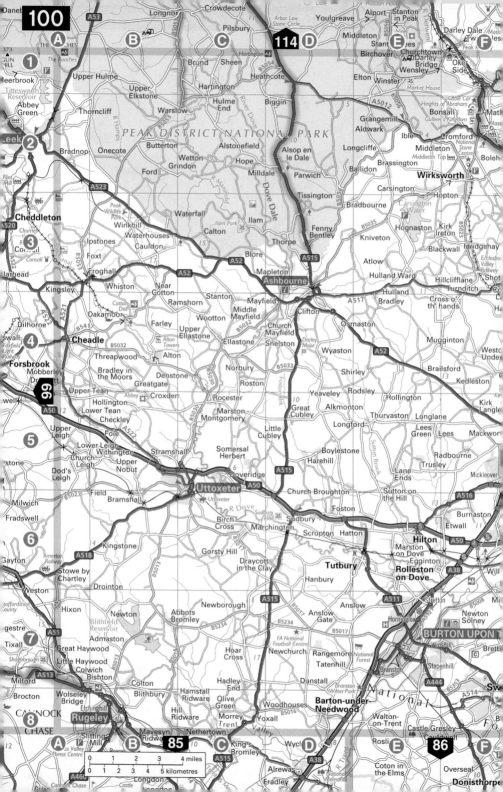

G H J K L M

1
2
3

North Norfolk
Heritage Coast

Holkham Bay

Brancaster
Bay

Scolt Head
Island

Peddars Way &
Norfolk Coast Path

Blakeney Point

Titchfield Marsh

Brancaster
Staithe

Burnham
Deepdale

Wells-
Harbour
Miniature
Railway

Holme
Dunes

Holme next
the Sea

Brancaster

Burnham
Overy
Staithe

Holkham

Wells-next-
the-Sea

4 Stif

Old
Hunstanton

Thornham

Titchwell

Branodunum
Roman Fort

Burnham
Norton

B1155

Holkham Hall

A149

Warham

nstanton

Ringstead

Burnham
Market

Burnham
Overy

Burnham
Thorpe

Wells &
Walsingham
Light Railway

Wighton

106

Heacham

Norfolk
Lavender

Summerfield

Peddars Way &
Norfolk Coast Path

B1153

North
Creake

B1355

Creake
Abbey

The Shrine of
Our Lady

Little
Walsingham

Great
Walsingham

5

Sedgeford

B1454

Docking

B1155

Stanhoe

South
Creake

10

North
Barsham

Hindringham

Houghton St Giles

Great
Snoring

Snettisham

Fring

B1153

Bircham
Newton

19

West
Barsham

East
Barsham

Thursford

Snettisham
Park

Ingoldisthorpe

12

Shernborne

B1440

Great
Bircham

Bircham
Tofts

Syderstone

Wicken Green
Village

Little
Snoring

A148

Croxte

Dersingham

B1455

Anmer

B1153

Houghton
Hall

Sculthorpe

Sculthorpe
Moor

Dunton
Coxford
Shereford

Kettlestone

Pensthorpe
Waterfo

6

Dersingham Bog

Sandringham

West
Newton

New
Houghton

West
Rudham

Hempton

Fakenham

Little Ryburgh

erton

A149

B1440

Flitcham

A148

East
Rudham

Tatterford

Toftrees

Great
Ryburgh

B1146

le Rising

Castle

A149

Hillington

Harpley

Helhoughton

East
Raynham

Colkirk

Gateley

River Wensu

A1067

Congham

Roydon

B1439

Little
Massingham

West
Raynham

Horningtoft

7

B1145

Roydon
Common

Grimston

Great
Massingham

South
Raynham

Weasenham
St Peter

Whissonsett

Wellingham

Brisley

North
Elmham

tle Rising

Fairstead

Gayton

B1145

Ashwicken

Gayton
Thorpe

B1153

Weasenham
All Saints

Rougham

A1065

Tittleshall

Stanfield

Litcham

East
Bilney

Old
Beetley

Mileham

B1145

Gressenhall

8

ng's Lynn

7

Fair Green

East
Winch

H

East
Walton

J 91

e Acre

Priory

K West
xham

Newton

L

Longham

M Gressenhall
Green
Gressenhall.

G Middleton

North

Blackborough
End

West
Bilney

15

B1153

J Ac

Castle

Great
Dunham

West
Lexham

East
Lexham

Bee

Derehar

tchey

South

Little

Dereha

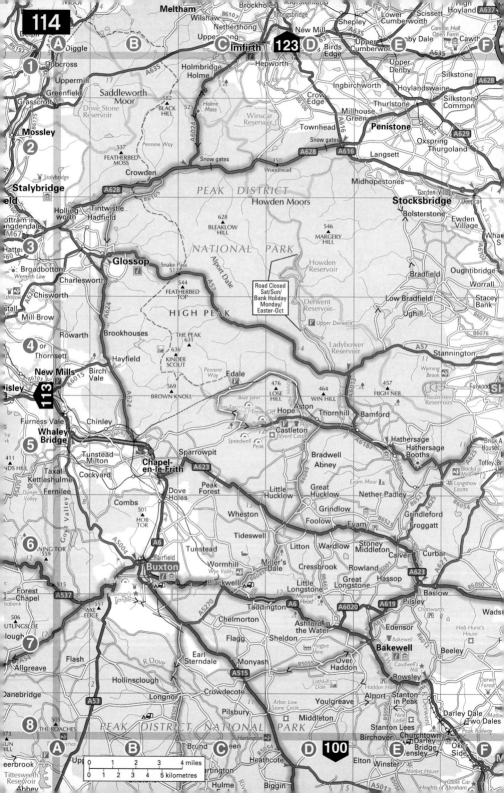

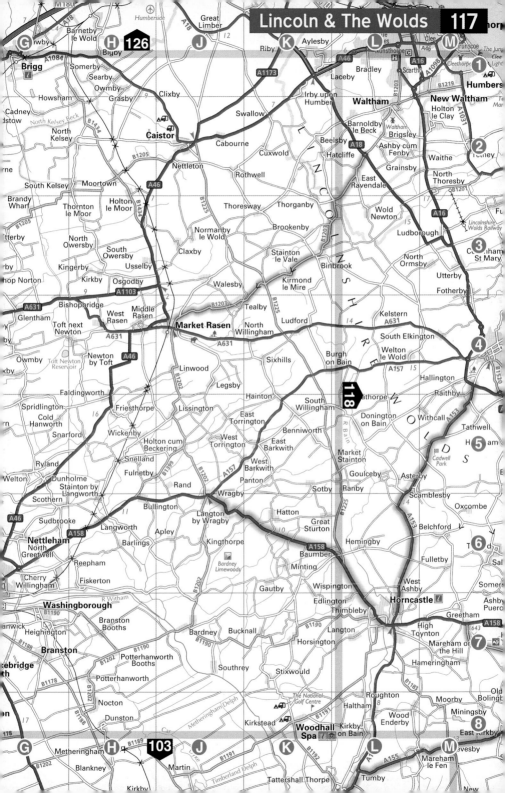

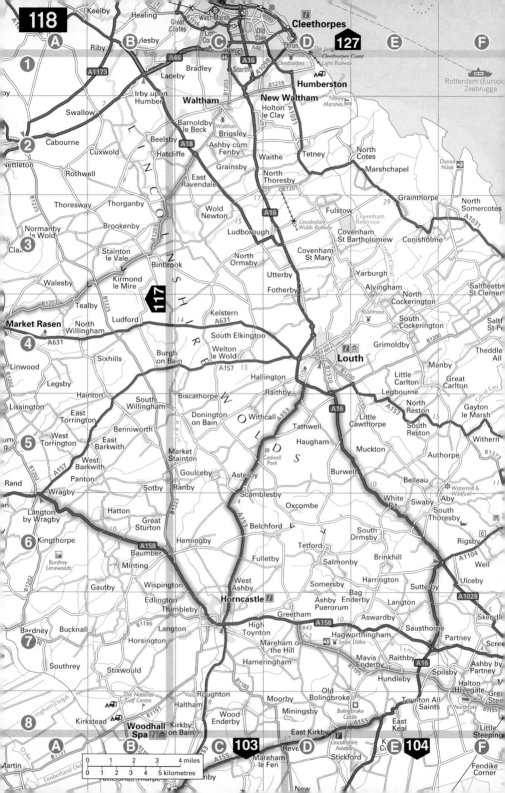

G   H   J   K   L   M

① ② ③ ④ ⑤ ⑥ ⑦ ⑧

eddlethorpe
Helen

y -
orpe Dunes

Seal Sanctuary &
Wildlife Centre

Mablethorpe

Trusthorpe

Sutton on Sea

Sandilands

Markby

Huttoft
hurlby

Anderby

esthorpe   Mumby

erworth   Chapel Point

Hogsthorpe   **Chapel
St Leonards**

ughby

Sloothby

Habertoft   Addlethorpe   Fantasy Island
on
rsh   **Ingoldmells**

Ingoldmells
Point

by   Lincolnshire Coast
Light Railway

Burgh le Marsh

ft   A158   Natureland Seal
Sanctuary

n the Marsh   **Skegness**

G   104   H   J   K   L   M

Croft

orpe St Peter   Wainfleet
Haven

Wainfleet

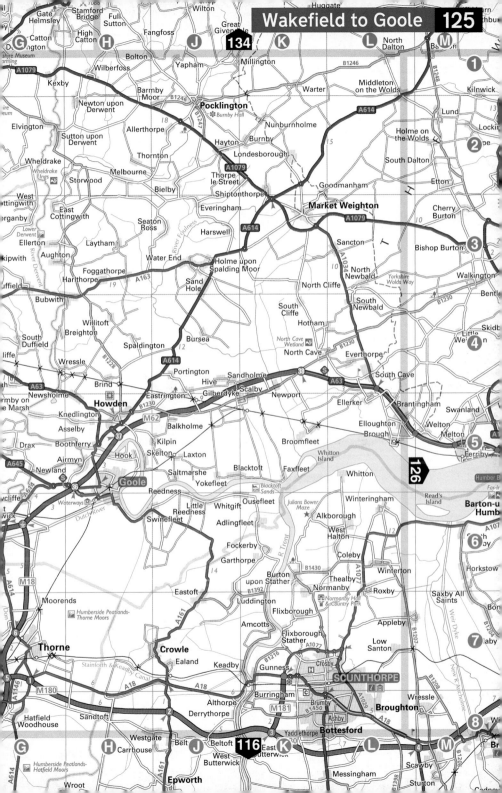

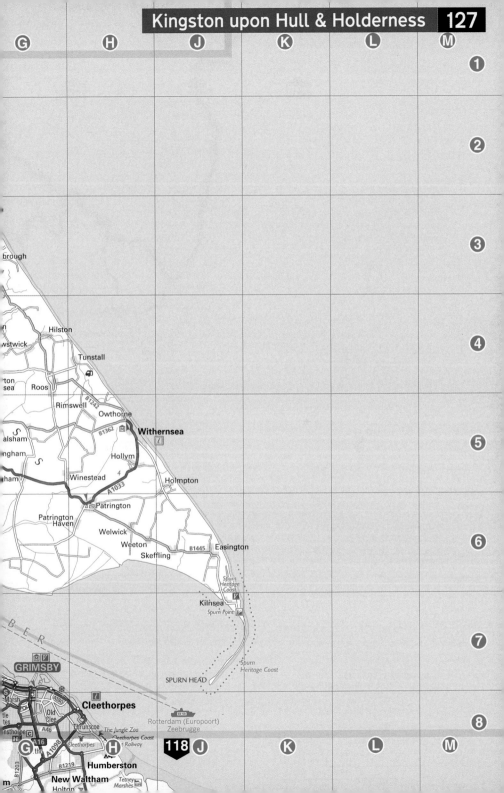

G   H   J   K   L   M

1
2
3
4
5
6
7
8

brough

Hilston

vstwick

Tunstall

ton
sea   Roos

Rimswell

Owthorne

alsham

ngham   **Withernsea**

Hollym

Winestead

ham

Holmpton

A1033

Patrington

Patrington
Haven

Welwick

Weeton

Skeffling   B1445   Easington

Spurn
Heritage
Coast

Kilnsea

Spurn Point

H B E R

GRIMSBY

Spurn
Heritage Coast

SPURN HEAD

Cleethorpes

Rotterdam (Europoort)
Zeebrugge

Marsh

Old
Clee

tes

A46

Thrunscoe

The Jungle Zoo
Cleethorpes Coast
t Railway

nsthorper

118   J

G   A1098

A116

the

Cleethorpes

H

Humberston

B1203

B1219

m

New Waltham

Holton

Tetney
Marshes

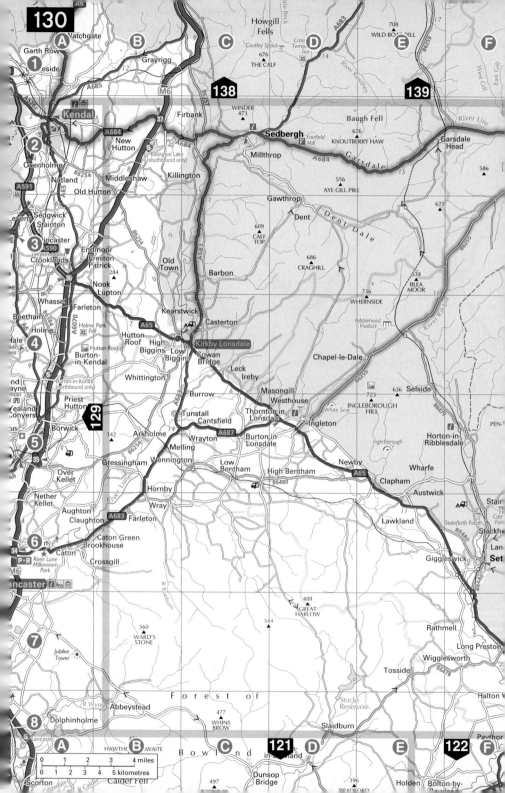

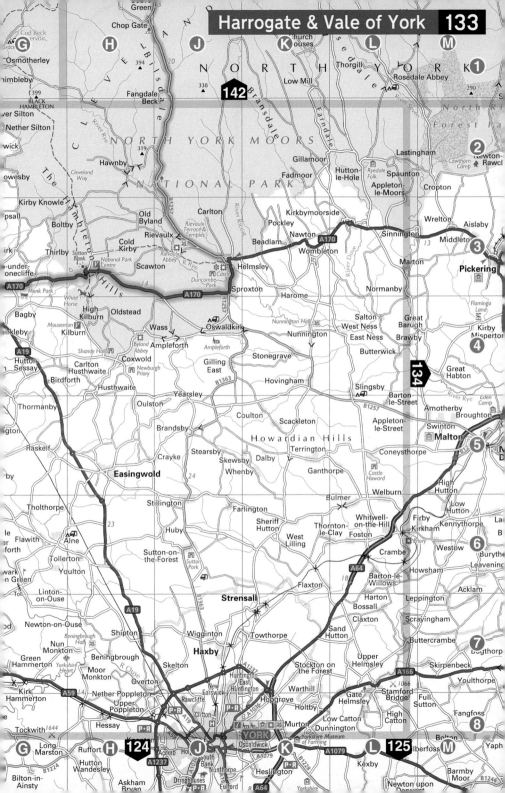

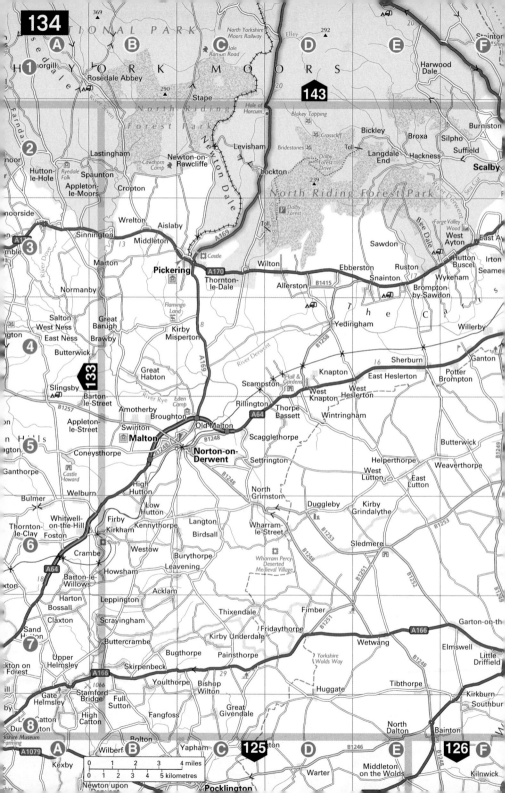

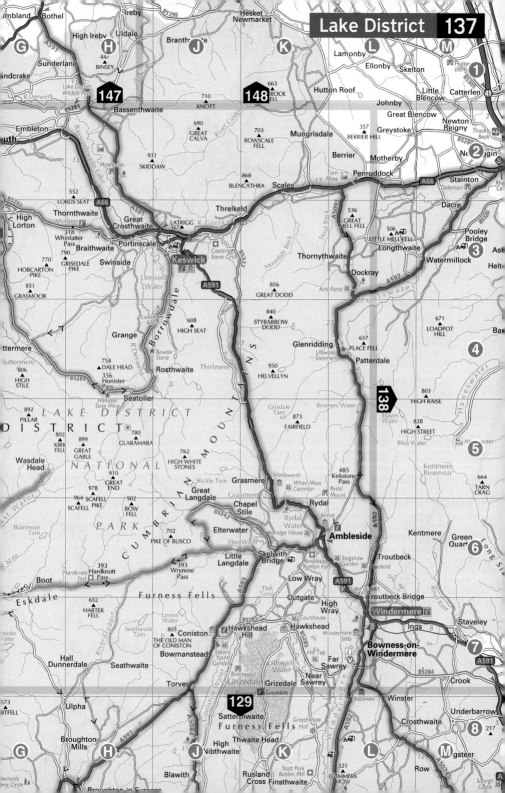

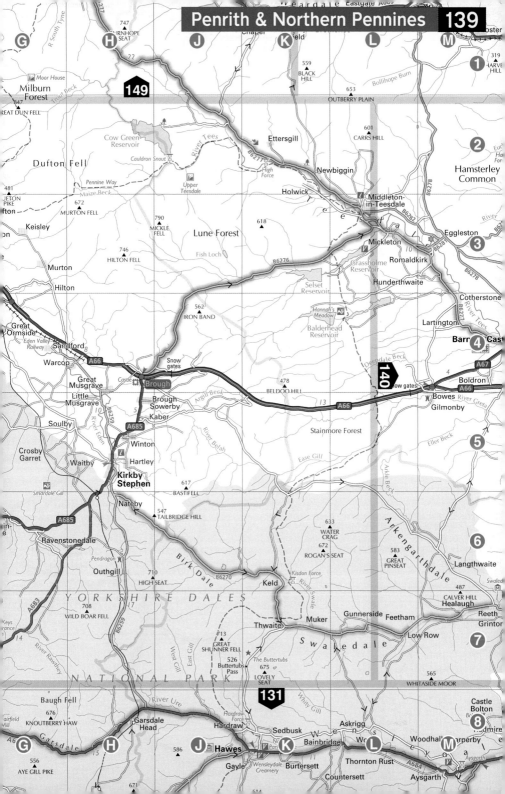

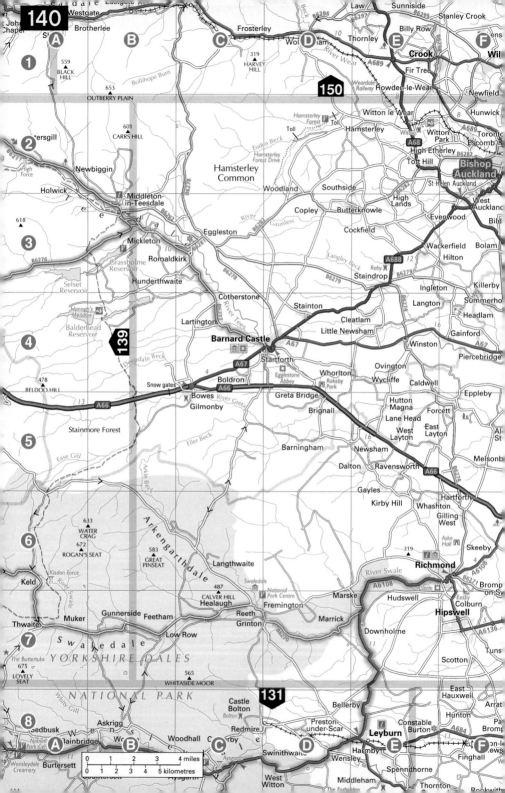

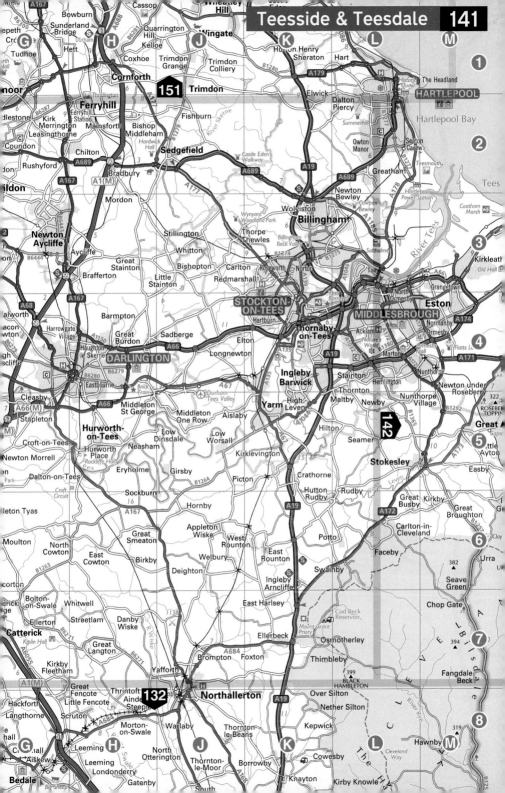

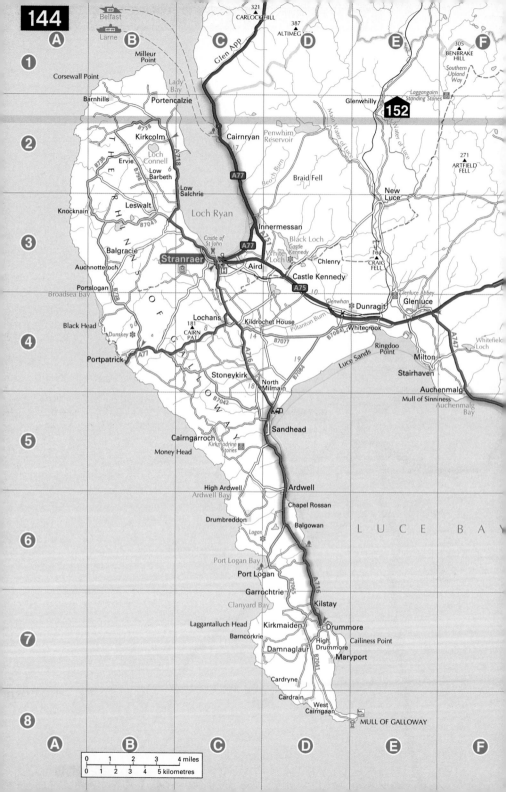

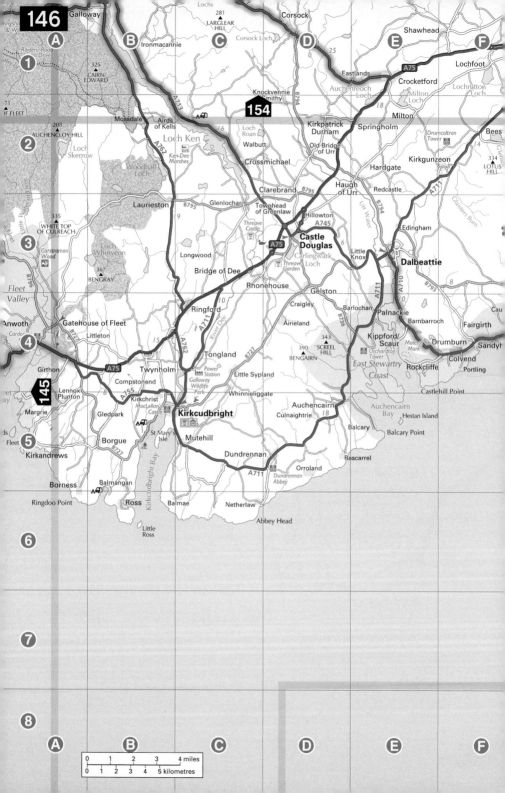

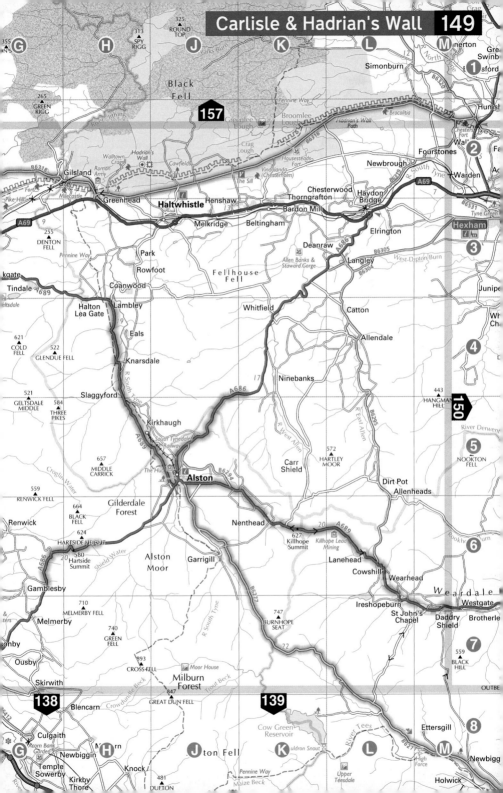

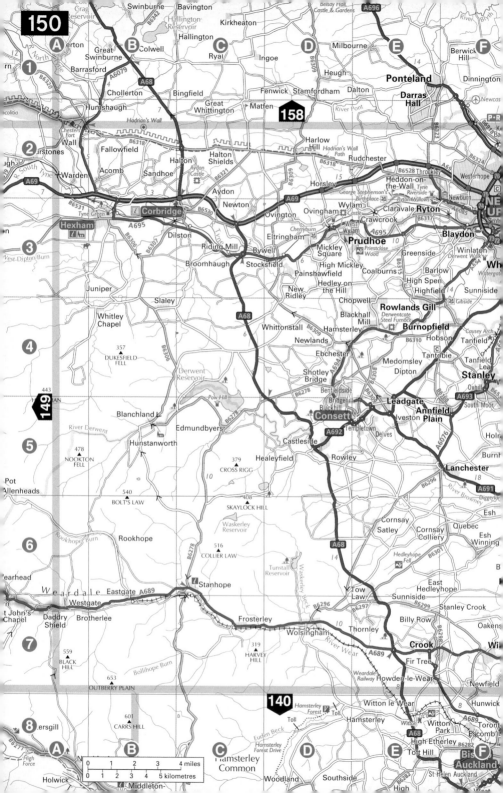

G A77 Grimmet H iltreehill J Ranl B730 K L M gbank Ne umr

Maybole Patna 489 KILMEIN HILL 1

Kirkmichael Loch Spallander Reservoir Waterside Scottish Industrial B741

Threave B045 163 306 KEIRS HILL Burnton 464 BENBEOCH 164 ILL 2 fton Reservoir

Crosshill Straiton B741 A713 High Pennyvenie Dalmellington

B741 Ness Glen Mossdale 536 Carsphairn Forest 697 WINDY STANDARD

320 MARATZ HILL 10 Drumjohn Bow Burn 796 CAIRNSMORE OF CARSPHAIRN 3

429 GARLEFFIN FELL Loch Finlas A713 Carsphairn

Linfern Loch Tallaminnock Loch Bradan 523 CRAIGLEE Loch Doon Castle 622 MEAUL The Glenkens Kendoon Loch 4 vehea B729

Dalquhairn River Stinchar Loch Recar 695 MEAUL 154

R R I C K Loch Macaterick Polmaddy Burn 9

Balloch 549 POLMADDIE HILL 768 SHALLOCH ON MINNOCH 813 CORSERINE 5

Knockeen Galloway 781 KIRRIEREOCH HILL 716 MILFIRE Loch Dungeon 2

Loch Moan 842 MERRICK Loch Enoch Knocksheen St J Tow

346 GARWALL HILL Forest Park Loch Neldricken Silver Flowe Garroch

Glen Trool Lodge Bruce Memorial Loch Dee 380 BENNAN A762 6

Glentrool Loch Trool Bruce's Stone New Galloway

Creebank Bargrennan Glentrool 716 LAMACHAN HILL Clatteringshaws Loch Clatteringshaws Forest & Wildlife Centre Raiders Road Forest Drive 325 CAIRN EDWAR

nlamford Loch Dornal 675 LARG HILL 654 MILLFORE 19 402 ROUND FELL 7

Loch Ochiltree Knowe 440 GARLICK HILL Galloway Deer Range Murray's 471 FELL OF FLEET Loch Fleet

A714 22 A712 Black Water of Dee

G A L L O W A Y 145 Loch Enoch 208 AUCHENCLOY HILL Loch Skerrow 8

Carseriggan Wood of Cree 710 CAIRNSMORE OF FLEET

Barfad Challoch Minnigaff Big Water Cairnsmore of Fleet

Newton Stewart B7079 Kirroughtree L 335 WHITE TOP OF CULREACH

Shennanton G H J K M A714 Palnure A75 15

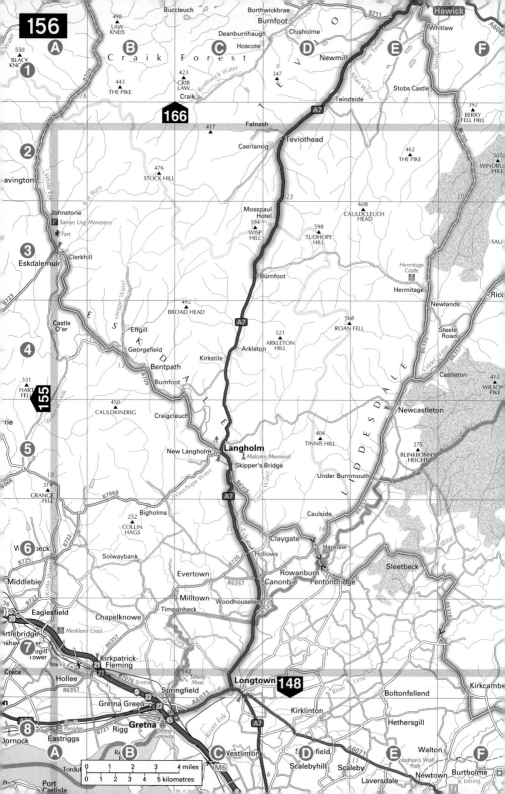

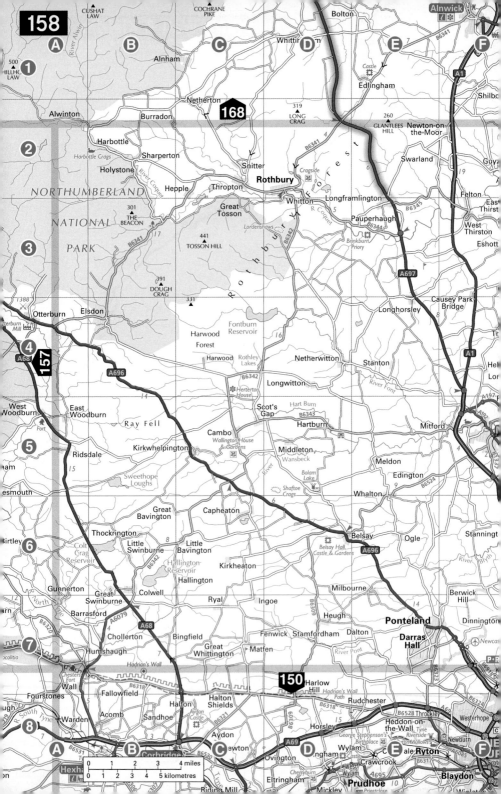

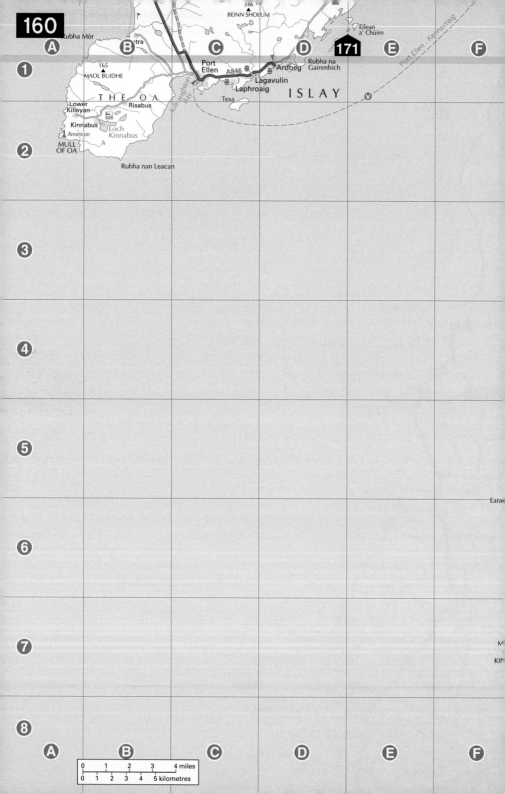

171

Rubha Mòr

A

B

ntra

C

Port
Ellen

A846

D

Ardbeg

Rubha na
Gainmhich

E

Eilean
a' Chùirn

Port Ellen – Kennacraig

F

1

165
MAOL BUIDHE

346
BEINN SHOLUM

3   Lagavulin
Laphroaig

Texa

ISLAY

T H E   O A

Lower
Killeyan

Risabus

Kilnaughton
Bay

2

Kinnabus

American

Loch
Kinnabus

MULL
OF OA

Rubha nan Leacan

3

4

5

Earad

6

7

M

KIN

8

A

B

C

D

E

F

0   1   2   3   4 miles
0 1 2 3 4   5 kilometres

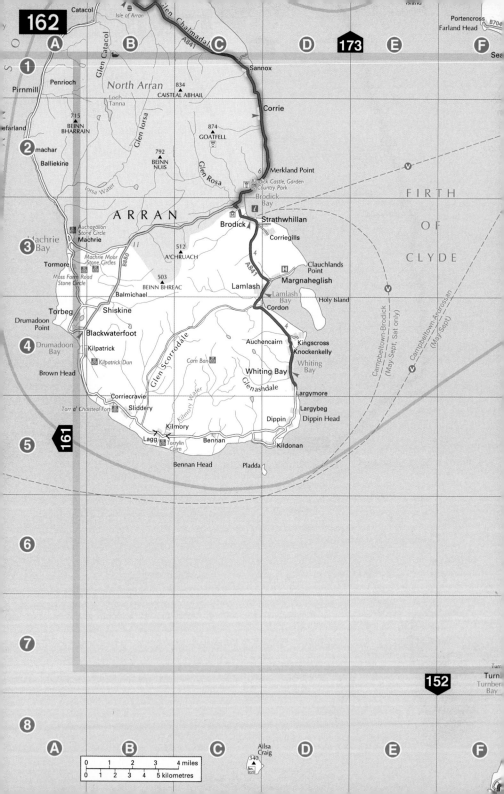

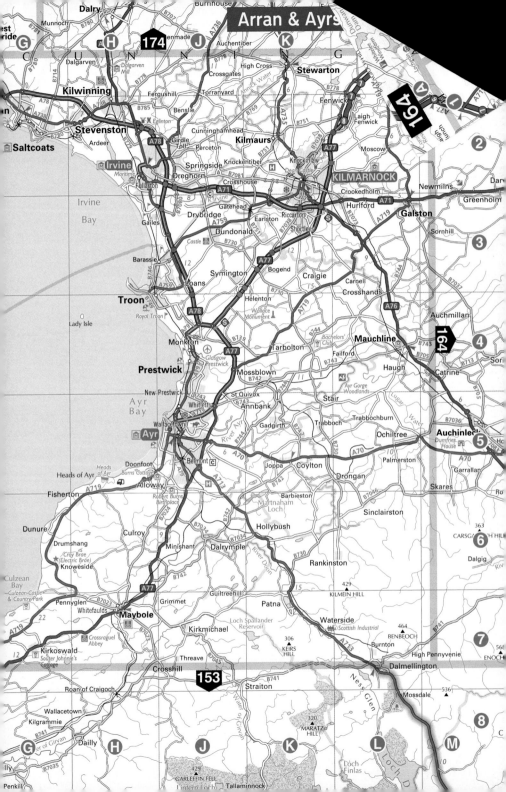

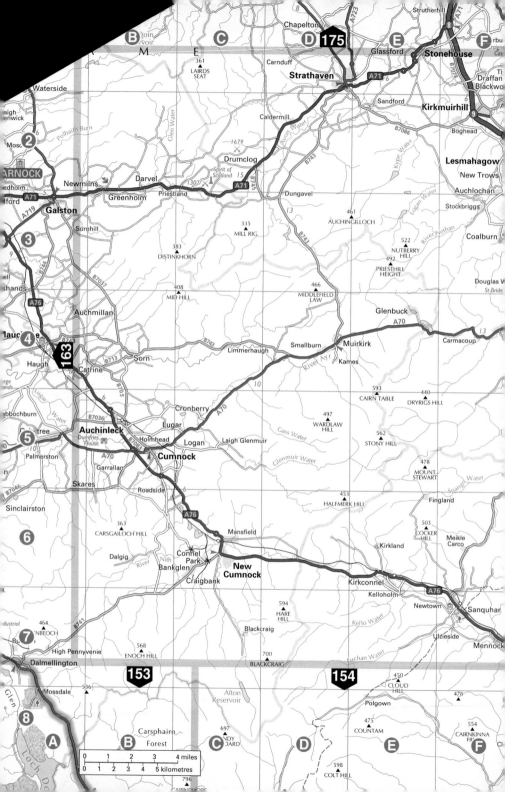

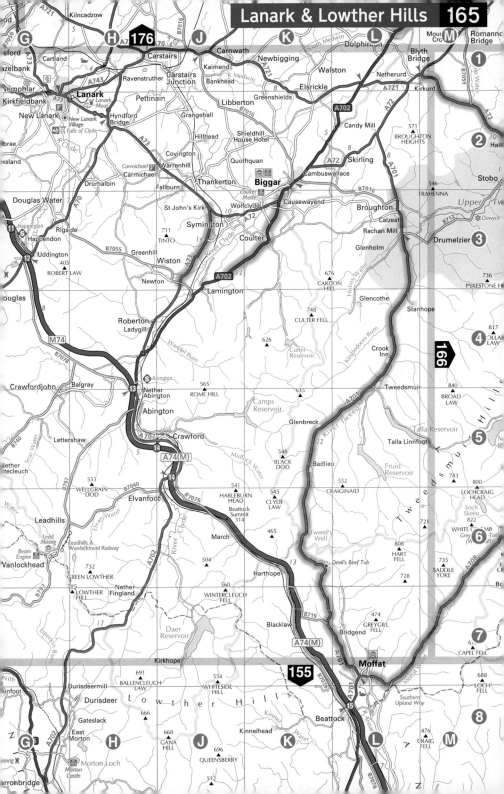

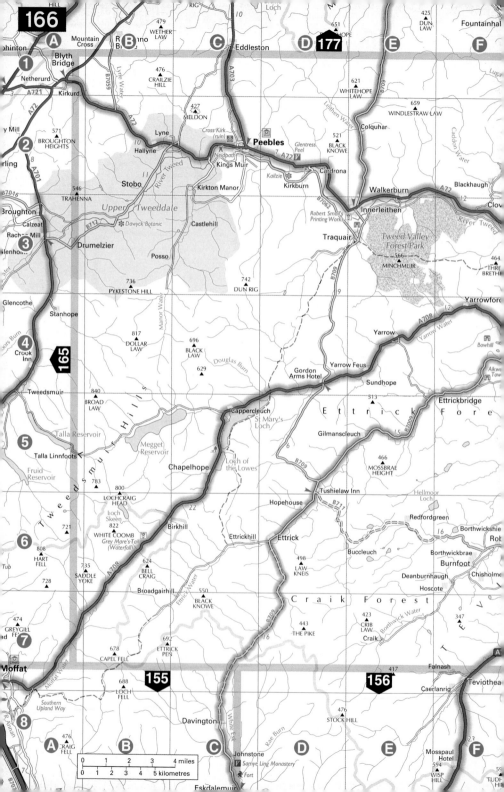

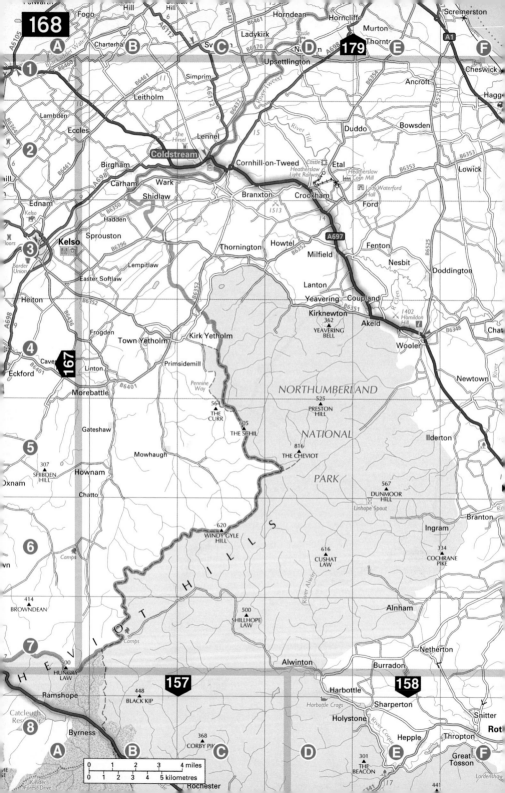

G H J K L M

1
2
3
4
5
6
7
8

Causeway flooded at high tide

HOLY ISLAND

Holy Island

Lindisfarne Priory

Lindisfarne Castle

Castle Point

Guile Point

Longstone

FARNE ISLANDS

Staple Sound

Inner Sound

North Northumberland Heritage Coast

Budle Bay

Bamburgh

B1342

B1340

Belford

B6349

B6348

Seahouses

Lucker

North Sunderland

Warenford

Beadnell

Swinhoe

Chathill

Tughall

Beadnell Bay

A1

Newstead

Ellingham

Preston

Pele Tower

Newton-by-the-Sea

Embleton & Newton Links

Christon Bank

Embleton

Embleton Bay

Ros Castle

267 CATERAN HILL

North Charlton

Fallodon

Dunstanburgh Castle

South Charlton

B6347

Dunstan

Craster

Eglingham

Rock

Rennington

Stamford

Howick Hall

Howick

B1340

B6341

B6346

B1339

Cullernose Point

Longhoughton

Denwick

River Aln

Boulmer

Bolton

Alnwick

Aln Valley Railway

Lesbury

Séaton Point

B6341

B6346

Alnmouth

Alnmouth Bay

Castle

Edlingham

A1

Shilbottle

A1068

260 GLANTLEES HILL

Newton-on-the-Moor

Warkworth Castle & Hermitage

Warkworth

Amble **159**

Coquet Island

Swarland

B63

Guyzance

Gloster Hill

High Hauxley

cramlington

Pauperhaugh

B6344

Brinkburn

Acklington

Togston

Broomhill

Felton

East Thirston

West Thirston

South Broomhill

Red Row

Druridge Bay

G H J K L M

Dub

Nave Island

Ardnave
Point

Tòn Mhòr

Kilnave

Sanaigmore

Eilean Mòr

Loch Gruinart

Rubha Lamanais

Loch
Gorr

Lecht Gruinart

B8017

Saligo Bay

Gruinart

Gleann Mòr

Loch
Gorm

B8018

Kilchoman

Sunderland

B8018

A847

Coul Point

Machir
Bay

Bruichladdich

Loch
Indaal

Bowmore

I   S   L   A   Y

Kilchiaran Bay

1.5
M

**Port
Charlotte**

231
▲
BEINN TART A'MHILL

Lossit Bay

R

H
I
N
N
S

Nerabus

Laggan
Point

Duich R

O
F

Rubha na
Faing

A847

L a g g a n

Portnahaven

Orsay

Port Wemyss

B a y

RHINNS
POINT

Rubha Mòr

K

165
▲
MAOL BU

0   1   2   3   4 miles
0 1 2 3 4 5 kilometres

Lower

T H E

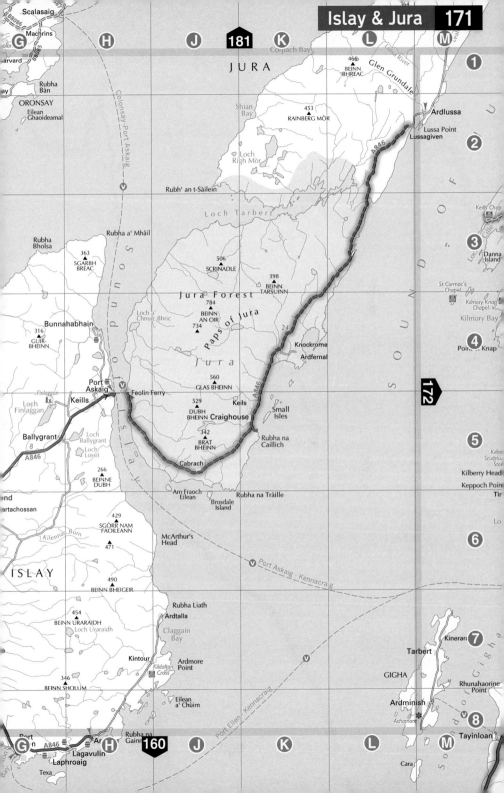

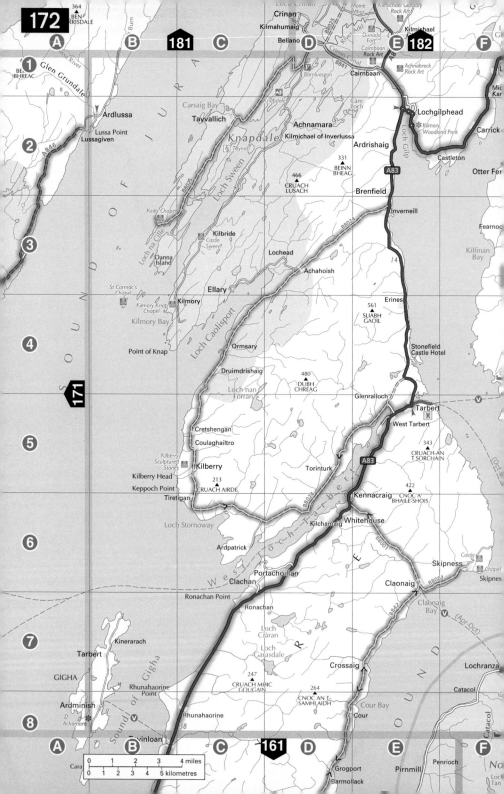

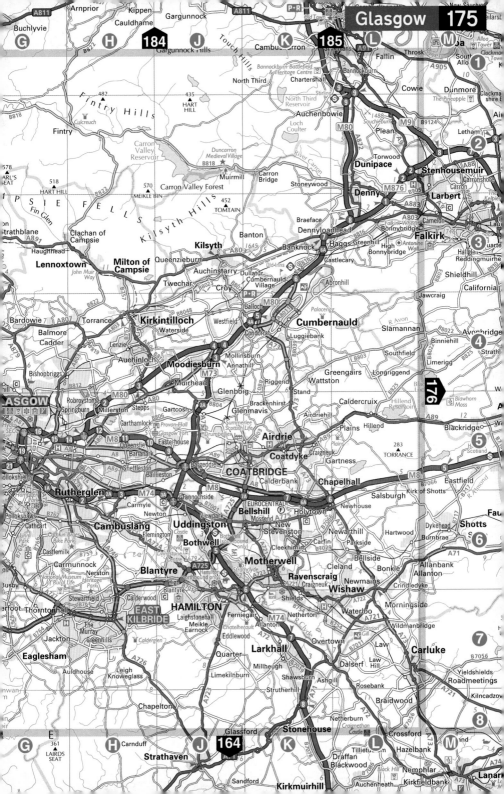

ULVA

Bac Mòr or Dutchman's Cap

1

Staffa   Little Colonsay   Inch Kenneth
Inchkenneth Chapel (ruin)

Fingal's

Loch na Keal
Isle of Mull

2

491
CREACH BHEINN

Fossil Tree

Burg

3

IONA

Iona Abbey & Nunnery

Baile Mòr

MacLean's Cross

Fionnphort

Sound of Iona

St Columba Exhibition Centre

Rubha nan Cearc

Kintra

Aridhglas

Loch na Lathaich

Bunessan

A849

Loch Assapol

LOC

CRU

ROSS OF MULL

4

Soa Island

Erraid

Ardchiavaig

Uisken

Rubh' Ardalanish

Rub
Brà

5

Torran Rocks

6

7

Eilean Dubh

Rubh

Kiloran Bay

143
CARNAN EOIN

COLONSAY

Kiloran

Kilchattan

Scalasaig

B8086

B8085

Machrins

Colonsay

8

Gar

Oronsay

Rubha Bàn

Dubh Eilean

0   1   2   3   4 miles
0   1   2   3   4   5 kilometres

ISLE

OF

MULL

G **H** **190** **J** **K** **L** **M**

1

2

3

4

182

5

6

7

8

Scallastle Bay
Rubha an
Ridire
Kilch

Macquarie
Mausoleum

BEINN
NAN LUS

Forsa

BEINN
MHEADHON

Craignure

Eorsa

BEINN A'CHAISIG

DUN DA
GHAOITHE
766

Duart
Bay
Torosay

Duart
Duart
Point

Lochdonhead
Lochdon

Gorsten

966
BEN
MORE

704
CRUACHAN
DEARG

A849

17

Loch Don

Grass Point

Strathcoil

A849

Glen More

698
BEN CREACH

247
CARN
BAN

KERRE

Aird of
Kinloch

Pennycross

Pennyghael

717
BEN
BUIE

Croggan

Loch
Fuaran

503
BEINN NA
CROISE

Lochbuie

Loch
Uisg

Rubha Seanach

Lussa Water

Carsaig

376
BEINN
CHREAGACH

Rubha
Dubh

Loch Buie

377
DRUIM
FADA

337
MAOL
BAN

Malcolm's
Point

FIRTH

OF

LORNE

Insh
Island

Clachan

Clachan-Seil

SEIL

Ellenabeich
Seafari

Easdale

Balvicar

B844

Easdale

Ardmaddy

Colonsay–Oban

Cuan

Seil Sound

Garbh Eileach

Cullipool

Torsa

Degnish

Loch Melfc

Eilean
Dubh Mór

GARVELLACHS
Monastery &
Beehive Cells

LUING

Toberonochy

Arduaine
Garden

Arduai

Eileach
an Naoimh

LUNGA

Scarba, Lunga

and the

Garvellachs

Sound of Luing

Shuna Sound

SHUNA

Shuna
Point

Craobh
Haven

Craigd

SCARBA

448
CRUACH SCARBA

Ardf

Ki

En M

En

Gulf of Corryvreckan

Aird

Loch Craignish

Glengarrisdale
Bay

295
CRUACH NA
SEILCHEIG

Craignish Point

Island
Macaskin

Stockave
Woo
rcles

Ti

Ri Cruin
Poltall

Glendebadel Bay

Loch Crinan

Crinan

JURA

364
BEN
GARRISDALE

Lealt Burn

Kilmahumaig

Bellanoch

B8025

Lussa River

Corpach Bay

G **H** **171** **J** **K** **L** **172** **M**

466
BEINN
BHREAC

Glen Grundale

Barnluasgan

Carsaig Bay

Knapdale

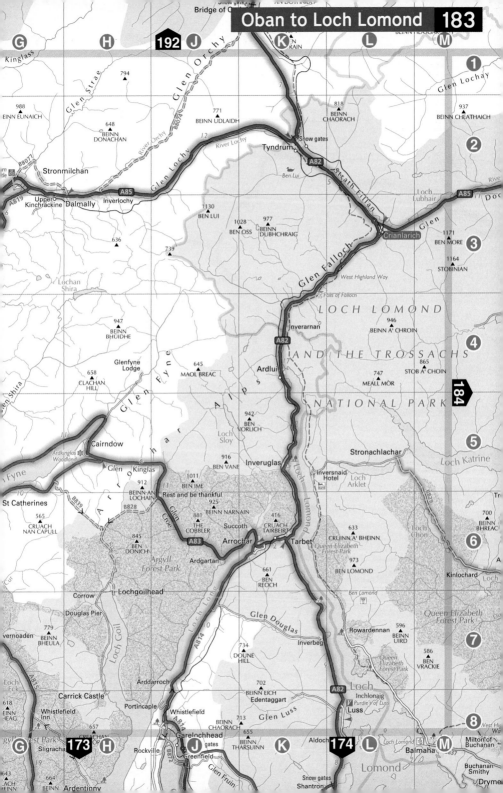

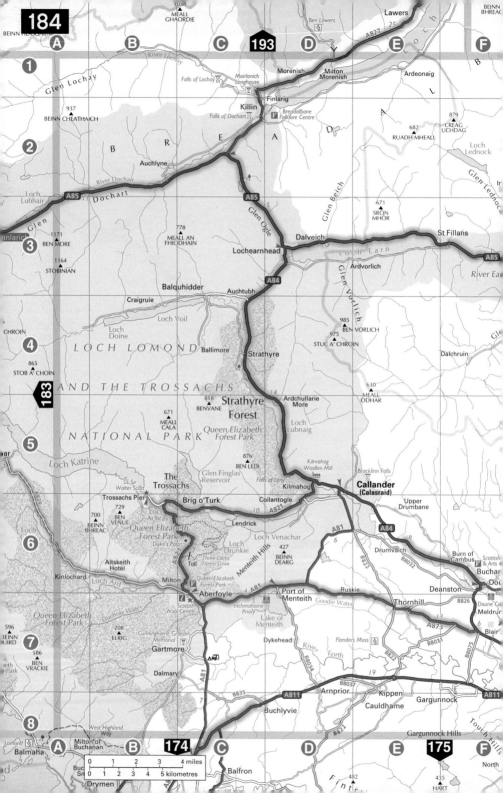

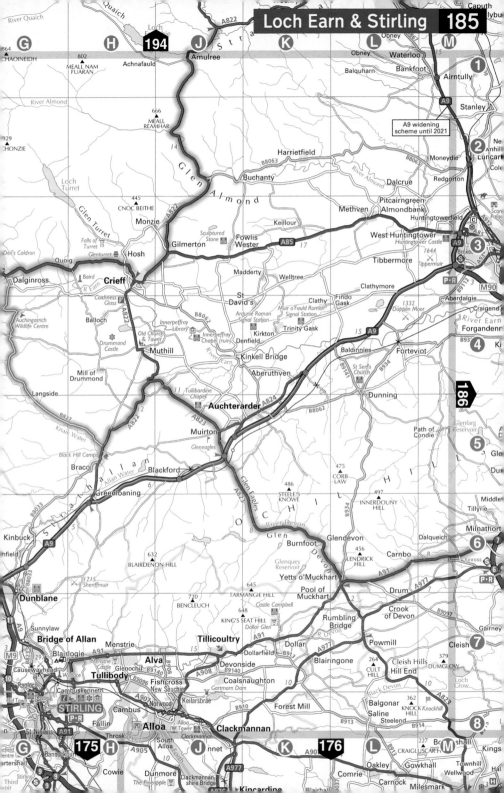

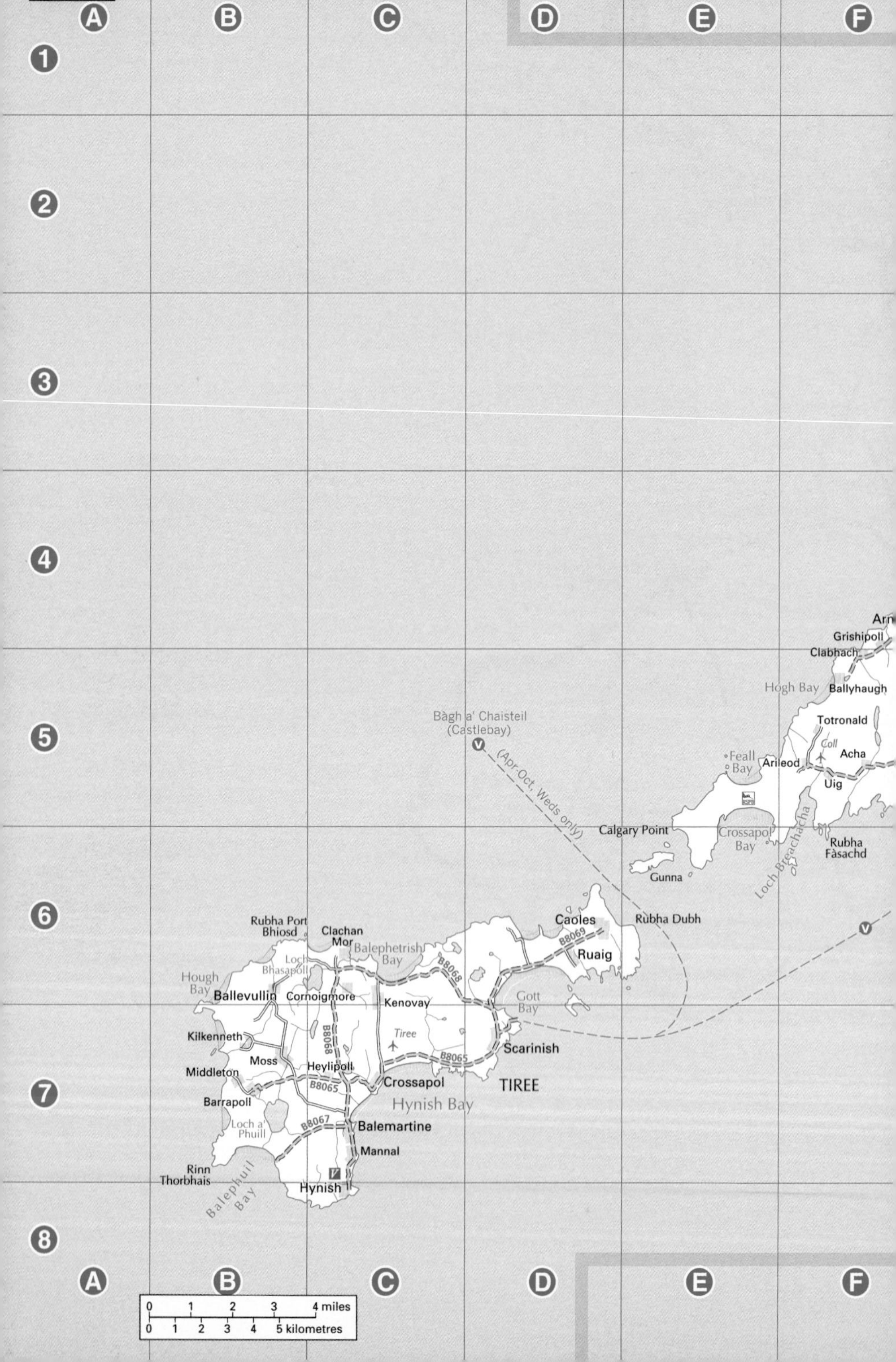

A   B   C   D   E   F

1

2

3

4

Arn
Grishipoll
Clabhach
Hogh Bay   Ballyhaugh
Totronald
Coll
Bàgh a' Chaisteil
(Castlebay)   Acha
Feall   Arileod
Bay
Uig
(Apr-Oct, Weds only)
Calgary Point   Crossapol   Rubha
Bay   Fàsachd

Gunna

6
Rubha Port   Caoles   Rùbha Dubh
Bhiosd   Clachan   B8069
Mor   Balephetrish   Ruaig
Loch   Bay
Hough   Bhasapoll   B8068
Bay   Ballevullin   Cornoigmore   Kenovay
Gott
Bay
Kilkenneth   *Tiree*
B8068   Scarinish
7   Moss   Heylipoll
Middleton   B8065
B8065   Crossapol   **TIREE**
Barrapoll
Loch a'   B8067   Balemartine
Phuill
Mannal
Rinn
Thorbhais   Hynish Bay
Balephuill   Hynish
Bay

8

A   B   C   D   E   F

0   1   2   3   4 miles
0 1 2 3 4 5 kilometres

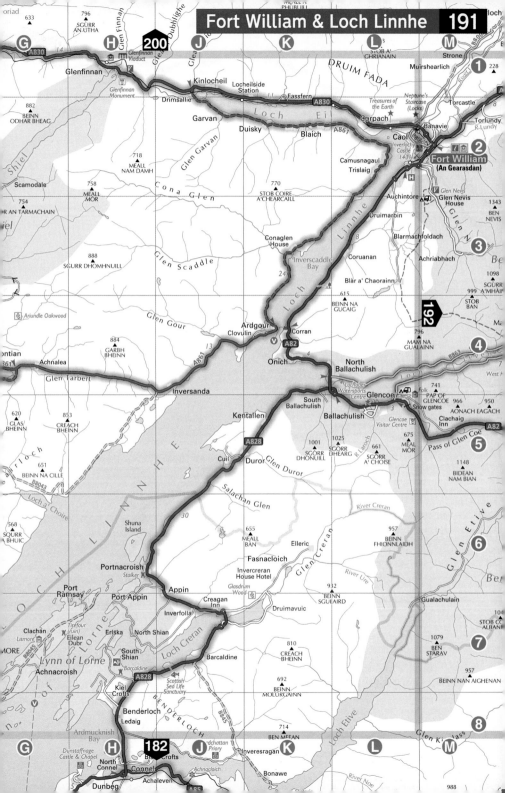

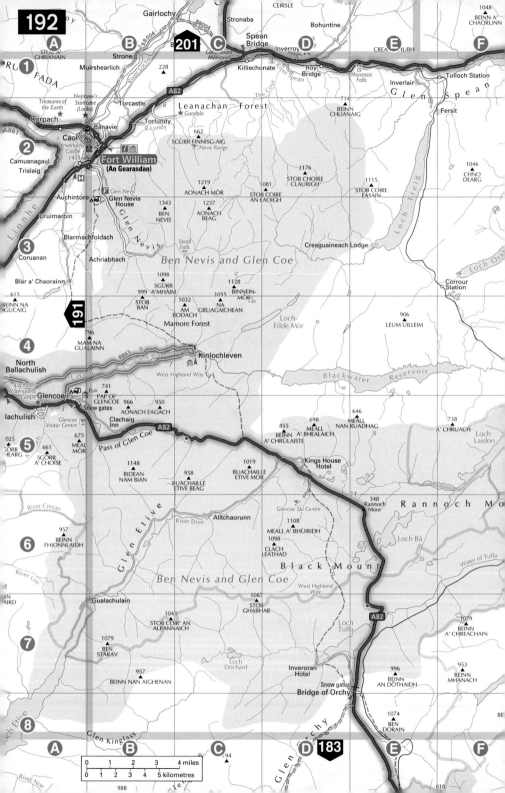

G 202 H J K L M

86

1

Snow gates

747
BINNEIN
SHUAS

1049
GEAL
CHÀRN

896
MEALL
CRUAIDH

769
CREAGAN
MÒR

94
CÀRN NA CAIM

Loch an Du

River Pa

Loch
Pattack

926
GLAS
MHEALL MÒR

Loch an Du

1

1088
BEINN
A' CHLACHAIR

1034
CÀRN
DEARG

975
A' MHARCONAICH

459
Drumochter
Summit

2

Loch Ericht

1101
BEINN
EIBHINN

1008
BEINN
UDLAMAIN

991
SGAIRNEACH
MHÒR

Dalnaspidal

1145
BEN
ALDER

Loch Garry

20

Snow gates
Dalnacardoch

3

844
MEALL A'BHEALAICH

Glen Garry

952
SGÒR
GAIBHRE

Loch
Con

Loch
Erroehty

Trinafour

B847

511
TORR
DUBH

R. Ericht

626
SRON A
CHLAONAIDH

841
BEINN
MHOLACH

Glen   rr

Tay Fo

4

BEINN PHARIAGAIN

864

892
BEINN
A' CHUALLAICH

194

Tay
Forest Park

7

B846

R Tummel

nnoch
ation

Dunan

B846

Finnart

Bridge
of Ericht

Killichonan

16

Loch Rannoch

Kinloch
Rannoch

Drumchastle

Dunalastair

Dunalastair
Water

Tummel
Bridge

Loch
Eigheach

Bridge
of Gaur

Inverhadden

Tempar

Camghouran

Carie

Tay Forest Park

1081
SCHIEHALLION

5

7

Glengoulandie
Deer Park

Loch Rannoch and Glen Lyon

745
MEALL A' MHUIC

1042
CÀRN
MAIRG

B846

4

931
MEALL
BUIDHE

860
CAM CHREAG

824
BEINN
DEARG

1027
CÀRN
GORM

Cos
Ke.

6

Loch an
Daimh

Fortingall
Yew ★

Fortingall

Tay
Forest
Park

Glen Lyon

Bridge of Balgie

River Lyon

Kenmore

780
MEALL
LUAIDHE

924
MEALL A' CHOIRE
LEITH

1116
MEALL
GARBH

1000
MEALL
GREIGH

Fearnan

The Scottish
Crannog Centre

aharn

7

Pubil

908
BEINN NAN OIGHREAG

1214
BEN LAWERS

Lochan na
Làirige

Leckbuie

713
BEINN
BHREAC

Loch Tay

1038
MEALL
GHAORDIE

Ben Lawers

Lawers

A827

25

8

86
SRON A' CH

River Lochay

Milton
Morenish

184

renish

Ardeo g

G H J K L M

en Lochay

Falls of Lochay

Mo   longhouse

Finlarig

Killin

937

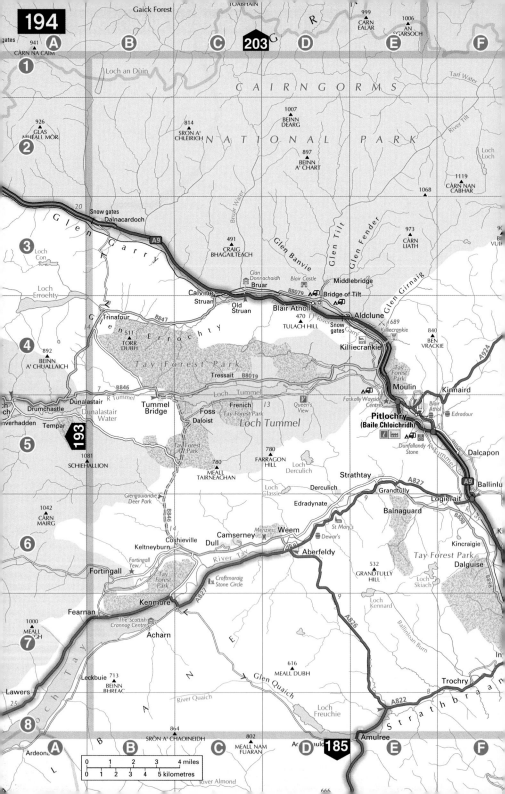

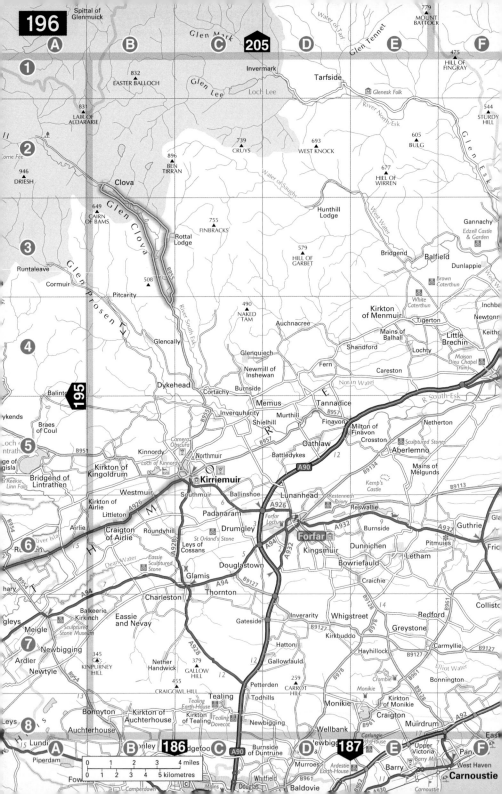

G | H | 206 | J | K | L | M

Goosecruives
Tanna
v Mill
Temple
of Fiddes
465
GOYLE
HILL
Drumlithie
10
Fowlsheugh
454
Cairn
O'Mount
Glenbervie
414 Auchenblae
Mondynes
Crawton
FINELLA
HILL
Catterline
Snow gates
Kinneff
Todhead Point
B966
Fordoun
Grassic Gibbon
Centre
A92
Pittarrow
Redmyre Arbuthnott
cairn
Mains of
Haulkerton
Inverbervie
Bervie
Bay
B9120
25
Laurencekirk
Gourdon
ogmuir
B9120
B974
Redford
Sauchieburn
ds
thermuir
Dykelands
Benholm
A90
B971
North
Marykirk
Johnshaven
Logie
Pert
Craigo
Lochside
Bush
Milton Ness
Logie
St Cyrus
Morphie
Hillside
A92
House of
Dun
Dun
Montrose Air Station
9 A935
onian
ay
ns of
aird
Montrose
Montrose
Basin
Scurdie Ness
Barnhead
Maryton
Ferryden
A934
Craig
Usan
Westerton
of Rossie
Boddin Point
DY
Braehead
Lunan
e
Lunan Bay
ack
Inverkeilor
n Water
13
hapelton
Cauldcots
Red Head
n
e
A92
Marywell
igeans
Auchmithie
Carlingheugh
Bay
The Deil's
Head
Arbroath

G | H | J | K | L | M

1 2 3 4 5 6 7 8

208

Taisker
Bay
Glen Eynort
Minginish
147
BEINN
BHREAC
Gr
Glen
Brittle
Brittle
Forest

Loch Eynort

434
AN CRUACHIN
Glenbrittle
Bualintur

Loch Brittle

Rubha an Dùnain

Ci

V
Loch Baghasdail
(Lochboisdale)

C U

210
CANNA CÀRN A' GHAILL
Garrisdale Point   A'Chill
Canna
Harbour
Kilmory
Bay
Rubha
Shamhnan
Insir

Sanday

Sound of Canna

302
MULLACH
MÒR

A' Bhrìdeanach

570
ORVAL

Kinloch

Oigh-sgeir

RÙM

810
ASKIVAL

Harris
Bay

763
SGÙRR NAN
GILLEAN

The Small Isles

Rubha nam
Meirleach

Sound

Eilean
nan Each

MU

189

Port M

0   1   2   3   4 miles
0 1 2 3 4 5 kilometres

Sligachan
GLAMAIG
ISLE
OF
SKYE
The Cuillin Hills
illin Hills
Loch Coruisk
SGURR SDAIR
GARS BHEINN 894
Mol-chlach
SOAY
h' hais
SOUND

Ard Dorch
396 MULLA NA CA
A87
Luib
Loch Ainort
17
Dunan
Strollamus
J 209
Scalpay
564
GLAS BHEIN MHOR

Corry
H
Broadford Bay
Lower Breakish
Waterloo
Broadford
732 BEINN NA CAILLICH
708 BEINN DEORG MHOR
B8083
Harrapool
Skulamus
Breakish
732 SGURR NA COINNICH
Otter Hide
605 BEN ASLAK

A87
Kyleakin
Bright Water
(Caol Loch A
Skye Bridge
Pabay
27
(Kyle of Loch
M
1
Kyl ea
2
Loch na Dal
Eila

927 BLAVEN
Torrin
Loch na Crèitheach
14
Kirkibost
B8083
Loch Slapin
300 BEINN NAN CARN
Heaste
Drumfearn
561 BEINN NA SEAMRAIG
Sandaig Islands
3
Rubha Buidhe

344 BEN MEABOST
Elgol
Glasnakille
Loch Scavaig
Suisnish
Rubha Suisnish
Loch Eishort
298 SGORACH BREAC
Ord River
Duisdalemore
Isleornsay
Ornsay
Rubha Àrd Slisneach
Invergus
4

Strathaird Point
Tokavaig
Tarskavaig
Achnacloich
Loch nam Uamph
Teangue
Knock
Knock Bay
SOUND OF SLEAT
Airor
200
518 DRUIM NA CLUAIN-AIRIDHE
5
erie

139 BEINN BHREAC
Loch Scavaig

Tarskavaig Bay
Ferrindonald
Kilmore
Kilbeg
Armadale Castle
Ardvasar
Calligarry
Armadale
Sandaig
Sandaig Bay
Rubha Raonuill
Inverie Bay
6

Aird of Sleat
Ard Thurinish
Point of Sleat
V

Courteachan
Mallaig (Malaig)
Glasnacardoch Bay
Mallaigvaig
547 CÀRN A'GHOBHAIR
Loch an Nostaire
437 SGURR BHUIDHE
Loch Ne

vehicles must have e relevant island rmit prior to travel The Small Isles. vices are seasonal, weather dependent.

B8008
Beoraidbeg
Morar
Bracorina
Bracora
Tarbet
Swordland
Loch Mo

Bay of Laig
Cleadale
299 AN CRUACHAN
Kildonnan
EIGG
393 AN SGURR
Galmisdale
Eilean Chathastail

Eilean Ighe
Back of Keppoch
Luinga Mhòr
Arisaig
Rubh' Arisaig
Glenancross
Bunacaimb
A830
503 CÀRN A' MHADAIDH-RUAIDH
Lettermorar
Loch nan Ceall
600 SIDHEAN MOR
Loch Mo
7

103 CRUACH DOIRE
Druimindarroch
Arisaig House
Prince Charlie's Cairn
Kinlochnanuagh
Polnish
Loch nan Uamh
Lochailort
Inverailort
8

Rubha Choalais

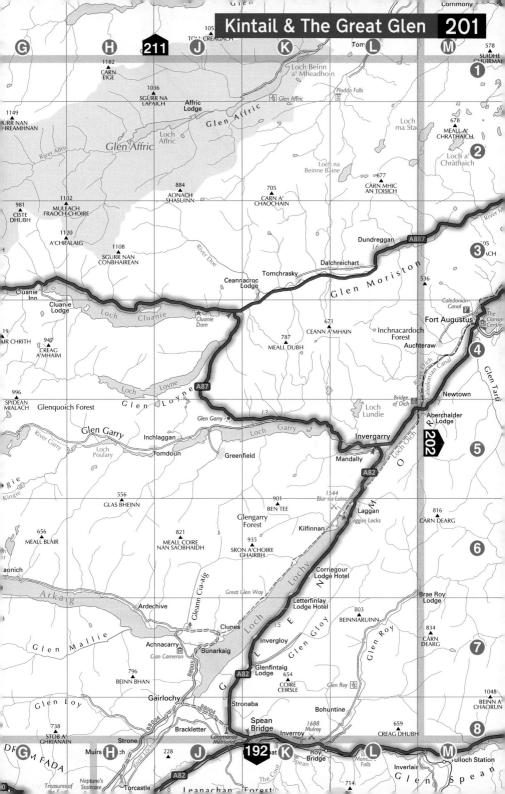

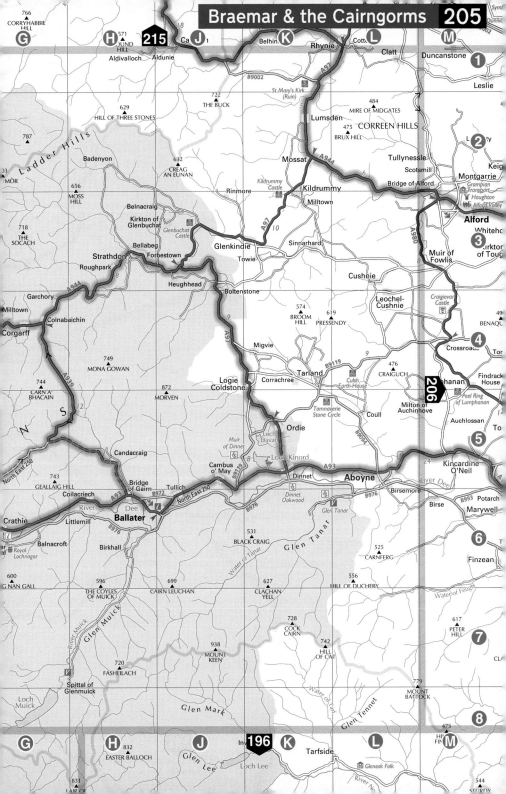

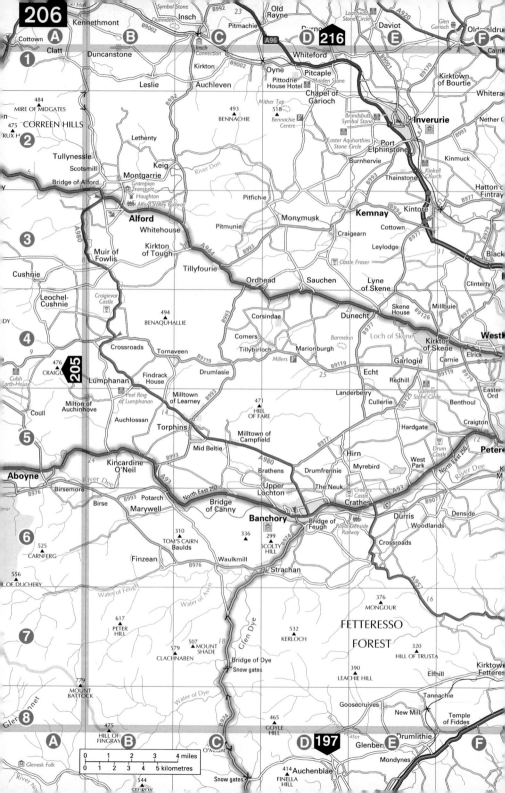

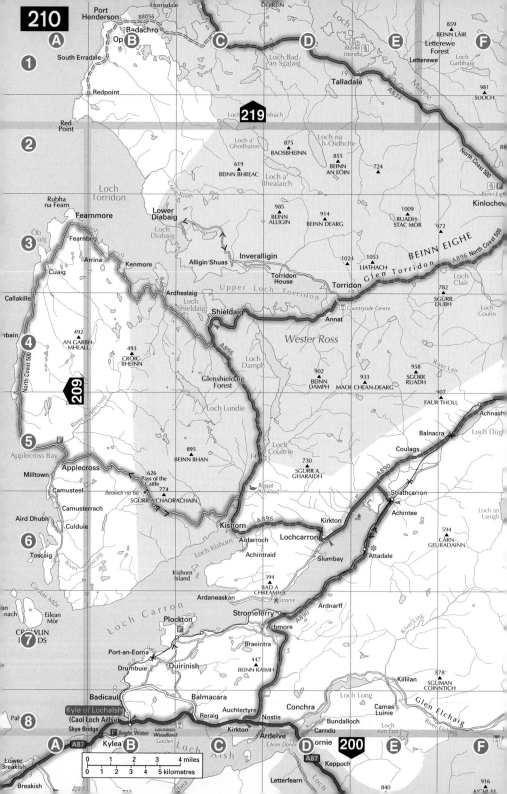

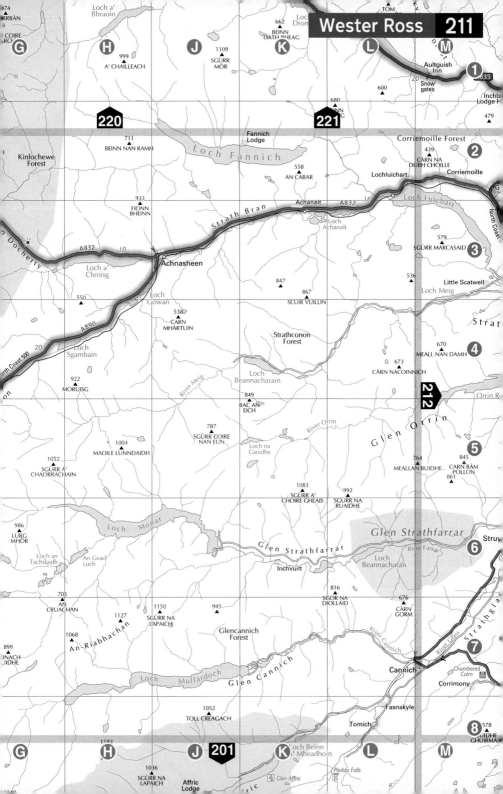

G
H
J
K
L
M

Loch a' Bhraoin
COIRE RCH
RBAN
74

TOM

662 BEINN LIATH BHEAG
Loch Dron

Aultguish Inn
835
1
Snow gates
600
20
Inchb Lodge F

999 A' CHAILLEACH
1109 SGÙRR MÒR
K
L
M

220

221

680 NN G

479

711 BEINN NAN RAMH

Fannich Lodge

Corriemoille Forest
439 CÀRN NA DUBH CHOILLE
2

Kinlochewe Forest

558 AN CABAR

Loch Fannich

Lochluichart
Corriemoille

North Coas

933 FIONN BHEINN

Strath Bran

Achanalt
A832
Loch Luichart
1.6

n Docherty
A832
10
Achnasheen
Loch Achanalt
579 SGÙRR MARCASAID
3

Loch a' Chroisg

847
536
Little Scatwell
Loch Meig

550
Loch Gowan

867 SCUIR VUILLIN

A890
538 CÀRN MHÀRTUIN

Strathconon Forest

Strat

Loch Sgamhain
North Coast 500
20

922 MORUISG

Loch Beannacharain

670 MEALL NAN DAMH
4

673 CÀRN NACOINNICH

River Meig
849 BAC AN EICH

212
Orrin R

787 SGÙRR COIRE NAN EUN

Loch na Caoidhe

River Orrin
Glen Orrin

1004 MAOILE LUNNDAIDH

5

1052 SGÙRR A' CHAORRACHAIN

764 MEALLAN BUIDHE
845 CÀRN BÀN POLLON
861

1083 SGÙRR A' CHOIRE GHLAIS

992 SGÙRR NA RUAIDHE

986 LURG MHÒR

Loch Monar

Glen Strathfarrar

Glen Strathfarrar
Struy

Loch an Tachdaidh
An Geadh Loch

Glen Strathfarrar
River Farrar
6

Inchvuilt
Loch Beannacharan

705 AN CRUACHAN

816 SGOR NA DIOLLAID

676 CÀRN GORM

899 ONACH UIDHE
1068 An-Riabhachan

1127 SGÙRR NA LAPAICH

945

Glencannich Forest

River Cannich

7

1150 SGÙRR NA L'APAICH

Loch Mullardoch
Glen Cannich

Cannich
Chambered Cairn

Corrimony

River Glass

Strathglass

Fasnakyle

1052 TOLL CREAGACH

Tomich

578 UIDHE GHUIRMAI
8

G
H
J
K
L
M

201

1182

1036 SGÙRR NA LAPAICH

Affric Lodge

Loch Beinn ' Mheadhoin

Plodda Falls

Glen Affric

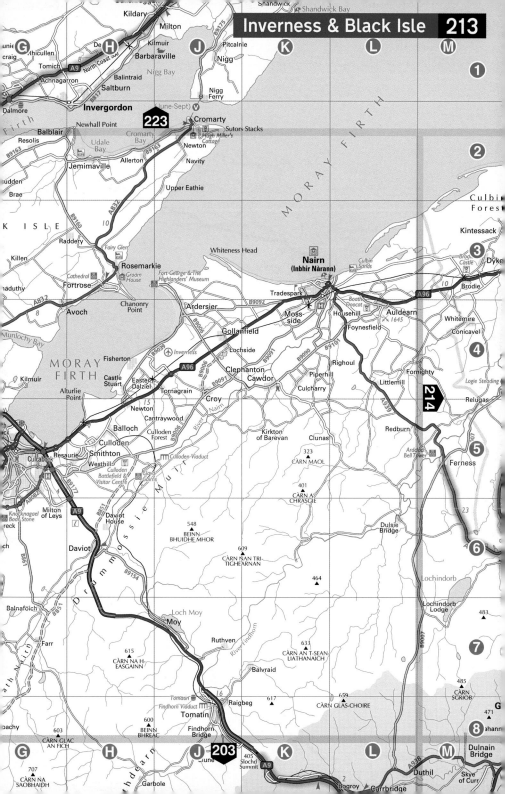

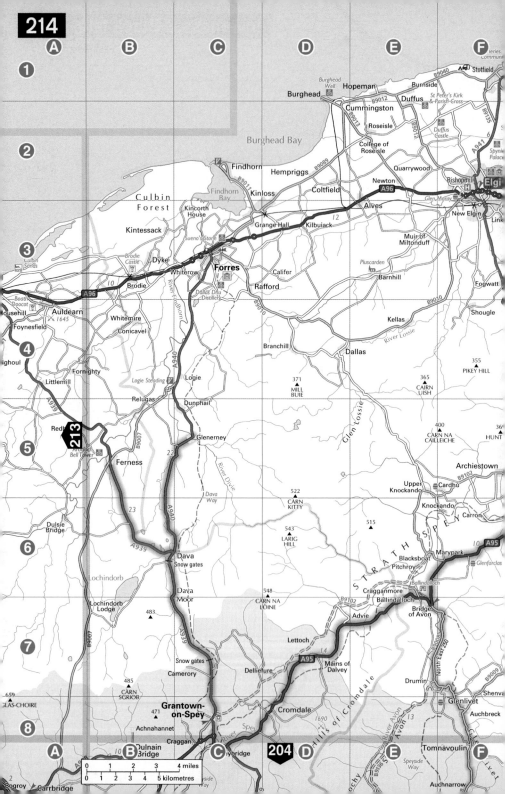

G   H   J   K   L   M

1

2

3

4

5

6

7

8

Rosehearty   Pittulie   Castle, Lighthouse & Museum   Kinnaird Head
Pitsligo   Sandhaven   **Fraserburgh**
Craigiefold   Peathill   Kirktown   Fraserburgh Bay
Aberdour Bay   Percyhorner   Pitblae   Cairnbulg   Inverallochy
Coburty   Mid Ardlaw   Maggie's Hoosie   Whitelinks Bay
New dour   Boyndlie   Memsie   St Combs
Tyrie
North East 250   A98   Rathen
Memsie Cairn   Crofts of Savoch
Newburgh   Lonmay
234 WAUGHTON HILL   Loch of Strathbeg   Rattray Head
ew sligo   Strichen   Crimond
Blackhill
nykelly   New Leeds   North East 250
Leys   Kirktown   St Fergus   Scotstown Head
Denhead   Backfolds
Fetterangus   Rora   A90
Deer Abbey   Dunshillock
Maud   Old Deer   Mintlaw   Longside   Inverugie   Buchanhaven   **Peterhead**
Railway   Aberdeenshire Farming   Peterhead
Blackhill of Clackriach   Stuartfield   Inverquhomery
ew eer   Drymuir   Bulwark   Millbreck   Nether Kinmundy   Hillhead of Cocklaw   Peterhead Bay
Nethermuir   Clola   Invernettie
Knaven   Kinnadie   Blackhill   **Boddam**
Auchnagatt   Stirling   Buchan Ness
Kinknockie   Lendrum Terrace
irnorrie rownhill   Inkhorn   Coldwells   Ardallie   Longhaven
ick   Arthrath   Muirtack   Hatton   A90   Auchiries   Bullers of Buchan   North Haven
han   Toll of Birness   Bogbrae   Slains   Cruden Bay
Ythanbank   Birness   Chapel Hill   Bay of Cruden
Auchedly   North East 250   Whinnyfold   The Skares
Altar Tomb of William Forbes   Artrochie
Kinharrachie   **Ellon**   P·R
Ythsie   Esslemont   Kirkton of Logie Buchan   Kirktown of Slains
Pitmedden   A920   Collieston
Housieside   Logierieve   Forvie
Ud Gre.   G   H   J   **207**   K   L   M
Udny Station   A90
Pettymuk   Foveran   Newburgh
Culterculten

A **B** **C** **D** **E** **F**

1

Loch Shell

2

Loch
Collum

SOUND OF SHIANT

SHIANT
ISLANDS

3

4

5

Fladda-chùain

Eilean Trodday

6

Rubha Hunish

Tairbeart
(Tarbert)

Duntulm   Kilmaluag

A855

Lùb Score

Skye Museum
of Island Life

Flodigarry

Eilean Flodigarry

Borneskitaig

Kilmuir   Heribusta

Kilvaxter   542
MEAL NA   Digg   Staffin Island
Balgown   SUIREAMACH

7

Loch am Madadh
(Lochmaddy)

Linicro

Staffin
Bay

Brogaig

Stenscholl   Staffin

208   209

Totscore   464
BIODA
BUIDHE   Kilt Rock
Ellishader

Trotternish

Idrigill   River Rha   Maligar

Marishader   Valtos

8   611   Garros   Rubha nam Brathairean
BEINN   Culnaknock
Uig Bay   Uig   Fairy
(Uige)   Glen   River Conon

Earl...   Le...   Tote

Loch S...ort   **A**   **B**   **C**   **D**   **E**   **F**

0   1   2   3   4 miles
0   1   2   3   4   5 kilometres

608
Peinlich   A855

G H J K L M

Badentarbat Bay

1

Tanera Beg

Tanera Mòr

Steornabhagh (Stornoway)

Hors Island

Glas-leac Beag

Eilean Dubh

2

Priest Island

Cailleach Head

Le

Scoraig

Greenstone Point

Rubha Beag

Stattic Point

Badluarach **3**

Littl

Rubha Rèidh

Foura

Rubha nan Sasan

Mellon Udrigle

GRUINARD ISLAND

A832

Badca

Cove

Mellon Charles

Ormiscaig

Laide

Gruinard Bay

Aultbea

Gruinard

296 AN CUAIDH

Loch a' Bhaid luachraich

Gruinard River

4

Melvaig

ISLE OF EWE

347 CREAG-MHEAL BEAG

Aultgrishin

Loch Ewe

Inverasdale

293 CNOC BREAC

Naast

Loch Fada

220

Fionn

681 BEINN A' CHAISGEIN BEAG

Wester Ross

5

field Fo

North Erradale

B8021

Inverewe Garden

13

Londubh

250 MEALL NA MEINE

Poolewe

Big Sand

Longa Island

Strath

A832

Heritage

Smithstown

Lonemore

Auchtercairn

Gairloch

Gairloch & Loch Ewe

Charlestown

421 MEALL AN DOIREIN

791 BEINN AIRIDH CHARR

Dubh Loch

6

Loch Gairloch

Loch

859 BEINN LÀIR

Port Henderson

Eilean Horrisdale

B8056

Badachro

Opinan

Maree Islands

Letterewe Forest

Letterewe

Loch Garbhaig

South Erradale

Loch Bad an Sgalaig

19

981 SLIOCH

7

Redpoint

Loch Ghaineamhach

Talladale

A832

Maree

Red Point

North Coast 500

8

210

Craig River

875 BAOSBHEINN

Loch na h-Oidhche

855 BEINN AN EOIN

724

619 BEINN BHREAC

Loch a' Bhealaich

Beinn E

Kinloche

Rubha na Fearn

Fearnn

Lower Diabaig

B. ALLIGIN

914 BEINN DEARG

1009 RUADH-STAC MÒR

972

Loch Torridon

G H J K L M

Òb Chuaig

Fearnbeg

Loch Diabaig

Inveralligin

1024 1053

BEINN EIGHE

A896 North Coast 500

G   H   J   K   L   M

1

Loch Urigill

307
CN GLAS MHEALL ▲ H

364
AN STICHD ▲ J

BEINN AN ▲ K

L   M

Cola

402
CNOC A' CHOIRE ▲

romalt Hills G

Rappach

Loch a' Chroisg

Loch na Claise Mòire

225

River Oykel

A 839

Rosehall
A 837

27

2

08
MANNAN ▲

Oykel Bridge

Doune

Strath Oykel

31

Altass

Linsiden

en Achall

Loch an Daimh

Strath Mulzie

Rappach Water

Glen Einig

493
BEINN ULBHAIDH ▲

412
CREAG LOISGTE ▲

Giasha Burn

701
CARN A' CHOIN DEIRG ▲

Croick

Amat Forest

506
MEALL DHEIRGIDH ▲

463
BREAC BHEINN ▲

Brealangwell Lodge

Strathcarron

3

642
MEALL DUBH ▲

677
MEALL NAM BRADHAN ▲

Loch a' Choire Mhòir

842
CARN BÀN ▲

River Carron

63
CÀRN BHREN ▲

4

verlael Forest

647
CÀRN MÒR ▲

Gleann Beag

Crom Loch

628 ▲

710
BEINN THARSUINN ▲

Glencalvie Forest

222

838
CARN CHUINNEAG ▲

60
CÀRN CAS NAN GABHAR ▲

5

River Lael

ael Forest

1081
BEINN DEARG ▲

Loch Coire Lair

771
MEALL A' GHRIANAIN ▲

Loch a' Chaorunn

E A

Corrieshalloch Gorge

Snow gates

618
MEALL LEACACHAIN ▲

Strathvaich Forest

Loch Vaich

742
BEINN NAN EUN ▲

Loch Morie

737
MEALL MÒR ▲

6

raemore Forest

742
TOM BÀN MÒR ▲

662
BEINN LIATH BHEAG ▲

Loch Droma

Loch Glascarnoch

Loch Glass

09
RR OR ▲

Aultguish Inn

20

Snow gates

600 ▲

A835

Inchbae Lodge Hotel

479 ▲

1045
BEN WYVIS ▲

Glen Gla

7

Fannich Lodge

211

680
BEINN DEARG ▲

Corriemoille Forest

Ben Wyvis

Strath Garve

558
AN CABAR ▲

Fannich

439
CARN NA DUBH CHOILLE ▲

Lochluichart

Corriemoille

212

761
LITTLE WYVIS ▲

484
CLOCH MHÒR ▲

8

Achanalt   A832   16

Loch Luichart

Gorstan

Garve

Loch Garve

Dingwall
(Inbhir Pheofharain)

G   H

Achanalt

J

579
SGÙRR MARCASAIDH ▲

North Coast 500

K

Rogie Falls

A835

L   Auchterneed

M

A834   Gower

Mou

Strathpeffer

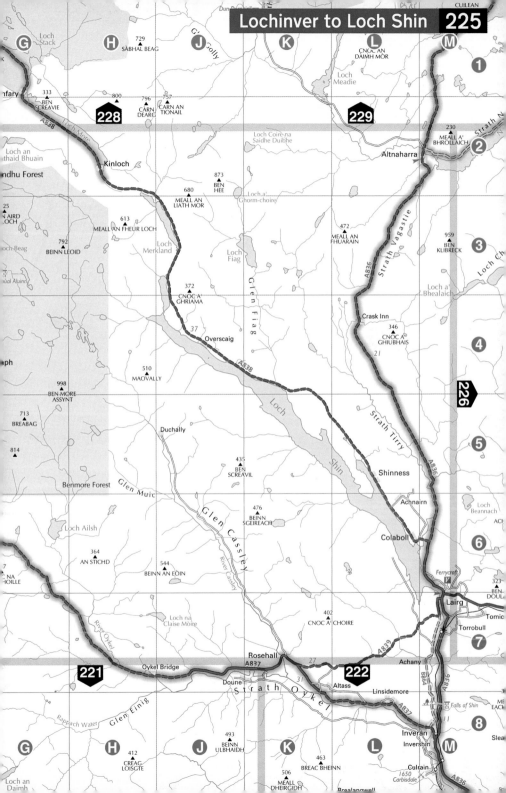

G   H   J   K   L   M

1

2

Whiten
Head

lean Hoan

408
BEN HUTIG

Strathan

Talmine

Melness
Midtown

Rabbit
Islands

Eilean
Nan Ròn

Neave or
Coomb Island

Ardmore
Point

Kirtomy Point

Farr Point

Armad... 3

Kirtomy

A838

North Coast 500

Tongue
Bay

Skerray

Achtoty

Torrisdale

Scullomie

Coldbackie

Torrisdale Farr
Bay   Bay

Invernaver

Borgie

Bettyhill

Farr

Swordly

Strathnaver

Bettyhill

Achina

Loch
Meadie

Farr Point

230
BEN
NABOLL

262
DRUIM
NAN CLIAR

Kyle of Tongue

Tongue

310
MEALL LEATHAD
NA CRAOIBHE

13

A836

Skelpick

Sleipick Burn

228
N
BÓ

4

230

Loch Mòr
na Cadrach

Kinloch

Loch na
Seilg

598
MEALLAN
LIATH

318
CNOC
CRAGGIE

17

Loch
Craggie

Strathnaver

12

Loch
nan C...

5

927
BEN
HOPE

763
BEN
LOYAL

527
BEINN
STUMANADH

213
CNOC
MALPELLY

River Borgie

B871

River Naver

Loch Strathy

335
MEALL BAD
NA CUAICHE

Strath More

Loch an
Deerie

Loch
Loyal

557
CNOC NAN
CUILEAN

Loch Loyal
Lodge

Loch
Syre

345
CNOC NAN
TRI-CHLAC

6

Syre

656
CNOC AN
DÀIMH MÒR

294
POLE
HILL

259
BEINN
ROSAIL

B871

404
BEINN
MHADADH

16

BE

7

Loch
Meadie

och Coire na
aidhe Duibhe

225

230
MEALL A'
BHROLLAICH

Altnaharra

Strath Naver

12

Loch Naver

B873

270
BEADAIG

226

Loch
Rimsdale

Loch
nan Clar

Loch an
Altan Fhéarna

Loch
Badanloch

Ba

8

h a'
-choire

G   H   J   K   L   M

472
MEALL AN
FHUARAIN

h Vagastie

959
BEN
KLIBRECK

-choire Forest

694

Loch
Truder

434
CNOC NA HAT...

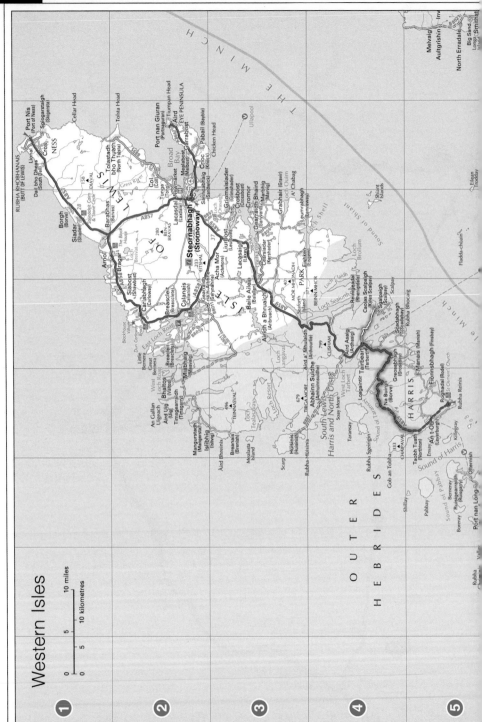

Western Isles

10 miles

10 kilometres

OUTER HEBRIDES

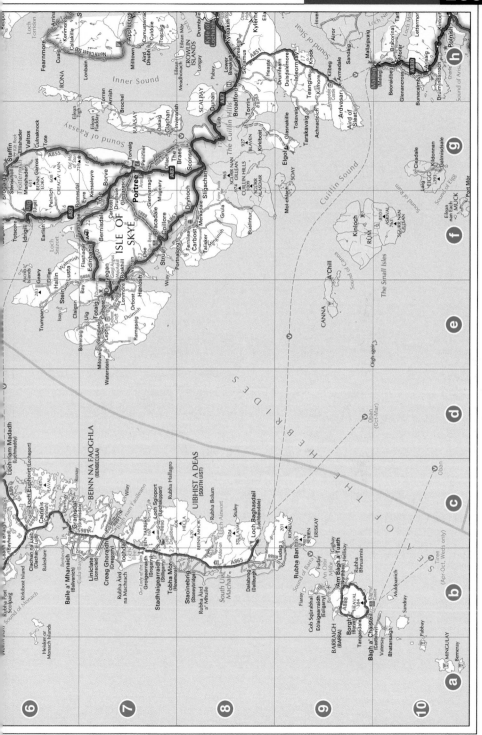

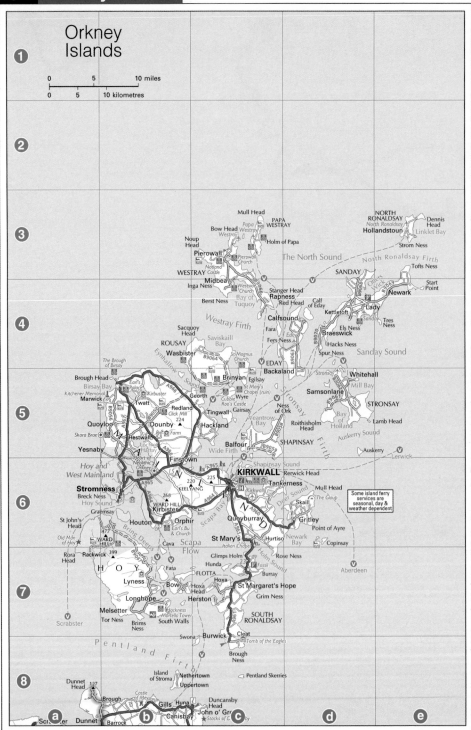

Orkney
Islands

| 0 | 5 | | 10 miles |
| 0 | 5 | | 10 kilometres |

Mull Head
Papa
Bow Head Westray **PAPA WESTRAY**
Westray
Noup
Head Holm of Papa

Pierowall
Pierowall
Church
Notland
Castle
WESTRAY
Midbea
Inga Ness Westside
Church
Berst Ness Bay of
Tuquoy

NORTH RONALDSAY
North Ronaldsay
Hollandstoun Dennis
Head
Linklet Bay
Strom Ness

The North Sound
North Ronaldsay Firth
Tofts Ness
SANDAY
Otters
Wick
Start
Point
Stanger Head **Newark**
Rapness Red Head Calf
of Eday Kettletoft
Sanday
Lady Tres
Ness

Calfsound
Fara
Fers Ness
EDAY
Backaland
Stronsay

Els Ness
Braeswick
Hacks Ness
Spur Ness **Sanday Sound**

Sacquoy
Head Saviskaill
Bay
ROUSAY
Wasbister B9064 St Magnus
Church
The Brough
of Birsay
Eynhallow Sound
Brinyan
Egilsay
St Mary's
Chapel (ruin)
Cubbie
Roo's Castle
Wyre

Whitehall
Mill Bay
Samsonlane
STRONSAY

Brough Head
Birsay Bay Earl's
Palace
Kitchener Memorial
Marwick
Twatt Kirbuster
Redland
Click Mill 224
Georth
Ness
of Ork
Lamb Head
Bay
of
Holland
Veantrow
Bay
Roithisholm
Head
Auskerry Sound
Tingwall
Gairsay

Lerwick

Quoyloo
Skara Brae
Hestwall
Dounby Farm
Hackland
SHAPINSAY
Auskery

Yesnaby
Loch Harray
Port of
Neolithic
Orkney
Balfour
Wide Firth
Finstown
Shapinsay Sound

Hoy and
West Mainland
A965 **KIRKWALL** Rerwick Head

220 225
Stromness
Breck Ness
Hoy Sound
KEELYANG
Kirkwall
Tankerness
Mull Head
The Gloup
Some island ferry
services are
seasonal, day &
weather dependent
268
WARD HILL
Kirbister
Deer Sound
Skaill

St John's
Head
477
WARD
HILL
Houton
Orphir
Earl's Bu
& Church
Quoyburray
Gritley
Point of Ayre

Old Man
of Hoy
Graemsay
Bring Deeps
Cava
Scapa
Flow
St Mary's
Italian Chapel
Hurtiso
Newark
Bay
Copinsay

Rora
Head
Rackwick 399
H O Y
Fara
Glimps Holm Rose Ness
Hunda
231
Fossil
Aberdeen

Lyness
FLOTTA
Hoxa
Bow
Hoxa
Head
Burray
St Margaret's Hope
Grim Ness

Longhope
Herston
SOUTH RONALDSAY

Melsetter
Tor Ness
Hackness
Martello Tower
South Walls
Brims
Ness
Swona **Burwick** Cleat
Tomb of the Eagles

Scrabster
Pentland Firth
Brough
Ness

Dunnet
Head 127
Island
of Stroma
Nethertown
Pentland Skerries
Uppertown

Brough
Castle
of Mey
Duncansby
Head
Scrabster **Dunnet**
Barrock
Gills Huna
Canisbay
John o' Gro
Stacks of

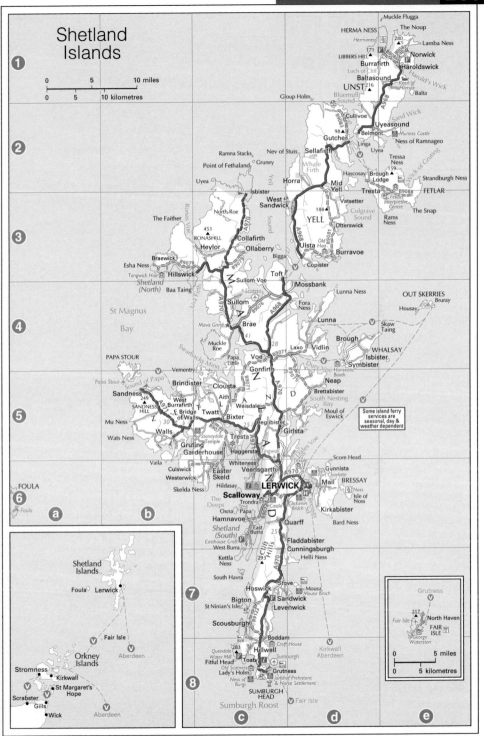

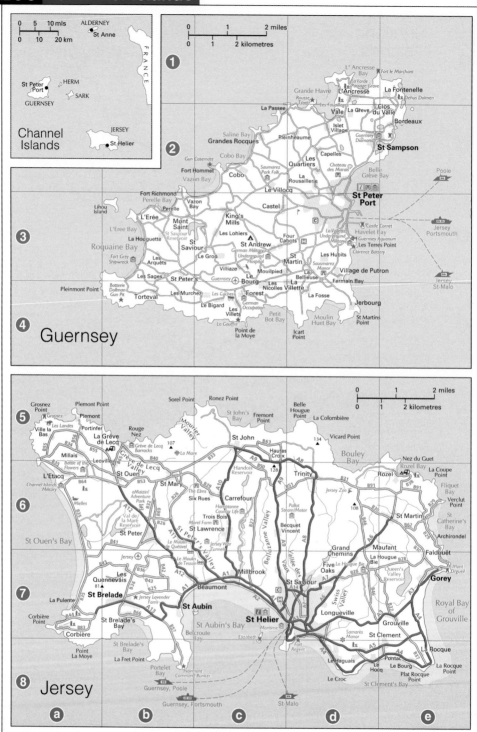

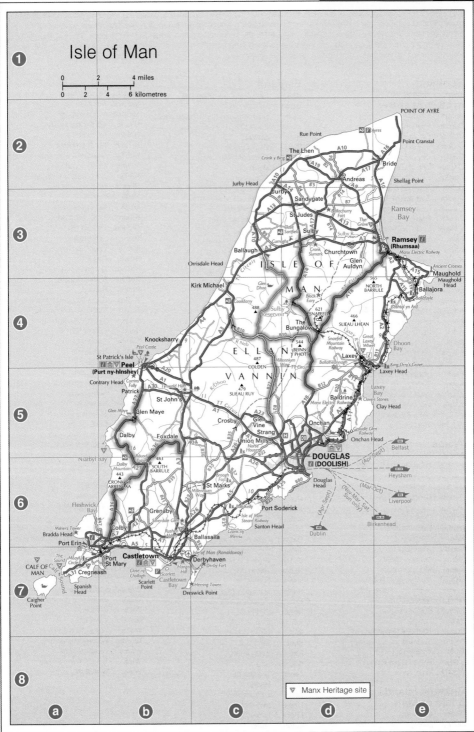

Isle of Man

```
0        2        4 miles
|----|----|----|----|
0    2    4    6 kilometres
```

POINT OF AYRE

Rue Point

The Lhen

Cronk y Bing

Point Cranstal

Bride

Jurby Head

Jurby

Sandygate

Andreas

Shellag Point

St Judes

Sulby

Ballachurry Fort

The Grove

Ramsey Bay

Churchtown

Ramsey (Rhumsaa)

Manx Electric Railway

Ballaugh

Cronk Sumark

Glen Auldyn

Orrisdale Head

ISLE OF MAN

Maughold

Maughold Head

Kirk Michael

Glen Dhoo

Black Eary

NORTH BARRULE

Ballajora

Cashtal yn Ard

Cooildarry

Sulby Reservoir

SNAEFELL

SLIEAU LHEAN

The Bungalow

Dhoon Bay

Knocksharry

Peel Castle

R Neb

BEINN Y PHOTT

Snaefell Mountain Railway

Great Laxey Wheel

St Patrick's Isle

Peel (Purt ny-hInshey)

ELLAN

COLDEN

Laxey

King Orry's Grave

Laxey Head

Contrary Head

Corrins Folly

VANNIN

SLIEAU RUY

TT Circuit

Bollaiheannagh

Patrick

St John's

Thwaild Hill

R Dhoo

Laxey Bay

Glen Maye

Glen Maye

Crosby

Glen Vine

Baldrine

Cloven Stones

Manx Electric Railway

Clay Head

Dalby

Foxdale

Strang

Union Mills

Noise Houses

Onchan

Groddle Glen Railway

Onchan Head

Niarbyl Bay

Dalby Mountain

Round Table

SOUTH BARRULE

Noble's Houses

Belfast

CRONK NY ARREY LAA

Brough Fort

DOUGLAS (DOOLISH)

Heysham

St Marks

Millennium Way

Douglas Head

Liverpool

Fleshwick Bay

Grenaby

Silverdale Glen

Port Soderick

Isle of Man Steam Railway

Santon Head

Birkenhead

Miners Tower

Bradda Head

Colby

Rushen Abbey

Cronk ny Merriu

Dublin

Port Erin

Ballasalla

Meayll Circle

Port St Mary

Castletown

Isle of Man (Ronaldsway)

Derbyhaven

Derby Fort

CALF OF MAN

The Sound

Cregneash

Close ny Chollagh

Scarlett Point

Castletown Bay

Hango Hill

Caigher Point

Spanish Head

Dreswick Point

Herring Tower

▽ Manx Heritage site

This index lists places appearing in the main map section of the atlas in alphabetical order. The reference following each name gives the atlas page number and grid reference of the square in which the place appears. The map shows counties, unitary authorities and administrative areas, together with a list of the abbreviated name forms used in the index. The top 100 places of tourist interest are indexed in red, World Heritage sites in **green**, motorway service areas in blue, airports in blue *italic* and National Parks in green *italic*.

Scotland

Abers	Aberdeenshire
Ag & B	Argyll and Bute
Angus	Angus
Border	Scottish Borders
C Aber	City of Aberdeen
C Dund	City of Dundee
C Edin	City of Edinburgh
C Glas	City of Glasgow
Clacks	Clackmannanshire (1)
D & G	Dumfries & Galloway
E Ayrs	East Ayrshire
E Duns	East Dunbartonshire (2)
E Loth	East Lothian
E Rens	East Renfrewshire (3)
Falk	Falkirk
Fife	Fife
Highld	Highland
Inver	Inverclyde (4)
Mdloth	Midlothian (5)
Moray	Moray
N Ayrs	North Ayrshire
N Lans	North Lanarkshire (6)
Ork	Orkney Islands
P & K	Perth & Kinross
Rens	Renfrewshire (7)
S Ayrs	South Ayrshire
S Lans	South Lanarkshire
Shet	Shetland Islands
Stirlg	Stirling
W Duns	West Dunbartonshire (8)
W Isls	Western Isles (Na h-Eileanan an Iar)
W Loth	West Lothian

Wales

Blae G	Blaenau Gwent (9)
Brdgnd	Bridgend (10)
Caerph	Caerphilly (11)
Cardif	Cardiff
Carmth	Carmarthenshire
Cerdgn	Ceredigion
Conwy	Conwy
Denbgs	Denbighshire
Flints	Flintshire
Gwynd	Gwynedd
IoA	Isle of Anglesey
Mons	Monmouthshire
Myr Td	Merthyr Tydfil (12)
Neath	Neath Port Talbot (13)
Newpt	Newport (14)
Pembks	Pembrokeshire
Powys	Powys
Rhondd	Rhondda Cynon Taf (15)
Swans	Swansea
Torfn	Torfaen (16)
V Glam	Vale of Glamorgan (17)
Wrexhm	Wrexham

Channel Islands & Isle of Man

Guern	Guernsey
Jersey	Jersey
IoM	Isle of Man

England

BaNES	Bath & N E Somerset (18)
Barns	Barnsley (19)
BCP	Bournemouth, Christchurch and Poole (20)
Bed	Bedford
Birm	Birmingham
Bl w D	Blackburn with Darwen (21)
Bolton	Bolton (22)
Bpool	Blackpool
Br & H	Brighton & Hove (23)
Br For	Bracknell Forest (24)
Bristl	City of Bristol
Bucks	Buckinghamshire
Bury	Bury (25)
C Beds	Central Bedfordshire
C Brad	City of Bradford
C Derb	City of Derby
C KuH	City of Kingston upon Hull
C Leic	City of Leicester
C Nott	City of Nottingham
C Pete	City of Peterborough
C Plym	City of Plymouth
C Port	City of Portsmouth
C Sotn	City of Southampton
C Stke	City of Stoke-on-Trent
C York	City of York
Calder	Calderdale (26)
Cambs	Cambridgeshire
Ches E	Cheshire East
Ches W	Cheshire West and Chester
Cnwll	Cornwall
Covtry	Coventry
Cumb	Cumbria
Darltn	Darlington (27)
Derbys	Derbyshire
Devon	Devon
Donc	Doncaster (28)
Dorset	Dorset
Dudley	Dudley (29)
Dur	Durham
E R Yk	East Riding of Yorkshire
E Susx	East Sussex
Essex	Essex
Gatesd	Gateshead (30)
Gloucs	Gloucestershire
Gt Lon	Greater London
Halton	Halton (31)
Hants	Hampshire
Hartpl	Hartlepool (32)
Herefs	Herefordshire
Herts	Hertfordshire
IoS	Isles of Scilly
IoW	Isle of Wight
Kent	Kent
Kirk	Kirklees (33)
Knows	Knowsley (34)
Lancs	Lancashire
Leeds	Leeds
Leics	Leicestershire
Lincs	Lincolnshire
Lpool	Liverpool
Luton	Luton
M Keyn	Milton Keynes

Manch	Manchester
Medway	Medway
Middsb	Middlesbrough
N Linc	North Lincolnshire
N Som	North Somerset
N Tyne	North Tyneside (35)
N u Ty	Newcastle upon Tyne
N York	North Yorkshire
NE Lin	North East Lincolnshire
Nhants	Northamptonshire
Norfk	Norfolk
Notts	Nottinghamshire
Nthumb	Northumberland
Oldham	Oldham (36)
Oxon	Oxfordshire
R & Cl	Redcar & Cleveland
Readg	Reading
Rochdl	Rochdale (37)
Rothm	Rotherham (38)
Rutlnd	Rutland
S Glos	South Gloucestershire (39)
S on T	Stockton-on-Tees (40)
S Tyne	South Tyneside (41)
Salfd	Salford (42)
Sandw	Sandwell (43)
Sefton	Sefton (44)
Sheff	Sheffield
Shrops	Shropshire
Slough	Slough (45)
Solhll	Solihull (46)
Somset	Somerset
St Hel	St Helens (47)
Staffs	Staffordshire
Sthend	Southend-on-Sea
Stockp	Stockport (48)
Suffk	Suffolk
Sundld	Sunderland
Surrey	Surrey
Swindn	Swindon
Tamesd	Tameside (49)
Thurr	Thurrock (50)
Torbay	Torbay
Traffd	Trafford (51)
W & M	Windsor & Maidenhead (52)
W Berk	West Berkshire
W Susx	West Sussex
Wakefd	Wakefield (53)
Warrtn	Warrington (54)
Warwks	Warwickshire
Wigan	Wigan (55)
Wilts	Wiltshire
Wirral	Wirral (56)
Wokham	Wokingham (57)
Wolves	Wolverhampton (58)
Worcs	Worcestershire
Wrekin	Telford & Wrekin (59)
Wsall	Walsall (60)

ORKNEY
ISLANDS

SHETLAND
ISLANDS

WESTERN ISLES (Na h-Eileanan an Iar)

HIGHLAND

MORAY

S C O T L A N D

Aberdeen

ABERDEENSHIRE

ANGUS

PERTH &
KINROSS

Dundee

ARGYLL
AND BUTE

STIRLING

FIFE

1
FALK
8   2
4 Glasgow
7
3
W
LOTH
6
Edinburgh
E LOTH
5

NORTH
AYRSHIRE

S LANS

SCOTTISH
BORDERS

E AYRS

S AYRS

DUMFRIES &
GALLOWAY

NORTHUMBERLAND

Newcastle
upon Tyne   35
41
30
Sunderland

DURHAM

32
27 40 R & CL
Middlesbrough

CUMBRIA

IoM

NORTH YORKSHIRE

Blackpool

LANCASHIRE

Bradford

York

EAST RIDING
OF YORKSHIRE

Kingston
upon Hull

Leeds

21
26
53
22 25 37
33
36
19
42
49
44
55
47
28
N LINC
NE
LIN

Liverpool
34
56
54
31
51
48
Manchester

38
Sheffield

IoA

CONWY

FLINTS

CHES
W

CHES
E

DERBYS

NOTTS

LINCOLNSHIRE

DENBGS

WREXHAM

Stoke-on-
Trent

Derby

Nottingham

GWYNEDD

STAFFS

LEICS

RUTLAND

NORFOLK

59

SHROPSHIRE

58 60
43
29   Birmingham
Coventry

Leicester

Peterborough

POWYS

46

NHANTS

CAMBS

CERDGN

WORCS

WARWKS

Milton
Keynes

BED

SUFFOLK

W A L E S

HEREFS

E N G L A N D

PEMBKS

CARMTH

MONS

GLOUCS

OXON

BUCKS

BEDS Luton

HERTS

ESSEX

9
12
16
13
15 11
11
10   14
Cardiff
17
Swansea

N
SOM
39
18
Bristol

Swindon

Reading
W BERK

52 45
57 24

GREATER
LONDON

50

Southend-
on-Sea

MEDWAY

SURREY

KENT

WILTSHIRE

HAMPSHIRE

W SUSX

E SUSX

23

SOMERSET

DORSET

Southampton

Portsmouth

20

IoW

DEVON

CORNWALL

Torbay

Plymouth

CHANNEL
ISLANDS

Guernsey

Jersey

IoS

A

Abbas Combe
Somset....................27 G6
Abberley Worcs..............70 D2
Abberley Common
Worcs......................70 D2
Abberton Essex..............62 B4
Abberton Worcs..............71 H4
Abbess Roding Essex.....60 F5
Abbeydale Sheff............114 F5
Abbey Dore Herefs.......54 B3
Abbey Green Staffs......99 L2
Abbey St Bathans
Border.....................178 F6
Abbeystead Lancs.......130 B8
Abbeytown Cumb........147 L5
Abbey Village Lancs....121 J6
Abbey Wood Gt Lon......45 J4
Abbotrule Border........167 J6
Abbots Bickington
Devon...........................9 K3
Abbots Bromley
Staffs......................100 B7
Abbotsbury Dorset......14 B5
Abbots Deuglie
P & K......................186 B5
Abbotsham Devon........22 F6
Abbotskerswell
Devon..........................7 K3
Abbots Langley
Herts........................59 H7
Abbots Leigh N Som.....38 D5
Abbotsley Cambs..........75 J3
Abbots Morton
Worcs.......................71 H4
Abbots Ripton Cambs...89 J7
Abbot's Salford
Warwks......................71 J4
Abbots Worthy Hants....29 J5
Abbotts Ann Hants.......29 G3
Abbott Street Dorset...15 J3
Abdon Shrops...............83 L6
Aberaeron Cerdgn.......66 B3
Aberaman Rhondd........52 F7
Aberangell Gwynd........81 J2
Aberarder Highld........202 F1
Aberargie P & K.........186 B4
Aberarth Cerdgn.........66 B2
Aberavon Neath...........51 L7
Abercanaid Myr Td......53 G7
Abercarn Caerph.........37 K2
Abercastle Pembks.......64 B7
Abercegir Powys...........81 H3
Aberchalder Lodge
Highld.....................202 B5
Aberchirder Abers......216 C4
Abercorn W Loth........176 E3
Abercraf Powys...........52 C5
Abercregan Neath........36 D2
Abercwmboi Rhondd.....52 F7
Abercych Pembks.........65 H6
Abercynon Rhondd.......37 G2
Aberdalgie P & K.......185 M4
Aberdare Rhondd.........52 F7
Aberdaron Gwynd.........94 C7
Aberdeen C Aber........207 H4
Aberdeen Airport
C Aber.....................207 G3
Aberdour Fife............177 G2
Aberdulais Neath........52 B7
Aberdyfi Gwynd...........80 E4
Aberedw Powys............68 C5
Abereiddy Pembks........48 D2
Abererch Gwynd..........95 G5
Aberfan Myr Td...........53 G7
Aberfeldy P & K........194 D6
Aberffraw IoA............108 D7
Aberford Leeds..........124 C3
Aberfoyle Stirlg.......184 C7
Abergavenny Mons........53 L5
Abergele Conwy..........110 C6
Abergorlech Carmth.....66 D7
Abergwesyn Powys........67 J4
Abergwili Carmth.........50 F2
Abergwynfi Neath.........36 D2

Abergwyngregyn
Gwynd.....................109 J6
Abergynolwyn Gwynd....80 F3
Aberkenfig Brdgnd.......36 D4
Aberlady E Loth.........178 B3
Aberlemno Angus.......196 E5
Aberllefenni Gwynd......81 G2
Aberllynfi Powys.........68 D6
Aberlour,
Charlestown of
Moray.....................215 G5
Abermule Powys..........82 D5
Abernant Carmth..........50 D2
Abernant Rhondd..........52 F7
Abernethy P & K........186 C4
Abernyte P & K..........186 D2
Aberporth Cerdgn.........65 J4
Abersoch Gwynd...........94 E6
Abersychan Torfn........53 K7
Aberthin V Glam..........36 F5
Abertillery Blae G......53 K7
Abertridwr Caerph.......37 H3
Abertridwr Powys.........97 G8
Aberuthven P & K......185 K4
Aberystwyth Cerdgn.....80 D6
Abingdon-on-
Thames Oxon..............41 J2
Abinger Common
Surrey......................31 J3
Abinger Hammer
Surrey......................31 H2
Abington Nhants..........73 L3
Abington S Lans.........165 H5
Abington Pigotts
Cambs.......................75 K5
Abington Services
S Lans....................165 H4
Abingworth W Susx.......18 F3
Ab Kettleby Leics......102 B7
Ablington Gloucs.........56 C6
Abney Derbys.............114 D5
Aboyne Abers............205 L5
Abhainn Suidhe
W Isls....................232 d4
Abram Wigan.............112 E2
Abriachan Highld.......212 E7
Abridge Essex.............45 J2
Abronhill N Lans.......175 K3
Abson S Glos.............39 G5
Abthorpe Nhants.........73 J5
Aby Lincs................118 F5
Acaster Malbis
C York.....................124 E2
Acaster Selby N York ..124 E3
Accrington Lancs.......121 L5
Acha Ag & B.............188 F5
Achahoish Ag & B.......172 D3
Achalader P & K........195 H7
Achaleven Ag & B.......182 D1
Acha Mor W Isls........232 f3
Achanalt Highld........211 K3
Achandunie Highld......222 E6
Achany Highld...........222 D2
Acharacle Highld.......190 D3
Acharn Highld...........190 E6
Acharn P & K............194 B7
Achavanich Highld......231 H6
Achduart Highld........224 C2
Achfary Highld..........228 D7
A'Chill Highld..........198 D4
Achiltibuie Highld.....224 C6
Achina Highld...........229 L4
Achinhoan Ag & B.......161 J6
Achintee Highld.........210 E6
Achintraid Highld......210 C6
Achmelvich Highld......224 C4
Achmore Highld.........210 D7
Achmore W Isls.........232 f3
Achnacarnin Highld....224 C3
Achnacarry Highld......201 J7
Achnacloich Highld.....199 J4
Achnaconeran Highld...202 C2
Achnacroish Ag & B....191 G2
Achnadrish House
Ag & B....................189 L6
Achnafauld P & K......185 J1
Achnagarron Highld....222 F7

Achnaha Highld.........189 L3
Achnahaird Highld......224 B5
Achnahannet Highld....214 B8
Achnairn Highld........225 L6
Achnalea Highld........191 G4
Achnamara Ag & B......172 D2
Achnasheen Highld.....211 J3
Achnashellach
Highld.....................210 F5
Achnastank Moray.......215 G7
Achosnich Highld.......189 K3
Achranich Highld.......190 E6
Achreamie Highld.......230 E3
Achriabhach Highld.....192 B3
Achriesgill Highld......228 C5
Achtoty Highld..........229 K3
Achurch Nhants...........88 E6
Achvaich Highld........222 F3
Achvarasdal Highld.....230 E3
Ackergill Highld........231 L5
Acklam Middsb...........141 L4
Acklam N York...........134 B7
Ackleton Shrops.........84 D4
Acklington Nthumb.....159 G2
Ackton Wakefd..........124 C6
Ackworth Moor Top
Wakefd....................124 C7
Acle Norfk................93 J2
Acock's Green Birm......85 K6
Acol Kent.................35 J2
Acomb C York...........124 E1
Acomb Nthumb..........150 B2
Aconbury Herefs........54 D2
Acton Ches E..............98 F2
Acton Gt Lon.............44 D4
Acton Staffs..............99 J4
Acton Suffk...............77 K5
Acton Wrexhm............97 M3
Acton Beauchamp
Herefs......................70 C4
Acton Bridge Ches W ...112 E6
Acton Burnell Shrops...83 K3
Acton Green Herefs......70 C4
Acton Round Shrops.....84 B4
Acton Scott Shrops......83 J5
Acton Trussell Staffs....99 J1
Acton Turville S Glos...39 J4
Adbaston Staffs..........99 H6
Adber Dorset..............26 E7
Adbolton Notts..........101 L5
Adderbury Oxon..........72 F7
Adderley Shrops..........98 F4
Addiewell W Loth.......176 D5
Addingham C Brad......123 G1
Addington Bucks.........58 C3
Addington Gt Lon........45 G7
Addington Kent...........33 H2
Addiscombe Gt Lon......45 G6
Addlestone Surrey.......43 H7
Addlethorpe Lincs......119 H7
Adeyfield Herts..........59 H6
Adfa Powys.................82 B4
Adforton Herefs..........69 H1
Adisham Kent..............35 G4
Adlestrop Gloucs.........56 E3
Adlingfleet E R Yk.....125 K6
Adlington Lancs.........121 J7
Admaston Staffs.........100 B7
Admaston Wrekin.........84 B2
Adpar Cerdgn.............65 J6
Adsborough Somset......25 L5
Adscombe Somset.........25 J4
Adstock Bucks.............58 C3
Adstone Nhants...........73 H4
Adversane W Susx........31 H6
Advie Highld.............214 D7
Adwick le Street
Donc......................124 E8
Adwick upon
Dearne Donc.............115 J2
Ae D & G.................155 H4
Ae Bridgend D & G....155 H5
Afan Forest Park
Neath.......................36 D2
Affleck Abers...........216 B6
Affpuddle Dorset........14 F4
Affric Lodge Highld....201 J2

Afon-wen Flints........110 F6
Afton IoW..................16 D5
Agglethorpe N York....131 K3
Aigburth Lpool..........111 L4
Aike E R Yk..............126 C2
Aiketgate Cumb.........148 E5
Aikton Cumb.............148 B4
Ailsworth C Pete.........89 G4
Ainderby Quernhow
N York....................132 E4
Ainderby Steeple
N York....................132 E2
Aingers Green Essex.....62 D4
Ainsdale Sefton........120 D7
Ainstable Cumb.........148 F5
Ainsworth Bury..........121 L8
Ainthorpe N York.......142 E5
Aintree Sefton..........111 L2
Ainville W Loth.........176 F5
Aird Ag & B.............181 M7
Aird D & G...............144 D3
Aird W Isls..............232 g2
Aird a' Mhulaidh
W Isls....................232 e3
Aird Asaig W Isls......232 e4
Aird Dhubh Highld.....209 L6
Airdeny Ag & B.........182 E2
Aird of Kinloch
Ag & B....................181 H2
Aird of Sleat Highld...199 J5
Airdrie N Lans..........175 K5
Airdriehill N Lans.....175 K5
Airds of Kells D & G....154 B7
Àird Uig W Isls.........232 d2
Airidh a bhruaich
W Isls....................232 e3
Airieland D & G........146 D4
Airlie Angus............195 L6
Airmyn E R Yk..........125 H5
Airntully P & K........186 A1
Airor Highld............199 L4
Airth Falk...............176 B2
Airton N York...........131 G7
Aisby Lincs..............103 G5
Aisby Lincs..............116 E5
Aish Devon.................7 G4
Aish Devon.................7 J4
Aisholt Somset...........25 J4
Aiskew N York...........132 D2
Aislaby N York..........134 B3
Aislaby N York..........143 H5
Aislaby S on T..........141 J5
Aisthorpe Lincs........116 F5
Aith Shet................235 c5
Akeld Nthumb...........168 E4
Akeley Bucks.............73 K6
Albaston Cnwll............6 B2
Alberbury Shrops........83 G1
Albourne W Susx.........19 H3
Albrighton Shrops.......84 E3
Albrighton Shrops.......98 C8
Alburgh Norfk............92 F6
Albury Herts..............60 C3
Albury Surrey.............31 H2
Albury Heath Surrey....31 H3
Alcaig Highld...........212 E3
Alcaston Shrops.........83 J6
Alcester Warwks.........71 K3
Alcester Lane End
Birm........................85 J7
Alciston E Susx..........20 B5
Alcombe Somset..........24 F3
Alconbury Cambs.........89 H7
Alconbury Weston
Cambs.......................89 H7
Aldborough N York.....132 F6
Aldborough Norfk......106 E5
Aldbourne Wilts..........40 E5
Aldbrough E R Yk.......127 G3
Aldbrough St John
N York....................140 F5
Aldbury Herts............58 F5
Aldcliffe Lancs.........129 K7
Aldclune P & K..........194 E4
Aldeburgh Suffk.........79 K3
Aldeby Norfk.............93 J5
Aldenham Herts..........44 D2

Alderbury Wilts 28 D6
Alderford Norfk............ 106 D8
Alderholt Dorset 28 C8
Alderley Gloucs 39 H3
Alderley Edge Ches E .. 113 J5
Aldermans Green
 Covtry.......................86 D6
Aldermaston W Berk.......41 L7
Alderminster Warwks...72 B5
Aldershot Hants.............30 E2
Alderton Gloucs 56 A2
Alderton Nhants............73 K5
Alderton Suffk 79 H6
Alderton Wilts 39 J4
Aldfield N York 132 D5
Aldford Ches W..............98 B2
Aldgate Rutlnd...............88 E3
Aldham Essex 61 L3
Aldham Suffk 78 C5
Aldingbourne W Susx ..18 C5
Aldingham Cumb 129 G5
Aldington Kent.............34 E7
Aldington Worcs 71 J5
Aldington Corner
 Kent...........................34 E7
Aldivalloch Moray 205 H1
Aldochlay Ag & B 174 C1
Aldreth Cambs 90 C8
Aldridge Wsall.............85 J4
Aldringham Suffk.........79 J3
Aldsworth Gloucs..........56 D6
Aldunie Moray 215 H8
Aldwark Derbys........... 100 E2
Aldwark N York 133 G6
Aldwick W Susx 18 C6
Aldwincle Nhants..........88 E6
Aldworth W Berk..........41 K4
Alexandria W Duns ... 174 D3
Aley Somset 25 J4
Alfington Devon 12 E3
Alfold Surrey 31 H5
Alfold Crossways
 Surrey 31 H4
Alford Abers 206 B3
Alford Lincs 118 F6
Alford Somset 26 E5
Alfreton Derbys........... 101 H2
Alfrick Worcs 70 D4
Alfrick Pound Worcs 70 D4
Alfriston E Susx 20 B5
Algarkirk Lincs 103 M5
Alhampton Somset.......26 F4
Alkborough N Linc....... 125 K6
Alkham Kent..................35 H6
Alkmonton Derbys...... 100 D5
Allaleigh Devon 7 J5
Allanaquoich Abers .. 204 D6
Allanbank N Lans....... 175 L6
Allanton Border 179 H7
Allanton N Lans........... 175 L6
Allanton S Lans 175 K7
Allaston Gloucs.............54 F6
Allbrook Hants 29 J7
All Cannings Wilts........40 B7
Allendale Nthumb 149 L4
Allen End Warwks.........85 L4
Allenheads Nthumb ... 149 L6
Allen's Green Herts......60 D5
Allensmore Herefs.......69 J7
Allenton C Derb 101 G6
Aller Devon 24 B6
Aller Somset 26 B5
Allerby Cumb 147 J6
Allercombe Devon........12 D4
Allerford Somset 24 D3
Allerston N York 134 D3
Allerthorpe E R Yk 125 J2
Allerton C Brad........... 123 G4
Allerton Highld 213 H2
Allerton Lpool 111 L4
Allerton Bywater
 Leeds.......................124 C5
Allerton Mauleverer
 N York......................132 F7
Allesley Covtry..............86 C7
Allestree C Derb 101 G5
Allexton Leics 88 B4

Allgreave Ches E 113 L7
Allhallows Medway......46 D4
Alligin Shuas Highld 210 C3
Allington Dorset............13 L4
Allington Lincs 102 E4
Allington Wilts 28 D4
Allington Wilts 39 K5
Allington Wilts 40 B7
Allithwaite Cumb 129 J4
Alloa Clacks 185 J8
Allonby Cumb.............. 147 J6
Alloway S Ayrs 163 J5
Allowenshay Somset......26 B8
All Stretton Shrops......83 J4
Alltchaorunn Highld... 192 C6
Alltwalis Carmth...........66 B7
Alltwen Neath...............51 K5
Alltyblaca Cerdgn 66 C5
Allweston Dorset 26 F8
Almeley Herefs.............69 G4
Almington Staffs...........99 G5
Almondbank P & K...... 185 M3
Almondbury Kirk 123 H7
Almondsbury S Glos 38 E4
Alne N York 133 G6
Alness Highld 222 E7
Alnham Nthumb......... 168 E7
Alnmouth Nthumb...... 169 J7
Alnwick Nthumb 169 J6
Alperton Gt Lon...........44 D4
Alphamstone Essex......77 K7
Alpheton Suffk 77 K4
Alphington Devon 11 L6
Alport Derbys 114 E8
Alpraham Ches E 98 E1
Alresford Essex............62 C4
Alrewas Staffs..............85 L1
Alsager Ches E..............99 H2
Alsop en le Dale
 Derbys.....................100 D2
Alston Cumb 149 J5
Alston Devon.................13 H2
Alstone Gloucs.............55 M2
Alstonefield Staffs 100 C2
Alston Sutton Somset.....26 B2
Alswear Devon...............23 L6
Altandhu Highld 224 B6
Altarnun Cnwll...............9 G8
Altass Highld 222 C2
Altcreich Ag & B......... 190 D8
Altgaltraig Ag & B...... 173 H4
Althorne Essex..............61 L7
Althorpe N Linc 125 K8
Altnabreac Station
 Highld......................230 E6
Altnaharra Highld 225 M2
Altofts Wakefd............ 124 B5
Alton Derbys............... 115 G8
Alton Hants 30 B4
Alton Staffs 100 B4
Alton Barnes Wilts.......40 C7
Alton Pancras Dorset....14 D3
Alton Priors Wilts.........40 C7
Alton Towers Staffs.... 100 B4
Altrincham Traffd....... 113 H4
Altskeith Hotel Stirlg.. 184 B6
Alva Clacks 185 J7
Alvanley Ches W.......... 112 D6
Alvaston C Derb......... 101 H5
Alvechurch Worcs........85 J8
Alvecote Warwks..........86 B3
Alvediston Wilts...........27 L6
Alveley Shrops..............84 D6
Alverdiscott Devon.......23 H6
Alverstoke Hants 17 H3
Alverstone IoW 17 H5
Alverthorpe Wakefd 123 L6
Alverton Notts............ 102 C4
Alves Moray 214 E3
Alvescot Oxon...............56 F6
Alveston S Glos 38 F3
Alveston Warwks..........72 B3
Alvingham Lincs 118 E4
Alvington Gloucs..........54 E7
Alwalton C Pete...........89 G4
Alwinton Nthumb...... 168 D7
Alwoodley Leeds........ 123 K3

Alyth P & K....................195 K6
Am Bàgh a Tuath
 W Isls........................233 b9
Ambergate Derbys 101 G3
Amberley Gloucs..........55 J7
Amberley W Susx.........18 D3
Amble Nthumb 159 G2
Amblecote Dudley........84 F6
Ambler Thorn C Brad... 123 G5
Ambleside Cumb......... 137 K6
Ambleston Pembks......49 G3
Ambrosden Oxon..........57 L4
Amcotts N Linc 125 K7
Amersham Bucks..........42 F2
Amersham
 Common Bucks..........42 F2
Amersham Old
 Town Bucks...............42 F2
Amersham on the
 Hill Bucks..................58 F7
Amesbury Wilts............28 D3
Amhuinnsuidhe
 W Isls........................232 d4
Amington Staffs...........86 B3
Amisfield D & G...........155 H5
Amlwch IoA 108 F3
Ammanford Carmth......51 J3
Amotherby N York 134 B5
Ampfield Hants 29 H6
Ampleforth N York 133 J4
Ampney Crucis
 Gloucs.......................56 B7
Ampney St Mary
 Gloucs.......................56 C7
Ampney St Peter
 Gloucs.......................56 B7
Amport Hants 28 F3
Ampthill C Beds............74 F6
Ampton Suffk 77 J1
Amroth Pembks............49 K6
Amulree P & K............. 185 J1
Amwell Herts.................59 K5
Anaheilt Highld 191 G4
Ancaster Lincs 103 G4
Ancells Farm Hants......30 D1
Ancroft Nthumb......... 168 E1
Ancrum Border 167 K4
Anderby Lincs 119 G6
Andover Hants...............29 G3
Andoversford Gloucs....56 A4
Andreas IoM 237 d2
Anerley Gt Lon 45 G6
Anfield Lpool 111 K3
Angarrack Cnwll............3 G4
Angelbank Shrops........83 L7
Angle Pembks 48 E6
Anglesey Abbey
 Cambs.......................76 D3
Angmering W Susx.......18 E5
Angram N York 124 D2
Ankerville Highld 223 H6
Anlaby E R Yk 126 C5
Anmer Norfk 105 H6
Anmore Hants 17 J1
Annan D & G................ 147 L2
Annandale Water
 Services D & G.........155 J4
Annat Highld 210 D4
Annathill N Lans......... 175 J4
Anna Valley Hants........29 G3
Annbank S Ayrs 163 K5
Anne Hathaway's
 Cottage Warwks.......71 L4
Annfield Plain Dur...... 150 F5
Anniesland C Glas 174 F5
Ansdell Lancs............. 120 D5
Ansford Somset 26 F5
Ansley Warwks..............86 C5
Anslow Staffs.............. 100 E7
Anslow Gate Staffs ... 100 D7
Anstey Herts.................60 C2
Anstey Leics 87 G2
Anstruther Fife 187 J6
Ansty W Susx 19 J2
Ansty Warwks...............86 E6

Ansty Wilts...................27 L6
Anthorn Cumb 147 L4
Antingham Norfk....... 106 F5
An t-Ob W Isls............. 232 d5
Antonine Wall 175 L3
Anton's Gowt Lincs ... 103 M3
Antony Cnwll..................6 B5
Antrobus Ches W 112 F5
Anwick Lincs 103 J3
Anwoth D & G 145 M4
Aperfield Gt Lon...........32 D2
Apethorpe Nhants 88 E4
Apley Lincs 117 J6
Apperknowle Derbys... 115 G5
Apperley Gloucs...........55 K3
Appin Ag & B...............191 J6
Appleby N Linc 126 B7
Appleby-in-
 Westmorland
 Cumb........................139 G3
Appleby Magna Leics...86 C2
Appleby Parva Leics...86 C2
Applecross Highld 209 L5
Appledore Devon.........23 G5
Appledore Devon.........25 G8
Appledore Kent............34 C8
Appleford Oxon.............41 K2
Applegarth Town
 D & G........................155 K5
Appleshaw Hants 28 F2
Appleton Halton 112 D4
Appleton Oxon 57 H7
Appleton Warrtn 112 F5
Appleton-le-Moors
 N York......................133 L3
Appleton-le-Street
 N York......................134 B5
Appleton Roebuck
 N York......................124 E3
Appleton Thorn
 Warrtn......................112 F5
Appleton Wiske
 N York......................141 J6
Appletreehall Border... 167 H6
Appletreewick N York... 131 K7
Appley Somset 25 G6
Appley Bridge Lancs... 121 G8
Apse Heath IoW 17 G5
Apsley End C Beds........59 J2
Apuldram W Susx 18 A5
Arabella Highld...........223 H6
Arbirlot Angus 196 F7
Arborfield Wokham......42 C6
Arborfield Cross
 Wokham....................42 C6
Arbourthorne Sheff ... 115 G4
Arbroath Angus 197 G7
Arbuthnott Abers 197 K2
Archddu Carmth...........50 F5
Archdeacon Newton
 Darltn.......................141 G4
Archencarroch
 W Duns.....................174 D3
Archiestown Moray..... 214 F5
Archirondel Jersey 236 e6
Arclid Ches E.................99 H1
Ardallie Abers 217 J6
Ardanaiseig Hotel
 Ag & B......................182 F3
Ardaneaskan Highld ...210 C7
Ardarroch Highld 210 C6
Ardbeg Ag & B 160 D1
Ardbeg Ag & B 173 J5
Ardbeg Ag & B 173 K2
Ardcharnich Highld 220 F4
Ardchiavaig Ag & B 180 E4
Ardchonnell Ag & B ... 182 D5
Ardchronie Highld 222 E4
Ardchullarie More
 Stirlg........................184 D5
Arddarroch Ag & B 183 J7
Arddleen Powys............82 F1
Ard Dorch Highld 209 J8
Ardechive Highld 201 H7
Ardeer N Ayrs 163 H2
Ardeley Herts................60 A3
Ardelve Highld 210 D8

Arden Ag & B...... 174 C2
Ardens Grafton
  Warwks..........71 K4
Ardentallen Ag & B.... 182 B3
Ardentinny Ag & B.... 173 L2
Ardentraive Ag & B ... 173 H4
Ardeonaig Stirlg..... 184 E1
Ardersier Highld...... 213 J4
Ardessie Highld........ 220 D4
Ardfern Ag & B........ 182 A6
Ardfernal Ag & B..... 171 K4
Ardgartan Ag & B.... 183 J6
Ardgay Highld 222 D4
Ardgour Highld 191 K4
Ardgowan Inver....... 173 L4
Ardhallow Ag & B 173 K4
Ardhasig W Isls....... 232 e4
Ardheslaig Highld..... 210 B3
Ardindrean Highld..... 220 F4
Ardingly W Susx 32 C7
Ardington Oxon........41 H3
Ardlamont Ag & B.... 173 G5
Ardleigh Essex 62 C3
Ardleigh Heath
  Essex..............62 C2
Ardler P & K 195 L7
Ardley Oxon...........57 K3
Ardlui Ag & B......... 183 K4
Ardlussa Ag & B...... 172 B2
Ardmair Highld........ 220 E2
Ardmaleish Ag & B ... 173 J5
Ardminish Ag & B..... 172 B8
Ardmolich Highld...... 190 E3
Ardmore Ag & B....... 174 C3
Ardmore Highld 222 F4
Ardnadam Ag & B..... 173 K3
Ardnagrask Highld.... 212 E4
Ardnamurchan
  Highld.............. 190 B3
Ardnarff Highld........ 210 D7
Ardnastang Highld..... 190 F4
Ardpatrick Ag & B.... 172 C6
Ardrishaig Ag & B..... 172 E2
Ardross Highld........ 222 E6
Ardrossan N Ayrs 163 G2
Ardsley East Leeds ... 123 K5
Ardslignish Highld.... 190 B4
Ardtalla Ag & B....... 171 J7
Ardtoe Highld......... 190 C3
Arduaine Ag & B...... 182 A5
Ardullie Highld........ 212 E2
Ardvasar Highld....... 199 K5
Ardvorlich P & K 184 D3
Ardvourlie W Isls..... 232 e3
Ardwell D & G 144 D5
Ardwick Manch........ 113 J3
Areley Kings Worcs...70 E1
Arevegaig Highld 190 D3
Arford Hants 30 D4
Argoed Caerph........53 J7
Argyll Forest Park
  Ag & B............. 183 J6
Aribruach W Isls...... 232 e3
Aridhglas Ag & B..... 180 D3
Arileod Ag & B........ 188 F5
Arinagour Ag & B..... 189 G5
Ariogan Ag & B....... 182 C3
Arisaig Highld......... 199 K7
Arisaig House Highld.. 199 L7
Arkendale N York 132 F7
Arkesden Essex........76 C7
Arkholme Lancs....... 130 B5
Arkleton D & G 156 C4
Arkley Gt Lon..........44 E2
Arksey Donc.......... 115 L1
Arkwright Town
  Derbys............. 115 H7
Arle Gloucs 55 L4
Arlecdon Cumb....... 136 E4
Arlesey C Beds........75 H7
Arleston Wrekin........84 B2
Arley Ches E.......... 112 F5
Arley Warwks..........86 C5
Arlingham Gloucs......55 G6
Arlington Devon........23 K4
Arlington E Susx 20 B4
Armadale Highld...... 199 K5

Armadale Highld 230 A3
Armadale W Loth 176 C5
Armathwaite Cumb...... 148 E5
Arminghall Norfk.......92 F3
Armitage Staffs........85 J1
Armley Leeds......... 123 H4
Armscote Warwks......72 B5
Armthorpe Donc...... 115 L1
Arnabost Ag & B...... 188 F4
Arncliffe N York....... 131 H5
Arncroach Fife........ 187 H6
Ardilly House
  Moray............... 215 G5
Arne Dorset 15 H5
Arnesby Leics..........87 H5
Arngask P & K 186 B5
Arnisdale Highld...... 200 C3
Arnish Highld 209 J5
Arniston Mdloth....... 177 K6
Arnol W Isls.......... 232 f1
Arnold E R Yk 126 E3
Arnold Notts.......... 101 L4
Arnprior Stirlg........ 184 D7
Arnside Cumb......... 129 K4
Aros Ag & B.......... 190 B7
Arrad Foot Cumb..... 129 G4
Arram E R Yk 126 C2
Arrathorne N York ... 132 C2
Arreton IoW...........17 G5
Arrina Highld......... 210 B3
Arrington Cambs.......75 K4
Arrochar Ag & B 183 K6
Arrow Warwks..........71 J3
Arscott Shrops.........83 J2
Artafallie Highld...... 212 F4
Arthington Leeds..... 123 K2
Arthingworth Nhants...87 L7
Arthrath Abers 217 H6
Artrochie Abers 217 J7
Arundel W Susx 18 D4
Asby Cumb........... 136 E3
Ascog Ag & B......... 173 J5
Ascot W & M..........42 F6
Ascott-under-
  Wychwood Oxon 56 F4
Asenby N York........ 132 F4
Asfordby Leics........ 102 B8
Asfordby Hill Leics... 102 B8
Asgarby Lincs......... 103 J4
Ash Kent 35 H3
Ash Kent 45 L6
Ash Somset 26 C7
Ash Surrey 30 E2
Ashampstead W Berk ...41 K5
Ashbocking Suffk......78 E4
Ashbourne Derbys.... 100 D3
Ashbrittle Somset......25 G6
Ashburton Devon 7 H2
Ashbury Devon 10 D5
Ashbury Oxon 40 E4
Ashby N Linc.......... 125 L8
Ashby by Partney
  Lincs............... 118 F7
Ashby cum Fenby
  NE Linc............. 118 C2
Ashby de la Launde
  Lincs............... 103 H2
Ashby-de-la-Zouch
  Leics................86 D1
Ashby Folville Leics...87 K2
Ashby Magna Leics....87 H5
Ashby Parva Leics.....87 G5
Ashby Puerorum
  Lincs............... 118 D7
Ashby St Ledgers
  Nhants...............73 H2
Ashby St Mary Norfk ..93 G3
Ashchurch Gloucs......55 L2
Ashcombe Devon 11 L8
Ashcombe N Som 37 M7
Ashcott Somset........26 C4
Ashdon Essex 76 E6
Ashdown Forest
  E Susx...............32 K6
Ashe Hants 29 K2
Asheldham Essex......62 A7

Ashen Essex...........77 H6
Ashendon Bucks........58 B5
Asheridge Bucks.......58 F6
Ashfield Stirlg........ 185 G6
Ashfield cum
  Thorpe Suffk.........78 E3
Ashfield Green Suffk...92 F8
Ashford Devon 7 G6
Ashford Devon 23 H4
Ashford Kent..........34 D6
Ashford Surrey 43 H6
Ashford Bowdler
  Shrops...............69 K1
Ashford Carbonell
  Shrops...............69 K1
Ashford Hill Hants.....41 K7
Ashford in the
  Water Derbys....... 114 D7
Ashgill S Lans........ 175 K7
Ash Green Surrey 30 E2
Ash Green Warwks.....86 D6
Ashill Devon 12 E1
Ashill Norfk............91 K3
Ashill Somset 25 L7
Ashingdon Essex......46 E2
Ashington Nthumb.... 159 G5
Ashington Somset.....26 E6
Ashington W Susx......18 F3
Ashkirk Border 167 G5
Ashleworth Gloucs.....55 J3
Ashleworth Quay
  Gloucs...............55 J3
Ashley Cambs..........77 G3
Ashley Ches E........ 113 H5
Ashley Devon..........10 F3
Ashley Gloucs.........39 L2
Ashley Hants 16 B4
Ashley Hants 29 G5
Ashley Kent 35 J5
Ashley Nhants 87 L5
Ashley Staffs..........99 H5
Ashley Wilts..........39 J6
Ashley Green Bucks...58 F6
Ash Magna Shrops.....98 E4
Ashmansworth Hants...41 H8
Ashmansworthy
  Devon...............22 E7
Ash Mill Devon 24 C6
Ashmore Dorset.......27 K7
Ashmore Green
  W Berk..............41 J6
Ashorne Warwks.......72 C3
Ashover Derbys....... 115 G8
Ashow Warwks.........72 C1
Ashperton Herefs......70 B6
Ashprington Devon 7 J4
Ash Priors Somset.....25 J5
Ashreigney Devon......10 F3
Ash Street Suffk.......78 B5
Ashtead Surrey........44 D8
Ash Thomas Devon 12 C1
Ashton Ches W........ 112 D7
Ashton Cnwll...........3 G5
Ashton Devon..........11 K7
Ashton Herefs..........69 K2
Ashton Inver.......... 173 L3
Ashton Nhants.........73 L5
Ashton Nhants........88 F5
Ashton Common
  Wilts................39 K8
Ashton-in-
  Makerfield Wigan... 112 E2
Ashton Keynes Wilts...40 B2
Ashton under Hill
  Worcs...............71 H6
Ashton-under-Lyne
  Tamesd............. 113 L2
Ashton Vale Bristl.....38 E6
Ashurst Hants.........16 D1
Ashurst Kent 32 F5
Ashurst Lancs........ 121 G8
Ashurst W Susx 19 G3
Ashurstwood W Susx ..32 D6
Ash Vale Surrey 30 E2
Ashwater Devon 9 K5
Ashwell Herts.........75 J6
Ashwell Rutlnd........88 C2

Ashwell End Herts 75 J6
Ashwellthorpe Norfk...92 D4
Ashwick Somset........26 F2
Ashwicken Norfk 105 H8
Askam in Furness
  Cumb............... 128 F4
Askern Donc.......... 124 E7
Askerswell Dorset 14 A4
Askett Bucks..........58 D6
Askham Cumb......... 138 D3
Askham Notts 116 C6
Askham Bryan
  C York.............. 124 E2
Askham Richard
  C York.............. 124 E2
Asknish Ag & B....... 172 F1
Askrigg N York........ 131 H2
Askwith N York....... 123 H2
Aslackby Lincs........ 103 H6
Aslacton Norfk.........92 D5
Aslockton Notts...... 102 C4
Aspatria Cumb........ 147 K6
Aspenden Herts........60 B3
Aspley Guise C Beds ..74 D7
Aspley Heath C Beds...74 D7
Aspull Wigan......... 121 J8
Asselby E R Yk....... 125 H5
Assington Suffk........77 L6
Assington Green
  Suffk................77 H4
Astbury Ches E........99 J1
Astcote Nhants........73 J4
Asterby Lincs......... 118 C5
Asterley Shrops........83 H3
Asterton Shrops........83 H5
Asthall Oxon...........56 F5
Asthall Leigh Oxon....56 F5
Astle Highld.......... 223 G3
Astley Shrops..........98 D8
Astley Warwks.........86 C5
Astley Wigan......... 113 G2
Astley Worcs..........70 D2
Astley Abbots Shrops...84 C4
Astley Bridge Bolton.. 121 K7
Astley Cross Worcs 70 E1
Aston Birm............85 J5
Aston Ches E..........98 E3
Aston Ches W........ 112 E5
Aston Derbys......... 114 D5
Aston Flints.......... 111 J7
Aston Herts...........59 L4
Aston Oxon...........57 G7
Aston Rothm......... 115 J4
Aston Shrops..........84 E5
Aston Shrops..........98 D6
Aston Staffs...........99 H4
Aston Staffs...........99 K7
Aston Wokham........42 C4
Aston Wrekin..........84 B2
Aston Abbotts Bucks...58 D4
Aston Botterell
  Shrops...............84 B6
Aston-by-Stone
  Staffs................99 K6
Aston Cantlow
  Warwks..............71 K3
Aston Clinton Bucks...58 E5
Aston Crews Herefs....54 F4
Aston End Herts.......59 L3
Aston Fields Worcs....71 H2
Aston Flamville Leics...86 F5
Aston Ingham Herefs...55 G4
Aston le Walls
  Nhants...............72 F4
Aston Magna Gloucs...71 L7
Aston Munslow
  Shrops...............83 K6
Aston on Clun
  Shrops...............83 H6
Aston Pigott Shrops....83 G3
Aston Rogers Shrops...83 G3
Aston Rowant Oxon....58 B7
Aston Somerville
  Worcs...............71 J6
Aston-sub-Edge
  Gloucs...............71 K6
Aston Tirrold Oxon....41 K3

Aston-upon-Trent
Derbys.......................101 H6
Aston Upthorpe
Oxon...........................41 K3
Astwick C Beds...............75 J6
Astwood M Keyn...............74 D5
Astwood Worcs................71 G2
Astwood Bank Worcs.....71 J3
Aswarby Lincs...............103 H4
Aswardby Lincs..............118 E7
Atcham Shrops................83 K2
Athelhampton Dorset....14 E4
Athelington Suffk..........78 E1
Athelney Somset...........25 M5
Athelstaneford
E Loth........................178 C3
Atherington Devon.........23 J6
Atherstone Warwks.......86 C4
Atherstone on Stour
Warwks........................72 B4
Atherton Wigan.............113 G2
Atlow Derbys.................100 E3
Attadale Highld............210 E6
Atterby Lincs................117 G3
Attercliffe Sheff...........115 G4
Atterton Leics................86 D4
Attingham Park
Shrops..........................83 K2
Attleborough Norfk......92 C4
Attleborough
Warwks........................86 D5
Attlebridge Norfk..........92 D1
Attleton Green Suffk....77 G4
Atwick E R Yk...............126 F1
Atworth Wilts.................39 J7
Auborn Lincs................116 F8
Auchbreck Moray..........214 F8
Auchedly Abers.............217 G7
Auchenblae Abers.........197 H1
Auchenbowie Stirlg......175 L2
Auchencairn D & G......146 D5
Auchencairn D & G......155 G5
Auchencairn N Ayrs.....162 D4
Auchencrow Border......179 H6
Auchendinny Mdloth.....177 H6
Auchengray S Lans.......176 D7
Auchenhalrig Moray.....215 J3
Auchenheath S Lans....164 F2
Auchenhessnane
D & G..........................154 E3
Auchenlochan
Ag & B........................173 G4
Auchenmade N Ayrs....174 C8
Auchenmalg D & G......144 F4
Auchentiber N Ayrs.....174 C8
Auchindrain Ag & B.....182 E6
Auchindrean Highld.....221 G5
Auchininna Abers.........216 C5
Auchinleck E Ayrs.......164 B5
Auchinloch N Lans.......175 H4
Auchinstarry N Lans....175 J3
Auchintore Highld........191 L2
Auchiries Abers............217 K6
Auchlean Highld...........203 K5
Auchlee Abers...............207 G6
Auchleven Abers...........206 C1
Auchlochan S Lans.......164 F3
Auchlossan Abers.........206 B5
Auchlyne Stirlg.............184 B2
Auchmillan E Ayrs.......164 A4
Auchmithie Angus........197 G7
Auchmuirbridge
Fife.............................186 C6
Auchnacree Angus.......196 D4
Auchnagatt Abers.........217 H6
Auchnarrow Moray.......204 F2
Auchnotteroch
D & G..........................144 B3
Auchroisk Moray...........215 H4
Auchterarder P & K......185 K5
Auchteraw Highld........202 B4
Auchterblair Highld.....203 L2
Auchtercairn Highld....219 J6
Auchterderran Fife.......186 C7
Auchterhouse Angus....196 B8
Auchterless Abers........216 D6
Auchtermuchty Fife......186 D5

Auchterneed Highld.....212 D3
Auchtertool Fife............177 H1
Auchtertyre Highld......210 C8
Auchtubh Stirlg............184 C4
Auckengill Highld.........231 L3
Auckley Donc................116 A2
Audenshaw Tamesd.....113 K3
Audlem Ches E...............98 F4
Audley Staffs.................99 J3
Audley End Essex..........76 D6
Audley End House
& Gardens Essex.......76 D6
Audnam Dudley.............84 F6
Aughton E R Yk...........125 G3
Aughton Lancs..............111 L1
Aughton Lancs..............129 L6
Aughton Rothm............115 J4
Aughton Wilts................28 E1
Aughton Park Lancs....112 B1
Auldearn Highld...........213 L4
Aulden Herefs................69 J4
Auldgirth D & G............154 F5
Auldhouse S Lans.........175 H7
Ault a' chruinn
Highld........................200 E2
Aultbea Highld.............219 K4
Aultgrishin Highld.......219 H4
Aultguish Inn Highld...221 J7
Ault Hucknall Derbys...115 J7
Aultmore Moray............215 J4
Aultnagoire Highld......202 E2
Aultnamain Highld.......222 F5
Aunsby Lincs................103 H5
Aust S Glos....................38 E3
Austerfield Donc..........115 M3
Austrey Warwks.............86 C3
Austwick N York...........130 E5
Authorpe Lincs.............118 E5
Avebury Wilts.................40 C6
Avebury Wilts................40 C6
Aveley Thurr.................45 L4
Avening Gloucs..............39 K2
Averham Notts.............102 C2
Aveton Gifford Devon....7 G6
Aviemore Highld..........203 L3
Avington W Berk..........41 G6
Avoch Highld................213 G4
Avon Hants....................15 L3
Avonbridge Falk...........176 B4
Avon Dassett Warwks...72 E4
Avonmouth Bristl..........38 D5
Avonwick Devon..............7 G4
Awbridge Hants.............28 F6
Awliscombe Devon........12 E3
Awre Gloucs...................55 G6
Awsworth Notts...........101 J4
Axbridge Somset...........26 B1
Axford Hants.................29 L3
Axford Wilts..................40 E6
Axminster Devon............13 H3
Axmouth Devon..............13 G4
Aycliffe Dur..................141 G3
Aydon Nthumb..............150 C2
Aylburton Gloucs..........54 E7
Aylesbeare Devon..........12 D4
Aylesbury Bucks............58 D5
Aylesby NE Lin............126 F8
Aylesford Kent...............33 J2
Aylesham Kent...............35 H4
Aylestone C Leic............87 H4
Aylestone Park
C Leic...........................87 H4
Aylmerton Norfk..........106 E5
Aylsham Norfk.............106 E6
Aylton Herefs................70 B6
Aylworth Gloucs............56 C4
Aymestrey Herefs..........69 H2
Aynho Nhants................57 K2
Ayot St Lawrence
Herts............................59 K5
Ayr S Ayrs....................163 J5
Aysgarth N York...........131 J2
Ayshford Devon.............25 G7
Ayside Cumb................129 J3
Ayston Rutlnd................88 C4
Ayton Border................179 J6
Azerley N York.............132 C5

B

Babbacombe Torbay.......7 L3
Babbs Green Herts.......60 C5
Babcary Somset.............26 E5
Babraham Cambs...........76 D4
Babworth Notts............116 B5
Backaland Ork..............234 d4
Backfolds Abers...........217 J4
Backford Ches W..........111 L6
Backies Highld..............223 H2
Back of Keppoch
Highld........................199 K7
Backwell N Som.............38 C6
Baconsthorpe Norfk....106 D5
Bacton Herefs................54 A2
Bacton Norfk................107 H5
Bacton Suffk..................78 C2
Bacup Lancs.................122 C6
Badachro Highld..........219 J6
Badanloch Highld.........226 E2
Badbury Swindn............40 D4
Badby Nhants................73 H3
Badcall Highld..............228 C4
Badcaul Highld..............220 D3
Baddeley Edge
C Stke...........................99 K3
Baddeley Green
C Stke...........................99 K3
Baddesley Clinton
Warwks........................86 B8
Baddesley Ensor
Warwks........................86 C4
Baddidarrach Highld...224 D4
Baddinsgill Border......176 F7
Badenscoth Abers........216 D6
Badentarbet Highld.....224 B6
Badenyon Abers...........205 H2
Badger Shrops...............84 D4
Badgeworth Gloucs......55 K4
Badgworth Somset........26 B2
Badicaul Highld...........210 B8
Badingham Suffk...........79 G2
Badlesmere Kent...........34 D4
Badlieu Border.............165 K5
Badlipster Highld.........231 J5
Badluarach Highld.......220 C3
Badninish Highld..........223 G3
Badrallach Highld........220 D3
Badsey Worcs.................71 J5
Badshot Lea Surrey.......30 E2
Badsworth Wakefd......124 C7
Badwell Ash Suffk.........78 B2
Bagber Dorset................27 H8
Bagby N York...............133 G4
Bag Enderby Lincs.......118 E6
Bagendon Gloucs..........56 A6
Bàgh a' Chaisteil
W Isls.........................233 b9
Bagillt Flints................111 H6
Baginton Warwks.........86 D8
Baglan Neath.................51 L6
Bagley Shrops...............98 B6
Bagley Somset...............26 C3
Bagnall Staffs................99 L3
Bagshot Surrey..............42 E7
Bagstone S Glos............39 G3
Bagworth Leics.............86 F2
Bagwy Llydiart
Herefs..........................54 C3
Baildon C Brad............123 H3
Baildon Green
C Brad.........................123 H3
Baile Ailein W Isls.......232 f3
Baile a' Mhanaich
W Isls.........................233 b6
Baile Mòr Ag & B........180 D3
Baillieston C Glas........175 J5
Bainbridge N York.......131 H2
Bainshole Abers...........216 B7
Bainton C Pete..............89 G3
Bainton E R Yk............134 E8
Baintown Fife...............186 F6
Bairnkine Border.........167 K6
Bakewell Derbys...........114 E7
Bala Gwynd...................96 E5

Balallan W Isls.............232 f3
Balbeg Highld..............212 C7
Balbeggie P & K...........186 C2
Balblair Highld.............212 D5
Balblair Highld.............213 G2
Balby Donc...................115 K2
Balcary D & G..............146 E5
Balchraggan Highld.....212 E5
Balchreick Highld........228 B4
Balcombe W Susx..........32 B6
Balcomie Links Fife....187 K5
Baldersby N York.........132 E4
Baldersby St James
N York........................132 E4
Balderstone Lancs.......121 J4
Balderton Notts...........102 D3
Baldinnie Fife..............187 G5
Baldinnies P & K..........185 L4
Baldock Herts.................75 J7
Baldock Services
Herts............................75 J6
Baldovie C Dund..........187 G2
Baldrine IoM.................237 d5
Baldslow E Susx...........20 E4
Bale Norfk....................106 B5
Baledgarno P & K.......186 D2
Balemartine Ag & B....188 C7
Balerno C Edin............177 G5
Balfarg Fife.................186 D6
Balfield Angus..............196 E3
Balfour Ork..................234 c5
Balfron Stirlg...............174 F1
Balgaveny Abers..........216 C6
Balgonar Fife...............185 L8
Balgowan D & G..........144 D6
Balgowan Highld.........202 F6
Balgown Highld...........218 B7
Balgracie D & G..........144 B3
Balgray S Lans.............165 H5
Balham Gt Lon...............44 F5
Balhary P & K..............195 L6
Balholmie P & K..........186 B1
Baligill Highld..............230 C3
Balintore Angus...........195 L5
Balintore Highld...........223 J6
Balintraid Highld.........223 G7
Balivanich W Isls.........233 b6
Balkeerie Angus...........196 B7
Balkholme E R Yk........125 J5
Ballabeg IoM................237 b6
Ballachulish Highld.....191 L5
Ballajora IoM................237 e4
Ballanlay Ag & B..........173 H6
Ballantrae S Ayrs........152 C5
Ballasalla IoM..............237 b6
Ballater Abers..............205 J6
Ballaugh IoM................237 c3
Ballchraggan Highld...223 G6
Ballencrieff E Loth......178 B3
Ballevullin Ag & B.......188 B6
Ball Green C Stke...........99 K3
Ball Hill Hants...............41 H7
Ballidon Derbys............100 D2
Balliekine N Ayrs.........161 L2
Balliemore Ag & B.......182 F7
Balligmorrie S Ayrs....152 F4
Ballimore Stirlg............184 C4
Ballindalloch Moray....214 E7
Ballindean P & K..........186 D2
Ballinger Common
Bucks...........................58 E7
Ballingham Herefs........54 E2
Ballingry Fife................186 C7
Ballinluig P & K............194 F5
Ballinshoe Angus.........196 C5
Ballintuim P & K..........195 H5
Balloch Highld..............213 H5
Balloch N Lans.............175 K4
Balloch P & K................185 H4
Balloch S Ayrs...............153 G3
Balloch W Duns...........174 D3
Balls Cross W Susx........31 G6
Balls Green E Susx.......32 E6
Ballygown Ag & B........189 K7
Ballygrant Ag & B........171 G5
Ballyhaugh Ag & B......188 F5
Balmacara Highld........210 C8
Balmaclellan D & G.....154 B6

Balmae D & G 146 C6
Balmaha Stirlg 174 D1
Balmalcolm Fife 186 E5
Balmangan D & G 146 B5
Balmedie Abers 207 H2
Balmerino Fife 186 F3
Balmichael N Ayrs 162 B3
Balmore E Duns 175 G4
Balmuchy Highld 223 J5
Balmule Fife 177 G2
Balmullo Fife 187 G4
Balnacoil Highld 226 E6
Balnacra Highld 210 F5
Balnacroft Abers 205 G6
Balnafoich Highld 213 G7
Balnaguard P & K 194 E6
Balnahard Ag & B 180 F1
Balnain Highld 212 C7
Balnakeil Highld 228 F2
Balne N York 124 F6
Balquharn P & K 185 L1
Balquhidder Stirlg 184 C3
Balsall Common
Solhll 86 B7
Balsall Heath Birm 85 J6
Balscote Oxon 72 E6
Balsham Cambs 76 E4
Baltasound Shet 235 e1
Baltersan D & G 145 J3
Balthangie Abers 216 F4
Baltonsborough
Somset 26 D4
Balvicar Ag & B 181 M4
Balvraid Highld 200 C3
Balvraid Highld 213 K7
Bamber Bridge
Lancs 121 H5
Bamber's Green
Essex 60 F4
Bamburgh Nthumb 169 H3
Bamburgh Castle
Nthumb 169 H3
Bamford Derbys 114 E6
Bampton Cumb 138 D4
Bampton Devon 24 E6
Bampton Oxon 56 F7
Bampton Grange
Cumb 138 D4
Banavie Highld 191 L2
Banbury Oxon 72 F6
Bancffosfelen
Carmth 50 F3
Banchory Abers 206 D6
Banchory-Devenick
Abers 207 G5
Bancycapel Carmth 50 E3
Bancyfelin Carmth 50 D2
Bandirran P & K 186 C2
Banff Abers 216 D2
Bangor Gwynd 109 H6
Bangor-on-Dee
Wrexhm 98 B4
Bangors Cnwll 9 G5
Banham Norfk 92 C6
Bank Hants 16 C2
Bankend D & G 147 H2
Bankfoot P & K 185 M1
Bankglen E Ayrs 164 C6
Bankhead C Aber 207 G4
Bankhead S Lans 165 J1
Banknock Falk 175 K3
Banks Lancs 120 E6
Bankshill D & G 155 L5
Banningham Norfk 106 F6
Bannister Green
Essex 61 H4
Bannockburn Stirlg 175 L1
Banstead Surrey 44 E7
Bantham Devon 6 F6
Banton N Lans 175 K3
Banwell N Som 38 B8
Bapchild Kent 34 C3
Bapton Wilts 27 M4
Barabhas W Isls 232 f1
Barassie S Ayrs 163 J3
Barbaraville Highld 223 G6
Barbieston S Ayrs 163 K5

Barbon Cumb 130 C3
Barbrook Devon 23 L2
Barby Nhants 73 G1
Barcaldine Ag & B 191 J7
Barcombe E Susx 19 L3
Barcombe Cross
E Susx 19 L3
Barden Park Kent 33 G4
Bardfield End Green
Essex 61 G2
Bardfield Saling
Essex 61 G3
Bardney Lincs 117 J2
Bardon Leics 86 F2
Bardon Mill Nthumb 149 K3
Bardowie E Duns 175 G4
Bardrainney Inver 174 C4
Bardsea Cumb 129 G5
Bardsey Leeds 124 B2
Bardsey Island
Gwynd 94 B7
Bardwell Suffk 91 L8
Bare Lancs 129 K6
Barfad D & G 145 G2
Barford Norfk 92 D3
Barford Warwks 72 C3
Barford St John
Oxon 57 H2
Barford St Martin
Wilts 28 B5
Barford St Michael
Oxon 57 H2
Barfrestone Kent 35 H5
Bargeddie N Lans 175 J5
Bargoed Caerph 53 J7
Bargrennan D & G 153 H6
Barham Cambs 89 G7
Barham Kent 35 G5
Barham Suffk 78 D4
Bar Hill Cambs 75 L2
Barholm Lincs 88 F2
Barkby Leics 87 J2
Barkby Thorpe Leics 87 J2
Barkestone-le-Vale
Leics 102 C5
Barkham Wokham 42 C6
Barking Gt Lon 45 H3
Barking Suffk 78 C4
Barkingside Gt Lon 45 H3
Barking Tye Suffk 78 C4
Barkisland Calder 122 F6
Barkla Shop Cnwll 3 J2
Barkston Lincs 102 F4
Barkston Ash N York 124 D4
Barkway Herts 75 L7
Barlanark C Glas 175 H5
Barlaston Staffs 99 K5
Barlavington W Susx 18 C3
Barlborough Derbys 115 J6
Barlby N York 124 F4
Barlestone Leics 86 E3
Barley Herts 76 B6
Barley Lancs 122 B3
Barleythorpe Rutlnd 88 B2
Barling Essex 46 F3
Barlings Lincs 117 H6
Barlochan D & G 146 E4
Barlow Derbys 115 G6
Barlow Gatesd 150 E3
Barlow N York 124 F5
Barmby Moor
E R Yk 125 J2
Barmby on the
Marsh E R Yk 125 G5
Barmollack Ag & B 161 K1
Barmouth Gwynd 80 E1
Barmpton Darltn 141 H4
Barmston E R Yk 135 J7
Barnacarry Ag & B 182 E8
Barnack C Pete 88 F3
Barnard Castle Dur 140 D4
Barnard Gate Oxon 57 H6
Barnardiston Suffk 77 G5
Barnbarroch D & G 146 E4
Barnburgh Donc 115 J2
Barnby Suffk 93 K5
Barnby Dun Donc 124 F8

Barnby in the
Willows Notts 102 E3
Barnby Moor Notts 116 A5
Barncorkrie D & G....... 144 D7
Barnes Gt Lon 44 E5
Barnes Street Kent 33 H4
Barnet Gt Lon 44 E2
Barnetby le Wold
N Linc 126 C8
Barney Norfk 106 B6
Barnham Suffk 91 K7
Barnham W Susx 18 C5
Barnham Broom
Norfk 92 C3
Barnhead Angus 197 G5
Barnhill C Dund 187 H2
Barnhill Moray 214 E3
Barnhills D & G 152 B7
Barningham Dur 140 D5
Barningham Suffk 91 L7
Barnoldby le Beck
NE Lin 118 C2
Barnoldswick Lancs 122 C2
Barns Green W Susx 31 J6
Barnsley Barns 115 G1
Barnsley Gloucs 56 B6
Barnstaple Devon 23 J5
Barnston Essex 61 G4
Barnston Wirral 111 J5
Barnstone Notts 102 B5
Barnt Green Worcs 85 H8
Barnton C Edin 177 G4
Barnton Ches W 112 F6
Barnwell All Saints
Nhants 88 F6
Barnwell St Andrew
Nhants 88 F6
Barnwood Gloucs 55 K4
Barr S Ayrs 153 G4
Barra W Isls 233 b9
Barra Airport W Isls 233 b9
Barrachan D & G 145 H5
Barraigh W Isls 233 b9
Barrananaoil Ag & B 182 B6
Barrapoll Ag & B 188 B7
Barrasford Nthumb 158 A7
Barrhead E Rens 174 F6
Barrhill S Ayrs 152 F5
Barrington Cambs 76 B5
Barrington Somset 26 B7
Barripper Cnwll 3 H4
Barrmill N Ayrs 174 C7
Barrock Highld 231 J2
Barrow Gloucs 55 K3
Barrow Lancs 121 L3
Barrow Rutlnd 88 C1
Barrow Somset 27 G5
Barrow Suffk 77 H2
Barrowby Lincs 102 E5
Barrowden Rutlnd 88 D4
Barrowford Lancs 122 C3
Barrow Gurney
N Som 38 D6
Barrow Haven N Linc ... 126 D6
Barrow-in-Furness
Cumb 128 E5
Barrow Island Cumb 128 E5
Barrow-upon-
Humber N Linc 126 D6
Barrow upon Soar
Leics 101 L8
Barrow upon Trent
Derbys 101 G6
Barry Angus 187 J1
Barry V Glam 37 H6
Barry Island V Glam 37 H6
Barsby Leics 87 K2
Barsham Suffk 93 H5
Barston Solhll 86 B7
Bartestree Herefs 69 L6
Barthol Chapel
Abers 216 F7
Bartholomew Green
Essex 61 H4
Barthomley Ches E 99 H3
Bartley Hants 28 F8
Bartley Green Birm 85 H6

Bartlow Cambs 76 E5
Barton Cambs 76 B4
Barton Ches W 98 C2
Barton Gloucs 56 C3
Barton Lancs 120 E3
Barton Lancs 121 G3
Barton N York 141 G5
Barton Oxon 57 K6
Barton Torbay 7 K3
Barton Bendish
Norfk 91 G3
Barton End Gloucs 39 J2
Barton Hartshorn
Bucks 57 M2
Barton in Fabis Notts 101 K6
Barton in the Beans
Leics 86 E3
Barton-le-Clay
C Beds 59 H2
Barton-le-Street
N York 133 L5
Barton-le-Willows
N York 133 L6
Barton Mills Suffk 91 G8
Barton-on-Sea
Hants 16 B4
Barton-on-the-
Heath Warwks 56 E2
Barton Park
Services N York 140 F5
Barton St David
Somset 26 D5
Barton Seagrave
Nhants 88 C7
Barton Stacey Hants 29 H3
Barton Town Devon 23 L4
Barton Turf Norfk 107 H7
Barton-under-
Needwood Staffs 100 D8
Barton-upon-
Humber N Linc 126 C6
Barton Waterside
N Linc 126 C6
Barvas W Isls 232 f1
Barway Cambs 90 D7
Barwell Leics 86 F4
Barwick Devon 10 E4
Barwick Somset 26 E8
Barwick in Elmet
Leeds 124 B3
Baschurch Shrops 98 B7
Bascote Warwks 72 E2
Bashall Eaves Lancs 121 K2
Basildon Essex 46 B3
Basingstoke Hants 29 M2
Baslow Derbys 114 E6
Bason Bridge Somset 25 M3
Bassaleg Newpt 37 L3
Bassendean Border 167 K1
Bassenthwaite
Cumb 137 H2
Bassett C Sotn 29 H7
Bassingbourn-cum-
Kneesworth
Cambs 75 L5
Bassingham Lincs 102 E1
Bassingthorpe Lincs 102 F6
Bassus Green Herts 60 A3
Baston Lincs 89 G2
Bastwick Norfk 107 J8
Batchworth Herts 43 H2
Batcombe Dorset 14 C2
Batcombe Somset 27 G4
Batford Herts 59 J5
Bath BaNES 39 H7
Bath BaNES 39 H7
Bathampton BaNES 39 H7
Bathealton Somset 25 G6
Batheaston BaNES 39 H6
Bathford BaNES 39 H6
Bathgate W Loth 176 D5
Bathley Notts 102 C2
Bathpool Cnwll 5 L2
Bathpool Somset 25 K6
Bath Side Essex 62 F2
Bathville W Loth 176 C5
Bathway Somset 26 E2

Batley Kirk 123 J5
Batsford Gloucs 71 L7
Battersby N York 142 D5
Battersea Gt Lon 44 F5
Battisford Tye Suffk......78 B4
Battle E Susx 20 F3
Battle Powys 52 F2
Battledykes Angus... 196 D5
Battlesbridge Essex.....46 C2
Battleton Somset 24 E6
Baughton Worcs 70 F6
Baughurst Hants...........41 L7
Baulds Abers............. 206 B6
Baulking Oxon 40 F3
Baumber Lincs 117 L6
Baunton Gloucs 56 A6
Baverstock Wilts...........28 B5
Bawburgh Norfk...........92 D2
Bawdeswell Norfk 106 C7
Bawdrip Somset 25 M4
Bawdsey Suffk 79 H6
Bawtry Donc............. 115 M3
Baxenden Lancs........ 122 B5
Baxterley Warwks 86 C4
Bay Highld................. 208 D4
Bayble W Isls 232 g2
Baybridge Hants...........29 K6
Baycliff Cumb............ 129 G5
Baydon Wilts 40 F5
Bayford Herts 60 A4
Bayford Somset 27 G5
Bayhead W Isls 233 b6
Baylham Suffk 78 D4
Baysham Herefs 54 E3
Bayston Hill Shrops......83 J2
Baythorne End Essex ...77 G6
Bayton Worcs 84 C8
Bayworth Oxon 57 J7
Beachampton Bucks.....73 L6
Beachamwell Norfk......91 H3
Beachy Head E Susx ...20 C6
Beacon Devon 12 F2
Beacon End Essex........62 A3
Beacon Hill Notts...... 102 D2
Beacon Hill Surrey.......30 E4
Beacon's Bottom
     Bucks 42 C2
Beaconsfield Bucks 42 F3
Beaconsfield
     Services Bucks......42 F3
Beadlam N York 133 K3
Beadlow C Beds 75 G6
Beadnell Nthumb 169 J4
Beaford Devon 10 E2
Beal N York 124 E5
Beal Nthumb 169 G2
Bealsmill Cnwll 6 A1
Beaminster Dorset 13 L3
Beamish Dur 151 G4
Beamish Museum
     Dur 150 F4
Beamsley N York 131 K8
Beanacre Wilts..............39 K7
Beanley Nthumb 169 G5
Beardon Devon 10 D7
Beare Green Surrey.....31 K3
Bearley Warwks............71 L3
Bearpark Dur 151 G6
Bearsden E Duns....... 174 F4
Bearsted Kent 33 K3
Bearstone Shrops 99 G5
Bearwood BCP 15 K3
Bearwood Birm.............85 H6
Bearwood Herefs..........69 H4
Beattock D & G........... 155 J2
Beauchamp Roding
     Essex 60 F6
Beauchief Sheff 115 G5
Beaufort Blae G.............53 J5
Beaulieu Hants..............16 E3
Beauly Highld............. 212 E5
Beaumaris Cumb 109 H6
Beaumaris Castle
     IoA 109 J4
Beaumont Cumb 148 C3
Beaumont Essex............62 E3
Beaumont Jersey 236 c7

Beaumont Leys
     C Leic 87 H2
Beausale Warwks.........72 B1
Beauworth Hants.........29 L6
Beaworthy Devon 10 C5
Beazley End Essex.......61 H3
Bebington Wirral 111 K5
Beccles Suffk 93 J5
Becconsall Lancs 120 F6
Beckbury Shrops..........84 D3
Beckenham Gt Lon 45 G6
Beckermet Cumb 136 E6
Beckfoot Cumb 147 J5
Beckford Worcs............71 H7
Beckhampton Wilts 40 C6
Beckingham Lincs...... 102 E2
Beckingham Notts ... 116 C4
Beckington Somset......27 J2
Beckjay Shrops.............83 H7
Beckley E Susx 21 G2
Beckley Oxon 57 K5
Beck Row Suffk 91 G7
Beck Side Cumb 128 F3
Beckton Gt Lon 45 H4
Beckwithshaw N York.. 132 D8
Becontree Gt Lon 45 J3
Becquet Vincent
     Jersey 236 c6
Bedale N York 132 D2
Bedchester Dorset 27 J7
Beddau Rhondd 37 G4
Beddgelert Gwynd.......95 K3
Beddingham E Susx 19 L4
Beddington Gt Lon 44 F6
Beddington Corner
     Gt Lon 44 F6
Bedfield Suffk 78 F2
Bedford Bed..................74 F5
Bedgrove Bucks 58 D5
Bedhampton Hants......17 K2
Bedingfield Suffk..........78 E2
Bedlam N York 132 D7
Bedlington Nthumb ... 159 G5
Bedlinog Myr Td 53 H7
Bedminster Bristl 38 E6
Bedminster Down
     Bristl 38 E6
Bedmond Herts.............59 J7
Bednall Staffs 99 L8
Bedrule Border 167 J5
Bedstone Shrops..........83 G7
Bedwas Caerph 37 J3
Bedwellty Caerph 53 J7
Bedworth Warwks 86 D6
Beeby Leics 87 J2
Beech Hants 30 B4
Beech Staffs 99 J5
Beech Hill W Berk 42 B7
Beechingstoke Wilts ...40 C8
Beedon W Berk.............41 J5
Beeford E R Yk 135 H8
Beeley Derbys 114 E7
Beelsby NE Lin 117 K2
Beenham W Berk.........41 L6
Beer Devon 13 G5
Beer Somset 26 B5
Beercrocombe
     Somset 25 L7
Beer Hackett Dorset... 14 B1
Beesands Devon 7 J7
Beesby Lincs 118 F5
Beeson Devon 7 J7
Beeston C Beds 75 H5
Beeston Ches W............98 D2
Beeston Leeds 123 K4
Beeston Norfk...............91 K1
Beeston Notts............. 101 K5
Beeston Regis Norfk.. 106 E4
Beeswing D & G 146 F2
Beetham Cumb 129 K4
Beetham Somset 25 L8
Beetley Norfk.............. 106 A8
Begbroke Oxon 57 J5
Begelly Pembks 49 J6
Beguildy Powys............82 D7
Beighton Norfk..............93 H2
Beighton Sheff 115 H5

Beinn Na Faoghla
     W Isls........................ 233 c7
Beith N Ayrs............... 174 C7
Bekesbourne Kent 35 G4
Belaugh Norfk 107 G8
Belbroughton Worcs....85 G7
Belchalwell Dorset........14 E1
Belchamp Otten
     Essex 77 J6
Belchamp St Paul
     Essex 77 H6
Belchamp Walter
     Essex 77 J6
Belchford Lincs 118 D6
Belford Nthumb 169 G3
Belgrave C Leic 87 H3
Belhaven E Loth 178 E3
Belhelvie Abers 207 H2
Belhinnie Abers 215 K8
Bellabeg Abers 205 H3
Bellanoch Ag & B....... 182 A8
Bellaty Angus............. 195 K4
Bell Busk N York 131 G7
Belleau Lincs 118 E5
Bell End Worcs.............85 G7
Bellerby N York 131 L2
Belle Vue Cumb 148 C4
Belle Vue Wakefd 123 L6
Bellfield S Lans........... 164 F3
Bellingdon Bucks.........58 F6
Bellingham Nthumb ... 157 L5
Belloch Ag & B........... 161 H2
Bellochantuy Ag & B.. 161 H3
Bell o' th' Hill Ches W .. 98 D4
Bellshill N Lans........... 175 J6
Bellside N Lans........... 175 L6
Bellsquarry W Loth..... 176 E5
Bells Yew Green
     E Susx 33 G6
Belluton BaNES............38 E7
Belmaduthy Highld.... 213 G3
Belmont Bl w D 121 K7
Belmont Gt Lon 44 E7
Belmont S Ayrs 163 J5
Belmont Shet.............. 235 d2
Belnacraig Abers 205 J3
Belper Derbys 101 G3
Belsay Nthumb 158 D6
Belses Border............. 167 J4
Belsford Devon 7 H4
Belsize Herts 59 G7
Belstead Suffk 78 D6
Belstone Devon 10 F6
Belthorn Bl w D 121 L5
Beltinge Kent................47 K6
Beltingham Nthumb ... 149 K3
Beltoft N Linc 116 D1
Belton Leics 101 H7
Belton Lincs 102 F4
Belton N Linc 116 C1
Belton Norfk............... 93 K3
Belton House Lincs.... 102 F5
Belton in Rutland
     Rutlnd...........................88 B3
Belvedere Gt Lon 45 J4
Belvoir Leics 102 D5
Bembridge IoW............17 J5
Bemerton Wilts 28 C5
Bempton E R Yk........ 135 J5
Benacre Suffk 93 K6
Benbecula W Isls...... 233 c7
Benbecula Airport
     W Isls........................ 233 c6
Benbuie D & G 154 C3
Benderloch Ag & B.... 191 H8
Benenden Kent.............33 K6
Benfieldside Dur 150 D4
Bengeo Herts................60 A5
Bengeworth Worcs......71 J5
Benhall Green Suffk.....79 H3
Benhall Street Suffk.....79 H3
Benholm Abers 197 L4
Beningbrough N York . 133 H7
Benington Herts............59 M4
Benington Lincs 104 C3
Benllech IoA............... 109 G5
Benmore Ag & B........ 173 K2

Bennan N Ayrs........... 162 C5
Ben Nevis Highld........ 192 B3
Benniworth Lincs 117 K5
Benover Kent................33 J4
Ben Rhydding C Brad.. 123 H2
Benslie N Ayrs............ 163 J2
Benson Oxon................41 L3
Benthoul C Aber........ 206 F5
Bentley Donc.............. 115 K1
Bentley E R Yk 126 C4
Bentley Hants...............30 C3
Bentley Suffk................78 D6
Bentley Warwks...........86 C4
Bentpath D & G.......... 156 B4
Bentwichen Devon......24 B5
Bentworth Hants 30 A4
Benvie Angus............. 186 E2
Benville Dorset.............14 A2
Benwick Cambs............89 L5
Beoley Worcs 71 J1
Beoraidbeg Highld 199 L6
Bepton W Susx 18 B3
Berden Essex................60 D3
Berea Pembks................48 D2
Bere Alston Devon 6 C3
Bere Ferrers Devon.......6 C3
Bere Regis Dorset 14 F4
Bergh Apton Norfk......93 G4
Berinsfield Oxon...........41 L2
Berkeley Gloucs............55 G7
Berkhamsted Herts 59 G6
Berkley Somset............27 J2
Berkswell Solhll 86 B7
Bermondsey Gt Lon 45 G4
Bernera Highld 200 C2
Bernisdale Highld...... 208 F4
Berrick Prior Oxon......41 L2
Berrick Salome Oxon... 41 L2
Berriedale Highld 227 K4
Berrier Cumb 137 L2
Berriew Powys 82 D4
Berrington Shrops.......83 K3
Berrington Worcs.........69 L2
Berrington Green
     Worcs.......................... 69 L2
Berrow Somset 25 L2
Berrow Green Worcs...70 D3
Berryfields Bucks 58 C5
Berryhillock Moray.... 215 L3
Berryhillock Moray.... 215 L4
Berrynarbor Devon......23 J3
Berry Pomeroy
     Devon 7 J4
Bersham Wrexhm........97 L3
Bersted W Susx 18 C5
Berwick E Susx 20 B5
Berwick Bassett
     Wilts.............................40 C5
Berwick Hill Nthumb.. 158 F6
Berwick St James
     Wilts.............................28 B4
Berwick St John
     Wilts.............................27 L6
Berwick St Leonard
     Wilts.............................27 L5
Berwick-upon-
     Tweed Nthumb....... 179 K7
Bescar Lancs.............. 120 E7
Besford Worcs..............71 G5
Bessacarr Donc......... 115 L2
Bessingby E R Yk...... 135 J6
Bessingham Norfk..... 106 E5
Besthorpe Norfk..........92 C4
Besthorpe Notts 116 D8
Bestwood Village
     Notts.......................... 101 K3
Beswick E R Yk 126 C2
Betchworth Surrey......31 K2
Bethel Gwynd............ 109 G7
Bethel IoA.................. 108 C7
Bethersden Kent..........34 C6
Bethesda Gwynd 109 J7
Bethesda Pembks........49 J4
Bethlehem Carmth 51 K1
Bethnal Green Gt Lon.. 45 G4
Betley Staffs..................99 H3
Betsham Kent...............45 L5

Betteshanger Kent.........35 J4
Bettiscombe Dorset......13 K3
Bettisfield Wrexhm......98 C5
Bettws Brdgnd 36 D3
Bettws Newpt................37 L3
Bettws Cedewain
Powys....................82 C4
Bettws Ifan Cerdgn.......65 J5
Bettws-Newydd
Mons 54 A6
Bettyhill Highld.............229 L3
Betws Bledrws
Cerdgn 66 D4
Betws Gwerfil Goch
Denbgs 97 G3
Betws-y-Coed
Conwy 96 C2
Betws-yn-Rhos
Conwy 110 C6
Beulah Cerdgn 65 J5
Beulah Powys 67 K4
Bevercotes Notts.........116 B6
Beverley E R Yk.............126 C3
Beverston Gloucs...........39 K2
Bewcastle Cumb 156 F7
Bewdley Worcs.............84 D7
Bewerley N York 132 B6
Bewholme E R Yk..........126 E1
Bexhill-on-Sea
E Susx 20 E4
Bexley Gt Lon 45 J5
Bexleyheath Gt Lon 45 J5
Bexwell Norfk...............90 F3
Beyton Suffk................77 L2
Beyton Green Suffk......77 L2
Bhaltos W Isls 232 d2
Bhatarsaigh W Isls....233b10
Bibury Gloucs...............56 C6
Bicester Oxon 57 L4
Bickenhill Solhll 85 L6
Bicker Lincs 103 L5
Bickerstaffe Lancs.......112 C2
Bickerton N York 124 C1
Bickford Staffs..............84 F2
Bickington Devon 7 J2
Bickington Devon 23 H5
Bickleigh Devon 6 D4
Bickleigh Devon 12 B2
Bickley Ches W 98 D3
Bickley Gt Lon 45 H6
Bickley N York 134 E2
Bicknacre Essex............61 J7
Bicknoller Somset.........25 H4
Bicknor Kent................33 L2
Bicton Shrops...............82 F6
Bicton Shrops...............83 J1
Bidborough Kent...........32 F5
Biddenden Kent...........33 L5
Biddenham Bed............74 E4
Biddestone Wilts..........39 K5
Biddisham Somset.........26 B2
Biddlesden Bucks...........73 J6
Biddulph Staffs.............99 K2
Biddulph Moor Staffs....99 K2
Bideford Devon 23 G6
Bidford-on-Avon
Warwks 71 K4
Bielby E R Yk.................125 J2
Bieldside C Aber 207 G5
Bierley IoW 17 G6
Bierton Bucks...............58 D5
Big Balcraig D & G 145 H6
Bigbury Devon 6 F6
Bigbury-on-Sea
Devon 6 F6
Bigby Lincs 117 H1
Biggar S Lans 165 K2
Biggin Derbys 100 D2
Biggin Hill Gt Lon 32 D2
Biggleswade C Beds 75 H5
Bigholms D & G 156 B6
Bighouse Highld..........230 C3
Bighton Hants.............29 L4
Biglands Cumb 148 A4
Bignor W Susx 18 D3
Bigrigg Cumb 136 D5
Big Sand Highld..........219 H5

Bigton Shet 235 c7
Bilborough C Nott 101 K4
Bilbrook Somset............25 G3
Bilbrough N York..........124 E2
Bilbster Highld............231 K5
Bildershaw Dur...........140 F3
Bildeston Suffk.............78 B5
Billericay Essex............46 B2
Billesdon Leics.............87 K3
Billesley Warwks..........71 K3
Billingborough Lincs....103 J5
Billinge St Hel............112 D2
Billingford Norfk...........92 E7
Billingford Norfk..........106 B7
Billingham S on T........141 K3
Billinghay Lincs..........103 J2
Billingley Barns..........115 H1
Billingshurst W Susx....31 H6
Billingsley Shrops.........84 C6
Billington C Beds...........58 F4
Billington Lancs..........121 L4
Billockby Norfk.............93 J2
Billy Row Dur..............150 E7
Bilsborrow Lancs..........121 G3
Bilsby Lincs 119 G6
Bilsham W Susx............18 D5
Bilsington Kent.............34 D7
Bilsthorpe Notts..........101 M1
Bilston Mdloth............177 H5
Bilston Wolves.............85 G4
Bilstone Leics...............86 D3
Bilton E R Yk...............126 E4
Bilton N York 132 D7
Bilton Warwks...............86 F8
Bilton-in-Ainsty
N York 124 D1
Binbrook Lincs 117 K3
Bincombe Dorset...........14 D5
Binegar Somset.............26 E2
Binfield Br For 42 D6
Binfield Heath Oxon....42 C5
Bingfield Nthumb........158 B7
Bingham Notts............102 B4
Bingley C Brad 123 G3
Binham Norfk...............106 B5
Binley Covtry................86 E7
Binley Hants.................29 H2
Binley Woods
Warwks 86 E7
Binnegar Dorset...........15 G5
Binniehill Falk.............176 B4
Binscombe Surrey.........30 F3
Binstead IoW 17 H4
Binsted Hants...............30 C3
Binsted W Susx.............18 D4
Binton Warwks..............71 K4
Bintree Norfk..............106 B7
Birch Essex..................61 M4
Bircham Newton
Norfk 105 J5
Bircham Tofts Norfk....105 J6
Birchanger Essex 60 E4
Birchgrove Green
Services Essex........60 E4
Birch Cross Staffs......100 C6
Bircher Herefs..............69 J2
Birchfield Highld...........85 J5
Birch Green Essex........61 M4
Birchgrove Cardif........37 J4
Birchgrove Swans........51 K5
Birchgrove W Susx........32 D7
Birchington Kent..........35 J2
Birchley Heath
Warwks 86 C5
Birchover Derbys........100 E1
Birch Services
Rochdl 122 K1
Birch Vale Derbys.......114 A4
Birchwood Lincs.........116 F7
Birch Wood Somset......25 K8
Birchwood Warrtn.......112 F4
Bircotes Notts............115 M3
Birdbrook Essex............77 G6
Birdforth N York 133 D4
Birdham W Susx...........17 M3
Birdingbury Warwks....72 E2
Birdlip Gloucs...............55 L5

Birdsall N York 134 C6
Birds Edge Kirk...........123 J8
Birds Green Essex..........60 F6
Birdsgreen Shrops........84 D6
Birdsmoorgate
Dorset 13 K3
Birdwell Barns............115 G2
Birgham Border...........168 B2
Birichin Highld............223 G3
Birkby N York 141 H6
Birkdale Sefton...........120 D7
Birkenbog Abers.........215 L2
Birkenhead Wirral.......111 K4
Birkenhead
(Queensway)
Tunnel Lpool 111 K4
Birkenhills Abers.........216 E5
Birkenshaw Kirk.........123 J5
Birkhall Abers.............205 H6
Birkhill Angus............186 F1
Birkhill D & G 166 B6
Birkin N York 124 E5
Birley Herefs................69 J4
Birley Carr Sheff..........115 G3
Birling Kent..................46 B7
Birlingham Worcs..........71 G5
Birmingham Birm..........85 J6
Birmingham Airport
Solhll 85 L6
Birnam P & K 195 G7
Birness Abers.............217 J7
Birse Abers.................206 B6
Birsemore Abers.........205 L5
Birstall Kirk 123 J5
Birstall Leics...............87 H2
Birstwith N York 132 C7
Birtley Gatesd............151 G4
Birtley Herefs................69 G2
Birtley Nthumb...........157 L6
Birts Street Worcs........70 D7
Bisbrooke Rutlnd.........88 C4
Biscathorpe Lincs.......118 C5
Bisham W & M 42 D4
Bishampton Worcs........71 H4
Bish Mill Devon 24 B6
Bishop Auckland
Dur 140 F2
Bishopbridge Lincs.....117 H3
Bishopbriggs E Duns...175 G4
Bishop Burton
E R Yk 126 B3
Bishop Middleham
Dur 141 H2
Bishopmill Moray........214 F2
Bishop Monkton
N York 132 E6
Bishop Norton Lincs....117 G3
Bishopsbourne Kent....35 G4
Bishops Cannings
Wilts 40 B7
Bishop's Castle
Shrops 83 G5
Bishop's Caundle
Dorset 27 G8
Bishop's Cleeve
Gloucs 55 L3
Bishop's Frome
Herefs 70 B5
Bishop's Green Essex...61 G4
Bishop's Hull Somset....25 J6
Bishop's Itchington
Warwks 72 E3
Bishops Lydeard
Somset 25 J5
Bishop's Norton
Gloucs 55 J3
Bishop's Nympton
Devon 24 B6
Bishop's Offley Staffs...99 H6
Bishop's Stortford
Herts 60 D4
Bishop's Sutton
Hants 29 L5
Bishop's Tachbrook
Warwks 72 C3
Bishop's Tawton
Devon 23 J5

Bishopsteignton
Devon 7 K2
Bishopstoke Hants.........29 J7
Bishopston Swans.........51 H7
Bishopstone Bucks........58 D6
Bishopstone E Susx......19 M5
Bishopstone Herefs.......69 H5
Bishopstone Kent..........47 K6
Bishopstone Swindn....40 E4
Bishopstone Wilts..........28 B6
Bishopstrow Wilts..........27 K3
Bishop Sutton BaNES....38 E7
Bishop's Waltham
Hants 29 K7
Bishopswood Somset....25 K8
Bishop's Wood Staffs....84 E2
Bishopsworth Bristl......38 E6
Bishop Thornton
N York 132 D6
Bishopthorpe C York....124 F2
Bishopton Darltn 141 J3
Bishopton Rens 174 E4
Bishop Wilton E R Yk....134 C7
Bishton Newpt..............38 B3
Bishton Staffs.............100 A7
Bisley Gloucs...............55 K6
Bisley Surrey................42 F8
Bissoe Cnwll 3 K3
Bisterne Hants.............15 L3
Bitchfield Lincs..........103 G6
Bittadon Devon............23 J3
Bittaford Devon 6 F4
Bitterley Shrops............83 L7
Bitterne C Sotn.............29 J8
Bitteswell Leics............87 G6
Bitton S Glos 39 G6
Bix Oxon 42 B4
Bixter Shet.................235 c5
Blaby Leics..................87 H4
Blackadder Border.......179 H7
Blackawton Devon 7 J5
Blackborough Devon....12 E1
Blackborough End
Norfk 90 F1
Black Bourton Oxon.....56 F6
Blackboys E Susx...........20 B2
Blackbrook Derbys......101 G3
Blackbrook St Hel.......112 D3
Blackbrook Staffs.........99 H5
Blackburn Abers.........206 F3
Blackburn Bl w D 121 K5
Blackburn W Loth.......176 D5
Blackburn with
Darwen Services
Bl w D 121 K5
Blackcraig E Ayrs........164 C7
Black Crofts Ag & B 182 D1
Blackdog Abers...........207 H3
Black Dog Devon 11 J3
Blackdown Dorset.........13 K2
Blacker Hill Barns........115 G2
Blackfen Gt Lon 45 J5
Blackfield Hants............16 E3
Blackford P & K 185 J5
Blackford Somset..........26 B2
Blackford Somset..........26 F6
Blackfordby Leics........101 G8
Blackhall C Edin..........177 H4
Blackhall Colliery
Dur 151 K6
Blackhall Mill Gatesd..150 E4
Blackheath Gt Lon........45 G5
Blackheath Sandw........85 H6
Blackheath Suffk..........93 J8
Blackheath Surrey.........31 G3
Blackhill Abers............217 K3
Blackhill Abers............217 K3
Blackhill Dur 150 D5
Blackhill of
Clackriach Abers...217 H5
Blackhorse Devon 12 C4
Blacklaw D & G 165 K7
Blackley Manch 113 J2
Blacklunans P & K.......195 J4
Blackmarstone
Herefs 69 K6

Blackmill Brdgnd 36 E3
Blackmoor Hants.............30 C5
Blackmoor N Som.............38 C7
Blackmoorfoot Kirk.....123 G7
Blackmore Essex.............60 F7
Blackmore End
    Essex.............................61 H2
Black Mountains 53 K3
Blackness Falk 176 E3
Blacknest Hants.............30 D3
Black Notley Essex 61 J4
Blacko Lancs.................122 C3
Black Pill Swans.............51 J7
Blackpool Bpool...........120 D4
Blackpool Devon..............7 K6
Blackpool Zoo Bpool... 120 D4
Blackridge W Loth.........176 B5
Blackrod Bolton............121 J4
Blacksboat Moray.........214 E6
Blackshaw D & G........147 J2
Blackshaw Head
    Calder.......................122 E5
Blackstone W Susx........19 H3
Black Street Suffk.........93 K6
Blackthorn Oxon...........57 L4
Blackthorpe Suffk.........77 K2
Blacktoft E R Yk...........125 J5
Blacktop C Aber...........207 G4
Black Torrington
    Devon.........................10 C4
Blackwall Bpool...........100 E3
Blackwall Tunnel
    Gt Lon........................45 H4
Blackwater Cnwll.............3 J3
Blackwater Hants...........42 D7
Blackwater IoW 17 G5
Blackwater Somset........25 K7
Blackwaterfoot
    N Ayrs......................162 A4
Blackwell Cumb 148 D4
Blackwell Derbys.........101 H2
Blackwell Derbys.........114 C6
Blackwell Warwks..........72 B5
Blackwell Worcs............71 H1
Blackwood Caerph.........37 J2
Blackwood D & G.........154 F5
Blackwood S Lans.........164 F1
Blacon Ches W...............111 L7
Bladnoch D & G..........145 J4
Bladon Oxon..................57 J5
Blaenannerch Cerdgn....65 H5
Blaenau Ffestiniog
    Gwynd........................96 A4
Blaenavon Torfn............53 K6
Blaenavon
    Industrial
    Landscape Torfn........53 K6
Blaencwm Rhondd........52 E7
Blaenffos Pembks..........65 H6
Blaengarw Brdgnd.........36 D2
Blaengwrach Neath........52 D6
Blaengwynfi Neath.........36 D2
Blaenpennal Cerdgn......66 E2
Blaenplwyf Cerdgn.........80 D7
Blaenporth Cerdgn.........65 J5
Blaenrhondda
    Rhondd......................52 E7
Blaenwaun Carmth.......50 B1
Blaen-y-coed
    Carmth......................65 K8
Blagdon N Som.............38 D8
Blagdon Somset............25 K7
Blagdon Torbay...............7 K4
Blagdon Hill Somset.....25 K7
Blaich Highld................191 K2
Blain Highld.................190 D3
Blaina Blae G.................53 J6
Blair Atholl P & K.........194 D4
Blair Drummond
    Stirlg........................184 F7
Blairgowrie P & K........195 J7
Blairhall Fife.................176 D2
Blairingone P & K.........185 K7
Blairlogie Stirlg............185 H7
Blairmore Ag & B.........173 L2
Blairmore Highld.........228 C4
Blair's Ferry Ag & B......173 G4

Blaisdon Gloucs..............55 G5
Blakebrook Worcs..........84 E7
Blakedown Worcs...........84 F7
Blake End Essex.............61 H4
Blakemere Ches W 112 D7
Blakemere Herefs..........69 G6
Blakenall Heath
    Wsall..........................85 H3
Blakeney Gloucs............54 F6
Blakeney Norfk............106 B4
Blakenhall Ches E..........99 G3
Blakenhall Wolves.........85 G4
Blakesley Nhants............73 J4
Blanchland Nthumb......150 B5
Blandford Forum
    Dorset.......................15 G2
Blandford St Mary
    Dorset.......................15 G2
Blanefield Stirlg............174 F3
Blankney Lincs.............103 H1
Blantyre S Lans............175 J6
Blàr a' Chaorainn
    Highld.......................191 J3
Blarghour Ag & B.........182 E5
Blargie Highld...............202 F6
Blarmachfoldach
    Highld.......................191 L3
Blaston Leics..................88 B4
Blatherwycke Nhants......88 D4
Blawith Cumb...............129 G2
Blawquhairn D & G.......154 B5
Blaxhall Suffk................79 H3
Blaxton Donc................116 A2
Blaydon Gatesd.............150 F3
Bleadney Somset............26 C3
Bleadon N Som..............25 M1
Blean Kent....................34 F3
Bleasby Notts...............102 B3
Blebocraigs Fife.............187 G4
Bleddfa Powys................68 E2
Bledington Gloucs..........56 E4
Bledlow Bucks................58 C7
Bledlow Ridge Bucks.....42 D2
Blegbie E Loth..............178 B6
Blencarn Cumb.............138 F2
Blencogo Cumb............147 L5
Blendworth Hants...........30 B8
Blenheim Palace
    Oxon..........................57 H5
Blennerhasset Cumb.....147 L6
Bletchingdon Oxon........57 J4
Bletchingley Surrey........32 B3
Bletchley M Keyn...........58 E2
Bletchley Shrops............98 F5
Bletchley Park
    Museum M Keyn.......74 C7
Bletherston Pembks.......49 H4
Bletsoe Bed...................74 E3
Blewbury Oxon..............41 K4
Blickling Norfk.............106 E6
Blidworth Notts............101 L2
Blidworth Bottoms
    Notts........................101 L2
Blindcrake Cumb..........147 K7
Blindley Heath
    Surrey........................32 C4
Blisland Cnwll.................5 H2
Blissford Hants..............28 D8
Bliss Gate Worcs............84 D8
Blisworth Nhants............73 K4
Blithbury Staffs.............100 B8
Blockley Gloucs..............71 L7
Blofield Norfk................93 G2
Blofield Heath Norfk 93 G2
Blo Norton Norfk...........92 B7
Bloomfield Border........167 J4
Blore Staffs..................100 C3
Bloxham Oxon................72 E7
Bloxholm Lincs.............103 H2
Bloxwich Wsall...............85 H3
Bloxworth Dorset...........15 G4
Blubberhouses
    N York......................132 B7
Blue Anchor Somset.....24 F3
Blue Bell Hill Kent........46 C7
Blue John Cavern
    Derbys.....................114 C5

Blundellsands Sefton .. 111 J2
Blundeston Suffk............93 L4
Blunham C Beds.............75 H4
Blunsdon St
    Andrew Swindn.........40 C3
Bluntington Worcs.........84 F8
Bluntisham Cambs.........89 L8
Blurton C Stke...............99 K4
Blyborough Lincs..........116 F3
Blyford Suffk.................93 J7
Blymhill Staffs................84 E2
Blyth Notts...................115 L4
Blyth Nthumb...............159 H5
Blyth Bridge Border......165 M1
Blythburgh Suffk...........93 J7
Blythe Border................178 D7
Blythe Bridge Staffs......99 L4
Blyth Services Notts.....115 L4
Blyton Lincs.................116 D3
Boarhills Fife...............187 J5
Boarhunt Hants............17 H2
Boarstall Bucks...............57 L5
Boath Highld................222 D6
Boat of Garten
    Highld.......................203 L2
Bobbing Kent................46 E6
Bobbington Staffs..........84 E5
Bocking Essex.................61 J4
Bocking
    Churchstreet
    Essex.........................61 J3
Boddam Abers..............217 L6
Boddam Shet................235 c7
Boddington Gloucs........55 K3
Bodedern IoA...............108 D5
Bodelwyddan Denbgs...110 D6
Bodenham Herefs..........69 K4
Bodenham Wilts.............28 D6
Bodenham Moor
    Herefs........................69 K4
Bodewryd IoA..............108 E4
Bodfari Denbgs.............110 F7
Bodffordd IoA..............108 F6
Bodham Norfk..............106 D4
Bodiam E Susx...............33 K7
Bodicote Oxon................72 F6
Bodinnick Cnwll..............5 H5
Bodle Street Green
    E Susx........................20 D3
Bodmin Cnwll..................5 G3
Bodmin Moor Cnwll........5 J1
Bodsham Kent................34 E5
Boduan Gwynd...............94 F5
Bodwen Cnwll..................5 G4
Bogallan Highld............212 F4
Bogbrae Abers..............217 J7
Bogend S Ayrs..............163 K3
Boggs Holdings
    E Loth......................177 L4
Boghall Mdloth.............177 H5
Boghall W Loth.............176 D5
Boghead S Lans............164 F2
Bogmoor Moray............215 H2
Bogmuir Abers..............197 G3
Bogniebrae Abers.........216 B5
Bognor Regis W Susx....18 C6
Bogroy Highld...............203 L2
Bogue D & G.................154 B6
Bohortha Cnwll................3 L5
Bohuntine Highld.........201 L8
Bolam Dur....................140 F3
Bolberry Devon...............7 H7
Boldmere Birm...............85 K5
Boldre Hants..................16 C3
Boldron Dur.................140 C4
Bole Notts....................116 C4
Bolehill Derbys.............100 F2
Bolham Devon................24 E7
Bolham Water Devon....25 J8
Bolingey Cnwll.................3 K1
Bollington Ches E..........113 L6
Bolney W Susx...............19 J2
Bolnhurst Bed................74 F3
Bolnore W Susx..............19 J2
Bolshan Angus.............197 G6
Bolsover Derbys...........115 J7
Bolsterstone Sheff........114 F3

Boltby N York...............133 G3
Boltenstone Abers........205 J3
Bolton Bolton................121 L8
Bolton Cumb.................138 F3
Bolton E Loth...............178 B4
Bolton E R Yk...............125 J1
Bolton Nthumb.............169 G6
Bolton Abbey N York....131 K8
Bolton-by-Bowland
    Lancs........................122 B1
Boltonfellend Cumb......148 E2
Boltongate Cumb..........147 M6
Bolton-le-Sands
    Lancs........................129 K6
Bolton Low Houses
    Cumb........................147 M6
Bolton-on-Swale
    N York.......................141 G7
Bolton Percy N York......124 E3
Bolton upon Dearne
    Barns.......................115 J2
Bolventor Cnwll...............5 J1
Bomere Heath
    Shrops........................98 C8
Bonar Bridge Highld....222 E3
Bonawe Ag & B............182 E2
Bonby N Linc................126 C7
Boncath Pembks............65 H6
Bonchester Bridge
    Border......................167 J6
Bondleigh Devon............10 F4
Bonds Lancs.................121 G2
Bo'ness Falk.................176 D3
Boney Hay Staffs............85 J2
Bonhill W Duns............174 D3
Boningale Shrops...........84 E3
Bonjedward Border.......167 K5
Bonkle N Lans..............175 L6
Bonnington Angus........196 F7
Bonnington Kent............34 E7
Bonnybank Fife............186 F6
Bonnybridge Falk.........175 L3
Bonnykelly Abers..........217 G4
Bonnyrigg Mdloth.........177 J5
Bonnyton Angus...........196 B8
Bonsall Derbys.............100 F2
Bonshaw Tower
    D & G........................155 M7
Bont-Dolgadfan
    Powys........................81 J4
Bont-goch Cerdgn.........80 F6
Bontnewydd Cerdgn......66 E2
Bontnewydd Gwynd.......95 H1
Bontuchel Denbgs.........97 G2
Bonvilston V Glam.........37 G5
Boode Devon..................23 H4
Booker Bucks..................42 D3
Boon Border.................167 J1
Boosbeck R & Cl...........142 E4
Boose's Green Essex......61 K2
Boot Cumb...................137 G6
Booth Calder................122 F5
Boothby Graffoe
    Lincs........................103 G2
Boothby Pagnell
    Lincs........................102 F6
Boothferry E R Yk........125 H5
Boothstown Salfd.........113 G2
Boothville Nhants..........73 L2
Bootle Cumb................128 D2
Bootle Sefton................111 K3
Boraston Shrops............70 B1
Bordeaux Guern...........236 e2
Borden Kent..................34 B3
Boreham Essex..............61 J6
Boreham Street
    E Susx........................20 D4
Borehamwood Herts.....44 D2
Boreland D & G...........155 L4
Boreraig Highld............208 C4
Borgh W Isls................232 f1
Borgh W Isls................233 b9
Borgie Highld...............229 K4
Borgue D & G...............146 B5
Borgue Highld..............227 L2
Borley Essex...................77 J6
Borneskitaig Highld......218 B7

Borness D & G 146 A5
Boroughbridge
  N York.................... 132 F6
Borough Green Kent......33 G2
Borrowash Derbys.... 101 H5
Borrowby N York..... 132 F2
Borrowdale Cumb 137 J4
Borrowstoun Falk...... 176 D3
Borstal Medway..............46 B6
Borth Cerdgn..............80 E5
Borthwick Mdloth.... 177 K6
Borthwickbrae
  Border...................... 166 F6
Borthwickshiels
  Border...................... 166 F6
Borth-y-Gest Gwynd... 95 K5
Borve W Isls.............. 209 G5
Borve W Isls.............. 232 d4
Borve W Isls.............. 232 f1
Borve W Isls.............. 233 b9
Borwick Lancs............ 129 L5
Bosbury Herefs..............70 C5
Boscastle Cnwll................8 E6
Boscombe BCP.............. 15 L4
Boscombe Wilts............28 D4
Bosham W Susx............ 17 L2
Bosherston Pembks.....49 G8
Bosley Ches E.............. 113 K7
Bossall N York............ 133 L7
Bossiney Cnwll................8 E6
Bossingham Kent..........34 F5
Bossington Somset 24 D2
Bostock Green
  Ches W.................... 112 F7
Boston Lincs.............. 104 B4
Boston Spa Leeds..... 124 C2
Boswinger Cnwll............ 4 F7
Botallack Cnwll 2 C5
Botany Bay Gt Lon.....59 M7
Botesdale Suffk............92 C7
Bothal Nthumb......... 159 G5
Bothamsall Notts..... 116 A6
Bothel Cumb.............. 147 L6
Bothenhampton
  Dorset......................13 L4
Bothwell S Lans......... 175 J6
Bothwell Services
  S Lans..................... 175 J6
Botley Bucks..............59 G7
Botley Hants............29 K8
Botley Oxon..............57 J6
Botolph Claydon
  Bucks......................58 B3
Botolphs W Susx.... 19 G4
Bottesford Leics..... 102 D5
Bottesford N Linc.... 125 L8
Bottisham Cambs.....76 D3
Bottomcraig Fife..... 186 F3
Bottoms Calder..... 122 D6
Botusfleming Cnwll...... 6 B4
Botwnnog Gwynd.....94 E6
Bough Beech Kent......32 E4
Boughrood Powys.....68 C6
Boughton Nhants.....73 L2
Boughton Norfk.....91 G3
Boughton Notts..... 116 B7
Boughton Aluph
  Kent......................34 D5
Boughton Green
  Kent......................33 K3
Boughton
  Monchelsea Kent......33 K3
Boughton Street
  Kent......................34 E3
Bouldon Shrops.....83 K6
Boulmer Nthumb.... 169 K6
Boultham Lincs..... 116 F7
Bourn Cambs..............75 K3
Bournbrook Birm.....85 J6
Bourne Lincs.............. 103 H7
Bournebridge Essex.....45 J2
Bourne End Bucks.....42 E3
Bourne End C Beds.....74 D5
Bourne End Herts.....59 G6
Bournemouth BCP...... 15 K4
Bournemouth
  Airport BCP 15 L3

Bournes Green
  Sthend...................... 46 E3
Bournheath Worcs.....85 G8
Bournmoor Dur..... 151 H5
Bournville Birm.....85 J7
Bourton Dorset..............27 H5
Bourton Oxon..............40 E3
Bourton Shrops.....83 L4
Bourton Wilts..............40 B7
Bourton on
  Dunsmore
  Warwks......................72 E1
Bourton-on-the-
  Hill Gloucs..............56 D2
Bourton-on-the-
  Water Gloucs..............56 D4
Bousd Ag & B.............. 189 G4
Bouth Cumb............. 129 H3
Bouthwaite N York.... 131 L5
Boveridge Dorset............28 B7
Bovey Tracey Devon........7 J1
Bovingdon Herts..............59 G7
Bow Devon.................. 11 G4
Bow Gt Lon..............45 G4
Bow Ork.................. 234 b7
Bow Brickhill M Keyn.....74 C7
Bowbridge Gloucs..............55 J6
Bowburn Dur..... 151 H7
Bowcombe IoW..............16 F5
Bowd Devon.................. 12 E4
Bowden Border..... 167 H4
Bowden Hill Wilts............39 L6
Bowdon Traffd..... 113 H4
Bower Highld..... 231 J3
Bowerchalke Wilts............28 A6
Bowermadden Highld.. 231 J3
Bowers Staffs..............99 J5
Bowers Gifford
  Essex......................46 C3
Bowershall Fife..... 176 F1
Bower's Row Leeds.... 124 B5
Bowes Dur..... 140 C4
Bowgreave Lancs..... 121 G2
Bowhouse D & G..... 147 H2
Bowland Border..... 167 G2
Bowley Herefs..............69 K4
Bowlhead Green
  Surrey....................30 E4
Bowling C Brad..... 123 H4
Bowling W Duns..... 174 E4
Bowmanstead Cumb.... 137 J7
Bowmore Ag & B..... 170 F6
Bowness-on-
  Solway Cumb..... 147 L3
Bowness-on-
  Windermere
  Cumb..... 137 L7
Bow of Fife Fife..... 186 E5
Bowriefauld Angus... 196 E6
Bowsden Nthumb..... 168 E2
Bow Street Cerdgn.....80 E6
Bowthorpe Norfk.....92 E2
Box Gloucs..............55 K7
Box Wilts..............39 J6
Boxford Suffk..............77 L6
Boxford W Berk..............41 H6
Boxgrove W Susx...... 18 B4
Boxley Kent..............33 K2
Boxmoor Herts..............59 H6
Boxted Essex......................62 B2
Boxted Essex......................62 B2
Boxted Suffk..............77 J4
Boxworth Cambs.....75 L2
Boyden Gate Kent.....47 L6
Boylestone Derbys.... 100 D5
Boyndie Abers..... 216 C2
Boyndlie Abers..... 217 G2
Boynton E R Yk..... 135 H6
Boysack Angus..... 197 G6
Boyton Cnwll.................. 9 J6
Boyton Suffk..............79 H5
Boyton Wilts..............27 L4
Boyton Cross Essex.....61 G6
Boyton End Suffk..............77 G5
Bozeat Nhants..............74 C3
Brabourne Kent..............34 E6

Brabourne Lees Kent....34 E6
Brabstermire Highld.... 231 K2
Bracadale Highld......... 208 E6
Braceborough Lincs.....88 F2
Bracebridge Heath
  Lincs...................... 117 G7
Bracebridge Low
  Fields Lincs...... 116 F7
Braceby Lincs..... 103 G5
Bracewell Lancs..... 122 C2
Brackenfield Derbys.... 101 G1
Brackenhirst N Lans.... 175 K5
Brackla Brdgnd..............36 E4
Bracklesham W Susx.... 17 L3
Brackletter Highld..... 201 J8
Brackley Nhants.....73 H6
Bracknell Br For..............42 E6
Braco P & K..... 185 H5
Bracobrae Moray..... 215 L4
Bracon Ash Norfk.....92 E4
Bracora Highld..... 199 L6
Bracorina Highld..... 199 L6
Bradbourne Derbys.... 100 D3
Bradbury Dur..... 141 H2
Bradden Nhants.....73 J5
Bradeley C Stke..............99 K3
Bradenham Bucks.....42 D2
Bradenstoke Wilts.....39 M4
Bradfield Devon.................. 12 D1
Bradfield Essex......................62 D2
Bradfield Norfk..... 106 F5
Bradfield Sheff..... 114 F3
Bradfield W Berk..............41 L6
Bradfield Combust
  Suffk......................77 K3
Bradfield Green
  Ches E..............99 G2
Bradfield Heath
  Essex......................62 D3
Bradfield St Clare
  Suffk......................77 K3
Bradfield St George
  Suffk......................77 K3
Bradford C Brad..... 123 H4
Bradford Devon.................. 9 L4
Bradford Abbas
  Dorset....................26 E8
Bradford Leigh Wilts.....39 J7
Bradford-on-Avon
  Wilts......................39 J7
Bradford-on-Tone
  Somset....................25 J6
Bradford Peverell
  Dorset....................14 C4
Bradiford Devon..............23 J5
Brading IoW..............17 H5
Bradley Derbys..... 100 E4
Bradley Hants............29 M3
Bradley NE Lin..... 118 C1
Bradley Staffs..............99 K8
Bradley Wolves.....85 G4
Bradley Worcs..............71 H3
Bradley Green Worcs.....71 H3
Bradley in the
  Moors Staffs..... 100 B4
Bradley Stoke S Glos.....38 E4
Bradmore Notts..... 101 L6
Bradninch Devon.................. 12 C2
Bradnop Staffs..... 100 A2
Bradpole Dorset.................. 13 L4
Bradshaw Calder..... 123 G4
Bradstone Devon.................. 9 K8
Bradwall Green
  Ches E...................... 113 H8
Bradwell Derbys..... 114 D5
Bradwell Essex......................61 J4
Bradwell M Keyn..............74 B6
Bradwell Norfk..............93 K3
Bradwell-on-Sea
  Essex......................62 B6
Bradwell Waterside
  Essex......................62 B6
Bradworthy Devon.................. 9 J3
Brae Highld..... 213 G2
Brae Shet..... 235 c4
Braeface Falk..... 175 K3
Braehead Angus..... 197 H5

Braehead D & G.............. 145 J4
Braehead S Lans..... 176 C7
Braeintra Highld..... 210 D7
Braemar Abers..... 204 E6
Braemore Highld..... 221 G5
Braemore Highld..... 227 J3
Brae Roy Lodge
  Highld..................... 201 L6
Braeside Inver..... 173 L4
Braes of Coul Angus... 195 L5
Braes of Enzie Moray.. 215 J3
Braeswick Ork..... 234 d4
Braevallich Ag & B..... 182 D6
Braewick Shet..... 235 b3
Brafferton Darltn..... 141 H3
Brafferton N York.... 132 F5
Brafield-on-the-
  Green Nhants..............74 B3
Bragar W Isls..... 232 f2
Bragbury End Herts.....59 L4
Braidwood S Lans..... 175 L8
Brailsford Derbys.... 100 E4
Braintree Essex......................61 J4
Braiseworth Suffk.....78 D1
Braishfield Hants.....29 G6
Braithwaite Cumb..... 137 H3
Braithwell Donc..... 115 K3
Bramber W Susx...... 19 G4
Bramcote Warwks.....86 E5
Bramdean Hants............29 L5
Bramerton Norfk.....93 G3
Bramfield Herts.....59 M5
Bramfield Suffk..............93 H8
Bramford Suffk..............78 D5
Bramhall Stockp..... 113 K5
Bramham Leeds..... 124 C2
Bramhope Leeds..... 123 K2
Bramley Hants......41 M8
Bramley Leeds..... 123 K4
Bramley Rothm..... 115 J3
Bramley Surrey............31 G3
Bramling Kent..............35 G4
Brampford Speke
  Devon...................... 11 L5
Brampton Cambs.....75 J1
Brampton Cumb..... 138 F3
Brampton Cumb..... 148 F3
Brampton Lincs..... 116 D5
Brampton Norfk..... 106 F7
Brampton Rothm..... 115 H2
Brampton Suffk..............93 J6
Brampton Abbotts
  Herefs....................54 E3
Brampton Ash
  Nhants....................87 L6
Brampton Bryan
  Herefs....................83 G8
Brampton-en-le-
  Morthen Rothm..... 115 J4
Bramshall Staffs..... 100 B6
Bramshaw Hants............28 F7
Bramshott Hants............30 D5
Bramwell Somset............26 B5
Branault Highld..... 190 B3
Brancaster Norfk..... 105 J4
Brancaster Staithe
  Norfk..................... 105 J4
Brancepeth Dur..... 150 F7
Branchill Moray..... 214 D4
Branderburgh Moray... 214 F1
Brandesburton
  E R Yk..................... 126 E2
Brandeston Suffk.....78 F3
Brandiston Norfk..... 106 D7
Brandon Dur..... 151 G6
Brandon Lincs..... 102 E3
Brandon Suffk..............91 H6
Brandon Warwks.....86 E7
Brandon Parva Norfk.....92 C2
Brandsby N York..... 133 J3
Brandy Wharf Lincs.... 117 G3
Bran End Essex......................61 G3
Branksome BCP...... 15 K4
Branksome Park
  BCP...................... 15 K4
Bransbury Hants............29 H3
Bransby Lincs..... 116 E5

Branscombe Devon........12 F5
Bransford Worcs.............70 E4
Bransgore Hants.............16 A3
Bransholme C KuH....... 126 D4
Bransley Shrops.............84 B7
Branston Leics 102 D6
Branston Lincs 117 G2
Branston Staffs 100 E7
Branston Booths
   Lincs........................ 117 H7
Branstone IoW 17 G5
Brant Broughton
   Lincs........................ 102 E2
Brantham Suffk.............78 D7
Branthwaite Cumb. 136 E3
Branthwaite Cumb. 148 B7
Brantingham E R Yk... 125 L5
Branton Donc.............. 115 M2
Branton Nthumb....... 168 F6
Branton Green
   N York...................... 132 F6
Branxton Nthumb....... 168 D2
Brassington Derbys... 100 E2
Brasted Kent.................32 E3
Brasted Chart Kent.......32 E3
Brathens Abers........... 206 D5
Bratoft Lincs 119 G8
Brattleby Lincs 116 F5
Bratton Wilts.................27 K2
Bratton Wrekin 84 B2
Bratton Clovelly
   Devon........................10 C6
Bratton Fleming
   Devon........................23 K4
Bratton Seymour
   Somset......................26 F5
Braughing Herts............60 C3
Braunston Nhants.........73 G2
Braunston RutInd.........88 B3
Braunton Devon............23 H4
Brawby N York 134 B4
Brawl Highld............... 230 B3
Bray W & M...................42 E4
Braybrooke Nhants.......87 L6
Brayford Devon.............23 L4
Bray Shop Cnwll 5 M2
Brayton N York 124 F4
Braywick W & M............42 E4
Breachwood Green
   Herts.........................59 J4
Breacleit W Isls........... 232 e2
Breaclete W Isls........... 232 e2
Breadsall Derbys......... 101 G5
Breadstone Gloucs......55 G7
Breage Cnwll...................3 G5
Breakachy Highld........ 212 D5
Breakish Highld........... 199 L2
Brealangwell Lodge
   Highld...................... 222 C3
Bream Gloucs................54 E6
Breamore Hants............28 D7
Brean Somset................25 L1
Breanais W Isls 232 a3
Brearton N York 132 E7
Breascleit W Isls......... 232 e2
Breasclete W Isls......... 232 e2
Breaston Derbys 101 J5
Brechfa Carmth.............66 C7
Brechin Angus 196 F4
Breckles Norfk...............91 L5
Brecon Powys...............53 G3
Brecon Beacons
   National Park 52 F3
Bredbury Stockp......... 113 L3
Brede E Susx.................21 G3
Bredenbury Herefs.......69 L3
Bredfield Suffk..............78 F4
Bredgar Kent.................34 B3
Bredhurst Kent..............46 D7
Bredon Worcs................71 G6
Bredon's Hardwick
   Worcs........................71 G7
Bredon's Norton
   Worcs........................71 G6
Bredwardine Herefs......69 G5
Breedon on the Hill
   Leics....................... 101 H7

Breich W Loth................ 176 C6
Breightmet Bolton...... 121 L8
Breighton E R Yk........ 125 G4
Breinton Herefs.............69 J6
Bremhill Wilts.................39 L5
Brenchley Kent 33 H5
Brendon Devon..............24 B2
Brenfield Ag & B 172 E2
Brenish W Isls 232 d3
Brent Cross Gt Lon......44 E3
Brent Eleigh Suffk.........77 L5
Brentford Gt Lon...........44 D5
Brentingby Leics......... 102 C8
Brent Knoll Somset......25 M2
Brent Mill Devon............7 G4
Brent Pelham Herts......60 C2
Brentwood Essex..........45 L2
Brenzett Kent 21 K1
Brenzett Green Kent....34 D8
Brereton Staffs..............85 J1
Brereton Green
   Ches E...................... 113 H8
Bressay Shet............... 235 d6
Bressingham Norfk.......92 C7
Bretby Derbys............. 100 F7
Bretford Warwks..........86 E7
Bretforton Worcs..........71 K5
Bretherton Lancs........ 121 G6
Brettabister Shet........ 235 d5
Brettenham Norfk.........91 L6
Brettenham Suffk.........77 L4
Bretton C Pete.............89 H4
Bretton Flints.............. 111 K8
Brewood Staffs.............84 F2
Briantspuddle Dorset.....14 F4
Brickendon Herts..........60 A6
Bricket Wood Herts......59 J7
Brick Houses Sheff 114 F5
Bricklehampton
   Worcs........................71 H6
Bride IoM 237 e2
Bridekirk Cumb. 147 K7
Bridestowe Devon........10 D6
Brideswell Abers......... 216 B6
Bridford Devon.............11 J7
Bridge Kent...................35 G4
Bridgefoot Angus....... 186 F1
Bridgehampton
   Somset......................26 E6
Bridge Hewick
   N York...................... 132 E5
Bridgehill Dur.............. 150 D5
Bridgemary Hants........17 H2
Bridgend Abers........... 215 L7
Bridgend Ag & B 161 K2
Bridgend Ag & B 171 G6
Bridgend Angus.......... 196 E3
Bridgend Brdgnd...........36 E4
Bridgend Cerdgn...........65 G5
Bridgend D & G........... 165 L7
Bridgend Devon..............6 E6
Bridgend Fife.............. 186 F5
Bridgend Moray........... 215 J7
Bridgend P & K............ 186 B3
Bridgend W Loth......... 176 E3
Bridgend of
   Lintrathen Angus.... 195 L5
Bridge of Alford
   Abers........................ 206 B2
Bridge of Allan Stirlg.. 185 G7
Bridge of Avon
   Moray....................... 204 D2
Bridge of Avon
   Moray....................... 214 E7
Bridge of Balgie
   P & K........................ 193 J6
Bridge of
   Brewlands Angus.... 195 J4
Bridge of Brown
   Highld...................... 204 D2
Bridge of Cally P & K.. 195 J6
Bridge of Canny
   Abers........................ 206 C6
Bridge of Craigisla
   Angus....................... 195 K5
Bridge of Dee D & G.... 146 C3
Bridge of Don C Aber.. 207 H4

Bridge of Dye Abers..... 206 C7
Bridge of Earn P & K.... 186 B4
Bridge of Ericht
   P & K........................ 193 H5
Bridge of Feugh
   Abers........................ 206 D6
Bridge of Gairn
   Abers........................ 205 H6
Bridge of Gaur P & K... 193 H5
Bridge of Marnoch
   Abers........................ 216 B4
Bridge of Muchalls
   Abers........................ 207 G6
Bridge of Orchy
   Ag & B...................... 192 E7
Bridge of Tilt P & K...... 194 D4
Bridge of Tynet
   Moray....................... 215 J3
Bridge of Walls Shet.. 235 b5
Bridge of Weir Rens.... 174 D5
Bridgerule Devon...........9 H4
Bridge Sollers
   Herefs.......................69 H6
Bridge Street Suffk.......77 K5
Bridgetown Somset......24 E5
Bridge Trafford
   Ches W..................... 112 C7
Bridgham Norfk.............91 L6
Bridgnorth Shrops........84 C5
Bridgwater Somset......25 L4
Bridgwater Services
   Somset......................25 L4
Bridlington E R Yk...... 135 J6
Bridport Dorset............13 L4
Bridstow Herefs............54 E3
Brierfield Lancs.......... 122 C3
Brierley Barns............. 124 C7
Brierley Gloucs.............54 F5
Brierley Hill Dudley......85 G6
Brigg N Linc................ 117 G1
Briggate Norfk............ 107 G6
Briggswath N York...... 143 H5
Brigham Cumb. 136 F2
Brigham E R Yk........... 135 G8
Brighouse Calder........ 123 H6
Brighstone IoW............17 G6
Brighthampton Oxon....57 G7
Brightley Devon.............10 E5
Brightling E Susx..........20 D2
Brightlingsea Essex......62 C5
Brighton Br & H.............19 J5
Brighton City
   Airport W Susx......... 19 G5
Brighton le Sands
   Sefton..................... 111 J2
Brightons Falk............ 176 C3
Brightwalton W Berk....41 H5
Brightwell Suffk............78 F5
Brightwell Baldwin
   Oxon........................41 M2
Brightwell-cum-
   Sotwell Oxon............41 L3
Brightwell
   Upperton Oxon........42 A2
Brignall Dur................ 140 D5
Brig o'Turk Stirlg........ 184 C6
Brigsley NE Lin............ 118 C2
Brigsteer Cumb. 129 K2
Brigstock Nhants..........88 D6
Brill Bucks....................58 A5
Brill Cnwll......................3 J5
Brilley Herefs................68 F5
Brimfield Herefs............69 K2
Brimfield Cross
   Herefs.......................69 K2
Brimington Derbys..... 115 H6
Brimley Devon................7 J1
Brimpsfield Gloucs......55 L5
Brimpton W Berk..........41 K7
Brimscombe Gloucs.....55 J7
Brimstage Wirral........ 111 J5
Brincliffe Sheff........... 115 F4
Brind E R Yk................ 125 H4
Brindister Shet........... 235 c5
Brindle Lancs.............. 121 J5
Brineton Staffs.............84 E2
Bringhurst Leics...........88 B5

Bringsty Common
   Herefs.......................70 C4
Brington Cambs 88 F7
Briningham Norfk....... 106 C5
Brinkhill Lincs 118 E6
Brinkley Cambs 76 F4
Brinklow Warwks.........86 E7
Brinkworth Wilts..........40 A4
Brinscall Lancs........... 121 J6
Brinsley Notts............. 101 J3
Brinsworth Rothm..... 115 H4
Brinton Norfk.............. 106 C5
Brinyan Ork................. 234 c5
Brisley Norfk............... 105 M7
Brislington Bristl..........38 F6
Brissenden Green
   Kent..........................34 C6
Bristol Bristl.................38 E5
Bristol Airport N Som.. 38 D7
Bristol Zoo Gardens
   Bristl........................38 E5
Briston Norfk.............. 106 C6
Britford Wilts................28 D5
Brithdir Caerph.............53 J7
Brithdir Gwynd.............96 B8
British Legion
   Village Kent..............33 J2
Briton Ferry Neath.......51 L6
Britwell Salome
   Oxon........................42 A2
Brixham Torbay..............7 L5
Brixton Devon.................6 E5
Brixton Gt Lon...............44 F5
Brixton Deverill Wilts....27 K4
Brixworth Nhants.........73 L1
Brize Norton Oxon........56 F6
Brize Norton
   Airport Oxon............ 56 F6
Broad Alley Worcs........70 F2
Broad Blunsdon
   Swindn.....................40 D3
Broadbottom Tamesd.. 113 M3
Broadbridge W Susx......17 M2
Broadbridge Heath
   W Susx......................31 J5
Broad Campden
   Gloucs......................71 L6
Broad Carr Calder...... 123 G6
Broad Chalke Wilts......28 B6
Broadclyst Devon.........12 C3
Broadfield Inver......... 174 C4
Broadford Highld........ 199 K2
Broadford Bridge
   W Susx......................31 H6
Broadgairhill Border ... 166 C7
Broad Green Worcs......70 D4
Broadhaugh Border.... 179 H7
Broad Haven Pembks....48 E5
Broadheath Traffd 113 H4
Broadhembury
   Devon........................12 E2
Broadhempston
   Devon..........................7 J3
Broad Hinton Wilts.......40 C5
Broadland Row
   E Susx......................21 G2
Broadley Moray.......... 215 J3
Broad Marston
   Worcs........................71 K5
Broadmayne Dorset.....14 D5
Broad Meadow
   Staffs........................99 J3
Broadmoor Pembks......49 J6
Broadoak Dorset..........13 K3
Broad Oak Cumb. 120 C2
Broad Oak E Susx.........21 G2
Broad Oak Herefs.........54 C4
Broad Oak Kent............35 G3
Broad Oak St Hel........ 112 D3
Broadsands Torbay........7 K4
Broad's Green Essex.....61 H5
Broadstairs Kent..........35 K2
Broadstone BCP...........15 J4
Broadstone Shrops.......83 K5
Broad Street E Susx......21 H3
Broad Street Kent.........33 L2
Broad Town Wilts..........40 C5

Broadwas Worcs 70 D4
Broadwater Herts.............59 L4
Broadwater W Susx........18 F5
Broadwaters Worcs 84 E7
Broadway Pembks........48 E5
Broadway Somset.........25 L7
Broadway Worcs..............71 K6
Broadwell Gloucs.........54 E5
Broadwell Gloucs.........56 D3
Broadwell Oxon..........56 E6
Broadwell Warwks........72 F2
Broadwindsor Dorset....13 K2
Broadwood Kelly
  Devon.........10 F4
Broadwoodwidger
  Devon.........9 K6
Brochel Highld.........209 J5
Brochroy Ag & B.......182 E2
Brockamin Worcs.......70 D4
Brockbridge Hants......29 L7
Brockdish Norfk........92 E7
Brockenhurst Hants.....16 C3
Brocketsbrae S Lans....164 F2
Brockford Street
  Suffk.........78 D2
Brockhall Nhants......73 J2
Brockham Surrey.......31 K2
Brockhampton
  Gloucs.........56 B4
Brockhampton Hants....17 K2
Brockhampton
  Herefs.........54 E2
Brockholes Kirk......123 H7
Brocklesby Lincs......126 E7
Brockley N Som........38 C6
Brockley Suffk........77 J1
Brockley Green Suffk...77 G5
Brockley Green Suffk...77 J4
Brockmoor Dudley......84 F5
Brockton Shrops.......83 G3
Brockton Shrops.......83 G6
Brockton Shrops.......83 L5
Brockweir Gloucs......54 D7
Brockworth Gloucs.....55 K5
Brocton Staffs........99 L8
Brodick N Ayrs.......162 C3
Brodie Moray.........214 B3
Brodsworth Donc......115 J1
Brogaig Highld.......218 C7
Brokenborough Wilts...39 K3
Broken Cross Ches E...113 K6
Brokerswood Wilts.....27 J2
Bromborough Wirral...111 K5
Brome Suffk..........92 D7
Brome Street Suffk....92 D7
Bromeswell Suffk......79 G4
Bromfield Cumb.......147 L5
Bromfield Shrops......83 J7
Bromham Bed..........74 E4
Bromham Wilts........39 L7
Bromley Dudley.......85 G6
Bromley Gt Lon........45 H6
Bromley Shrops.......84 D4
Bromley Cross Bolton..121 L7
Brompton Medway......46 C6
Brompton N York......141 J7
Brompton-by-
  Sawdon N York.....134 E3
Brompton-on-
  Swale N York......140 F7
Brompton Ralph
  Somset.........25 G5
Brompton Regis
  Somset.........24 E5
Bromsberrow Gloucs....70 D7
Bromsberrow Heath
  Gloucs.........55 G2
Bromsgrove Worcs.....71 G1
Bromyard Herefs......70 B4
Bronant Cerdgn.......66 E2
Brongest Cerdgn......65 K5
Bronington Wrexhm....98 C4
Bronllys Powys........68 D7
Bronwydd Carmth......50 E2
Brongarth Shrops......97 K5
Brook Hants..........28 F8
Brook IoW...........16 E5

Brook Kent..........34 E6
Brook Surrey.........30 F4
Brooke Norfk.........93 G4
Brooke Rutlnd........88 B3
Brookenby Lincs......117 K3
Brookfield Rens......174 D5
Brookhampton
  Somset.........26 F5
Brook Hill Hants......28 F8
Brookhouse Lancs.....129 L6
Brookhouse Rothm....115 K4
Brookhouse Green
  Ches E.........99 J1
Brookhouses Derbys...114 B4
Brookland Kent.......21 K1
Brooklands Traffd....113 H4
Brookmans Park
  Herts.........59 L7
Brook Street Essex....45 L2
Brook Street Kent.....34 C7
Brookthorpe Gloucs....55 J5
Brookwood Surrey.....42 F8
Broom C Beds........75 H6
Broom Rothm.........115 H3
Broom Warwks........71 K4
Broome Norfk.........93 H5
Broome Shrops.......83 H7
Broome Worcs........84 F7
Broomedge Warrtn....113 G4
Broomfield Essex......61 H5
Broomfield Kent.......33 L3
Broomfield Kent.......47 K6
Broomfield Somset....25 K5
Broomfleet E R Yk....125 K5
Broomhaugh Nthumb...150 C3
Broom Hill Barns......115 H2
Broom Hill Notts......101 K3
Broomhill Nthumb.....159 G3
Broompark Dur.......151 G6
Brora Highld.........226 F7
Broseley Shrops......84 C3
Brotherlee Dur.......150 A7
Brotherton N York....124 D5
Brotton R & Cl.......142 E4
Broubster Highld.....230 F4
Brough Cumb.........139 H4
Brough E R Yk.......125 L5
Brough Highld........231 J2
Brough Notts.........102 D2
Brough Shet.........235 d4
Broughall Shrops......98 E4
Brough Lodge Shet....235 d2
Brough Sowerby
  Cumb.........139 H5
Broughton Border.....165 L3
Broughton Cambs......89 K7
Broughton Flints.....111 K8
Broughton Hants......28 F5
Broughton Lancs......121 G4
Broughton M Keyn....74 C6
Broughton N Linc.....126 B8
Broughton N York....122 D1
Broughton N York....134 B5
Broughton Nhants.....88 B7
Broughton Oxon......72 E6
Broughton Salfd......113 J2
Broughton V Glam.....36 E6
Broughton Astley
  Leics.........87 G5
Broughton Gifford
  Wilts.........39 K7
Broughton Green
  Worcs.........71 G3
Broughton Hackett
  Worcs.........71 G4
Broughton-in-
  Furness Cumb......128 F3
Broughton Mains
  D & G.........145 J6
Broughton Mills
  Cumb.........128 F2
Broughton Moor
  Cumb.........147 J7
Broughton Poggs
  Oxon.........56 E7
Broughty Ferry
  C Dund.........187 H2

Brown Candover
  Hants.........29 L4
Brown Edge Staffs....99 K2
Brownhill Abers.....217 G6
Brownhills Fife......187 H4
Brownhills Wsall......85 J3
Browninghill Green
  Hants.........41 L7
Brown Lees Staffs....99 K2
Brownsea Island
  Dorset.........15 J5
Brown's Green Birm...85 J5
Browns Hill Gloucs....55 K7
Brownston Devon.......7 G5
Broxa N York.........134 E2
Broxbourne Herts......60 B6
Broxburn E Loth.....178 E3
Broxburn W Loth.....176 E4
Broxted Essex........60 F3
Bruan Highld........231 K7
Bruar P & K.........194 C3
Bruchag Ag & B......173 J6
Bruichladdich Ag & B..170 E6
Bruisyard Suffk......79 G2
Bruisyard Street
  Suffk.........79 G2
Brumby N Linc......125 K8
Brund Staffs.........100 C1
Brundall Norfk........93 G2
Brundish Suffk........78 F1
Brundish Street
  Suffk.........78 F1
Brunery Highld......190 E3
Brunswick Village
  N u Ty.........159 G7
Brunthwaite C Brad...122 F2
Bruntingthorpe Leics...87 H5
Brunton Fife........186 E3
Brunton Wilts........28 E1
Brushford Devon......11 G4
Brushford Somset.....24 E6
Bruton Somset........27 G4
Bryan's Green Worcs...70 F2
Bryanston Dorset......15 G2
Brydekirk D & G......155 L7
Bryher IoS...........2 a1
Brympton Somset.....26 D7
Bryn Carmth.........51 G5
Bryn Neath..........36 C3
Bryn Wigan.........112 E2
Brynamman Carmth....51 K3
Brynberian Pembks....64 F7
Bryncir Gwynd........95 H4
Bryn-côch Neath......51 L5
Bryncroes Gwynd......94 D6
Bryncrug Gwynd.......80 E3
Bryneglwys Denbgs....97 H3
Brynford Flints.....111 G6
Bryn Gates Wigan....112 E2
Bryngwran IoA.......108 D6
Bryngwyn Mons.......54 B6
Bryngwyn Powys.......68 D5
Bryn-Henllan
  Pembks.........64 E6
Brynhoffnant Cerdgn...65 K4
Brynmawr Blae G......53 J5
Bryn-mawr Gwynd......94 D5
Brynmenyn Brdgnd.....36 D4
Brynmill Swans.......51 J6
Brynna Rhondd........36 F4
Brynrefail Gwynd....109 H8
Brynsadler Rhondd.....37 G4
Bryn Saith Marchog
  Denbgs.........97 G3
Brynsiencyn IoA.....108 F7
Brynteg IoA........109 G5
Bryn-y-Maen Conwy...110 B6
Bualintur Highld.....198 F2
Bubbenhall Warwks....86 D8
Bubwith E R Yk......125 H4
Buccleuch Border....166 E6
Buchanan Smithy
  Stirlg.........174 E1
Buchanhaven Abers...217 L5
Buchanty P & K.......185 J2
Buchany Stirlg......184 F6
Buchlyvie Stirlg.....184 C8

Buckabank Cumb......148 C5
Buckden Cambs........75 H2
Buckden N York.....131 H4
Buckenham Norfk......93 H3
Buckerell Devon.......12 E3
Buckfast Devon........7 H3
Buckfastleigh Devon...7 H3
Buckhaven Fife......186 F7
Buckholt Mons.......54 D5
Buckhorn Weston
  Dorset.........27 H6
Buckhurst Hill Essex...45 H2
Buckie Moray........215 J2
Buckingham Bucks....73 K7
Buckland Bucks.......58 E5
Buckland Devon........7 G6
Buckland Gloucs......71 J7
Buckland Herts.......75 L7
Buckland Kent........35 J6
Buckland Oxon.......41 G2
Buckland Surrey......31 K2
Buckland Brewer
  Devon.........22 F7
Buckland Common
  Bucks.........58 F6
Buckland Dinham
  Somset.........27 H2
Buckland Filleigh
  Devon.........10 C3
Buckland in the
  Moor Devon........7 G2
Buckland
  Monachorum
  Devon.........6 D3
Buckland Newton
  Dorset.........14 D2
Buckland Ripers
  Dorset.........14 C6
Buckland St Mary
  Somset.........25 L8
Buckland-Tout-
  Saints Devon.......7 H6
Bucklebury W Berk....41 K6
Bucklers Hard Hants...16 E3
Bucklesham Suffk......78 F6
Buckley Flints.......111 J8
Bucklow Hill Ches E...113 G5
Buckminster Leics....102 E7
Bucknall C Stke.......99 K3
Bucknall Lincs......117 K7
Bucknell Oxon........57 K3
Bucknell Shrops......83 G8
Buckpool Moray.....215 J2
Bucksburn C Aber....207 G4
Buck's Cross Devon....22 E6
Bucks Green W Susx...31 H5
Buckshaw Village
  Lancs.........121 H6
Bucks Horn Oak
  Hants.........30 D3
Buck's Mills Devon....22 E6
Buckton E R Yk.....135 J5
Buckton Nthumb.....169 G2
Buckworth Cambs......89 G7
Budby Notts........115 L7
Bude Cnwll...........9 G4
Budge's Shop Cnwll....5 M4
Budleigh Salterton
  Devon.........12 D6
Budock Water Cnwll....3 K5
Buerton Ches E.......99 G4
Bugbrooke Nhants.....73 J3
Bugle Cnwll...........4 F4
Bugley Dorset........27 H6
Bugthorpe E R Yk....134 B7
Buildwas Shrops......84 B3
Builth Wells Powys....68 B4
Bulbridge Wilts......28 C5
Bulford Wilts........28 D3
Bulkeley Ches E......98 D2
Bulkington Warwks....86 E6
Bulkington Wilts......39 L8
Bulkworthy Devon......9 K3
Bullbrook Br For......42 E6
Bullington Hants.....29 J3
Bullington Lincs....117 H6
Bulmer Essex........77 J6

Bulmer N York.............. 133 L6
Bulmer Tye Essex.............77 J6
Bulphan Thurr.................45 M3
Bulwark Abers 217 H5
Bulwell C Nott.............. 101 K4
Bulwick Nhants 88 D5
Bumble's Green
    Essex.................60 C6
Bunacaimb Highld 199 K7
Bunarkaig Highld........ 201 J7
Bunbury Ches E............98 E2
Bunchrew Highld 212 F5
Bundalloch Highld...... 210 D8
Bunessan Ag & B........ 180 E3
Bungay Suffk.................93 G5
Bunnahabhain
    Ag & B 171 H4
Bunny Notts 101 L6
Buntait Highld 212 C7
Buntingford Herts........60 B3
Bunwell Norfk..............92 D5
Burbage Leics..............86 F5
Burbage Wilts..............40 E7
Burchett's Green
    W & M.................42 D4
Burcombe Wilts 28 B5
Burcott Bucks 58 E4
Bures Essex...................77 K7
Burford Oxon 56 E5
Burford Shrops 69 L2
Burg Ag & B 189 J7
Burgess Hill W Susx......19 J2
Burgh Suffk...................78 F4
Burgh by Sands
    Cumb 148 B3
Burgh Castle Norfk 93 K3
Burghclere Hants..........41 J7
Burghead Moray 214 D1
Burghfield W Berk 42 A6
Burghfield Common
    W Berk 42 A6
Burgh Heath Surrey 44 E7
Burghill Herefs..............69 J5
Burgh Island Devon 6 F6
Burgh le Marsh Lincs.. 119 G7
Burgh next Aylsham
    Norfk 106 F7
Burgh on Bain Lincs.... 117 L4
Burgh St Margaret
    Norfk 93 J4
Burgh St Peter Norfk 93 K5
Burghwallis Donc 124 E7
Burham Kent.................46 B7
Buriton Hants 30 C7
Burland Ches E..............98 E2
Burlawn Cnwll 4 F2
Burleigh Gloucs.............55 K7
Burlescombe Devon 25 G7
Burleston Dorset 14 E4
Burley Hants 16 B2
Burley Rutlnd..............88 C2
Burleydam Ches E 98 E4
Burley Gate Herefs.........69 L5
Burley in
    Wharfedale
    C Brad 123 H2
Burley Street Hants 16 B2
Burley Wood Head
    C Brad 123 H2
Burlton Shrops 98 C7
Burmarsh Kent...............34 E7
Burmington Warwks......72 C6
Burn N York.................. 124 F5
Burnage Manch 113 K3
Burnaston Derbys........ 100 F6
Burnbrae N Lans 176 B6
Burnby E R Yk............. 125 K2
Burneside Cumb 138 D7
Burneston N York........ 132 D3
Burnett BaNES.............38 F7
Burnfoot Border 166 F6
Burnfoot Border 167 H6
Burnfoot D & G........... 155 G4
Burnfoot D & G........... 156 C3
Burnfoot D & G........... 156 C4
Burnfoot P & K........... 185 K6
Burnham Bucks..............42 F4

Burnham Deepdale
    Norfk 105 J4
Burnham Market
    Norfk 105 K4
Burnham Norton
    Norfk 105 K4
Burnham-on-
    Crouch Essex....... 46 F2
Burnham-on-Sea
    Somset 25 L2
Burnham Overy
    Norfk 105 K4
Burnham Overy
    Staithe Norfk...... 105 K4
Burnham Thorpe
    Norfk 105 K4
Burnhead D & G....... 154 E3
Burnhervie Abers 206 D2
Burnhill Green Staffs....84 E4
Burnhope Dur............. 150 F5
Burnhouse N Ayrs...... 174 D7
Burniston N York........ 134 F2
Burnley Lancs 122 C4
Burnmouth Border 179 K6
Burn of Cambus
    Stirlg 184 F6
Burnopfield Dur......... 150 F4
Burnsall N York........... 131 J7
Burnside Angus 196 C4
Burnside Angus 196 E6
Burnside Fife.............. 186 B5
Burnside Moray.......... 214 E1
Burnside W Loth......... 176 E3
Burnside of
    Duntrune Angus .. 187 G1
Burntisland Fife......... 177 H2
Burnton E Ayrs........... 163 L7
Burntwood Staffs.........85 J2
Burntwood Green
    Staffs..................85 J2
Burnt Yates N York 132 C7
Burnworthy Somset 25 J7
Burpham Surrey...........31 G2
Burpham W Susx..........18 E4
Burradon Nthumb 168 E7
Burrafirth Shet........... 235 e1
Burravoe Shet............ 235 d3
Burrells Cumb............ 138 F4
Burrelton P & K.......... 195 K8
Burridge Devon 13 H2
Burridge Hants............17 G1
Burrill N York.............. 132 C3
Burringham N Linc...... 125 K8
Burrington Devon 10 F2
Burrington Herefs........69 J1
Burrington N Som 38 C8
Burrough Green
    Cambs 76 F4
Burrough on the
    Hill Leics 87 L2
Burrow Lancs 130 C4
Burrow Somset 24 E3
Burrow Bridge
    Somset 25 M5
Burrowhill Surrey.........42 F7
Burry Green Swans......50 F7
Burry Port Carmth 50 F5
Burscough Lancs 120 F7
Burscough Bridge
    Lancs 120 F7
Bursea E R Yk............. 125 J4
Bursledon Hants 16 F1
Burstall Suffk...............78 D5
Burstock Dorset 13 K2
Burston Norfk...............92 D6
Burstow Surrey 32 B5
Burswick E R Yk........... 126 F5
Burtersett N York........ 131 G2
Burtholme Cumb 148 F3
Burthorpe Green
    Suffk...................77 H2
Burtoft Lincs 103 L5
Burton BCP..................15 M4
Burton Ches W............ 111 K6
Burton Ches W............ 112 D8
Burton Pembks............49 G6
Burton Somset 25 J3

Burton Wilts..................39 J4
Burton Agnes E R Yk... 135 H6
Burton Bradstock
    Dorset 13 L4
Burton-by-Lincoln
    Lincs................. 116 F6
Burton Coggles Lincs.. 103 G7
Burton End Essex..........60 E4
Burton Fleming
    E R Yk................ 135 G5
Burton Hastings
    Warwks................86 E5
Burton-in-Kendal
    Cumb 129 L4
Burton-in-Kendal
    Services Cumb ... 129 L4
Burton in Lonsdale
    N York................ 130 C5
Burton Joyce Notts.... 101 M4
Burton Latimer
    Nhants.................88 C8
Burton Lazars Leics......87 L1
Burton Leonard
    N York................ 132 E6
Burton on the
    Wolds Leics 101 L7
Burton Overy Leics......87 J4
Burton Pedwardine
    Lincs................. 103 J4
Burton Pidsea E R Yk... 127 G4
Burton Salmon
    N York................ 124 D5
Burton's Green Essex..... 61 K3
Burton upon
    Stather N Linc.... 125 K6
Burton upon Trent
    Staffs................. 100 E7
Burton Waters Lincs.. 116 F6
Burtonwood Warrtn.... 112 E3
Burtonwood
    Services Warrtn.... 112 E4
Burwardsley Ches W......98 D2
Burwarton Shrops........84 B6
Burwash E Susx............33 H7
Burwash Common
    E Susx 20 D2
Burwash Weald
    E Susx 20 D2
Burwell Cambs.............76 E2
Burwell Lincs.............. 118 E5
Burwen IoA................ 108 E3
Burwick Ork................ 234 c8
Bury Cambs..................89 K6
Bury Somset 24 E6
Bury W Susx.................18 D3
Bury Green Herts 60 D4
Bury St Edmunds
    Suffk...................77 J2
Burythorpe N York..... 134 C6
Busby E Rens.............. 175 G6
Buscot Oxon 40 E2
Bush Bank Herefs.........69 J4
Bushbury Wolves..........85 G3
Bushey Herts.................43 J2
Bushey Heath Herts......43 J2
Bush Hill Park Gt Lon.....45 G2
Bushley Worcs...............70 F7
Bushmoor Shrops.........83 J6
Bushton Wilts...............40 B5
Bussage Gloucs.............55 K7
Bussex Somset 26 A4
Butcombe N Som 38 D7
Bute Ag & B............... 173 H4
Butleigh Somset 26 D5
Butleigh Wootton
    Somset 26 D4
Butlers Marston
    Warwks................72 D4
Butley Suffk..................79 H4
Buttercrambe N York... 133 L7
Butterdean Border 179 G5
Butterknowle Dur...... 140 E3
Butterleigh Devon 12 C2
Buttermere Cumb 137 G4
Buttershaw C Brad 123 H5

Butterstone P & K 195 G7
Butterton Staffs 99 J8
Butterton Staffs 100 B2
Butterwick Lincs......... 104 C4
Butterwick N York...... 133 L4
Butterwick N York...... 134 F5
Buttington Powys..........82 E2
Buttonoak Shrops........84 D7
Buxhall Suffk................78 B3
Buxted E Susx...............20 A2
Buxton Derbys............ 114 B6
Buxton Norfk.............. 106 F7
Buxton Heath Norfk... 106 E7
Bwlch Powys.................53 J4
Bwlchgwyn Wrexhm......97 K2
Bwlch-y-cibau Cerdgn ..66 D3
Bwlchtocyn Gwynd.......94 E7
Bwlch-y-cibau
    Powys...................97 J3
Bwlch-y-ffridd
    Powys...................82 B4
Bwlch-y-groes
    Pembks 65 H7
Bwlch-y-sarnau
    Powys...................82 B8
Byers Green Dur........ 150 F7
Byfield Nhants..............73 G4
Byfleet Surrey 43 H7
Byford Herefs................69 H6
Byker N u Ty............... 151 G3
Bylchau Conwy.......... 110 D8
Byley Ches W.............. 113 G7
Byrness Nthumb 157 K2
Bystock Devon 12 D5
Bythorn Cambs............88 F7
Byton Herefs.................69 G2
Bywell Nthumb 150 D3
Byworth W Susx...........31 G7

C

Cabourne Lincs.......... 117 J2
Cabrach Ag & B.......... 171 J5
Cabrach Moray........... 215 J8
Cabus Lancs............... 121 G2
Cadbury Devon 11 L4
Cadbury World Birm....85 J7
Cadder E Duns 175 G4
Caddington C Beds 59 H4
Caddonfoot Border 167 G3
Cadeby Donc.............. 115 K2
Cadeby Leics................86 E3
Cadeleigh Devon 11 L4
Cade Street E Susx........20 C2
Cadgwith Cnwll 3 J7
Cadham Fife............... 186 D6
Cadishead Salfd......... 113 G3
Cadle Swans.................51 J6
Cadley Lancs.............. 121 G4
Cadley Wilts.................28 E2
Cadley Wilts.................40 E6
Cadmore End Bucks......42 C3
Cadnam Hants..............28 F8
Cadney N Linc............ 117 G2
Cadoxton V Glam 37 H6
Cadoxton Juxta-
    Neath Neath.........51 L5
Caeathro Gwynd...........95 J1
Caenby Lincs.............. 117 G4
Caerau Brdgnd............36 D7
Caerau Cardif...............37 H5
Caer Farchell
    Pembks 48 D3
Caergeiliog IoA.......... 108 D5
Caergwrle Flints 97 L2
Caerlanrig Border 156 D2
Caerleon Newpt...........37 M3
Caernarfon Gwynd.... 108 F8
Caernarfon Castle
    Gwynd................ 108 F8
Caerphilly Caerph........37 J3
Caersws Powys.............82 B5
Caerwedros Cerdgn 65 L4
Caerwent Mons............38 C3
Caerwys Flints............ 110 F6

Caio Carmth.....66 F6
Cairinis W Isls.....233 c6
Cairnbaan Ag & B.....172 E1
Cairnbulg Abers.....217 J2
Cairncross Border.....179 J5
Cairncurran Inver.....174 C4
Cairndow Ag & B.....183 H5
Cairneyhill Fife.....176 E2
Cairngarroch D & G.....144 C5
Cairngorms
National Park.....204 L2
Cairnie Abers.....215 K5
Cairnorrie Abers.....217 J2
Cairnryan D & G.....144 C2
Cairnty Moray.....215 H4
Caister-on-Sea
Norfk.....93 L2
Caistor Lincs.....117 J2
Caistor St Edmund
Norfk.....92 F3
Calanais W Isls.....232 e2
Calbourne IoW.....16 E5
Calceed Flints.....111 G6
Calcot Gloucs.....56 C6
Calcot Row W Berk.....42 A6
Calcots Moray.....215 G2
Caldbeck Cumb.....148 B6
Caldecote Cambs.....75 L3
Caldecote Cambs.....89 G5
Caldecote
Highfields Cambs.....75 L3
Caldecott Nhants.....74 E2
Caldecott Oxon.....41 J2
Caldecott Rutlnd.....88 C5
Calderbank N Lans.....175 K5
Calder Bridge Cumb.....136 E6
Caldercruix N Lans.....175 L5
Calder Grove Wakefd.....123 L6
Caldermill S Lans.....164 D2
Calder Vale Lancs.....121 G2
Calderwood S Lans.....175 H7
Caldey Island
Pembks.....49 K7
Caldmore Wsall.....85 H4
Caldwell N York.....140 E5
Calf of Man IoM.....237 a7
Calfsound Ork.....234 d4
Calgary Ag & B.....189 J6
Califer Moray.....214 D3
California Falk.....176 B3
California Norfk.....93 K1
Calke Derbys.....101 G7
Calke Abbey Derbys.....101 G7
Callakille Highld.....209 L4
Callander Stirlg.....184 D5
Callanish W Isls.....232 e2
Callestick Cnwll.....3 K2
Calligarry Highld.....199 K5
Callington Cnwll.....6 A3
Callow Herefs.....69 J7
Callow End Worcs.....70 E4
Callow Hill Wilts.....40 B4
Calmore Hants.....29 G7
Calmsden Gloucs.....56 B6
Calne Wilts.....39 M6
Calshot Hants.....16 F3
Calstock Cnwll.....6 C3
Calstone Wellington
Wilts.....40 B6
Calthorpe Norfk.....106 E6
Calthorpe Street
Norfk.....107 J7
Calthwaite Cumb.....148 E6
Calton Staffs.....100 C3
Calveley Ches E.....98 E2
Calver Derbys.....114 E6
Calverhall Shrops.....98 E5
Calverleigh Devon.....11 L3
Calverton M Keyn.....73 L6
Calverton Notts.....101 L4
Calvine P & K.....194 C3
Calzeat Border.....165 L3
Cam Gloucs.....55 H7
Camasachoirce
Highld.....190 F4
Camasine Highld.....190 F4

Camas Luinie Highld.....210 E8
Camastianavaig
Highld.....209 H6
Camault Muir Highld.....212 D6
Camber E Susx.....21 J2
Camberley Surrey.....42 E7
Camberwell Gt Lon.....44 F5
Camblesforth N York.....124 F5
Cambo Nthumb.....158 C5
Camborne Cnwll.....3 H4
Camborne &
Redruth Mining
District Cnwll.....3 H4
Cambourne Cambs.....75 K3
Cambridge Cambs.....76 C3
Cambridge Gloucs.....55 H7
Cambridge Airport
Cambs.....76 C3
Cambrose Cnwll.....3 H3
Cambus Clacks.....185 H8
Cambusavie Highld.....223 G3
Cambusbarron Stirlg.....185 G8
Cambuskenneth
Stirlg.....185 G8
Cambuslang S Lans.....175 H6
Cambus o' May
Abers.....205 J5
Cambuswallace
S Lans.....165 K2
Camden Town Gt Lon.....44 F4
Cameley BaNES.....38 E8
Camelford Cnwll.....8 E7
Camelon Falk.....176 B3
Camerory Highld.....214 C7
Camerton BaNES.....39 G8
Camerton Cumb.....136 E2
Camghouran P & K.....193 J5
Camieston Border.....167 J4
Cammachmore
Abers.....207 G6
Cammeringham
Lincs.....116 F5
Camore Highld.....223 G4
Campbeltown Ag & B.....161 J5
Campbeltown
Airport Ag & B.....161 H5
Cample D & G.....154 F4
Campmuir P & K.....195 K8
Camps W Loth.....176 E5
Campsall Donc.....124 E7
Campsea Ash Suffk.....79 G4
Campton C Beds.....75 G6
Camptown Border.....167 K6
Camrose Pembks.....48 F4
Camserney P & K.....194 C6
Camusnagaul Highld.....191 L2
Camusnagaul Highld.....220 D4
Camusteel Highld.....209 L6
Camusterrach Highld.....209 L6
Canada Hants.....28 F7
Candacraig Abers.....205 H5
Candlesby Lincs.....118 F7
Candy Mill Border.....165 L2
Cane End Oxon.....42 B4
Canewdon Essex.....46 E2
Canford Cliffs BCP.....15 K5
Canford Heath BCP.....15 J4
Canisbay Highld.....231 L2
Canley Covtry.....86 C7
Cann Dorset.....27 K7
Canna Highld.....198 C4
Cann Common
Dorset.....27 K7
Cannich Highld.....211 L7
Cannington Somset.....25 K4
Canning Town Gt Lon.....45 H4
Cannock Staffs.....85 H2
Cannock Chase
Staffs.....99 M8
Cannon Bridge
Herefs.....69 H6
Canonbie D & G.....156 C6
Canon Frome Herefs.....70 B5
Canon Pyon Herefs.....69 J5
Canons Ashby
Nhants.....73 H4
Canonstown Cnwll.....2 F4

Canterbury Kent.....34 F3
Canterbury
Cathedral Kent.....34 F3
Cantley Norfk.....93 H3
Canton Cardif.....37 J5
Cantraywood Highld.....213 J5
Cantsfield Lancs.....130 C5
Canvey Island Essex.....46 D4
Canwick Lincs.....117 G7
Canworthy Water
Cnwll.....9 G6
Caol Highld.....191 L2
Caolas Scalpaigh
W Isls.....232 e4
Caoles Ag & B.....188 D6
Caonich Highld.....201 G6
Capel Kent.....33 H4
Capel Surrey.....31 K4
Capel Bangor Cerdgn.....80 E7
Capel Coch IoA.....108 F5
Capel Curig Highld.....96 A2
Capel Dewi Carmth.....50 F2
Capel Dewi Cerdgn.....66 B6
Capel-Dewi Cerdgn.....80 E6
Capel Garmon Conwy.....96 C2
Capel Hendre Carmth.....51 H4
Capel Iwan Carmth.....65 J7
Capel-le-Ferne Kent.....35 H6
Capelles Guern.....236 d2
Capel Parc IoA.....108 F4
Capel St Andrew
Suffk.....79 H5
Capel St Mary Suffk.....78 C6
Capel Seion Cerdgn.....80 E7
Capelulo Conwy.....109 L6
Capenhurst Ches W.....111 K6
Cape Wrath Highld.....228 D1
Capheaton Nthumb.....158 C6
Caplaw E Rens.....174 E6
Cappercleuch Border.....166 C5
Capton Devon.....7 J5
Caputh P & K.....195 H7
Caradon Mining
District Cnwll.....5 L2
Carbeth Inn Stirlg.....174 F3
Carbis Bay Cnwll.....2 F4
Carbost Highld.....208 F5
Carbost Highld.....208 F7
Carbrook Sheff.....115 G4
Carbrooke Norfk.....91 L3
Car Colston Notts.....102 B4
Carcroft Donc.....124 E8
Cardenden Fife.....186 C7
Cardhu Moray.....214 F5
Cardiff Cardif.....37 J5
Cardiff Airport
V Glam.....37 G6
Cardiff Gate
Services Cardif.....37 K4
Cardiff West
Services Cardif.....37 H4
Cardigan Cerdgn.....65 G5
Cardington Bed.....74 F5
Cardington Shrops.....83 K4
Cardinham Cnwll.....5 H3
Cardrain D & G.....144 D8
Cardrona Border.....166 D2
Cardross Ag & B.....174 C3
Cardryne D & G.....144 D7
Cardurnock Cumb.....147 L3
Careby Lincs.....88 E1
Careston Angus.....196 E4
Carew Pembks.....49 H6
Carew Cheriton
Pembks.....49 H6
Carew Newton
Pembks.....49 H6
Carey Herefs.....54 E2
Carfin N Lans.....175 K6
Carfraemill Border.....178 B7
Cargate Green Norfk.....93 H2
Cargenbridge D & G.....155 G7
Cargill P & K.....195 J8
Cargo Cumb.....148 C3
Cargreen Cnwll.....6 C4
Carham Nthumb.....168 B2
Carhampton Somset.....24 F3

Carharrack Cnwll.....3 J3
Carie P & K.....193 K5
Carinish W Isls.....233 c6
Carisbrooke IoW.....16 F5
Cark Cumb.....129 H4
Carkeel Cnwll.....6 B4
Càrlabhagh W Isls.....232 e2
Carlbury Darltn.....140 F4
Carlby Lincs.....88 F2
Carleen Cnwll.....3 G5
Carleton Forehoe
Norfk.....92 C3
Carleton-in-Craven
N York.....122 E1
Carleton Rode Norfk.....92 D5
Carleton St Peter
Norfk.....93 H3
Carlincraig Abers.....216 D5
Carlingcott BaNES.....39 G8
Carlisle Cumb.....148 D4
Carlisle Airport
Cumb.....148 E3
Carlops Border.....177 G6
Carloway W Isls.....232 e2
Carlton Barns.....124 B7
Carlton Bed.....74 D4
Carlton Cambs.....76 F4
Carlton Leeds.....123 L5
Carlton Leics.....86 E3
Carlton N York.....124 F5
Carlton N York.....131 K3
Carlton N York.....133 J3
Carlton Notts.....101 L4
Carlton S on T.....141 J3
Carlton Suffk.....79 H2
Carlton Colville Suffk.....93 K5
Carlton Curlieu Leics.....87 K4
Carlton Green Cambs.....76 F4
Carlton Husthwaite
N York.....133 G4
Carlton-in-
Cleveland N York.....142 B6
Carlton in Lindrick
Notts.....115 L5
Carlton-le-
Moorland Lincs.....102 E2
Carlton Miniott
N York.....132 F4
Carlton-on-Trent
Notts.....116 D8
Carlton Scroop Lincs.....102 F4
Carluke S Lans.....175 L7
Carmacoup S Lans.....164 F4
Carmarthen Carmth.....50 E2
Carmel Carmth.....51 H3
Carmel Flints.....111 G6
Carmel Gwynd.....95 H2
Carmichael S Lans.....165 H2
Carmunnock C Glas.....175 G6
Carmyle C Glas.....175 H6
Carmyllie Angus.....196 E7
Carnaby E R Yk.....135 H6
Carnbee Fife.....187 J6
Carnbo P & K.....185 L6
Carn Brea Cnwll.....3 H3
Carnbrogie Abers.....216 F8
Carndu Highld.....210 D8
Carnduff S Lans.....164 D1
Carnell E Ayrs.....163 L3
Carnforth Lancs.....129 K5
Carn-gorm Highld.....200 E2
Carnhell Green Cnwll.....3 G4
Carnie Abers.....206 F4
Carnkie Cnwll.....3 H4
Carnkie Cnwll.....3 J4
Carno Powys.....81 K4
Carnock Fife.....176 E1
Carnon Downs Cnwll.....4 C7
Carnousie Abers.....216 C4
Carnoustie Angus.....187 J1
Carnwath S Lans.....176 D8
Carol Green Solhll.....86 C7
Carperby N York.....131 J2
Carradale Ag & B.....161 K2
Carrbridge Highld.....203 L2
Carrefour Jersey.....236 c6
Carreglefn IoA.....108 E4

Carr Gate Wakefd........ 123 L5
Carrhouse N Linc.......... 116 C1
Carrick Ag & B 172 F2
Carrick Castle Ag & B.. 183 H8
Carriden Falk............... 176 D3
Carrington Mdloth....... 177 J6
Carrington Traffd....... 113 H3
Carrog Denbgs.............97 H4
Carron Falk 176 B2
Carron Moray.............. 214 F6
Carronbridge D & G.... 154 F3
Carron Bridge Stirlg... 175 K2
Carronshore Falk 176 B2
Carr Shield Nthumb.... 149 K5
Carrutherstown
  D & G................... 155 J7
Carruth House Inver.. 174 C5
Carrville Dur 151 H6
Carsaig Ag & B............ 181 H3
Carseriggan D & G 145 G2
Carsethorn D & G....... 147 H3
Carshalton Gt Lon.......44 F6
Carsington Derbys...... 100 E2
Carskey Ag & B........... 161 H7
Carsluith D & G.......... 145 K4
Carsphairn D & G 153 L4
Carstairs S Lans 165 H1
Carstairs Junction
  S Lans.............. 165 J1
Carterton Oxon 56 F6
Carthew Cnwll............... 4 F5
Carthorpe N York 132 D3
Cartland S Lans 165 G1
Cartmel Cumb............. 129 H4
Carway Carmth............50 F4
Cashe's Green Gloucs...55 J6
Cassington Oxon 57 J5
Cassop Dur................. 151 J7
Castel Guern 236 c3
Casterton Cumb........... 130 C4
Castle Acre Norfk 91 J1
Castle Ashby Nhants....74 C3
Castlebay W Isls.......... 233 b9
Castle Bolton N York... 131 J2
Castle Bromwich
  Solhll 85 K5
Castle Bytham Lincs.... 103 G8
Castlebythe Pembks....49 H2
Castle Caereinion
  Powys...................82 D3
Castle Camps Cambs...76 F6
Castle Carrock Cumb .. 148 F4
Castlecary Falk 175 K3
Castle Cary Somset 26 F5
Castle Combe Wilts 39 J5
Castle Donington
  Leics 101 H6
Castle Douglas D &G.. 146 D3
Castle Eaton Swindn....40 C2
Castle Eden Dur 151 K7
Castleford Wakefd 124 C5
Castle Frome Herefs ...70 C5
Castle Gresley
  Derbys................. 100 F8
Castle Hedingham
  Essex....................77 H7
Castlehill Border.......... 166 C3
Castlehill Highld.......... 231 H2
Castle Hill Suffk...........78 D5
Castlehill W Duns....... 174 D3
Castle Howard
  N York.................. 133 L5
Castle Kennedy
  D & G.................. 144 D3
Castle Lachlan
  Ag & B................. 182 E7
Castlemartin Pembks...48 F7
Castlemilk C Glas 175 G6
Castlemorton Worcs....70 E6
Castlemorton
  Common Worcs.........70 E6
Castle O'er D & G....... 156 A4
Castle Rising Norfk.... 105 G7
Castleside Dur 150 D5
Castle Stuart Highld... 213 H4
Castlethorpe M Keyn..74 B5
Castleton Ag & B......... 172 E4

Castleton Border.......... 156 E4
Castleton Derbys......... 114 D5
Castleton N York 142 E5
Castleton Newpt...........37 K4
Castleton Rochdl......... 122 D7
Castletown Highld....... 231 H3
Castletown IoM 237 b7
Castletown Sundld..... 151 J4
Castley N York............ 123 K2
Caston Norfk................91 L4
Castor C Pete...............89 G4
Catacol N Ayrs 172 F7
Catcliffe Rothm 115 H4
Catcomb Wilts..............39 M5
Catcott Somset...........26 B4
Catcott Burtle
  Somset....................26 B3
Caterham Surrey........32 C3
Catfield Norfk............ 107 H7
Catford Gt Lon..............45 G5
Catforth Lancs........... 121 G4
Cathcart C Glas.......... 175 G6
Cathedine Powys.........53 H3
Catherington Hants.....30 B8
Catherston
  Leweston Dorset......13 J4
Catisfield Hants...........17 G2
Catlodge Highld.......... 202 F6
Catmere End Essex.....76 C6
Catmore W Berk...........41 J4
Caton Lancs................ 129 L6
Caton Green Lancs..... 129 L6
Catrine E Ayrs............ 164 B4
Catsfield E Susx...........20 E3
Catsgore Somset........26 D6
Catshill Worcs..............85 G8
Cattadale Ag & B........ 161 H7
Cattal N York.............. 133 G8
Cattawade Suffk..........62 D2
Catterall Lancs........... 121 G3
Catterick N York 141 G7
Catterick Bridge
  N York.................. 141 G7
Catterlen Cumb........... 148 E7
Catterline Abers........ 197 L2
Catterton N York 124 D2
Catteshall Surrey........31 G3
Catthorpe Leics...........87 G7
Cattistock Dorset........14 B3
Catton N York............ 132 E4
Catton Nthumb........... 149 L4
Catwick E R Yk........... 126 E2
Catworth Cambs..........88 F8
Caudle Green Gloucs...55 L6
Caulcott Oxon..............57 K3
Cauldcots Angus......... 197 G6
Cauldhame Stirlg........ 184 E8
Cauldmill Border........ 167 H6
Cauldon Staffs........... 100 B3
Cauldwell Derbys.........86 B1
Caulkerbush D & G..... 147 G4
Caulside D & G............ 156 D6
Caundle Marsh
  Dorset...................27 G8
Caunton Notts........... 102 C1
Causeway End D & G.. 145 J3
Causeway End Essex...61 G4
Causewayend S Lans.. 165 K3
Causewayhead Stirlg.. 185 G7
Causeyend Abers........ 207 H2
Causey Park Bridge
  Nthumb 158 F3
Cavendish Suffk...........77 J5
Cavenham Suffk...........77 H1
Caversfield Oxon..........57 L3
Caversham Readg.......42 B5
Caverswall Staffs.........99 L4
Caverton Mill Border.. 167 M4
Cawdor Highld............ 213 K4
Cawood N York........... 124 E3
Cawsand Cnwll..............6 C5
Cawston Norfk........... 106 D7
Cawthorne Barns....... 123 K8
Caxton Cambs..............75 K3
Caynham Shrops.........83 K8
Caythorpe Lincs.......... 102 F3
Caythorpe Notts......... 102 B4

Cayton N York............ 135 G3
Ceannabeinne Highld.. 228 F3
Ceann a Bhaigh
  W Isls.................. 233 b6
Ceannacroc Lodge
  Highld.................. 201 K3
Cearsiadar W Isls...... 232 f3
Cefn Newpt................37 L3
Cefn-brîth Conwy.........96 E3
Cefn-bryn-brain
  Carmth...................51 L3
Cefn Cribwr Brdgnd....36 D4
Cefneithin Carmth.......51 G3
Cefngorwydd Powys....67 J5
Cefn-mawr Wrexhm.....97 L4
Cefn-y-pant Carmth.....49 K3
Cellardyke Fife............ 187 J6
Cellarhead Staffs.........99 L3
Cemaes IoA 108 E3
Cemmaes Powys...........81 H3
Cemmaes Road
  Powys....................81 H3
Cenarth Cerdgn...........65 J6
Ceres Fife................... 186 F5
Cerne Abbas Dorset....14 C3
Cerney Wick Gloucs.....40 B2
Cerrigydrudion
  Conwy....................96 E3
Ceunant Gwynd..........95 J1
Chaceley Gloucs...........55 J2
Chacewater Cnwll 3 K3
Chackmore Bucks.........73 K7
Chacombe Nhants........72 F5
Chadbury Worcs...........71 H5
Chadderton Oldham ... 113 K1
Chaddesden C Derb.... 101 G5
Chaddesley Corbett
  Worcs....................84 F8
Chaddlehanger
  Devon.....................6 C1
Chaddleworth
  W Berk...................41 H5
Chadlington Oxon........57 G4
Chadshunt Warwks......72 D4
Chadwell Leics........... 102 C7
Chadwell Heath
  Gt Lon....................45 J3
Chadwell St Mary
  Thurr.....................45 M4
Chadwick Worcs...........70 E2
Chadwick End Solhll....86 B8
Chaffcombe Somset....13 J1
Chafford Hundred
  Thurr.....................45 L4
Chagford Devon...........11 G7
Chailey E Susx.............19 K2
Chainhurst Kent..........33 J4
Chaldon Surrey...........32 B3
Chaldon Herring
  Dorset...................14 E5
Chale IoW...................16 F6
Chale Green IoW..........16 F6
Chalfont Common
  Bucks.....................43 G3
Chalfont St Giles
  Bucks.....................43 G2
Chalfont St Peter
  Bucks.....................43 G3
Chalford Gloucs...........55 K7
Chalford Wilts.............27 K2
Chalgrove Oxon...........41 M2
Chalk Kent..................46 A5
Chalkwell Kent............34 B2
Challacombe Devon.....23 L3
Challoch D & G........... 145 H2
Challock Kent..............34 D5
Chalton C Beds............59 G3
Chalton Hants.............30 B7
Chalvey Slough............42 F4
Chalvington E Susx......20 B4
Chandler's Cross
  Herts.....................43 H3
Chandler's Ford
  Hants.....................29 H7
Channel Tunnel
  Terminal Kent........35 G6
Chantry Somset..........27 G3

Chantry Suffk...............78 D5
Chapel Fife................. 186 D8
Chapel Allerton
  Leeds................... 123 L3
Chapel Allerton
  Somset....................26 B2
Chapel Amble Cnwll......4 F2
Chapel Brampton
  Nhants...................73 K2
Chapel Chorlton
  Staffs....................99 J5
Chapelend Way
  Essex....................77 G6
Chapel-en-le-Frith
  Derbys................. 114 B5
Chapel Green
  Warwks..................72 F3
Chapel Haddlesey
  N York.................. 124 E5
Chapelhall N Lans 175 K5
Chapel Hill Abers....... 217 K7
Chapel Hill Lincs........ 103 K2
Chapel Hill N York 123 L2
Chapelhope Shrops..... 166 C5
Chapelknowe D & G ... 156 B7
Chapel Lawn Shrops....82 F7
Chapel-le-Dale
  N York.................. 130 E4
Chapel Leigh Somset...25 H5
Chapel of Garioch
  Abers................... 206 D1
Chapel Rossan D & G.. 144 D6
Chapel Row W Berk 41 L6
Chapel St Leonards
  Lincs.................... 119 H6
Chapel Stile Cumb 137 K6
Chapelton Abers........ 207 G6
Chapelton Angus........ 197 G6
Chapelton Devon.........23 J6
Chapelton S Lans 175 J8
Chapeltown Bl w D..... 121 L7
Chapeltown Moray..... 204 F2
Chapeltown Sheff...... 115 G3
Chapmanslade Wilts....27 J2
Chapmans Well
  Devon.....................9 J6
Chapmore End Herts...60 B5
Chappel Essex.............61 L3
Chard Somset.............13 H2
Chard Junction
  Somset....................13 J2
Chardleigh Green
  Somset....................13 H1
Chardstock Devon.......13 H2
Charfield S Glos...........39 G3
Charing Kent...............34 C5
Charingworth Gloucs...71 L6
Charlbury Oxon...........57 G4
Charlcombe BaNES......39 H6
Charlcutt Wilts............39 M5
Charlecote Warwks......72 C3
Charlemont Sandw......85 H5
Charles Devon..............23 L5
Charleston Angus....... 196 C7
Charlestown C Aber.... 207 H5
Charlestown C Brad.... 123 H3
Charlestown Calder.... 122 E5
Charlestown Cnwll........ 5 G5
Charlestown Cnwll........ 5 G5
Charlestown Fife........ 176 E2
Charlestown Highld.... 213 G5
Charlestown Highld.... 219 J6
Charlestown Salfd..... 113 J2
Charlestown of
  Aberlour Moray 215 G5
Charles Tye Suffk........78 B4
Charlesworth Derbys.. 114 A3
Charlinch Somset........25 K4
Charlottetown Fife..... 186 E5
Charlton Gt Lon...........45 H4
Charlton Nhants..........73 G7
Charlton Nthumb........ 157 L5
Charlton Oxon.............41 H3
Charlton Somset.........25 L6
Charlton Somset.........27 G2
Charlton W Susx..........18 B3
Charlton Wilts.............27 K6

Charlton Wilts.....39 L3
Charlton Worcs.....71 H5
Charlton Wrekin.....83 L2
Charlton Abbots
  Gloucs.....56 B3
Charlton Adam
  Somset.....26 D5
Charlton All Saints
  Wilts.....28 D6
Charlton Down
  Dorset.....14 D4
Charlton Horethorne
  Somset.....26 F6
Charlton Kings
  Gloucs.....55 L4
Charlton Mackrell
  Somset.....26 D5
Charlton Marshall
  Dorset.....15 G2
Charlton Musgrove
  Somset.....27 G5
Charlton-on-Otmoor Oxon.....57 K5
Charlton on the Hill
  Dorset.....15 G2
Charlton St Peter
  Wilts.....28 C1
Charlwood Hants.....30 A5
Charlwood Surrey.....31 L3
Charminster Dorset.....14 D4
Charmouth Dorset.....13 J4
Charndon Bucks.....58 A3
Charney Bassett
  Oxon.....41 G2
Charnock Richard
  Lancs.....121 H7
Charnock Richard
  Services Lancs.....121 H7
Charsfield Suffk.....78 F3
Charter Alley Hants.....41 L8
Charterhall Border.....179 G8
Charterhouse Somset.....26 D1
Chartershall Stirlg.....175 K1
Chartham Kent.....34 E4
Chartham Hatch
  Kent.....34 E4
Chartridge Bucks.....58 F7
Chart Sutton Kent.....33 K4
Charvil Wokham.....42 C5
Charwelton Nhants.....73 G4
Chase Terrace Staffs.....85 J2
Chasetown Staffs.....85 J2
Chastleton Oxon.....56 E3
Chasty Devon.....9 J4
Chatburn Lancs.....121 L2
Chatcull Staffs.....99 H5
Chatham Medway.....46 C6
Chatham Green
  Essex.....61 H5
Chathill Nthumb.....169 J4
Chatsworth House
  Derbys.....114 E7
Chattenden Medway.....46 C5
Chatteris Cambs.....90 B6
Chatterton Lancs.....122 B6
Chattisham Suffk.....78 C6
Chatto Border.....168 B5
Chatton Nthumb.....168 F4
Chawleigh Devon.....11 G3
Chawton Hants.....30 B4
Cheadle Staffs.....100 A4
Cheadle Stockp.....113 K4
Cheadle Hulme
  Stockp.....113 K4
Cheam Gt Lon.....44 E7
Chearsley Bucks.....58 B6
Chebsey Staffs.....99 G6
Checkendon Oxon.....41 M4
Checkley Ches E.....99 G4
Checkley Staffs.....100 B5
Chedburgh Suffk.....77 H3
Cheddar Somset.....26 C2
Cheddington Bucks.....58 F4
Cheddleton Staffs.....99 L3
Cheddon Fitzpaine
  Somset.....25 K6

Chedgrave Norfk.....93 H4
Chedington Dorset.....13 L2
Chediston Suffk.....93 H7
Chedworth Gloucs.....56 B5
Chedzoy Somset.....25 M4
Cheetham Hill Manch..113 J2
Cheldon Devon.....11 H3
Chelford Ches E.....113 J6
Chellaston C Derb.....101 G6
Chellington Bed.....74 D4
Chelmarsh Shrops.....84 C5
Chelmondiston Suffk..78 E6
Chelmorton Derbys.....114 C7
Chelmsford Essex.....61 H6
Chelmsley Wood
  Solhll.....85 L6
Chelsea Gt Lon.....44 F4
Chelsfield Gt Lon.....45 J7
Chelsworth Suffk.....77 L5
Cheltenham Gloucs.....55 L4
Chelveston Nhants.....74 E1
Chelvey N Som.....38 C6
Chelwood BaNES.....38 F7
Chelwood Gate
  E Susx.....32 D6
Cheney Longville
  Shrops.....83 H6
Chenies Bucks.....43 G2
Chepstow Mons.....38 D2
Cherhill Wilts.....40 B6
Cherington Gloucs.....55 K7
Cherington Warwks.....72 C6
Cheriton Hants.....29 L5
Cheriton Kent.....35 G4
Cheriton Pembks.....49 G7
Cheriton Swans.....50 F6
Cheriton Bishop
  Devon.....11 H6
Cheriton Fitzpaine
  Devon.....11 K4
Cherrington Wrekin...98 F8
Cherry Burton E R Yk..126 B3
Cherry Hinton Cambs..76 C3
Cherry Orchard
  Worcs.....70 F4
Cherry Willingham
  Lincs.....117 G6
Chertsey Surrey.....43 H6
Cherwell Valley
  Services Oxon.....57 K3
Cheselbourne Dorset..14 D3
Chesham Bucks.....58 F7
Chesham Bury.....122 B7
Chesham Bois Bucks..58 F7
Cheshunt Herts.....60 B7
Chesil Beach Dorset..14 B6
Cheslyn Hay Staffs.....85 H3
Chessetts Wood
  Warwks.....85 L8
Chessington Gt Lon......44 D7
Chessington World
  of Adventures
  Gt Lon.....44 D7
Chester Ches W.....112 B7
Chesterblade Somset..26 F3
Chesterfield Derbys..115 G7
Chesterfield Staffs.....85 K3
Chesterhill Mdloth.....177 K5
Chester-le-Street
  Dur.....151 G5
Chester Moor Dur..151 G5
Chesters Border.....167 J5
Chesters Border.....167 K7
Chester Services
  Ches W.....112 C6
Chesterton Cambs.....76 C3
Chesterton Cambs.....89 G4
Chesterton Gloucs.....56 A7
Chesterton Oxon.....57 K4
Chesterton Shrops.....84 D4
Chesterton Staffs.....99 J3
Chesterton Green
  Warwks.....72 D3
Chesterwood Nthumb.149 L2
Chester Zoo Ches W...112 B7
Chestfield Kent.....47 J6
Cheston Devon.....7 G4

Cheswardine Shrops.....99 G6
Cheswick Nthumb.....168 F1
Chetnole Dorset.....14 B2
Chettisham Cambs.....90 D6
Chettle Dorset.....27 L8
Chetton Shrops.....84 B5
Chetwynd Wrekin.....99 G7
Chetwynd Aston
  Wrekin.....99 H8
Cheveley Cambs.....76 F3
Chevening Kent.....32 E2
Chevington Suffk.....77 H3
Cheviot Hills.....168 A7
Chevithorne Devon.....24 F7
Chew Magna BaNES.....38 E7
Chew Stoke BaNES.....38 E7
Chewton Keynsham
  BaNES.....38 F6
Chewton Mendip
  Somset.....26 E2
Chicheley M Keyn.....74 C5
Chichester W Susx.....18 B5
Chickerell Dorset.....14 C6
Chicklade Wilts.....27 K4
Chidden Hants.....30 A7
Chiddingfold Surrey..30 F4
Chiddingly E Susx.....20 B3
Chiddingstone Kent..32 E4
Chiddingstone
  Causeway Kent.....32 F4
Chideock Dorset.....13 K4
Chidham W Susx.....17 L2
Chidswell Kirk.....123 K6
Chieveley W Berk.....41 J5
Chieveley Services
  W Berk.....41 J6
Chignall St James
  Essex.....61 G6
Chignall Smealy
  Essex.....61 G5
Chigwell Essex.....45 H2
Chigwell Row Essex..45 J2
Chilbolton Hants.....29 H4
Chilcomb Hants.....29 J5
Chilcombe Dorset.....13 M4
Chilcompton Somset..26 F2
Chilcote Leics.....86 C2
Childer Thornton
  Ches W.....111 K6
Child Okeford Dorset..27 J8
Childrey Oxon.....41 G3
Child's Ercall Shrops..98 F7
Childswickham
  Worcs.....71 J6
Childwall Lpool.....112 B4
Chilfrome Dorset.....14 B3
Chilgrove W Susx.....18 A3
Chilham Kent.....34 E4
Chillaton Devon.....10 C8
Chillenden Kent.....35 H4
Chillerton IoW.....16 F5
Chillesford Suffk.....79 H4
Chillington Devon.....7 J7
Chillington Somset.....13 K1
Chilmark Wilts.....27 L5
Chilmington Green
  Kent.....34 C6
Chilson Oxon.....56 F4
Chilsworthy Cnwll.....6 B2
Chilsworthy Devon.....9 J4
Chiltern Hills.....42 C2
Chilthorne Domer
  Somset.....26 D7
Chilton Bucks.....58 B5
Chilton Dur.....141 H2
Chilton Oxon.....41 J4
Chilton Candover
  Hants.....29 L4
Chilton Cantelo
  Somset.....26 E6
Chilton Foliat Wilts..40 F6
Chilton Polden
  Somset.....26 B4
Chilton Street Suffk..77 H5
Chilton Trinity
  Somset.....25 L4
Chilwell Notts.....101 K5

Chilworth Hants.....29 H7
Chilworth Surrey.....31 G3
Chimney Oxon.....57 G7
Chineham Hants.....30 A1
Chingford Gt Lon.....45 G2
Chinley Derbys.....114 B5
Chinnor Oxon.....58 C7
Chipnall Shrops.....99 G6
Chippenham Cambs..76 F1
Chippenham Wilts.....39 L5
Chipperfield Herts.....59 H7
Chipping Herts.....60 B2
Chipping Lancs.....121 J2
Chipping Campden
  Gloucs.....71 L6
Chipping Norton
  Oxon.....56 F3
Chipping Ongar
  Essex.....60 E7
Chipping Sodbury
  S Glos.....39 G4
Chipping Warden
  Nhants.....72 F5
Chipstable Somset.....25 G6
Chipstead Kent.....32 E3
Chipstead Surrey.....32 B2
Chirbury Shrops.....82 F4
Chirk Wrexhm.....97 L5
Chirnside Border.....179 H6
Chirnsidebridge
  Border.....179 H7
Chirton Wilts.....40 B8
Chisbury Wilts.....40 F6
Chiselborough
  Somset.....26 C8
Chiseldon Swindn.....40 D4
Chiselhampton Oxon..57 L7
Chisholme Border.....166 F6
Chislehurst Gt Lon.....45 H6
Chislet Kent.....47 L6
Chisley Calder.....122 F5
Chiswell Green Herts..59 J6
Chiswick Gt Lon.....44 E4
Chisworth Derbys.....113 M3
Chithurst W Susx.....30 D6
Chittering Cambs.....76 C1
Chitterne Wilts.....27 M3
Chittlehamholt
  Devon.....23 K7
Chittlehampton
  Devon.....23 K6
Chittoe Wilts.....39 L6
Chivelstone Devon.....7 H7
Chivenor Devon.....23 H4
Chlenry D & G.....144 D3
Chobham Surrey.....42 F7
Cholderton Wilts.....28 E3
Cholesbury Bucks.....58 F6
Chollerford Nthumb..158 B7
Chollerton Nthumb..158 B7
Cholsey Oxon.....41 L3
Cholstrey Herefs.....69 J3
Chop Gate N York.....142 C7
Choppington Nthumb..159 G5
Chopwell Gatesd.....150 E4
Chorley Ches E.....98 E3
Chorley Lancs.....121 H6
Chorley Shrops.....84 C6
Chorleywood Herts...43 H2
Chorleywood West
  Herts.....43 G2
Chorlton Ches E.....99 G3
Chorlton-cum-
  Hardy Manch.....113 J3
Chorlton Lane
  Ches W.....98 C3
Choulton Shrops.....83 H5
Chrishall Essex.....76 C6
Chriswell Inver.....173 L4
Christchurch BCP.....15 M4
Christchurch Cambs..90 C4
Christchurch Newpt...37 M3
Christian Malford
  Wilts.....39 L5
Christon N Som.....38 B8
Christon Bank
  Nthumb.....169 J5
Christow Devon.....11 J7

Chudleigh Devon 11 K8
Chudleigh Knighton
  Devon............................7 J1
Chulmleigh Devon.........11 G3
Church Lancs 121 L5
Churcham Gloucs 55 H4
Church Aston Wrekin ...99 H8
Church Brampton
  Nhants........................73 K2
Church Broughton
  Derbys........................100 D5
Church Cove Cnwll.........3 J8
Church Crookham
  Hants..........................30 D2
Churchdown Gloucs 55 K4
Church Eaton Staffs 99 J8
Church Green Devon 12 F3
Church Hanborough
  Oxon...........................57 H5
Church Houses
  N York........................142 E7
Churchill Devon 13 H3
Churchill N Som.............38 C7
Churchill Oxon 56 F3
Churchill Worcs.............71 G4
Churchill Worcs.............84 F7
Churchinford Somset ...25 K8
Church Knowle
  Dorset.........................15 H6
Church Langton
  Leics............................87 K5
Church Lawford
  Warwks.......................86 F7
Church Leigh Staffs.....100 A5
Church Lench Worcs 71 H4
Church Mayfield
  Staffs..........................100 D4
Church Minshull
  Ches E..........................98 F1
Church Norton
  W Susx.........................18 B6
Churchover Warwks.......87 G2
Church Preen Shrops.....83 K4
Church Pulverbatch
  Shrops.........................83 H3
Churchstanton
  Somset........................25 J8
Churchstoke Powys 82 F5
Churchstow Devon 7 G6
Church Stowe
  Nhants........................73 J3
Church Street Kent.......46 B5
Church Stretton
  Shrops.........................83 J5
Churchtown Cnwll.........5 H1
Churchtown Derbys 114 E8
Churchtown IoM 237 d3
Churchtown Lancs 121 G2
Church Village
  Rhondd........................37 H3
Church Warsop
  Notts..........................115 K7
Churston Ferrers
  Torbay...........................7 K5
Churt Surrey..................30 D4
Churton Ches W 98 B2
Churwell Leeds 123 K5
Chwilog Gwynd.............95 G5
Chyandour Cnwll 2 E5
Cilcain Flints 111 G7
Cilcennin Cerdgn 66 C3
Cilfrew Neath................52 B7
Cilfynydd Rhondd.........37 G3
Cilgerran Pembks 65 H6
Cilmaengwyn Neath 51 L4
Cilmery Powys 67 L4
Cilsan Carmth...............51 H2
Ciltalgarth Gwynd........96 D4

Cilycwm Carmth............67 G6
Cimla Neath 36 B2
Cinderford Gloucs 54 F5
Cinder Hill Wolves........85 G5
Cippenham Slough........42 F4
Cirencester Gloucs......56 A7
City Gt Lon 45 G4
City Airport Gt Lon 45 H4
Clabhach Ag & B 188 F5
Clachaig Ag & B 173 J3
Clachaig Inn Highld....192 B5
Clachan Ag & B...........172 C6
Clachan Ag & B...........182 A4
Clachan Ag & B...........182 F6
Clachan Ag & B...........191 G7
Clachan Highld............209 H6
Clachan-a-Luib
  W Isls.........................233 c6
Clachan Mor Ag & B ...188 C6
Clachan na Luib
  W Isls.........................233 c6
Clachan of Campsie
  E Duns........................175 G3
Clachan-Seil Ag & B...181 M4
Clachnaharry Highld...213 G5
Clachtoll Highld...........224 C3
Clackavoid P & K 195 J4
Clacket Lane
  Services Surrey.........32 D3
Clackmannan Clacks ...185 J8
Clackmannanshire
  Bridge Fife...............176 C2
Clackmarras Moray 214 F3
Clacton-on-Sea
  Essex...........................62 E5
Cladich Ag & B 182 F3
Cladswell Worcs 71 J3
Claggan Highld............190 E6
Claigan Highld.............208 C4
Clanfield Hants.............30 B7
Clanfield Oxon...............56 F7
Clanville Hants.............28 F2
Clanville Somset 26 F5
Claonaig Ag & B 172 E6
Clapgate Herts..............60 C3
Clapham Bed.................74 F4
Clapham Gt Lon............44 F5
Clapham N York...........130 E5
Clapham W Susx...........18 F4
Clapton Somset 13 K2
Clapton Somset 26 F2
Clapton-in-
  Gordano N Som..........38 C5
Clapton-on-the-
  Hill Gloucs................56 D4
Claravale Gatesd.........150 E3
Clarbeston Pembks 49 H3
Clarbeston Road
  Pembks.......................49 H4
Clarborough Notts......116 B5
Clare Suffk...................77 H5
Clarebrand D & G 146 D2
Clarencefield D & G.....147 J2
Clarilaw Border...........167 H5
Clarkston E Rens.........175 G6
Clashmore Highld........223 G4
Clashmore Highld........224 C3
Clashnessie Highld......224 C3
Clashnoir Moray..........204 F2
Clathy P & K 185 K4
Clathymore P & K 185 L3
Clatt Abers..................205 L1
Clatter Powys...............81 L5
Claughton Lancs 121 G3
Claughton Lancs 130 B6
Claughton Wirral 111 J4
Claverdon Warwks........71 L2
Claverham N Som.........38 C6
Clavering Essex 60 D2
Claverley Shrops 84 E5
Claverton BaNES..........39 H7
Clawdd-coch V Glam....37 G5
Clawdd-newydd
  Denbgs.......................97 G3
Clawton Devon 9 J5
Claxby Lincs 117 J3

Claxton N York............133 L7
Claxton Norfk................93 H3
Claybrooke Magna
  Leics............................86 F5
Clay Coton Nhants........87 H7
Clay Cross Derbys.......115 H8
Claydon Oxon 72 F4
Claydon Suffk................78 D5
Claygate D & G 156 D6
Claygate Kent................33 J4
Claygate Surrey.............44 D7
Clayhall Gt Lon 45 H3
Clayhanger Devon.........24 F6
Clayhidon Devon...........25 J7
Clayhill E Susx..............21 G2
Clayock Highld.............231 H4
Claypits Gloucs 55 H6
Claypole Lincs 102 D3
Clayton C Brad............123 G4
Clayton Donc...............124 C8
Clayton W Susx.............19 J3
Clayton-le-Moors
  Lancs.........................121 L4
Clayton-le-Woods
  Lancs.........................121 H6
Clayton West Kirk 123 K7
Clayworth Notts..........116 B4
Cleadale Highld...........199 G7
Cleadon S Tyne............151 J3
Clearbrook Devon 6 D3
Clearwell Gloucs..........54 E6
Cleasby N York............141 G5
Cleat Ork.....................234 c8
Cleatlam Dur...............140 E4
Cleator Cumb..............136 D4
Cleator Moor Cumb.....136 E4
Cleckheaton Kirk 123 J5
Cleehill Shrops..............83 L7
Cleekhimin N Lans......175 K6
Clee St Margaret
  Shrops.........................83 L6
Cleethorpes NE Lin 127 H8
Cleeton St Mary
  Shrops.........................84 B7
Cleeve N Som................38 C7
Cleeve Oxon..................41 L4
Cleeve Hill Gloucs........55 M3
Cleeve Prior Worcs........71 J5
Cleghornie E Loth.......178 D2
Clehonger Herefs..........69 J6
Cleish P & K 186 A7
Cleland N Lans............175 L6
Clenamacrie Ag & B....182 C2
Clenchwarton Norfk....104 F7
Clenerty Abers.............216 E3
Clent Worcs...................85 G7
Cleobury Mortimer
  Shrops.........................84 C7
Cleobury North
  Shrops.........................84 B6
Cleongart Ag & B 161 H3
Clephanton Highld......213 J4
Clerkhill D & G 156 A3
Cleuch-head D & G......154 E3
Clevancy Wilts..............40 B5
Clevedon N Som............38 B6
Cleveleys Lancs 120 D2
Cleverton Wilts............39 L4
Clewer Somset..............26 C2
Cley next the Sea
  Norfk.........................106 C4
Cliburn Cumb..............138 E3
Cliddesden Hants.........29 M2
Cliffe Medway...............46 C5
Cliffe N York...............125 G4
Cliff End E Susx............21 H3
Cliffe Woods Medway...46 C5
Clifford Herefs..............68 E5
Clifford Leeds.............124 C2
Clifford Chambers
  Warwks.......................71 L4
Clifford's Mesne
  Gloucs.........................55 G4
Clifton Bristl................38 E5
Clifton C Beds...............75 H6
Clifton C Nott..............101 K5
Clifton C York..............133 J8

Clifton Calder..............123 H6
Clifton Cumb...............138 D2
Clifton Derbys.............100 D4
Clifton Devon 23 J3
Clifton Donc................115 K3
Clifton Lancs................120 F4
Clifton N York..............123 J2
Clifton Oxon..................57 J2
Clifton Worcs................70 F5
Clifton Campville
  Staffs..........................86 B2
Clifton Hampden
  Oxon...........................41 K2
Clifton Reynes
  M Keyn.......................74 C4
Clifton upon
  Dunsmore
  Warwks.......................87 G7
Clifton upon Teme
  Worcs.........................70 C3
Cliftonville Kent...........35 K1
Climping W Susx...........18 D5
Clink Somset 27 H2
Clint N York................132 D7
Clinterty C Aber..........206 F3
Clint Green Norfk 92 B2
Clintmains Border......167 J3
Clippesby Norfk 93 J2
Clipsham Rutlnd...........88 D1
Clipston Nhants............87 K7
Clipston Notts.............101 M5
Clipstone C Beds...........58 F3
Clipstone Notts...........115 L8
Clitheroe Lancs 121 L3
Clive Shrops 98 D7
Cliveden Bucks.............42 E4
Clixby Lincs 117 J2
Cloatley Wilts...............39 M3
Clocaenog Denbgs........97 G2
Clochan Moray............215 J3
Clodock Herefs..............53 L3
Clola Abers..................217 J5
Clophill C Beds..............74 F6
Clopton Nhants.............88 F7
Clopton Suffk................78 F4
Clopton Corner Suffk...78 F4
Clos du Valle Guern....236 d2
Closeburn D & G 154 F4
Closeburnmill D & G ...154 F3
Closworth Somset 14 B1
Clothall Herts................59 L2
Clotton Ches W 112 D8
Clough Foot Calder....122 D5
Clough Head Calder....123 G6
Cloughton N York.......143 K7
Clousta Shet................235 c5
Clova Angus................196 B2
Clovelly Devon..............22 E6
Clovenfords Border....167 G3
Clovulin Highld...........191 K4
Clowne Derbys............115 J6
Clows Top Worcs...........70 C1
Cluanie Inn Highld......201 G3
Cluanie Lodge Highld..201 G3
Clugston D & G...........145 H4
Clun Shrops 82 F7
Clunas Highld..............213 K5
Clunbury Shrops 83 G7
Clunderwen Carmth.....49 J4
Clune Highld................203 J1
Clunes Highld..............201 J7
Clungunford Shrops.....83 H7
Clunie P & K 195 H7
Clunton Shrops.............83 G7
Cluny Fife....................186 D7
Clutton BaNES..............38 F8
Clutton Ches W 98 C2
Clutton Hill BaNES.......38 F8
Clydach Mons...............53 K5
Clydach Swans..............51 K5
Clydach Vale Rhondd....36 F2
Clydebank W Duns.....174 F4
Clyffe Pypard Wilts......40 B5
Clynder Ag & B 174 A2
Clyne Neath...................52 C7
Clynnog Fawr Gwynd...95 G3
Clyro Powys..................68 E5

Clyst Honiton Devon......12 C4
Clyst Hydon Devon.........12 D3
Clyst St George
Devon........................12 C5
Clyst St Lawrence
Devon........................12 D3
Clyst St Mary Devon 12 C4
Cnoc W Isls 232 g2
Cnwch Coch Cerdgn 80 F8
Coad's Green Cnwll..........5 L1
Coalburn S Lans............164 F3
Coalburns Gatesd.........150 E3
Coaley Gloucs 55 H7
Coalhill Essex 61 J7
Coalpit Heath S Glos 38 F4
Coal Pool Wsall..............85 H4
Coalport Wrekin.............84 C3
Coalsnaughton
Clacks.....................185 J7
Coaltown of
Balgonie Fife 186 E7
Coaltown of
Wemyss Fife............186 E7
Coalville Leics 86 E2
Coanwood Nthumb 149 H3
Coat Somset 26 C7
Coatbridge N Lans 175 J5
Coatdyke N Lans 175 K5
Coate Swindn 40 D4
Coate Wilts....................40 B7
Coates Cambs................89 K4
Coates Gloucs 55 L7
Coates Lincs 116 E5
Coates W Susx 18 D3
Cobbaton Devon 23 K6
Coberley Gloucs.............55 L5
Cobham Kent................46 A6
Cobham Surrey 43 J7
Cobham Services
Surrey 43 J8
Cobnash Herefs 69 J3
Cobo Guern 236 c2
Cobridge C Stke 99 K3
Coburby Abers 217 H2
Cockayne Hatley
C Beds........................75 J5
Cock Bridge Abers......205 G4
Cockburnspath
Border......................179 G4
Cock Clarks Essex.........61 K7
Cockenzie and Port
Seton E Loth.............177 L4
Cockerham Lancs 120 F1
Cockermouth Cumb.....136 F2
Cockernhoe Herts..........59 J4
Cockett Swans................51 J6
Cockfield Dur 140 E3
Cockfield Suffk..............77 K4
Cockfosters Gt Lon........44 F2
Cock Green Essex 61 H4
Cocking W Susx..............18 B3
Cocking Causeway
W Susx.......................18 B2
Cockington Torbay 7 K3
Cocklake Somset...........26 C2
Cockley Cley Norfk.........91 H3
Cock Marling E Susx......21 H2
Cockpole Green
Wokham....................42 D4
Cockshutt Shrops 98 B6
Cockthorpe Norfk........106 B4
Cockwood Devon 12 C6
Cockyard Derbys.........114 B5
Coddenham Suffk..........78 D4
Coddington Herefs........70 C6
Coddington Notts........102 D2
Codford St Mary
Wilts..........................27 L4
Codford St Peter
Wilts..........................27 L4
Codicote Herts................59 K4
Codmore Hill W Susx.....31 H7
Codnor Derbys..............101 H3
Codrington S Glos..........39 G5
Codsall Staffs................84 F3
Codsall Wood Staffs.......84 F3
Coedpoeth Wrexhm.......97 L3

Coed Talon Flints 97 L2
Coed-y-paen Mons 53 M7
Coffinswell Devon 7 K3
Cofton Devon 12 C6
Cofton Hackett
Worcs........................85 H7
Cogan V Glam 37 J6
Cogenhoe Nhants..........74 B3
Cogges Oxon.................57 G6
Coggeshall Essex 61 K4
Coignafearn Highld.......203 H2
Coilacriech Abers.........205 H6
Coilantogle Stirlg..........184 D6
Coillore Highld.............208 E6
Coity Brdgnd..................36 E4
Col W Isls....................232 g2
Colaboll Highld.............225 L6
Colan Cnwll 4 D4
Colaton Raleigh
Devon........................12 D5
Colbost Highld.............208 C5
Colburn N York 140 F7
Colby Cumb 138 F3
Colby IoM 237 b6
Colchester Essex...........62 B3
Colchester Zoo
Essex........................62 A4
Cold Ash W Berk 41 K6
Cold Ashby Nhants........87 J7
Cold Ashton S Glos 39 H6
Cold Aston Gloucs.........56 C4
Coldbackie Highld.........229 J4
Cold Brayfield
M Keyn 74 D4
Coldean Br & H..............19 J4
Coldeast Devon 7 J2
Colden Calder 122 E5
Colden Common
Hants.........................29 J6
Cold Hanworth Lincs....117 G5
Coldharbour Surrey........31 J3
Cold Higham Nhants......73 J4
Coldingham Border 179 J3
Cold Kirby N York.........133 H3
Coldmeece Staffs...........99 J6
Cold Norton Essex.........61 K7
Cold Overton Leics........88 B2
Coldred Kent..................35 H5
Coldridge Devon 11 G4
Coldstream Border.......168 C2
Coldwaltham W Susx......18 D3
Coldwells Abers............217 H6
Cole Somset 26 F5
Colebatch Shrops 83 G6
Colebrook Devon 12 C2
Colebrooke Devon..........11 H5
Coleby Lincs 102 F1
Coleby N Linc 125 L6
Coleford Devon 11 H5
Coleford Gloucs.............54 E6
Coleford Somset 27 G2
Colegate End Norfk 92 E6
Colehill Dorset 15 J3
Coleman's Hatch
E Susx........................32 D6
Colemere Shrops 98 B6
Colemore Hants.............30 B5
Colenden P & K...........186 B2
Colerne Wilts.................39 J6
Colesbourne Gloucs.......56 A5
Coleshill Bucks 42 F2
Coleshill Oxon...............40 E2
Coleshill Warwks...........85 L5
Coley BaNES..................26 E1
Colgate W Susx..............31 L5
Colinsburgh Fife...........187 H6
Colinton C Edin............177 H5
Colintraive Ag & B.........173 H4
Colkirk Norfk 105 L7
Coll Ag & B...................189 G5
Coll W Isls 232 g2
Collace P & K................186 C2
Collafirth Shet.............235 c3
Collaton Devon 7 G7
Collaton St Mary
Torbay.........................7 K4

College of Roseisle
Moray......................214 E2
College Town Br For 42 D7
Collessie Fife...............186 E5
Collier Row Gt Lon.........45 J2
Collier's End Herts.........60 B4
Collier Street Kent.........33 J4
Colliston Abers.............217 K8
Collin D & G..................155 H6
Collingbourne
Ducis Wilts...............28 E2
Collingbourne
Kingston Wilts 28 E1
Collingham Leeds 124 B2
Collingham Notts.........102 D1
Collington Herefs..........70 B3
Collingtree Nhants........73 L4
Collins Green Warrtn....112 E3
Colliston Angus...........196 F7
Colliton Devon..............12 E2
Collyweston Nhants.......88 E3
Colmonell S Ayrs.........152 D5
Colmworth Bed..............75 G3
Colnabaichin Abers......205 G4
Colnbrook Slough..........43 G5
Colne Cambs.................89 L7
Colne Lancs 122 D3
Colne Engaine
Essex........................61 K3
Colney Norfk 92 E3
Colney Heath Herts........59 K6
Coln Rogers Gloucs 56 B6
Coln St Aldwyns
Gloucs.......................56 C6
Coln St Dennis
Gloucs.......................56 B5
Colonsay Ag & B..........180 E7
Colonsay Airport
Ag & B 180 E8
Colpy Abers 216 C7
Colquhar Border 166 E2
Colsterworth Lincs........102 F7
Colston Bassett
Notts.......................102 B5
Coltfield Moray 214 D2
Coltishall Norfk............106 F8
Colton Cumb 129 G3
Colton Leeds 124 B4
Colton N York 124 E2
Colton Norfk.................92 D2
Colton Staffs................100 B7
Colt's Hill Kent..............33 H4
Colvend D & G.............146 F4
Colwall Herefs...............70 D6
Colwell Nthumb 158 B6
Colwich Staffs..............100 A7
Colwinston V Glam........36 E5
Colworth W Susx...........18 C5
Colwyn Bay Conwy......110 B5
Colyford Devon 13 G4
Colyton Devon 13 G4
Combe Oxon.................57 H5
Combe W Berk 41 G7
Combe Down BaNES......39 H7
Combe Fishacre
Devon..........................7 J3
Combe Florey
Somset 25 J5
Combe Hay BaNES 39 G7
Combeinteignhead
Devon..........................7 K2
Combe Martin Devon 23 J3
Combe Raleigh
Devon........................12 F3
Comberbach Ches W 112 F6
Comberford Staffs.........85 L3
Comberton Cambs.........75 L4
Comberton Herefs.........69 K2
Combe St Nicholas
Somset 13 H1
Combrook Warwks........72 C4
Combs Derbys..............114 B6
Combs Suffk..................78 C3
Combs Ford Suffk..........78 C3
Combwich Somset.........25 K3
Comers Abers 206 D4
Comhampton Worcs......70 E2

Commins Coch
Powys.........................81 J3
Commondale N York 142 E5
Common End Cumb......136 D3
Common Moor Cnwll 5 K2
Compstall Stockp.........113 L4
Compstonend D & G.....146 B4
Compton Devon 7 K3
Compton Hants.............29 J6
Compton Staffs..............84 E6
Compton Surrey............30 F3
Compton W Berk...........41 K4
Compton W Susx...........30 C7
Compton Wilts..............28 C2
Compton Abbas
Dorset........................27 K7
Compton Abdale
Gloucs.......................56 B5
Compton Bassett
Wilts..........................40 B6
Compton
Beauchamp Oxon....40 F3
Compton Bishop
Somset 26 B1
Compton
Chamberlayne
Wilts..........................28 B5
Compton Dando
BaNES........................38 F7
Compton Dundon
Somset 26 C5
Compton Durville
Somset 26 B7
Compton Greenfield
S Glos........................38 E4
Compton Martin
BaNES........................38 D8
Compton
Pauncefoot
Somset 26 F6
Compton Valence
Dorset........................14 B4
Comrie Fife..................176 D1
Comrie P & K...............185 G3
Conaglen House
Highld......................191 K3
Conchra Highld............210 D8
Concraigie P & K..........195 H7
Conderton Worcs..........71 G6
Condicote Gloucs 56 D3
Condorrat N Lans 175 K4
Condover Shrops 83 J3
Coney Hill Gloucs..........55 J4
Coneyhurst
Common W Susx 31 J6
Coneysthorpe N York...133 L5
Coney Weston Suffk......91 L7
Congerstone Leics.........86 D3
Congham Norfk...........105 H7
Congleton Ches E.........113 J8
Congresbury N Som.......38 C7
Conheath D & G...........147 H2
Conicavel Moray 214 B4
Coningsby Lincs...........103 L2
Conington Cambs..........75 K2
Conington Cambs..........89 H6
Conisbrough Donc.......115 K2
Conisholme Lincs.........118 E3
Coniston Cumb 137 J7
Coniston E R Yk............126 E4
Coniston Cold N York ...131 G8
Conistone N York.........131 J6
Connah's Quay Flints....111 J7
Connel Ag & B.............182 C1
Connel Park E Ayrs 164 C6
Connor Downs Cnwll......3 G4
Conon Bridge Highld....212 E4
Cononley N York..........122 E2
Consall Staffs.................99 M3
Consett Dur 150 E5
Constable Burton
N York......................132 B2
Constable Lee Lancs....122 B5
Constantine Cnwll...........3 J5
Constantine Bay
Cnwll 4 D2
Contin Highld 212 C3

Conwy Conwy.............. 109 L6
Conwy Castle Conwy ... 109 L6
Conyer's Green Suffk......77 K2
Cooden E Susx............20 E4
Cookbury Devon............. 9 K4
Cookham W & M.........42 E4
Cookham Dean
W & M.................42 E4
Cookham Rise
W & M.................42 E4
Cookhill Worcs.............71 J3
Cookley Suffk...............93 H7
Cookley Worcs..............84 E7
Cookley Green Oxon....42 B3
Cookney Abers............ 207 G6
Cook's Green E Susx.....62 E4
Cooks Green Suffk......77 L4
Cooksmill Green
Essex....................61 G6
Coolham W Susx............31 J6
Cooling Medway...........46 C5
Coombe Cnwll............. 4 E5
Coombe Devon.............. 7 L2
Coombe Devon 12 E4
Coombe Gloucs 39 H2
Coombe Hants.............30 A7
Coombe Bissett
Wilts....................28 C6
Coombe Cellars
Devon.................... 7 K2
Coombe Hill Gloucs 55 K3
Coombe Keynes
Dorset 14 F5
Coombe Pafford
Torbay................... 7 L3
Coombes W Susx.........19 G4
Coombes-Moor
Herefs...................69 G2
Coombeswood
Dudley..................85 H6
Coopersale
Common Essex......60 D7
Copdock Suffk.............78 D6
Copford Green Essex....61 L4
Copgrove N York 132 E6
Copister Shet............. 235 d3
Cople Bed...................75 G5
Copley Dur 140 D3
Copmanthorpe
C York.................. 124 E2
Copmere End Staffs 99 J6
Copp Lancs 120 F3
Coppenhall Staffs........99 K8
Copperhouse Cnwll 2 F4
Coppingford Cambs....89 H7
Copplestone Devon......11 H4
Coppull Lancs 121 H7
Copsale W Susx............31 K6
Copster Green Lancs... 121 K4
Copston Magna
Warwks................86 F5
Cop Street Kent...........35 J3
Copt Hewick N York.....132 E5
Copthorne W Susx........32 B5
Copt Oak Leics...........86 F2
Copythorne Hants........28 F8
Corbets Tey Gt Lon......45 K3
Corbière Jersey........ 236 a7
Corbridge Nthumb...... 150 C3
Corby Nhants...............88 C5
Corby Glen Lincs 103 G7
Cordon N Ayrs............ 162 D4
Coreley Shrops.............84 B8
Corfe Somset..............25 K7
Corfe Castle Dorset 15 H6
Corfe Mullen Dorset....15 J3
Corfton Shrops............83 J6
Corgarff Abers........... 205 G4
Corlae D & G 154 B3
Corley Warwks............86 C6
Corley Services
Warwks................86 C6
Cormuir Angus 195 L3
Cornard Tye Suffk.......77 K6
Cornforth Dur 151 H7
Cornhill Abers........... 216 B3

Cornhill-on-Tweed
Nthumb 168 C2
Cornholme Calder 122 D5
Cornoigmore Ag & B ... 188 C6
Cornsay Dur............... 150 E6
Cornsay Colliery
Dur..................... 150 F6
Corntown Highld........ 212 E3
Corntown V Glam........36 E5
Cornwall Airport
Newquay Cnwll 4 D3
Cornwell Oxon.............56 F3
Cornwood Devon 6 E4
Cornworthy Devon 7 J5
Corpach Highld.......... 191 L2
Corpusty Norfk.......... 106 D6
Corrachree Abers...... 205 K4
Corran Highld............ 191 K4
Corran Highld............ 200 C4
Corrie D & G.............. 155 L5
Corrie N Ayrs............. 162 C2
Corriecravie N Ayrs... 162 B5
Corriegills N Ayrs..... 162 D3
Corriegour Lodge
Hotel Highld........... 201 K6
Corriemoillie Highld ... 212 B2
Corrimony Highld....... 212 B7
Corringham Lincs....... 116 E4
Corringham Thurr 46 B4
Corris Gwynd.............81 G2
Corris Uchaf Gwynd......81 G2
Corrow Ag & B............ 183 H7
Corry Highld............... 199 K1
Corscombe Devon 10 F5
Corscombe Dorset......13 M2
Corse Gloucs 55 H3
Corse Lawn Gloucs......55 J2
Corsham Wilts............39 K6
Corsindae Abers....... 206 D4
Corsley Wilts..............27 J3
Corsley Heath Wilts.....27 J3
Corsock D & G 154 D6
Corston BaNES............39 G7
Corston Wilts..............39 L4
Corstorphine C Edin... 177 G4
Cortachy Angus........ 196 C4
Corton Suffk................93 L4
Corton Wilts................27 L4
Corton Denham
Somset..................26 F6
Coruanan Highld....... 191 L3
Corwen Denbgs..........97 G4
Coryton Devon 10 C7
Coryton Thurr 46 C4
Cosby Leics 87 G4
Coseley Dudley..........85 G5
Cosgrove Nhants........73 L6
Cosham C Port............17 J2
Cosheston Pembks......49 G6
Coshieville P & K 194 C6
Cossall Notts............. 101 J4
Cossington Leics 87 H2
Cossington Somset 26 A4
Costessey Norfk..........92 E2
Costock Notts........... 101 L7
Coston Leics 102 D7
Coston Norfk..............92 C3
Cote Oxon...................57 G7
Cotebrook Ches W...... 112 E7
Cotehill Cumb............ 148 E5
Cotes Leics 101 K7
Cotesbach Leics.........87 G6
Cotford St Luke
Somset..................25 J6
Cotgrave Notts......... 101 M5
Cothal Abers............. 207 G3
Cotham Notts............ 102 C3
Cotherstone Dur 140 C4
Cothill Oxon................57 J7
Cotleigh Devon...........13 G3
Cotmanhay Derbys.... 101 J4
Coton Cambs..............76 B3
Coton Nhants..............73 J1
Coton Staffs................99 J7
Coton Clanford
Staffs....................99 K7
Coton Hill Shrops.......83 J2

Coton in the Elms
Derbys..................86 B1
Cotswolds 55 M6
Cotswold Wildlife
Park & Gardens
Oxon....................56 E6
Cott Devon 7 H4
Cottam Lancs 121 G4
Cottam Notts............. 116 D5
Cottenham Cambs.......76 C2
Cottered Herts............60 A3
Cotteridge Birm..........85 J7
Cotterstock Nhants........88 F5
Cottesbrooke Nhants....87 K8
Cottesmore Rutlnd......88 C2
Cottingham E R Yk..... 126 C4
Cottingham Nhants......88 B5
Cottingley C Brad...... 123 G3
Cottisford Oxon..........57 L2
Cotton Suffk................78 C2
Cottown Abers........... 206 E3
Cottown Abers........... 215 L8
Cottown of Gight
Abers.................. 216 F6
Cotts Devon 6 C3
Coughton Warwks.......71 J3
Coulaghailtro Ag & B...172 C5
Coulags Highld 210 E5
Coull Abers............... 205 L5
Coulport Ag & B......... 173 L2
Coulsdon Gt Lon.........32 B2
Coulston Wilts.............27 L2
Coulter S Lans............ 165 K3
Coulton N York.......... 133 K5
Coultra Fife............... 186 F3
Cound Shrops............83 L3
Coundon Dur 141 G2
Countersett N York... 131 H2
Countess Wear
Devon...................12 B4
Countesthorpe Leics....87 H4
Countisbury Devon......24 B2
Coupar Angus P & K...195 K7
Coupland Nthumb...... 168 D3
Cour Ag & B............... 172 D8
Courteachan Highld... 199 L6
Courteenhall Nhants....73 L4
Court Henry Carmth....51 H2
Courtsend Essex.........47 G2
Courtway Somset........25 J5
Cousland Mdloth...... 177 K5
Cousley Wood E Susx...33 H6
Cove Ag & B............... 173 L2
Cove Border............... 179 G4
Cove Devon 24 E7
Cove Hants.................30 E1
Cove Highld............... 219 J3
Cove Bay C Aber....... 207 H5
Covehithe Suffk..........93 L6
Coven Staffs...............85 G3
Coveney Cambs..........90 C6
Covenham St
Bartholomew
Lincs................... 118 D3
Covenham St Mary
Lincs................... 118 D3
Coventry Covtry..........86 D7
Coverack Cnwll 3 K7
Coverack Bridges
Cnwll..................... 3 H5
Coverham N York....... 131 L3
Covington Cambs.......74 F1
Covington S Lans...... 165 J2
Cowan Bridge Lancs... 130 C4
Cowbeech E Susx........20 C3
Cowbit Lincs............. 103 L8
Cowbridge V Glam......36 F5
Cowden Kent..............32 E5
Cowdenbeath Fife..... 177 G1
Cowers Lane Derbys... 100 F3
Cowes IoW...................16 F3
Cowesby N York......... 133 G2
Cowfold W Susx...........31 K6
Cowhill S Glos.............38 E3
Cowie Stirlg............... 175 L1
Cowley Devon 11 K5
Cowley Gloucs 55 L5

Cowley Gt Lon.............43 H4
Cowley Oxon 57 K7
Cowling Lancs 121 H6
Cowling N York 122 E2
Cowling N York 132 C3
Cowlinge Suffk............77 G4
Cowpen Nthumb........ 159 H5
Cowplain Hants...........17 K1
Cowshill Dur 149 L6
Cowslip Green
N Som....................38 C7
Cowthorpe N York..... 132 E4
Coxbank Ches E...........98 F4
Coxbench Derbys....... 101 G4
Coxford Cnwll 8 F5
Coxford Norfk............ 105 K6
Coxheath Kent............33 J3
Coxhoe Dur 151 H7
Coxley Somset............26 D3
Coxley Wick Somset....26 D3
Coxtie Green Essex......45 K2
Coxwold N York......... 133 H4
Coychurch Brdgnd......36 E4
Coylton S Ayrs........... 163 K5
Coylumbridge Highld... 203 L3
Coytrahen Brdgnd.......36 D4
Crabbs Cross Worcs....71 J2
Crabtree W Susx..........31 K6
Crackenthorpe Cumb.. 138 F3
Crackington Haven
Cnwll..................... 8 F5
Crackley Staffs............99 J3
Crackleybank Shrops.....84 D2
Cracoe N York............ 131 J7
Craddock Devon.........25 G8
Cradley Dudley...........85 G6
Cradley Herefs............70 D5
Cradley Heath Sandw...85 G6
Cradoc Powys.............52 F2
Crafthole Cnwll 6 B5
Craggan Highld.......... 204 C1
Cragganmore Moray ... 214 E6
Craghead Dur 150 F5
Cragside House &
Garden Nthumb...... 158 D2
Crai Powys..................52 D3
Craibstone Moray..... 215 L3
Craichie Angus......... 196 E6
Craig Angus.............. 197 H5
Craig Highld.............. 211 G4
Craigbank E Ayrs...... 164 C6
Craigburn Border 177 H7
Craigcleuch D & G 156 C5
Craigdam Abers........ 216 F7
Craigdhu Ag & B....... 182 B6
Craigearn Abers....... 206 D3
Craigellachie Moray ... 215 G5
Craigend P & K.......... 186 B4
Craigend Rens........... 174 E4
Craigendoran Ag & B ... 174 C3
Craigends Rens......... 174 D5
Craighlaw D & G........ 145 G3
Craighouse Ag & B..... 171 K5
Craigie P & K............. 195 H7
Craigie S Ayrs........... 163 K3
Craigiefold Abers...... 217 H2
Craigley D & G 146 D4
Craig Llangiwg
Neath................... 51 K4
Craiglockhart C Edin... 177 H4
Craigmillar C Edin..... 177 J4
Craigneston D & G..... 154 D5
Craigneuk N Lans...... 175 K5
Craigneuk N Lans...... 175 K6
Craignure Ag & B...... 190 E6
Craigo Angus............ 197 H4
Craigrothie Fife........ 186 F5
Craigruie Stirlg......... 184 B4
Craigton Angus......... 196 E8
Craigton C Aber........ 206 F5
Craigton E Rens........ 174 F7
Craigton of Airlie
Angus................. 196 B6
Craik Border............. 166 E7
Crail Fife.................. 187 K5
Crailing Border......... 167 L4
Craiselound N Linc.... 116 C2

Crakehall N York 132 C2
Crambe N York 133 L6
Cramlington Nthumb ... 159 G6
Cramond C Edin 177 G3
Cramond Bridge
 C Edin 177 G4
Cranage Ches E 113 H7
Cranberry Staffs 99 J5
Cranborne Dorset 28 B8
Cranbourne Br For 42 F5
Cranbrook Devon 12 C4
Cranbrook Kent 33 K6
Cranfield C Beds 74 D6
Cranford Gt Lon 43 J5
Cranford St Andrew
 Nhants 88 D7
Cranford St John
 Nhants 88 D7
Cranham Gloucs 55 K5
Crank St Hel 112 D2
Cranleigh Surrey 31 H4
Cranmore Somset 26 F3
Cranoe Leics 87 L4
Cransford Suffk 79 G2
Cranshaws Border 178 E6
Crantock Cnwll 4 C4
Cranwell Lincs 103 G3
Cranwich Norfk 91 H4
Cranworth Norfk 92 B3
Craobh Haven Ag & B.. 182 A6
Crarae Ag & B 182 E7
Crask Inn Highld 225 L4
Crask of Aigas Highld.. 212 D6
Craster Nthumb 169 K5
Cratfield Suffk 93 G7
Crathes Abers 206 E6
Crathie Abers 205 G6
Crathie Highld 202 E6
Crathorne N York 141 K5
Craven Arms Shrops.... 83 H6
Crawcrook Gatesd...... 150 E3
Crawford S Lans 165 J5
Crawfordjohn S Lans ... 165 G5
Crawley Hants 29 H4
Crawley Oxon 57 G5
Crawley W Susx 31 L4
Crawley Down
 W Susx 32 C5
Crawton Abers 197 L1
Cray N York 131 H4
Crayford Gt Lon 45 K5
Crayke N York 133 H5
Crays Hill Essex 46 B2
Creacombe Devon 24 C7
Creagan Inn Ag & B.... 191 J7
Creag Ghoraidh
 W Isls 233 c7
Creagorry W Isls 233 c7
Creaguaineach
 Lodge Highld 192 E3
Creaton Nhants 73 K1
Creca D & G 155 M7
Credenhill Herefs 69 J5
Crediton Devon 11 J5
Creebank D & G 153 H6
Creebridge D & G 145 J2
Creech Heathfield
 Somset 25 L6
Creech St Michael
 Somset 25 L6
Creed Cnwll 4 E6
Creekmouth Gt Lon...... 45 J4
Creeting St Mary
 Suffk 78 D3
Creeton Lincs 103 G8
Creetown D & G 145 K3
Cregneash IoM 237 a7
Creich Fife 186 E3
Creigiau Cardif 37 G4
Cremyll Cnwll 6 C5
Cressage Shrops 83 L3
Cressbrook Derbys 114 D6
Cresselly Pembks........ 49 H6
Cressex Bucks.............. 42 D3
Cressing Essex 61 J4
Cresswell Nthumb 159 H4
Cresswell Pembks........ 49 H6

Cresswell Staffs 99 L5
Creswell Derbys 115 K6
Cretingham Suffk 78 F3
Cretshengan Ag & B.... 172 C5
Crewe Ches E 99 G2
Crewe-by-Farndon
 Ches W 98 B2
Crewe Green Ches E.... 99 G2
Crew Green Powys........ 83 G1
Crewkerne Somset 13 K1
Crewton C Derb 101 G5
Crianlarich Stirlg 183 L3
Cribyn Cerdgn 66 C4
Criccieth Gwynd............ 95 J5
Crich Derbys 101 G2
Crichton Mdloth 177 K6
Crick Nhants 87 H8
Crickadarn Powys 68 C6
Cricket St Thomas
 Somset 13 J2
Crickhowell Powys........ 53 K4
Cricklade Wilts.............. 40 D2
Cricklewood Gt Lon 44 E3
Crieff P & K 185 H3
Criggion Powys 82 F1
Crigglestone Wakefd .. 123 L7
Crimond Abers 217 K3
Crimplesham Norfk 90 F3
Crimscote Warwks 72 B5
Crinaglack Highld........ 212 C6
Crinan Ag & B 182 A8
Crindledyke N Lans 175 L6
Cringleford Norfk.......... 92 E3
Crinow Pembks.............. 49 J5
Croachy Highld............ 213 G8
Crockenhill Kent............ 45 J6
Crocker End Oxon 42 B3
Crockernwell Devon 11 H6
Crockerton Wilts.......... 27 K3
Crocketford D & G........ 154 E7
Crockham Hill Kent...... 32 D3
Croeserw Neath............ 36 D2
Croes-goch Pembks 48 D2
Croes-lan Cerdgn 65 L5
Croesor Gwynd 95 L4
Croesyceiliog Carmth.. 50 E3
Croesyceiliog Torfn...... 37 L2
Croft Leics 87 G4
Croft Lincs 104 E1
Croft Warrtn 112 F3
Croftamie Stirlg 174 E2
Crofton Wakefd 124 B6
Croft-on-Tees
 N York 141 H5
Croftown Highld 220 F5
Crofts Moray 215 G4
Crofts Bank Traffd 113 H3
Crofts of Dipple
 Moray 215 H3
Crofts of Savoch
 Abers 217 K3
Crofty Swans................ 51 G6
Croggan Ag & B 181 L3
Croglin Cumb 148 F5
Croick Highld 222 B3
Cromarty Highld 223 H7
Crombie Fife 176 E2
Cromdale Highld 214 D8
Cromer Herts 59 M3
Cromer Norfk 106 F4
Cromford Derbys 100 F2
Cromhall S Glos 39 G3
Cromor W Isls 232 f3
Cromwell Notts 102 C1
Cronberry E Ayrs 164 C5
Crondall Hants 30 C2
Cronton Knows............ 112 C4
Crook Cumb 138 C7
Crookedholm E Ayrs.... 163 L3
Crookes Sheff 114 F4
Crookham Nthumb...... 168 D2
Crookham W Berk 41 K7
Crookham Village
 Hants 30 C2
Crook Inn Border 165 L4
Crooklands Cumb 129 L3

Crook of Devon
 P & K 185 L7
Cropredy Oxon 72 F5
Cropston Leics 87 G2
Cropthorne Worcs........ 71 H5
Cropton N York 134 B2
Cropwell Bishop
 Notts 102 B5
Cropwell Butler
 Notts 102 B5
Cros W Isls 232 g1
Crosbost W Isls 232 f3
Crosby Cumb 147 J7
Crosby IoM 237 c5
Crosby N Linc 125 K7
Crosby Sefton 111 J2
Crosby Garret Cumb .. 139 G5
Crosby Ravensworth
 Cumb 138 F4
Croscombe Somset 26 E3
Cross Somset 26 B1
Crossaig Ag & B.......... 172 E7
Crossapol Ag & B........ 188 C7
Cross Ash Mons 54 B4
Cross-at-Hand Kent...... 33 K4
Crossbost W Isls 232 f3
Crosscanonby Cumb .. 147 J6
Crossdale Street
 Norfk 106 F5
Cross Flatts C Brad 123 G3
Crossford Fife 176 E2
Crossford S Lans 175 L8
Crossgatehall E Loth.. 177 K5
Crossgates E Ayrs 163 J1
Crossgates Fife 176 F1
Cross Gates Leeds 124 B4
Crossgates N York...... 134 F3
Crossgill Lancs 129 L6
Cross Green Leeds 123 L4
Cross Green Suffk 77 K4
Cross Green Suffk 78 B4
Cross Hands Carmth...... 51 H3
Crosshands E Ayrs 163 L4
Crosshill Fife 186 C7
Crosshill S Ayrs 163 J7
Crosshouse E Ayrs 163 K2
Cross Houses Shrops.... 83 K3
Cross in Hand E Susx .. 20 B2
Cross Inn Cerdgn 65 L3
Cross Keys Ag & B 174 C2
Crosskeys Caerph.......... 37 K3
Crosskirk Highld.......... 230 F2
Cross Lane IoW 17 G4
Cross Lane Head
 Shrops 84 C4
Crosslee Rens.............. 174 D5
Crossmichael D & G .. 146 C2
Cross of Jackston
 Abers 216 E7
Cross o' th' hands
 Derbys 100 F4
Crossroads Abers 206 B4
Crossroads Abers 206 E6
Cross Street Suffk 92 E7
Crosston Angus 196 E5
Cross Town Ches E...... 113 H5
Crossway Green
 Worcs 70 E2
Crossways Dorset 14 E5
Crosswell Pembks........ 64 F6
Crosthwaite Cumb 129 J2
Croston Lancs 121 G6
Crostwick Norfk............ 92 F1
Crouch End Gt Lon 44 F3
Croucheston Wilts........ 28 B6
Crouch Hill Dorset........ 14 D1
Croughton Nhants 73 G7
Crovie Abers 216 F2
Crowan Cnwll 3 H4
Crowborough E Susx.. 32 F6
Crowborough
 Warren E Susx............ 32 E6
Crowcombe Somset 25 H4
Crowdecote Derbys 114 C7
Crowden Derbys 114 B2
Crow Edge Barns........ 114 D2
Crowell Oxon 58 C7

Crowfield Suffk 78 D3
Crowhill E Loth 178 F4
Crow Hill Herefs 54 F3
Crowhurst E Susx 20 F3
Crowhurst Surrey 32 D4
Crowland Lincs.............. 89 J2
Crowland Suffk.............. 78 B1
Crowlas Cnwll 2 F5
Crowle N Linc 125 J7
Crowle Worcs................ 71 G4
Crowle Green Worcs.... 71 G3
Crowmarsh Gifford
 Oxon 41 L3
Crown Corner Suffk...... 78 F1
Crownhill C Plym............ 6 C4
Crownpits Surrey.......... 30 F3
Crownthorpe Norfk...... 92 C3
Crowntown Cnwll 3 H5
Crows-an-Wra Cnwll 2 D5
Crowther Wokham 42 D7
Crowton Ches W.......... 112 E6
Croxdale Dur 151 G7
Croxden Staffs 100 B5
Croxley Green Herts.... 43 H2
Croxteth Lpool 111 L3
Croxton Cambs............ 75 J3
Croxton N Linc 126 D7
Croxton Norfk 91 K6
Croxton Norfk 106 B6
Croxton Staffs 99 H6
Croxton Kerrial Leics .. 102 D6
Croy Highld 213 J4
Croy N Lans 175 J3
Croyde Devon................ 23 G4
Croydon Cambs............ 75 K5
Croydon Gt Lon............ 44 F6
Crubenmore Highld...... 203 G7
Cruckmeole Shrops...... 83 H2
Cruckton Shrops 83 H2
Cruden Bay Abers 217 K6
Crudgington Wrekin 98 F8
Crudie Abers 216 E3
Crudwell Wilts.............. 39 L2
Crumlin Caerph 37 K2
Crumplehorn Cnwll........ 5 K5
Crumpsall Manch........ 113 J2
Crundale Kent 34 E5
Crux Easton Hants 29 H1
Crwbin Carmth.............. 50 F3
Cryers Hill Bucks 42 E2
Crymych Pembks.......... 65 G7
Crynant Neath 52 C6
Crystal Palace Gt Lon.... 45 G5
Cuaig Highld 209 L3
Cuan Ag & B 181 L4
Cubert Cnwll 4 C4
Cublington Bucks.......... 58 D4
Cublington Herefs........ 69 H6
Cuckfield W Susx 32 B7
Cucklington Somset...... 27 H6
Cuckney Notts 115 K7
Cuddesdon Oxon 57 L7
Cuddington Bucks........ 58 C5
Cuddington Ches W 112 E7
Cuddington Heath
 Ches W 98 C3
Cudham Gt Lon 32 D2
Cudliptown Devon.......... 6 D1
Cudnell BCP.................. 15 K3
Cudworth Barns.......... 124 B8
Cudworth Somset.......... 13 J1
Cuffley Herts................ 59 M7
Cuil Highld 191 J5
Culbokie Highld 212 F3
Culburnie Highld.......... 212 D6
Culcabock Highld........ 213 G5
Culcharry Highld.......... 213 K4
Culcheth Warrtn.......... 112 F3
Culdrain Abers 215 L7
Culduie Highld 209 L6
Culford Suffk 77 J1
Culgaith Cumb............ 138 E2
Culham Oxon 41 J2
Culkein Highld 224 C2
Culkein Drumbeg
 Highld 224 D2
Culkerton Gloucs 39 L2

Cullen Moray.............. 215 L2
Cullercoats N Tyne...... 159 J7
Cullerlie Abers............ 206 E5
Cullicudden Highld...... 213 G2
Cullingworth C Brad... 123 G3
Cuillin Hills Highld 199 G2
Cullipool Ag & B......... 181 L5
Cullivoe Shet 235 d2
Culloden Highld.......... 213 H5
Cullompton Devon......12 C2
**Cullompton
  Services** Devon.........12 D2
Culm Davy Devon 25 H7
Culmington Shrops......83 J6
Culmstock Devon.........25 H8
Culnacraig Highld...... 224 C7
Culnaightrie D & G.... 146 D5
Culnaknock Highld...... 209 H2
Culrain Highld............ 222 D3
Culross Fife................ 176 D2
Culroy S Ayrs............. 163 H6
Culsalmond Abers...... 216 C7
Culscadden D & G...... 145 K5
Culshabbin D & G...... 145 G5
Culswick Shet............. 235 b6
Cultercullen Abers...... 207 H1
Cults C Aber............... 207 G5
Culverstone Green
  Kent......................45 M7
Culverthorpe Lincs 103 G4
Culworth Nhants...........73 G5
**Culzean Castle &
  Country Park**
  S Ayrs..................... 163 G7
Cumbernauld N Lans... 175 K4
**Cumbernauld
  Village** N Lans....... 175 K3
Cumberworth Lincs...... 119 G6
Cuminestown Abers...... 216 F4
Cumledge Border 179 G6
Cummersdale Cumb.... 148 D4
Cummertrees D & G.... 147 K2
Cummingston
  Moray.................... 214 E1
Cumnock E Ayrs......... 164 B5
Cumnor Oxon..............57 J7
Cumrew Cumb............ 148 F5
Cumrue D & G 155 J5
Cumwhinton Cumb...... 148 D4
Cumwhitton Cumb...... 148 E4
Cundall N York............ 132 F5
Cunninghamhead
  N Ayrs.................... 163 J2
Cunningsburgh Shet... 235 c7
Cupar Fife.................. 186 F4
Cupar Muir Fife......... 186 F5
Curbar Derbys............ 114 E6
Curbridge Hants...........17 G1
Curbridge Oxon............57 G6
Curdridge Hants...........29 K8
Curdworth Warwks.......85 L5
Curland Somset...........25 L7
Curridge W Berk 41 J6
Currie C Edin............. 177 G5
Curry Mallet Somset......25 L6
Curry Rivel Somset......26 B6
Curtisden Green
  Kent........................33 J5
Curtisknowle Devon 7 H5
Cury Cnwll.....................3 H6
Cushnie Abers............ 205 L3
Cutcloy D & G............ 145 J7
Cutcombe Somset.........24 E4
Cuthill Highld............. 223 G4
Cutnall Green Worcs.....70 F2
Cutsdean Gloucs...........56 C3
Cutthorpe Derbys........ 115 G6
Cuxham Oxon..............42 A2
Cuxton Medway............46 B6
Cuxwold Lincs............ 117 K2
Cwm Denbgs............... 110 E6
Cwmafan Neath...........36 B3
Cwmaman Rhondd.........52 F7
Cwmbach Carmth...........50 B1
Cwmbâch Powys..........68 D6
Cwmbach Rhondd.........52 F7

Cwmbach Llechrhyd
  Powys......................68 B4
Cwmbran Torfn.............37 L2
Cwmcarn Caerph..........37 K2
Cwmcarvan Mons..........54 C6
Cwm-cou Cerdgn..........65 J6
Cwm Crawnon
  Powys......................53 H4
Cwmdare Rhondd..........52 F7
Cwmdu Powys..............53 J4
Cwmdu Swans..............51 J6
Cwmduad Carmth..........65 L7
Cwmfelin Brdgnd..........36 D3
Cwmfelin Myr Td...........53 H7
Cwmfelin Boeth
  Carmth.....................49 K4
Cwmfelinfach Caerph....37 J3
Cwmffrwd Carmth..........50 E3
Cwmgiedd Powys..........52 C5
Cwmgorse Carmth..........51 K4
Cwmgwili Carmth..........51 H4
Cwmhiraeth Carmth........65 K6
Cwm Llinau Powys.......81 J2
Cwmllynfell Neath........51 L3
Cwmmawr Carmth..........51 G3
Cwmparc Rhondd..........36 E2
Cwmpengraig
  Carmth.....................65 K7
Cwmtillery Blae G........53 K6
Cwm-twrch Isaf
  Powys......................52 B6
Cwm-twrch Uchaf
  Powys......................51 L4
Cwm-y-glo Gwynd....... 109 H8
Cwmystwyth Cerdgn....81 H8
**Cyfarthfa Castle
  Museum** Myr Td......53 G6
Cyffylliog Denbgs..........97 G2
Cylibebyll Neath...........51 L5
Cymmer Neath...............36 D2
Cymmer Rhondd............36 F3
Cynghordy Carmth.........67 H6
Cynonville Neath...........36 C2
Cynwyd Denbgs............97 G4
Cynwyl Elfed Carmth 65 L8

D

Daccombe Devon 7 K3
Dacre Cumb................ 138 C2
Dacre N York............... 132 B7
Dacre Banks N York... 132 B6
Daddry Shield Dur...... 149 M7
Dadford Bucks..............73 J6
Dadlington Leics..........86 E4
Dafen Carmth...............51 G5
Dagenham Gt Lon.........45 J3
Daglingworth Gloucs....55 M6
Dagnall Bucks..............59 G5
Dail bho Dheas
  W Isls.................... 232 g1
Dailly S Ayrs............... 152 F2
Dairsie Fife................ 187 G4
Dalabrog W Isls.......... 233 b8
Dalavich Ag & B.......... 182 D5
Dalbeattie D & G........ 146 E3
Dalby IoM................... 237 b5
Dalby N York............... 133 K5
Dalcapon P & K........... 194 F5
Dalchalm Highld......... 226 F7
Dalchreichart Highld... 201 L3
Dalchruin P & K.......... 184 F4
Dalcrue P & K............. 185 L2
Dalditch Devon.............12 D5
Dale Derbys................ 101 H5
Dale Pembks................48 D6
Dalelia Highld............ 190 E3
Dalgarven N Ayrs....... 163 H1
Dalgety Bay Fife........ 177 G2
Dalgig E Ayrs.............. 164 B6
Dalginross P & K........ 185 K3
Dalguise P & K........... 194 F6
Dalhalvaig Highld...... 230 C5
Dalham Suffk...............77 G3

Daliburgh W Isls.......... 233 b8
Dalkeith Mdloth.......... 177 K5
Dallas Moray............... 214 D4
Dallinghoo Suffk...........78 F4
Dallington E Susx.........20 D2
Dallington Nhants.........73 K3
Dalmally Ag & B......... 183 H3
Dalmary Stirlg............. 184 C7
Dalmellington E Ayrs... 153 K2
Dalmeny C Edin.......... 176 F3
Dalmore Highld........... 222 F7
Dalmuir W Duns......... 174 E4
Dalnabreck Highld...... 190 E3
Dalnacardoch P & K ... 194 B3
Dalnahaitnach Highld.. 203 K2
Dalnaspidal P & K....... 193 K2
Dalnawillan Lodge
  Highld.................... 230 F7
Daloist P & K.............. 194 C5
Dalqueich P & K......... 185 M6
Dalquharn S Ayrs........ 153 G3
Dalreavoch Highld...... 226 D6
Dalry N Ayrs............... 174 B7
Dalrymple E Ayrs........ 163 J6
Dalserf S Lans............ 175 L7
Dalsmeran Ag & B...... 161 G6
Dalston Cumb............. 148 C5
Dalston Gt Lon............45 G3
Dalswinton D & G....... 155 G5
Dalton D & G.............. 155 K7
Dalton N York............. 132 F4
Dalton N York............. 140 E5
Dalton Nthumb........... 158 E7
Dalton-in-Furness
  Cumb..................... 128 F5
Dalton-le-Dale Dur 151 K5
Dalton-on-Tees
  N York.................... 141 H5
Dalton Piercy Hartpl... 141 L2
Dalveich Stirlg........... 184 D3
Dalwhinnie Highld...... 202 F7
Dalwood Devon.............13 G3
Damerham Hants..........28 C7
Damgate Norfk............93 J2
Damnaglaur D & G...... 144 D7
Danbury Essex.............61 J6
Danby N York.............. 142 F5
Danby Wiske N York... 141 H7
Dandaleith Moray....... 215 G5
Danderhall Mdloth...... 177 J4
Danebridge Ches E 113 L7
Dane End Herts............60 B4
Danehill E Susx............32 D7
Dane Hills C Leic..........87 H3
Dane Street Kent..........34 E4
Danshillock Abers....... 216 D3
Danskine E Loth.......... 178 C5
Darenth Kent................45 K5
Daresbury Halton....... 112 E5
Darfield Barns............ 115 H1
Dargate Kent................34 E3
Dargavel Rens............ 174 D4
Darite Cnwll...................5 K3
Darlaston Wsall............85 H4
Darlaston Green
  Wsall.......................85 H4
Darley N York............. 132 C7
Darley Abbey C Derb... 101 G5
Darley Bridge
  Derbys.................... 100 E1
Darley Dale Derbys..... 114 F8
Darley Green Solhll......85 L8
Darleyhall Herts...........59 J4
Darley Head N York... 132 B7
Darlingscott Warwks.....72 B6
Darlington Darltn........ 141 H4
Darlton Notts.............. 116 C6
Darnick Border........... 167 H3
Darowen Powys............81 H3
Darra Abers................ 216 E5
Darracott Devon.............9 G2
Darracott Devon............23 G4
Darras Hall Nthumb.... 158 E7
Darrington Wakefd..... 124 D6
Darsham Suffk.............79 J1
Darshill Somset............26 E3
Dartford Kent...............45 K5

Dartford Crossing
  Kent........................45 K5
Dartington Devon 7 H4
**Dartmoor National
  Park** Devon..............10 F7
Dartmouth Devon 7 K5
Darton Barns.............. 123 L7
Darvel E Ayrs.............. 164 B2
Darwen Bl w D........... 121 K6
Datchet W & M............43 G5
Datchworth Herts.........59 L4
Daubhill Bolton.......... 121 K8
**Daugh of
  Kinermony** Moray .. 214 F6
Dauntsey Wilts.............39 M4
Dava Highld................ 214 C6
Davenham Ches W...... 112 F7
Daventry Nhants..........73 H3
Davidson's Mains
  C Edin.................... 177 G4
Davidstow Cnwll.............8 F7
Davington Devon 155 M7
Davington Hill Kent.....34 D3
Daviot Abers............... 216 E8
Daviot Highld.............. 213 H6
Daviot House Highld... 213 H6
Davoch of Grange
  Moray.................... 215 K4
Davyhulme Traffd...... 113 H3
Daw End Wsall............85 J4
Dawesgreen Surrey......31 K3
Dawley Wrekin............84 C2
Dawlish Devon.............12 B6
Dawlish Warren
  Devon......................12 C6
Daybrook Notts......... 101 L4
Daylesford Gloucs........56 E3
Deal Kent....................35 K4
Dean Cumb................. 136 E3
Dean Devon 7 G3
Dean Devon 23 L2
Dean Hants...................29 K7
Dean Oxon...................57 G4
Dean Somset................26 F3
Dean Bottom Kent.......45 L6
Deanburnhaugh
  Border.................... 166 F6
Deancombe Devon 7 G3
Dean Court Oxon..........57 J6
Deane Bolton............. 121 K8
Deane Hants................29 K2
Deanhead Kirk........... 122 F7
Deanland Dorset..........27 M7
Dean Prior Devon 7 H3
Deanraw Nthumb........ 149 L3
Deans W Loth............. 176 D5
Deanscales Cumb....... 136 F2
Deanshanger Nhants.....73 L6
Deanshaugh Moray..... 215 H4
Deanston Stirlg.......... 184 F6
Dearham Cumb........... 147 J7
Debach Suffk...............78 F4
Debden Essex...............45 H2
Debden Essex...............60 E2
Debenham Suffk..........78 E2
Deblin's Green Worcs...70 E5
Dechmont W Loth....... 176 E4
Dechmont Road
  W Loth.................... 176 D4
Deddington Oxon.........57 J2
Dedham Essex..............62 C2
Dedworth W & M..........42 F5
Deene Nhants..............88 D5
Deenethorpe Nhants.....88 D5
Deepcar Sheff............ 114 F3
Deeping Gate C Pete....89 G2
Deeping St James
  Lincs......................89 H2
Deeping St Nicholas
  Lincs......................89 J1
Deerhurst Gloucs.........55 K3
Defford Worcs..............71 G5
Defynnog Powys...........52 E3
Deganwy Conwy......... 109 L5
Degnish Ag & B.......... 182 A5
Deighton C York......... 124 F2
Deighton N York......... 141 J6

Deiniolen Gwynd............ 109 H8
Delabole Cnwll.................... 8 E7
Delamere Ches W 112 E7
Delfrigs Abers 207 H2
Delliefure Highld............. 214 D7
Dell Quay W Susx.........18 A5
Delnabo Moray............ 204 E3
Delny Highld................. 223 G6
Delph Oldham.............. 122 E8
Delves Dur..................... 150 E5
Dembleby Lincs 103 H5
Denaby Donc................. 115 J2
Denbigh Denbgs............ 110 E7
Denbrae Fife................. 186 F4
Denbury Devon................. 7 J3
Denby Derbys............... 101 H4
Denby Dale Kirk 123 J8
Denchworth Oxon......41 G3
Dendron Cumb 128 F5
Denfield P & K............. 185 K4
Denford Nhants.............88 E7
Dengie Essex...................62 B7
Denham Bucks 43 H3
Denham Suffk.................77 H3
Denham Suffk.................92 E8
Denham Green
   Bucks.......................43 H3
Denhead Abers 217 J4
Denhead Fife................. 187 G5
Denhead of Gray
   C Dund 186 F2
Denholm Border 167 J5
Denholme C Brad 123 G4
Denmead Hants 30 A8
Denmore C Aber 207 H3
Dennington Suffk..........79 G2
Denny Falk 175 L2
Dennyloanhead Falk ... 175 L3
Den of Lindores Fife... 186 D4
Denshaw Oldham 122 E7
Denside Abers 206 F6
Densole Kent..................35 G6
Denston Suffk.................77 H4
Denstone Staffs 100 C4
Denstroude Kent 34 E2
Dent Cumb 130 D3
Denton Cambs..............89 G6
Denton Darltn............. 140 F4
Denton E Susx...............19 L5
Denton Kent...................35 G5
Denton Lincs 102 E6
Denton N York 123 H2
Denton Nhants..............74 B3
Denton Norfk.................93 G5
Denton Tamesd 113 L3
Denver Norfk..................90 E3
Denwick Nthumb 169 J6
Deopham Norfk............92 C4
Deopham Green
   Norfk.......................92 C4
Depden Suffk.................77 H3
Deptford Gt Lon............45 G4
Deptford Wilts...............28 A4
Derby C Derb 101 G5
Derby Devon...................23 J5
Derbyhaven IoM........... 237 b7
Derculich P & K............ 194 D5
Dereham Norfk..............92 B2
Deri Caerph....................53 H7
Derringstone Kent 35 G5
Derrington Staffs...........99 K7
Derry Hill Wilts...............39 L6
Derrythorpe N Linc...... 125 J4
Dersingham Norfk......... 105 H6
Dervaig Ag & B 189 K6
Derwen Denbgs...............97 G3
Derwenlas Powys..........80 F4
Derwent Valley Mills
   Derbys......................100 F2
Derwent Water Cumb.. 137 J3
Desborough Nhants......88 B6
Desford Leics................86 F3
Deskford Moray 215 L3
Detling Kent...................33 K2
Devauden Mons..............54 C2
Devil's Bridge Cerdgn...81 G7
Devizes Wilts..................40 A7

Devonport C Plym............. 6 C5
Devonside Clacks 185 J7
Devoran Cnwll................. 4 C7
Devoran & Perran
   Cnwll........................ 3 K4
Dewarton Mdloth 177 K5
Dewlish Dorset................14 E3
Dewsbury Kirk.............. 123 K6
Dewsbury Moor Kirk.... 123 J6
Deytheur Powys............97 K8
Dibden Hants.................16 E2
Dibden Purlieu
   Hants.......................16 E2
Dickleburgh Norfk 92 E6
Didbrook Gloucs 56 B2
Didcot Oxon 41 K3
Diddington Cambs........75 H2
Diddlebury Shrops 83 K6
Didling W Susx 18 A3
Didmarton Gloucs.........39 J3
Didsbury Manch............ 113 J3
Digby Lincs.................. 103 H2
Digg Highld................. 218 C7
Diggle Oldham.............. 122 F8
Digmoor Lancs............ 112 C1
Dihewyd Cerdgn..............66 C4
Dilham Norfk............... 107 G7
Dilhorne Staffs..............99 L4
Dill Hall Lancs 121 L4
Dillington Cambs..........75 G2
Dilston Nthumb............ 150 B3
Dilton Wilts...................27 K2
Dilton Marsh Wilts........27 J2
Dilwyn Herefs................69 H4
Dinas Gwynd..................94 E5
Dinas Cross Pembks......64 E6
Dinas-Mawddwy
   Gwynd......................81 J1
Dinas Powys V Glam.......37 J6
Dinder Somset................26 E3
Dinedor Herefs...............69 K6
Dingestow Mons............54 C6
Dingle Lpool 111 K4
Dingley Nhants...............87 L6
Dingwall Highld........... 212 E3
Dinnet Abers............... 205 K5
Dinnington N u Ty......... 158 F7
Dinnington Rothm........ 115 K4
Dinnington Somset........26 B8
Dinorwic Gwynd............95 K1
Dinton Bucks.................58 C5
Dinton Wilts...................28 A5
Dinwoodie D & G......... 155 K4
Dinworthy Devon............. 9 J2
Dipford Somset..............25 J6
Dippen Ag & B 161 K2
Dippertown Devon.........10 C7
Dippin N Ayrs............... 162 D5
Dipple S Ayrs............... 152 E2
Diptford Devon................. 7 G4
Dipton Dur.................. 150 E4
Dirleton E Loth 178 B2
Dirt Pot Nthumb 149 L5
Diseworth Leics........... 101 J7
Dishforth N York.......... 132 F5
Disley Ches E................ 113 L5
Diss Norfk..................... 92 D7
Distington Cumb.......... 136 D3
Ditcheat Somset.............26 F4
Ditchingham Norfk 93 G5
Ditchling E Susx............19 J3
Ditherington Shrops......83 K2
Ditteridge Wilts.............39 J6
Dittisham Devon............. 7 K5
Ditton Kent...................33 J2
Ditton Green Cambs......76 F3
Ditton Priors Shrops......83 L5
Dixton Mons...................54 D5
Dobcross Oldham......... 113 M1
Dobwalls Cnwll................. 5 K3
Doccombe Devon...........11 H7
Dochgarroch Highld..... 212 F6
Docking Norfk.............. 105 J5
Docklow Herefs...............69 L3
Dockray Cumb.............. 137 L3

Doddinghurst Essex 60 F7
Doddington Cambs........90 B5
Doddington Kent............34 C4
Doddington Lincs 116 E7
Doddington Nthumb..... 168 E3
Doddington Shrops........84 B7
Doddiscombsleigh
   Devon......................11 K7
Dodd's Green Ches E......98 E4
Dodford Nhants..............73 H3
Dodford Worcs..............85 G8
Dodington S Glos...........39 H4
Dodington Somset..........25 J4
Dodleston Ches W..........98 A1
Dodside E Rens.............. 174 F7
Dod's Leigh Staffs........ 100 A5
Dodworth Barns........... 114 F1
Doe Bank Birm..............85 K4
Dogdyke Lincs............. 103 K2
Dogmersfield Hants........30 C2
Dogsthorpe C Pete.........89 H4
Dolanog Powys...............82 B2
Dolbenmaen Gwynd.......95 J4
Dolfach Powys................81 K3
Dolfor Powys..................82 C6
Dolgarrog Conwy......... 109 L7
Dolgellau Gwynd............96 B8
Doll Highld.................. 226 F7
Dollar Clacks............... 185 K7
Dollarfield Clacks........ 185 K7
Dolphin Flints............. 111 H6
Dolphinholme Lancs 129 L8
Dolphinton S Lans....... 176 F8
Dolton Devon.................10 E3
Dolwen Conwy............. 110 B6
Dolwyddelan Conwy......96 B3
Domgay Powys...............97 L8
Doncaster Donc........... 115 L2
Doncaster North
   Services Donc......... 125 G7
Doncaster Sheffield
   Airport Donc.......... 115 M2
Donhead St Andrew
   Wilts.......................27 K6
Donhead St Mary
   Wilts.......................27 K6
Donibristle Fife 177 G2
Doniford Somset............25 G3
Donington Lincs.......... 103 K5
Donington on Bain
   Lincs....................... 118 C5
Donington Park
   Services Leics........ 101 J7
Donisthorpe Leics..........86 C2
Donnington Gloucs........56 D3
Donnington Shrops........83 L2
Donnington W Berk.......41 J6
Donnington W Susx........18 B5
Donnington Wrekin........84 C2
Donnington Wood
   Wrekin.....................84 C2
Donyatt Somset..............25 M8
Doonfoot S Ayrs........... 163 H5
Dorback Lodge
   Highld.................... 204 D3
Dorchester Dorset.........14 D4
Dorchester-on-
   Thames Oxon...........41 L2
Dordon Warwks..............86 C4
Dore Sheff................... 114 F5
Dores Highld................ 212 F7
Dorking Surrey...............31 K2
Dormansland Surrey 32 D5
Dormington Herefs.........69 L6
Dornston Worcs...............71 H3
Dorney Bucks.................42 F5
Dornie Highld............... 200 D1
Dornoch Highld............ 223 H4
Dornock D & G............. 147 M2
Dorrery Highld............. 230 F5
Dorridge Solhll..............85 L8
Dorrington Lincs.......... 103 H2
Dorrington Shrops..........83 J3
Dorrington Shrops..........99 G4
Dorsington Warwks........71 K4
Dorstone Herefs.............69 G6
Dorton Bucks.................58 B5

Douglas IoM................. 237 d6
Douglas S Lans............. 165 G4
Douglas and Angus
   C Dund 187 G2
Douglas Pier Ag & B.... 183 H7
Douglastown Angus..... 196 C6
Douglas Water
   S Lans..................... 165 G3
Douglas West
   S Lans..................... 164 F3
Doulting Somset..............26 F3
Dounby Ork.................. 234 b5
Doune Highld............... 221 L2
Doune Stirlg................. 184 F6
Dounepark S Ayrs........ 152 E3
Dounie Highld.............. 222 D4
Dousland Devon............... 6 D3
Dove Dale Derbys........ 100 D3
Dove Holes Derbys....... 114 B6
Dovenby Cumb............ 147 J7
Dover Kent 35 J6
Dover Castle Kent.........35 J6
Dovercourt Essex..........62 F2
Doverdale Worcs............70 F2
Doveridge Derbys........ 100 C5
Doversgreen Surrey.......31 L2
Dowally P & K.............. 194 F6
Dowdeswell Gloucs........55 M4
Dowlais Myr Td..............53 G6
Dowland Devon..............10 E3
Dowlish Wake
   Somset......................26 A8
Down Ampney
   Gloucs......................40 C2
Downderry Cnwll............. 5 L5
Downe Gt Lon................45 H7
Downend Gloucs............55 J7
Downend S Glos.............38 F5
Downfield C Dund........ 186 F1
Downgate Cnwll............... 6 A2
Downham Essex.............46 B2
Downham Gt Lon 45 H5
Downham Lancs........... 122 B2
Downham Market
   Norfk.......................90 E3
Down Hatherley
   Gloucs......................55 K4
Downhead Somset..........26 E6
Downhead Somset..........27 G3
Downhill P & K............. 186 A2
Downholme N York...... 140 E7
Downies Abers.............. 207 H6
Downley Bucks...............42 D2
Down St Mary Devon.....11 H4
Downside Surrey 43 J8
Down Thomas Devon....... 6 D6
Downton Wilts................28 D6
Dowsby Lincs............... 103 J6
Doynton S Glos..............39 G5
Draethen Caerph............37 K3
Draffan S Lans.............. 164 F1
Drakeholes Notts......... 116 B4
Drakemyre N Ayrs....... 174 B7
Drakes Broughton
   Worcs......................71 G5
Draughton N York........ 131 K8
Draughton Nhants.........87 L7
Drax N York................. 125 G5
Draycote Warwks..........72 F1
Draycott Derbys........... 101 H6
Draycott Gloucs.............71 L7
Draycott Somset............26 C2
Draycott in the Clay
   Staffs...................... 100 D6
Draycott in the
   Moors Staffs............99 M4
Drayton C Port...............17 J2
Drayton Leics................88 B5
Drayton Norfk................92 E2
Drayton Oxon................72 E6
Drayton Oxon................41 J3
Drayton Somset..............26 B6
Drayton Worcs...............85 G7
Drayton Bassett
   Staffs.......................85 L4
Drayton Beauchamp
   Bucks......................58 E5

Drayton Manor Park
Staffs.....................85 L4
Drayton Parslow
Bucks 58 D3
Drayton St Leonard
Oxon.....................41 L2
Dreen Hill Pembks......48 F5
Drefach Carmth.........51 G3
Drefach Carmth.........65 K6
Drefach Cerdgn 66 C5
Dreghorn N Ayrs 163 J2
Drellingore Kent........35 H6
Drem E Loth...............178 B3
Dresden C Stke.........99 K4
Drewsteignton
Devon 11 H6
Driffield E R Yk 134 F7
Driffield Gloucs 56 B7
Drift Cnwll..................2 D5
Drigg Cumb 136 E7
Drighlington Leeds....123 J5
Drimnin Highld 190 B5
Drimpton Dorset........13 K2
Drimsallie Highld 191 J1
Dringhouses C York...124 E2
Drinkstone Suffk........77 L3
Drinkstone Green
Suffk......................77 L3
Droitton Staffs..........100 A6
Droitwich Spa Worcs...70 F2
Dron P & K.................186 B4
Dronfield Derbys.......115 G5
Drongan E Ayrs.........163 K5
Dronley Angus 186 E1
Droop Dorset 14 E2
Droxford Hants...........29 L7
Droylsden Tamesd....113 K2
Druid Denbgs 97 G4
Druidston Pembks......48 E4
Druimarbin Highld....191 L3
Druimavuic Ag & B...191 K7
Druimdrishaig
Ag & B 172 C4
Druimindarroch
Highld....................199 L7
Drum Ag & B 172 F3
Drum P & K.................185 L7
Drumalbin S Lans 165 H2
Drumbeg Highld 224 D3
Drumblade Abers......216 B6
Drumbreddon D & G..144 C6
Drumbuie Highld......210 B7
Drumburgh Cumb.....148 A3
Drumburn D & G.......146 F4
Drumburn D & G.......147 G3
Drumchapel C Glas ..174 F4
Drumchastle P & K ...193 L5
Drumclog S Lans 164 C2
Drumeldrie Fife.........187 G6
Drumelzier Border 165 M3
Drumfearn Highld.....199 L3
Drumfrennie Abers....206 D5
Drumgley Angus 196 C6
Drumguish Highld 203 J5
Drumin Moray 214 E7
Drumjohn D & G 153 L3
Drumlamford S Ayrs..153 G6
Drumlasie Abers.......206 C4
Drumleaning Cumb....148 A5
Drumlemble Ag & B...161 H5
Drumlithie Abers.......197 J1
Drummoddie D & G...145 H6
Drummore D & G.......144 D7
Drummuir Moray 215 J5
Drumnadrochit
Highld....................212 D7
Drumnagorrach
Moray....................215 L4
Drumpark D & G........154 F6
Drumruie Highld.......224 E7
Drumshang S Ayrs....163 G6
Drumuie Highld 209 G5
Drumuillie Highld 204 B2
Drumvaich Stirlg 184 E6
Drunzie P & K............186 B5
Drybeck Cumb 138 F4
Drybridge Moray......215 K2

Drybridge N Ayrs........163 J3
Drybrook Gloucs 54 F4
Dryburgh Border.......167 J3
Dry Doddington
Lincs.......................102 D3
Dry Drayton Cambs.....75 L3
Drymen Stirlg 174 E2
Drymuir Abers...........217 G5
Drynoch Highld.........208 F7
Dubford Abers...........216 F2
Duchally Highld 225 J5
Ducklington Oxon......57 G6
Duddenhoe End
Essex......................76 C7
Duddingston C Edin ..177 J4
Duddington Nhants....88 B4
Duddlestone Somset...25 K7
Duddo Nthumb..........168 D2
Duddon Ches W........112 D8
Dudleston Shrops......97 M5
Dudleston Heath
Shrops....................98 A5
Dudley Dudley...........85 G5
Dudley N Tyne..........159 G7
Dudley Port Sandw ...85 G5
Dudsbury Dorset........15 K3
Duffield Derbys........101 G4
Duffryn Neath............36 C2
Dufftown Moray........215 H6
Duffus Moray 214 E2
Dufton Cumb 139 G3
Duggleby N York 134 D6
Duirinish Highld 210 B7
Duisdalemore Highld..199 L3
Duisky Highld 191 K2
Dukestown Blae G.....53 H6
Duke Street Suffk......78 C6
Dukinfield Tamesd....113 L2
Dulcote Somset.........26 E3
Dulford Devon............12 D2
Dull P & K.................194 C6
Dullatur N Lans 175 K3
Dullingham Cambs.....76 F3
Dulnain Bridge
Highld....................204 B1
Duloe Bed..................75 H3
Duloe Cnwll..................5 K4
Dulsie Bridge Highld ..213 L6
Dulverton Somset......24 E5
Dulwich Gt Lon..........45 G5
Dumbarton W Duns...174 D4
Dumbleton Gloucs......71 H7
Dumfries D & G.........155 G6
Dumgoyne Stirlg.......174 F2
Dummer Hants...........29 L3
Dumpton Kent............35 K2
Dun Angus 197 G4
Dunalastair P & K 193 L5
Dunan Ag & B...........173 K4
Dunan Highld 209 J8
Dunan P & K.............193 G5
Dunaverty Ag & B 161 H7
Dunball Somset.........25 L3
Dunbar E Loth..........178 E3
Dunbeath Highld......227 L3
Dunbeg Ag & B 182 C2
Dunblane Stirlg 185 G6
Dunbog Fife..............186 E4
Duncanston Highld....212 F3
Duncanstone Abers...206 B1
Dunchideock Devon...11 K7
Dunchurch Warwks....72 F1
Duncow D & G 155 G5
Duncrievie P & K 186 B5
Duncton W Susx........18 C3
Dundee C Dund........186 F2
Dundee Airport
C Dund...................186 F2
Dundon Somset.........26 C5
Dundonald S Ayrs.....163 J3
Dundonnell Highld....220 E4
Dundraw Cumb 147 L5
Dundreggan Highld...201 L3
Dundrennan D & G....146 D5
Dundry N Som...........38 E6
Dunecht Abers..........206 E4
Dunfermline Fife.......176 F2

Dunfield Gloucs..........40 C2
Dungavel S Lans 164 D3
Dungeness Kent.........21 L3
Dunham Massey
Traffd......................113 H4
Dunham-on-the-
Hill Ches W 112 C6
Dunham-on-Trent
Notts......................116 D6
Dunhampton Worcs....70 F2
Dunham Town Traffd...113 H4
Dunham
Woodhouses
Traffd......................113 G4
Dunholme Lincs........117 G5
Dunino Fife..............187 J5
Dunipace Falk 175 L2
Dunkeld P & K 195 G7
Dunkerton BaNES......39 G8
Dunkeswell Devon......12 E2
Dunkeswick N York...123 L2
Dunkirk Kent..............34 E3
Dunkirk S Glos...........39 H4
Dunk's Green Kent.....33 G3
Dunlappie Angus 196 F3
Dunley Worcs.............70 E2
Dunlop E Ayrs 174 D8
Dunmaglass Highld ...202 F2
Dunmore Falk...........176 B1
Dunnet Highld..........231 J2
Dunnichen Angus 196 E6
Dunning P & K..........185 L4
Dunnington C York....133 K8
Dunnington E R Yk...126 E1
Dunnington Warwks ...71 J4
Dunoon Ag & B 173 K3
Dunphail Moray 214 C5
Dunragit D & G.........144 E4
Duns Border 179 G7
Dunsby Lincs............103 J6
Dunscore D & G 154 F5
Dunscroft Donc.........124 F8
Dunsdale R & Cl.......142 D4
Dunsden Green Oxon...42 C5
Dunsdon Devon 9 J3
Dunsfold Surrey.........31 G4
Dunsford Devon 11 J6
Dunshalt Fife............186 D5
Dunshillock Abers....217 J5
Dunsill Notts............101 J1
Dunsley N York.........143 H5
Dunsley Staffs...........84 F6
Dunsmore Bucks........58 E6
Dunsop Bridge Lancs..121 K1
Dunstable C Beds.....59 G4
Dunstall Staffs..........100 D7
Dunstan Nthumb 169 K5
Dunster Somset.........24 F3
Duns Tew Oxon..........57 J3
Dunston Gatesd........151 G3
Dunston Lincs...........117 H8
Dunston Norfk...........92 F3
Dunston Staffs...........99 L8
Dunstone Devon 6 E5
Dunstone Devon 7 G2
Dunsville Donc.........124 F8
Dunswell E R Yk.......126 D4
Dunsyre S Lans........176 E8
Dunterton Devon 6 B1
Duntisbourne
Abbots Gloucs........55 L6
Duntisbourne
Rouse Gloucs.........55 M6
Duntish Dorset...........14 D2
Duntocher W Duns ...174 E4
Dunton Bucks............58 D3
Dunton C Beds...........75 J5
Dunton Norfk...........105 L6
Dunton Bassett Leics...87 G5
Dunton Green Kent 32 F2
Duntulm Highld........218 C6
Dunure S Ayrs..........163 G6
Dunvant Swans..........51 H6
Dunvegan Highld 208 D5
Dunwich Suffk...........79 K1
Durgan Cnwll..............3 K5
Durham Dur..............151 G6

Durham Cathedral
Dur.........................151 G6
Durham Services
Dur.........................151 H7
Durham Tees Valley
Airport on T 141 J5
Durisdeer D & G........154 F2
Durisdeermill D & G...154 F2
Durleigh Somset........25 L4
Durley Hants.............29 K7
Durley Wilts..............40 E7
Durley Street Hants...29 K7
Durlock Kent..............35 H3
Durlock Kent..............35 J2
Durness Highld 228 F3
Durno Abers.............216 D8
Duror Highld.............191 K5
Durran Ag & B..........182 D5
Durrington W Susx....18 F5
Durrington Wilts........28 D3
Durris Abers.............206 E6
Dursley Gloucs...........39 H2
Dursley Cross Gloucs..55 G4
Durston Somset..........25 L5
Durweston Dorset.......15 G2
Duston Nhants..........73 K3
Duthil Highld 203 L1
Dutton Ches W 112 E5
Duxford Cambs..........76 C5
Duxford Oxon............57 G7
Duxford IWM Cambs...76 C5
Dwygyfylchi Conwy...109 L6
Dwyran IoA..............108 F7
Dyce C Aber 207 G3
Dyffryn Ardudwy
Gwynd....................95 K7
Dyffryn Cellwen
Neath......................52 D6
Dyke Lincs...............103 J7
Dyke Moray..............214 B3
Dykehead Angus 195 K5
Dykehead Angus 196 C4
Dykehead N Lans.....176 B6
Dykehead Stirlg........184 D7
Dykelands Abers.......197 J3
Dykends Angus 195 K5
Dykeside Abers.........216 D5
Dymchurch Kent.........34 E8
Dymock Gloucs...........55 G2
Dyrham S Glos...........39 H5
Dysart Fife...............186 E8
Dyserth Denbgs.........110 E5

E

Eagland Hill Lancs.....120 F2
Eagle Lincs...............116 E7
Eaglesfield Cumb......136 F2
Eaglesfield D & G......155 M7
Eaglesham E Rens....175 G7
Eagley Bolton..........121 L7
Eakring Notts...........102 A1
Ealand N Linc...........125 J7
Ealing Gt Lon............44 D4
Eals Nthumb............149 H4
Eamont Bridge
Cumb......................138 D2
Earby Lancs..............122 D2
Earcroft Bl w D.........121 K5
Eardington Shrops.....84 C5
Eardisland Herefs......69 H3
Eardisley Herefs........68 F5
Eardiston Shrops........98 A7
Eardiston Worcs.........70 C2
Earith Cambs.............89 L8
Earlestown St Hel.....112 E3
Earley Wokham..........42 C6
Earlham Norfk...........92 E2
Earlish Highld...........208 F3
Earls Barton Nhants...74 C2
Earls Colne Essex......61 K3
Earls Common Worcs..71 G3
Earl's Croome Worcs...70 F6
Earlsdon Covtry.........86 D7
Earlsferry Fife...........187 H7

Earlsfield Gt Lon..............44 E5
Earlsford Abers............216 F7
Earlsheaton Kirk..........123 K6
Earl Shilton Leics..........86 F4
Earl Soham Suffk..........78 F2
Earl Sterndale
 Derbys..............114 C7
Earlston Border.............167 J2
Earlston E Ayrs.............163 K3
Earlswood Surrey 32 B4
Earlswood Warwks.....85 K8
Earnley W Susx............17 M3
Earsdon N Tyne.............159 H7
Earsham Norfk.............93 G5
Eartham W Susx............18 C4
Easby N York.............142 C5
Easdale Ag & B...........181 L4
Easebourne W Susx....30 E6
Easenhall Warwks........86 F7
Eashing Surrey............30 F3
Easington Bucks...........58 B6
Easington Dur............151 K6
Easington E R Yk.........127 J6
Easington R & Cl........142 F4
Easington Colliery
 Dur................151 K6
Easington Lane
 Sundld.............151 J5
Easingwold N York....133 H5
Eassie and Nevay
 Angus..............196 B7
East Aberthaw
 V Glam..............37 G6
East Allington Devon.........7 H6
East Anstey Devon.........24 D6
East Ashey IoW............17 H5
East Ashling W Susx....17 M2
East Ayton N York....134 F3
East Barkwith Lincs......117 K5
East Barming Kent......33 J3
East Barnby N York...143 G5
East Barnet Gt Lon......44 F2
East Barns E Loth......178 F3
East Barsham Norfk....105 L5
East Beckham Norfk...106 E4
East Bedfont Gt Lon...43 H5
East Bergholt Suffk....78 C7
East Bilney Norfk......106 A8
East Blatchington
 E Susx..............20 A5
East Boldon S Tyne....151 J3
East Boldre Hants......16 D3
Eastbourne Darltn....141 H4
Eastbourne E Susx......20 C5
East Bradenham
 Norfk................91 L2
East Brent Somset......25 M2
Eastbridge Suffk........79 J2
East Bridgford Notts...102 B4
East Buckland Devon....23 L5
East Budleigh Devon....12 D5
Eastburn C Brad..........122 F2
Eastbury W Berk.........41 G5
East Butterwick
 N Linc..............116 D1
Eastby N York...........131 J8
East Calder W Loth...176 E5
East Carleton Norfk....92 E3
East Carlton Leeds....123 J2
East Carlton Nhants....88 B5
East Chaldon Dorset....14 E5
East Challow Oxon.........41 G3
East Charleton
 Devon................7 H7
East Chelborough
 Dorset................14 A2
East Chiltington
 E Susx..............19 K3
East Chinnock
 Somset...............26 C8
East Chisenbury
 Wilts................28 C2
Eastchurch Kent.........47 G5
East Clandon Surrey......31 H2
East Claydon Bucks....58 C3
East Coker Somset.....26 D8
Eastcombe Gloucs.....55 K6

East Compton
 Somset...............26 E3
East Cornworthy
 Devon..................7 J5
Eastcote Gt Lon..........43 J3
Eastcote Nhants.........73 K4
Eastcote Solhll.........85 L7
Eastcott Wilts..........28 A1
East Cottingwith
 E R Yk..............125 G3
Eastcourt Wilts.........40 E7
East Cowes IoW...........16 F4
East Cowick E R Yk....125 G6
East Cowton N York...141 H6
East Cranmore
 Somset...............27 G3
East Dean E Susx........20 B6
East Dean Gloucs............54 F4
East Dean Hants........28 F6
East Dean W Susx........18 B3
East Drayton Notts....116 C6
East Dulwich Gt Lon....45 G5
East Dundry N Som.......38 E7
East Ella C KuH........126 C5
Eastend Essex..........46 F2
East End Hants........16 D3
East End Hants........41 H7
East End Kent.........33 L6
East End Oxon.........57 H5
East End Somset.......26 F3
Easter Balmoral
 Abers...............205 G6
Easter Compton
 S Glos...............38 E4
Easter Dalziel Highld...213 H4
Eastergate W Susx.....18 C5
Easterhouse C Glas...175 J5
Easter Howgate
 Mdloth..............177 H5
Easter Kinkell Highld...212 E4
Easter Moniack
 Highld..............212 E5
Eastern Green Covtry...86 C7
Easter Ord Abers.....206 F4
Easter Pitkierie Fife...187 J6
Easter Skeld Shet....235 c6
Easter Softlaw
 Border..............168 A3
Easterton Wilts.............28 A1
East Everleigh Wilts...28 D2
East Farleigh Kent......33 J3
East Farndon Nhants...87 K6
East Ferry Lincs.......116 D2
Eastfield N Lans.......176 B5
Eastfield N York.......135 G3
East Fortune E Loth...178 C3
East Garston W Berk...41 G5
Eastgate Dur...........150 B7
Eastgate Lincs.........103 J8
Eastgate Norfk.........106 D7
East Goscote Leics....87 J2
East Grafton Wilts...........40 E7
East Grimstead Wilts...28 E5
East Grinstead
 W Susx................32 D5
East Guldeford
 E Susx..............21 J2
East Haddon Nhants....73 J2
East Hagbourne
 Oxon.................41 K3
East Halton N Linc...126 E6
East Ham Gt Lon.......45 H4
Easthampton Herefs....69 H2
East Hanney Oxon......41 H2
East Hanningfield
 Essex................61 J7
East Hardwick
 Wakefd..............124 C6
East Harling Norfk....92 B6
East Harlsey N York..141 K7
East Harnham Wilts....28 C5
East Harptree BaNES...38 E1
East Harting W Susx...30 D7
East Hatch Wilts......27 L5
East Hatley Cambs.....75 K4
East Hauxwell N York.132 B2
East Haven Angus.....187 J1

East Heckington
 Lincs...............103 K4
East Hedleyhope
 Dur.................150 E6
East Helmsdale
 Highld..............227 H5
East Hendred Oxon.....41 J3
East Heslerton
 N York..............134 E4
East Hoathly E Susx...20 B3
East Holme Dorset.....15 G5
Easthope Shrops.......83 L4
Easthorpe Essex.............61 L4
East Horrington
 Somset...............26 E3
East Horsley Surrey...31 H2
East Howe BCP.........15 K4
East Huntington
 C York..............133 J7
East Huntspill
 Somset...............26 A3
East Ilsley W Berk....41 J4
Eastington Devon........11 H3
Eastington Gloucs.....55 H6
Eastington Gloucs.....56 C5
East Keal Lincs......118 E8
East Kennett Wilts....40 C6
East Keswick Leeds...124 B2
East Kilbride S Lans.175 H7
East Kirkby Lincs....118 D8
East Knighton Dorset..14 F5
East Knoyle Wilts.....27 K5
East Lambrook
 Somset...............26 B7
Eastlands D & G......154 E7
East Langdon Kent.....35 J5
East Langton Leics....87 K5
East Lavant W Susx....18 B4
East Lavington
 W Susx...............18 C3
East Layton N York...140 E5
Eastleach Martin
 Gloucs...............56 D6
Eastleach Turville
 Gloucs...............56 D6
East Leake Notts.....101 K7
Eastleigh Devon.......23 H5
Eastleigh Hants.......29 J7
East Lexham Norfk....105 K8
Eastling Kent.........34 C4
East Linton E Loth...178 D3
East Lockinge Oxon....41 H3
East Lound N Linc....116 C2
East Lulworth Dorset..15 G6
East Lutton N York...134 E5
East Lydford Somset...26 E5
East Malling Kent.....33 J2
East Marden W Susx....30 D8
East Markham Notts...116 C6
East Martin Hants.....28 B7
East Marton N York...122 D1
East Meon Hants.......30 B6
East Mersea Essex.....62 C5
East Midlands
 Airport Leics......101 J7
East Molesey Surrey...43 J6
East Morden Dorset....15 G4
East Morton C Brad...123 G3
East Morton D & G....154 F3
East Ness N York.....133 L4
Eastney C Port........17 J3
Eastnor Herefs........70 D6
East Norton Leics.....87 L4
Eastoft N Linc......125 J7
East Ogwell Devon......7 J2
Easton Cambs..........75 G1
Easton Devon..........11 G6
Easton Dorset.........14 D7
Easton Hants..........29 K5
Easton Lincs.........102 F7
Easton Norfk..........92 D2
Easton Somset.........26 D3
Easton Suffk..........79 G3
Easton Wilts..........39 K6
Easton Grey Wilts.....39 K3
Easton-in-Gordano
 N Som................38 D5

Easton Maudit
 Nhants...............74 C3
Easton-on-the-Hill
 Nhants...............88 E3
East Orchard Dorset...27 J7
East Peckham Kent.....33 H4
East Pennard Somset...26 E4
East Perry Cambs......75 G2
East Portlemouth
 Devon.................7 H7
East Prawle Devon......7 H8
East Preston W Susx...18 E5
East Putford Devon....9 K2
East Quantoxhead
 Somset...............25 H3
East Rainton Sundld..151 H5
East Ravendale
 NE Lin..............118 C2
East Raynham Norfk...105 L7
Eastrea Cambs.........89 K4
East Rigton Leeds....124 B2
Eastrington E R Yk...125 J4
Eastrop Swindn........40 D2
East Rounton N York..141 K6
East Rudham Norfk....105 K6
East Runton Norfk....106 E4
East Ruston Norfk....107 H6
Eastry Kent...........35 J4
East Saltoun E Loth..178 B5
East Sheen Gt Lon.....44 D5
East Shefford W Berk..41 H5
East Stockwith Lincs.116 C3
East Stoke Dorset.....15 G5
East Stoke Notts.....102 C3
East Stour Dorset.....27 J6
East Stourmouth
 Kent.................35 H3
East Stowford Devon...23 K6
East Stratton Hants...29 K4
East Studdal Kent.....35 J5
East Taphouse Cnwll....5 J3
East-the-Water
 Devon................23 G6
East Thirston Nthumb.158 F3
East Tilbury Thurr....46 B4
East Tisted Hants.....30 B5
East Torrington Lincs..117 J5
East Tuddenham
 Norfk................92 C2
East Tytherley Hants..28 F5
East Tytherton Wilts..39 L5
East Village Devon....11 J4
Eastville Bristl......38 E5
Eastville Lincs......104 C2
East Walton Norfk.....91 G1
East Week Devon.......10 F6
Eastwell Leics.......102 C6
East Wellow Hants.....28 F7
East Wemyss Fife.....186 E7
East Whitburn
 W Loth..............176 C5
Eastwick Herts........60 C5
East Wickham Gt Lon...45 J5
East Williamston
 Pembks...............49 J6
East Winch Norfk......91 G1
East Winterslow
 Wilts................28 E5
East Wittering
 W Susx...............17 L3
East Witton N York...131 L3
Eastwood Notts......101 J3
Eastwood Sthend.......46 D3
East Woodburn
 Nthumb..............158 A5
East Woodhay Hants....41 H7
East Worldham
 Hants................30 C4
East Wretham Norfk....91 K5
Eathorpe Warwks.......72 E2
Eaton Ches E.........113 K7
Eaton Ches W.........112 E8
Eaton Leics..........102 D6
Eaton Norfk...........92 E3
Eaton Notts..........116 B6

Eaton Oxon................57 H7
Eaton Shrops..............83 K5
Eaton Bray C Beds........58 F4
Eaton Constantine
    Shrops................83 L3
Eaton Green C Beds.......58 F4
Eaton Hastings Oxon......56 E7
Eaton Mascott
    Shrops................83 K3
Eaton Socon Cambs........75 H3
Eaton upon Tern
    Shrops................98 F7
Ebberston N York.........134 D3
Ebbesborne Wake
    Wilts................27 M6
Ebbw Vale Blae G.........53 J6
Ebchester Dur...........150 D4
Ebford Devon.............12 C5
Ebley Gloucs.............55 J6
Ebnal Ches W.............98 C3
Ebrington Gloucs.........71 L6
Ecchinswell Hants........41 J8
Ecclaw Border...........178 F5
Ecclefechan D & G.......155 L7
Eccles Border...........168 A2
Eccles Kent..............46 B7
Eccles Salfd...........113 H2
Ecclesall Sheff.........114 F5
Ecclesfield Sheff.......115 G3
Eccleshall Staffs........99 J6
Eccleshill C Brad.......123 H4
Ecclesmachan
    W Loth..............176 E4
Eccles Road Norfk........92 B5
Eccleston Ches W........112 B8
Eccleston Lancs.........121 G6
Eccleston St Hel........112 C3
Echt Abers.............206 E4
Eckford Border..........167 L4
Eckington Derbys........115 H5
Eckington Worcs..........71 G6
Ecton Nhants.............74 B2
Edale Derbys...........114 C4
Eday Ork...............234 d4
Eday Airport Ork........234 d4
Edburton W Susx..........19 H4
Edderton Highld.........222 F4
Eddleston Border........177 H8
Eddlewood S Lans........175 J7
Edenbridge Kent..........32 D4
Edenfield Lancs.........122 B6
Edenhall Cumb...........138 E2
Edenham Lincs...........103 H7
Eden Park Gt Lon.........45 G6
Eden Project Cnwll........5 G5
Edensor Derbys..........114 E7
Edentaggart Ag & B......183 K8
Edenthorpe Donc.........115 L1
Edern Gwynd..............94 E5
Edgbaston Birm...........85 J6
Edgcott Bucks............58 B4
Edgcott Somset...........24 D4
Edge Gloucs..............55 J6
Edgefield Norfk........106 C5
Edgefield Green
    Norfk..............106 D5
Edgerton Kirk...........123 H6
Edgeworth Gloucs.........55 L6
Edgmond Wrekin...........99 G8
Edgton Shrops............83 H6
Edgware Gt Lon...........44 D2
Edgworth Bl w D.........121 L6
Edinbane Highld.........208 E4
Edinburgh C Edin........177 H4
Edinburgh Airport
    C Edin.............176 F4
Edinburgh Castle
    C Edin.............177 H4
Edinburgh Old &
    New Town C Edin....177 H4
Edinburgh Royal
    Botanic Gardens
    C Edin.............177 H4
Edinburgh Zoo
    RZSS C Edin........177 G4
Edingale Staffs..........86 B2
Edingham D & G..........146 E3

Edingley Notts..........102 A2
Edingthorpe Norfk.......107 G6
Edingthorpe Green
    Norfk..............107 G6
Edington Border.........179 J7
Edington Nthumb.........158 E5
Edington Somset..........26 B4
Edington Wilts...........27 L2
Edington Burtle
    Somset..............26 B3
Edingworth Somset.......26 A2
Edithmead Somset.........25 L2
Edith Weston Rutlnd......88 D3
Edlesborough Bucks.......58 F4
Edlingham Nthumb.......169 G7
Edlington Lincs.........118 C7
Edmondsham Dorset........15 K1
Edmondsley Dur..........151 G5
Edmondthorpe Leics.......88 C1
Edmonton Gt Lon..........45 G2
Edmundbyers Dur........150 C5
Ednam Border...........167 L2
Ednaston Derbys.........100 E4
Edradynate P & K........194 D6
Edrom Border...........179 H7
Edstaston Shrops.........98 D6
Edstone Warwks...........71 L3
Edwalton Notts..........101 L5
Edwinstowe Notts........115 L7
Edworth C Beds...........75 J6
Edwyn Ralph Herefs.......70 B3
Edzell Angus...........196 F3
Edzell Woods Abers......197 G3
Efail-fach Neath.........36 B2
Efail Isaf Rhondd........37 G4
Efailnewydd Gwynd........94 F5
Efailwen Carmth..........49 K3
Efenechtyd Denbgs........97 H2
Effgill D & G..........156 B4
Effingham Surrey.........31 J2
Egerton Bolton.........121 K7
Egerton Kent.............34 B5
Eggborough N York......124 E5
Eggbuckland C Plym........6 D4
Eggesford Devon..........11 G3
Eggington C Beds.........58 F3
Egginton Derbys.........100 E6
Eggleston Dur..........140 C3
Egham Surrey.............43 G6
Egleton Rutlnd...........88 C3
Eglingham Nthumb.......169 G5
Egloshayle Cnwll..........4 F2
Egloskerry Cnwll..........9 H7
Eglwysbach Conwy.......109 M7
Eglwys Cross
    Wrexhm...............98 C4
Eglwyswrw Pembks.........65 G6
Egmanton Notts.........116 B7
Egremont Cumb..........136 D5
Egremont Wirral........111 K3
Egton N York...........143 G6
Egton Bridge N York....143 G6
Egypt Bucks..............42 F3
Eigg Highld............199 G7
Eight Ash Green
    Essex................61 M3
Eilanreach Highld......200 C2
Eilean Donan Castle
    Highld.............200 D1
Eisgein W Isls.........232 f3
Eishken W Isls.........232 f3
Elan Valley Powys........67 J2
Elan Village Powys.......67 K2
Elberton S Glos..........38 E3
Elburton C Plym...........6 D5
Elcombe Swindn...........40 C4
Eldersfield Worcs........55 H2
Elderslie Rens.........174 E5
Eldon Dur..............141 G2
Elerch Cerdgn............80 F6
Elfhill Abers..........206 F7
Elford Staffs............85 L2
Elgin Moray............214 F2
Elgol Highld...........199 H3
Elham Kent...............35 G6
Elie Fife..............187 H7
Elim IoA...............108 D4
Eling Hants..............29 G8

Elkesley Notts.........116 B6
Elkstone Gloucs..........55 L5
Ella Abers.............216 C3
Ellacombe Torbay.........7 L3
Elland Calder..........123 G6
Ellary Ag & B..........172 C3
Ellastone Staffs.......100 C4
Ellel Lancs............129 K7
Ellemford Border.......178 F6
Ellenabeich Ag & B.....181 L4
Ellenhall Staffs.........99 J7
Ellen's Green Surrey.....31 H4
Ellerbeck N York.......141 K7
Ellerby N York.........143 G4
Ellerdine Heath
    Wrekin..............98 F7
Elleric Ag & B.........191 K6
Ellerker E R Yk.........125 L5
Ellerton E R Yk........125 G3
Ellerton N York........141 G7
Ellesborough Bucks.......58 D6
Ellesmere Shrops.........98 B5
Ellesmere Port
    Ches W.............111 L6
Ellingham Norfk..........93 H5
Ellingham Nthumb.......169 H4
Ellingstring N York....132 B3
Ellington Cambs..........75 H1
Ellington Nthumb.......159 G4
Elliots Green Somset.....27 J3
Ellisfield Hants.........29 M3
Ellishader Highld......209 H2
Ellistown Leics..........86 E2
Ellon Abers............217 H7
Ellonby Cumb...........148 D7
Elloughton E R Yk......125 L5
Ellwood Gloucs...........54 E6
Elm Cambs...............90 C3
Elmbridge Worcs..........70 F2
Elmdon Essex............76 C6
Elmdon Solhll............85 L6
Elmer W Susx.............18 D5
Elmers End Gt Lon........45 G6
Elmer's Green Lancs....112 D1
Elmesthorpe Leics........86 F4
Elmhurst Staffs..........85 K2
Elmley Castle Worcs......71 H6
Elmley Lovett Worcs......70 F1
Elmore Gloucs............55 H5
Elmore Back Gloucs.......55 H5
Elm Park Gt Lon..........45 K3
Elmsett Suffk............78 C5
Elmstead Market
    Essex................62 C3
Elmsted Kent.............34 F5
Elmstone Kent............35 H3
Elmstone
    Hardwicke Gloucs.....55 K3
Elmswell E R Yk........134 F7
Elmswell Suffk...........78 B2
Elmton Derbys..........115 J6
Elphin Highld..........224 F6
Elphinstone E Loth.....177 K4
Elrick Abers...........206 F4
Elrig D & G............145 G5
Elrington Nthumb.......149 L3
Elsdon Nthumb..........158 B4
Elsenham Essex...........60 E3
Elsfield Oxon............57 K6
Elsham N Linc..........126 C7
Elsing Norfk.............92 C1
Elslack N York.........122 D2
Elson Hants..............17 H3
Elsrickle S Lans.......165 K2
Elstead Surrey...........30 E3
Elsted W Susx............30 D7
Elsthorpe Lincs........103 H7
Elston Notts...........102 C3
Elstow Bed...............74 F5
Elstree Herts............44 D2
Elstronwick E R Yk.....126 F4
Elswick Lancs..........120 F3
Elswick N u Ty.........151 G3
Elsworth Cambs...........75 K3
Elterwater Cumb........137 K6
Eltham Gt Lon............45 H5
Eltisley Cambs...........75 J3

Elton Cambs.............88 F5
Elton Ches W...........112 C6
Elton Derbys...........100 E1
Elton Herefs............69 J1
Elton S on T...........141 J4
Elton-on-the-Hill
    Notts..............102 C5
Eltringham Nthumb......150 D3
Elvanfoot S Lans.......165 J6
Elvaston Derbys........101 H6
Elveden Suffk............91 J7
Elvetham Heath
    Hants................30 D1
Elvingston E Loth......178 A4
Elvington C York.......125 G2
Elvington Kent...........35 H5
Elwick Hartpl..........141 K2
Elworth Ches E...........99 H1
Elworthy Somset..........25 G4
Ely Cambs...............90 D7
Ely Cardiff..............37 H5
Emberton M Keyn..........74 C5
Embleton Cumb..........137 G2
Embleton Nthumb........169 J5
Embo Highld............223 H3
Emborough Somset.........26 E2
Embo Street Highld.....223 H3
Embsay N York..........131 J8
Emery Down Hants.........16 C2
Emley Kirk.............123 K7
Emmington Oxon...........58 C7
Emneth Norfk.............90 C3
Emneth Hungate
    Norfk................90 D3
Empingham Rutlnd.........88 D2
Empshott Hants...........30 C5
Emsworth Hants...........17 K2
Enborne W Berk...........41 H7
Enborne Row W Berk.......41 H7
Enderby Leics............87 G4
Endmoor Cumb...........129 L3
Endon Staffs.............99 L2
Endon Bank Staffs........99 L2
Enfield Gt Lon...........60 B7
Enfield Lock Gt Lon......60 B7
Enfield Wash Gt Lon......60 B7
Enford Wilts.............28 C2
Engine Common
    S Glos...............39 G4
Englefield W Berk........41 L6
Englefield Green
    Surrey...............43 G6
English Bicknor
    Gloucs...............54 E5
Englishcombe BaNES.......39 G7
English Frankton
    Shrops...............98 C6
Enham Alamein
    Hants................29 G2
Enmore Somset............25 K4
Enmore Green
    Dorset...............27 J6
Ennerdale Bridge
    Cumb...............136 E4
Enochdhu P & K.........195 G4
Ensay Ag & B...........189 J6
Ensbury BCP.............15 K3
Ensdon Shrops............83 H1
Enstone Oxon.............57 G3
Enterkinfoot D & G.....154 E2
Enville Staffs...........84 E6
Eòlaigearraidh
    W Isls.............233 b9
Eoligarry W Isls.......233 b9
Epney Gloucs.............55 H5
Epperstone Notts.......102 A3
Epping Essex.............60 D7
Epping Green Essex.......60 C6
Epping Upland Essex......60 C6
Eppleby N York.........140 F5
Epsom Surrey.............44 E7
Epwell Oxon.............72 D6
Epworth N Linc.........116 C2
Erbistock Wrexhm........97 M4
Erdington Birm...........85 K5
Eridge Green E Susx......32 F6
Erines Ag & B..........172 E4

Eriska Ag & B 191 H7
Eriskay W Isls 233 c9
Eriswell Suffk................. 91 G7
Erith Gt Lon................... 45 K4
Erlestoke Wilts............... 27 L2
Ermington Devon............... 6 F5
Erpingham Norfk............ 106 E6
Errogie Highld............... 202 E2
Errol P & K................... 186 D3
Erskine Rens................. 174 E4
Erskine Bridge Rens ... 174 E4
Ervie D & G.................. 144 B2
Erwarton Suffk................ 78 F7
Erwood Powys................. 68 C6
Eryholme N York............ 141 H5
Eryrys Denbgs................ 97 J2
Escomb Dur................... 140 F2
Escrick N York.............. 124 F2
Esgairgeiliog Powys....81 G3
Esh Devon..................... 150 F6
Esher Surrey.................. 43 J7
Eshott Nthumb.............. 158 F3
Esh Winning Dur.......... 150 F6
Eskadale Highld............ 212 C6
Eskbank Mdloth............. 177 J5
Eskdale Green
Cumb...................... 137 G6
Eskdalemuir D & G.... 155 M3
Esprick Lancs.............. 120 E3
Essendine Rutlnd.......... 88 F2
Essendon Herts.............. 59 L6
Essich Highld............... 213 G6
Essington Staffs............ 85 G3
Esslemont Abers........... 217 H7
Eston R & Cl................ 142 C4
Etal Nthumb................ 168 D2
Etchilhampton Wilts.... 40 B7
Etchingham E Susx 33 J7
Etchinghill Kent........... 34 F6
Etchinghill Staffs........ 100 B8
Eton W & M.................. 42 F5
Eton Wick W & M......... 42 F5
Etruria C Stke................ 99 K3
Etteridge Highld........... 203 G6
Ettersgill Dur.............. 139 K2
Ettiley Heath Ches E ... 99 G1
Ettingshall Wolves........ 85 G4
Ettington Warwks......... 72 C5
Etton C Pete.................. 89 G3
Etton E R Yk................. 126 B2
Ettrick Border............. 166 D6
Ettrickbridge Border ... 166 F4
Ettrickhill Border...... 166 C6
Etwall Derbys.............. 100 F6
Euston Suffk................. 91 K7
Euxton Lancs................ 121 H6
Evanton Highld............ 212 F2
Evedon Lincs............... 103 H3
Evelix Highld............... 223 G4
Evenjobb Powys............. 68 F3
Evenley Nhants.............. 73 H7
Evenlode Gloucs............ 56 E3
Evenwood Dur.............. 140 E3
Evercreech Somset........ 26 F4
Everingham E R Yk..... 125 J3
Everleigh Wilts............. 28 D2
Eversholt C Beds........... 59 G2
Evershot Dorset............ 14 B2
Eversley Hants.............. 42 C7
Eversley Cross Hants.... 42 C7
Everthorpe E R Yk....... 125 L4
Everton C Beds.............. 75 H4
Everton Hants............... 16 C4
Everton Lpool.............. 111 K3
Everton Notts.............. 116 B4
Evertown D & G........... 156 C6
Evesbatch Herefs........... 70 C5
Evesham Worcs.............. 71 J5
Evington C Leic............. 87 J3
Ewden Village Sheff.... 114 F3
Ewell Surrey................. 44 E7
Ewell Minnis Kent........ 35 H6
Ewelme Oxon................ 41 M3
Ewen Gloucs................. 40 A2
Ewenny V Glam............. 36 D5
Ewerby Lincs.............. 103 J3
Ewhurst Surrey............. 31 H4

Ewhurst Green
    E Susx 20 F2
Ewhurst Green
    Surrey........................ 31 H4
Ewloe Flints................ 111 J7
Ewood Bl w D............. 121 K5
Eworthy Devon............... 10 C6
Ewshot Hants................. 30 D2
Ewyas Harold Herefs.... 54 B3
Exbourne Devon............. 10 E4
Exbury Hants................. 16 E3
Exebridge Somset........... 24 E6
Exelby N York 132 D3
Exeter Devon................. 11 L6
Exeter Airport Devon......12 C4
Exeter Services
    Devon 12 C4
Exford Somset................ 24 D4
Exfordsgreen Shrops.... 83 J3
Exhall Warwks............... 71 K4
Exhall Warwks............... 86 D6
Exlade Street Oxon........ 42 A4
Exminster Devon............. 12 B5
Exmoor National
    Park 24 D4
Exmouth Devon............... 12 C6
Exning Suffk................. 76 E2
Exton Devon.................. 12 C5
Exton Hants.................. 29 L7
Exton Rutlnd................ 88 D2
Exton Somset................ 24 E5
Exwick Devon................. 11 K6
Eyam Derbys............... 114 E6
Eydon Nhants................ 73 G4
Eye C Pete.................... 89 J3
Eye Herefs..................... 69 J2
Eye Suffk..................... 92 D8
Eyemouth Border......... 179 K5
Eyeworth C Beds........... 75 J5
Eyhorne Street Kent...... 33 L3
Eyke Suffk..................... 79 G4
Eynesbury Cambs.......... 75 H3
Eynsford Kent............... 45 K6
Eynsham Oxon............... 57 H6
Eype Dorset.................. 13 L4
Eyre Highld................. 208 F2
Eythorne Kent............... 35 H5
Eyton Herefs.................. 69 J3
Eyton Shrops................. 98 C7
Eyton on Severn
    Shrops....................... 83 L3
Eyton upon the
    Weald Moors
    Wrekin...................... 84 B1

F

Faccombe Hants............. 41 H8
Faceby N York............. 141 L6
Fachwen Powys.............. 82 B1
Faddiley Ches E............. 98 E3
Fadmoor N York 133 K2
Faerdre Swans............... 51 K5
Faifley W Duns............ 174 F4
Failand N Som 38 D6
Failford S Ayrs 163 L4
Failsworth Oldham 113 K2
Fairbourne Gwynd........ 80 E2
Fairburn N York 124 D5
Fairfield Derbys........... 114 B6
Fairfield Worcs............. 85 G7
Fairford Gloucs............. 56 D7
Fairgirth D & G........... 146 F4
Fair Green Norfk............ 90 F1
Fairhaven Lancs.......... 120 D5
Fair Isle Shet 235 e7
Fair Isle Airport Shet .. 235 e7
Fairlands Surrey............ 30 F2
Fairlie N Ayrs 173 L7
Fairlight E Susx 21 G4
Fairmile Devon.............. 12 E3
Fairmile Surrey............. 43 J7
Fairnilee Border 167 G3
Fair Oak Hants............. 29 J7
Fairoak Staffs............... 99 H6

Fair Oak Green
    Hants......................... 42 A7
Fairseat Kent................ 45 L7
Fairstead Essex............. 61 J5
Fairstead Norfk 105 G8
Fairwarp E Susx 32 E7
Fairwater Cardif............ 37 H5
Fairy Cross Devon 22 F6
Fakenham Norfk 105 L6
Fakenham Magna
    Suffk......................... 91 K7
Fala Mdloth................ 177 L6
Fala Dam Mdloth......... 177 L6
Faldingworth Lincs..... 117 H5
Faldouët Jersey........... 236 e7
Falfield S Glos.............. 39 G2
Falkenham Suffk........... 79 G6
Falkirk Falk.................. 176 B3
Falkirk Wheel Falk...... 176 A3
Falkland Fife.............. 186 D6
Fallburn S Lans 165 J2
Fallin Stirlg................ 175 L1
Fallodon Nthumb......... 169 J5
Fallowfield Manch....... 113 J3
Fallowfield Nthumb..... 150 B2
Falmer E Susx 19 K4
Falmouth Cnwll 3 K5
Falnash Border 156 D2
Falsgrave N York 134 F2
Falstone Nthumb......... 157 J5
Fanagmore Highld...... 228 B5
Fancott C Beds.............. 59 G3
Fanellan Highld.......... 212 D5
Fangdale Beck
    N York 142 C7
Fangfoss E R Yk.......... 134 B8
Fanmore Ag & B.......... 189 K7
Fannich Lodge
    Highld...................... 211 K2
Fans Border 167 J2
Far Bletchley M Keyn... 74 C7
Farcet Cambs................ 89 H5
Far Cotton Nhants......... 73 L3
Fareham Hants.............. 17 H2
Farewell Staffs............. 85 J2
Faringdon Oxon............ 40 F2
Farington Lancs.......... 121 H5
Farlam Cumb.............. 148 F3
Farleigh N Som............. 38 D6
Farleigh Surrey 32 C2
Farleigh
    Hungerford
    Somset 39 J8
Farleigh Wallop
    Hants......................... 29 L3
Farlesthorpe Lincs 119 G6
Farleton Cumb............ 129 L4
Farleton Lancs.......... 130 B6
Farley Staffs............... 100 B4
Farley Wilts.................. 28 E5
Farley Green Surrey...... 31 H3
Farley Hill Wokham...... 42 C7
Farleys End Gloucs...... 55 H5
Farlington C Port.......... 17 J2
Farlington N York........ 133 J6
Farlow Shrops............... 84 B7
Farmborough BaNES...... 38 F7
Farmcote Gloucs............ 56 B3
Farmington Gloucs....... 56 C5
Farmoor Oxon............... 57 J6
Far Moor Wigan........... 112 D2
Farmtown Moray 215 L4
Farnah Green Derbys.... 101 G3
Farnborough Gt Lon..... 45 H7
Farnborough Hants....... 30 E2
Farnborough W Berk..... 40 F4
Farnborough Warwks.... 72 E5
Farnborough Park
    Hants......................... 30 E1
Farncombe Surrey......... 31 G3
Farndish Bed................ 74 D2
Farndon Ches W............ 98 B2
Farndon Notts............ 102 C3
Farne Islands
    Nthumb.................... 169 J2
Farnell Angus............. 197 G5
Farnham Dorset............ 27 L7
Farnham Essex.............. 60 D3

Farnham N York......... 132 E7
Farnham Suffk............... 79 H3
Farnham Surrey 30 D3
Farnham Common
    Bucks......................... 42 F4
Farnham Royal
    Bucks......................... 42 F4
Farningham Kent 45 K6
Farnley Leeds............. 123 K4
Farnley N York........... 123 J2
Farnley Tyas Kirk 123 H7
Farnsfield Notts......... 102 A2
Farnworth Bolton....... 113 G1
Farnworth Halton....... 112 D4
Far Oakridge Gloucs.... 55 L7
Farr Highld................ 203 K5
Farr Highld................ 213 G7
Farr Highld................ 229 L3
Farraline Highld......... 202 C2
Farringdon Devon 12 C4
Farrington Gurney
    BaNES........................ 26 F1
Far Sawrey Cumb 137 K7
Farthinghoe Nhants..... 73 G6
Farthingstone
    Nhants........................ 73 H4
Fartown Kirk.............. 123 H6
Fasnacloich Ag & B.... 191 K6
Fasnakyle Highld....... 211 L8
Fassfern Highld.......... 191 K2
Fatfield Sundld............ 151 H4
Fauldhouse W Loth ... 176 C6
Faulkbourne Essex....... 61 J5
Faulkland Somset......... 27 H1
Fauls Shrops................ 98 E6
Faversham Kent........... 34 D3
Fawdington N York...... 132 F5
Fawdon N u Ty........... 151 G2
Fawkham Green
    Kent.......................... 45 L6
Fawler Oxon................. 57 G4
Fawley Bucks............... 42 C3
Fawley Hants............... 16 F2
Fawley W Berk............. 41 H4
Faxfleet E R Yk.......... 125 K5
Faygate W Susx 31 K4
Fazakerley Lpool........ 111 K3
Fazeley Staffs.............. 85 L3
Fearby N York............ 132 B4
Fearn Highld............. 223 H6
Fearnan P & K 194 B7
Fearnbeg Highld 210 B3
Fearnmore Highld...... 209 L3
Fearnoch Ag & B........ 172 F3
Featherstone Staffs...... 85 G3
Featherstone Wakefd.. 124 C6
Feckenham Worcs........ 71 H3
Feering Essex................ 61 L4
Feetham N York.......... 140 C7
Felbridge Surrey 32 C5
Felbrigg Norfk 106 E5
Felcourt Surrey 32 C5
Felindre Carmth........... 51 G2
Felindre Carmth........... 65 K6
Felindre Powys............. 82 D7
Felindre Swans.............. 51 J5
Felindre Farchog
    Pembks....................... 64 F6
Felinfoel Carmth........... 51 G5
Felingwm Isaf
    Carmth....................... 51 G2
Felingwm Uchaf
    Carmth....................... 51 G1
Felixkirk N York......... 133 G3
Felixstowe Suffk.......... 79 G7
Felling Gatesd............ 151 G3
Felmersham Bed.......... 74 E3
Felmingham Norfk..... 106 F6
Felpham W Susx........... 18 C5
Felsham Suffk.............. 77 L3
Felsted Essex................ 61 G4
Feltham Gt Lon............. 43 J5
Felthamhill Surrey....... 43 H6
Felthorpe Norfk 106 E8
Felton Herefs................ 69 L5
Felton N Som................ 38 D7
Felton Nthumb............ 158 F3

Felton Butler Shrops 98 B8
Feltwell Norfk.................. 91 G5
Fence Lancs 122 C3
Fence Rothm 115 H4
Fencott Oxon 57 L5
Fendike Corner Lincs.. 104 D1
Fen Ditton Cambs........ 76 C3
Fen Drayton Cambs 75 L2
Feniscliffe Bl w D 121 K5
Feniscowles Bl w D 121 J5
Feniton Devon 12 E3
Fenn Green Shrops 84 D6
Fenn Street Medway 46 D5
Fenny Bentley
　Derbys..................... 100 D3
Fenny Bridges Devon 12 E3
Fenny Compton
　Warwks.......................72 E4
Fenny Drayton Leics....... 86 D4
Fenstanton Cambs........ 75 K2
Fen Street Norfk 92 B4
Fenton Cambs.............. 89 K7
Fenton Cumb.................. 148 E4
Fenton Lincs 102 E3
Fenton Lincs 116 D6
Fenton Notts 116 C5
Fenton Nthumb 168 E3
Fenton Barns E Loth 178 B3
Fenwick Donc............ 124 F7
Fenwick E Ayrs 163 L2
Fenwick Nthumb 158 D7
Fenwick Nthumb 169 G2
Feock Cnwll................... 4 C7
Feolin Ferry Ag & B.... 171 H4
Fergushill N Ayrs 163 J2
Feriniquarrie Highld.. 208 B4
Fermain Bay Guern.... 236 d3
Fern Angus 196 D4
Ferndale Rhondd........ 36 F2
Ferndown Dorset........ 15 K3
Ferness Highld............ 214 B5
Fernham Oxon............ 40 F3
Fernhill Heath Worcs.... 70 F3
Fernhurst W Susx 30 E5
Fernie Fife.................. 186 E4
Ferniegair S Lans 175 K7
Fernilea Highld.......... 208 F7
Fernilee Derbys........ 114 A5
Fernwood Notts........ 102 D3
Ferrensby N York 132 E7
Ferrindonald Highld.... 199 K4
Ferring W Susx 18 F5
Ferrybridge
　Services Wakefd 124 D6
Ferryden Angus........ 197 H5
Ferryhill Dur.............. 141 H2
Ferryhill Station Dur.. 141 H2
Ferry Point Highld........ 223 G4
Ferryside Carmth........ 50 D4
Ferrytown Highld........ 223 G4
Fersfield Norfk............ 92 C6
Fersit Highld.............. 192 F2
Feshiebridge Highld 203 K4
Fetcham Surrey............ 31 J1
Fetlar Shet.................. 235 e2
Fetterangus Abers 217 J4
Fettercairn Abers 197 G2
Fewston N York........ 132 B8
Ffairfach Carmth........ 51 J2
Ffair Rhos Cerdgn........ 67 G2
Ffarmers Carmth........ 66 E5
Ffestiniog Gwynd........ 96 A4
Ffestiniog Railway
　Gwynd 95 L4
Fforest Carmth............ 51 H5
Ffostrasol Cerdgn........ 65 L5
Ffrith Flints.................. 97 L2
Ffynnongroyw Flints.... 110 F5
Fickleshole Surrey........ 32 C2
Fiddington Somset........ 25 K4
Fiddleford Dorset........ 27 J8
Fiddlers Green Cnwll 4 C5
Field Staffs 100 A5
Field Dalling Norfk 106 B5
Field Head Leics........ 86 F2
Fifehead Magdalen
　Dorset.....................27 H6

Fifehead Neville
　Dorset......................14 E1
Fifehead St Quintin
　Dorset......................14 E1
Fife Keith Moray 215 J4
Fifield Oxon................ 56 E4
Fifield W & M.............. 42 E5
Figheldean Wilts 28 D3
Filby Norfk.................. 93 K2
Filey N York.............. 135 H4
Filgrave M Keyn........ 74 C5
Filkins Oxon.............. 56 E6
Filleigh Devon............ 23 K5
Fillingham Lincs........ 116 F4
Fillongley Warwks........ 86 C6
Filton S Glos.............. 38 E5
Fimber E R Yk............ 134 D7
Finavon Angus........ 196 D5
Fincham Norfk............ 91 G3
Finchampstead
　Wokham 42 D7
Fincharn Ag & B.... 182 C6
Finchdean Hants............ 30 C8
Finchingfield Essex 61 G2
Finchley Gt Lon.............. 44 F2
Findern Derbys.......... 100 F6
Findhorn Moray 214 C2
Findhorn Bridge
　Highld.................. 213 J8
Findochty Moray 215 K2
Findo Gask P & K.... 185 L4
Findon Abers............ 207 H6
Findon W Susx............ 18 F4
Findon Mains Highld ... 212 F3
Findrack House
　Abers 206 B4
Finedon Nhants........ 88 D8
Fingask P & K........ 186 C4
Fingest Bucks.............. 42 C3
Finghall N York 132 B2
Fingland D & G.......... 164 E6
Finglesham Kent............ 35 J4
Fingringhoe Essex........ 62 B4
Finlarig Stirlg............ 184 C1
Finmere Oxon............ 57 M2
Finnart P & K............ 193 H5
Finningham Suffk........ 78 C1
Finningley Donc........ 116 A2
Finsbay W Isls.......... 232 d5
Finstall Worcs............ 71 H2
Finsthwaite Cumb........ 129 H2
Finstock Oxon............ 57 G5
Finstown Ork............ 234 b6
Fintry Abers............ 216 E4
Fintry Stirlg.............. 175 H2
Finzean Abers........ 206 B6
Fionnphort Ag & B.... 180 D3
Fionnsbhagh W Isls... 232 d5
Firbank Cumb............ 130 C2
Firbeck Rothm 115 K4
Firby N York............ 132 D3
Firby N York............ 134 B6
Firle E Susx.............. 19 M4
Firsby Lincs.............. 118 F8
Fir Tree Dur.............. 150 E7
Fishbourne IoW............ 17 G4
Fishbourne W Susx 18 A5
Fishbourne Roman
　Palace W Susx 18 A5
Fishburn Dur.............. 141 J2
Fishcross Clacks........ 185 J7
Fisherford Abers........ 216 C7
Fisherrow E Loth........ 177 K4
Fisher's Pond Hants 29 J7
Fisherton Highld........ 213 H4
Fisherton S Ayrs........ 163 H6
Fisherton de la
　Mere Wilts............ 27 M4
Fishery Estate W & M.... 42 E4
Fishguard Pembks........ 64 D6
Fishlake Donc............ 125 G7
Fishnish Pier Ag & B... 190 D7
Fishponds Bristl........ 38 F5
Fishtoft Lincs............ 104 B4
Fishtoft Drove Lincs 104 A3
Fishwick Lancs............ 121 H4
Fiskavaig Highld........ 208 E7

Fiskerton Lincs............ 117 H6
Fiskerton Notts............ 102 C3
Fittleton Wilts.............. 28 D2
Fittleworth W Susx....... 18 D2
Fitz Shrops.................... 98 C8
Fitzhead Somset........ 25 H5
Fitzwilliam Wakefd........ 124 C7
Five Ash Down
　E Susx 19 M2
Five Ashes E Susx........ 32 F7
Fivehead Somset........ 26 A6
Fivelanes Cnwll.............. 9 G8
Five Oak Green Kent....... 33 H4
Five Oaks Jersey........ 236 d7
Five Oaks W Susx........ 31 H5
Five Roads Carmth........ 50 F4
Flackwell Heath
　Bucks........................42 E3
Fladbury Worcs............ 71 H5
Fladdabister Shet........ 235 c6
Flagg Derbys.............. 114 C7
Flamborough E R Yk 135 K5
Flamborough Head
　E R Yk 135 K5
Flamingo Land
　Theme Park
　N York.................. 134 B4
Flamstead Herts............ 59 H5
Flamstead End Herts 60 B7
Flansham W Susx........ 18 C5
Flanshaw Wakefd........ 123 L6
Flasby N York............ 131 H7
Flash Staffs.............. 114 A7
Flashader Highld........ 208 E4
Flaunden Herts............ 59 G7
Flawborough Notts........ 102 C4
Flawith N York............ 133 G6
Flax Bourton N Som...... 38 D6
Flaxby N York............ 132 F7
Flaxley Gloucs............ 55 G5
Flaxpool Somset........ 25 H4
Flaxton N York............ 133 K6
Fleckney Leics............ 87 J5
Flecknoe Warwks........ 73 G2
Fledborough Notts 116 D6
Fleet Dorset.............. 14 C6
Fleet Hants................ 30 D2
Fleet Lincs................ 104 C7
Fleet Hargate Lincs 104 C7
Fleet Services Hants 30 D1
Fleetwood Lancs........ 120 D2
Fleggburgh Norfk........ 93 J2
Flemington S Lans 175 H6
Flempton Suffk............ 77 J1
Fletchertown Cumb 147 L6
Fletching E Susx.......... 19 L2
Flexbury Cnwll.............. 9 H4
Flexford Surrey............ 30 F2
Flimby Cumb............ 147 H7
Flimwell E Susx............ 33 J6
Flint Flints................ 111 H6
Flintham Notts............ 102 C4
Flinton E R Yk............ 126 F4
Flitcham Norfk............ 105 H6
Flitton C Beds.............. 74 F7
Flitwick C Beds............ 74 F7
Flixborough N Linc...... 125 K7
Flixborough Stather
　N Linc 125 K7
Flixton N York............ 135 G4
Flixton Suffk.............. 93 G6
Flixton Traffd............ 113 H3
Flockton Kirk............ 123 J7
Flockton Green Kirk.... 123 K7
Flodigarry Highld........ 218 C6
Flookburgh Cumb........ 129 H4
Flordon Norfk............ 92 E4
Flore Nhants.............. 73 J3
Flowton Suffk.............. 78 C5
Flushing Cnwll.............. 3 L4
Fluxton Devon............ 12 E4
Flyford Flavell Worcs 71 H4
Fobbing Thurr............ 46 B4
Fochabers Moray........ 215 H3
Fochriw Caerph............ 53 H6
Fockerby N Linc............ 125 K6

Foddington Somset........ 26 E5
Foel Powys................ 81 L2
Foggathorpe
　E R Yk 125 H3
Fogo Border 179 G8
Fogwatt Moray 214 F3
Foindle Highld............ 228 B5
Folda Angus 195 J4
Fole Staffs.................. 100 B5
Foleshill Covtry............ 86 D6
Folke Dorset.............. 26 F8
Folkestone Kent............ 35 H7
Folkingham Lincs........ 103 H5
Folkington E Susx........ 20 B5
Folksworth Cambs........ 89 G5
Folkton N York............ 135 G4
Folla Rule Abers........ 216 D7
Follifoot N York............ 124 A1
Folly Gate Devon........ 10 E5
Fonthill Bishop Wilts....... 27 L5
Fonthill Gifford Wilts...... 27 L5
Fontmell Magna
　Dorset.....................27 K7
Fontmell Parva
　Dorset.....................27 J8
Fontwell W Susx........ 18 C4
Foolow Derbys.......... 114 D6
Forbestown Abers........ 205 H3
Forcett N York............ 140 F5
Ford Ag & B 182 C6
Ford Bucks................ 58 C6
Ford Derbys.............. 115 H5
Ford Devon................ 22 F6
Ford Gloucs................ 56 C3
Ford Nthumb.............. 168 E2
Ford Somset................ 25 H5
Ford Staffs.................. 100 B2
Ford W Susx................ 18 D5
Ford Wilts.................. 39 J5
Fordcombe Kent............ 32 F5
Fordell Fife................ 177 G2
Forden Powys.............. 82 E4
Ford End Essex............ 61 G5
Forder Green Devon........ 7 H3
Fordham Cambs............ 76 F1
Fordham Essex............ 61 L3
Fordham Norfk............ 90 E4
Fordingbridge
　Hants....................28 D8
Fordon E R Yk............ 135 G4
Fordoun Abers............ 197 J2
Fordstreet Essex........ 61 L3
Ford Street Somset........ 25 J7
Fordwich Kent............ 35 G3
Fordyce Abers............ 216 B2
Forebridge Staffs........ 99 L7
Forest Guern 236 c4
Forest Chapel
　Ches E 113 L6
Forest Gate Gt Lon........ 45 H3
Forest Green Surrey...... 31 J3
Forest Hall N Tyne........ 151 G2
Forest Hill Oxon............ 57 L6
Forest Lane Head
　N York.................. 132 E7
Forest Mill Clacks........ 185 K8
Forest of Bowland
　Lancs 130 C8
Forest of Dean
　Gloucs 54 F5
Forest Row E Susx........ 32 D6
Forestside W Susx........ 30 C8
Forfar Angus............ 196 D6
Forgandenny P & K...... 186 A4
Forge Hammer Torfn...... 37 L2
Forgie Moray............ 215 J4
Forgieside Moray 215 J4
Forgue Abers............ 216 B5
Formby Sefton 111 J1
Forncett End Norfk........ 92 D5
Forncett St Mary
　Norfk......................92 E5
Forncett St Peter
　Norfk......................92 E5
Fornham All Saints
　Suffk......................77 J2

Fornham St Martin
Suffk..............................77 J2
Fornighty Highld..........213 L4
Forres Moray................214 C3
Forsbrook Staffs..............99 L4
Forse Highld.................227 M2
Forsinard Highld...........230 C6
Forss Highld.................230 F2
Fort Augustus
Highld..........................202 B4
Forteviot P & K............185 L4
Forth S Lans.................176 C7
Forthampton Gloucs......55 K2
Fort Hommet Guern....236 c2
Forth Rail Bridge
C Edin........................176 F3
Forth Road Bridge
Fife.............................176 F3
Fortingall P & K............194 B6
Fort le Marchant
Guern.........................236 d1
Forton Hants...................29 H3
Forton Lancs.................121 G1
Forton Shrops.................83 H1
Forton Somset................13 J2
Forton Staffs..................99 H7
Fortrie Abers................216 C5
Fortrose Highld.............213 H3
Fortuneswell
Dorset............................14 D7
Fort William Highld.....191 L2
Forty Hill Gt Lon............60 B7
Fosbury Wilts..................40 F8
Foscot Oxon....................56 E4
Fosdyke Lincs...............104 A5
Foss P & K....................194 C5
Fossebridge Gloucs.......56 B5
Foster Street Essex........60 D6
Foston Derbys...............100 D6
Foston Leics...................87 H4
Foston Lincs.................102 E4
Foston N York................133 L6
Foston on the
Wolds E R Yk...............135 H7
Fotherby Lincs...............118 D3
Fotheringhay
Nhants............................88 F5
Foula Shet.....................235 a6
Foula Airport Shet........235 a6
Foulden Border..............179 J7
Foulden Norfk................91 H4
Foul End Warwks...........86 B4
Foulness Island
Essex..............................47 G2
Foulridge Lancs.............122 D3
Foulsham Norfk.............106 B7
Fountainhall Border.....177 L8
Four Ashes Suffk...........78 B1
Four Cabots Guern......236 c3
Four Crosses
Powys.............................97 K8
Four Elms Kent...............32 E4
Four Forks Somset.........25 K4
Four Gotes Cambs..........90 C1
Four Lanes Cnwll..............3 J4
Four Marks Hants............30 A4
Four Mile Bridge
IoA.................................108 C5
Four Oaks Birm................85 K4
Four Oaks Solhll.............86 B7
Fourpenny Highld.........223 H3
Four Roads Carmth.........50 F4
Fourstones Nthumb.....149 M2
Four Throws Kent............33 K7
Fovant Wilts....................28 A5
Foveran Abers................207 H2
Fowey Cnwll......................5 H5
Fowlhall Kent...................33 J4
Fowlis Angus.................186 E2
Fowlis Wester
P & K.............................185 J3
Fowlmere Cambs............76 B5
Fownhope Herefs...........69 L7
Foxbar Rens..................174 E6
Foxcote Somset..............27 G1
Foxdale IoM...................237 b5
Foxearth Essex...............77 J5

Foxfield Cumb................128 F3
Foxhole Cnwll....................4 F5
Foxholes N York.............134 F5
Foxley Norfk..................106 C7
Foxt Staffs.....................100 B3
Foxton Cambs..................76 B5
Foxton Leics....................87 K5
Foxton N York................141 K7
Foxwood Shrops.............84 B7
Foy Herefs.......................54 E3
Foyers Highld.................202 D2
Foynesfield Highld........213 L4
Fraddon Cnwll...................4 E4
Fradley Staffs..................85 L2
Fradswell Staffs...............99 M6
Fraisthorpe E R Yk........135 J7
Framfield E Susx..............20 A2
Framingham Earl
Norfk..............................92 F3
Framingham Pigot
Norfk..............................92 F3
Framlingham Suffk..........79 G2
Frampton Dorset..............14 C4
Frampton Lincs..............104 B5
Frampton Cotterell
S Glos..............................38 F4
Frampton Mansell
Gloucs............................55 L7
Frampton-on-
Severn Gloucs...............55 H6
Framsden Suffk................78 E3
Framwellgate Moor
Dur...............................151 G6
Franche Worcs................84 E7
Frankby Wirral...............111 H4
Frankley Worcs................85 H7
Frankley Services
Worcs.............................85 H7
Frankton Warwks............72 E1
Frant E Susx....................33 G6
Fraserburgh Abers.......217 J2
Frating Essex...................62 C4
Frating Green Essex......62 C4
Fratton C Port.................17 J3
Freathy Cnwll.....................6 B5
Freckenham Suffk...........76 F1
Freckleton Lancs..........120 F5
Freeby Leics...................102 D7
Freefolk Hants.................29 J2
Freeland Oxon.................57 H5
Freethorpe Norfk............93 J3
Freethorpe
Common Norfk..............93 J3
Freiston Lincs................104 B4
Fremington Devon...........23 H5
Fremington N York.......140 D7
Frenchay S Glos...............38 F5
Frenich P & K.................194 C5
Frensham Surrey.............30 D3
Freshfield Sefton..........120 C8
Freshford Wilts...............39 H7
Freshwater IoW...............16 D5
Fressingfield Suffk.........92 F7
Freston Suffk...................78 E6
Freswick Highld.............231 L3
Fretherne Gloucs............55 G6
Frettenham Norfk..........106 F8
Freuchie Fife.................186 E6
Freystrop Pembks...........49 G5
Friar Park Sandw............85 H4
Friday Bridge Cambs......90 C3
Friday Street Suffk..........79 H3
Fridaythorpe E R Yk......134 D7
Friern Barnet
Gt Lon.............................44 F2
Friesthorpe Lincs..........117 H5
Frieston Lincs................102 F3
Frieth Bucks.....................42 D3
Frilford Oxon...................41 H2
Frilsham W Berk...............41 K5
Frimley Surrey.................42 E8
Frindsbury Medway.......46 C6
Fring Norfk.....................105 H5
Fringford Oxon................57 L3
Frinsted Kent...................34 B4
Frinton-on-Sea
Essex..............................62 F4

Friockheim Angus.........196 F6
Frisby on the
Wreake Leics...............102 B8
Friskney Lincs................104 D2
Friston E Susx..................20 B6
Friston Suffk....................79 J3
Fritchley Derbys............101 G3
Fritham Hants..................28 E8
Frithelstock Devon.........23 G7
Frithelstock Stone
Devon.............................23 G7
Frithville Lincs..............104 A3
Frittenden Kent...............33 K5
Frittiscombe Devon...........7 J6
Fritton Norfk....................92 F5
Fritton Norfk....................93 K4
Fritwell Oxon...................57 K3
Frizinghall C Brad.........123 H4
Frizington Cumb...........136 E4
Frocester Gloucs.............55 H7
Frodesley Shrops............83 K3
Frodsham Ches W..........112 D6
Frogden Border.............168 B4
Frog End Cambs..............76 B5
Froggatt Derbys.............114 E6
Froghall Staffs...............100 A3
Frogmore Devon................7 H7
Frognall Lincs..................89 H2
Frog Pool Worcs..............70 E2
Frogwell Cnwll...................6 A3
Frolesworth Leics...........87 G5
Frome Somset..................27 H2
Frome St Quintin
Dorset............................14 B2
Fromes Hill Herefs..........70 C5
Froncysyllte Wrexhm......97 L4
Fron-goch Gwynd...........96 D5
Fron Isaf Wrexhm............97 L4
Frosterley Dur...............150 C7
Froxfield Wilts.................40 F6
Froxfield Green
Hants..............................30 B6
Fryern Hill Hants.............29 H7
Fryerning Essex...............61 G7
Fuinary Highld...............190 C6
Fulbeck Lincs.................102 F3
Fulbourn Cambs..............76 D4
Fulbrook Oxon.................56 E5
Fulflood Hants.................29 J5
Fulford C York................124 F2
Fulford Somset................25 K5
Fulford Staffs...................99 L5
Fulham Gt Lon.................44 E5
Fulking W Susx................19 H4
Fullarton N Ayrs.............163 H2
Fuller Street Essex.........61 H5
Fullerton Hants................29 G4
Fulletby Lincs................118 D6
Fullready Warwks............72 C5
Full Sutton E R Yk.........134 B7
Fullwood E Ayrs.............174 E7
Fulmer Bucks...................43 G4
Fulmodeston Norfk.......106 B6
Fulnetby Lincs...............117 H5
Fulney Lincs...................103 L7
Fulstow Lincs.................118 D3
Fulwell Sundld...............151 J3
Fulwood Lancs..............121 H4
Fulwood Sheff................114 F4
Fundenhall Norfk............92 D4
Funtington W Susx.........17 L2
Funtullich P & K............184 F3
Furley Devon....................13 H2
Furnace Ag & B..............182 E7
Furnace Carmth...............51 G5
Furness Vale Derbys.....114 A5
Furneux Pelham
Herts..............................60 C3
Furzley Hants...................28 F7
Fyfield Essex....................60 F6
Fyfield Hants....................28 F3
Fyfield Oxon....................57 H7
Fyfield Wilts....................40 C6
Fyfield Wilts....................40 D7
Fylingthorpe N York....143 J6
Fyning W Susx.................30 D6
Fyvie Abers....................216 E6

G

Gabroc Hill E Ayrs........174 E7
Gaddesby Leics................87 K2
Gaddesden Row
Herts..............................59 H5
Gadgirth S Ayrs.............163 K5
Gaerllwyd Mons..............38 C2
Gaerwen IoA..................108 F7
Gailes N Ayrs.................163 H3
Gailey Staffs.....................85 G2
Gainford Dur.................140 F4
Gainsborough Lincs.....116 D4
Gainsford End Essex......77 G7
Gairloch Highld.............219 J6
Gairlochy Highld...........201 J8
Gairneybridge P & K....186 B7
Gaitsgill Cumb...............148 C5
Galashiels Border.........167 G3
Galgate Lancs.................129 K7
Galhampton Somset........26 F5
Gallanachbeg Ag & B...182 B2
Gallanachmore
Ag & B...........................182 B3
Gallatown Fife...............186 E8
Galleywood Essex............61 H7
Gallovie Highld..............202 E7
Galloway Forest
Park.............................153 J5
Gallowfauld Angus.......196 D7
Gallowhill P & K............186 B1
Galltair Highld...............200 C2
Galmisdale Highld.........199 G8
Galmpton Devon................7 G7
Galmpton Torbay...............7 K5
Galphay N York..............132 C5
Galston E Ayrs................163 L3
Gamblesby Cumb..........149 G6
Gamlingay Cambs............75 J4
Gamlingay Great
Heath Cambs................75 J4
Gamrie Abers.................216 F2
Gamston Notts...............101 L5
Gamston Notts...............116 B6
Ganavan Bay Ag & B....182 B2
Ganllwyd Gwynd.............96 B7
Gannachy Angus............196 F3
Ganstead E R Yk............126 E4
Ganthorpe N York.........133 L5
Ganton N York...............134 F4
Garbity Moray...............215 H4
Garboldisham Norfk.......92 B7
Garchory Abers.............205 G4
Gardeners Green
Wokham.........................42 D6
Gardenstown Abers......216 F2
Garden Village Sheff....114 E2
Garderhouse Shet.........235 c5
Gare Hill Somset.............27 H4
Garelochhead Ag & B...173 L1
Garford Oxon...................41 H2
Garforth Leeds...............124 B4
Gargrave N York............131 H8
Gargunnock Stirlg........184 F8
Garlic Street Norfk..........92 E6
Garlieston D & G............145 K5
Garlinge Kent...................35 J2
Garlinge Green Kent......34 F4
Garlogie Abers...............206 E4
Garmond Abers.............216 F4
Garmouth Moray...........215 H2
Garmston Shrops............83 L3
Garndolbenmaen
Gwynd............................95 J4
Garrabost W Isls...........232 g2
Garrallan E Ayrs............164 B5
Garras Cnwll......................3 J6
Garreg Gwynd..................95 K4
Garrigill Cumb...............149 G5
Garroch D & G...............153 M6
Garrochtie D & G...........144 D7
Garrochty Ag & B...........173 J7
Garros Highld................209 H2
Garsdale Head Cumb....130 E2
Garsdon Wilts..................39 L3

Garshall Green Staffs.....99 L5
Garsington Oxon..............57 L7
Garstang Lancs 121 G2
Garston Herts...................59 J7
Garston Lpool 112 B5
Gartachossan Ag & B... 171 G6
Gartcosh N Lans 175 J5
Garth Powys......................67 K5
Garth Wrexhm.................97 K4
Garthamlock C Glas...... 175 H5
Garthmyl Powys..............82 E4
Garthorpe Leics 102 D7
Garthorpe N Linc 125 K6
Garth Row Cumb............138 D7
Gartly Abers 215 L7
Gartmore Stirlg 184 C7
Gartness N Lans 175 K5
Gartness Stirlg 174 F2
Gartocharn W Duns......174 D2
Garton-on-the-
    Wolds E R Yk..............134 F7
Gartymore Highld 227 H5
Garva Bridge Highld 202 E6
Garvald Border 176 F8
Garvald E Loth 178 D4
Garvan Highld 191 J2
Garvard Ag & B..............171 G1
Garve Highld...................212 B3
Garvellachs Ag & B...... 181 K5
Garvestone Norfk............92 B3
Garvock Inver 174 B4
Garway Herefs..................54 C4
Garynahine W Isls........232 e2
Garyvard W Isls.............232 f3
Gasper Wilts.....................27 H5
Gastard Wilts 39 K6
Gasthorpe Norfk..............91 L7
Gaston Green Essex 60 D5
Gatcombe IoW 16 F5
Gate Burton Lincs 116 D5
Gateforth N York 124 E5
Gatehead E Ayrs............163 K3
Gate Helmsley N York...133 L7
Gatehouse Nthumb........157 K4
Gatehouse of Fleet
    D & G...........................146 A4
Gateley Norfk..................106 A7
Gatenby N York 132 E3
Gateshaw Border 168 B5
Gateshead Gatesd 151 G3
Gateside Angus 196 D7
Gateside E Rens 174 E6
Gateside Fife..................186 C5
Gateside N Ayrs.............174 C7
Gateslack D & G.............154 F2
Gatley Stockp 113 J4
Gattonside Border 167 H3
Gatwick Airport
    W Susx 32 B5
Gaulby Leics....................87 K4
Gauldry Fife 186 F3
Gauldswell P & K...........195 K6
Gautby Lincs 117 K6
Gavinton Border 179 G7
Gawcott Bucks.................58 B2
Gawsworth Ches E 113 K7
Gawthrop Cumb..............130 D3
Gawthwaite Cumb..........129 G3
Gaydon Warwks................72 D4
Gayhurst M Keyn.............74 B5
Gayle N York 131 G2
Gayles N York 140 E5
Gayton Nhants 73 K4
Gayton Norfk..................105 H8
Gayton Staffs 99 M6
Gayton le Marsh
    Lincs 118 F5
Gayton Thorpe Norfk....105 H8
Gaywood Norfk 105 G7
Gazeley Suffk...................77 G2
Gearraidh Bhaird
    W Isls..........................232 f3
Gearraidh na
    h-Aibhne W Isls......232 e2
Geary Highld...................208 D3
Gedding Suffk...................77 L3
Geddington Nhants.........88 C6

Gedling Notts 101 L4
Gedney Lincs 104 C7
Gedney Broadgate
    Lincs............................104 C7
Gedney Drove End
    Lincs............................104 D6
Gedney Dyke Lincs.......104 C7
Gedney Hill Lincs............89 L2
Geeston Rutlnd................88 E3
Geldeston Norfk...............93 H5
Gellifor Denbgs..............110 F8
Gelligaer Caerph.............37 H2
Gellilydan Gwynd............95 M4
Gellinudd Neath..............51 K5
Gellyburn P & K.............195 H8
Gellywen Carmth.............50 C2
Gelston D & G................146 D3
Gelston Lincs 102 E4
Gembling E R Yk............135 H7
Gentleshaw Staffs..........85 J2
Georgefield D & G.........156 B4
George Green Bucks...... 43 G4
Georgeham Devon 23 G4
Georgemas
    Junction Station
    Highld..........................231 H4
George Nympton
    Devon............................23 L6
Georth Ork 234 b5
Germansweek Devon 10 C6
Gerrans Cnwll 4 D8
Gerrards Cross
    Bucks............................43 G3
Gerrick R & Cl...............142 E5
Gestingthorpe Essex......77 J6
Geuffordd Powys.............82 E2
Gidea Park Gt Lon 45 K3
Giffnock E Rens 175 G6
Gifford E Loth................178 C5
Giffordtown Fife.............186 E5
Giggleswick N York 130 F6
Gigha Ag & B..................171 L7
Gilberdyke E R Yk..........125 K5
Gilchriston E Loth..........178 B5
Gilcrux Cumb..................147 K7
Gildersome Leeds 123 K5
Gildingwells Rothm........115 K4
Gilesgate Moor Dur 151 H6
Gileston V Glam..............36 F6
Gilfach Caerph.................53 J7
Gilfach Goch Brdgnd......36 F3
Gilfachrheda Cerdgn......65 L3
Gilgarran Cumb..............136 E3
Gillamoor N York...........133 K2
Gillen Highld..................208 D3
Gillesbie D & G..............155 K4
Gilling East N York.........133 J4
Gillingham Dorset...........27 J6
Gillingham Medway........46 C6
Gillingham Norfk............93 J5
Gilling West N York 140 F6
Gillock Highld 231 J4
Gills Highld 231 K2
Gilmanscleuch
    Border.........................166 E5
Gilmerton C Edin...........177 J5
Gilmerton P & K.............185 J3
Gilmonby Dur 140 C5
Gilmorton Leics 87 H6
Gilsland Nthumb............149 G2
Gilston Border 177 L6
Gilston Herts....................60 D5
Gilwern Mons 53 K5
Gimingham Norfk...........107 G5
Gipping Suffk...................78 C2
Gipsey Bridge Lincs......103 M3
Girdle Toll N Ayrs 163 J2
Girlsta Shet 235 c5
Girsby N York 141 K5
Girthon D & G................146 A4
Girton Cambs...................76 B3
Girton Notts 116 D7
Girvan S Ayrs.................152 E3
Gisburn Lancs 122 C2
Gisleham Suffk................93 K5
Gislingham Suffk.............78 C1
Gissing Norfk...................92 D6

Gittisham Devon 12 E3
Gladestry Powys.............68 E4
Gladsmuir E Loth 177 M4
Glais Swans 51 K5
Glaisdale N York 143 G6
Glamis Angus 196 C6
Glanaman Carmth...........51 J3
Glandford Norfk.............106 C4
Glandwr Pembks 49 K2
Glandyfi Cerdgn...............80 F4
Glanllynfi Brdgnd............36 D3
Glan-rhyd Powys.............52 B6
Glanton Nthumb.............169 G6
Glanvilles Wootton
    Dorset............................14 D2
Glan-y-don Flints...........111 G5
Glapthorn Nhants............88 E5
Glapwell Derbys.............115 J7
Glasbury Powys...............68 D6
Glascote Staffs................86 B3
Glascwm Powys...............68 D4
Glasfryn Conwy 96 E3
Glasgow C Glas..............175 G5
Glasgow Airport
    Rens............................174 E5
Glasgow Prestwick
    Airport S Ayrs.............163 J4
Glasgow Science
    Centre C Glas.............175 G5
Glasinfryn Gwynd...........109 H7
Glasnacardoch Bay
    Highld..........................199 L6
Glasnakille Highld 199 H3
Glasphein Highld............208 B4
Glassford S Lans 175 J8
Glasshouse Gloucs..........55 G4
Glasshouses N York......132 B6
Glasslaw Abers...............216 F3
Glasson Cumb.................148 A3
Glasson Lancs.................129 K7
Glassonby Cumb.............149 G7
Glasterlaw Angus...........196 F6
Glaston Rutlnd.................88 C4
Glastonbury Somset.......26 D4
Glatton Cambs.................89 H6
Glazebrook Warrtn.........113 G3
Glazebury Warrtn...........112 F3
Glazeley Shrops...............84 C5
Gleaston Cumb...............128 F5
Glebe Highld 202 D2
Gledhow Leeds...............123 L3
Gledpark D & G..............146 B5
Gledrid Shrops.................97 L5
Glemsford Suffk..............77 J5
Glenallachie Moray........215 G6
Glenancross Highld........199 K6
Glenaros House
    Ag & B..........................190 B7
Glen Auldyn IoM 237 d3
Glenbarr Ag & B.............161 H3
Glenbarry Abers.............216 B4
Glenbeg Highld..............190 C4
Glenbervie Abers...........197 J1
Glenbog N Lans.............175 J5
Glenborrodale Highld.....190 C4
Glenbranter Ag & B.......183 G7
Glenbreck Border 165 K5
Glenbrittle Highld...........198 F2
Glenbuck E Ayrs.............164 E4
Glencally Angus 196 B4
Glencaple D & G.............147 H2
Glencarse P & K.............186 C3
Glencoe Highld 191 L5
Glencothe Border 165 L4
Glencraig Fife.................186 C7
Glencrosh D & G............154 D4
Glendale Highld 208 B4
Glendaruel Ag & B.........173 G2
Glendevon P & K 185 K6
Glendoe Lodge
    Highld..........................202 C4
Glendoick P & K.............186 C3
Glenduckie Fife..............186 C5
Glenegedale Ag & B.......170 F7
Glenelg Highld................200 C2
Glenernie Moray............214 C5
Glenfarg P & K................186 B5

Glenfield Leics 87 G3
Glenfinnan Highld..........191 H1
Glenfintaig Lodge
    Highld..........................201 K7
Glenfoot P & K................186 C4
Glenfyne Lodge
    Ag & B..........................183 H4
Glengarnock N Ayrs.......174 C7
Glengolly Highld.............231 G3
Glengorm Castle
    Ag & B..........................189 K5
Glengrasco Highld..........209 G5
Glenholm Border 165 L3
Glenhoul D & G 154 A5
Glenisla Angus................195 K4
Glenkin Ag & B 173 K3
Glenkindie Abers............205 K3
Glenlivet Moray...............214 F6
Glenlochar D & G 146 C3
Glenlomond P & K..........186 C6
Glenluce D & G...............144 E4
Glenmassen Ag & B 173 J2
Glenmavis N Lans..........175 K5
Glen Maye IoM................237 b5
Glenmore Highld.............209 G6
Glenmore Lodge
    Highld..........................204 B4
Glen Nevis House
    Highld..........................192 B3
Glenochil Clacks.............185 H7
Glen Parva Leics.............87 H4
Glenquiech Angus 196 C4
Glenralloch Ag & B........172 E5
Glenridding Cumb..........137 L4
Glenrothes Fife...............186 D7
Glenshero Lodge
    Highld..........................202 E6
Glenstriven Ag & B........173 J3
Glentham Lincs...............117 G4
Glentrool D & G..............153 H6
Glen Trool Lodge
    D & G...........................153 J6
Glentruim Highld............203 G6
Glentworth Lincs 116 F4
Glenuig Highld................190 D2
Glenvarragill Highld.......209 G6
Glen Vine IoM.................237 c5
Glenwhilly D & G............152 E7
Glespin S Lans 164 F4
Glewstone Herefs............54 E4
Glinton C Pete.................89 H3
Glooston Leics.................87 L4
Glossop Derbys...............114 B3
Gloster Hill Nthumb.......159 G2
Gloucester Gloucs...........55 J4
Gloucester Services
    Gloucs.........................55 J5
Gloucestershire
    Airport Gloucs.............55 K4
Glusburn N York 122 F2
Glutt Lodge Highld........227 H2
Glympton Oxon................57 H4
Glynarthen Cerdgn..........65 K5
Glyn Ceiriog Wrexhm......97 J5
Glyncoch Rhondd............37 G3
Glyncorrwg Neath...........52 D7
Glynde E Susx 19 L4
Glyndyfrdwy Denbgs.......97 J4
Glynneath Neath..............52 D6
Glyntawe Powys...............52 D5
Glynteg Carmth................65 K6
Gnosall Staffs 99 J8
Gnosall Heath Staffs.......99 J7
Goadby Leics 87 L4
Goadby Marwood
    Leics 102 C7
Goatacre Wilts.................40 A5
Goathill Dorset................26 F7
Goathland N York 143 H6
Goathurst Somset............25 K5
Goat Lees Kent................34 D5
Gobowen Shrops.............97 L5
Godalming Surrey 30 F3
Goddard's Green
    Kent..............................33 L6
Godmanchester
    Cambs..........................75 J1

Godmanstone Dorset.....14 C3
Godmersham Kent.........34 E5
Godney Somset.............26 C3
Godolphin Cross
Cnwll.........................3 G5
Godre'r-graig Neath.....51 L4
Godshill IoW 17 G6
Godstone Surrey 32 C3
Goetre Mons 53 L6
Goff's Oak Herts...........60 B7
Gogar C Edin 177 G4
Goginan Cerdgn 80 F7
Golan Gwynd 95 J4
Golant Cnwll 5 H5
Golberdon Cnwll 5 M2
Golborne Wigan 112 E3
Golcar Kirk 123 G7
Goldcliff Newpt............38 A4
Golden Green Kent.......33 H4
Goldenhill C Stke..........99 J2
Golden Pot Hants.........30 B3
Golders Green Gt Lon...44 E3
Goldhanger Essex.........61 L6
Goldington Bed 74 F4
Goldsborough N York ..132 F7
Goldsborough N York ..143 H4
Golds Green Sandw.......85 H5
Goldsithney Cnwll 2 F5
Goldthorpe Barns........115 J2
Goldworthy Devon.........22 F6
Gollanfield Highld........213 J4
Golspie Highld.............223 H2
Gomeldon Wilts............28 D4
Gomshall Surrey 31 H2
Gonalston Notts..........102 B3
Gonerby Hill Foot
Lincs........................102 E5
Gonfirth Shet..............235 c4
Good Easter Essex........60 F5
Gooderstone Norfk.......91 H3
Goodleigh Devon...........23 J5
Goodmanham E R Yk...125 K2
Goodmayes Gt Lon.......45 J3
Goodnestone Kent........34 D3
Goodnestone Kent........35 H4
Goodrich Herefs............54 E4
Goodrington Torbay........7 K4
Goodshaw Lancs..........122 B5
Goodwick Pembks.........64 C6
Goodworth Clatford
Hants........................29 G3
Goole E R Yk...............125 H5
Goom's Hill Worcs.........71 H4
Goonbell Cnwll 3 J2
Goonhavern Cnwll 3 K1
Goonvrea Cnwll 3 J2
Goosecruives Abers 206 E8
Gooseford Devon..........11 G6
Goose Green Essex.......62 D3
Goose Green S Glos......38 F5
Gooseham Cnwll............9 G2
Goosey Oxon................41 G3
Goosnargh Lancs.........121 H3
Goostrey Ches E..........113 H7
Gordano Services
N Som.......................38 D5
Gordon Border............167 K2
Gordon Arms Hotel
Border.....................166 D4
Gordonstown Abers....216 B3
Gordonstown Abers....216 D6
Gorebridge Mdloth.....177 K6
Gorefield Cambs...........90 B2
Gores Wilts..................40 C8
Gorey Jersey...............236 e7
Goring Oxon................41 L4
Goring-by-Sea
W Susx.....................18 F5
Gorleston on Sea
Norfk........................93 L3
Gorrachie Abers 216 E3
Gorran Churchtown
Cnwll.........................4 F7
Gorran Haven Cnwll 4 F7
Gorsedd Flints............111 G6
Gorse Hill Swindn........40 D3
Gorseinon Swans.........51 H5

Gorsgoch Cerdgn..........66 C4
Gorslas Carmth............51 H3
Gorsley Gloucs.............55 G3
Gorsley Common
Herefs.......................54 F3
Gorstan Highld............212 B2
Gorsten Ag & B...........181 L2
Gorsty Hill Staffs........100 C6
Gorthleck Highld.........202 E2
Gorton Manch.............113 K3
Gosbeck Suffk..............78 D4
Gosberton Lincs..........103 L6
Gosfield Essex..............61 J3
Gosforth Cumb...........136 E6
Gosforth N u Ty...........151 G2
Gosport Hants..............17 H3
Gossington Gloucs.......55 H7
Gotham Notts.............101 K6
Gotherington Gloucs....55 L3
Gotton Somset.............25 K5
Goudhurst Kent...........33 J5
Goulceby Lincs............118 C5
Gourdas Abers 216 E6
Gourdie C Dund 186 F2
Gourdon Abers 197 K3
Gourock Inver 173 L3
Govan C Glas...............174 F5
Goveton Devon..............7 H6
Govilon Mons...............53 K5
Gowdall E R Yk...........124 F6
Gower Highld 212 D3
Gower Swans...............51 G7
Gowerton Swans..........51 H6
Gowkhall Fife.............176 E1
Goxhill E R Yk............126 F2
Goxhill N Linc............126 D6
Grabhair W Isls..........232 f3
Graffham W Susx..........18 C3
Grafham Cambs............75 H2
Grafham Surrey............31 G3
Grafton N York...........132 F6
Grafton Oxon...............56 F7
Grafton Shrops............98 B8
Grafton Worcs..............71 H6
Grafton Flyford
Worcs........................71 G4
Grafton Regis Nhants.....73 L5
Grafton Underwood
Nhants.......................88 D7
Grafty Green Kent........34 B5
Graig Conwy...............109 M6
Graigfechan Denbgs......97 J2
Grain Medway...............46 E5
Grainsby Lincs............118 C2
Grainthorpe Lincs.......118 E3
Grampound Cnwll..........4 E6
Grampound Road
Cnwll.........................4 E5
Gramsdal W Isls..........233 c6
Gramsdale W Isls........233 c6
Granborough Bucks......58 C3
Granby Notts..............102 C5
Grandborough
Warwks......................72 F2
Grand Chemins
Jersey......................236 d7
Grandes Rocques
Guern.......................236 c2
Grandtully P & K.........194 E5
Grange Cumb..............137 H4
Grange Medway............46 D6
Grange P & K..............186 D3
Grange Crossroads
Moray.......................215 K4
Grange Hall Moray......214 C3
Grangehall S Lans.......165 J2
Grange Hill Essex.........45 H2
Grangemill Derbys......100 E2
Grange Moor Kirk.......123 J7
Grangemouth Falk......176 C3
Grange of Lindores
Fife.........................186 D4
Grange-over-Sands
Cumb.......................129 J4
Grangepans Falk.........176 D3
Grange Park Nhants.....73 L4
Grangetown R & Cl.....142 C3

Grangetown Sundld 151 K4
Grange Villa Dur.........151 G4
Gransmoor E R Yk.......135 H7
Granston Pembks.........64 C7
Grantchester Cambs.....76 B4
Grantham Lincs..........102 E5
Granton C Edin 177 H3
Grantown-on-Spey
Highld......................214 C8
Grantshouse Border ...179 G5
Grasby Lincs...............117 H1
Grasmere Cumb..........137 K5
Grasscroft Oldham......113 L1
Grassendale Lpool......111 L4
Grassington N York....131 J6
Grassmoor Derbys......115 H7
Grassthorpe Notts......116 C7
Grateley Hants.............28 F3
Graveley Cambs...........75 J2
Graveley Herts.............59 L3
Gravelly Hill Birm........85 K5
Graveney Kent.............34 E3
Gravesend Kent...........46 A5
Gravir W Isls..............232 f3
Grayingham Lincs.......116 F3
Grayrigg Cumb...........138 E7
Grays Thurr..................45 L4
Grayshott Hants...........30 E4
Grayswood Surrey........30 E4
Greasbrough Rothm....115 H3
Greasby Wirral...........111 H4
Great Abington
Cambs......................76 D5
Great Addington
Nhants.......................88 D7
Great Alne Warwks......71 K3
Great Altcar Lancs......111 K1
Great Amwell Herts......60 B5
Great Asby Cumb........138 F5
Great Ashfield Suffk....78 B2
Great Ayton N York....142 C5
Great Baddow Essex.....61 H6
Great Badminton
S Glos......................39 J4
Great Bardfield
Essex........................61 G2
Great Barford Bed 75 G4
Great Barr Sandw........85 J4
Great Barrington
Gloucs......................56 E5
Great Barrow Ches W..112 C7
Great Barton Suffk.......77 K2
Great Barugh N York..134 B4
Great Bavington
Nthumb....................158 C6
Great Bealings Suffk....78 F5
Great Bedwyn Wilts.....40 F7
Great Bentley Essex.....62 D4
Great Billing Nhants.....74 B3
Great Bircham Norfk..105 J6
Great Blakenham
Suffk........................78 D4
Great Blencow Cumb ..138 C2
Great Bolas Wrekin.....98 F7
Great Bookham
Surrey......................31 J1
Great Bourton Oxon ...72 F5
Great Bowden Leics.....87 L5
Great Bradley Suffk.....76 F4
Great Braxted Essex.....61 K5
Great Bricett Suffk......78 C4
Great Brickhill Bucks..58 E3
Great Bridgeford
Staffs........................99 K6
Great Brington
Nhants.......................73 J2
Great Bromley Essex...62 C3
Great Broughton
Cumb.......................136 E2
Great Broughton
N York......................142 C6
Great Budworth
Ches W.....................112 F6
Great Burdon Darltn..141 H4
Great Burstead
Essex........................46 B2
Great Busby N York....142 B6

Great Carlton Lincs......118 E4
Great Casterton
Rutlnd........................88 E2
Great Chalfield Wilts....39 K7
Great Chart Kent.........34 C4
Great Chatwell Staffs...84 E1
Great Chell C Stke........99 K3
Great Chesterford
Essex........................76 D6
Great Cheverell Wilts....27 M1
Great Chishill Cambs....76 B6
Great Clacton Essex.....62 E5
Great Clifton Cumb ...136 E2
Great Coates NE Lin...126 F8
Great Comberton
Worcs........................71 G6
Great Corby Cumb.....148 E4
Great Cornard Suffk....77 K6
Great Cowden E R Yk..126 F3
Great Coxwell Oxon....40 F2
Great Cransley
Nhants.......................88 B7
Great Cressingham
Norfk........................91 J3
Great Crosthwaite
Cumb.......................137 J3
Great Cubley Derbys..100 D5
Great Cumbrae
Island N Ayrs...........173 K6
Great Dalby Leics.........87 L2
Great Denham Bed......74 E5
Great Doddington
Nhants.......................74 C2
Great Dunham Norfk....91 K1
Great Dunmow Essex...61 G4
Great Durnford Wilts....28 C4
Great Easton Essex......60 F3
Great Easton Leics.......88 B5
Great Eccleston
Lancs......................120 F3
Great Ellingham
Norfk........................92 B4
Great Elm Somset.......27 H2
Great Everdon
Nhants.......................73 H3
Great Eversden
Cambs......................75 L4
Great Fencote N York..132 D2
Great Finborough
Suffk........................78 B3
Greatford Lincs............88 F2
Great Fransham
Norfk........................91 K2
Great Gaddesden
Herts........................59 G5
Greatgate Staffs........100 B4
Great Gidding Cambs...89 G6
Great Givendale
E R Yk......................134 C8
Great Glemham
Suffk........................79 H3
Great Glen Leics..........87 J4
Great Gonerby Lincs....102 E5
Great Gransden
Cambs......................75 J4
Great Green Cambs......75 K5
Great Green Suffk........77 K4
Great Habton N York..134 B4
Great Hale Lincs.........103 J4
Great Hallingbury
Essex........................60 E4
Greatham Hants...........30 C5
Greatham Hartpl........141 L2
Greatham W Susx........18 E3
Great Hampden
Bucks........................58 D7
Great Harrowden
Nhants.......................74 C1
Great Harwood
Lancs......................121 L4
Great Haseley Oxon......57 M7
Great Hatfield E R Yk..126 F3
Great Haywood
Staffs......................100 A7
Great Heck N York......124 E6
Great Henny Essex.......77 K6
Great Hinton Wilts......39 K8

Great Hockham
Norfk.....................**91** L5
Great Holland Essex......**62** E4
Great Hollands
Br For.................**42** E6
Great Horkesley
Essex.....................**62** B2
Great Hormead
Herts.....................**60** C3
Great Horton C Brad.... **123** H4
Great Horwood
Bucks.....................**58** C2
Great Houghton
Barns.....................**115** H1
Great Houghton
Nhants.....................**73** L3
Great Hucklow
Derbys.....................**114** D6
Great Kelk E R Yk........**135** H7
Great Kimble Bucks.....**58** D6
Great Kingshill Bucks....**42** E2
Great Langdale
Cumb.....................**137** J6
Great Langton N York.. **141** H7
Great Leighs Essex......**61** H4
Great Limber Lincs.......**126** E8
Great Linford M Keyn...**74** C6
Great Livermere
Suffk.....................**77** K1
Great Longstone
Derbys.....................**114** D6
Great Lumley Dur........**151** H5
Great Malvern Worcs....**70** D5
Great Maplestead
Essex.....................**77** J7
Great Marton Bpool... **120** D4
Great Massingham
Norfk.....................**105** J7
Great Milton Oxon......**57** L7
Great Missenden
Bucks.....................**58** E7
Great Mitton Lancs......**121** K3
Great Mongeham
Kent.....................**35** K4
Great Moulton Norfk.. **92** E5
Great Musgrave
Cumb.....................**139** H4
Great Ness Shrops........**98** B8
Great Notley Essex......**61** H4
Great Oak Mons.........**54** B6
Great Oakley Essex......**62** E3
Great Oakley Nhants....**88** C6
Great Offley Herts......**59** J3
Great Ormside Cumb... **139** G4
Great Orton Cumb.....**148** B4
Great Ouseburn
N York.....................**133** G6
Great Oxendon
Nhants.....................**87** K6
Great Park N u Ty........**158** F7
Great Parndon Essex....**60** C6
Great Paxton Cambs.....**75** H2
Great Plumpton
Lancs.....................**120** E4
Great Plumstead
Norfk.....................**93** G2
Great Ponton Lincs....**102** F6
Great Preston Leeds.....**124** B5
Great Raveley Cambs....**89** J7
Great Rissington
Gloucs.....................**56** D5
Great Rollright Oxon....**56** F2
Great Ryburgh Norfk... **106** A6
Great Ryton Shrops......**83** J3
Great Saling Essex.......**61** H3
Great Salkeld Cumb....**148** F7
Great Sampford
Essex.....................**76** F7
Great Saughall
Ches W.....................**111** K7
Great Shefford
W Berk.....................**41** G5
Great Shelford
Cambs.....................**76** C4
Great Smeaton
N York.....................**141** H6
Great Snoring Norfk.. **105** M5

Great Somerford
Wilts.....................**39** L4
Great Soudley
Shrops.....................**99** G6
Great Stainton Darltn.. **141** H3
Great Stambridge
Essex.....................**46** E2
Great Staughton
Cambs.....................**75** G2
Great Steeping Lincs... **118** F8
Great Stoke S Glos......**38** F4
Greatstone-on-Sea
Kent.....................**21** L2
Great Strickland
Cumb.....................**138** D3
Great Stukeley
Cambs.....................**89** J8
Great Sturton Lincs **117** K6
Great Swinburne
Nthumb.....................**158** B6
Great Tew Oxon..........**57** H3
Great Tey Essex...........**61** L3
Great Thurlow Suffk.....**76** F4
Great Torrington
Devon.....................**23** H7
Great Tosson Nthumb... **158** C3
Great Totham Essex......**61** K5
Great Totham Essex......**61** L5
Great Urswick Cumb ... **129** G5
Great Wakering
Essex.....................**46** F3
Great Waldingfield
Suffk.....................**77** K5
Great Walsingham
Norfk.....................**105** M5
Great Waltham Essex....**61** H5
Great Warley Essex......**45** L2
Great Washbourne
Gloucs.....................**71** H7
Great Weeke Devon **11** G7
Great Wenham Suffk....**78** C6
Great Whittington
Nthumb.....................**158** C7
Great Wigborough
Essex.....................**62** A5
Great Wilbraham
Cambs.....................**76** D3
Great Wishford Wilts....**28** B4
Great Witcombe
Gloucs.....................**55** K5
Great Witley Worcs......**70** D2
Great Wolford
Warwks.....................**72** B7
Greatworth Nhants......**73** G6
Great Wratting Suffk....**77** G5
Great Wymondley
Herts.....................**59** K3
Great Wyrley Staffs......**85** H3
Great Yarmouth
Norfk.....................**93** L3
Great Yeldham
Essex.....................**77** H6
Greenburn W Loth.......**176** C6
Green End Herts..........**60** B2
Green End Herts..........**60** B4
Greenfield Ag & B........**173** M1
Greenfield C Beds.........**74** F7
Greenfield Flints..........**111** H6
Greenfield Highld..........**201** J5
Greenfield Oldham.......**113** M2
Greenford Gt Lon..........**43** J4
Greengairs N Lans........**175** K4
Greengates C Brad........**123** J3
Greenham Somset.........**25** G7
Green Hammerton
N York.....................**133** G7
Greenhaugh Nthumb... **157** L5
Greenhead Nthumb......**149** H3
Green Heath Staffs......**85** H2
Greenhill D & G...........**155** J6
Greenhill Falk...............**175** L3
Greenhill Kent..............**47** K6
Greenhills S Lans..........**165** H3
Greenhills S Lans..........**175** H7
Greenhithe Kent..........**45** L5
Greenholm E Ayrs........**164** B3
Greenhouse Border......**167** H5

Greenhow Hill N York.. **131** L6
Greenland Highld..........**231** J3
Greenland Sheff...........**115** H4
Greenlaw Border..........**167** L1
Greenlea D & G.............**155** H6
Greenloaning P & K....**185** H6
Greenmount Bury........**122** B7
Greenock Inver...........**174** B3
Greenodd Cumb...........**129** G3
Green Ore Somset.........**26** E2
Green Quarter Cumb... **138** C6
Greenshields S Lans.....**165** K2
Greenside Gatesd.........**150** E3
Greenside Kirk.............**123** H7
Greens Norton
Nhants.....................**73** J4
Greenstead Green
Essex.....................**61** K3
Green Street Herts........**59** K7
Green Street Herts........**60** D4
Green Tye Herts...........**60** C4
Greenway Somset..........**25** L6
Greenwich Gt Lon.........**45** G4
Greenwich
Maritime Gt Lon.......**45** H4
Greet Gloucs.................**56** B3
Greete Shrops..............**69** L1
Greetham Lincs............**118** D7
Greetham RutInd.........**88** D2
Greetland Calder..........**123** G6
Greinton Somset..........**26** B4
Grenaby IoM................**237** b6
Grendon Nhants...........**74** C3
Grendon Warwks..........**86** C4
Grendon
Underwood Bucks...**58** B4
Grenoside Sheff............**115** G3
Greosabhagh W Isls... **232** e4
Gresford Wrexhm.........**97** M2
Gresham Norfk.............**106** E5
Greshornish Highld...... **208** E4
Gressenhall Norfk.........**91** L1
Gressenhall Green
Norfk.....................**91** L1
Gressingham Lancs **130** B5
Greta Bridge Dur.........**140** D5
Gretna D & G...............**148** B2
Gretna Green D & G.....**148** B2
Gretna Services
D & G.....................**148** B2
Gretton Gloucs.............**56** A2
Gretton Nhants.............**88** C5
Gretton Shrops..............**83** K4
Grewelthorpe N York... **132** C4
Greyrigg D & G.............**155** J4
Greys Green Oxon........**42** B4
Greysouthen Cumb......**136** E2
Greystoke Cumb...........**138** B2
Greystone Angus..........**196** E7
Greywell Hants.............**30** B2
Griff Warwks.................**86** D5
Griffithstown Torfn......**53** L7
Grimeford Village
Lancs.....................**121** J7
Grimesthorpe Sheff..... **115** G4
Grimethorpe Barns......**124** C8
Grimley Worcs..............**70** E3
Grimmet S Ayrs............**163** H7
Grimoldby Lincs...........**118** E4
Grimpo Shrops.............**98** A7
Grimsargh Lancs...........**121** H4
Grimsby NE Lin.............**127** G7
Grimscote Nhants.........**73** J4
Grimscott Cnwll..............**9** H4
Grimshader W Isls........**232** f3
Grimsthorpe Lincs.......**103** H7
Grimston Leics.............**102** B7
Grimston Norfk.............**105** H7
Grimstone Dorset..........**14** C4
Grimstone End Suffk.....**77** L2
Grindale E R Yk............**135** H5
Grindleford Derbys...... **114** E6
Grindleton Lancs..........**121** L2
Grindley Brook
Shrops.....................**98** D4
Grindlow Derbys...........**114** D6
Grindon Staffs.............**100** B2

Gringley on the Hill
Notts.....................**116** C4
Grinsdale Cumb **148** C4
Grinshill Shrops.............**98** D7
Grinton N York.............**140** D7
Griomaisiader W Isls.. **232** f3
Grishipoll Ag & B.........**188** F4
Gristhorpe N York........**135** H3
Griston Norfk...............**91** L4
Gritley Ork...................**234** d6
Grittenham Wilts..........**40** B4
Grittleton Wilts............**39** K4
Grizebeck Cumb...........**128** F3
Grizedale Cumb...........**137** K7
Groby Leics...................**87** G3
Groes Conwy................**110** D8
Groes-faen Rhondd........**37** G4
Groeslon Gwynd............**95** H2
Groes-Wen Caerph........**37** H3
Grogarry W Isls............**233** b7
Grogport Ag & B...........**161** K1
Groigearraidh W Isls...**233** b7
Gronant Flints..............**110** F5
Groombridge E Susx......**32** F5
Grosebay W Isls...........**232** e4
Grosmont Mons............**54** B3
Grosmont N York..........**143** H6
Groton Suffk.................**77** L6
Grouville Jersey............**236** e7
Grove Notts..................**116** C5
Grove Oxon....................**41** H3
Grove Green Kent..........**33** K3
Grove Park Gt Lon.........**45** H5
Grovesend Swans..........**51** H5
Gruinard Highld...........**219** L4
Gruinart Ag & B............**170** F5
Grula Highld..................**208** F8
Gruline Ag & B..............**190** B7
Grundisburgh Suffk......**78** F4
Gruting Shet.................**235** c5
Grutness Shet..............**235** c8
Gualachulain Highld ... **192** B7
Guardbridge Fife..........**187** G4
Guarlford Worcs...........**70** E5
Guay P & K...................**194** F6
Guernsey Guern.............**236** c3
Guernsey Airport
Guern.....................**236** c3
Guestling Green
E Susx.....................**21** G3
Guestling Thorn
E Susx.....................**21** G3
Guestwick Norfk...........**106** C6
Guide Bridge Tamesd... **113** L3
Guilden Morden
Cambs.....................**75** K5
Guilden Sutton
Ches W.....................**112** C7
Guildford Surrey............**31** G2
Guildtown P & K...........**186** B2
Guilsborough Nhants **87** J8
Guilsfield Powys............**82** E2
Guiltreehill S Ayrs........**163** J7
Guineaford Devon..........**23** J4
Guisborough R & Cl.....**142** D4
Guiseley Leeds.............**123** J3
Guist Norfk..................**106** B7
Guiting Power
Gloucs.....................**56** C3
Gullane E Loth.............**178** B2
Gulval Cnwll....................**2** E5
Gulworthy Devon...........**6** C2
Gumfreston Pembks......**49** J7
Gumley Leics.................**87** K5
Gunby Lincs..................**102** F7
Gunby Lincs..................**118** F7
Gundleton Hants...........**29** L5
Gun Hill E Susx.............**20** C3
Gunn Devon...................**23** K5
Gunnerside N York....... **139** L7
Gunnerton Nthumb...... **158** A7
Gunness N Linc............**125** K7
Gunnislake Cnwll............**6** C2
Gunnista Shet...............**235** d6
Gunthorpe C Pete.........**89** H3
Gunthorpe N Linc........**116** D3
Gunthorpe Norfk..........**106** B5

Gunthorpe Notts.......... 102 B4
Gunwalloe Cnwll............. 3 H6
Gurnard IoW 16 F4
Gurney Slade Somset .. 26 F2
Gurnos Powys...............52 B6
Gussage All Saints
Dorset 15 J1
Gussage St Andrew
Dorset 27 L8
Gussage St Michael
Dorset 15 J1
Guston Kent................35 J5
Gutcher Shet 235 d2
Guthrie Angus.......... 196 F6
Guyhirn Cambs...........90 B3
Guyzance Nthumb .. 158 F2
Gwaenysgor Flints ... 110 F5
Gwalchmai IoA 108 E6
Gwaun-Cae-
Gurwen Carmth....51 K3
Gweek Cnwll 3 J6
Gwenddwr Powys....68 B6
Gwennap Cnwll 3 J4
Gwennap Mining
District Cnwll............. 3 K3
Gwernaffield Flints 111 H7
Gwernesney Mons....54 B7
Gwernogle Carmth 66 C7
Gwernymynydd
Flints...............97 J1
Gwespyr Flints........... 110 F5
Gwinear Cnwll 3 G4
Gwithian Cnwll 3 G3
Gwyddelwern
Denbgs.................97 G3
Gwyddgrug Carmth......66 B7
Gwytherin Conwy...........96 D1

Habberley Shrops........83 H3
Habberley Worcs........84 E7
Habergham Lancs ... 122 B4
Habertoft Lincs 119 G7
Habrough NE Lin....... 126 E7
Hacconby Lincs......... 103 J7
Haceby Lincs.............. 103 G5
Hacheston Suffk 79 G3
Hackbridge Gt Lon 44 F6
Hackenthorpe Sheff .. 115 H5
Hackford Norfk...........92 C3
Hackforth N York...... 132 C2
Hackland Ork 234 c5
Hackleton Nhants......74 B4
Hacklinge Kent 35 J4
Hackness N York 134 F2
Hackney Gt Lon 45 G3
Hackthorn Lincs........ 117 G5
Hackthorpe Cumb .. 138 D3
Hadden Border 168 B3
Haddenham Bucks....58 C6
Haddenham Cambs....90 C7
Haddington E Loth ... 178 B4
Haddington Lincs 116 E8
Haddiscoe Norfk.........93 J4
Haddo Abers 216 F6
Haddon Cambs...........89 G5
Hadfield Derbys 114 A3
Hadham Ford Herts....60 C4
Hadleigh Essex 46 D3
Hadleigh Suffk............78 B6
Hadley Worcs...............70 F2
Hadley Wrekin............84 C2
Hadley End Staffs... 100 C7
Hadley Wood Gt Lon....44 E1
Hadlow Kent 33 H3
Hadlow Down E Susx..20 B2
Hadnall Shrops............98 D7
Hadrian's Wall......... 150 B2
Hadstock Essex..........76 D5
Hadzor Worcs 71 G3
Haggersta Shet........ 235 c5
Haggerston Nthumb .. 168 F2
Haggs Falk................. 175 L3
Hagley Herefs..............69 L6

Hagley Worcs 85 G7
Hagworthingham
Lincs....................... 118 D7
Haile Cumb 136 E5
Hailey Oxon 57 G5
Hailsham E Susx.............20 C4
Hail Weston Cambs.....75 H3
Hainault Gt Lon 45 J2
Hainford Norfk 106 F8
Hainton Lincs............. 117 K5
Haisthorpe E R Yk 135 H6
Hakin Pembks 48 F6
Halam Notts............... 102 B2
Halbeath Fife.............. 176 F1
Halberton Devon..........24 F8
Halcro Highld 231 J4
Hale Cumb 129 K4
Hale Halton.................. 112 C5
Hale Hants.....................28 D7
Hale Surrey.....................30 D2
Hale Traffd 113 H4
Hale Barns Traffd..... 113 H4
Hales Norfk.....................93 H4
Hales Staffs....................99 G5
Halesowen Dudley......85 G6
Hales Place Kent...........34 F3
Hale Street Kent...........33 H4
Halesworth Suffk..........93 H7
Halewood Knows....... 112 C4
Halford Devon.................7 J2
Halford Warwks............72 C5
Halfpenny Green
Staffs......................84 E5
Halfway House
Shrops......................83 G2
Halfway Houses Kent....46 F5
Halifax Calder 123 G5
Halket E Ayrs.............. 174 D7
Halkirk Highld............. 231 G4
Halkyn Flints............... 111 H7
Hall E Rens.................. 174 D7
Halland E Susx...............20 A3
Hallaton Leics...............87 L4
Hallatrow BaNES...........38 F8
Hallbankgate Cumb .. 149 G3
Hall Dunnerdale
Cumb....................... 137 H7
Hallen S Glos.................38 D4
Hallgarth Dur.............. 151 H6
Hallglen Falk............... 176 B3
Hall Green Birm...........85 K7
Hallin Highld............... 208 D3
Halling Medway.............46 B7
Hallington Lincs......... 118 D4
Hallington Nthumb .. 158 C6
Halliwell Bolton.......... 121 K7
Halloughton Notts.... 102 B3
Hallow Worcs.................70 E3
Hall's Green Herts........59 L3
Hallyne Border............ 166 B2
Halmore Gloucs............55 G7
Halnaker W Susx...........18 B4
Halsall Lancs.............. 120 E7
Halse Nhants................73 H6
Halse Somset................25 H5
Halsetown Cnwll............. 2 E4
Halsham E R Yk.......... 127 G5
Halstead Essex..............61 K2
Halstead Kent................45 J7
Halstead Leics..............87 L3
Halstock Dorset............14 A2
Haltham Lincs............. 118 C8
Halton Bucks.................58 E6
Halton Halton.............. 112 D5
Halton Lancs............... 129 K6
Halton Leeds............... 123 L4
Halton Nthumb 150 C2
Halton Wrexhm.............97 L4
Halton East N York..... 131 K8
Halton Gill N York 131 G4
Halton Holegate
Lincs....................... 118 F7
Halton Lea Gate
Nthumb.................. 149 H4
Halton Shields
Nthumb.................. 150 C2
Halton West N York ... 130 F8

Haltwhistle Nthumb...... 149 J3
Halvergate Norfk 93 J3
Halwell Devon.....................7 H5
Halwill Devon.....................10 C5
Halwill Junction
Devon.......................10 C5
Ham Devon......................13 G3
Ham Gloucs.....................55 G7
Ham Gt Lon.......................44 D5
Ham Kent..........................35 J4
Ham Somset 25 L6
Ham Wilts..........................41 G7
Hambleden Bucks.........42 C3
Hambledon Hants.........29 M7
Hambledon Surrey.........30 F4
Hamble-le-Rice
Hants.......................16 F2
Hambleton Lancs.......... 120 E3
Hambleton N York 124 E4
Hambridge Somset......26 B6
Hambrook W Susx.........17 L2
Hameringham Lincs ... 118 D7
Hamerton Cambs.........89 G7
Ham Green Worcs.........71 H2
Hamilton S Lans.......... 175 J7
Hamilton Services
S Lans...................... 175 J6
Hamlet Dorset................14 B2
Hammersmith Gt Lon....44 E4
Hammerwich Staffs....85 J3
Hammoon Dorset 27 J8
Hamnavoe Shet 235 c6
Hampden Park
E Susx......................20 C5
Hampnett Gloucs..........56 C5
Hampole Donc............. 124 D7
Hampreston Dorset.....15 K3
Hampstead Gt Lon..........44 E3
Hampstead Norreys
W Berk......................41 K5
Hampsthwaite N York.. 132 C7
Hampton C Pete...........89 H5
Hampton Gt Lon...........43 J6
Hampton Kent................47 K6
Hampton Shrops..........84 D6
Hampton Swindn.........40 D3
Hampton Worcs.............71 H5
Hampton Bishop
Herefs......................69 L6
Hampton Court
Palace Gt Lon...........44 D6
Hampton Heath
Ches W......................98 D3
Hampton-in-Arden
Solhll.......................86 B7
Hampton Lovett
Worcs.......................70 F2
Hampton Lucy
Warwks.....................72 B3
Hampton Magna
Warwks.....................72 C2
Hampton Poyle Oxon....57 J5
Hampton Wick
Gt Lon......................44 D6
Hamptworth Wilts........28 E7
Hamsey E Susx...............19 L3
Hamstall Ridware
Staffs..................... 100 C8
Hamstead Birm...........85 J5
Hamstead Marshall
W Berk......................41 H7
Hamsterley Dur.......... 140 E2
Hamsterley Dur.......... 150 E4
Hamstreet Kent............34 D7
Ham Street Somset....26 C6
Hamworthy BCP...........15 J4
Hanbury Staffs.......... 100 D6
Hanbury Worcs.............71 G2
Hanchurch Staffs.........99 J4
Handa Island Highld .. 228 A6
Hand and Pen Devon...12 D4
Handbridge Ches W.... 112 B7
Handcross W Susx........31 L5
Handforth Ches E....... 113 J5
Handley Ches W.............98 C2
Handley Derbys.......... 101 G1
Handsworth Birm........85 J5

Handsworth Sheff........ 115 H4
Hanford C Stke...............99 K4
Hanging Heaton Kirk.. 123 K6
Hanging Houghton
Nhants......................87 L8
Hanging Langford
Wilts.........................28 B4
Hangleton Br & H........19 H4
Hanham S Glos...........38 F6
Hankelow Ches E..........98 F4
Hankerton Wilts..........39 L3
Hanley C Stke................99 K3
Hanley Castle Worcs....70 E6
Hanley Child Worcs......70 B2
Hanley Swan Worcs......70 E6
Hanley William
Worcs.......................70 C2
Hanlith N York............ 131 G7
Hanmer Wrexhm.........98 C4
Hannaford Devon.........23 J5
Hannington Hants.......29 K1
Hannington Nhants 74 B1
Hannington Swindn.....40 D2
Hannington Wick
Swindn......................40 D2
Hanslope M Keyn.........74 B5
Hanthorpe Lincs 103 H7
Hanwell Gt Lon.............44 D4
Hanwell Oxon...............72 E5
Hanwood Shrops.........83 J2
Hanworth Gt Lon.........43 J6
Hanworth Norfk......... 106 E5
Happendon S Lans 165 G3
Happendon
Services S Lans...... 165 G3
Happisburgh Norfk ... 107 H6
Happisburgh
Common Norfk...... 107 H6
Hapsford Ches W 112 C6
Hapton Lancs.............. 122 B4
Hapton Norfk................92 E4
Harberton Devon...........7 H4
Harbertonford Devon...7 H5
Harbledown Kent.........34 F3
Harborne Birm.............85 H6
Harborough Magna
Warwks.....................86 F2
Harbottle Nthumb 158 B2
Harbourneford
Devon.........................7 G4
Harbury Warwks..........72 D3
Harby Leics................. 102 C6
Harby Notts................. 116 E7
Harcombe Devon...........11 K8
Harcombe Devon...........12 F4
Harcombe Bottom
Devon.........................13 J4
Harden C Brad............ 123 G3
Harden Wsall................85 H4
Hardenhuish Wilts.......39 K5
Hardgate Abers......... 206 E5
Hardgate D & G......... 146 D4
Hardgate W Duns....... 174 F4
Hardham W Susx..........18 E3
Hardingham Norfk........92 C3
Hardingstone Nhants ...73 L3
Hardington Somset......27 H2
Hardington
Mandeville
Somset.....................13 M1
Hardington Marsh
Somset.....................13 M1
Hardington Moor
Somset.....................13 M1
Hardisworthy Devon....22 C7
Hardley Hants...............16 E2
Hardley Street Norfk 93 H4
Hardraw N York 131 G2
Hardstoft Derbys....... 115 H8
Hardway Hants.............17 H3
Hardway Somset..........27 G5
Hardwick Bucks...........58 D4
Hardwick Cambs..........75 L3
Hardwick Nhants.........74 B1
Hardwick Norfk............92 F5
Hardwick Oxon.............57 G6
Hardwick Oxon.............57 L3

Hardwick Wsall 85 J4
Hardwicke Gloucs........55 H5
Hardwicke Gloucs........55 K3
Hardwick Hall
  Derbys....................... 115 J8
Hardy's Green Essex......61 M4
Hare Croft C Brad 123 G4
Harefield Gt Lon 43 H3
Hare Green Essex...........62 D3
Hare Hatch Wokham....42 D5
Harehill Derbys 100 D5
Harehills Leeds 123 L4
Harelaw Border 167 H5
Harelaw D & G 156 D6
Harescombe Gloucs.......55 J6
Haresfield Gloucs.........55 J6
Harestock Hants 29 J5
Hare Street Essex...........60 C6
Hare Street Herts...........60 C3
Harewood Leeds 123 L2
Harewood End
  Herefs 54 D3
Harford Devon 6 F4
Hargrave Ches W 98 C1
Hargrave Nhants...........74 F1
Hargrave Suffk..............77 H3
Harkstead Suffk............78 E7
Harlaston Staffs............86 B2
Harlaxton Lincs 102 E6
Harlech Gwynd 95 K6
Harlech Castle
  Gwynd 95 K6
Harlescott Shrops.........83 K1
Harlesden Gt Lon 44 E4
Harlesthorpe Derbys ... 115 J6
Harleston Devon 7 J6
Harleston Norfk............92 F6
Harleston Suffk.............78 B3
Harlestone Nhants........73 K2
Harle Syke Lancs 122 C4
Harley Rothm 115 G2
Harley Shrops...............83 L3
Harlington C Beds 59 G2
Harlington Donc 115 J2
Harlington Gt Lon 43 H5
Harlosh Highld........... 208 D6
Harlow Essex 60 D6
Harlow Carr RHS
  N York..................... 132 D8
Harlow Hill Nthumb...... 150 D2
Harlthorpe E R Yk 125 H3
Harlton Cambs..............75 L4
Harlyn Cnwll................. 4 D2
Harman's Cross
  Dorset 15 J6
Harmby N York........... 131 L2
Harmer Green Herts......59 L5
Harmer Hill Shrops........98 C7
Harmston Lincs 116 F8
Harnage Shrops 83 L3
Harnhill Gloucs..............56 B7
Harold Hill Gt Lon.........45 K2
Haroldston West
  Pembks....................48 E4
Haroldswick Shet....... 235 e1
Harold Wood Gt Lon 45 K3
Harome N York............ 133 K3
Harpenden Herts...........59 J5
Harpford Devon 12 E4
Harpham E R Yk.......... 135 H7
Harpley Norfk............ 105 J7
Harpley Worcs...............70 C3
Harpole Nhants.............73 K3
Harpsdale Highld........ 231 G4
Harpswell Lincs.......... 116 F4
Harpurhey Manch....... 113 K2
Harraby Cumb............ 148 D4
Harracott Devon 23 J6
Harrapool Highld........ 199 K2
Harrietfield P & K...... 185 K2
Harrietsham Kent.........33 L3
Harringay Gt Lon 44 F3
Harrington Cumb........ 136 D3
Harrington Lincs......... 118 E6
Harrington Nhants........88 D4
Harringworth Nhants....88 D4
Harris W Isls 232 d4

Harrogate N York 132 D7
Harrold Bed 74 D3
Harrow Gt Lon...............44 D3
Harrowbarrow Cnwll...... 6 B2
Harrowgate Village
  Darltn...................... 141 H4
Harrow Green Suffk......77 J4
Harrow on the Hill
  Gt Lon.......................44 D3
Harrow Weald Gt Lon 44 D2
Harston Cambs..............76 B4
Harston Leics............. 102 D6
Harswell E R Yk 125 J3
Hart Hartpl................. 151 L7
Hartburn Nthumb 158 D5
Hartburn S on T.......... 141 K4
Hartest Suffk................77 J4
Hartfield E Susx...........32 E6
Hartford Cambs............89 J8
Hartford Ches W.......... 112 F6
Hartfordbridge
  Hants........................42 C8
Hartford End Essex......61 G4
Harthill N York........... 140 F6
Hartgrove Dorset..........27 J7
Harthill Ches W............98 D2
Harthill N Lans........... 176 B5
Harthill Rothm 115 J5
Harthope D & G.......... 165 K6
Hartington Derbys..... 100 C1
Hartland Devon 22 D6
Hartland Quay Devon ...22 C6
Hartlebury Worcs..........70 E1
Hartlepool Hartpl 151 L7
Hartley Cumb 139 H5
Hartley Kent.................33 K6
Hartley Kent.................45 L6
Hartley Wespall
  Hants........................42 B8
Hartley Wintney
  Hants........................30 C1
Hartlip Kent.................46 D7
Harton N York............ 133 L6
Harton S Tyne............ 151 J2
Hartpury Gloucs...........55 J3
Hartshead Kirk........... 123 J6
Hartshead Moor
  Services Calder....... 123 H5
Hartshill C Stke............99 K4
Hartshill Warwks..........86 D5
Hartshorne Derbys..... 100 F7
Hartwell Nhants............73 L4
Hartwith N York......... 132 C6
Hartwood N Lans....... 175 L6
Hartwoodmyres
  Border 166 F4
Harvel Kent..................46 A7
Harvington Worcs.........71 J5
Harvington Worcs.........84 F8
Harwell Notts............ 116 B3
Harwell Oxon...............41 J3
Harwich Essex..............62 F2
Harwood Nthumb....... 158 C4
Harwood Dale N York... 143 K7
Harworth Notts.......... 115 L3
Hasbury Dudley...........85 G6
Hascombe Surrey.........31 G4
Haselbech Nhants........87 K7
Haselbury Plucknett
  Somset 13 L1
Haseley Warwks...........72 B2
Haselor Warwks...........71 K3
Hasfield Gloucs.............55 J3
Haskayne Lancs 120 E8
Hasketon Suffk.............78 F4
Haslemere Surrey.........30 E5
Haslingden Lancs....... 122 B6
Haslingfield Cambs......76 B4
Haslington Ches E.........99 G2
Hassingham Norfk.......93 H3
Hassocks W Susx..........19 J3
Hassop Derbys........... 114 E6
Haster Highld............. 231 K5
Hastingleigh Kent.........34 E5
Hastings E Susx............21 G4
Hastingwood Essex......60 D6
Hastoe Herts.................58 F6

Haswell Dur............... 151 J6
Haswell Plough Dur... 151 J6
Hatch Beauchamp
  Somset 25 L7
Hatch End Gt Lon.........43 J3
Hatchmere Ches W..... 112 D6
Hatcliffe NE Lin 117 K2
Hatfield Donc............ 125 G8
Hatfield Herefs............69 L3
Hatfield Herts..............59 L6
Hatfield Broad Oak
  Essex........................60 E5
Hatfield Heath Essex....60 E5
Hatfield Peverel
  Essex........................61 J5
Hatfield Woodhouse
  Donc....................... 125 G8
Hatford Oxon...............41 G2
Hatherden Hants..........29 G2
Hatherleigh Devon 10 D4
Hathern Leics............. 101 J7
Hatherop Gloucs...........56 D6
Hathersage Derbys 114 E5
Hathersage Booths
  Derbys..................... 114 E5
Hatherton Ches E.........99 G3
Hatherton Staffs..........85 G2
Hatley St George
  Cambs.......................75 K4
Hatt Cnwll..................... 6 B4
Hattersley Tamesd 113 M3
Hatton Abers.............. 217 K6
Hatton D & G 196 D7
Hatton Derbys............ 100 E6
Hatton Gt Lon..............43 J5
Hatton Lincs............... 117 K6
Hatton Shrops..............83 J5
Hatton Warrtn........... 112 E5
Hatton Warwks............72 B2
Hatton of Fintray
  Abers....................... 206 F3
Haugh E Ayrs.............. 163 L4
Haugham Lincs........... 118 D5
Haughhead E Duns..... 175 G3
Haughley Suffk.............78 B3
Haughley Green
  Suffk........................78 B2
Haugh of Glass
  Moray....................... 215 J6
Haugh of Urr D & G... 146 E2
Haughs of Kinnaird
  Angus...................... 197 G5
Haughton Ches E.........98 E2
Haughton Shrops.........98 B6
Haughton Staffs...........99 K7
Haughton le Skerne
  Darltn...................... 141 H4
Haultwick Herts............60 B4
Haunton Staffs.............86 B2
Hautes Croix Jersey ... 236 c6
Hauxton Cambs............76 B4
Havant Hants...............17 K2
Havenstreet IoW...........17 G4
Havercroft Wakefd..... 124 B7
Haverfordwest
  Pembks....................48 F4
Haverhill Suffk.............76 F5
Haverigg Cumb.......... 128 E4
Havering-atte-
  Bower Gt Lon 45 K2
Haversham M Keyn........74 B6
Haverthwaite Cumb ... 129 H3
Havyatt N Som..............38 C7
Hawarden Flints......... 111 J7
Hawbush Green
  Essex........................61 J4
Hawen Cerdgn 65 K5
Hawes N York............ 131 G2
Hawe's Green Norfk.....92 F4
Hawford Worcs.............70 E3
Hawick Border............ 167 G6
Hawkchurch Devon.......13 J3
Hawkedon Suffk..........77 H4
Hawkeridge Wilts.........27 K2
Hawkesbury S Glos.......39 H3
Hawkesbury Upton
  S Glos.......................39 H3

Hawkhurst Kent............33 K6
Hawkinge Kent............35 G6
Hawkley Hants 30 C5
Hawkridge Somset 24 D5
Hawkshead Cumb....... 137 K7
Hawkshead Hill
  Cumb....................... 137 K7
Hawksland S Lans...... 165 G2
Hawkstone Shrops........98 E6
Hawkswick N York...... 131 H5
Hawksworth Leeds..... 123 H3
Hawksworth Notts...... 102 C4
Hawkwell Essex............46 E2
Hawley Hants...............42 E8
Hawling Gloucs.............56 B4
Hawnby N York........... 133 H2
Haworth C Brad.......... 122 F3
Hawstead Suffk............77 J3
Hawthorn Dur............ 151 K5
Hawthorn Hill Lincs.... 103 K2
Hawton Notts............ 102 C3
Haxby C York.............. 133 J7
Haxey N Linc............. 116 C2
Haydock St Hel.......... 112 E3
Haydon Bridge
  Nthumb.................... 149 L3
Haydon Wick Swindn...40 C3
Hayes Gt Lon...............43 J4
Hayes Gt Lon...............45 H6
Hayes End Gt Lon.........43 H4
Hayfield Ag & B.......... 182 F3
Hayfield Derbys.......... 114 B4
Hayhillock Angus....... 196 E7
Hayle Cnwll..................... 2
Hayle Port Cnwll............ 2 F4
Hayley Green Cnwll.......85 G6
Hayling Island Hants....17 K3
Hayne Devon 11 H7
Haynes C Beds 75 G6
Haynes Church End
  C Beds 74 F6
Haynes West End
  C Beds 74 F6
Hay-on-Wye Powys.......68 E6
Hayscastle Pembks......48 F3
Hayscastle Cross
  Pembks....................48 F3
Hay Street Herts...........60 C3
Hayton Cumb............. 147 K6
Hayton Cumb............. 148 E4
Hayton E R Yk............ 125 J2
Hayton Notts............. 116 B5
Haytor Vale Devon 7 H1
Haytown Devon 9 K3
Haywards Heath
  W Susx......................19 J2
Haywood Donc............ 124 E7
Hazelbank S Lans...... 165 G1
Hazelbury Bryan
  Dorset 14 E2
Hazeleigh Essex...........61 K7
Hazel Grove Stockp.... 113 L4
Hazelton Walls Fife.... 186 E3
Hazelwood Derbys..... 101 G4
Hazlemere Bucks..........42 E2
Hazlerigg N u Ty......... 159 G7
Hazleton Gloucs...........56 B4
Heacham Norfk.......... 105 G5
Headbourne Worthy
  Hants........................29 J5
Headcorn Kent............33 L4
Headingley Leeds....... 123 K4
Headington Oxon 57 K6
Headlam Dur.............. 140 F4
Headlesscross
  N Lans..................... 176 B6
Headless Cross
  Worcs........................71 J2
Headley Hants 30 D4
Headley Hants 41 K7
Headley Surrey............31 K1
Headley Down Hants....30 D4
Headon Notts............. 116 C6
Heads Nook Cumb...... 148 E4
Heage Derbys............ 101 G3
Healaugh N York........ 124 D2
Healaugh N York........ 140 C7

Heald Green Stockp..... 113 J4
Heale Somset............25 K7
Heale Somset............26 B6
Healey N York............132 B4
Healeyfield Dur..........150 D5
Healing NE Lin...........126 F7
Heamoor Cnwll 2 E5
Heanor Derbys...........101 H3
Heanton
  Puchardon
  Devon...................23 H4
Heapham Lincs...........116 E4
Heart of Scotland
  Services N Lans 176 B5
Heasley Mill Devon 24 B5
Heaste Highld............199 K2
Heath Derbys.............115 H7
Heath Wakefd............123 L6
Heath and Reach
  C Beds...................58 F3
Heathcote Derbys........100 D1
Heather Leics.............86 E2
Heathfield E Susx 20 C2
Heathfield Somset........25 J6
Heath Green Worcs.......71 J1
Heath Hall D & G 155 H6
Heath Hayes &
  Wimblebury
  Staffs....................85 H2
Heath Hill Shrops 84 D2
Heathrow Airport
  Gt Lon..................43 H5
Heathton Shrops..........84 E5
Heath Town Wolves 85 G4
Heatley Warrtn 113 G4
Heaton C Brad 123 H4
Heaton N u Ty............151 G2
Heaton Staffs............113 L8
Heaton Chapel
  Stockp..................113 K3
Heaton Mersey
  Stockp..................113 K4
Heaton Norris Stockp... 113 K4
Heaton's Bridge
  Lancs...................120 E7
Heaverham Kent..........33 G2
Heavitree Devon 12 B4
Hebburn S Tyne..........151 H3
Hebden N York...........131 J6
Hebden Bridge
  Calder 122 E5
Hebing End Herts.........60 A4
Hebron Carmth............49 K3
Hebron Nthumb..........158 F4
Heckfield Hants...........42 B7
Heckfield Green
  Suffk....................92 E7
Heckfordbridge
  Essex....................61 M4
Heckington Lincs.........103 J4
Heckmondwike Kirk.....123 J5
Heddington Wilts 39 M6
Heddon-on-the-
  Wall Nthumb...........150 E2
Hedenham Norfk..........93 G5
Hedge End Hants..........29 J8
Hedgerley Bucks...........42 F3
Hedging Somset...........25 L5
Hedley on the Hill
  Nthumb.................150 D3
Hednesford Staffs.........85 H2
Hedon E R Yk............126 F5
Hedsor Bucks..............42 E3
Heeley Sheff.............115 G5
Heglibister Shet 235 c5
Heighington Darltn 141 G3
Heighington Lincs........117 G7
Heightington Worcs.......70 D1
Heiton Border 167 L4
Hele Devon 12 C2
Hele Devon 23 H3
Helensburgh Ag & B ... 174 B2
Helenton S Ayrs 163 K3
Helford Cnwll 3 K6
Helford Passage
  Cnwll......................3 K6
Helhoughton Norfk 105 K7

Helions Bumpstead
  Essex....................76 F6
Helland Cnwll 5 G2
Hellescott Cnwll............9 H6
Hellesdon Norfk..........92 E2
Hellidon Nhants 73 G3
Hellifield N York 131 G7
Hellingly E Susx 20 C4
Helmdon Nhants 73 H5
Helme Kirk...............123 G7
Helmingham Suffk........78 E3
Helmsdale Highld 227 H5
Helmshore Lancs.........122 B6
Helmsley N York 133 J3
Helperby N York 133 G5
Helperthorpe N York ... 134 E5
Helpringham Lincs........103 J4
Helpston C Pete 89 G3
Helsby Ches W 112 C6
Helston Cnwll................3 H5
Helstone Cnwll 8 E8
Helton Cumb 138 D3
Hemel Hempstead
  Herts....................59 H6
Hemerdon Devon...........6 E4
Hemingbrough
  N York..................125 G4
Hemingby Lincs 118 C6
Hemingford Abbots
  Cambs...................75 K1
Hemingford Grey
  Cambs...................75 K1
Hemingstone Suffk.......78 D4
Hemington Leics 101 J6
Hemington Nhants 88 F6
Hemington Somset........27 G2
Hemley Suffk..............79 G6
Hemlington Middsb......142 B4
Hempnall Norfk...........92 F5
Hempnall Green
  Norfk....................92 F5
Hempriggs Moray........214 D2
Hempstead Essex.........76 F6
Hempstead Medway......46 C6
Hempstead Norfk........106 D5
Hempstead Norfk........107 J6
Hempton Norfk..........105 L6
Hempton Oxon...........57 H2
Hemsby Norfk...........107 K8
Hemswell Lincs..........116 F4
Hemswell Cliff Lincs ... 116 F4
Hemsworth Wakefd......124 C7
Hemyock Devon...........25 H8
Henbury Bristl............38 E5
Hendon Gt Lon...........44 E3
Hendon Sundld..........151 K4
Hendy Carmth............51 H5
Henfield W Susx 19 G3
Hengoed Caerph 37 J2
Hengoed Powys...........68 E4
Hengrave Suffk............77 J2
Henham Essex............60 E3
Heniarth Powys...........82 C2
Henlade Somset...........25 L6
Henley Dorset............14 D2
Henley Somset............26 B5
Henley Suffk...............78 E4
Henley W Susx 30 E6
Henley Green Covtry......86 D6
Henley-in-Arden
  Warwks..................71 L2
Henley-on-Thames
  Oxon....................42 C4
Henley's Down
  E Susx...................20 E3
Henllan Cerdgn 65 K6
Henllan Denbgs 110 E7
Henllys Torfn..............37 K3
Henlow C Beds 75 H6
Hennock Devon...........11 J8
Henny Street Essex.......77 K4
Henryd Conwy...........109 L6
Henry's Moat
  (Castell Hendre)
  Pembks..................49 H3
Hensall N York...........124 F5
Henshaw Nthumb........149 J3

Hensingham Cumb.......136 D4
Henstead Suffk............93 K6
Hensting Hants 29 J6
Henstridge Somset........27 G7
Henstridge Ash
  Somset...................27 G7
Henton Oxon..............58 C7
Henton Somset............26 C3
Henwick Worcs 70 E4
Henwood Cnwll 5 L2
Heol-y-Cyw Brdgnd......36 E4
Hepple Nthumb..........158 C2
Hepscott Nthumb........158 F5
Hepstonstall Calder 122 E5
Hepworth Kirk...........114 D1
Hepworth Suffk...........92 B8
Herbrandston
  Pembks..................48 E6
Hereford Herefs...........69 K6
Hereson Kent..............35 K2
Heribusta Highld 218 B7
Heriot Border 177 L7
Hermiston C Edin........177 G4
Hermitage Border 156 E3
Hermitage Dorset........14 C2
Hermitage W Berk........41 J5
Hermon Carmth...........65 K7
Hermon Pembks...........49 L2
Herne Kent................47 K6
Herne Bay Kent...........47 K6
Herne Hill Gt Lon.........44 F5
Herne Pound Kent........33 H3
Hernhill Kent..............34 E3
Herodsfoot Cnwll...........5 K4
Heronsford S Ayrs 152 D5
Herriard Hants............30 A3
Herringfleet Suffk.........93 K4
Herringswell Suffk........77 G1
Herringthorpe Rothm...115 J3
Herrington Sundld........151 J4
Hersden Kent.............35 G3
Hersham Surrey...........43 J7
Herstmonceux
  E Susx...................20 D3
Herston Ork..............234 c7
Hertford Herts............60 B5
Hertford Heath Herts....60 B5
Hertingfordbury
  Herts....................60 A5
Hesket Bank Lancs......120 F5
Hesket Lane Lancs.......121 J3
Hesket Newmarket
  Cumb...................148 C7
Hesleden Dur............151 K7
Heslington C York 124 F1
Hessay C York............133 H8
Hessenford Cnwll 5 L4
Hessett Suffk..............77 L3
Hessle E R Yk............126 C5
Hessle Wakefd...........124 C6
Hest Bank Lancs.........129 K6
Heston Gt Lon............43 J5
Heston Services
  Gt Lon..................43 J5
Hestwall Ork.............234 b5
Heswall Wirral...........111 J5
Hethe Oxon...............57 L3
Hethersett Norfk..........92 D3
Hethersgill Cumb.........148 E2
Hett Dur..................151 G7
Hetton N York...........131 H7
Hetton-le-Hole
  Sundld..................151 J5
Heugh Nthumb..........158 D7
Heughhead Abers 205 J3
Heugh Head Border 179 H6
Heveningham Suffk.......93 G8
Hever Kent................32 E4
Heversham Cumb........129 K3
Hevingham Norfk........106 E7
Hewas Water Cnwll.........4 F6
Hewelsfield Gloucs........54 E7
Hewish Somset............13 K2
Hewood Dorset...........13 J2
Hexham Nthumb.........150 B3
Hextable Kent..............45 K6
Hexthorpe Donc.........115 K2

Hexton Herts..............59 J2
Hexworthy Cnwll 9 K8
Hexworthy Devon 6 F2
Heybridge Essex...........61 G7
Heybridge Essex...........61 K6
Heybrook Bay Devon 6 D6
Heydon Cambs............76 B6
Heydon Norfk............106 D6
Heydour Lincs...........103 G5
Heylipoll Ag & B 188 C7
Heylor Shet 235 c3
Heysham Lancs...........129 J7
Heyshott W Susx 18 B3
Heytesbury Wilts 27 L3
Heythrop Oxon............57 G3
Heywood Rochdl 122 C7
Heywood Wilts 27 K2
Hibaldstow N Linc.......116 F2
Hickleton Donc 115 J1
Hickling Norfk............107 J7
Hickling Notts...........102 B6
Hickling Green Norfk.. 107 J7
Hickstead W Susx 31 L7
Hidcote Bartrim
  Gloucs...................71 L6
Hidcote Boyce
  Gloucs...................71 L6
High Ackworth
  Wakefd..................124 C6
Higham Barns............114 F1
Higham Derbys...........101 H2
Higham Kent..............33 G4
Higham Kent..............46 B5
Higham Lancs...........122 B3
Higham Suffk..............77 H2
Higham Suffk..............78 B7
Higham Ferrers
  Nhants...................74 D2
Higham Gobion
  C Beds....................59 J2
Higham Hill Gt Lon.......45 G3
Higham on the Hill
  Leics.....................86 E4
Highampton Devon.......10 C4
Highams Park Gt Lon 45 H2
High Ardwell D & G 144 C6
High Auldgirth D & G...154 F5
High Bankhill Cumb......148 F6
High Beach Essex.........60 C7
High Bentham N York..130 C5
High Bickington
  Devon...................23 J7
High Biggins Cumb 130 B4
High Blantyre S Lans...175 J6
High Bonnybridge
  Falk.....................175 L2
High Bray Devon 23 L5
Highbridge Somset 25 L3
Highbrook W Susx 32 C7
High Brooms Kent 33 G5
Highburton Kirk..........123 J7
Highbury Gt Lon..........44 F3
Highbury Somset..........27 G2
High Catton E R Yk.......133 L8
Highclere Hants............41 H8
Highcliffe BCP..............16 B4
High Coniscliffe
  Darltn...................141 G4
High Crosby Cumb 148 E3
High Cross E Ayrs 163 K1
High Cross Hants..........30 B6
High Cross Herts...........60 B4
High Cross Warwks.......71 L2
High Drummore
  D & G...................144 D7
High Easter Essex.........60 F5
High Ellington N York..132 B3
Higher Ansty Dorset.....14 E2
Higher Bartle Lancs.....121 G4
Higher
  Bockhampton
  Dorset...................14 D4
Higher Brixham
  Torbay....................7 L5
High Ercall Wrekin........98 E8
Higher Chillington
  Somset...................13 K1

Higher Folds Wigan 113 G2
Higher Gabwell
　Devon 7 L3
Higher Heysham
　Lancs 129 J7
Higher Irlam Salfd 113 G3
Higher Kinnerton
　Flints 97 L1
Higher Muddiford
　Devon 23 J4
Higher Penwortham
　Lancs 121 G5
Higher Prestacott
　Devon 9 K5
Higher Town Cnwll 4 C6
Higher Town Cnwll 4 H4
Higher Town IoS 2 b1
Higher Walton Lancs .. 121 H5
Higher Walton
　Warrtn 112 E4
Higher Wambrook
　Somset 13 H2
Higher Waterston
　Dorset 14 D4
Higher Wheelton
　Lancs 121 J6
Higher Whitley
　Ches W 112 F5
Higher Wincham
　Ches W 113 G6
Higher Wraxhall
　Dorset 14 B3
Higher Wych Ches W 98 C4
High Etherley Dur 140 F2
Highfield Gatesd 150 E3
Highfield N Ayrs 174 C7
High Garrett Essex 61 J3
Highgate Gt Lon 44 F3
Highgate Kent 33 K6
High Grantley N York .. 132 C5
High Green Norfk 92 D3
High Green Norfk 92 E5
High Green Sheff 115 G3
High Halden Kent 34 B7
High Halstow
　Medway 46 C5
High Ham Somset 26 B5
High Harrington
　Cumb 136 D3
High Harrogate
　N York 132 D7
High Hatton Shrops 98 E7
High Hauxley Nthumb .. 159 G2
High Hawsker N York ... 143 J5
High Hesket Cumb 148 E6
High Hoyland Barns 123 K8
High Hurstwood
　E Susx 32 E7
High Hutton N York 134 B5
High Ireby Cumb 147 M7
High Kilburn N York ... 133 H4
High Lands Dur 140 E3
Highlane Derbys 115 H5
High Lane Stockp 113 L4
High Lanes Cnwll 3 G4
Highleadon Gloucs 55 H4
High Legh Ches E 113 G5
Highleigh W Susx 18 A6
High Leven S on T 141 K5
Highley Shrops 84 C5
High Littleton BaNES ... 38 F8
High Lorton Cumb 137 G3
High Marnham Notts .. 116 D7
High Melton Donc 115 K2
High Mickley
　Nthumb 150 D3
Highmoor Oxon 42 B4
Highmoor Cross
　Oxon 42 B4
Highnam Gloucs 55 H4
High Newport Sundld .. 151 J4
High Newton Cumb 129 J3
High Nibthwaite
　Cumb 129 G2
High Offley Staffs 99 H7
High Ongar Essex 60 E7
High Onn Staffs 84 E1

High Park Corner
　Essex 62 C4
High Pennyvenie
　E Ayrs 163 L7
High Roding Essex 60 F4
High Salvington
　W Susx 18 F4
High Spen Gatesd 150 E3
Highsted Kent 34 B3
High Street Cnwll 4 F5
Highstreet Kent 34 E3
Highstreet Green
　Surrey 31 G4
Hightae D & G 155 J6
Highter's Heath Birm ... 85 J7
Hightown Sefton 111 J2
Hightown Green
　Suffk 77 L4
High Toynton Lincs 118 C7
High Valleyfield Fife .. 176 D2
Highweek Devon 7 J2
Highwood Essex 61 G7
Highwood Hill Gt Lon ... 44 E2
Highworth Swindn 40 D2
High Wray Cumb 137 K7
High Wych Herts 60 D5
High Wycombe
　Bucks 42 E2
Hilborough Norfk 91 J4
Hilcott Wilts 40 C8
Hildenborough Kent 32 F4
Hilden Park Kent 33 G4
Hildersham Cambs 76 D5
Hilderstone Staffs 99 L5
Hilderthorpe E R Yk ... 135 J6
Hilgay Norfk 90 E4
Hill S Glos 38 F2
Hill Warwks 72 F2
Hillam N York 124 D5
Hill Brow Hants 30 C6
Hillbutts Dorset 15 J3
Hill Chorlton Staffs 99 H5
Hillclifflane Derbys ... 100 F3
Hill Common Somset 25 H6
Hilldyke Lincs 104 B3
Hillend Fife 176 F2
Hill End Fife 185 L7
Hill End Gloucs 70 F6
Hillend Mdloth 177 H5
Hillend N Lans 175 L5
Hillesden Bucks 58 B3
Hillesley Gloucs 39 H3
Hillfarrance Somset 25 J6
Hill Green Kent 46 D7
Hillhead Abers 216 B7
Hill Head Hants 17 G2
Hillhead S Lans 165 J2
Hillhead of Cocklaw
　Abers 217 K5
Hillclay Highld 231 H3
Hillingdon Gt Lon 43 H4
Hillington C Glas 174 F5
Hillington Norfk 105 H7
Hillmorton Warwks 87 G8
Hill of Beath Fife 176 F1
Hill of Fearn Highld .. 223 H5
Hillowton D & G 146 D3
Hill Ridware Staffs 100 B8
Hillside Abers 207 H5
Hillside Angus 197 H4
Hill Side Kirk 123 H6
Hills Town Derbys 115 J7
Hillstreet Hants 29 G7
Hillswick Shet 235 c3
Hill Top Sandw 85 H5
Hill Top Wakefd 123 L7
Hillwell Shet 235 c8
Hilmarton Wilts 40 A5
Hilperton Wilts 39 K8
Hilsea C Port 17 J2
Hilston E R Yk 127 G4
Hilton Border 179 H7
Hilton Cambs 75 K2
Hilton Cumb 139 G3
Hilton Derbys 100 E6
Hilton Dorset 14 E2
Hilton Dur 140 F3

Hilton Highld 223 J6
Hilton S on T 141 K5
Hilton Shrops 84 D4
Hilton Park
　Services Staffs 85 G3
Himbleton Worcs 71 G3
Himley Staffs 84 F5
Hincaster Cumb 129 L3
Hinchley Wood
　Surrey 44 D6
Hinckley Leics 86 E5
Hinderclay Suffk 92 B7
Hinderwell N York 143 G4
Hindhead Surrey 30 E4
Hindhead Tunnel
　Surrey 30 E4
Hindley Wigan 112 F1
Hindlip Worcs 70 F3
Hindolveston Norfk ... 106 C6
Hindon Wilts 27 K5
Hindringham Norfk ... 106 B5
Hingham Norfk 92 B3
Hinstock Shrops 99 G7
Hintlesham Suffk 78 C5
Hinton Herefs 69 G6
Hinton S Glos 39 G5
Hinton Shrops 83 H2
Hinton Ampner
　Hants 29 L6
Hinton Blewett
　BaNES 26 E1
Hinton
　Charterhouse
　BaNES 39 H8
Hinton-in-the-
　Hedges Nhants 73 H6
Hinton Martell
　Dorset 15 J2
Hinton on the
　Green Worcs 71 H6
Hinton Parva Swindn .. 40 E4
Hinton St George
　Somset 26 B8
Hinton St Mary
　Dorset 27 H7
Hinton Waldrist
　Oxon 57 G7
Hints Staffs 85 L3
Hinwick Bed 74 D3
Hinxhill Kent 34 D6
Hinxton Cambs 76 C5
Hinxworth Herts 75 J7
Hipperholme Calder .. 123 H5
Hipswell N York 140 F7
Hirn Abers 206 D5
Hirnant Powys 97 G7
Hirst Nthumb 159 G5
Hirst Courtney N York. 124 F5
Hirwaun Rhondd 52 E6
Hiscott Devon 23 J6
Histon Cambs 76 B2
Hitcham Suffk 78 B4
Hitcham Causeway
　Suffk 78 B4
Hitcham Street Suffk 78 B4
Hitchin Herts 59 K3
Hither Green Gt Lon 45 H5
Hittisleigh Devon 11 H5
Hive E R Yk 125 J4
Hixon Staffs 100 A7
Hoaden Kent 35 H3
Hoar Cross Staffs 100 C7
Hoarwithy Herefs 54 D3
Hoath Kent 47 K7
Hobarris Shrops 82 F7
Hobkirk Border 167 J7
Hobson Dur 150 F4
Hoby Leics 102 A8
Hockering Norfk 92 C2
Hockerton Notts 102 B2
Hockley Essex 46 D2
Hockley Heath Solhll ... 85 L8
Hockliffe C Beds 58 F3
Hockwold cum
　Wilton Norfk 91 G6
Hockworthy Devon 25 G7
Hoddesdon Herts 60 B6

Hoddlesden Bl w D 121 L6
Hoddom Cross D & G .. 155 L7
Hoddom Mains
　D & G 155 K7
Hodgeston Pembks 49 H7
Hodnet Shrops 98 E6
Hodsock Notts 115 L4
Hodsoll Street Kent 45 M7
Hodson Swindn 40 D4
Hodthorpe Derbys 115 K6
Hoe Norfk 92 B1
Hogben's Hill Kent 34 D4
Hoggeston Bucks 58 D3
Hoggrill's End
　Warwks 86 B5
Hoghton Lancs 121 J5
Hognaston Derbys 100 E3
Hogsthorpe Lincs 119 H6
Holbeach Lincs 104 B7
Holbeach Bank Lincs .. 104 B6
Holbeach Clough
　Lincs 104 B6
Holbeach Drove
　Lincs 89 K2
Holbeach Hurn Lincs .. 104 C6
Holbeach St Johns
　Lincs 104 B8
Holbeach St Mark's
　Lincs 104 B6
Holbeach St
　Matthew Lincs 104 C6
Holbeck Notts 115 K6
Holberrow Green
　Worcs 71 H3
Holbeton Devon 6 F5
Holborn Gt Lon 44 F4
Holbrook Derbys 101 G4
Holbrook Suffk 78 E6
Holbrooks Covtry 86 D6
Holbury Hants 16 E2
Holcombe Devon 12 B7
Holcombe Somset 26 F2
Holcombe Rogus
　Devon 25 G7
Holcot Nhants 73 L1
Holden Lancs 122 B1
Holdenby Nhants 73 K2
Holder's Green Essex ... 61 G3
Holdgate Shrops 83 L5
Holdingham Lincs 103 H3
Holditch Dorset 13 J2
Holemoor Devon 10 B4
Holford Somset 25 J3
Holgate C York 124 E1
Holker Cumb 129 H4
Holkham Norfk 105 L4
Hollacombe Devon 9 K4
Holland Fen Lincs 103 L3
Holland-on-Sea
　Essex 62 E5
Hollandstoun Ork 234 e3
Hollee D & G 148 A2
Hollesley Suffk 79 H5
Hollicombe Torbay 7 K4
Hollingbourne Kent 33 L3
Hollingbury Br & H 19 J4
Hollingdon Bucks 58 E3
Hollington Derbys 100 E5
Hollington Staffs 100 B5
Hollingworth Tamesd .. 114 A3
Hollinsclough Staffs .. 114 B7
Hollins End Sheff 115 G5
Hollins Green
　Warrtn 113 G4
Hollinswood Wrekin 84 C2
Hollocombe Devon 10 F3
Holloway Derbys 100 F2
Holloway Gt Lon 44 F3
Hollowell Nhants 73 K1
Hollowmoor Heath
　Ches W 112 C7
Hollows D & G 156 C6
Hollybush Caerph 53 J7
Hollybush E Ayrs 163 K6
Hollybush Herefs 70 D6
Hollym E R Yk 127 H5
Holmbridge Kirk 114 C1

Holmbury St Mary
Surrey 31 J3
Holmbush Cnwll...............5 G5
Holmcroft Staffs 99 K7
Holme Cambs...............89 H6
Holme Cumb 129 L4
Holme Kirk 114 C1
Holme N York 132 E3
Holme Notts.................102 D2
Holme Chapel Lancs ...122 C5
Holme Hale Norfk 91 K3
Holme Lacy Herefs.........69 L7
Holme Marsh Herefs.....69 G4
Holme next the Sea
Norfk 105 H4
Holme on the Wolds
E R Yk 126 B2
Holme Pierrepont
Notts 101 L5
Holmer Herefs...............69 K6
Holmer Green Bucks 42 E2
Holme St Cuthbert
Cumb 147 J5
Holmes Chapel
Ches E 113 H7
Holmesfield Derbys 114 F6
Holmeswood Lancs......120 F6
Holmethorpe Surrey....32 B3
Holme upon
Spalding Moor
E R Yk 125 J3
Holmewood Derbys 115 H7
Holmfirth Kirk 123 H8
Holmhead E Ayrs 164 B5
Holmpton E R Yk 127 J5
Holmrook Cumb 136 E7
Holmside Dur..............150 F5
Holne Devon 7 G3
Holnicote Somset 24 E3
Holsworthy Devon 9 J4
Holsworthy Beacon
Devon 9 K3
Holt Dorset 15 J2
Holt Norfk 106 C5
Holt Wilts 39 K7
Holt Worcs 70 E3
Holtby C York 133 K8
Holt End Worcs 71 J1
Holt Heath Worcs.......70 E2
Holton Oxon 57 L6
Holton Somset 27 G6
Holton Suffk 93 J7
Holton cum
Beckering Lincs 117 J5
Holton le Clay Lincs......118 C2
Holton le Moor Lincs ...117 H3
Holton St Mary Suffk...78 C6
Holwell Dorset.............14 D1
Holwell Herts................59 K2
Holwell Leics 102 B7
Holwell Oxon 56 E6
Holwick Dur................139 K2
Holybourne Hants 30 B4
Holyhead IoA 108 C5
Holystone Nthumb 158 B2
Holytown N Lans 175 K6
Holywell C Beds 59 G5
Holywell Cambs...........75 L1
Holywell Cnwll...............4 B4
Holywell Dorset...........14 B2
Holywell Flints 111 G6
Holywell Green
Calder 123 G6
Holywell Lake
Somset 25 H7
Holywell Row Suffk......91 G7
Holywood D & G 155 G6
Holywood Village
D & G 155 G6
Homer Shrops...............84 B3
Homersfield Suffk........93 H6

Homington Wilts 28 C6
Honeybourne Worcs.......71 K5
Honeychurch Devon 10 F4
Honeystreet Wilts 40 C7
Honey Tye Suffk..............77 L7
Honiley Warwks.............86 B8
Honing Norfk 107 G6
Honingham Norfk..........92 D2
Honington Lincs..........102 F4
Honington Suffk............91 K8
Honington Warwks........72 C6
Honiton Devon...............12 F3
Honley Kirk.................123 H7
Hooe C Plym 6 D5
Hooe E Susx..................20 E4
Hoo Green Ches E 113 G5
Hoohill Bpool 120 D3
Hook E R Yk 125 H5
Hook Gt Lon.................44 D7
Hook Hants...................30 B1
Hook Pembks 49 G5
Hook Wilts 40 B4
Hooke Dorset 14 A3
Hook Green Kent..........33 H6
Hook Norton Oxon.......57 G2
Hookway Devon 11 K5
Hooley Surrey...............32 B3
Hoo St Werburgh
Medway 46 C5
Hooton Levitt Rothm ...115 K3
Hooton Pagnell Donc..124 D8
Hooton Roberts
Rothm........................115 J3
Hope Derbys 114 D5
Hope Devon 7 G7
Hope Flints 97 L2
Hope Staffs.................100 C2
Hope Bagot Shrops.......83 L8
Hope Bowdler
Shrops........................83 J5
Hopehouse Border 166 D6
Hopeman Moray 214 E1
Hope Mansell Herefs 54 F4
Hopesay Shrops 83 H6
Hope under
Dinmore Herefs.......69 K4
Hopgrove C York 133 K8
Hopperton N York 132 F7
Hopstone Shrops..........84 D5
Hopton Derbys............100 E2
Hopton Staffs...............99 L7
Hopton Suffk.................92 B7
Hopton Cangeford
Shrops........................83 K7
Hopton Castle
Shrops........................83 G7
Hoptonheath Shrops 83 H7
Hopton on Sea Norfk ...93 L4
Hopton Wafers
Shrops........................84 B7
Hopwas Staffs 85 L3
Hopwood Worcs...........85 J7
Hopwood Park
Services Worcs 85 J8
Horam E Susx...............20 C3
Horbling Lincs.............103 J5
Horbury Wakefd 123 K6
Horden Dur..................151 K6
Hordle Hants................16 C4
Hordley Shrops............98 B6
Horfield Bristl..............38 E5
Horham Suffk 92 E8
Horkesley Heath
Essex...........................62 B3
Horkstow N Linc.........126 B6
Horley Oxon 72 E5
Horley Surrey................32 B5
Hornblotton Green
Somset 26 E5
Hornby Lancs 130 B5
Hornby N York 132 C2
Hornby N York 141 J6
Horncastle Lincs.........118 C7
Hornchurch Gt Lon......45 K3
Horncliffe Nthumb 179 J7
Horndean Border 179 J8
Horndean Hants...........30 B8

Horndon Devon 10 D8
Horndon on the Hill
Thurr 46 A4
Horne Surrey................32 C4
Horner Somset..............24 D3
Horning Norfk 107 H8
Horninghold Leics........88 B4
Horninglow Staffs 100 E7
Horningsea Cambs.......76 C3
Horningsham Wilts......27 J3
Horningtoft Norfk.......105 M7
Horns Cross Devon 22 F6
Hornsea E R Yk 126 F2
Hornsey Gt Lon............44 F3
Hornton Oxon 72 E5
Horra Shet 235 d2
Horrabridge Devon 6 D2
Horringer Suffk..............77 J3
Horrocksford Lancs 121 L2
Horsebridge Devon 6 B2
Horsebridge E Susx 20 C4
Horsebridge Hants 29 G5
Horsehay Wrekin..........84 C3
Horseheath Cambs.......76 E5
Horsehouse N York 131 K4
Horsell Surrey...............43 G8
Horseman's Green
Wrexhm 98 C4
Horsey Norfk 107 K7
Horsey Somset..............25 L4
Horsford Norfk 92 E1
Horsforth Leeds 123 J3
Horsham W Susx..........31 K5
Horsham Worcs.............70 D3
Horsham St Faith
Norfk 92 E1
Horsington Lincs 117 K7
Horsington Somset 27 G6
Horsley Derbys 101 G4
Horsley Gloucs.............39 J2
Horsley Nthumb 150 D2
Horsley Nthumb 157 L3
Horsleycross Street
Essex...........................62 D3
Horsleyhill Border 167 H5
Horsley Woodhouse
Derbys.......................101 H4
Horsmonden Kent.........33 J5
Horspath Oxon 57 L6
Horstead Norfk...........106 F8
Horsted Keynes
W Susx 32 C7
Horton Bucks 58 F4
Horton Dorset 15 J2
Horton Lancs 122 C1
Horton Nhants 74 B4
Horton S Glos................39 H4
Horton Somset 25 L7
Horton Staffs................99 L2
Horton Swans 50 F7
Horton W & M 43 G5
Horton Wilts.................40 B7
Horton Wrekin.............84 C1
Horton-cum-
Studley Oxon 57 L5
Horton Green
Ches W 98 C3
Horton-in-
Ribblesdale
N York 130 F5
Horton Kirby Kent........45 K6
Horwich Bolton...........121 J7
Horwood Devon 23 H6
Hoscote Border 166 F6
Hose Leics 102 B6
Hosh P & K 185 H3
Hoswick Shet 235 c7
Hotham E R Yk 125 L4
Hothfield Kent..............34 C5
Hoton Leics 101 L7
Hough Ches E...............99 G3
Hougham Lincs 102 E4
Hough Green Halton.....112 C4
Hough-on-the-Hill
Lincs 102 F3
Houghton Cambs 75 K1
Houghton Hants 29 G5

Houghton Pembks 49 G6
Houghton W Susx 18 D4
Houghton Conquest
C Beds.........................74 F6
Houghton Green
E Susx 21 H2
Houghton-le-
Spring Sundld 151 H5
Houghton on the
Hill Leics 87 J3
Houghton Regis
C Beds.........................59 G4
Houghton St Giles
Norfk 105 L5
Hound Green Hants......42 B8
Houndslow Border 178 D8
Houndwood Border....179 H5
Hounslow Gt Lon..........43 J5
Househill Highld..........213 L4
Houses Hill Kirk.........123 J6
Housieside Abers 207 G1
Houston Rens 174 D5
Houstry Highld............227 K2
Houton Ork 234 b6
Hove Br & H 19 J5
Hoveringham Notts....102 B3
Hoveton Norfk 107 G8
Hovingham N York 133 K4
How Caple Herefs 54 E3
Howden E R Yk 125 H5
Howden-le-Wear
Dur 150 E7
Howe Highld 231 K3
Howe N York 132 E4
Howe Norfk 92 F4
Howe Green Essex 61 J7
Howegreen Essex..........61 K7
Howell Lincs................103 J4
Howe of Teuchar
Abers.........................216 E5
Howes D & G 147 L2
Howe Street Essex........61 H5
Howe Street Essex........77 G7
Howey Powys................68 B3
Howgate Cumb 136 D3
Howgate Mdloth..........177 H6
Howick Nthumb 169 K5
Howlett End Essex........76 E7
Howley Somset 13 H1
How Mill Cumb 148 E4
Howmore W Isls 233 b7
Hownam Border 168 B5
Howsham N Linc 117 H2
Howsham N York 133 L6
Howtel Nthumb 168 D3
How Wood Herts..........59 J7
Howwood Rens 174 D6
Hoxa Ork 234 c7
Hoxne Suffk 92 E7
Hoy Ork 234 b6
Hoylake Wirral 111 H4
Hoyland Barns 115 G2
Hoylandswaine
Barns.........................114 E1
Hubberston Pembks.....48 E6
Huby N York 123 K2
Huby N York 133 J6
Hucclecote Gloucs 55 K4
Hucking Kent 33 L2
Hucknall Notts 101 K3
Huddersfield Kirk.......123 H7
Huddington Worcs.......71 G3
Hudswell N York 140 E7
Huggate E R Yk 134 D3
Hughenden Valley
Bucks.........................42 E2
Hughley Shrops...........83 L4
Hugh Town IoS 2 b2
Huish Devon 10 D3
Huish Wilts 40 C7
Huish Champflower
Somset 25 G5
Huish Episcopi
Somset 26 B6
Hùisinis W Isls 232 d3
Huisinish W Isls 232 d3
Hulcott Bucks 58 D5

Hulham Devon 12 C5
Hulland Derbys 100 E3
Hulland Ward Derbys .. 100 E3
Hullavington Wilts 39 K4
Hullbridge Essex 46 D2
Hull, Kingston upon
   C KuH 126 D5
Hulme Manch 113 J3
Hulme Staffs 99 L4
Hulme Warrtn 112 E4
Hulme End Staffs 100 C2
Hulme Walfield
   Ches E 113 J7
Hulverstone IoW 16 E5
Hulver Street Suffk 93 K6
Humber Bridge
   N Linc 126 C5
Humberside Airport
   N Linc 126 D7
Humberston NE Lin 118 D1
Humberstone C Leic 87 J3
Humbie E Loth 178 B5
Humbleton E R Yk 126 F4
Humby Lincs 103 G6
Hume Border 167 L2
Humshaugh Nthumb 158 A7
Huna Highld 231 L2
Huncote Leics 87 G4
Hundalee Border 167 K5
Hunderthwaite Dur 140 C3
Hundleby Lincs 118 E7
Hundleton Pembks 49 G7
Hundon Suffk 77 G5
Hundred House
   Powys 68 C4
Hungarton Leics 87 K3
Hungerford Somset 25 G4
Hungerford W Berk 41 G6
Hungerford
   Newtown W Berk 41 G6
Hungerstone Herefs 69 J7
Hunmanby N York 135 H4
Hunningham Warwks ... 72 D2
Hunsbury Hill Nhants ... 73 K3
Hunsdon Herts 60 C5
Hunsingore N York 132 F8
Hunslet Leeds 123 L4
Hunsonby Cumb 149 G7
Hunstanton Norfk 105 G4
Hunstanworth Dur 150 B5
Hunsterson Ches E 99 G4
Hunston Suffk 77 L2
Hunston W Susx 18 B5
Hunstrete BaNES 38 F7
Hunsworth Kirk 123 J5
Hunter's Quay Ag & B .. 173 K3
Huntham Somset 25 M6
Hunthill Lodge
   Angus 196 D3
Huntingdon Cambs 89 J8
Huntingfield Suffk 93 G8
Huntington C York 133 J7
Huntington Ches W 112 B8
Huntington E Loth 178 B4
Huntington Herefs 68 E4
Huntington Staffs 85 H2
Huntingtowerfield
   P & K 185 M3
Huntley Gloucs 55 G4
Huntly Abers 215 L6
Hunton Kent 33 J4
Hunton N York 132 B2
Huntscott Somset 24 E3
Huntsham Devon 24 F7
Huntshaw Devon 23 H6
Huntspill Somset 25 L3
Huntstile Somset 25 K5
Huntworth Somset 25 L4
Hunwick Dur 140 F2
Hunworth Norfk 106 C5
Hurdcott Wilts 28 D5
Hurdsfield Ches E 113 L6
Hurley W & M 42 D4
Hurley Warwks 86 B4
Hurley Common
   Warwks 86 B4
Hurlford E Ayrs 163 L3

Hurn BCP 15 L3
Hursley Hants 29 H6
Hurst Wokham 42 C5
Hurstbourne Priors
   Hants 29 H3
Hurstbourne Tarrant
   Hants 29 G2
Hurst Green E Susx 33 J7
Hurst Green Essex 62 C5
Hurst Green Lancs 121 K3
Hurst Green Surrey 32 D3
Hurst Hill Dudley 85 G5
Hurstpierpoint
   W Susx 19 J3
Hurstwood Lancs 122 C4
Hurtiso Ork 234 c6
Hurworth-on-Tees
   Darltn 141 H5
Hurworth Place
   Darltn 141 H5
Husbands Bosworth
   Leics 87 J6
Husborne Crawley
   C Beds 74 D7
Husthwaite N York 133 H4
Huthwaite Notts 101 J2
Huttoft Lincs 119 G6
Hutton Border 179 J7
Hutton E R Yk 134 F8
Hutton Essex 45 M2
Hutton Lancs 121 G5
Hutton N Som 37 M8
Hutton Buscel N York .. 134 F3
Hutton Conyers
   N York 132 E5
Hutton Cranswick
   E R Yk 126 C1
Hutton End Cumb 148 D7
Hutton Henry Dur 151 K7
Hutton-le-Hole
   N York 133 L2
Hutton Lowcross
   R & Cl 142 D4
Hutton Magna Dur 140 E5
Hutton Roof Cumb 130 B4
Hutton Roof Cumb 148 C7
Hutton Rudby N York .. 141 K6
Hutton Sessay N York .. 133 G4
Hutton Wandesley
   N York 124 D1
Huxham Devon 12 B3
Huxley Ches W 98 D1
Huyton Knows 112 C4
Hycemoor Cumb 128 D2
Hyde Tamesd 113 L3
Hyde Heath Bucks 58 F7
Hyde Lea Staffs 99 K8
Hylands House &
   Park Essex 61 G7
Hyndford Bridge
   S Lans 165 H2
Hynish Ag & B 188 C8
Hyssington Powys 82 F5
Hythe Essex 62 B3
Hythe Hants 16 E2
Hythe Kent 34 F7
Hythe End W & M 43 G6

I

Ibberton Dorset 14 E2
Ible Derbys 100 E2
Ibsley Hants 15 L1
Ibstock Leics 86 E2
Ibstone Bucks 42 C2
Ibthorpe Hants 29 G2
Iburndale N York 143 H5
Ibworth Hants 29 K1
Ichrachan Ag & B 182 E2
Ickburgh Norfk 91 J4
Ickenham Gt Lon 43 H3
Ickford Bucks 57 M6
Ickham Kent 35 G3
Ickleford Herts 59 K2
Icklesham E Susx 21 H3

Ickleton Cambs 76 C5
Icklingham Suffk 91 H8
Ickornshaw N York 122 E2
Ickwell Green C Beds ... 75 G5
Icomb Gloucs 56 E4
Idbury Oxon 56 E4
Iddesleigh Devon 10 E3
Ide Devon 11 K6
Ideford Devon 7 K1
Ide Hill Kent 32 E3
Iden E Susx 21 H2
Iden Green Kent 33 J5
Iden Green Kent 33 K6
Idle C Brad 123 H3
Idless Cnwll 4 C6
Idlicote Warwks 72 C5
Idmiston Wilts 28 D4
Idole Carmth 50 E3
Idridgehay Derbys 100 F3
Idrigill Highld 208 F2
Idstone Oxon 40 E4
Iffley Oxon 57 K7
Ifield W Susx 31 L4
Ifold W Susx 31 G5
Iford BCP 15 L4
Iford E Susx 19 L4
Ifton Mons 38 C3
Ightfield Shrops 98 E5
Ightham Kent 33 G2
Ilam Staffs 100 C3
Ilchester Somset 26 D6
Ilderton Nthumb 168 F5
Ilford Gt Lon 45 H3
Ilford Somset 26 A7
Ilfracombe Devon 23 H2
Ilkeston Derbys 101 J4
Ilketshall St Andrew
   Suffk 93 H6
Ilketshall St
   Margaret Suffk 93 H6
Ilkley C Brad 123 G2
Illand Cnwll 5 L1
Illey Dudley 85 H7
Illogan Cnwll 3 H3
Illston on the Hill
   Leics 87 K4
Ilmer Bucks 58 C6
Ilmington Warwks 72 B5
Ilminster Somset 26 A8
Ilsington Devon 7 H2
Ilston Swans 51 H7
Ilton N York 132 B4
Ilton Somset 25 M7
Imachar N Ayrs 161 L2
Immingham NE Lin 126 F7
Immingham Dock
   NE Lin 126 F7
Impington Cambs 76 C2
Ince Ches W 112 C6
Ince Blundell Sefton .. 111 K2
Ince-in-Makerfield
   Wigan 112 E1
Inchbae Lodge
   Hotel Highld 221 K7
Inchbare Angus 196 F4
Inchberry Moray 215 G4
Incheril Highld 211 G3
Inchinnan Rens 174 E5
Inchlaggan Highld 201 J5
Inchmichael P & K 186 D3
Inchmore Highld 212 E5
Inchnadamph Highld .. 224 F4
Inchture P & K 186 D2
Inchvuilt Highld 211 K6
Inchyra P & K 186 C4
Indian Queens Cnwll 4 E4
Ingatestone Essex 61 G7
Ingbirchworth
   Barns 114 E1
Ingestre Staffs 99 L7
Ingham Lincs 116 F5
Ingham Norfk 107 H7
Ingham Suffk 77 J1
Ingham Corner Norfk. 107 H6
Ingleby Derbys 101 G6
Ingleby Arncliffe
   N York 141 K6

Ingleby Barwick
   S on T 141 K4
Ingleby Greenhow
   N York 142 C6
Ingleigh Green
   Devon 10 E4
Inglesbatch BaNES 39 G7
Inglesham Swindn 56 D7
Ingleston D & G 147 G2
Ingleton Dur 140 F3
Ingleton N York 130 D5
Inglewhite Lancs 121 H3
Ingoe Nthumb 158 C7
Ingol Lancs 121 G4
Ingoldisthorpe Norfk. 105 G6
Ingoldmells Lincs 119 H7
Ingoldsby Lincs 103 G6
Ingram Nthumb 168 F6
Ingrave Essex 45 M2
Ingrow C Brad 122 F3
Ings Cumb 138 C7
Ingworth Norfk 106 E6
Inkberrow Worcs 71 H3
Inkhorn Abers 217 H6
Inkpen W Berk 41 G7
Inkstack Highld 231 J2
Innellan Ag & B 173 K4
Innerleithen Border ... 166 E3
Innerleven Fife 186 F7
Innermessan D & G ... 144 C3
Innerwick E Loth 178 F4
Innesmill Moray 215 G2
Insch Abers 216 C8
Insh Highld 203 J5
Inskip Lancs 120 F3
Instow Devon 23 G5
Intake Sheff 115 H5
Inver Abers 204 F6
Inver Highld 223 J5
Inver P & K 194 F7
Inverailort Highld 190 F1
Inveralligin Highld 210 C3
Inverallochy Abers 217 K2
Inveran Highld 222 D2
Inveraray Ag & B 182 F5
Inverarish Highld 209 J7
Inverarity Angus 196 D7
Inverarnan Stirlg 183 K4
Inverasdale Highld 219 J4
Inverbeg Ag & B 183 K7
Inverbervie Abers 197 K2
Inverboyndie Abers ... 216 C2
Invercreran House
   Hotel Ag & B 191 K6
Inverdruie Highld 203 L3
Inveresk E Loth 177 K4
Inveresragan Ag & B .. 182 E1
Inverey Abers 204 D7
Inverfarigaig Highld .. 202 D2
Inverfolla Ag & B 191 J7
Invergarry Highld 201 L5
Invergeldie P & K 184 F2
Invergloy Highld 201 K7
Invergordon Highld ... 222 F7
Invergowrie P & K 186 F2
Inverguseran Highld .. 200 B4
Inverhadden P & K 193 L5
Inverie Highld 200 B5
Inverinan Ag & B 182 E4
Inverinate Highld 200 E2
Inverkeilor Angus 197 G6
Inverkeithing Fife 176 F2
Inverkeithny Abers ... 216 C5
Inverkip Inver 173 L4
Inverkirkaig Highld ... 224 C4
Inverlael Highld 220 F4
Inverlair Highld 192 E1
Inverliever Lodge
   Ag & B 182 C6
Inverlochy Ag & B 183 H2
Invermark Angus 196 D1
Invermoriston Highld. 202 C3
Invernaver Highld 229 L4
Inverneill Ag & B 172 E3
Inverness Highld 213 G5

Inverness Airport
 Highld.................213 J4
Invernettie Abers.........217 L5
Invernoaden Ag & B.....183 G7
Inveroran Hotel
 Ag & B.................192 D7
Inverquharity Angus 196 C5
Inverquhomery
 Abers.................217 J5
Inverroy Highld 201 K8
Inversanda Highld.........191 J4
Invershiel Highld...........200 E2
Invershin Highld............222 D3
Invershore Highld 231 J8
Inversnaid Hotel
 Stirlg 183 K5
Inverugie Abers.............217 L5
Inveruglas Ag & B 183 K5
Inveruglass Highld..........203 J5
Inverurie Abers..............206 E2
Inwardleigh Devon.........10 E5
Inworth Essex................61 L4
Iochdar W Isls 233 b7
Iona Ag & B..................180 D3
Iping W Susx...................30 D6
iPort Logistics Park
 Donc.................115 L2
Ipplepen Devon 7 J3
Ipsden Oxon..................41 M4
Ipstones Staffs 100 A3
Ipswich Suffk 78 E5
Irby Wirral 111 J5
Irby in the Marsh
 Lincs.................118 F8
Irby upon Humber
 NE Lin.................117 K1
Irchester Nhants 74 D2
Ireby Cumb...................147 M7
Ireby Lancs 130 C4
Ireleth Cumb 128 F4
Ireshopeburn Dur 149 L7
Irlam Salfd 113 G3
Irnham Lincs 103 G7
Iron Acton S Glos............39 G4
Ironbridge Wrekin...........84 C3
Ironbridge Gorge
 Wrekin.................84 C3
Ironmacannie D & G....154 B6
Ironville Derbys..............101 H3
Irstead Norfk.................107 H7
Irthington Cumb............148 E3
Irthlingborough
 Nhants.................74 D1
Irton N York...................134 F3
Irvine N Ayrs..................163 H2
Isauld Highld 230 E3
Isbister Shet..................235 c2
Isbister Shet..................235 d4
Isfield E Susx...................19 L3
Isham Nhants..................88 C8
Isington Hants................30 C3
Islay Ag & B..................171 G4
Islay Airport Ag & B 170 F7
Isle Abbotts
 Somset.................26 A7
Isle Brewers
 Somset.................26 A7
Isleham Cambs 90 F8
Isle of Dogs Gt Lon.........45 G4
Isle of Grain Medway.....46 E5
Isle of Lewis W Isls.........232 f2
Isle of Man IoM 237 c4
Isle of Man
 Ronaldsway
 Airport IoM 237 b7
Isle of Mull Ag & B 181 J1
Isle of Purbeck
 Dorset.................15 J5
Isle of Sheppey Kent......46 F6
Isle of Skye Highld 208 F6
Isle of Thanet Kent.........35 J2
Isle of Walney Cumb....128 E6
Isle of Whithorn
 D & G.................145 K7
Isle of Wight IoW...17 G5
Isleornsay Highld...........199 L3
Isles of Scilly IoS.............2 b1

Isles of Scilly St
 Mary's Airport
 IoS.......................2 b2
Islesteps D & G.............155 G7
Islet Village Guern..........236 d2
Isleworth Gt Lon...........44 D5
Isley Walton Leics 101 H7
Islibhig W Isls.................232 d3
Islington Gt Lon............44 F3
Islip Nhants.....................88 E7
Islip Oxon......................57 K5
Islivig W Isls..................232 d3
Isombridge Wrekin.........83 L2
Istead Rise Kent.............45 M6
Itchen Abbas Hants 29 K5
Itchen Stoke Hants.........29 K5
Itchingfield W Susx.........31 J5
Itteringham Norfk 106 D6
Itton Mons 38 C2
Itton Common Mons.....38 C2
Ivegill Cumb 148 D6
Iver Bucks 43 G4
Iver Heath Bucks............43 G4
Iveston Dur 150 E5
Ivinghoe Bucks...............58 F5
Ivinghoe Aston
 Bucks.................58 F4
Ivington Herefs 69 J3
Ivybridge Devon 6 F5
Ivychurch Kent...............21 K1
Ivy Hatch Kent.................33 G3
Iwade Kent.....................46 E6
Iwerne Courtney
 Dorset.................27 K8
Iwerne Minster
 Dorset.................27 K8
Ixworth Suffk.................77 L1
Ixworth Thorpe Suffk....91 K8

J

Jack-in-the-Green
 Devon.................12 C4
Jackton S Lans 175 G2
Jacobstow Cnwll..............9 G5
Jacobstowe Devon.........10 E4
Jameston Pembks 49 H7
Jamestown Highld.........212 D3
Jamestown W Duns.......174 D3
Janetstown Highld 227 L3
Janetstown Highld 231 L5
Jardine Hall D & G.........155 J5
Jarrow S Tyne................151 H3
Jasper's Green
 Essex.................61 H3
Jawcraig Falk...............175 L4
Jaywick Essex.................62 D5
Jedburgh Border 167 K5
Jeffreyston Pembks........49 J6
Jemimaville Highld 213 H2
Jerbourg Guern..............236 d4
Jersey Jersey..................236 c6
Jersey Airport Jersey...236 b7
Jesmond N u Ty..............151 G2
Jevington E Susx............20 B5
Jockey End Herts............59 H5
Johnby Cumb.................148 D7
John Lennon
 Airport Lpool......112 B5
John o' Groats Highld....231 L2
Johnshaven Abers 197 J3
Johnston Pembks 48 F5
Johnstone D & G 155 M3
Johnstone Rens..............174 D5
Johnstonebridge
 D & G.................155 J4
Johnstown Carmth.........50 E2
Johnstown Wrexhm.......97 L4
Joppa C Edin 177 J4
Joppa Cerdgn.................66 D2
Joppa S Ayrs 163 K5
Jordanston Pembks........64 C7
Joyden's Wood Kent......45 K5
Juniper Nthumb............150 B3
Juniper Green C Edin...177 G5

Jura Ag & B...................171 J2
Jurassic Coast Devon.....13 H4
Jurby IoM......................237 c2

K

Kaber Cumb...................139 H5
Kaimend S Lans 165 J1
Kames Ag & B 173 G4
Kames E Ayrs 164 D4
Kea Cnwll 4 C7
Keadby N Linc...............125 K7
Keal Cotes Lincs 104 B1
Kearsley Bolton 113 H1
Kearsney Kent.................35 H6
Kearstwick Cumb 130 B4
Kedington Suffk..............77 G5
Kedleston Derbys 100 F4
Keelby Lincs..................126 E8
Keele Staffs 99 J4
Keele Services Staffs......99 J4
Keelham C Brad 123 G4
Keeston Pembks..............48 F4
Keevil Wilts....................39 L8
Kegworth Leics 101 J7
Kehelland Cnwll 3 G3
Keig Abers....................206 B2
Keighley C Brad.............122 F3
Keilarsbrae Clacks.........185 J8
Keillour P & K................185 K3
Keilloch Abers...............204 E6
Keils Ag & B..................171 K5
Keinton Mandeville
 Somset.................26 D5
Keir Mill D & G..............154 E4
Keisley Cumb.................139 G3
Keiss Highld...................231 L4
Keith Moray...................215 J4
Keithick P & K................195 K8
Keithock Angus..............196 F4
Keithtown Highld...........212 E3
Kelbrook Lancs..............122 D2
Kelby Lincs....................103 G4
Keld N York....................139 K6
Kelfield N York...............124 F3
Kelham Notts.................102 C2
Kelhead D & G 147 K2
Kellamergh Lancs..........120 E5
Kellas Angus..................187 G1
Kellas Moray..................214 E4
Kellaton Devon 7 J7
Kelling Norfk.................106 C4
Kellington N York...........124 E5
Kelloe Dur.....................151 J7
Kelloholm D & G............164 E6
Kells Cumb....................136 D4
Kelly Devon......................9 K8
Kelmarsh Nhants 87 K7
Kelmscott Oxon..............56 E7
Kelsale Suffk...................79 H2
Kelsall Ches W...............112 D7
Kelshall Herts..................75 K7
Kelsick Cumb.................147 L5
Kelso Border..................167 L3
Kelstedge Derbys...........115 G8
Kelstern Lincs................118 C4
Kelston BaNES...............39 G6
Keltneyburn P & K........194 B6
Kelton D & G..................155 H7
Kelty Fife......................186 B8
Kelvedon Essex...............61 K4
Kelvedon Hatch
 Essex.................60 F7
Kelynack Cnwll................2 C5
Kemback Fife.................187 G4
Kemberton Shrops..........84 D3
Kemble Gloucs................39 M2
Kemerton Worcs.............71 G6
Kemeys
 Commander
 Mons.................53 M6
Kemnay Abers...............206 E3
Kempley Gloucs...............54 F3
Kempley Green
 Gloucs.................55 G3

Kempsey Worcs...............70 F5
Kempsford Gloucs 40 D2
Kempshott Hants............29 L2
Kempston Bed.................74 F5
Kempton Shrops 83 G6
Kemp Town Br & H 19 J5
Kemsing Kent.................32 F2
Kenardington Kent.........34 C7
Kenchester Herefs 69 J6
Kencot Oxon...................56 E6
Kendal Cumb.................129 L2
Kenfig Brdgnd.................36 C4
Kenilworth Warwks........72 C1
Kenley Gt Lon.................32 B2
Kenley Shrops.................83 L4
Kenmore Highld 210 B3
Kenmore P & K..............194 B7
Kenn Devon 11 L7
Kenn N Som...................38 B6
Kennacraig Ag & B........172 D5
Kennall Vale Cnwll...........3 J4
Kennerleigh Devon.........11 J4
Kennet Clacks 176 C1
Kennethmont Abers.....215 L8
Kennett Cambs 77 G2
Kennford Devon 11 L7
Kenninghall Norfk..........92 C6
Kennington Kent.............34 D5
Kennington Oxon............57 K7
Kennoway Fife...............186 F6
Kenny Somset.................25 L7
Kenny Hill Suffk..............90 F7
Kennythorpe N York......134 C6
Kenovay Ag & B.............188 C6
Kensaleyre Highld.........208 F4
Kensington Gt Lon..........44 E4
Kensington Palace
 Gt Lon.................44 E4
Kensworth Common
 C Beds.................59 G4
Kentallen Highld 191 K5
Kentchurch Herefs..........54 B3
Kentford Suffk 77 G2
Kentisbeare Devon 12 D2
Kentisbury Devon 23 K3
Kentish Town Gt Lon......44 F3
Kentmere Cumb 138 C2
Kenton Devon 12 B5
Kenton Gt Lon................44 D3
Kenton N u Ty................150 F2
Kenton Suffk 78 E2
Kenton Bankfoot
 N u Ty.................150 F2
Kentra Highld 190 D3
Kent's Green Gloucs........55 H4
Kent's Oak Hants 28 F6
Kenwyn Cnwll...................4 C6
Keoldale Highld 228 F3
Keppoch Highld.............200 D1
Kepwick N York..............133 G2
Keresley Covtry...............86 D6
Kerrera Ag & B..............182 B2
Kerry Powys.....................82 D5
Kerrycroy Ag & B...........173 J6
Kersall Notts.................116 B8
Kersbrook Devon 12 D5
Kersey Suffk....................78 B5
Kershader W Isls............232 f3
Kerswell Devon 12 D2
Kerswell Green
 Worcs.................70 F5
Kesgrave Suffk................78 F5
Kessingland Suffk...........93 L6
Kestle Cnwll......................4 F6
Kestle Mill Cnwll..............4 D4
Keston Gt Lon.................45 H7
Keswick Cumb...............137 J3
Keswick Norfk 92 E3
Kettering Nhants.............88 C7
Ketteringham Norfk........92 E3
Kettins P & K.................195 K8
Kettlebaston Suffk..........77 L4
Kettlebridge Fife...........186 E6
Kettlebrook Staffs..........86 B3
Kettleburgh Suffk............79 G3
Kettleholm D & G..........155 K6
Kettleshulme Ches E......113 M5

Kettlesing N York 132 C7
Kettlesing Bottom
  N York........................ 132 C7
Kettlestone Norfk.......... 106 A6
Kettlethorpe Lincs........ 116 D6
Kettletoft Ork 234 d4
Kettlewell N York 131 H5
Ketton Rutlnd 88 E3
Kew Gt Lon.....................44 D6
Kew Royal Botanic
  Gardens Gt Lon 44 D5
Kewstoke N Som 37 M7
Kexby C York................ 125 G1
Kexby Lincs.................. 116 E4
Key Green Ches E 113 K8
Keyham Leics.................87 J3
Keyhaven Hants..............16 C4
Keyingham E R Yk........ 127 G5
Keymer W Susx...............19 J3
Keynsham BaNES............38 F6
Keysoe Bed 74 F3
Keysoe Row Bed 74 F3
Keyston Cambs...............88 F7
Keyworth Notts 101 L6
Kibblesworth Gatesd... 151 G4
Kibworth
  Beauchamp Leics......87 K5
Kibworth Harcourt
  Leics...........................87 K5
Kidbrooke Gt Lon..........45 H5
Kidderminster Worcs....84 E7
Kidlington Oxon.............57 J5
Kidmore End Oxon........42 B5
Kidsdale D & G 145 J7
Kidsgrove Staffs 99 J2
Kidwelly Carmth............50 E4
Kiel Crofts Ag & B........ 191 H8
Kielder Nthumb............ 157 G4
Kielder Forest 157 G5
Kiells Ag & B................ 171 H5
Kilbarchan Rens 174 D5
Kilbeg Highld................ 199 K4
Kilberry Ag & B 172 C5
Kilbirnie N Ayrs 174 C7
Kilbride Ag & B 172 C3
Kilbride Ag & B 173 H5
Kilbuiack Moray........... 214 D3
Kilburn Derbys............. 101 G4
Kilburn Gt Lon..............44 E4
Kilburn N York............. 133 H4
Kilby Leics.....................87 J4
Kilchamaig Ag & B 172 D6
Kilchattan Ag & B 173 J7
Kilchattan Ag & B 180 E7
Kilcheran Ag & B.......... 191 G8
Kilchoan Highld........... 189 L4
Kilchoman Ag & B 170 D5
Kilchrenan Ag & B 182 E3
Kilconquhar Fife 187 H6
Kilcot Gloucs 55 G3
Kilcoy Highld............... 212 E4
Kilcreggan Ag & B 173 L3
Kildale N York 142 D5
Kildalloig Ag & B......... 161 J5
Kildary Highld 223 G6
Kildavaig Ag & B 173 G5
Kildavanan Ag & B....... 173 H5
Kildonan Highld........... 227 G4
Kildonan N Ayrs 162 D5
Kildonan Lodge
  Highld....................... 226 F4
Kildonnan Highld 199 G7
Kildrochet House
  D & G........................ 144 C4
Kildrummy Abers 205 K2
Kildwick N York 122 F2
Kilfinan Ag & B 172 F3
Kilfinnan Highld 201 K6
Kilgetty Pembks............49 J6
Kilgrammie S Ayrs 152 F2
Kilgwrrwg Common
  Mons 38 C2
Kilham E R Yk.............. 135 G6
Kilkenneth Ag & B 188 B7
Kilkenzie Ag & B 161 H4
Kilkerran Ag & B 161 J5
Kilkhampton Cnwll..........9 H3

Killamarsh Derbys........ 115 J5
Killay Swans 51 H6
Killearn Stirlg 174 F2
Killen Highld................ 213 G3
Killerby Darltn............. 140 F3
Killerton Devon 12 C3
Killichonan P & K 193 J5
Killiechonate Highld 192 D1
Killiechronan Ag & B .. 190 B7
Killiecrankie P & K...... 194 E4
Killilan Highld.............. 210 E7
Killimster Highld......... 231 K4
Killin Stirlg.................. 184 C2
Killinghall N York 132 D7
Killinghall N Yorks 132 D7
Killington Cumb 130 C2
Killington Lake
  Services Cumb ... 130 B2
Killingworth N Tyne.... 159 G7
Killochyett Border 167 G1
Kilmacolm Inver.......... 174 C4
Kilmahog Stirlg 184 D5
Kilmahumaig Ag & B .. 182 A8
Kilmaluag Highld 218 C6
Kilmany Fife 186 F3
Kilmarnock E Ayrs...... 163 K2
Kilmartin Ag & B 182 B7
Kilmaurs E Ayrs 163 K2
Kilmelford Ag & B 182 B5
Kilmersdon Somset.......27 G2
Kilmeston Hants 29 L6
Kilmichael Ag & B....... 161 H5
Kilmichael Glassary
  Ag & B 182 B8
Kilmichael of
  Inverlussa Ag & B... 172 D2
Kilmington Devon 13 H3
Kilmington Wilts...........27 H4
Kilmington
  Common Wilts 27 H4
Kilmington Street
  Wilts...........................27 H4
Kilmorack Highld......... 212 D5
Kilmore Ag & B............ 182 C3
Kilmore Highld............. 199 K4
Kilmory Ag & B 172 C4
Kilmory Highld............. 190 B3
Kilmory N Ayrs............ 162 B5
Kilmuir Highld............. 208 D5
Kilmuir Highld............. 213 G4
Kilmuir Highld............. 218 B7
Kilmuir Highld............. 223 G6
Kilmun Ag & B 173 K3
Kilnave Ag & B 170 F4
Kilncadzow S Lans...... 176 B8
Kilndown Kent...............33 J6
Kilninver Ag & B 182 B3
Kilnsea E R Yk.............. 127 J7
Kilnsey N York 131 H6
Kilnwick E R Yk........... 126 C1
Kiloran Ag & B 180 E7
Kilpatrick N Ayrs......... 162 A4
Kilpeck Herefs...............54 C3
Kilpin E R Yk............... 125 J5
Kilrenny Fife 187 J6
Kilsby Nhants 73 H1
Kilspindie P & K.......... 186 C3
Kilstay D & G 144 D7
Kilsyth N Lans 175 J3
Kiltarlity Highld 212 D6
Kilton R & Cl............... 142 E4
Kilton Thorpe R & Cl... 142 E4
Kilvaxter Highld........... 218 B7
Kilve Somset..................25 H3
Kilvington Notts.......... 102 D4
Kilwinning N Ayrs....... 163 H2
Kimberley Norfk............92 C3
Kimberley Notts.......... 101 J4
Kimberworth Rothm... 115 H3
Kimblesworth Dur...... 151 G5
Kimbolton Cambs..........75 G2
Kimbolton Herefs..........69 K3
Kimcote Leics................87 H6
Kimmeridge Dorset 15 H6
Kimpton Hants 28 F3
Kimpton Herts...............59 K4
Kinbrace Highld........... 226 F3
Kinbuck Stirlg.............. 185 G6

Kincaple Fife 187 G4
Killay Fife 176 C2
Kincardine Fife 176 C2
Kincardine Highld........ 222 E4
Kincardine Bridge
  Fife............................ 176 C2
Kincardine O'Neil
  Abers......................... 206 B5
Kinclaven P & K 195 J8
Kincorth C Aber........... 207 H5
Kincorth House
  Moray........................ 214 C3
Kincraig Highld............ 203 K4
Kincraigie P & K.......... 194 F6
Kindallachan P & K..... 194 F6
Kinerarach Ag & B...... 172 B7
Kineton Gloucs.............56 C3
Kineton Warwks 72 D4
Kinfauns P & K 186 C3
Kingarth Ag & B 173 J6
Kingcausie Abers 207 G5
Kingcoed Mons 54 B6
Kingerby Lincs............. 117 H3
Kingham Oxon...............56 E3
Kingholm Quay
  D & G........................ 155 G7
Kinghorn Fife 177 H2
Kinglassie Fife 186 D7
Kingoodie P & K 186 E2
Kingsand Cnwll...............6 C5
Kingsbarns Fife 187 K5
Kingsbridge Devon........7 H6
Kingsbridge Somset......24 F4
King's Bromley Staffs... 85 K1
Kingsburgh Highld....... 208 F4
Kingsbury Gt Lon..........44 D3
Kingsbury Warwks........86 B4
Kingsbury Episcopi
  Somset........................26 B7
King's Caple Herefs......54 E3
Kingsclere Hants...........41 K8
King's Cliffe Nhants......88 E4
Kings Clipstone
  Notts......................... 115 L8
Kingscote Gloucs..........39 J2
Kingscott Devon 23 H7
King's Coughton
  Warwks.......................71 J3
Kingscross N Ayrs....... 162 D4
Kingsdon Somset...........26 C6
Kingsdown Kent.............35 K5
Kingsdown Swindn........40 D3
Kingsdown Wilts............39 J6
Kingseat Abers 207 G2
Kingseat Fife 176 F1
Kingsey Bucks................58 C6
Kingsfold W Susx 31 K4
Kingsford C Aber......... 206 F4
Kingsford E Ayrs 174 E8
Kingsgate Kent..............35 K1
Kingshall Street
  Suffk...........................77 K3
King's Heath Birm.........85 J7
Kings Hill Kent..............33 H4
King's Hill Wsall...........85 H4
Kings House Hotel
  Highld....................... 192 D5
Kingshurst Solhll 85 L6
Kingskerswell Devon......7 K3
Kingskettle Fife 186 E5
Kingsland Herefs..........69 J3
Kingsland IoA.............. 108 C5
Kings Langley Herts.....59 H7
Kingsley Ches W.......... 112 D6
Kingsley Hants 30 C4
Kingsley Staffs 100 A3
Kingsley Green
  W Susx........................30 E5
Kingsley Park Nhants...73 L3
King's Lynn Norfk 104 F8
Kings Meaburn
  Cumb......................... 138 E3
King's Mills Guern.........6 b2
Kingsmuir Angus......... 196 D6
Kings Muir Border....... 166 C2
Kingsmuir Fife 187 J5
Kingsnorth Kent............34 D6
King's Norton Birm.......85 J7

King's Norton Leics......87 K4
Kings Nympton
  Devon.........................23 L7
King's Pyon Herefs.......69 J4
Kings Ripton Cambs.....89 J7
King's Somborne
  Hants..........................29 G5
King's Stag Dorset........14 D1
King's Stanley Gloucs...55 J7
King's Sutton Nhants....72 F7
Kingstanding Birm........85 J4
Kingsteignton Devon......7 K2
Kingsthorne Herefs......54 D2
Kingsthorpe Nhants.....73 L2
Kingston Cambs............75 L4
Kingston Cnwll 6 A2
Kingston Devon 6 F6
Kingston Dorset............14 E1
Kingston Dorset............15 H6
Kingston E Loth 178 C3
Kingston IoW.................16 F6
Kingston Kent................35 G4
Kingston Bagpuize
  Oxon..........................57 H7
Kingston Blount
  Oxon..........................58 C7
Kingston Deverill
  Wilts...........................27 J4
Kingstone Herefs..........69 H7
Kingstone Somset.........26 B8
Kingstone Staffs 100 B6
Kingston Lacy
  House &
  Gardens Dorset.......15 J3
Kingston Lisle Oxon 40 F3
Kingston near
  Lewes E Susx 19 K4
Kingston on Soar
  Notts......................... 101 J6
Kingston on Spey
  Moray........................ 215 H2
Kingston Russell
  Dorset........................14 B4
Kingston St Mary
  Somset........................25 K5
Kingston Seymour
  N Som.........................38 B6
Kingston upon Hull
  C KuH 126 D5
Kingston upon
  Thames Gt Lon........44 D6
King's Walden Herts.....59 K4
Kingswear Devon...........7 K5
Kingswells C Aber 207 G4
Kings Weston Bristl......38 D5
Kingswinford Dudley....84 F5
Kingswood Bucks..........58 B4
Kingswood Gloucs........39 H3
Kingswood S Glos.........38 F5
Kingswood Somset........25 H4
Kingswood Surrey.........31 L1
Kingswood Warwks.......71 L1
Kingswood
  Common Staffs........84 E3
Kings Worthy Hants......29 J5
Kingthorpe Lincs......... 117 J6
Kington Herefs..............68 F3
Kington S Glos..............38 F3
Kington Worcs...............71 H4
Kington Langley
  Wilts...........................39 L5
Kington Magna
  Dorset........................27 H6
Kington St Michael
  Wilts...........................39 K5
Kingussie Highld......... 203 H5
Kingweston Somset......26 D5
Kinharrachie Abers 217 H7
Kinharvie D & G 147 G2
Kinkell Bridge P & K.... 185 J4
Kinknockie Abers 217 J6
Kinleith C Edin 177 G5
Kinlet Shrops................84 C7
Kinloch Highld............. 198 F5
Kinloch Highld............. 225 H2
Kinloch Highld............. 229 H5
Kinloch P & K............... 195 J7

Kinlochard Stirlg 184 B6
Kinlochbervie Highld... 228 C4
Kinlocheil Highld 191 J1
Kinlochewe Highld 210 F3
Kinloch Hourn Highld.. 200 E4
Kinlochlaggan Highld.. 202 E7
Kinlochleven Highld... 192 C4
Kinlochmoidart
        Highld............................ 190 E2
Kinlochnanuagh
        Highld............................ 200 B8
Kinloch Rannoch
        P & K........................... 193 L5
Kinloss Moray 214 C3
Kinmel Bay Conwy...... 110 D5
Kinmuck Abers.............. 206 F2
Kinmundy Abers 207 G2
Kinnabus Ag & B 160 B2
Kinnadie Abers.............. 217 H5
Kinnaird P & K............. 194 F5
Kinneff Abers................ 197 K2
Kinnelhead D & G........ 155 H2
Kinnell Angus............... 196 F6
Kinnerley Shrops..........97 M7
Kinnersley Herefs......... 69 G5
Kinnersley Worcs..........70 F5
Kinnerton Powys........... 68 E2
Kinnesswood P & K...... 186 C6
Kinnordy Angus............ 196 B5
Kinoulton Notts 102 B6
Kinross P & K................ 186 B6
Kinrossie P & K............ 186 C2
Kinross Services
        P & K........................... 186 B6
Kinsham Herefs.............. 69 G2
Kinsham Worcs.............. 71 G7
Kinsley Wakefd 124 C7
Kinson BCP 15 K3
Kintail Highld 200 F2
Kintbury W Berk........... 41 G6
Kintessack Moray 214 B3
Kintillo P & K............... 186 B4
Kinton Herefs................ 83 H4
Kinton Shrops................ 98 A8
Kintore Abers............... 206 E3
Kintour Ag & B............ 171 H7
Kintra Ag & B 170 F8
Kintra Ag & B 180 D3
Kintraw Ag & B 182 B6
Kintyre Ag & B 161 J2
Kinveachy Highld......... 203 L2
Kinver Staffs 84 E6
Kippax Leeds................ 124 C4
Kippen Stirlg 184 E7
Kippford D & G............ 146 E4
Kipping's Cross Kent.....33 H5
Kirbister Ork............... 234 b6
Kirby Bedon Norfk.......93 G3
Kirby Bellars Leics..... 102 B8
Kirby Cane Norfk..........93 H5
Kirby Cross Essex.........62 E4
Kirby Grindalythe
        N York......................... 134 D6
Kirby Hill N York......... 132 F5
Kirby Hill N York......... 140 E6
Kirby Knowle N York... 133 G3
Kirby-le-Soken
        Essex.............................62 F4
Kirby Misperton
        N York......................... 134 B4
Kirby Muxloe Leics 87 G3
Kirby Underdale
        E R Yk.......................... 134 C7
Kirby Wiske N York..... 132 E3
Kirdford W Susx 31 G6
Kirk Highld.................. 231 K4
Kirkabister Shet 235 d6
Kirkandrews D & G 146 A5
Kirkandrews upon
        Eden Cumb.................. 148 C4
Kirkbampton Cumb..... 148 B4
Kirkbean D & G............ 147 G3
Kirk Bramwith Donc... 124 F7
Kirkbride Cumb........... 147 M4
Kirkbuddo Angus........ 196 E7
Kirkburn Border.......... 166 D2
Kirkburn E R Yk 134 F7

Kirkburton Kirk........... 123 J7
Kirkby Knows 111 L2
Kirkby Lincs................. 117 H3
Kirkby N York............. 142 C6
Kirkby Fleetham
        N York......................... 141 G7
Kirkby Green Lincs....... 103 H2
Kirkby-in-Ashfield
        Notts 101 J2
Kirkby-in-Furness
        Cumb.......................... 128 F3
Kirkby la Thorpe
        Lincs........................... 103 J4
Kirkby Lonsdale
        Cumb.......................... 130 B4
Kirkby Malham
        N York......................... 131 G7
Kirkby Mallory Leics.......86 F4
Kirkby Malzeard
        N York......................... 132 C5
Kirkbymoorside
        N York......................... 133 L3
Kirkby on Bain Lincs ... 118 C8
Kirkby Overblow
        N York......................... 123 L2
Kirkby Stephen
        Cumb.......................... 139 H5
Kirkby Thore Cumb...... 138 F3
Kirkby Underwood
        Lincs........................... 103 H6
Kirkby Wharf N York... 124 D3
Kirkcaldy Fife............. 186 D8
Kirkcambeck
        Cumb.......................... 148 F2
Kirkchrist D & G.......... 146 B5
Kirkcolm D & G........... 144 B2
Kirkconnel D & G........ 164 E6
Kirkconnell D & G 147 G2
Kirkcowan D & G........ 145 G3
Kirkcudbright D & G... 146 B5
Kirkdale Lpool 111 K3
Kirk Deighton N York... 124 B1
Kirk Ella E R Yk........... 126 C5
Kirkfieldbank S Lans ... 165 G4
Kirkgunzeon D & G..... 146 F2
Kirk Hallam Derbys..... 101 J4
Kirkham Lancs............. 120 F4
Kirkham N York........... 134 B6
Kirkhamgate Wakefd... 123 K6
Kirk Hammerton
        N York......................... 133 G7
Kirkhaugh Nthumb..... 149 H5
Kirkheaton Kirk........... 123 H6
Kirkheaton Nthumb..... 158 C6
Kirkhill Highld 212 E5
Kirkhope S Lans........... 165 J7
Kirkibost Highld 199 H2
Kirkinch P & K............. 195 L7
Kirkinner D & G.......... 145 J5
Kirkintilloch E Duns... 175 H4
Kirk Ireton Derbys...... 100 E3
Kirkland Cumb............. 136 E4
Kirkland D & G............ 154 E4
Kirkland D & G............ 155 H4
Kirkland D & G............ 164 E6
Kirk Langley Derbys.... 100 F5
Kirkleatham R & Cl...... 142 D3
Kirklevington S on T ... 141 K5
Kirkley Suffk.................93 L5
Kirklington N York...... 132 D4
Kirklington Notts........ 102 B2
Kirkliston C Edin......... 176 F4
Kirkmabreck D & G..... 145 K4
Kirkmaiden D & G 144 D7
Kirk Merrington Dur... 141 G2
Kirk Michael IoM........ 237 c4
Kirkmichael P & K....... 195 H4
Kirkmichael S Ayrs..... 163 J7
Kirkmuirhill S Lans 164 F2
Kirknewton Nthumb... 168 D4
Kirknewton W Loth.... 176 F5
Kirkney Abers.............. 215 L7
Kirk of Shotts N Lans... 175 L5
Kirkoswald Cumb........ 148 F6
Kirkoswald S Ayrs....... 163 G5
Kirkpatrick D & G........ 154 F4

Kirkpatrick Durham
        D & G........................... 154 D7
Kirkpatrick-
        Fleming D & G............. 156 B7
Kirk Sandall Donc 124 F8
Kirksanton Cumb......... 128 D4
Kirk Smeaton N York ... 124 D7
Kirkstall Leeds.............. 123 K4
Kirkstead Lincs............. 103 K1
Kirkstile Abers............. 215 L7
Kirkstile D & G............. 156 C4
Kirkstyle Highld........... 231 L2
Kirkthorpe Wakefd 124 B6
Kirkton Abers.............. 206 C1
Kirkton D & G.............. 155 G6
Kirkton Fife................. 186 F3
Kirkton Highld............ 210 C8
Kirkton Highld............ 210 D6
Kirkton P & K.............. 185 K4
Kirkton Manor
        Border.......................... 166 C2
Kirkton of Airlie
        Angus.......................... 195 L6
Kirkton of
        Auchterhouse
        Angus.......................... 196 B8
Kirkton of Barevan
        Highld.......................... 213 K5
Kirkton of Collace
        P & K........................... 186 C2
Kirkton of
        Glenbuchat Abers.. 205 J3
Kirkton of
        Kingoldrum
        Angus.......................... 196 B5
Kirkton of Lethendy
        P & K........................... 195 H7
Kirkton of Logie
        Buchan Abers.......... 217 J7
Kirkton of
        Maryculter Abers... 207 G5
Kirkton of Menmuir
        Angus.......................... 196 E4
Kirkton of Monikie
        Angus.......................... 196 E8
Kirkton of Rayne
        Abers............................ 216 D7
Kirkton of Skene
        Abers............................ 206 F4
Kirkton of Tealing
        Angus.......................... 196 C8
Kirkton of Tough
        Abers............................ 206 C3
Kirktown Abers............ 217 J2
Kirktown Abers............ 217 K4
Kirktown of Alvah
        Abers............................ 216 D3
Kirktown of Bourtie
        Abers............................ 206 F1
Kirktown of
        Fetteresso Abers... 206 F7
Kirktown of
        Mortlach Moray...... 215 H6
Kirktown of Slains
        Abers............................ 217 K8
Kirkurd Border............ 165 M1
Kirkwall Ork................ 234 c6
Kirkwall Airport Ork ... 234 c6
Kirkwhelpington
        Nthumb........................ 158 C5
Kirk Yetholm Border 168 C4
Kirmington N Linc 126 D7
Kirmond le Mire
        Lincs........................... 117 K3
Kirn Ag & B 173 K3
Kirriemuir Angus........ 196 C5
Kirstead Green
        Norfk.............................93 G4
Kirtlebridge D & G 155 M7
Kirtling Cambs..............77 G3
Kirtling Green Cambs...76 F4
Kirtlington Oxon...........57 J4
Kirtomy Highld........... 229 M3
Kirton Lincs................. 104 A5
Kirton Notts................ 116 B7
Kirton Suffk..................78 F6
Kirtonhill W Duns....... 174 D4

Kirton in Lindsey
        N Linc.......................... 116 F2
Kirwaugh D & G.......... 145 J4
Kishorn Highld............ 210 C6
Kislingbury Nhants........73 K3
Kittisford Somset.........25 G6
Kitt's Green Birm..........85 L6
Kittybrewster C Aber.... 207 H4
Kivernoll Herefs...........54 C2
Kiveton Park Rothm.... 115 J5
Knaith Lincs................ 116 D5
Knap Corner Dorset.......27 J6
Knaphill Surrey.............42 F8
Knapp Somset..............25 L6
Knapton C York........... 124 E1
Knapton N York........... 134 D4
Knapton Norfk............ 107 G5
Knapwell Cambs 75 K2
Knaresborough
        N York......................... 132 E7
Knarsdale Nthumb...... 149 H4
Knaven Abers............... 217 G5
Knayton N York........... 132 F2
Knebworth Herts..........59 L4
Knedlington E R Yk..... 125 H5
Kneesall Notts............. 116 B8
Kneeton Notts............. 102 B4
Knelston Swans.............50 F7
Knenhall Staffs..............99 L5
Knightcote Warwks......72 E4
Knightley Staffs............99 J7
Knighton C Leic...........87 H4
Knighton Dorset..........14 C1
Knighton Powys............68 F1
Knighton Somset 25 J3
Knighton Staffs............99 G6
Knighton Staffs............99 H6
Knighton on Teme
        Worcs.............................70 B1
Knightwick Worcs.........70 D4
Knill Herefs...................68 F3
Knipoch Ag & B.......... 182 B3
Knipton Leics............... 102 D6
Kniveton Derbys......... 100 E3
Knock Cumb................ 138 F2
Knock Highld............... 199 K4
Knock Moray............... 215 L4
Knock W Isls................ 232 g2
Knockally Highld........ 227 K3
Knockan Highld.......... 224 F6
Knockando Moray...... 214 F6
Knockbain Highld....... 212 E5
Knockbain Highld....... 212 F3
Knock Castle N Ayrs ... 173 L5
Knockdee Highld........ 231 H4
Knockdow Ag & B....... 173 J4
Knockdown Wilts.........39 J3
Knockeen S Ayrs.......... 153 G3
Knockenkelly N Ayrs... 162 D4
Knockentiber E Ayrs... 163 K2
Knockholt Kent............32 C2
Knockholt Pound
        Kent..............................32 E2
Knockin Shrops............97 M7
Knockinlaw E Ayrs...... 163 K2
Knocknain D & G........ 144 B3
Knockrome Ag & B..... 171 K4
Knocksharry IoM........ 237 b4
Knocksheen D & G...... 153 M5
Knockvennie
        Smithy D & G............. 154 D7
Knodishall Suffk...........79 J3
Knodishall Common
        Suffk.............................79 J3
Knole Somset...............26 C6
Knolls Green Ches E.... 113 J6
Knolton Wrexhm..........98 B5
Knook Wilts...................27 L3
Knossington Leics.........88 B2
Knott End-on-Sea
        Lancs.......................... 120 E2
Knotting Bed...............74 E2
Knotting Green Bed......74 E2
Knottingley Wakefd.... 124 D5
Knotty Ash Lpool........ 112 B3
Knowbury Shrops.........83 L7
Knowe D & G............... 153 G7

Knowehead D & G....... 154 A4
Knoweside S Ayrs.... 163 G6
Knowle Bristl................38 E6
Knowle Devon............11 H5
Knowle Devon............12 C2
Knowle Devon............12 D6
Knowle Devon............23 H4
Knowle Shrops............83 L8
Knowle Solhll.............85 L7
Knowle Somset.........24 E3
Knowlefield Cumb..... 148 D4
Knowle Green Lancs ... 121 J3
Knowle St Giles
  Somset...............13 J1
Knowl Hill W & M..........42 D4
Knowsley Knows......... 112 C3
Knowsley Safari
  Park Knows.............. 112 C3
Knowstone Devon.......24 C6
Knox Bridge Kent........33 K5
Knoydart Highld......... 200 C5
Knucklas Powys.........82 F8
Knuston Nhants........74 D2
Knutsford Ches E...... 113 H5
Knutsford Services
  Ches E............... 113 G6
Krumlin Calder......... 122 F6
Kuggar Cnwll.............. 3 J7
Kyleakin Highld........ 200 B1
Kyle of Lochalsh
  Highld.............. 210 B8
Kylerhea Highld........ 200 B2
Kylesku Highld......... 224 F2
Kylesmorar Highld..... 200 C6
Kyles Scalpay W Isls ... 232 e4
Kylestrome Highld..... 224 F2
Kynnersley Wrekin......84 C1
Kyrewood Worcs.........69 L2

L

La Bellieuse Guern.... 236 d3
Lacasaigh W Isls...... 232 f3
Lacasdal W Isls....... 232 f2
Laceby NE Lin......... 117 K1
Lacey Green Bucks.....58 D7
Lach Dennis Ches W ... 113 G6
Lackford Suffk........77 H1
Lackford Green Suffk...77 H1
Lacock Wilts...........39 K6
Ladbroke Warwks......72 E3
Laddingford Kent.......33 J4
Ladock Cnwll............. 4 D5
Lady Ork............... 234 d4
Ladybank Fife......... 186 E5
Ladygill S Lans....... 165 H4
Lady Hall Cumb........ 128 E3
Ladykirk Border...... 179 J8
Ladywood Birm.........85 J6
Ladywood Worcs.......70 F3
La Fontenelle Guern... 236 e1
La Fosse Guern........ 236 d4
Lag D & G............. 154 F5
Laga Highld........... 190 D4
Lagavulin Ag & B...... 160 C1
Lagg N Ayrs........... 162 B5
Laggan Highld......... 201 L6
Laggan Highld......... 202 F6
Lagganlia Highld...... 203 K5
La Greve Guern........ 236 d2
La Grève de Lecq
  Jersey.............. 236 b5
La Hougue Bie
  Jersey.............. 236 d7
La Houguette Guern... 236 b3
Laid Highld........... 228 F4
Laide Highld.......... 219 L3
Laig Highld........... 199 G7
Laigh Clunch E Ayrs... 174 E8
Laigh Fenwick E Ayrs.. 163 L2
Laigh Glenmuir
  E Ayrs.............. 164 C5
Laighstonehall
  S Lans.............. 175 J7
Laindon Essex 46 B3

Lairg Highld.......... 225 M7
Laisterdyke C Brad 123 J4
Lake IoW...............17 H5
Lake Wilts.............28 C4
Lake District Cumb.... 137 H5
Lake District
  National Park
  Cumb............... 137 H5
Lakenheath Suffk......91 G6
Lakes End Norfk........90 D4
Laleston Brdgnd.......36 D4
Lamarsh Essex.........77 K7
Lamas Norfk.......... 106 F7
Lambden Border....... 167 L2
Lamberhurst Kent......33 H6
Lamberhurst Down
  Kent..................33 H6
Lamberton Border..... 179 K6
Lambeth Gt Lon........44 F4
Lambfair Green Suffk...77 G4
Lambley Notts........ 101 M4
Lambley Nthumb...... 149 H4
Lambourn W Berk......40 F5
Lambourne End
  Essex................45 J2
Lambs Green W Susx....31 L4
Lamerton Devon........ 6 C1
Lamesley Gatesd..... 151 G4
Lamington S Lans..... 165 J3
Lamlash N Ayrs....... 162 C3
Lamonby Cumb........ 148 D7
Lamorna Cnwll.......... 2 E6
Lamorran Cnwll......... 4 D7
Lampeter Cerdgn......66 D5
Lampeter Velfrey
  Pembks...............49 K5
Lamphey Pembks........49 H7
Lamplugh Cumb....... 136 F3
Lamport Nhants........87 L8
Lamyatt Somset........26 F4
Lanark S Lans........ 165 G2
Lancaster Lancs...... 129 K7
Lancaster Services
  Lancs............... 121 G1
Lanchester Dur....... 150 F5
Lancing W Susx........19 G5
L'Ancresse Guern..... 236 d1
Landbeach Cambs.......76 C2
Landcross Devon.......23 G6
Landerberry Abers.... 206 E4
Landford Wilts........28 E7
Land-hallow Highld ... 227 L2
Landimore Swans......50 F6
Landkey Devon.........23 J5
Landore Swans.........51 J6
Landrake Cnwll......... 6 B4
Land's End Airport
  Cnwll................. 2 C5
Landulph Cnwll......... 6 C4
Lane Cnwll............. 4 C4
Laneast Cnwll.......... 9 G7
Lane End Bucks........42 D3
Lane End Wilts........27 J3
Lane Ends Derbys..... 100 E5
Laneham Notts....... 116 D6
Lane Head Devon...... 140 E5
Lanehead Dur......... 149 L6
Lane Head Wsall.......85 H4
Lane Side Lancs...... 122 B6
Langal Highld......... 190 E3
Langaller Somset......25 K6
Langar Notts......... 102 B5
Langbank Rens....... 174 D4
Langbar N York....... 123 G1
Langcliffe N York..... 130 F6
Langdale End N York .. 134 E2
Langdown Hants........16 E2
Langdyke Fife........ 186 E6
Langenhoe Essex......62 B4
Langford C Beds.......75 H6
Langford Devon........12 D2
Langford Essex........61 K6
Langford Notts....... 102 D2
Langford Oxon.........56 E7
Langford Budville
  Somset...............25 H6
Langham Essex.........62 B2

Langham Norfk....... 106 B4
Langham Rutlnd........88 B2
Langham Suffk.........77 L1
Langho Lancs......... 121 K4
Langholm D & G....... 156 C5
Langland Swans.......51 H7
Langlee Border....... 167 H3
Langley Hants.........16 F3
Langley Herts.........59 K4
Langley Kent..........33 K3
Langley Nthumb...... 149 L3
Langley Slough........43 G5
Langley Somset........25 G5
Langley W Susx........30 D5
Langley Warwks........71 L3
Langley Burrell Wilts...39 L5
Langley Green Essex...61 L4
Langley Marsh
  Somset...............25 G5
Langley Mill Derbys.. 101 H3
Langley Park Dur..... 150 F6
Langley Street Norfk... 93 H3
Langley Upper
  Green Essex..........76 C7
Langney E Susx........20 D5
Langold Notts........ 115 L4
Langore Cnwll.......... 9 J7
Langport Somset......26 B6
Langrick Lincs....... 103 L3
Langridge BaNES.......39 H6
Langrigg Cumb....... 147 K5
Langrish Hants........30 B6
Langsett Barns....... 114 E2
Langside P & K....... 185 G5
Langstone Hants.......17 K2
Langthorne N York ... 132 C2
Langthorpe N York ... 132 F6
Langthwaite N York... 140 C6
Langtoft E R Yk...... 134 F6
Langtoft Lincs........89 G2
Langton Dur.......... 140 F4
Langton Lincs........ 118 C7
Langton Lincs........ 118 E7
Langton N York....... 134 C6
Langton by Wragby
  Lincs............... 117 J6
Langton Green Kent....32 F5
Langton Herring
  Dorset...............14 C6
Langton Matravers
  Dorset...............15 J6
Langtree Devon........10 C2
Langwathby Cumb..... 148 F7
Langwell House
  Highld.............. 227 K4
Langwith Derbys..... 115 K7
Langwith Junction
  Derbys.............. 115 K7
Langworth Lincs...... 117 H6
Lanhydrock House
  & Gardens Cnwll...... 5 H3
Lanivet Cnwll.......... 5 G3
Lanlivery Cnwll........ 5 G4
Lanner Cnwll........... 3 J4
Lanreath Cnwll......... 5 J4
Lansallos Cnwll........ 5 J5
Lanteglos Cnwll........ 8 E7
Lanteglos Highway
  Cnwll................. 5 J5
Lanton Border........ 167 J5
Lanton Nthumb....... 168 D3
La Passee Guern...... 236 d2
Lapford Devon.........11 H3
Laphroaig Ag & B..... 160 C1
Lapley Staffs.........84 F2
La Pulente Jersey.... 236 a7
Lapworth Warwks......71 L1
Larachbeg Highld..... 190 E6
Larbert Falk......... 176 B3
Largie Abers......... 216 B7
Largiemore Ag & B.... 172 F2
Largoward Fife....... 187 H5
Largs N Ayrs......... 173 L6
Largybeg N Ayrs...... 162 D5
Largymore N Ayrs..... 162 D4
Larkfield Inver...... 173 L4
Larkfield Kent.........33 J2

Larkhall S Lans...... 175 K7
Larkhill Wilts........28 C3
Larling Norfk.........92 B5
La Rocque Jersey..... 236 e8
La Rousaillerie
  Guern.............. 236 d2
Lartington Dur....... 140 C4
Lasham Hants..........30 A3
Lasswade Mdloth..... 177 J5
Lastingham N York ... 133 L2
Latchford Warrtn..... 112 F4
Latchingdon Essex......61 L7
Latchley Cnwll......... 6 B2
Lathbury M Keyn.......74 C5
Latheron Highld...... 227 L2
Latheronwheel
  Highld.............. 227 L3
Lathones Fife........ 187 H5
Latimer Bucks.........59 G7
Latteridge S Glos......38 F4
Lattiford Somset......27 G6
Latton Wilts..........40 C2
Lauder Border........ 178 C8
Laugharne Carmth......50 C4
Laughterton Lincs ... 116 D6
Laughton E Susx.......20 A3
Laughton Leics........87 J5
Laughton Lincs....... 103 H6
Laughton Lincs....... 116 D3
Laughton-en-le-
  Morthen Rothm..... 115 K4
Launceston Cnwll....... 9 J7
Launton Oxon..........57 L4
Laurencekirk Abers... 197 H3
Laurieston D & G..... 146 B3
Laurieston Falk...... 176 B3
Lavendon M Keyn.......74 D4
Lavenham Suffk........77 K5
Lavernock V Glam......37 J6
Laversdale Cumb..... 148 E3
Laverstock Wilts......28 D5
Laverstoke Hants......29 J2
Laverton Gloucs.......71 J7
Laverton N York...... 132 C5
Laverton Somset......27 H2
La Villette Guern.... 236 d4
Lavister Wrexhm.......98 A2
Law S Lans........... 175 L7
Lawers P & K......... 193 L7
Lawford Essex.........62 C2
Lawford Somset........25 H4
Law Hill S Lans...... 175 L7
Lawhitton Cnwll........ 9 J7
Lawkland N York...... 130 E6
Lawrence Weston
  Bristl...............38 D5
Lawrenny Pembks.......49 H6
Lawshall Suffk........77 K4
Laxay W Isls......... 232 f3
Laxdale W Isls....... 232 f2
Laxey IoM............ 237 d4
Laxfield Suffk........93 G8
Laxford Bridge
  Highld.............. 228 C6
Laxo Shet............ 235 d4
Laxton E R Yk........ 125 J5
Laxton Nhants.........88 D4
Laxton Notts......... 116 B7
Laycock C Brad....... 122 F3
Layer Breton Essex....61 M4
Layer-de-la-Haye
  Essex................62 A4
Layer Marney Essex....61 L4
Layham Suffk..........78 B6
Laymore Dorset........13 K2
Laytham E R Yk....... 125 H3
Lazonby Cumb......... 148 F6
Lea Derbys........... 101 G2
Lea Herefs............54 F4
Lea Lincs............ 116 D4
Lea Shrops............83 G5
Lea Wilts.............39 L3
Leachkin Highld...... 212 F5
Leadburn Border...... 177 H7
Leadenham Lincs...... 102 F3
Leaden Roding Essex...60 F5
Leadgate Dur......... 150 E5

Leadhills S Lans 165 G6
Leafield Oxon........56 F5
Leagrave Luton.............59 H4
Leake Common
  Side Lincs......... 104 C3
Lealholm N York.......142 F5
Lealt Highld..........209 H3
Lea Marston Warwks......86 B5
Leamington
  Hastings Warwks.......72 F2
Leamington Spa
  Warwks...........72 D2
Leap Cross E Susx 20 C4
Leasgill Cumb..........129 K3
Leasingham Lincs......103 H3
Leasingthorne Dur.....141 G2
Leatherhead Surrey....31 K1
Leathley N York.............123 J2
Leaton Shrops.........98 C8
Leaveland Kent........34 D4
Leavenheath Suffk....77 L6
Leavening N York.....134 C6
Leaves Green Gt Lon...45 H7
Lebberston N York....135 G3
Le Bigard Guern.......236 c4
Le Bourg Guern........236 c4
Le Bourg Jersey.......236 e8
Lechlade on
  Thames Gloucs........56 E7
Lecht Gruinart
  Ag & B............170 E5
Leck Lancs.............130 C4
Leckbuie P & K........193 L7
Leckford Hants.........29 G4
Leckhampstead
  Bucks............73 K6
Leckhampstead
  W Berk............41 H5
Leckhampstead
  Thicket W Berk..........41 H5
Leckhampton Gloucs....55 L4
Leckmelm Highld......220 F4
Leconfield E R Yk....126 C2
Ledaig Ag & B........191 H8
Ledburn Bucks.........58 E4
Ledbury Herefs........70 C6
Ledgemoor Herefs.....69 H4
Ledmore Highld........224 F6
Ledsham Leeds........124 C4
Ledston Leeds.........124 C5
Ledwell Oxon..........57 H3
Lee Devon.............23 H3
Lee Gt Lon............45 H5
Leebotwood Shrops....83 J4
Lee Brockhurst
  Shrops............98 D6
Leece Cumb...........128 F5
Lee Chapel Essex......46 B3
Lee Clump Bucks......58 E6
Leeds Kent............33 L3
Leeds Leeds..........123 K4
Leeds Bradford
  Airport Leeds......123 J3
Leeds Castle Kent.......33 L3
Leedstown Cnwll.........3 G4
Leek Staffs..........99 M2
Leek Wootton
  Warwks...........72 C2
Lee Mill Devon........6 E5
Leeming N York......132 D2
Leeming Bar N York...132 D2
Lee-on-the-Solent
  Hants............17 G3
Lees Derbys.........100 E5
Lees Oldham..........113 L2
Lees Green Derbys...100 E5
Leesthorpe Leics......87 L2
Leeswood Flints......97 K1
Leetown P & K........186 C3
Leftwich Ches W......112 F6
Legbourne Lincs......118 E5
Legerwood Border......167 J2
Legoland W & M........42 F5
Le Gron Guern........236 c3
Legsby Lincs.........117 J4
Le Haguais Jersey....236 d8
Le Hocq Jersey.......236 d8

Leicester C Leic.......87 H3
Leicester Forest
  East Services
  Leics.............87 G3
Leigh Dorset..........14 C2
Leigh Gloucs..........55 K3
Leigh Kent............32 F4
Leigh Surrey..........31 L3
Leigh Wigan.........112 F2
Leigh Wilts...........40 B3
Leigh Worcs...........70 D4
Leigh Beck Essex......46 D4
Leigh Delamere
  Wilts.............39 K5
Leigh Delamere
  Services Wilts......39 K5
Leigh Green Kent......34 B7
Leigh Knoweglass
  S Lans...........175 H7
Leigh-on-Sea Sthend..46 D3
Leigh Park Dorset....15 J3
Leigh Park Hants.....17 K2
Leigh Sinton Worcs...70 D4
Leighswood Wsall.....85 J3
Leighterton Gloucs...39 J3
Leighton Powys.......82 E3
Leighton Shrops......84 B3
Leighton
  Bromswold
  Cambs............89 G7
Leighton Buzzard
  C Beds............58 F3
Leigh upon Mendip
  Somset...........27 G3
Leigh Woods N Som....38 E6
Leinthall Earls
  Herefs...........69 J2
Leinthall Starkes
  Herefs...........69 J1
Leintwardine Herefs..83 H8
Leire Leics...........87 G5
Leiston Suffk.........79 J3
Leith C Edin.........177 H3
Leitholm Border.....168 B1
Lelant Cnwll...........2 F4
Lelley E R Yk........126 F4
Lempitlaw Border....168 B3
Lemreway W Isls.....232 f3
Lemsford Herts.......59 L5
Lenchwick Worcs......71 J5
Lendalfoot S Ayrs...152 D4
Lendrick Stirlg.....184 C6
Lendrum Terrace
  Abers............217 L6
Lenham Kent..........34 B4
Lenham Heath Kent...34 B5
Lenie Highld........202 D1
Lennel Border.......168 C2
Lennox Plunton
  D & G............146 A5
Lennoxtown E Duns...175 H3
Lenton C Nott.......101 K5
Lenton Lincs........103 G6
Lenwade Norfk......106 D8
Lenzie E Duns.......175 H4
Leochel-Cushnie
  Abers............205 L4
Leominster Herefs....69 K3
Leonard Stanley
  Gloucs...........55 J7
Leoville Jersey......236 b6
Lephin Highld.......208 B4
Leppington N York...134 B7
Lepton Kirk.........123 J7
Lerags Ag & B.......182 B3
L'Erée Guern........236 b3
Lerryn Cnwll..........5 J4
Lerwick Shet........235 d6
Les Arquets Guern...236 b3
Lesbury Nthumb......169 a6
Les Hubits Guern....236 d3
Leslie Abers........206 B1
Leslie Fife.........186 D6
Les Lohiers Guern...236 c3
Lesmahagow S Lans...164 F2
Les Murchez Guern...236 c4
Lesnewth Cnwll........8 F6

Les Nicolles Guern......236 c4
Les Quartiers Guern......236 d2
Les Quennevais
  Jersey...........236 b7
Les Sages Guern.....236 b3
Lessingham Norfk....107 H6
Lessonhall Cumb.....147 L5
Les Villets Guern...236 c4
Leswalt D & G.......144 B3
L'Etacq Jersey......236 a6
Letchmore Heath
  Herts.............43 J2
Letchworth Garden
  City Herts........59 L2
Letcombe Bassett
  Oxon.............41 G4
Letcombe Regis
  Oxon.............41 G3
Letham Angus.......196 E6
Letham Border......167 K7
Letham Falk.........176 B2
Letham Fife........186 E4
Letham Grange
  Angus............197 G7
Lethenty Abers.....206 B2
Lethenty Abers.....216 F6
Letheringham Suffk...78 F3
Letheringsett Norfk.106 C5
Lettaford Devon......9 L7
Letterewe Highld....219 L7
Letterfearn Highld..200 D2
Letterfinlay Lodge
  Hotel Highld.....201 K6
Lettermorar Highld..199 M7
Letters Highld......220 F4
Lettershaw S Lans...165 H5
Letterston Pembks....48 F2
Lettoch Highld......204 C2
Lettoch Highld......214 D7
Letton Herefs.......69 G5
Letty Green Herts....59 M5
Letwell Rothm......115 K4
Leuchars Fife......187 G3
Leumrabhagh W Isls..232 f3
Leurbost W Isls.....232 f3
Levedale Staffs......84 F1
Leven E R Yk.......126 D2
Leven Fife.........186 F7
Levens Cumb.........129 K3
Levens Green Herts...60 B4
Levenshulme Manch...113 K3
Levenwick Shet......235 c7
Leverburgh W Isls...232 d5
Leverington Cambs....90 C2
Leverstock Green
  Herts.............59 H6
Leverton Lincs......104 C3
Le Villocq Guern....236 c2
Levington Suffk......78 F6
Levisham N York....134 C2
Lew Oxon............56 F6
Lewannick Cnwll......9 H8
Lewdown Devon.......10 C7
Lewes E Susx........19 L4
Leweston Pembks.....48 F3
Lewisham Gt Lon....45 G5
Lewiston Highld....212 D8
Lewistown Brdgnd....36 E3
Lewknor Oxon........42 B2
Lewson Street Kent..34 C3
Lewtrenchard Devon..10 C7
Lexden Essex........62 A3
Lexworthy Somset....25 K4
Leybourne Kent......33 H2
Leyburn N York.....131 L2
Leygreen Herts......59 K3
Ley Hill Bucks......59 G7
Leyland Lancs......121 H6
Leylodge Abers.....206 E3
Leys Abers.........217 J4
Leys P & K.........195 K8
Leysdown-on-Sea
  Kent.............47 G6
Leysmill Angus.....197 G6
Leys of Cossans
  Angus............196 C6
Leysters Herefs.....69 L2
Leyton Gt Lon.......45 G3

Leytonstone Gt Lon 45 H3
Lezant Cnwll..........5 M1
Lhanbryde Moray 215 G3
Libanus Powys........52 F3
Libberton S Lans....165 J2
Liberton C Edin.....177 J4
Lichfield Staffs.....85 K2
Lickey Worcs.........85 H7
Lickey End Worcs....85 H8
Lickfold W Susx......30 F6
Liddesdale Highld..190 F4
Liddington Swindn...40 E4
Lidgate Suffk........77 G3
Lidlington C Beds...74 E6
Liff Angus.........186 E2
Lifford Birm.........85 J7
Lifton Devon.........9 K7
Liftondown Devon.....9 K7
Lighthorne Warwks...72 D4
Lighthorne Heath
  Warwks...........72 D4
Lightwater Surrey...42 F7
Lightwater Valley
  Theme Park
  N York..........132 D4
Lightwood C Stke....99 L4
Lilbourne Nhants....87 H7
Lilleshall Wrekin...84 D1
Lilley Herts........59 J3
Lilliesleaf Border.167 H4
Lillingstone Dayrell
  Bucks............73 K6
Lillingstone Lovell
  Bucks............73 K6
Lillington Dorset...26 F8
Lilliput BCP........15 K4
Lilstock Somset.....25 J3
Limbury Luton.......59 H3
Limekilnburn S Lans.175 J7
Limekilns Fife.....176 E2
Limerigg Falk......176 B4
Limerstone IoW......16 E6
Lime Street Worcs...55 J2
Limington Somset....26 D6
Limmerhaugh E Ayrs.164 C4
Limpenhoe Norfk.....93 H3
Limpley Stoke Wilts..39 H7
Limpsfield Surrey...32 D3
Limpsfield Chart
  Surrey...........32 D3
Linby Notts........101 K3
Linchmere W Susx....30 E5
Lincluden D & G....155 G6
Lincoln Lincs......116 F7
Lincomb Worcs.......70 E2
Lindale Cumb.......129 J4
Lindal in Furness
  Cumb............128 F4
Lindfield W Susx....32 C7
Lindford Hants......30 D4
Lindley Kirk.......123 G6
Lindores Fife......186 D4
Lindridge Worcs.....70 C2
Lindsell Essex......61 G3
Lindsey Suffk.......77 L5
Lindsey Tye Suffk...78 B5
Lingdale R & Cl....142 E4
Lingen Herefs.......69 G2
Lingfield Surrey....32 C4
Lingwood Norfk......93 H2
Liniclate W Isls...233 b7
Linicro Highld.....218 B7
Linkend Worcs.......55 J2
Linkenholt Hants....41 G8
Linkinhorne Cnwll....5 L2
Linktown Fife......177 J1
Linkwood Moray.....214 F3
Linley Shrops.......83 G5
Linley Green Herefs.70 C4
Linlithgow W Loth..176 D3
Linsidemore Highld.222 D2
Linslade C Beds.....58 E3
Linstead Parva Suffk.93 G7
Linstock Cumb......148 D4
Linthurst Worcs.....85 H8
Linthwaite Kirk....123 G7
Lintlaw Border.....179 H6

Lintmill Moray 215 L2
Linton Border 168 B4
Linton Cambs 76 E5
Linton Derbys................. 86 C1
Linton Herefs.................. 54 F3
Linton Kent....................... 33 K3
Linton Leeds 124 B2
Linton N York............... 131 J6
Linton Hill Herefs......... 54 F3
Linton-on-Ouse
    N York...................... 133 G7
Linwood Lincs............... 117 J4
Linwood Rens............... 174 E5
Lionacleit W Isls......... 233 b7
Lional W Isls................ 232 g1
Liphook Hants 30 D5
Liscard Wirral 111 J3
Liscombe Somset......... 24 D5
Liskeard Cnwll 5 K3
Lismore Ag & B........... 191 G7
Liss Hants 30 C5
Lissett E R Yk............... 135 H7
Lissington Lincs........... 117 J5
Lisvane Cardif................ 37 J4
Liswerry Newpt............ 37 M3
Litcham Norfk.............. 105 L8
Litchborough Nhants.... 73 J4
Litchfield Hants 29 J2
Litherland Sefton......... 111 K2
Litlington Cambs........... 75 K6
Litlington E Susx........... 20 B5
Little Abington
    Cambs...................... 76 D5
Little Addington
    Nhants...................... 88 D8
Little Airies D & G 145 J5
Little Alne Warwks....... 71 K3
Little Altcar Sefton...... 111 J1
Little Amwell Herts 60 B5
Little Aston Staffs....... 85 K4
Little Ayton N York..... 142 C5
Little Baddow Essex...... 61 J6
Little Badminton
    S Glos...................... 39 J4
Little Bampton Cumb .. 148 A4
Little Bardfield Essex.... 61 G2
Little Barford Bed........ 75 H3
Little Barningham
    Norfk...................... 106 D5
Little Barrington
    Gloucs....................... 56 D5
Little Barrow Ches W... 112 C7
Little Bavington
    Nthumb.................... 158 C6
Little Bedwyn Wilts........ 40 F7
Little Bentley Essex...... 62 D3
Little Berkhamsted
    Herts........................ 59 M6
Little Billing Nhants....74 B3
Little Billington
    C Beds...................... 58 F4
Little Birch Herefs........ 54 D2
Little Blakenham
    Suffk......................... 78 D5
Little Blencow Cumb ... 148 E7
Little Bognor W Susx..... 31 G7
Little Bollington
    Ches W................... 113 G4
Little Bookham
    Surrey....................... 31 J1
Littleborough Notts..... 116 D5
Littleborough Rochdl.. 122 D7
Littlebourne Kent......... 35 G3
Little Bourton Oxon..... 72 F5
Little Braxted Essex...... 61 K5
Little Brechin Angus.... 196 F4
Littlebredy Dorset........ 14 B5
Little Brickhill
    M Keyn..................... 58 E2
Little Brington
    Nhants...................... 73 J2
Little Bromley Essex..... 62 C3
Little Budworth
    Ches W.................... 112 E7
Littleburn Highld......... 212 F4
Little Burstead Essex.... 46 A2
Littlebury Essex 76 D6

Littlebury Green
    Essex........................ 76 C6
Little Bytham Lincs..... 103 G8
Little Carlton Lincs...... 118 E4
Little Casterton
    Rutlnd....................... 88 E2
Little Cawthorpe
    Lincs....................... 118 E5
Little Chalfont Bucks.... 43 G2
Little Chart Kent.......... 34 C5
Little Chesterford
    Essex........................ 76 D6
Little Cheverell Wilts..... 27 M2
Little Chishill Cambs..... 76 B6
Little Clacton Essex..... 62 E4
Little Clifton Cumb..... 136 E2
Little Coates NE Lin.... 127 G8
Little Comberton
    Worcs....................... 71 G5
Little Common
    E Susx....................... 20 E4
Little Compton
    Warwks..................... 56 E3
Little Cornard Suffk...... 77 K6
Little Cowarne
    Herefs....................... 69 L4
Little Coxwell Oxon...... 40 F2
Little Crakehall
    N York..................... 132 C2
Little Cressingham
    Norfk........................ 91 K4
Little Crosby Sefton.... 111 K2
Little Cubley Derbys 100 D5
Little Dalby Leics......... 87 L2
Littledean Gloucs......... 54 F5
Little Dewchurch
    Herefs....................... 54 D2
Little Ditton Cambs....... 76 F3
Little Downham
    Cambs....................... 90 D6
Little Driffield E R Yk... 134 F7
Little Dunham Norfk..... 91 K2
Little Dunkeld P & K... 195 G7
Little Dunmow
    Essex........................ 61 G4
Little Durnford Wilts..... 28 C5
Little Easton Essex....... 60 F3
Little Eaton Derbys 101 G4
Little Ellingham
    Norfk........................ 92 B4
Little Everdon Nhants.... 73 H3
Little Eversden
    Cambs....................... 75 L4
Little Faringdon
    Oxon........................ 56 E7
Little Fencote N York.. 132 D2
Little Fenton N York.... 124 D4
Littleferry Highld........ 223 H3
Little Fransham
    Norfk........................ 91 K2
Little Gaddesden
    Herts......................... 59 G5
Little Glemham Suffk.... 79 H3
Little Gorsley Herefs..... 55 G3
Little Gransden
    Cambs....................... 75 J4
Little Green Somset....... 27 G2
Little Hadham Herts...... 60 C4
Little Hale Lincs.......... 103 J4
Little Hallam Derbys.. 101 J4
Little Hallingbury
    Essex........................ 60 D4
Littleham Devon........... 12 D6
Littleham Devon........... 23 G6
Littlehampton
    W Susx....................... 18 D5
Little Harrowden
    Nhants...................... 74 C1
Little Haseley Oxon....... 57 M7
Little Haven Pembks..... 48 E5
Littlehaven W Susx....... 31 K5
Little Hay Staffs........... 85 K3
Little Haywood Staffs.. 100 A7
Littlehempston
    Devon......................... 7 J4
Little Hereford
    Herefs....................... 69 K2

Little Horkesley
    Essex........................ 62 A2
Little Hormead Herts.... 60 C3
Little Horsted E Susx.... 19 M3
Little Horton C Brad 123 H4
Little Horwood Bucks.... 58 C2
Little Houghton
    Barns....................... 115 H1
Little Houghton
    Nhants...................... 74 B3
Little Hucklow
    Derbys..................... 114 D5
Little Hutton N York 133 G4
Little Irchester
    Nhants...................... 74 C2
Little Keyford Somset.... 27 H3
Little Kimble Bucks....... 58 D6
Little Kineton
    Warwks..................... 72 D4
Little Kingshill Bucks.... 58 E7
Little Knox D & G....... 146 E3
Little Langdale
    Cumb...................... 137 J6
Little Langford Wilts..... 28 B4
Little Leigh Ches W 112 F6
Little Leighs Essex........ 61 H5
Little Lever Bolton...... 121 L8
Little Linford M Keyn.... 74 B5
Little Load Somset........ 26 C6
Little London Cambs..... 90 B4
Little London E Susx...... 20 C2
Little London Hants...... 29 G2
Little London Hants...... 41 L8
Little Longstone
    Derbys..................... 114 D6
Little Maplestead
    Essex........................ 77 J7
Little Marcle Herefs...... 70 C7
Little Marlow Bucks...... 42 E3
Little Massingham
    Norfk...................... 105 J7
Little Melton Norfk....... 92 E3
Littlemill Abers............ 205 H6
Littlemill Highld.......... 213 L4
Little Milton Oxon........ 57 L7
Little Missenden
    Bucks....................... 58 F7
Littlemore Oxon............ 57 K7
Little Musgrave
    Cumb...................... 139 H5
Little Ness Shrops......... 98 B8
Little Newcastle
    Pembks..................... 49 G2
Little Newsham Dur 140 E4
Little Norton Somset..... 26 C7
Little Oakley Essex........ 62 F3
Little Oakley Nhants..... 88 C6
Little Orton Cumb....... 148 C4
Littleover C Derb......... 101 G5
Little Packington
    Warwks..................... 86 B6
Little Paxton Cambs..... 75 H3
Little Petherick
    Cnwll........................ 4 E2
Little Plumstead
    Norfk........................ 93 G2
Little Ponton Lincs...... 102 F6
Littleport Cambs.......... 90 E6
Little Preston Nhants.... 73 H4
Little Raveley Cambs..... 89 J7
Little Reedness
    E R Yk...................... 125 J6
Little Ribston N York.... 132 F8
Little Rissington
    Gloucs...................... 56 D4
Little Rollright Oxon...... 56 F3
Little Ryburgh Norfk.... 106 A6
Little Salkeld Cumb..... 148 F7
Little Sampford
    Essex........................ 76 F7
Little Saughall
    Ches W.................... 111 K7
Little Saxham Suffk....... 77 H2
Little Scatwell Highld.. 212 B3
Little Shelford
    Cambs....................... 76 C4

Little Singleton
    Lancs....................... 120 E3
Little Skipwith N York.. 125 G3
Little Smeaton
    N York..................... 124 D6
Little Snoring Norfk.... 106 A6
Little Sodbury S Glos.... 39 H4
Little Somborne
    Hants........................ 29 G5
Little Somerford
    Wilts......................... 39 L4
Little Soudley Shrops.... 99 G6
Little Stainton Darltn .. 141 J3
Little Stanney
    Ches W.................... 112 B6
Little Staughton Bed..... 75 G3
Little Steeping Lincs.... 118 F8
Little Stoke Staffs........ 99 K6
Littlestone-on-Sea
    Kent......................... 21 L2
Little Stonham Suffk..... 78 D3
Little Stretton Leics...... 87 J4
Little Stretton Shrops..... 83 J5
Little Strickland
    Cumb...................... 138 E4
Little Stukeley
    Cambs....................... 89 H7
Little Sugnall Staffs...... 99 J6
Little Swinburne
    Nthumb.................... 158 B6
Little Sypland D & G... 146 C4
Little Tew Oxon............ 57 G3
Little Tey Essex............. 61 L4
Little Thetford Cambs.... 90 D7
Little Thorpe Dur......... 151 K6
Littlethorpe Leics......... 87 G4
Littlethorpe N York.... 132 E5
Little Thurlow Suffk...... 76 F4
Little Thurrock Thurr 45 L4
Littleton Angus............ 196 B6
Littleton Ches W......... 112 C7
Littleton D & G........... 146 B4
Littleton Hants............. 29 J5
Littleton Somset.......... 26 C5
Littleton Surrey............ 43 H6
Littleton Drew Wilts...... 39 J4
Littleton-on-Severn
    S Glos...................... 38 E3
Littleton Pannell
    Wilts......................... 27 M2
Little Torrington
    Devon....................... 10 D2
Littletown Dur.......... 151 H6
Little Town Lancs........ 121 K4
Little Urswick Cumb ... 128 F5
Little Wakering
    Essex........................ 46 F3
Little Walden Essex...... 76 D6
Little Waldingfield
    Suffk......................... 77 K5
Little Walsingham
    Norfk...................... 105 M5
Little Waltham Essex.... 61 H5
Little Weighton
    E R Yk...................... 126 B4
Little Wenlock
    Wrekin...................... 84 B3
Little Weston Somset.... 26 F6
Little Whitefield IoW..... 17 H4
Littlewick Green
    W & M...................... 42 D4
Little Wilbraham
    Cambs....................... 76 D3
Little Witcombe
    Gloucs...................... 55 K5
Little Witley Worcs....... 70 D2
Little Wittenham
    Oxon........................ 41 K2
Little Wolford
    Warwks..................... 72 C7
Little Woodcote
    Gt Lon...................... 44 F7
Littleworth Oxon.......... 40 F2
Littleworth Staffs......... 99 L7
Littleworth Worcs........ 70 F4
Little Wymington
    Bed.......................... 74 D2

Little Wymondley
Herts.................................59 K3
Little Wyrley Staffs.........85 H3
Little Yeldham Essex......77 H6
Littley Green Essex.......61 H4
Litton Derbys................114 D6
Litton N York.................131 G5
Litton Somset..................26 E1
Litton Cheney Dorset......14 A4
Liurbost W Isls............. 232 f3
Liverpool Lpool............ 111 K4
Liverpool Maritime
Mercantile City
Lpool....................... 111 K4
Liversedge Kirk........... 123 J5
Liverton Devon.................7 J2
Liverton R & Cl........... 142 F4
Livingston W Loth........ 176 E5
Livingston Village
W Loth....................176 E5
Lixwm Flints...............111 G7
Lizard Cnwll......................3 J8
Llanaelhaearn Gwynd....95 G4
Llanafan Cerdgn...........80 F8
Llanafan-Fawr
Powys...........................67 L4
Llanallgo IoA.............. 109 G4
Llanarmon Dyffryn
Ceiriog Wrexhm.........97 J6
Llanarmon-yn-Ial
Denbgs........................97 J2
Llanarth Cerdgn...........65 L3
Llanarth Mons..............54 B5
Llanarthne Carmth........51 G2
Llanasa Flints.............110 F5
Llanbadarn Fawr
Cerdgn.........................80 E7
Llanbadarn Fynydd
Powys..........................82 C7
Llanbadoc Mons............54 B7
Llanbeder Newpt...........38 B3
Llanbedr Gwynd............95 K6
Llanbedr Powys.............53 K4
Llanbedr-Dyffryn-
Clwyd Denbgs.............97 H2
Llanbedrgoch IoA....... 109 G5
Llanbedrog Gwynd.........94 F6
Llanbedr-y-Cennin
Conwy....................... 109 L7
Llanberis Gwynd............95 K1
Llanbethêry V Glam.......37 G6
Llanbister Powys...........82 C8
Llanblethian V Glam......36 F5
Llanboidy Carmth..........49 L3
Llanbradach Caerph.......37 J3
Llanbrynmair Powys......81 J3
Llancadle V Glam..........37 G6
Llancarfan V Glam.........37 G6
Llancloudy Herefs.........54 D4
Llandaff Cardif..............37 J5
Llandanwg Gwynd.........95 K6
Llanddaniel Fab IoA.... 109 G7
Llanddarog Carmth.......51 G3
Llanddeiniol Cerdgn......66 D1
Llanddeiniolen
Gwynd....................... 109 H7
Llandderfel Gwynd.........96 F5
Llanddeusant IoA....... 108 D4
Llanddew Powys............53 G2
Llanddewi Swans..........50 F7
Llanddewi Brefi
Cerdgn.........................66 F4
Llanddewi
Rhydderch Mons......53 M5
Llanddewi Velfrey
Pembks........................49 K4
Llanddewi
Ystradenni Powys.....68 C2
Llanddoged Conwy...... 109 M8
Llanddona IoA............. 109 H5
Llanddowror Carmth......50 B3
Llanddulas Conwy....... 110 C6
Llanddwywe Gwynd.......95 K7
Llanddyfnan IoA......... 109 G5
Llandefaelog-Tre'r-
Graig Powys.............53 H3
Llandefalle Powys.........68 C7

Llandegfan IoA........... 109 H6
Llandegla Denbgs.........97 J3
Llandegley Powys.........68 D2
Llandegveth Mons.........37 M2
Llandeilo Carmth...........51 J2
Llandeilo Graban
Powys...........................68 C5
Llandeloy Pembks.........48 E3
Llandenny Mons............54 B7
Llandevaud Newpt.........38 B3
Llandevenny Mons.........38 B3
Llandinam Powys...........82 B5
Llandissilio Pembks.......49 J3
Llandogo Mons...............54 D7
Llandough V Glam.........36 F6
Llandough V Glam.........37 J5
Llandovery Carmth.........67 G7
Llandow V Glam.............36 E5
Llandre Carmth..............66 F6
Llandre Cerdgn..............80 E6
Llandre Isaf Pembks......49 J2
Llandrillo Denbgs...........97 G5
Llandrillo-yn-Rhos
Conwy........................ 110 B5
Llandrindod Wells
Powys...........................68 B3
Llandrinio Powys...........97 L8
Llandudno Conwy........ 109 L5
Llandudno Junction
Conwy........................ 109 M6
Llandulas Powys............67 J6
Llandwrog Gwynd...........95 H2
Llandybie Carmth..........51 J3
Llandyfaelog Carmth......50 E3
Llandyfriog Cerdgn........65 K6
Llandygai Gwynd.......... 109 H7
Llandygwydd Cerdgn.....65 H5
Llandyrnog Denbgs...... 110 F8
Llandyssil Powys...........82 E4
Llandysul Cerdgn..........65 L6
Llanedeyrn Cardif.........37 K4
Llaneglwys Powys.........68 B6
Llanegryn Gwynd...........80 D3
Llanegwad Carmth........51 G2
Llaneilian IoA.............. 108 F3
Llanelian-yn-Rhôs
Conwy........................ 110 B6
Llanelidan Denbgs.........97 H3
Llanelieu Powys............68 D7
Llanellen Mons..............53 L5
Llanelli Carmth..............51 G5
Llanelltyd Gwynd...........96 A8
Llanelwedd Powys.........68 B4
Llanenddwyn Gwynd......95 K7
Llanengan Gwynd...........94 E6
Llanerchymedd IoA..... 108 E5
Llanerfyl Powys.............82 B2
Llanfachraeth IoA........ 108 D5
Llanfachreth Gwynd......96 B7
Llanfaelog IoA............. 108 D6
Llanfaelrhys Gwynd.......94 D7
Llanfaethlu IoA............ 108 D4
Llanfair Gwynd..............95 K6
Llanfair Caereinion
Powys...........................82 C3
Llanfair Clydogau
Cerdgn.........................66 E4
Llanfair Dyffryn
Clwyd Denbgs.............97 H2
Llanfairfechan
Conwy........................ 109 K6
Llanfairpwllgwyngyll
IoA............................ 109 G6
Llanfair Talhaiarn
Conwy........................ 110 C7
Llanfair Waterdine
Shrops.........................82 E7
Llanfairynghornwy
IoA............................ 108 D4
Llanfair-yn-
Neubwll IoA............. 108 C6
Llanfallteg Carmth.........49 K4
Llanfallteg West
Carmth.........................49 K4
Llanfarian Cerdgn.........80 D7
Llanfechain Powys.........97 J7
Llanfechell IoA............ 108 E3

Llanferres Denbgs.........97 J1
Llanfihangel-ar-
arth Carmth................66 B6
Llanfihangel Glyn
Myfyr Conwy..............96 F3
Llanfihangel Nant
Bran Powys................67 K7
Llanfihangel
Rhydithon Powys......68 D2
Llanfihangel Rogiet
Mons............................38 C3
Llanfihangel-y-
Creuddyn Cerdgn.....80 F7
Llanfihangel-yng-
Ngwynfa Powys.........82 C1
Llanfihangel yn
Nhowyn IoA............. 108 D6
Llanfihangel-y-
traethau Gwynd.......95 K5
Llanfilo Powys...............53 H2
Llanfoist Mons...............53 L5
Llanfor Gwynd................96 E5
Llanfrechfa Torfn...........37 L2
Llanfrynach Powys.........53 G3
Llanfwrog Denbgs.........97 H2
Llanfwrog IoA.............. 108 C5
Llanfyllin Powys.............97 H8
Llanfynydd Carmth........66 D8
Llanfynydd Flints...........97 L2
Llanfyrnach Pembks......49 L2
Llangadfan Powys.........81 L2
Llangadog Carmth.........66 F8
Llangadwaladr IoA...... 108 E7
Llangaffo IoA............... 108 F7
Llangammarch
Wells Powys..............67 K5
Llangan V Glam.............36 E5
Llangarron Herefs.........54 D4
Llangathen Carmth........51 H2
Llangattock Powys.........53 K4
Llangattock
Lingoed Mons...........54 A4
Llangedwyn Powys.........97 J7
Llangefni IoA............... 108 F6
Llangeinor Brdgnd.........36 E3
Llangeitho Cerdgn.........66 E3
Llangeler Carmth...........65 L6
Llangelynin Gwynd........80 D3
Llangendeirne
Carmth.........................50 F3
Llangennech Carmth.....51 H5
Llangennith Swans........50 E7
Llangernyw Conwy....... 110 B7
Llangian Gwynd.............94 E6
Llangloffan Pembks.......64 C7
Llanglydwen Carmth......49 K3
Llangoed IoA............... 109 J5
Llangollen Denbgs.........97 K4
Llangolman Pembks......49 J3
Llangors Powys.............53 H3
Llangower Gwynd...........96 D6
Llangrannog Cerdgn......65 K4
Llangristiolus IoA......... 108 F6
Llangrove Herefs...........54 D4
Llangunllo Powys...........68 E1
Llangunnor Carmth.......50 E2
Llangurig Powys.............81 K7
Llangwm Conwy............96 F4
Llangwm Mons...............54 B7
Llangwm Pembks...........49 G5
Llangwnnadl Gwynd.......94 D6
Llangwyryfon Cerdgn.....66 D1
Llangybi Cerdgn.............66 E4
Llangybi Gwynd.............95 G4
Llangybi Mons...............38 A2
Llangynhafal Denbgs.... 110 F8
Llangynidr Powys...........53 J4
Llangynin Carmth...........50 B2
Llangynog Carmth..........50 D3
Llangynog Powys...........97 G7
Llangynwyd Brdgnd.......36 D3
Llanhamlach Powys.......53 H3
Llanharan Rhondd..........36 F4
Llanharry Rhondd...........36 F4
Llanhennock Mons.........38 A2
Llanhilleth Blae G..........53 K7
Llanidloes Powys...........81 K6

Llaniestyn Gwynd...........94 E5
Llanigon Powys..............68 E6
Llanilar Cerdgn..............80 E8
Llanilid Rhondd..............36 F4
Llanina Cerdgn...............65 L3
Llanishen Cardif.............37 J4
Llanishen Mons..............54 C7
Llanllechid Gwynd........ 109 J7
Llanllowell Mons............54 B7
Llanllugan Powys...........82 B3
Llanllwch Carmth...........50 E2
Llanllwchaiarn
Powys...........................82 C5
Llanllwni Carmth............66 C6
Llanllyfni Gwynd.............95 H3
Llanmadoc Swans..........50 F6
Llanmaes V Glam...........36 F6
Llanmartin Newpt...........38 B3
Llanmiloe Carmth...........50 B4
Llannefydd Conwy........ 110 D7
Llannon Carmth..............51 G4
Llannor Gwynd................94 F5
Llanon Cerdgn................66 C2
Llanover Mons................53 L6
Llanpumsaint Carmth.....65 L8
Llanrhaeadr-ym-
Mochnant Powys.......97 H7
Llanrhian Pembks..........48 D2
Llanrhidian Swans.........50 F6
Llanrhychwyn Conwy.....96 B1
Llanrhyddlad IoA.......... 108 D4
Llanrhystud Cerdgn.......66 C1
Llanrug Gwynd.............. 109 G8
Llanrumney Cardif.........37 K4
Llanrwst Conwy.............96 C1
Llansadurnen Carmth.....50 C4
Llansadwrn Carmth........66 F7
Llansadwrn IoA............ 109 H6
Llansaint Carmth............50 E4
Llansamlet Swans..........51 K6
Llansanffraid Glan
Conwy Conwy........... 110 A6
Llansannan Conwy....... 110 C7
Llansanffraed
Powys...........................53 H4
Llansanffraed-
Cwmdeuddwr
Powys...........................67 L2
Llansanffraed-in-
Elvel Powys...............68 C4
Llansanffraid
Cerdgn.........................66 C2
Llansanffraid-ym-
Mechain Powys.........97 K7
Llansawel Carmth..........66 E7
Llansilin Powys..............97 K6
Llansoy Mons.................54 C7
Llanspyddid Powys........52 F3
Llanstadwell Pembks.....48 F6
Llansteffan Carmth........50 D4
Llantarnam Torfn...........37 L2
Llanteg Pembks.............49 K5
Llanthewy Skirrid
Mons............................53 M5
Llanthony Mons.............53 L3
Llantilio-Crossenny
Mons............................54 B5
Llantilio Pertholey
Mons............................53 L5
Llantrisant Mons............38 B2
Llantrisant Rhondd.........37 G4
Llantrithyd V Glam.........37 G6
Llantwit Fardre
Rhondd.........................37 G3
Llantwit Major
V Glam.........................36 F6
Llanuwchllyn Gwynd......96 D6
Llanvaches Newpt..........38 B3
Llanvair Discoed
Mons............................38 C3
Llanvapley Mons............54 A5
Llanvetherine Mons.......54 A5
Llanvihangel
Crucorney Mons.......53 L4
Llanwddyn Powys...........96 F8
Llanwenog Cerdgn.........66 C5
Llanwern Newpt.............38 A3

Llanwinio Carmth 50 C1
Llanwnda Gwynd............95 H2
Llanwnda Pembks........64 C6
Llanwnnen Cerdgn 66 C5
Llanwnog Powys............82 B5
Llanwrda Carmth............66 F7
Llanwrin Powys............81 H3
Llanwrthwl Powys........67 L2
Llanwrtyd Wells
  Powys............................67 J5
Llanwyddelan Powys......82 C4
Llanyblodwel Shrops......97 K7
Llanybri Carmth............50 D3
Llanybydder Carmth......66 C6
Llanycefn Pembks........49 J3
Llanychaer Pembks......64 D7
Llanymawddwy
  Gwynd..........................96 D8
Llanymynech Powys......97 K7
Llanynghenedl IoA......108 D5
Llanynys Denbgs 110 F8
Llanyre Powys................68 B3
Llanystumdwy
  Gwynd..........................95 H5
Llanwern Powys............53 H3
Llawhaden Pembks......49 H4
Llawryglyn Powys........81 K5
Llay Wrexhm..................97 M2
Llechrhyd Caerph 53 H6
Llechryd Cerdgn............65 H5
Lledrod Cerdgn..............66 E1
Lleyn Peninsula
  Gwynd..........................94 E5
Llithfaen Gwynd 94 F4
Lloc Flints 111 G6
Llowes Powys................68 D6
Llwydcoed Rhondd 52 F6
Llwydiarth Powys........82 B1
Llwyncelyn Cerdgn......66 B3
Llwyndafydd Cerdgn....65 K4
Llwyngwril Gwynd........80 D2
Llwynmawr Wrexhm......97 K5
Llwynypia Rhondd........36 F2
Llynclys Shrops............97 L7
Llynfaes IoA................108 E5
Llysfaen Conwy 110 B6
Llyswen Powys..............68 C6
Llysworney V Glam........36 E5
Llys-y-frân Pembks......49 H3
Llywel Powys................52 D3
Loan Falk 176 C3
Loanhead Mdloth........177 J5
Loaningfoot D & G 147 G4
Loans S Ayrs................163 J3
Lobhillcross Devon 10 C7
Lochailort Highld........200 B8
Lochaline Highld........190 D7
Lochans D & G............144 C4
Locharbriggs D & G......155 H6
Lochavich Ag & B........182 D4
Lochawe Ag & B..........183 G2
Loch Baghasdail
  W Isls........................233 c8
Lochboisdale W Isls....233 c8
Lochbuie Ag & B 181 J3
Lochcarron Highld......210 D6
Lochdon Ag & B..........181 L2
Lochdonhead
  Ag & B........................181 L2
Lochead Ag & B..........172 D3
Lochearnhead Stirlg....184 D3
Lochee C Dund............186 F2
Locheilside Station
  Highld........................191 K1
Lochend Highld..........212 F6
Lochport W Isls..........233 c6
Loch Euphoirt W Isls ..233 c6
Lochfoot D & G............154 F7
Lochgair Ag & B..........172 F1
Lochgelly Fife 186 C8
Lochgilphead Ag & B....172 E2
Lochgoilhead Ag & B....183 H6
Lochieheads Fife........186 D5
Lochill Moray..............215 G2
Lochindorb Lodge
  Highld........................214 B7
Lochinver Highld........224 D4

Loch Lomond and
  The Trossachs
  National Park 184 A5
Loch Loyal Lodge
  Highld........................229 J6
Lochluichart Highld 211 L2
Lochmaben D & G........155 J5
Lochmaddy W Isls......233 c6
Loch nam Madadh
  W Isls........................233 c6
Loch Ness Highld........202 E1
Lochore Fife 186 C7
Lochranza N Ayrs........172 F7
Loch Sgioport W Isls ..233 c7
Lochside Abers 197 H4
Lochside D & G............155 G6
Lochside Highld..........213 J4
Lochskipport W Isls 233 c7
Lochslin Highld..........223 J5
Lochton S Ayrs............152 F6
Lochty Angus..............196 E4
Lochty Fife 187 H5
Lochuisge Highld 190 F5
Lochwinnoch Rens......174 C6
Lochwood D & G..........155 J3
Lockengate Cnwll..........5 G4
Lockerbie D & G..........155 K5
Lockeridge Wilts..........40 C6
Lockerley Hants............28 F6
Locking N Som..............38 A8
Locking Stumps
  Warrtn........................112 F3
Lockington E R Yk........126 B2
Locklewood Shrops........99 G6
Locksbottom Gt Lon......45 H6
Locks Heath Hants........17 G2
Lockton N York............134 C2
Loddington Leics..........87 L3
Loddington Nhants........88 B7
Loddiswell Devon 7 G6
Loddon Norfk................93 H4
Lode Cambs..................76 D3
Lode Heath Solhll..........85 L7
Loders Dorset................13 L4
Lodsworth W Susx........30 F6
Lofthouse Leeds..........123 L5
Lofthouse N York........131 L5
Lofthouse Gate
  Wakefd......................123 L5
Loftus R & Cl..............142 F4
Logan E Ayrs..............164 C5
Loganlea W Loth........176 C6
Loggerheads Staffs......99 G5
Logie Angus................197 H4
Logie Fife 186 F4
Logie Moray................214 C4
Logie Coldstone
  Abers..........................205 K4
Logie Newton Abers....216 C6
Logie Pert Angus........197 G4
Logierait P & K............194 F6
Logierieve Abers........217 H8
Login Carmth................49 K3
Lolworth Cambs............75 L2
Lonbain Highld............209 L4
Londesborough
  E R Yk........................125 K2
London Gt Lon..............45 G4
London Apprentice
  Cnwll..............................4 F6
London Colney Herts....59 K7
Londonderry N York....132 D2
London Gateway
  Services Gt Lon..........44 D2
London Gatwick
  Airport W Susx..........32 B5
London Heathrow
  Airport Gt Lon............43 H5
London Luton
  Airport Luton..............59 J4
London Oxford
  Airport Oxon..............57 J5
London Southend
  Airport Essex..............46 E3
London Stansted
  Airport Essex..............60 E4
Londonthorpe Lincs 102 F5

London Zoo ZSL
  Gt Lon..........................44 F4
Londubh Highld..........219 K5
Lonemore Highld........219 J6
Long Ashton N Som......38 D6
Long Bank Worcs..........84 D8
Long Bennington
  Lincs..........................102 D4
Longbenton N Tyne....151 G2
Longborough Gloucs....56 D3
Long Bredy Dorset........14 B4
Longbridge Birm..........85 H7
Longbridge Deverill
  Wilts............................27 K4
Long Buckby Nhants....73 J2
Longburton Dorset........26 F8
Long Clawson Leics....102 B6
Longcliffe Derbys 100 E2
Longcombe Devon 7 J4
Long Compton Staffs....99 J7
Long Compton
  Warwks........................56 F2
Longcot Oxon................40 F3
Long Crendon Bucks....58 B6
Long Crichel Dorset......15 J1
Longden Shrops............83 J3
Long Ditton Surrey........44 D6
Longdon Staffs..............85 J2
Longdon Worcs..............70 E7
Longdon Green
  Staffs............................85 J2
Longdon upon Tern
  Wrekin..........................84 B1
Longdown Devon..........11 K6
Longdowns Cnwll............3 J4
Long Duckmanton
  Derbys........................115 H7
Long Eaton Derbys......101 J5
Longfield Kent..............45 L6
Longford Covtry............86 D6
Longford Derbys..........100 E5
Longford Gloucs............55 J4
Longford Shrops............98 F5
Longford Wrekin............99 G8
Longforgan P & K........186 E2
Longformacus
  Border........................178 E6
Longframlington
  Nthumb......................158 E3
Long Green Ches W 112 C7
Longham Dorset............15 K3
Longham Norfk..............91 L1
Long Hanborough
  Oxon............................57 H5
Longhaven Abers........217 L6
Longhirst Nthumb......158 F4
Longhope Gloucs..........55 G4
Longhope Ork............234 b7
Longhorsley Nthumb....158 E4
Longhoughton
  Nthumb......................169 J6
Long Itchington
  Warwks........................72 E2
Longlane Derbys..........100 E5
Long Lawford
  Warwks........................86 F7
Longleat Safari &
  Adventure Park
  Wilts............................27 J3
Longlevens Gloucs........55 J4
Longleys P & K............195 L7
Long Load Somset........26 C6
Longmanhill Abers......216 E2
Long Marston Herts......58 E5
Long Marston N York....124 D1
Long Marston
  Warwks........................71 L5
Long Marton Cumb....138 F3
Long Melford Suffk........77 J5
Longmoor Camp
  Hants............................30 C5
Longmorn Moray........214 F3
Longmoss Ches E........113 K6
Long Newton
  Gloucs..........................39 K3
Longnewton Border....167 J4
Long Newton E Loth....178 B5

Longnewton S on T......141 J4
Longney Gloucs............55 H5
Longniddry E Loth......177 L3
Longnor Shrops............83 J4
Longnor Staffs............114 C8
Longparish Hants..........29 H3
Long Preston N York....130 F7
Longridge Lancs..........121 J3
Longridge W Loth......176 C5
Longriggend N Lans....175 L4
Long Riston E R Yk......126 E3
Longrock Cnwll................2 E5
Longsdon Staffs............99 L2
Longside Abers............217 K5
Longstanton Cambs......76 B2
Longstock Hants............29 G4
Longstowe Cambs........75 K4
Long Stratton Norfk......92 E5
Long Street M Keyn......74 B5
Longstreet Wilts............28 C2
Long Sutton Hants........30 C3
Long Sutton Lincs........104 C7
Long Sutton Somset......26 C6
Longthorpe C Pete........89 H4
Long Thurlow Suffk......78 B2
Longthwaite Cumb......138 B3
Longton Lancs............121 G5
Longtown Cumb..........148 C2
Longtown Herefs..........53 L3
Longueville Jersey......236 d7
Longville in the
  Dale Shrops................83 K5
Long Waste Wrekin......84 B1
Long Whatton Leics....101 J7
Longwick Bucks............58 C6
Long Wittenham
  Oxon............................41 K2
Longwitton Nthumb....158 D4
Longwood D & G..........146 C3
Longworth Oxon............57 G7
Longyester E Loth......178 C5
Lonmay Abers............217 J3
Lonmore Highld..........208 D5
Looe Cnwll......................5 K5
Loose Kent....................33 K3
Loosley Row Bucks........58 D7
Lootcherbrae Abers....216 B4
Lopen Somset................26 B8
Loppington Shrops........98 C6
Lordshill C Sotn............29 H7
Lords Wood Medway......46 C2
Lornty P & K................195 J6
Loscoe Derbys............101 H3
Losgaintir W Isls........232 d4
Lossiemouth Moray....214 F1
Lostock Gralam
  Ches W........................113 G6
Lostock Green
  Ches W........................113 G6
Lostwithiel Cnwll............5 H4
Lothbeg Highld..........227 G6
Lothersdale N York......122 E2
Lothmore Highld........227 G6
Loudwater Bucks..........42 E3
Loughborough Leics 101 K8
Lougher Swans..............51 H6
Loughton Essex............45 H2
Loughton M Keyn..........74 B6
Lound Lincs................103 H8
Lound Notts................116 B4
Lound Suffk..................93 K4
Lount Leics..................101 G8
Louth Lincs................118 D4
Lover Wilts....................28 E7
Loversall Donc............115 L2
Loveston Pembks..........49 J5
Lovington Somset........26 E5
Low Ackworth
  Wakefd......................124 C6
Low Barbeth D & G......144 B2
Low Bentham N York....130 C5
Low Biggins Cumb......130 B4
Low Borrowbridge
  Cumb..........................138 E6
Low Bradfield Sheff....114 E3
Low Bradley N York......122 F2
Low Burnham N Linc....116 C2

Lowca Cumb............136 D3
Low Catton E R Yk.....133 L8
Low Crosby Cumb........148 D3
Lowdham Notts..........102 A3
Low Dinsdale Darltn....141 J5
Lower Aisholt
  Somset................25 J4
Lower Ansty Dorset....14 E2
Lower Apperley
  Gloucs................55 J3
Lower Arboll Highld...223 J6
Lower Ashton Devon....11 J7
Lower Assendon
  Oxon..................42 C4
Lower Badcall Highld..228 B6
Lower Bartle Lancs....121 G4
Lower Basildon
  W Berk................41 L5
Lower Beeding
  W Susx................31 L6
Lower Benefield
  Nhants................88 E5
Lower Bentley Worcs...71 H2
Lower Boddington
  Nhants................72 F4
Lower Bourne Surrey...30 D3
Lower Brailes
  Warwks................72 C6
Lower Breakish
  Highld...............199 L2
Lower Broadheath
  Worcs.................70 E3
Lower Broxwood
  Herefs................69 G4
Lower Bullingham
  Herefs................69 K6
Lower Burgate Hants...28 D7
Lower Caldecote
  C Beds................75 H5
Lower Chapel Powys....68 B7
Lower Chicksgrove
  Wilts.................27 L5
Lower Chute Wilts.....28 F2
Lower Clapton
  Gt Lon................45 G3
Lower Clent Worcs.....85 G7
Lower
  Cumberworth
  Kirk.................123 J8
Lower Darwen
  Bl w D...............121 K5
Lower Dean Bed........74 F2
Lower Diabaig Highld..210 C3
Lower Dicker E Susx...20 B4
Lower Down Shrops.....83 G6
Lower Dunsforth
  N York...............133 G6
Lower Egleton
  Herefs................70 B5
Lower End M Keynes....74 D6
Lower Eythorne Kent...35 H5
Lower Failand N Som...38 D5
Lower Farringdon
  Hants.................30 B4
Lower Feltham
  Gt Lon................43 H6
Lower Froyle Hants....30 C3
Lower Gabwell
  Devon..................7 L2
Lower Gledfield
  Highld...............222 D4
Lower Godney
  Somset................26 C3
Lower Gornal Dudley...85 G5
Lower Gravenhurst
  C Beds................75 G7
Lower Green Kent......32 F5
Lower Green Kent......33 G5
Lower Halstow Kent....46 E6
Lower Hamworthy
  BCP...................15 J4
Lower Hardres Kent....34 F4
Lower Hartwell
  Bucks.................58 C5
Lower Hergest
  Herefs................68 F4
Lower Heyford Oxon....57 J3

Lower Heysham
  Lancs................129 J7
Lower Houses Kirk....123 H7
Lower Irlam Salfd....113 G3
Lower Killeyan
  Ag & B...............160 A2
Lower Langford
  N Som.................38 C7
Lower Largo Fife.....187 G6
Lower Leigh Staffs...100 A5
Lower Loxhore
  Devon.................23 K4
Lower Lydbrook
  Gloucs................54 E5
Lower Lye Herefs......69 H2
Lower Machen
  Newpt.................37 K3
Lower Merridge
  Somset................25 J4
Lower Middleton
  Cheney Nhants........73 G6
Lower Moor Worcs......71 H5
Lower Morton S Glos...38 F3
Lower Nazeing Essex...60 C6
Lower Penarth
  V Glam................37 J4
Lower Penn Staffs.....84 F4
Lower Peover Ches E..113 H6
Lower Place Rochdl...122 D7
Lower Quinton
  Warwks................71 L5
Lower Raydon Suffk...78 C6
Lower Roadwater
  Somset................25 G4
Lower Seagry Wilts....39 L4
Lower Shelton
  C Beds................74 E6
Lower Shiplake Oxon...42 C4
Lower Shuckburgh
  Warwks................72 F3
Lower Slaughter
  Gloucs................56 D4
Lower Standen Kent....35 H6
Lower Stanton St
  Quintin Wilts........39 L4
Lower Stoke Medway....46 D5
Lower Stondon
  C Beds................75 H7
Lower Stone Gloucs....38 F2
Lower Stow Bedon
  Norfk.................91 L5
Lower Street Norfk...106 F5
Lower Street Suffk....78 D4
Lower Swanwick
  Hants.................16 F1
Lower Swell Gloucs....56 D3
Lower Tasburgh
  Norfk.................92 E4
Lower Tean Staffs....100 A5
Lower Town Devon.......7 G2
Lower Town Pembks.....64 D6
Lower Upham Hants.....29 K7
Lower Weare Somset....26 B2
Lower Welson Herefs...68 F4
Lower Westmancote
  Worcs.................71 G6
Lower Whatley
  Somset................27 H3
Lower Whitley
  Ches W...............112 E5
Lower Wield Hants.....29 M4
Lower Willingdon
  E Susx................20 C5
Lower Withington
  Ches E...............113 J7
Lower Woodford
  Wilts.................28 C4
Lower Wraxall
  Dorset................14 B3
Lowesby Leics.........87 K3
Lowestoft Suffk.......93 L5
Loweswater Cumb......137 G3
Low Fell Gatesd......151 G3
Lowfield Heath
Low Gartachorrans
  Stirlg...............174 E2

Low Grantley N York..132 C5
Low Ham Somset........26 B5
Low Harrogate
  N York...............132 D7
Low Hesket Cumb.......148 E5
Low Hutton N York....134 B6
Lowick Nhants.........88 E7
Lowick Nthumb........168 F2
Lowick Green Cumb....129 G3
Low Lorton Cumb......137 G3
Low Marnham Notts....116 D7
Low Mill N York......142 E7
Low Moorsley Sundld..151 H5
Low Moresby Cumb.....136 D3
Low Newton Cumb......129 J3
Low Row Cumb.........149 G3
Low Row N York.......140 B7
Low Salchrie D & G...144 B2
Low Santon N Linc....125 L7
Lowsonford Warwks.....71 L2
Low Tharston Norfk....92 E4
Lowther Cumb.........138 D3
Lowthorpe E R Yk.....135 G7
Lowton Somset.........25 J7
Low Torry Fife.......176 D2
Low Worsall N York...141 J5
Low Wray Cumb........137 K6
Loxbeare Devon........11 L2
Loxhill Surrey........31 G4
Loxhore Devon.........23 K4
Loxley Warwks.........72 C4
Loxton N Som..........26 A1
Loxwood W Susx........31 H5
Lubenham Leics........87 K6
Luccombe Somset.......24 E3
Luccombe Village
  IoW...................17 H6
Lucker Nthumb........169 H4
Luckett Cnwll..........6 B2
Lucking Street Essex..77 J7
Luckington Wilts......39 J4
Lucklawhill Fife.....187 G3
Luckwell Bridge
  Somset................24 E4
Lucton Herefs.........69 J2
Ludag W Isls.........233 b9
Ludborough Lincs.....118 D3
Ludbrook Devon.........6 F5
Ludchurch Pembks......49 K5
Luddenden Calder.....122 F5
Luddenden Foot
  Calder..............122 F5
Luddesdown Kent.......46 A6
Luddington N Linc....125 J7
Luddington Warwks.....71 L4
Luddington in the
  Brook Nhants.........89 G6
Ludford Lincs........117 K4
Ludford Shrops........83 K8
Ludgershall Bucks.....58 A4
Ludgershall Wilts.....28 E2
Ludgvan Cnwll..........2 E5
Ludham Norfk.........107 H8
Ludlow Shrops.........83 K7
Ludney Somset.........26 B8
Ludwell Wilts.........27 K6
Ludworth Dur.........151 J6
Luffness E Loth......178 B3
Lugar E Ayrs.........164 C5
Luggate Burn E Loth..178 D4
Luggiebank N Lans....175 K4
Lugton E Ayrs........174 D7
Lugwardine Herefs.....69 K6
Luib Highld..........209 J8
Luing Ag & B.........181 L5
Lulham Herefs.........69 H6
Lullington Derbys.....86 B2
Lullington Somset.....27 H2
Lulsgate Bottom
  N Som.................38 D7
Lulsley Worcs.........70 D4
Lumb Calder..........122 F6
Lumby N York.........124 D4
Lumphanan Abers......206 B4
Lumphinnans Fife.....186 C8
Lumsden Abers........205 K2
Lunan Angus..........197 H6

Lunanhead Angus......196 D6
Luncarty P & K.......186 A2
Lund E R Yk..........126 B2
Lund N York..........125 G4
Lundie Angus.........186 E1
Lundin Links Fife....187 G6
Lundin Mill Fife.....187 G6
Lundy Devon...........22 B3
Lunga Ag & B.........181 L5
Lunna Shet...........235 d4
Lunsford Kent.........33 J2
Lunsford's Cross
  E Susx................20 E4
Lunt Sefton..........111 K2
Luppitt Devon.........12 F2
Lupset Wakefd........123 L6
Lupton Cumb..........129 L4
Lurgashall W Susx.....30 F6
Lurley Devon..........11 L2
Luscombe Devon.........7 J4
Luss Ag & B..........183 L8
Lussagiven Ag & B....171 G2
Lusta Highld.........208 D3
Lustleigh Devon.......11 H8
Luston Herefs.........69 J2
Luthermuir Abers.....197 G3
Luthrie Fife.........186 E4
Luton Devon............7 K1
Luton Devon...........12 D2
Luton Luton...........59 H4
Luton Medway..........46 C6
Luton Airport Luton...59 J4
Lutterworth Leics.....87 G6
Lutton Devon...........6 E4
Lutton Devon...........7 G4
Lutton Lincs.........104 C7
Lutton Nhants.........89 G6
Luxborough Somset.....24 F4
Luxulyan Cnwll.........5 G4
Luxulyan Valley Cnwll..5 G4
Lybster Highld.......231 J7
Lydbury North
  Shrops................83 G6
Lydd Kent.............21 K2
Lydd Airport Kent.....21 L2
Lydden Kent...........35 H5
Lydden Kent...........35 K2
Lyddington Rutlnd.....88 C4
Lydeard St
  Lawrence Somset......25 H5
Lydford Devon.........10 D7
Lydford on Fosse
  Somset................26 E5
Lydgate Calder.......122 F6
Lydham Shrops.........83 G5
Lydiard Millicent
  Wilts.................40 C3
Lydiard Tregoze
  Swindn................40 C4
Lydiate Sefton.......111 K2
Lydiate Ash Worcs.....85 F7
Lydlinch Dorset.......27 H8
Lydney Gloucs.........54 F7
Lydstep Pembks........49 J7
Lye Dudley............85 G6
Lye Green E Susx......32 F6
Lye Green Warwks......71 L2
Lye's Green Wilts.....27 J3
Lyford Oxon...........41 H2
Lymbridge Green
  Kent..................34 F6
Lyme Regis Dorset.....13 J4
Lyminge Kent..........34 F6
Lymington Hants.......16 C2
Lyminster W Susx......18 D5
Lymm Warrtn..........113 G4
Lymm Services
  Warrtn...............112 F4
Lympne Kent...........34 F7
Lympsham Somset.......25 M1
Lympstone Devon.......12 C5
Lynchat Highld.......203 J5
Lynch Green Norfk.....92 D3
Lyndhurst Hants.......16 C2
Lyndon Rutlnd.........88 C4
Lyndon Green Birm.....85 K6
Lyne Border..........166 B2

Lyne Surrey.................43 G7
Lyneal Shrops................98 C6
Lyneham Oxon..............56 F4
Lyneham Wilts..............40 A5
Lynemouth Nthumb.....159 H4
Lyne of Skene Abers ...206 E4
Lyness Ork...................234 b7
Lyng Norfk 106 C8
Lyng Somset.................25 M5
Lynmouth Devon..........23 L2
Lynsted Kent...............34 C3
Lynton Devon...............23 L2
Lyon's Gate Dorset........14 C2
Lyonshall Herefs...........69 G4
Lytchett Matravers
   Dorset......................15 H4
Lytchett Minster
   Dorset......................15 H4
Lyth Highld.................231 K3
Lytham Lancs..............120 E5
Lytham St Annes
   Lancs......................120 D5
Lythe N York 143 H5
Lythmore Highld.........230 F3

M

Mabe Burnthouse
   Cnwll..........................3 K4
Mablethorpe Lincs......119 G4
Macclesfield Ches E.....113 K6
Macduff Abers.............216 D2
Macharioch Ag & B.....161 J7
Machen Caerph.............37 K3
Machrie N Ayrs...........162 A3
Machrihanish Ag & B...161 G5
Machrins Ag & B.........180 E8
Machynlleth Powys........81 G4
Machynys Carmth..........51 G5
Mackworth Derbys.......100 F5
Macmerry E Loth.........177 L4
Madderty P & K...........185 K3
Maddiston Falk............176 C3
Madeley Staffs..............99 H4
Madeley Wrekin............84 C3
Madingley Cambs..........76 B3
Madley Herefs...............69 H6
Madresfield Worcs.........70 E5
Madron Cnwll.................2 E5
Maenclochog
   Pembks......................49 J3
Maendy V Glam............36 F5
Maentwrog Gwynd........95 L4
Maen-y-groes
   Cerdgn.......................65 L3
Maer Staffs..................99 H5
Maerdy Conwy.............96 F4
Maerdy Rhondd............36 F2
Maesbrook Shrops.........97 L7
Maesbury Shrops..........97 L7
Maesbury Marsh
   Shrops.......................97 L7
Maesllyn Cerdgn...........65 K5
Maesteg Brdgnd............36 D3
Maesybont Carmth.........51 H3
Maesycwmmer
   Caerph......................37 J2
Maggieknockater
   Moray.....................215 H5
Magham Down
   E Susx......................20 C4
Maghull Sefton............111 K2
Magna Park Leics..........87 G6
Magor Mons..................38 B3
Magor Services
   Mons.........................38 B3
Maidenbower W Susx....32 B6
Maiden Bradley Wilts.....27 J4
Maidencombe Torbay......7 L3
Maidenhayne Devon......13 H4
Maiden Head N Som......38 B8
Maidenhead W & M......42 E4
Maiden Newton
   Dorset......................14 B3
Maidens S Ayrs...........163 G7

Maiden's Green
   Br For.......................42 E5
Maiden Wells
   Pembks.....................49 G7
Maidford Nhants...........73 H4
Maids Moreton
   Bucks.......................73 K7
Maidstone Kent 33 K3
Maidstone Services
   Kent.........................33 L3
Maidwell Nhants...........87 L7
Mail Shet...................235 d6
Maindee Newpt............37 L3
Mainland Ork..............234 c6
Mainland Shet............235 c5
Mainsforth Dur...........141 H2
Mains of Balhall
   Angus......................196 E4
Mains of
   Balnakettle Abers ...197 G2
Mains of Dalvey
   Highld......................214 D7
Mains of Haulkerton
   Abers.......................197 H2
Mains of Lesmoir
   Abers.......................215 K8
Mains of Melgunds
   Angus......................196 E5
Mainsriddle D & G.......147 G4
Mainstone Shrops.........82 F6
Maisemore Glouss.........55 J4
Major's Green Worcs......85 K7
Malborough Devon.........7 G7
Maldon Essex................61 K6
Malham N York...........131 G6
Maligar Highld...........209 G2
Mallaig Highld............199 L6
Mallaigvaig Highld.....199 L5
Malleny Mills C Edin....177 G5
Malltraeth IoA............108 E7
Mallwyd Gwynd............81 J2
Malmesbury Wilts.........39 L3
Malmsmead Devon........24 C2
Malpas Ches W..............98 C3
Malpas Cnwll.................4 D7
Malpas Newpt...............37 L3
Maltby Rothm.............115 K3
Maltby S on T.............141 L5
Maltby le Marsh
   Lincs.......................118 F5
Maltman's Hill Kent.......34 B6
Malton N York.............134 C5
Malvern Worcs.............70 D5
Malvern Hills...............70 D5
Malvern Link Worcs.......70 E5
Malvern Wells Worcs.....70 D6
Mamble Worcs..............70 C1
Mamhilad Mons............53 L7
Manaccan Cnwll..............3 K6
Manafon Powys............82 C3
Manais W Isls.............232 d5
Manaton Devon.............11 H8
Manby Lincs................118 E4
Mancetter Warwks.........86 D4
Manchester Manch.......113 J3
Manchester Airport
   Manch.....................113 J5
Mancot Flints.............111 K7
Mandally Highld.........201 L5
Manea Cambs................90 C5
Maney Birm..................85 K4
Manfield N York...........140 F4
Mangerista W Isls........232 d2
Mangotsfield S Glos......38 F5
Mangurstadh W Isls.....232 d2
Manish W Isls.............232 d5
Manley Ches W............112 D7
Manmoel Caerph...........53 J7
Mannal Ag & B...........188 C7
Manningford
   Bohune Wilts...........40 C8
Manningford Bruce
   Wilts........................40 C8
Manningham C Brad....123 H4
Mannings Heath
   W Susx......................31 K5
Mannington Dorset.......15 K2

Manningtree Essex.......62 D2
Mannofield C Aber.......207 H4
Manorbier Pembks........49 H7
Manorbier Newton
   Pembks.....................49 H7
Manorhill Border.........167 K3
Manorowen Pembks......64 C7
Manor Park Gt Lon.......45 H3
Mansell Gamage
   Herefs......................69 H5
Mansell Lacy Herefs......69 H5
Mansfield E Ayrs.........164 C6
Mansfield Notts..........101 K1
Mansfield
   Woodhouse Notts...115 K8
Manston Dorset............27 J7
Manston Kent...............35 J2
Manston Leeds............124 B4
Manswood Dorset.........15 J2
Manthorpe Lincs...........88 F1
Manton N Linc............116 F2
Manton Rutlnd..............88 C3
Manton Wilts................40 D6
Manuden Essex.............60 D3
Maperton Somset..........26 F6
Maplebeck Notts.........102 B1
Mapledurham Oxon.......42 A5
Mapledurwell Hants......30 B2
Maplehurst W Susx........31 K6
Maplescombe Kent........45 K7
Mapleton Derbys.........100 D3
Mapperley Derbys........101 H4
Mapperley Park
   C Nott.....................101 L4
Mapperton Dorset.........13 L3
Mappleborough
   Green Warwks...........71 J2
Mappleton E R Yk.......126 F2
Mapplewell Barns.......123 L7
Mappowder Dorset........14 E2
Marazion Cnwll..............2 F5
Marbhig W Isls...........232 f3
Marbury Ches E............98 E4
March Cambs................90 B4
March S Lans..............165 J6
Marcham Oxon.............41 J2
Marchamley Shrops......98 E6
Marchington Staffs.....100 C6
Marchros Gwynd............94 F7
Marchwiel Wrexhm........98 A3
Marchwood Hants..........16 D1
Marcross V Glam...........36 E6
Marden Herefs...............69 K5
Marden Kent.................33 J4
Marden Wilts................40 C8
Marden Thorn Kent........33 K5
Mardy Mons..................53 L5
Mareham le Fen
   Lincs.......................103 L1
Mareham on the
   Hill Lincs................118 C7
Marehill W Susx...........18 E3
Maresfield E Susx........19 M2
Marfleet C KuH...........126 E5
Marford Wrexhm...........98 A2
Margam Neath..............36 B3
Margaret Marsh
   Dorset......................27 J7
Margaretting Essex.......61 G7
Margaretting Tye
   Essex........................61 G7
Margate Kent................35 K1
Margnaheglish
   N Ayrs.....................162 D3
Margrie D & G.............145 M5
Margrove Park
   R & Cl.....................142 E4
Marham Norfk..............91 G2
Marhamchurch Cnwll......9 G4
Marholm C Pete...........89 G3
Mariansleigh Devon......24 B6
Marine Town Kent.........46 F5
Marionburgh Abers......206 D4
Marishader Highld.......209 H2
Maristow Devon..............6 C3
Marjoriebanks D & G....155 J5
Mark Somset.................26 B2

Markbeech Kent............32 E5
Markby Lincs..............119 G5
Mark Cross E Susx.......33 G6
Market Bosworth
   Leics........................86 E3
Market Deeping
   Lincs........................89 G2
Market Drayton
   Shrops......................98 F5
Market Harborough
   Leics........................87 K6
Market Lavington
   Wilts........................28 A1
Market Overton
   Rutlnd......................88 C1
Market Rasen Lincs....117 J4
Market Stainton
   Lincs.......................118 B5
Market Warsop
   Notts......................115 K7
Market Weighton
   E R Yk....................125 K3
Market Weston Suffk....92 B7
Markfield Leics.............86 F2
Markham Caerph...........53 J7
Markham Moor
   Notts......................116 B6
Markinch Fife.............186 E6
Markington N York.......132 D6
Markle E Loth.............178 C3
Marksbury BaNES.........38 F7
Marks Tey Essex...........61 L4
Markyate Herts.............59 H5
Marlborough Wilts........40 D6
Marlcliff Warwks...........71 K4
Marldon Devon...............7 K3
Marlesford Suffk...........79 G3
Marlingford Norfk.........92 D2
Marloes Pembks............48 D5
Marlow Bucks................42 D3
Marlow Bottom
   Bucks.......................42 D3
Marlpit Hill Kent...........32 D4
Marnhull Dorset............27 H7
Marple Stockp.............113 L4
Marr Donc.................115 K1
Marrick N York...........140 D7
Marsden Kirk..............122 F7
Marsden S Tyne...........151 J3
Marshalswick Herts.......59 K6
Marsham Norfk............106 E7
Marsh Baldon Oxon.......57 K7
Marshborough Kent.......35 J3
Marshbrook Shrops........83 J5
Marshchapel Lincs......118 E2
Marsh Farm Luton........59 H3
Marshfield Newpt..........37 K4
Marshfield S Glos..........39 H5
Marshgate Cnwll............8 F6
Marsh Gibbon Bucks.....57 M4
Marsh Green Devon.......12 D4
Marsh Green Kent.........32 D4
Marshland St
   James Norfk..............90 D2
Marsh Lane Derbys.....115 H5
Marsh Street Somset.....24 F3
Marshwood Dorset........13 J3
Marske N York............140 D6
Marske-by-the-Sea
   R & Cl.....................142 D3
Marston Herefs.............69 G3
Marston Lincs.............102 E4
Marston Oxon...............57 K6
Marston Staffs..............99 L6
Marston Wilts...............27 L1
Marston Green Solhll....85 L6
Marston Magna
   Somset......................26 E6
Marston Meysey
   Wilts........................40 C2
Marston
   Montgomery
   Derbys.....................100 C5
Marston Moretaine
   C Beds......................74 E6
Marston on Dove
   Derbys.....................100 E6

Marston St
  Lawrence Nhants........73 G6
Marston Trussell
  Nhants...............87 K6
Marstow Herefs 54 D4
Marsworth Bucks.............58 F5
Marten Wilts 40 F7
Martham Norfk.............107 J8
Martin Hants..................28 B7
Martin Kent...................35 J5
Martin Lincs 103 J1
Martinhoe Devon............23 L2
Martin Hussingtree
  Worcs...................70 F3
Martinstown Dorset......14 C5
Martlesham Suffk..........78 F5
Martlesham Heath
  Suffk....................78 F5
Martletwy Pembks.........49 H5
Martley Worcs.................70 D3
Martock Somset 26 C7
Marton Ches E 113 J7
Marton E R Yk 126 F3
Marton Lincs 116 D5
Marton Middsb 142 B4
Marton N York...............132 F6
Marton N York...............134 B3
Marton Shrops................82 F3
Marton Warwks..............72 E2
Marton-le-Moor
  N York..................132 E5
Martyr Worthy Hants 29 K5
Marvig W Isls................232 f3
Marwell Wildlife
  Hants....................29 J6
Marwick Ork.................234 b5
Marwood Devon..............23 H4
Marybank Highld..........212 D4
Maryburgh Highld.........212 E3
Marygold Border...........179 G6
Maryhill C Glas.............175 G4
Marykirk Abers..............197 H3
Marylebone Gt Lon........44 F4
Marylebone Wigan.......121 H8
Marypark Moray 214 F6
Maryport Cumb............147 H7
Maryport D & G.............144 D7
Marystow Devon..............10 C7
Mary Tavy Devon..............6 D1
Maryton Angus..............197 H5
Marywell Abers.............206 B6
Marywell Abers.............207 H5
Marywell Angus...........197 G7
Masham N York.............132 C4
Masongill N York..........130 C4
Mastin Moor Derbys......115 J6
Matching Green
  Essex....................60 E5
Matching Tye Essex 60 E5
Matfen Nthumb............158 C7
Matfield Kent..................33 H5
Mathern Mons................38 D3
Mathon Herefs................70 D5
Mathry Pembks...............48 E2
Matlask Norfk................106 D5
Matlock Derbys.............100 F1
Matlock Bath Derbys....100 F2
Matson Gloucs................55 J5
Mattersey Notts............116 B4
Mattingley Hants............42 B8
Mattishall Norfk.............92 C2
Mattishall Burgh
  Norfk....................92 C2
Mauchline E Ayrs..........163 L4
Maud Abers...................217 H5
Maufant Jersey..............236 d6
Maugersbury Gloucs.......56 D3
Maughold IoM...............237 e3
Mauld Highld.................212 C6
Maulden C Beds..............74 F6
Maulds Meaburn
  Cumb..................138 F4
Maunby N York.............132 E3
Maundown Somset..........25 G5
Mautby Norfk..................93 K2
Mavesyn Ridware
  Staffs....................85 J1

Mavis Enderby Lincs ... 118 E7
Mawbray Cumb 147 J5
Mawdesley Lancs 121 G7
Mawdlam Brdgnd............36 C4
Mawgan Cnwll 3 J6
Mawgan Porth Cnwll........4 D3
Mawla Cnwll 3 J3
Mawnan Cnwll 3 K5
Mawnan Smith Cnwll 3 K5
Mawsley Nhants...............88 B7
Maxey C Pete 89 G2
Maxstoke Warwks............86 B6
Maxton Border...............167 J4
Maxton Kent...................35 J6
Maxwelltown D & G......155 G6
Maxworthy Cnwll..............9 H6
May Bank Staffs..............99 J3
Maybole S Ayrs.............163 H7
Maybury Surrey...............43 G8
Mayfield E Susx...............33 G7
Mayfield Mdloth 177 K5
Mayfield Staffs..............100 D4
Mayford Surrey................31 G1
May Hill Gloucs...............55 G4
Mayland Essex.................61 L7
Maylandsea Essex...........61 L7
Maynard's Green
  E Susx...................20 C3
Maypole Birm...................85 J7
Maypole Green Norfk......93 J4
Maypole Green Suffk 77 K3
Meadgate BaNES.............39 G8
Meadle Bucks...................58 D6
Meadowfield Dur...........151 G6
Meadwell Devon 9 K8
Mealabost W Isls..........232 g2
Meanwood Leeds 123 K3
Meare Somset..................26 C3
Meare Green Somset......25 L6
Meare Green Somset......25 M5
Mearns E Rens...............174 F7
Mears Ashby Nhants......74 B2
Measham Leics...............86 D2
Meath Green Surrey.......32 B4
Meathop Cumb..............129 J4
Meavaig W Isls.............232 d2
Meavy Devon 6 D3
Medbourne Leics............88 B5
Meddon Devon..................9 H2
Meden Vale Notts..........115 L7
Medmenham Bucks........42 D4
Medomsley Dur.............150 E4
Medstead Hants..............30 A4
Medway Services
  Medway....................46 D7
Meerbrook Staffs............99 M1
Meesden Herts................60 C2
Meeth Devon..................10 E3
Meeting House Hill
  Norfk..................107 G6
Meidrim Carmth..............50 C2
Meifod Powys..................82 D2
Meigle P & K.................195 L7
Meikle Carco D & G......164 F6
Meikle Earnock
  S Lans.................175 J7
Meikle Kilmory
  Ag & B................173 H6
Meikle Obney P & K.....195 G8
Meikleour P & K............195 J7
Meikle Wartle Abers 216 D7
Meinciau Carmth............50 F4
Meir C Stke.....................99 L4
Melbost W Isls..............232 g2
Melbourn Cambs.............75 L5
Melbourne Derbys........101 G7
Melbourne E R Yk 125 H2
Melbury Abbas
  Dorset...................27 K7
Melbury Bubb Dorset.....14 B2
Melbury Osmond
  Dorset...................14 B2
Melchbourne Bed............74 E2
Melcombe Bingham
  Dorset...................14 E2
Meldon Devon..................10 E6
Meldon Nthumb............158 E5

Meldreth Cambs..............75 L5
Meldrum Stirlg...............184 F7
Melfort Ag & B...............182 B5
Meliden Denbgs.............110 E5
Melin-y-wig Denbgs.......97 G3
Melkinthorpe Cumb......138 D3
Melkridge Nthumb........149 J3
Melksham Wilts...............39 K7
Melling Lancs................130 B5
Melling Sefton...............111 L2
Mellis Suffk......................92 C8
Mellon Charles
  Highld.................219 K3
Mellon Udrigle
  Highld.................219 K3
Mellor Lancs.................121 J4
Mellor Stockp................113 M4
Mellor Brook Lancs 121 J4
Mells Somset...................27 G2
Melmerby Cumb............149 G7
Melmerby N York..........131 K3
Melmerby N York..........132 E4
Melness Highld.............229 J3
Melplash Dorset.............13 L3
Melrose Border..............167 H3
Melsetter Ork................234 b7
Melsonby N York..........140 F5
Meltham Kirk.................123 G7
Melton E R Yk...............126 B5
Melton Suffk...................79 G4
Melton Constable
  Norfk..................106 C6
Melton Mowbray
  Leics...................102 C8
Melton Ross N Linc......126 D7
Melvaig Highld..............219 H4
Melverley Shrops...........83 G1
Melvich Highld..............230 C3
Membury Devon..............13 H2
Membury Services
  W Berk...................40 F5
Memsie Abers................217 H2
Memus Angus................196 C5
Menai Bridge IoA..........109 H6
Mendham Suffk...............92 F6
Mendip Hills....................26 D2
Mendlesham Suffk.........78 D2
Mendlesham Green
  Suffk....................78 D2
Menheniot Cnwll..............5 L4
Mennock D & G............164 F7
Menston C Brad............123 H2
Menstrie Clacks.............185 H7
Mentmore Bucks.............58 E4
Meoble Highld...............200 C7
Meole Brace Shrops......83 J2
Meonstoke Hants............29 L7
Meopham Kent................45 M6
Mepal Cambs...................90 B7
Meppershall C Beds.......75 G7
Mere Ches E...................113 G5
Mere Wilts.......................27 J5
Mere Brow Lancs..........120 F6
Mereclough Lancs.........122 C4
Mere Green Birm............85 K4
Mereworth Kent..............33 H3
Meriden Solhll.................86 B6
Merkadale Highld..........208 F7
Merley BCP......................15 J3
Merrion Pembks...............48 F7
Merriott Somset..............26 C8
Merrow Surrey.................31 G2
Merry Hill Herts..............43 J2
Merryhill Wolves.............84 F4
Merrymeet Cnwll..............5 L3
Mersea Island Essex......62 B5
Mersey Crossing
  Halton................112 D5
Mersham Kent.................34 E6
Merstham Surrey............32 B3
Merston W Susx..............18 B5
Merstone IoW..................17 G5
Merthyr Cynog
  Powys...................67 L6
Merthyr Mawr
  Brdgnd...................36 D5
Merthyr Tydfil Myr Td...53 G6

Merthyr Vale Myr Td......53 G7
Merton Devon..................10 D3
Merton Gt Lon................44 E6
Merton Norfk...................91 K4
Merton Oxon....................57 L4
Meshaw Devon.................24 B7
Messing Essex.................61 L4
Messingham N Linc.......116 E2
Metfield Suffk...................93 G7
Metherell Cnwll..................6 B3
Metheringham Lincs 103 H1
Methil Fife.......................186 F7
Methilhill Fife................186 F7
Methlick Abers...............217 G6
Methven P & K...............185 L3
Methwold Norfk...............91 G4
Methwold Hythe
  Norfk....................91 G4
Mettingham Suffk...........93 H5
Metton Norfk.................106 E5
Mevagissey Cnwll............4 F6
Mexborough Donc.......115 J2
Mey Highld....................231 K2
Meysey Hampton
  Gloucs..................56 C7
Miabhaig W Isls............232 d2
Michaelchurch
  Herefs..................54 D3
Michaelchurch
  Escley Herefs.........69 G7
Michaelstone-y-
  Fedw Newpt...........37 K4
Michaelston-le-Pit
  V Glam..................37 J5
Michaelstow Cnwll...........5 G1
Michaelwood
  Services Gloucs.....39 G2
Micheldever Hants..........29 K4
Micheldever Station
  Hants....................29 K3
Michelmersh Hants.........29 G6
Mickfield Suffk................78 D3
Micklebring Donc..........115 K3
Mickleby N York............143 G5
Micklefield Leeds..........124 C4
Mickleham Surrey...........31 K2
Mickleover C Derb.........100 F5
Mickleton Dur...............140 B3
Mickleton Gloucs............71 L5
Mickletown Leeds.........124 B5
Mickle Trafford
  Ches W................112 C7
Mickley N York..............132 C4
Mickley Square
  Nthumb................150 D3
Mid Ardlaw Abers 217 H2
Midbea Ork...................234 c4
Mid Beltie Abers...........206 C5
Mid Calder W Loth........176 E5
Mid Clyth Highld..........231 K7
Mid Culbeuchly
  Abers..................216 C3
Middle Aston Oxon.........57 J3
Middle Barton Oxon.......57 H3
Middlebie D & G............155 L6
Middlebridge P & K.......194 D3
Middle Chinnock
  Somset..................26 C8
Middle Claydon
  Bucks....................58 B3
Middleham N York.........131 L2
Middle Handley
  Derbys................115 H6
Middlehill Wilts................39 J6
Middlehope Shrops.........83 K5
Middle Kames
  Ag & B.................172 F1
Middle Littleton
  Worcs....................71 J5
Middlemarsh Dorset......14 C2
Middle Mayfield
  Staffs..................100 C4
Middle Rasen Lincs 117 H4
Middle Rocombe
  Devon.....................7 K2
Middlesbrough
  Middsb................141 L4

Middleshaw Cumb 129 L2
Middlesmoor N York 131 K5
Middle Stoke
Medway 46 D5
Middlestone Dur 141 G2
Middlestown Wakefd 123 K6
Middlethird Border 167 K2
Middleton Ag & B 188 B7
Middleton Derbys 100 F2
Middleton Derbys 114 D8
Middleton Essex 77 K6
Middleton Hants 29 H3
Middleton Herefs 69 K1
Middleton Leeds 123 L5
Middleton N York 123 G2
Middleton N York 134 B3
Middleton Nhants 88 B5
Middleton Norfk 90 F1
Middleton Nthumb 158 D5
Middleton P & K 186 B6
Middleton Rochdl 113 K1
Middleton Shrops 83 K7
Middleton Suffk 79 J2
Middleton Swans 50 E7
Middleton Warwks 85 L4
Middleton Cheney
Nhants 73 G6
Middleton-in-
Teesdale Dur 139 L3
Middleton Moor
Suffk 79 J2
Middleton One Row
Darltn 141 J5
Middleton-on-Sea
W Susx 18 C5
Middleton on the
Hill Herefs 69 K2
Middleton on the
Wolds E R Yk 125 L2
Middleton Park
C Aber 207 H3
Middleton
Quernhow N York 132 E4
Middleton St
George Darltn 141 J5
Middleton Scriven
Shrops 84 C6
Middleton Stoney
Oxon 57 K4
Middleton Tyas
N York 141 G6
Middle Town IoS 2 a2
Middletown Powys 82 F2
Middle Tysoe Warwks 72 D5
Middle Wallop Hants 28 F4
Middlewich Ches E 113 G7
Middle Winterslow
Wilts 28 E5
Middlewood Cnwll 5 L2
Middle Woodford
Wilts 28 C4
Middlewood Green
Suffk 78 D3
Middlezoy Somset 26 B5
Midford BaNES 39 H7
Midgham W Berk 41 K6
Midgley Calder 122 F5
Midgley Wakefd 123 K7
Midhopestones Sheff 114 E2
Midhurst W Susx 30 E6
Mid Lavant W Susx 18 B4
Midlem Border 167 H4
Mid Mains Highld 212 C6
Midpark Ag & B 173 H6
Midsomer Norton
BaNES 26 F1
Midtown Highld 229 J4
Mid Yell Shet 235 d3
Migdale Highld 222 E3
Migvie Abers 205 K4
Milborne Port
Somset 26 F7
Milborne St Andrew
Dorset 14 F3
Milborne Wick
Somset 26 F7
Milbourne Nthumb 158 E6

Milbourne Wilts 39 L3
Milburn Cumb 138 F2
Milbury Heath S Glos 38 F3
Milby N York 132 F6
Milcombe Oxon 72 E7
Milden Suffk 77 L5
Mildenhall Suffk 91 G8
Mildenhall Wilts 40 E6
Mileham Norfk 105 L8
Mile Oak Br & H 19 H4
Milesmark Fife 176 E2
Miles Platting Manch 113 J2
Mile Town Kent 46 F5
Milfield Nthumb 168 D3
Milford Derbys 101 G4
Milford Devon 22 C6
Milford Staffs 99 L7
Milford Surrey 30 F3
Milford Haven
Pembks 48 F6
Milford on Sea Hants 16 C4
Milkwall Gloucs 54 E6
Millais Jersey 236 a5
Milland W Susx 30 D5
Mill Bank Calder 122 F6
Millbreck Abers 217 J5
Millbridge Surrey 30 D3
Millbrook C Beds 74 E6
Millbrook C Sotn 29 G8
Millbrook Cnwll 6 B5
Millbrook Jersey 236 c7
Mill Brow Stockp 113 L4
Millbuie Abers 206 F4
Millbuie Highld 212 E4
Millcorner E Susx 21 G2
Millcraig Highld 222 E7
Milldale Staffs 100 C2
Mill End Bucks 42 C4
Mill End Herts 60 B2
Millerhill Mdloth 177 J4
Miller's Dale Derbys 114 C6
Millerston C Glas 175 H5
Mill Green Cambs 76 F5
Mill Green Essex 61 G7
Mill Green Lincs 103 L7
Mill Green Suffk 77 L6
Mill Green Suffk 78 B3
Mill Green Suffk 78 D3
Millhalf Herefs 68 F5
Millheugh S Lans 175 K7
Mill Hill Gt Lon 44 E2
Millhouse Ag & B 173 G4
Millhousebridge
D & G 155 K5
Millhouse Green
Barns 114 E2
Millhouses Sheff 115 G5
Milliken Park Rens 174 D6
Millington E R Yk 125 J1
Millmeece Staffs 99 J5
Mill of Drummond
P & K 185 H4
Mill of Haldane
W Duns 174 D2
Millom Cumb 128 E4
Millport N Ayrs 173 K7
Mill Street Suffk 78 C1
Millthrop Cumb 130 C2
Milltimber C Aber 207 G5
Milltown Abers 205 G4
Milltown Abers 205 K3
Milltown D & G 156 C2
Milltown Devon 23 J4
Milltown Highld 209 L5
Milltown of
Auchindoun
Moray 215 H6
Milltown of
Campfield Abers 206 C5
Milltown of
Edinvillie Moray 215 G6
Milltown of Learney
Abers 206 C5
Milltown of
Rothiemay Moray 215 M5
Milnathort P & K 186 B6
Milngavie E Duns 175 G4

Milnrow Rochdl 122 D7
Milnthorpe Cumb 129 K3
Milovaig Highld 208 B4
Milson Shrops 84 B8
Milstead Kent 34 B3
Milston Wilts 28 D3
Milthorpe Nhants 73 H5
Milton C Stke 99 K3
Milton Cambs 76 C2
Milton Cumb 148 F3
Milton D & G 144 F4
Milton D & G 154 E7
Milton Derbys 100 F7
Milton Highld 212 D7
Milton Highld 212 E4
Milton Highld 223 G6
Milton Highld 231 L5
Milton Inver 174 C5
Milton Kent 46 A5
Milton Moray 204 E2
Milton Moray 215 L2
Milton N Som 37 M7
Milton Notts 116 B6
Milton Oxon 41 J3
Milton Oxon 72 F7
Milton P & K 195 G4
Milton Pembks 49 H6
Milton Somset 26 C6
Milton Stirlg 184 B6
Milton W Duns 174 D4
Milton Abbas Dorset 14 F3
Milton Abbot Devon 9 K8
Milton Bridge Mdloth 177 H5
Milton Bryan C Beds 58 F3
Milton Clevedon
Somset 26 F4
Milton Combe Devon 6 D3
Milton Damerel
Devon 9 K3
Milton Ernest Bed 74 E4
Milton Green Ches W 98 C2
Milton Hill Oxon 41 J3
Milton Keynes
M Keyn 74 C6
Milton Lilbourne
Wilts 40 D7
Milton Malsor
Nhants 73 K4
Milton Morenish
P & K 193 K8
Milton of
Auchinhove
Abers 206 B5
Milton of Balgonie
Fife 186 E7
Milton of Buchanan
Stirlg 174 E1
Milton of Campsie
E Duns 175 H3
Milton of Finavon
Angus 196 D5
Milton of Leys Highld 213 G6
Milton of Murtle
C Aber 207 G5
Milton on Stour
Dorset 27 J5
Milton Regis Kent 46 E6
Milton-under-
Wychwood Oxon 56 E4
Milverton Somset 25 H6
Milverton Warwks 72 C2
Milwich Staffs 99 L6
Minard Ag & B 182 D7
Minchinhampton
Gloucs 55 K7
Minehead Somset 24 F3
Minera Wrexhm 97 L3
Minety Wilts 40 A3
Minffordd Gwynd 95 K5
Mingarrypark Highld 190 D2
Miningsby Lincs 118 D8
Minions Cnwll 5 L2
Minishant S Ayrs 163 J6
Minllyn Gwynd 81 J2
Minnigaff D & G 145 J2
Minnonie Abers 216 E3
Minskip N York 132 F6

Minstead Hants 16 C1
Minsted W Susx 30 D7
Minster Kent 35 J2
Minsterley Shrops 83 G3
Minster Lovell Oxon 56 F5
Minster-on-Sea
Kent 46 F5
Minsterworth Gloucs 55 H5
Minterne Magna
Dorset 14 C2
Minting Lincs 117 K6
Mintlaw Abers 217 J5
Minto Border 167 H5
Minton Shrops 83 H5
Mirehouse Cumb 136 D4
Mireland Highld 231 K4
Mirfield Kirk 123 J6
Miserden Gloucs 55 L6
Miskin Rhondd 37 G4
Misson Notts 116 B3
Misterton Notts 116 C3
Misterton Somset 13 L2
Mistley Essex 62 D2
Mitcham Gt Lon 44 F6
Mitcheldean Gloucs 54 F4
Mitchell Cnwll 4 D5
Mitchellslacks D & G 155 G3
Mitchel Troy Mons 54 C6
Mitford Nthumb 158 F5
Mithian Cnwll 3 J2
Mixbury Oxon 73 H7
Mobberley Ches E 113 H5
Mobberley Staffs 100 A4
Mochdre Powys 82 B5
Mochrum D & G 145 H5
Mockbeggar Kent 33 J4
Mockerkin Cumb 136 F3
Modbury Devon 6 F5
Moddershall Staffs 99 L5
Moelfre IoA 109 G4
Moelfre Powys 97 J6
Moffat D & G 155 J2
Moggerhanger
C Beds 75 G5
Moira Leics 86 C1
Molash Kent 34 D4
Mol-chlach Highld 199 G3
Mold Flints 111 H8
Moldgreen Kirk 123 H7
Molehill Green Essex 60 E3
Molescroft E R Yk 126 C3
Molesworth Cambs 88 F7
Moll Highld 209 J7
Molland Devon 24 C5
Mollington Ches W 111 L7
Mollington Oxon 72 F5
Mollinsburn N Lans 175 J4
Mondynes Abers 197 J1
Monewden Suffk 78 F3
Moneydie P & K 185 M2
Moniaive D & G 154 D4
Monifieth Angus 187 H2
Monikie Angus 196 E8
Monimail Fife 186 E5
Monken Hadley
Gt Lon 44 E1
Monk Fryston N York 124 D5
Monkhide Herefs 70 B5
Monkhill Cumb 148 C3
Monkhopton Shrops 84 B5
Monkland Herefs 69 J3
Monkleigh Devon 23 G7
Monknash V Glam 36 E6
Monkokehampton
Devon 10 E4
Monkseaton N Tyne 159 H7
Monks Eleigh Suffk 77 L5
Monk's Gate W Susx 31 K6
Monks Heath Ches E 113 J6
Monk Sherborne
Hants 29 L1
Monksilver Somset 25 G4
Monks Kirby Warwks 86 F6
Monk Soham Suffk 78 E2
Monks Risborough
Bucks 58 D6
Monksthorpe Lincs 118 F7

Monk Street Essex.........60 F3
Monkswood Mons....53 M7
Monkton Devon........12 F2
Monkton Kent........47 M6
Monkton S Ayrs....163 J4
Monkton S Tyne....151 H3
Monkton Combe
  BaNES.........39 H7
Monkton Deverill
  Wilts.........27 J4
Monkton Farleigh
  Wilts.........39 J7
Monkton Heathfield
  Somset........25 K6
Monkton Wyld
  Dorset........13 J3
Monkwearmouth
  Sundld.......151 J4
Monkwood Hants....29 M5
Monmore Green
  Wolves......85 G4
Monmouth Mons....54 D5
Monnington on Wye
  Herefs......69 G5
Monreith D & G...145 H6
Montacute Somset....26 D7
Montford Shrops....83 H1
Montford Bridge
  Shrops......83 H1
Montgarrie Abers...206 B2
Montgomery Powys...82 E4
Montrose Angus....197 H5
Mont Saint Guern...236 b3
Monxton Hants....28 F3
Monyash Derbys...114 D7
Monymusk Abers....206 D3
Monzie P & K....185 H3
Moodiesburn N Lans...175 J4
Moonzie Fife....186 E4
Moor Allerton Leeds..123 L3
Moorby Lincs....118 D8
Moor Crichel Dorset...15 J2
Moordown BCP....15 K4
Moore Halton....112 E5
Moor End Calder....122 F5
Moorends Donc....125 G7
Moorhead C Brad...123 H3
Moorhouse Cumb...148 B4
Moorhouse Notts...116 C7
Moorhouse Bank
  Surrey......32 D3
Moorlinch Somset...26 B4
Moor Monkton
  N York......133 H7
Moorsholm R & Cl..142 E4
Moorside Dorset....27 H7
Moor Street Birm...85 H6
Moorswater Cnwll....5 K3
Moorthorpe Wakefd..124 C7
Moortown Leeds...123 K3
Moortown Lincs...117 H2
Morangie Highld...223 G5
Morar Highld....199 L6
Morborne Cambs...89 G5
Morchard Bishop
  Devon......11 H4
Morcombelake
  Dorset......13 K4
Morcott Rutlnd....88 D4
Morda Shrops....97 L6
Morden Dorset....15 H4
Morden Gt Lon....44 E6
Mordiford Herefs...69 L6
Mordon Dur....141 H2
More Shrops....83 G5
Morebath Devon...24 E6
Morebattle Border...168 B4
Morecambe Lancs...129 J6
Moredon Swindn....40 C3
Morefield Highld...220 E3
Morehall Kent....35 G7
Moreleigh Devon....7 H5
Morenish P & K....184 D1
Morestead Hants...29 K6
Moreton Dorset....14 F4
Moreton Essex....60 E6
Moreton Herefs...69 K2

Moreton Oxon........58 B6
Moreton Wirral....111 J4
Moreton Corbet
  Shrops......98 E7
Moretonhampstead
  Devon......11 H7
Moreton-in-Marsh
  Gloucs......56 D2
Moreton Jeffries
  Herefs......69 L5
Moreton Morrell
  Warwks......72 C4
Moreton on Lugg
  Herefs......69 K5
Moreton Pinkney
  Nhants......73 H5
Moreton Say Shrops..98 F5
Moreton Valence
  Gloucs......55 H6
Morfa Nefyn Gwynd...94 E4
Morham E Loth...178 C4
Morland Cumb....138 E3
Morley Ches E....113 J3
Morley Derbys...101 H4
Morley Leeds...123 K5
Morley Green Ches E..113 J5
Morley St Botolph
  Norfk......92 C4
Morningside C Edin..177 H4
Morningside N Lans..175 L7
Morningthorpe Norfk..92 F5
Morpeth Nthumb...158 F5
Morphie Abers...197 H4
Morrey Staffs...100 C8
Morriston Swans...51 J6
Morston Norfk...106 B4
Mortehoe Devon....23 G3
Morthen Rothm...115 J4
Mortimer W Berk....41 M7
Mortimer West End
  Hants......41 M7
Mortlake Gt Lon....44 E5
Morton Cumb....148 C4
Morton Derbys...101 H1
Morton Lincs....103 H7
Morton Lincs....116 D3
Morton Notts...102 B3
Morton Shrops....97 L7
Morton-on-Swale
  N York......132 E2
Morton on the Hill
  Norfk......92 D1
Morvah Cnwll.....2 D4
Morvich Highld...200 E2
Morville Shrops....84 C5
Morwenstow Cnwll....9 G2
Mosborough Sheff..115 H5
Moscow E Ayrs...163 L2
Moseley Birm....85 J6
Moseley Wolves...85 G4
Moseley Worcs....70 E3
Moss Ag & B....188 B7
Moss Donc....124 F7
Mossat Abers...205 K2
Mossbank Shet...235 d4
Moss Bank St Hel...112 D3
Mossbay Cumb....136 D2
Mossblown S Ayrs..163 K4
Mossburnford Border..167 K6
Mossdale D & G...154 B7
Mossdale E Ayrs...153 K2
Moss Edge Lancs...120 F2
Mossend N Lans...175 K6
Mossley Tamesd...113 L2
Mosspaul Hotel
  Border......156 D3
Moss-side Highld...213 K4
Mosstodloch Moray..215 H3
Mossyard D & G...145 L5
Mossy Lea Lancs...121 H7
Mosterton Dorset...13 L2
Moston Manch...113 K2
Mostyn Flints...111 G5
Motcombe Dorset...27 J6
Mothecombe Devon....6 F7
Motherby Cumb...138 B2
Motherwell N Lans..175 K6

Motspur Park Gt Lon....44 E6
Mottingham Gt Lon....45 H5
Mottisfont Hants...28 F6
Mottisfont Hants...28 F6
Mottistone IoW....16 E5
Mottram in
  Longdendale
    Tamesd.....113 M3
Mottram St Andrew
  Ches E......113 K5
Mouilpied Guern...236 c3
Mouldsworth
  Ches W......112 D7
Moulin P & K....194 E4
Moulsecoomb
  Br & H......19 J4
Moulsford Oxon....41 L4
Moulsoe M Keyn....74 C6
Moultavie Highld...222 E7
Moulton Ches W....112 F7
Moulton Lincs....104 A7
Moulton N York....141 G6
Moulton Nhants....73 L2
Moulton Suffk....77 G2
Moulton V Glam....37 G6
Moulton Chapel
  Lincs......103 M8
Moulton St Mary
  Norfk......93 H3
Moulton Seas End
  Lincs......104 A6
Mount Cnwll.....5 J3
Mountain C Brad...123 G4
Mountain Ash
  Rhondd......53 G7
Mountain Cross
  Border......176 F8
Mount Ambrose
  Cnwll.......3 J3
Mount Bures Essex...61 L2
Mountfield E Susx...20 E2
Mountgerald Highld..212 E3
Mount Hawke Cnwll....3 J2
Mountjoy Cnwll.....4 D4
Mount Lothian
  Mdloth......177 H6
Mountnessing Essex...60 F8
Mounton Mons...38 D2
Mount Pleasant
  Derbys......101 G3
Mount Pleasant
  Suffk......77 G5
Mountsorrel Leics...87 H2
Mount Tabor Calder..122 F5
Mousehole Cnwll.....2 E6
Mouswald D & G...155 J7
Mow Cop Ches E....99 J2
Mowhaugh Border...168 B5
Mowmacre Hill
  C Leic......87 H3
Mowsley Leics....87 J5
Moy Highld....202 C8
Moy Highld....213 J7
Moyle Highld....200 D2
Moylegrove Pembks...64 F5
Muasdale Ag & B...161 H2
Muchalls Abers...207 G6
Much Birch Herefs...54 D3
Much Cowarne
  Herefs......70 B5
Much Dewchurch
  Herefs......54 C2
Muchelney Somset...26 B6
Muchelney Ham
  Somset......26 C6
Much Hadham Herts...60 C4
Much Hoole Lancs...120 F6
Muchlarnick Cnwll....5 K5
Much Marcle Herefs...54 F2
Much Wenlock
  Shrops......84 B4
Muck Highld....189 K1
Muckleburgh
  Collection Norfk..106 D4
Mucklestone Staffs...99 G5
Muckton Lincs....118 E5
Muddiford Devon....23 J4

Muddles Green
  E Susx......20 B3
Mudeford BCP....16 A4
Mudford Somset....26 E7
Mudford Sock
  Somset......26 E7
Mugdock Stirlg...175 G3
Mugeary Highld...209 G6
Mugginton Derbys..100 F4
Muirden Abers...216 D4
Muirdrum Angus...196 F8
Muiresk Abers...216 D5
Muirhead Angus...186 E1
Muirhead Fife...186 E6
Muirhead N Lans...175 J4
Muirhouses Falk...176 D3
Muirkirk E Ayrs...164 D4
Muirmill Stirlg...175 J2
Muir of Fowlis
  Abers......206 B3
Muir of Miltonduff
  Moray......214 E3
Muir of Ord Highld..212 E4
Muirshearlich Highld..192 B1
Muirtack Abers...217 J6
Muirton P & K....185 J5
Muirton Mains
  Highld......212 C4
Muirton of Ardblair
  P & K......195 J7
Muker N York....139 K7
Mulbarton Norfk....92 E4
Mulben Moray...215 H4
Mull Ag & B....181 J1
Mullion Cnwll.....3 H7
Mullion Cove Cnwll....3 H7
Mumby Lincs....119 G6
Munderfield Row
  Herefs......70 B4
Munderfield Stocks
  Herefs......70 B4
Mundesley Norfk...107 G5
Mundford Norfk....91 H5
Mundham Norfk....93 G4
Mundon Hill Essex...61 K7
Mungrisdale Cumb..137 K2
Munlochy Highld...213 H4
Munnoch N Ayrs...174 B8
Munsley Herefs...70 B6
Munslow Shrops...83 K6
Murchington Devon...11 G7
Murcott Oxon....57 L5
Murkle Highld....231 H2
Murlaggan Highld...200 F6
Murroes Angus...187 G1
Murrow Cambs....89 L3
Mursley Bucks....58 D3
Murthill Angus...196 D5
Murthly P & K....195 H8
Murton C York....133 K8
Murton Cumb....139 G3
Murton Dur....151 J5
Murton Nthumb...179 K8
Musbury Devon....13 H4
Musselburgh E Loth...177 K4
Muston Leics....102 D5
Muston N York....135 H4
Muswell Hill Gt Lon...44 F3
Mutehill D & G...146 C5
Mutford Suffk....93 K6
Muthill P & K....185 H4
Mybster Highld...231 H5
Myddfai Carmth....52 B3
Myddle Shrops....98 C7
Mydroilyn Cerdgn...66 B4
Mylor Cnwll.....4 C8
Mylor Bridge Cnwll....4 C8
Mynachlog ddu
  Pembks......49 K2
Mynydd-bach Mons...38 C2
Mynydd-Bach Swans...51 J4
Mynyddgarreg
  Carmth......50 E4
Mynydd Isa Flints...111 J8
Myrebird Abers...206 E5
Myredykes Border...157 G3
Mytchett Surrey....30 E1

Mytholm Calder............ 122 E5
Mytholmroyd Calder 122 F5
Myton-on-Swale
  N York...................... 132 F6

N

Naast Highld 219 J5
Na Buirgh W Isls........ 232 d4
Naburn C York.............. 124 F2
Nackington Kent 34 F4
Nacton Suffk 78 F6
Nafferton E R Yk........ 135 G7
Nailsbourne Somset 25 K5
Nailsea N Som 38 C6
Nailstone Leics............86 E3
Nailsworth Gloucs 55 J7
Nairn Highld 213 K3
Nannerch Flints.......... 111 G7
Nanpantan Leics........ 101 K8
Nanpean Cnwll 4 E3
Nanstallon Cnwll............. 5 G3
Nanternis Cerdgn..........65 L3
Nantgaredig Carmth 50 F2
Nantglyn Denbgs..........96 F1
Nantmel Powys 68 B2
Nantmor Gwynd 95 K4
Nant Peris Gwynd........95 K2
Nantwich Ches E...........98 F3
Nantyglo Blae G 53 J6
Nant-y-moel Brdgnd....36 E2
Naphill Bucks.................42 D2
Napton on the Hill
  Warwks.......................72 F3
Narberth Pembks...........49 J4
Narborough Leics..........87 G4
Narborough Norfk..........91 H2
Nasareth Gwynd...........95 H3
Naseby Nhants..............87 K7
Nash Bucks....................73 L7
Nash Newpt 37 M4
Nash Shrops 69 L1
Nassington Nhants........88 F4
Nateby Cumb 139 H6
Nateby Lancs 120 F2
National Memorial
  Arboretum Staffs 85 L1
National Motor
  Museum
  (Beaulieu) Hants.......16 E2
National Space
  Centre C Leic............87 H3
Natland Cumb 129 L2
Naughton Suffk.............78 B5
Naunton Gloucs............56 C4
Naunton Worcs..............70 F6
Naunton
  Beauchamp
  Worcs.........................71 G4
Navenby Lincs 103 G2
Navestock Essex............45 K1
Navestock Side
  Essex..........................60 E8
Navidale Highld 227 J5
Navity Highld................ 213 J2
Nawton N York 133 K3
Nayland Suffk................77 L7
Nazeing Essex 60 C6
Neap Shet..................... 235 d5
Near Cotton Staffs...... 100 B4
Near Sawrey Cumb 137 K7
Neasden Gt Lon 44 E3
Neasham Darltn 141 H5
Neath Neath...................51 L6
Neatham Hants 30 C4
Neatishead Norfk....... 107 H7
Nebo Cerdgn 66 D2
Nebo Conwy 96 C2
Nebo Gwynd 95 H3
Nebo IoA...................... 108 F4
Necton Norfk.................91 K2
Nedd Highld................. 224 D3
Nedging Suffk................78 B5
Nedging Tye Suffk........78 B4
Needham Norfk.............92 F6

Needham Market
  Suffk...........................78 C4
Needingworth Cambs....75 L1
Neen Savage Shrops.....84 C7
Neen Sollars Shrops.....84 B8
Neenton Shrops.............84 B6
Nefyn Gwynd 94 E4
Neilston E Rens............ 174 E6
Nelson Caerph 37 H2
Nelson Lancs............... 122 C3
Nemphlar S Lans........ 165 G1
Nempnett Thrubwell
  BaNES.........................38 D7
Nenthead Cumb 149 K6
Nenthorn Border.......... 167 K2
Nerabus Ag & B.......... 170 E7
Nercwys Flints..............97 K1
Nerston S Lans............ 175 H6
Nesbit Nthumb 168 E3
Nesfield N York 123 G1
Nesscliffe Shrops..........98 B8
Neston Ches W 111 J6
Neston Wilts..................39 K6
Netchwood Shrops........84 B5
Nether Abington
  S Lans....................... 165 H5
Nether Alderley
  Ches E....................... 113 J6
Netheravon Wilts..........28 D2
Nether Blainslie
  Border....................... 167 H2
Netherbrae Abers........ 216 F3
Nether Broughton
  Leics......................... 102 B7
Netherbury Dorset 13 L3
Netherby N York.......... 123 L2
Nether Cerne Dorset.....14 C3
Nethercleuch D & G.... 155 K5
Nether Compton
  Dorset........................26 E7
Nether Crimond
  Abers......................... 206 F2
Nether Dallachy
  Moray....................... 215 H2
Netherend Gloucs.........54 E7
Netherfield E Susx........20 E2
Netherfield Notts........ 101 L4
Nether Fingland
  S Lans....................... 165 H7
Netherhampton
  Wilts..........................28 C5
Nether Handwick
  Angus....................... 196 B7
Nether Haugh Rothm .. 115 H3
Netherhay Dorset..........13 K2
Nether Headon Notts.. 116 C6
Nether Heage Derbys.. 101 G3
Nether Heyford
  Nhants........................73 J3
Nether Kellet Lancs.... 129 K6
Nether Kinmundy
  Abers......................... 217 K5
Nether Langwith
  Notts........................ 115 K7
Netherlaw D & G........ 146 C6
Netherley Abers.......... 207 G6
Nethermill D & G........ 155 H5
Nethermuir Abers....... 217 G5
Netherne-on-the-
  Hill Surrey..................32 B3
Netheroyd Hill Kirk.... 123 H6
Nether Padley
  Derbys...................... 114 E6
Nether Poppleton
  C York....................... 133 J8
Netherseal Derbys........86 C2
Nether Silton N York.. 133 G2
Nether Stowey
  Somset........................25 J4
Netherthong Kirk....... 123 H8
Netherton Angus 196 E5
Netherton Devon 7 K2
Netherton Dudley 85 G6
Netherton Kirk........... 123 H7
Netherton N Lans....... 175 K7
Netherton Nthumb..... 168 E7

Netherton P & K.......... 195 J6
Netherton Sefton....... 111 K2
Netherton Stirlg......... 175 G3
Netherton Wakefd 123 K6
Netherton Cumb 136 D5
Nethertown Highld..... 231 L1
Nethertown Staffs..... 100 C8
Netherurd Border....... 165 L1
Nether Wallop Hants....28 F4
Nether Wasdale
  Cumb........................ 136 F6
Nether Westcote
  Gloucs........................56 E4
Nether Whitacre
  Warwks.......................86 B5
Nether Whitecleuch
  S Lans....................... 165 G5
Nether Winchendon
  Bucks.........................58 B5
Netherwitton Nthumb. 158 D4
Nethy Bridge Highld ... 204 B2
Netley Hants.................16 F2
Netley Marsh Hants......29 G8
Nettlebed Oxon.............42 B3
Nettlebridge Somset....26 F2
Nettlecombe Dorset.....13 M4
Nettleden Herts.............59 G6
Nettleham Lincs.......... 117 G6
Nettlestead Kent...........33 H3
Nettlestead Green
  Kent............................33 H3
Nettlestone IoW............17 H4
Nettlesworth Dur....... 151 G5
Nettleton Lincs........... 117 J2
Nettleton Wilts.............39 J5
Netton Wilts..................28 C4
Nevern Pembks.............64 F6
Nevill Holt Leics............88 B5
New Abbey D & G........ 147 G2
New Aberdour Abers... 217 G2
New Addington
  Gt Lon.......................45 G7
Newall Leeds 123 J2
New Alresford Hants....29 L5
New Alyth P & K........ 195 K6
Newark C Pete...............89 H4
Newark Ork.................. 234 e4
Newark-on-Trent
  Notts........................ 102 D2
Newarthill N Lans....... 175 K6
New Ash Green Kent.....45 L6
New Balderton Notts.. 102 D3
New Barn Kent...............45 L6
New Barnet Gt Lon.......44 F2
Newbattle Mdloth 177 J5
New Bewick Nthumb... 169 G5
Newbie D & G.............. 147 L3
Newbiggin Cumb......... 138 C2
Newbiggin Cumb......... 138 F2
Newbiggin Cumb......... 148 F5
Newbiggin Dur............ 139 K2
Newbiggin N York....... 131 J3
Newbiggin-by-the-
  Sea Nthumb.............. 159 H5
Newbigging Angus..... 187 H1
Newbigging Angus..... 195 L7
Newbigging Angus..... 196 C8
Newbigging S Lans.... 165 K1
Newbiggin-on-
  Lune Cumb............... 139 G6
New Bilton Warwks......86 F7
Newbold Derbys.......... 115 G6
Newbold on Avon
  Warwks.......................86 F7
Newbold on Stour
  Warwks.......................72 B5
Newbold Pacey
  Warwks.......................72 C3
Newbold Verdon
  Leics..........................86 F3
New Bolingbroke
  Lincs........................ 104 A2
Newborough C Pete......89 H3
Newborough IoA 108 E7
Newborough Staffs.... 100 C7
New Boultham Lincs.. 116 F7
Newbourne Suffk..........78 F6

New Bradwell
  M Keyn........................74 B6
New Brampton
  Derbys...................... 115 G7
New Brancepeth Dur.. 151 G6
Newbridge C Edin....... 176 F4
Newbridge Caerph 37 K2
Newbridge Cnwll............. 2 D5
Newbridge D & G........ 155 G6
Newbridge Hants..........28 F7
Newbridge IoW.............16 E5
Newbridge Green
  Worcs.........................70 E6
Newbridge-on-Wye
  Powys........................67 L3
New Brighton Wirral.. 111 J3
Newbrough Nthumb... 149 L2
New Buckenham
  Norfk..........................92 C5
Newbuildings Devon ...11 J4
Newburgh Abers......... 207 J1
Newburgh Abers......... 217 H3
Newburgh Fife............ 186 D4
Newburgh Lancs......... 121 G7
Newburn N u Ty......... 150 F2
Newbury Somset...........27 G2
Newbury W Berk...........41 J6
Newbury Park Gt Lon....45 J3
Newby Cumb 138 E3
Newby Lancs............... 122 B2
Newby N York............. 130 D5
Newby N York............. 142 B5
Newby Bridge Cumb... 129 H3
Newby East Cumb....... 148 E4
New Byth Abers.......... 216 F4
Newby West Cumb..... 148 C4
Newcastle Mons...........54 C5
Newcastle Shrops........82 E6
Newcastle Airport
  Nthumb.................... 158 F7
Newcastle Emlyn
  Carmth.......................65 J6
Newcastleton Border.. 156 E5
Newcastle-under-
  Lyme Staffs................99 J4
Newcastle upon
  Tyne N u Ty.............. 151 G3
Newchapel Pembks......65 H6
Newchapel Surrey........32 C5
Newchurch IoW.............17 G5
Newchurch Kent...........34 E7
Newchurch Mons..........38 C2
Newchurch Powys........68 E4
Newchurch Staffs...... 100 D7
New Costessey Norfk...92 E2
Newcraighall C Edin... 177 J4
New Crofton Wakefd.. 124 B6
New Cross Gt Lon.........45 G5
New Cross Somset........26 B7
New Cumnock E Ayrs.. 164 C6
New Deer Abers.......... 217 G5
New Denham Bucks......43 H4
Newdigate Surrey.........31 K3
New Duston Nhants......73 K3
New Earswick C York.. 133 J7
New Edlington Donc ... 115 K2
New Elgin Moray......... 214 F3
New Ellerby E R Yk..... 126 E3
Newell Green Br For......42 E6
New Eltham Gt Lon......45 H5
New End Worcs.............71 J3
Newenden Kent............33 L7
New England C Pete......89 H4
Newent Gloucs..............55 G3
New Ferry Wirral........ 111 K4
Newfield Dur.............. 150 F7
Newfield Highld.......... 223 H6
New Fletton C Pete......89 H4
New Forest
  National Park............16 C2
Newgale Pembks...........48 E3
New Galloway D & G .. 154 B6
Newgate Street
  Herts..........................59 M6
New Gilston Fife......... 187 G5
New Grimsby IoS............. 2 a1
Newhall Ches E.............98 E4

New Hartley Nthumb.... 159 H6
Newhaven C Edin 177 H3
Newhaven E Susx 19 L5
New Haw Surrey 43 H7
New Hedges Pembks.....49 J6
New Holland N Linc ... 126 D5
Newholm N York 143 H5
New Houghton
  Derbys.....................115 J7
New Houghton Norfk.. 105 J6
Newhouse N Lans....... 175 L6
New Hutton Cumb 130 B2
Newick E Susx 19 L2
Newington Kent............ 35 G6
Newington Kent............ 46 E6
Newington Oxon............ 41 L2
New Inn Carmth 66 B6
New Inn Torfn 53 L7
New Invention
  Shrops......................82 F7
New Lakenham
  Norfk........................92 F3
New Lanark S Lans.... 165 G2
New Lanark Village
  S Lans 165 G2
Newland C KuH 126 D4
Newland Gloucs 54 D6
Newland N York 125 G5
Newland Somset 24 C4
Newland Worcs 70 E5
Newlandrig Mdloth....... 177 K6
Newlands Border 156 E4
Newlands Nthumb........ 150 D4
Newlands of
  Dundurcas Moray.... 215 G4
New Langholm D & G..156 C5
New Leake Lincs 104 C2
New Leeds Abers.......... 217 J4
New Lodge Barns........ 123 L8
New Longton Lancs ... 121 G5
New Luce D & G.......... 144 E3
Newlyn Cnwll 2 E5
Newmachar Abers 207 G2
Newmains N Lans 175 L6
New Malden Gt Lon 44 E6
Newman's Green
  Suffk.......................77 K5
Newmarket Suffk..........76 F2
Newmarket W Isls...... 232 f2
New Marske R & Cl.... 142 D3
New Marston Oxon........57 K6
New Mill Abers............ 206 E8
Newmill Border 167 G7
New Mill Cnwll................2 E4
New Mill Kirk............... 123 H8
Newmill Moray............ 215 K4
Newmillerdam
  Wakefd.................. 123 L7
Newmill of
  Inshewan Angus ... 196 C4
Newmills C Edin 177 G5
New Mills Derbys....... 113 M4
Newmills Fife 176 D2
Newmills Mons 54 D6
New Mills Powys..........82 C4
Newmilns P & K........... 186 B2
Newmilns E Ayrs........ 164 B2
New Milton Hants 16 B4
New Mistley Essex........62 D2
New Moat Pembks........49 H3
Newney Green Essex....61 G6
Newnham Hants 30 B2
Newnham Herts.............75 J6
Newnham Kent 34 C3
Newnham Nhants..........73 H3
Newnham Bridge
  Worcs......................70 B2
Newnham on
  Severn Gloucs 55 G5
New Ollerton Notts..... 116 A7
New Oscott Birm...........85 K5
New Pitsligo Abers 217 G3
Newport Cnwll.................9 J7
Newport E R Yk........... 125 K4
Newport Essex 76 D7
Newport Gloucs............39 G2
Newport Highld 227 K4

Newport IoW...................16 F5
Newport Newpt...............37 L3
Newport Pembks............64 E6
Newport Wrekin.............99 H8
Newport-on-Tay
  Fife........................ 187 G2
Newport Pagnell
  M Keyn...................74 C5
Newport Pagnell
  Services M Keyn......74 C5
New Prestwick
  S Ayrs..................... 163 J4
New Quay Cerdgn..........65 L3
Newquay Cnwll................4 C4
Newquay Zoo Cnwll..........4 C4
New Rackheath
  Norfk........................93 G2
New Radnor Powys........68 E3
New Ridley Nthumb..... 150 D3
New Romney Kent.........21 L2
New Rossington
  Donc...................... 115 L2
New Sauchie Clacks ... 185 J7
Newseat Abers............ 216 D7
Newsham Lancs.......... 121 G4
Newsham N York......... 132 E3
Newsham N York......... 140 E5
Newsham Nthumb....... 159 H6
New Sharlston
  Wakefd.................. 124 B6
Newsholme E R Yk..... 125 H5
New Silksworth
  Sundld.................... 151 J4
Newsome Kirk............. 123 H7
New Somerby
  Lincs...................... 102 F5
Newstead Border 167 H3
Newstead Notts 101 K3
Newstead Nthumb 169 H4
New Stevenston
  N Lans.................... 175 K6
Newthorpe Notts......... 101 J4
New Thundersley
  Essex.......................46 C3
Newton Ag & B 182 F7
Newton Border 167 J5
Newton Brdgnd............ 36 C5
Newton C Beds 75 J5
Newton Cambs..............76 B5
Newton Cambs..............90 B1
Newton Ches W 98 D1
Newton Ches W 112 B7
Newton Cumb 128 F5
Newton Derbys............ 101 H2
Newton Herefs.............53 M2
Newton Herefs.............69 K4
Newton Highld............ 212 F4
Newton Highld............ 213 H5
Newton Highld............ 213 J2
Newton Highld............ 231 L5
Newton Lincs.............. 103 H5
Newton Mdloth............ 177 J4
Newton Moray............ 214 E2
Newton Moray............ 215 H2
Newton Nhants............ 88 C6
Newton Norfk...............91 J1
Newton Notts.............. 102 B4
Newton Nthumb.......... 150 C3
Newton S Lans............ 165 H3
Newton S Lans............ 175 H6
Newton Sandw.............85 J5
Newton Staffs............. 100 B7
Newton Suffk...............77 K6
Newton W Loth........... 176 E3
Newton Warwks...........87 G7
Newton Abbot Devon 7 K2
Newton Arlosh Cumb... 147 L4
Newton Aycliffe Dur ... 141 G3
Newton Bewley
  Hartpl.................... 141 K2
Newton
  Blossomville
  M Keyn...................74 D4
Newton Bromswold
  Nhants.....................74 E2
Newton Burgoland
  Leics........................86 D2

Newton-by-the-
  Sea Nthumb............ 169 J4
Newton by Toft Lincs.... 117 H4
Newton Ferrers
  Devon........................6 E6
Newton Ferry W Isls... 232 c5
Newton Flotman
  Norfk........................92 E4
Newtongrange
  Mdloth.................... 177 J5
Newton Green Mons 38 D3
Newton Harcourt
  Leics........................87 J4
Newton Heath Manch.. 113 K2
Newtonhill Abers........ 207 G6
Newton-in-
  Bowland Lancs....... 121 K1
Newton Kyme N York... 124 C2
Newton-le-Willows
  N York.................... 132 C2
Newton-le-Willows
  St Hel..................... 112 E3
Newtonloan Mdloth.... 177 J5
Newton Longville
  Bucks........................58 D2
Newton Mearns
  E Rens.................... 174 F7
Newtonmill Angus..... 196 F4
Newtonmore Highld.... 203 H5
Newton Morrell
  N York.................... 141 G5
Newton of
  Balcanquhal
  P & K...................... 186 B5
Newton of
  Balcormo Fife........ 187 H6
Newton-on-Ouse
  N York.................... 133 H7
Newton-on-
  Rawcliffe N York ... 134 C2
Newton-on-the-
  Moor Nthumb......... 158 F2
Newton on Trent
  Lincs...................... 116 D6
Newton Poppleford
  Devon........................12 E4
Newton Purcell Oxon....57 L3
Newton Regis
  Warwks....................86 C3
Newton Reigny
  Cumb...................... 138 C2
Newton St Cyres
  Devon........................11 K5
Newton St Faith
  Norfk........................92 F1
Newton St Loe
  BaNES.....................39 G7
Newton St Petrock
  Devon..........................9 K3
Newton Solney
  Derbys.................... 100 F7
Newton Stacey Hants...29 H4
Newton Stewart
  D & G..................... 145 J3
Newton Tony Wilts 28 E4
Newton Tracey Devon....23 H6
Newton under
  Roseberry R & Cl.... 142 C5
Newton upon
  Derwent E R Yk..... 125 H2
Newton Valence
  Hants......................30 B5
Newton Wamphray
  D & G..................... 155 K3
Newton with Scales
  Lancs.................... 120 F4
Newtown BCP 15 K4
Newtown Cumb........... 147 J5
Newtown Cumb........... 148 E3
Newtown D & G.......... 164 F7
Newtown Devon...........12 D3
Newtown Devon...........24 B6
New Town E Susx 19 M2
Newtown Gloucs...........54 F7
Newtown Hants............29 L8
Newtown Herefs...........70 B5
Newtown Highld......... 202 B4

Newtown IoW.................16 E4
Newtown Nthumb....... 168 F4
Newtown Powys...........82 C5
Newtown Shrops...........98 C6
Newtown Somset..........25 L8
Newtown Staffs............99 K1
Newtown Wigan......... 112 E1
Newtown Worcs 70 F4
Newtown Linford
  Leics........................87 G2
Newtown of
  Beltrees Rens........ 174 D6
Newtown St
  Boswells Border 167 J3
New Tredegar Caerph...53 H7
New Trows S Lans...... 164 F2
Newtyle Angus........... 195 L7
New Walsoken
  Cambs.....................90 C2
New Waltham NE Lin... 118 C1
New Winton E Loth 177 L4
Newyork Ag & B 182 D5
New York Lincs 103 L2
New York N Tyne....... 159 H7
Neyland Pembks...........49 G6
Nicholashayne Devon....25 H7
Nicholaston Swans.......51 G7
Nidd N York............... 132 D7
Nigg C Aber 207 H5
Nigg Highld................ 223 H6
Nigg Ferry Highld 223 H7
Ninebanks Nthumb.... 149 K4
Nine Elms Swindn........40 C3
Ninfield E Susx............20 E3
Ningwood IoW...............16 E5
Nisbet Border 167 K4
Nisbet Hill Border...... 179 G7
Niton IoW.....................17 F6
Nitshill C Glas............ 174 F6
Nocton Lincs.............. 117 H8
Noke Oxon....................57 K5
Nolton Pembks.............48 E4
Nolton Haven
  Pembks....................48 E4
No Man's Heath
  Ches W.....................98 D3
No Man's Heath
  Warwks....................86 C2
Nomansland Devon.......11 J3
Nomansland Wilts........28 E7
Noneley Shrops............98 C6
Nonington Kent............35 H4
Nook Cumb................. 129 L3
Norbiton Gt Lon...........44 D6
Norbury Ches E 98 E3
Norbury Derbys.......... 100 C4
Norbury Gt Lon............44 F6
Norbury Shrops............83 G5
Norbury Staffs.............99 H7
Norchard Worcs 70 F2
Nordelph Norfk............90 D4
Nordley Shrops............84 C4
Norfolk Broads Norfk....93 K2
Norham Nthumb.......... 179 J8
Norley Ches W............ 112 E6
Norleywood Hants 16 D3
Normanby Lincs......... 117 G4
Normanby N Linc....... 125 K7
Normanby N York....... 134 B3
Normanby R & Cl....... 142 C4
Normanby le Wold
  Lincs...................... 117 J3
Normandy Surrey.........30 F2
Norman's Green
  Devon.......................12 D2
Normanton C Derb..... 101 G5
Normanton Leics........ 102 D4
Normanton Notts........ 102 B2
Normanton Wakefd.... 124 B6
Normanton le
  Heath Leics............86 D2
Normanton on
  Cliffe Lincs........... 102 F4
Normanton on Soar
  Notts...................... 101 K7
Normanton on the
  Wolds Notts 101 L6

Normanton on Trent
Notts 116 C7
Norris Green Lpool....... 111 L3
Norris Hill Leics...............86 D1
Norristhorpe Kirk........ 123 J6
Northall Bucks................58 F4
Northallerton N York .. 141 J7
Northam C Sotn.............29 H8
Northam Devon 23 G5
Northampton Nhants....73 L3
Northampton Worcs 70 E2
Northampton
Services Nhants........73 K3
North Anston Rothm... 115 K5
North Ascot Br For........42 E6
North Aston Oxon...........57 J3
Northaw Herts.................59 L7
Northay Somset...............13 H1
North Baddesley
Hants............................29 H7
North Ballachulish
Highld....................... 191 L4
North Barrow Somset.....26 E5
North Barsham Norfk.. 105 L5
Northbay W Isls 233 b9
North Benfleet Essex.....46 C3
North Berwick E Loth.. 178 C2
North Boarhunt
Hants............................17 H1
Northborough C Pete....89 H3
Northbourne Kent..........35 J4
North Bovey Devon 11 H7
North Bradley Wilts........27 J1
North Brentor Devon......10 C8
North Brewham
Somset..........................27 G4
Northbrook Hants 29 K4
North Buckland
Devon...........................23 G4
North Burlingham
Norfk...........................93 H2
North Cadbury
Somset..........................26 F6
North Carlton Lincs 116 F6
North Carlton Notts.... 115 L4
North Cave E R Yk........ 125 K4
North Cerney Gloucs 56 A6
North Chailey E Susx......19 K2
Northchapel W Susx.......30 F5
North Charford
Hants............................28 D7
North Charlton
Nthumb 169 H5
North Cheam Gt Lon......44 E6
North Cheriton
Somset..........................27 G6
North Chideock
Dorset 13 K4
Northchurch Herts.........58 F6
North Cliffe E R Yk...... 125 K3
North Clifton Notts.... 116 D6
North Cockerington
Lincs........................... 118 E4
North Connel Ag & B... 182 C1
North Cornelly
Brdgnd..........................36 C4
North Cotes Lincs........ 118 E2
Northcott Devon 9 J6
Northcourt Oxon............57 J7
North Cove Suffk............93 K5
North Cowton N York... 141 G6
North Crawley
M Keyn..........................74 D5
North Creake Norfk 105 K5
North Curry Somset........25 L6
North Dalton E R Yk.... 125 L1
North Deighton
N York......................... 124 B1
Northdown Kent............35 K2
North Downs 34 B4
North Duffield N York. 125 G3
North Elmham Norfk..... 106 B7
North Elmsall Wakefd. 124 D7
North End C Port............17 J3
North End Essex.............61 G4
North End Hants.............28 C7
North End Nhants..........74 D2

North End W Susx...........18 D5
Northend Warwks...........72 E4
Northenden Manch 113 J4
North Erradale
Highld........................ 219 H5
North Evington
C Leic............................87 J3
North Fambridge
Essex............................61 K7
North Ferriby E R Yk... 126 B5
Northfield Birm...............85 H7
Northfield C Aber......... 207 G4
Northfield E R Yk........ 126 C5
Northfields Lincs...........88 E2
Northfleet Kent..............45 M5
North Frodingham
E R Yk......................... 135 H8
North Gorley Hants.........15 M1
North Green Suffk..........79 G3
North Greetwell
Lincs........................... 117 G6
North Grimston
N York......................... 134 C6
North Haven Shet 235 e7
North Hayling Hants......17 K2
North Hill Cnwll 5 L1
North Hillingdon
Gt Lon..........................43 H4
North Hinksey
Village Oxon 57 J6
North Holmwood
Surrey...........................31 K3
North Huish Devon.......... 7 G5
North Hykeham Lincs.. 116 F7
Northiam E Susx 21 G2
Northill C Beds 75 G5
Northington Hants..........29 K4
North Kelsey Lincs....... 117 H2
North Kessock Highld.. 213 G5
North Killingholme
N Linc......................... 126 E6
North Kilvington
N York......................... 132 F3
North Kilworth Leics....87 H6
North Kyme Lincs........ 103 J3
North Landing E R Yk.. 135 K5
Northlands Lincs......... 104 B2
Northleach Gloucs.........56 C5
North Lee Bucks 58 D6
Northleigh Devon 12 F3
North Leigh Oxon...........57 H5
North Leverton with
Habblesthorpe
Notts........................... 116 C5
Northlew Devon 10 D5
North Littleton
Worcs...........................71 J5
North Lopham Norfk.....92 C6
North Luffenham
Rutlnd..........................88 D3
North Marden
W Susx..........................30 D7
North Marston Bucks.....58 C4
North Middleton
Mdloth........................ 177 K6
North Millbrex Abers .. 216 F5
North Milmain D & G... 144 C4
North Molton Devon......24 B5
Northmoor Oxon............57 H7
North Moreton Oxon.....41 K3
Northmuir Angus........ 196 C5
North Mundham
W Susx..........................18 B5
North Muskham
Notts........................... 102 D2
North Newbald
E R Yk......................... 125 L3
North Newington
Oxon.............................72 E6
North Newnton Wilts....40 C8
North Newton
Somset..........................25 L5
Northney Hants..............17 K2
North Nibley Gloucs......39 H2
Northolt Gt Lon..............43 J4
Northolt Airport
Gt Lon..........................43 H4

Northop Flints 111 H7
Northop Hall Flints 111 J7
North Ormesby
Middsb 142 B4
North Ormsby Lincs.... 118 C3
Northorpe Kirk........... 123 J6
Northorpe Lincs........... 103 K5
Northorpe Lincs........... 116 E3
North Otterington
N York......................... 132 E2
North Owersby Lincs... 117 H3
Northowram Calder..... 123 G5
North Perrott Somset..... 13 L1
North Petherton
Somset..........................25 L5
North Petherwin
Cnwll............................. 9 H6
North Pickenham
Norfk...........................91 J3
North Piddle Worcs 71 G4
North Poorton
Dorset 13 M3
Northport Dorset 15 H5
North Queensferry
Fife............................. 176 F3
North Rauceby Lincs... 103 G3
Northrepps Norfk 106 F5
North Reston Lincs...... 118 E5
North Rigton N York... 123 K1
North Rode Ches E...... 113 K7
North Ronaldsay Ork.. 234 e3
North Ronaldsay
Airport Ork 234 e3
North Runcton Norfk....90 F1
North Scarle Lincs...... 116 D7
North Shian Ag & B..... 191 H7
North Shields N Tyne.. 151 J2
North Shoebury
Sthend..........................46 F3
North Shore Bpool...... 120 D3
North Side C Pete..........89 K4
North Somercotes
Lincs........................... 118 F3
North Stainley N York. 132 D4
North Stifford Thurr.....45 L4
North Stoke BaNES........39 G6
North Stoke Oxon..........41 L3
North Stoke W Susx.......18 D4
North Street Kent..........34 D3
North Street W Berk......41 M6
North Sunderland
Nthumb 169 J3
North Tamerton
Cnwll............................. 9 J5
North Tawton Devon.....10 F4
North Third Stirlg........ 175 K1
North Thoresby Lincs.. 118 D2
North Tolsta W Isls..... 232 g2
Northton W Isls.......... 232 d5
North Town Devon.........10 D3
North Town Somset.......26 E3
North Town W & M........42 E4
North Tuddenham
Norfk...........................92 C2
North Uist W Isls........ 233 b6
Northumberland
National Park
Nthumb 157 K5
North Walsham
Norfk......................... 107 G6
North Waltham
Hants............................29 K3
North Warnborough
Hants............................30 B2
North Weald
Bassett Essex...............60 D7
North Wheatley
Notts........................... 116 C4
Northwich Ches W...... 112 F6
Northwick Worcs...........70 E3
North Widcombe
BaNES...........................38 E8
North Willingham
Lincs........................... 117 K4
North Wingfield
Derbys........................ 115 H8
North Witham Lincs.... 102 F7

Northwold Norfk............91 H4
Northwood C Stke 99 K3
Northwood Gt Lon..........43 H3
Northwood IoW...............16 F4
Northwood Shrops..........98 C6
Northwood Green
Gloucs...........................55 G5
North Wootton
Dorset 26 F8
North Wootton Norfk.. 105 G7
North Wootton
Somset..........................26 E3
North Wraxall Wilts.......39 J5
North York Moors
National Park 142 F6
Norton Donc................. 124 E7
Norton E Susx 19 M5
Norton Gloucs................55 J3
Norton Halton.............. 112 D5
Norton Nhants...............73 H2
Norton Notts................ 115 L6
Norton Powys.................68 F2
Norton S on T............... 141 K3
Norton Sheff................ 115 G5
Norton Shrops...............84 D4
Norton Suffk..................77 L2
Norton Swans................51 H7
Norton W Susx................18 C4
Norton Wilts...................39 K4
Norton Worcs..................70 F4
Norton Worcs..................71 J5
Norton Bavant Wilts.......27 K3
Norton Canes Staffs......85 H2
Norton Canes
Services Staffs........85 H3
Norton Canon Herefs.....69 H5
Norton Disney Lincs.... 102 E2
Norton Fitzwarren
Somset..........................25 J6
Norton Green IoW..........16 D5
Norton Hawkfield
BaNES...........................38 E7
Norton Heath Essex 60 F6
Norton in Hales
Shrops...........................99 G5
Norton-Juxta-
Twycross Leics...........86 D3
Norton-le-Clay
N York......................... 132 F5
Norton-le-Moors
C Stke 99 K3
Norton Lindsey
Warwks..........................72 B2
Norton Little Green
Suffk.............................77 L2
Norton Malreward
BaNES...........................38 E7
Norton-on-Derwent
N York......................... 134 C5
Norton St Philip
Somset..........................27 H1
Norton Subcourse
Norfk...........................93 J4
Norton sub Hamdon
Somset..........................26 C7
Norwell Notts.............. 102 C1
Norwell Woodhouse
Notts........................... 116 B8
Norwich Norfk...............92 F2
Norwich Airport
Norfk...........................92 E2
Norwick Shet............... 235 e1
Norwood Clacks.......... 185 J8
Norwood Green
Gt Lon..........................43 J5
Norwood Hill Surrey......31 L3
Norwoodside Cambs......90 B4
Noss Mayo Devon 6 E6
Nosterfield N York...... 132 D4
Nostie Highld.............. 210 D8
Notgrove Gloucs............56 C4
Nottage Brdgnd.............36 C5
Nottingham C Nott...... 101 L5
Notton Wakefd............ 123 L7
Notton Wilts...................39 K6
Noutard's Green
Worcs...........................70 E2

Nuffield Oxon.................42 A3
Nunburnholme
E R Yk.....................125 K2
Nuneaton Warwks..........86 D5
Nunhead Gt Lon.............45 G5
Nun Monkton N York ... 133 H7
Nunney Somset...............27 G3
Nunnington N York........133 K4
Nunsthorpe NE Lin 127 G8
Nunthorpe C York 124 F1
Nunthorpe Middsb........142 C4
Nunthorpe Village
Middsb......................142 C5
Nunton Wilts..................28 D6
Nunwick N York 132 E5
Nursling Hants...............29 G7
Nutbourne W Susx..........17 L2
Nutbourne W Susx..........18 E3
Nutfield Surrey...............32 B3
Nuthall Notts................101 K4
Nuthampstead Herts......76 B7
Nuthurst W Susx............31 K6
Nutley E Susx.................32 D7
Nuttall Bury.................122 B7
Nybster Highld.............231 L3
Nyetimber W Susx..........18 B6
Nyewood W Susx.............30 D6
Nymans W Susx.................31 L5
Nymet Rowland
Devon.........................11 G4
Nymet Tracey Devon 11 G5
Nympsfield Gloucs..........55 J7
Nynehead Somset...........25 H6
Nyton W Susx..................18 C5

O

Oadby Leics...................87 J4
Oad Street Kent.............34 B3
Oakamoor Staffs..........100 B4
Oakbank W Loth...........176 E5
Oak Cross Devon............10 D5
Oakdale Caerph.............37 J2
Oake Somset..................25 J6
Oaken Staffs..................84 F3
Oakenclough Lancs.......121 H2
Oakengates Wrekin........84 C2
Oakenshaw Dur............150 F7
Oakenshaw Kirk...........123 H5
Oakford Cerdgn.............66 B3
Oakford Devon...............24 E6
Oakham Rutlnd..............88 C2
Oakhanger Hants...........30 C4
Oakhill Somset...............26 F3
Oakington Cambs...........76 B2
Oakle Street Gloucs.......55 H4
Oakley Bed....................74 E4
Oakley Bucks.................57 M5
Oakley Fife...................176 D1
Oakley Hants.................29 K2
Oakley Suffk..................92 E7
Oakridge Lynch
Gloucs........................55 K7
Oaksey Wilts..................39 M2
Oakthorpe Leics.............86 D2
Oakwood C Derb...........101 G5
Oakworth C Brad.........122 F3
Oare Kent.....................34 D3
Oare Somset..................24 C3
Oare Wilts.....................40 D7
Oasby Lincs.................103 G5
Oath Somset..................26 B6
Oathlaw Angus.............196 D5
Oatlands Park Surrey.....43 H7
Oban Ag & B.................182 B2
Oban Airport Ag & B...182 C1
Obley Shrops.................83 G7
Obney P & K................195 G8
Oborne Dorset...............26 F7
Occold Suffk..................78 D1
Occumster Highld........231 J7
Ochiltree E Ayrs...........163 L5
Ockbrook Derbys..........101 H5
Ocker Hill Sandw...........85 H5
Ockham Surrey...............31 H1

Ockle Highld.................190 B3
Ockley Surrey.................31 J4
Ocle Pychard Herefs 69 L5
Odcombe Somset............26 D7
Odd Down BaNES...........39 H7
Oddingley Worcs............71 G3
Oddington Gloucs...........56 E3
Oddington Oxon.............57 K5
Odell Bed......................74 D3
Odiham Hants.................30 C2
Odsal C Brad................123 H5
Odsey Cambs..................75 K6
Odstock Wilts.................28 D6
Odstone Leics................86 E3
Offchurch Warwks..........72 D2
Offenham Worcs.............71 J5
Offerton Stockp............113 K4
Offham E Susx................19 L3
Offham Kent...................33 H2
Offham W Susx...............18 D4
Offord Cluny Cambs........75 J2
Offord D'Arcy Cambs......75 J2
Offton Suffk...................78 C5
Offwell Devon.................12 F3
Ogbourne Maizey
Wilts...........................40 D6
Ogbourne St
Andrew Wilts..............40 D6
Ogbourne St
George Wilts...............40 D5
Ogle Nthumb................158 E6
Oglet Lpool..................112 C5
Ogmore V Glam.............36 D7
Ogmore-by-Sea
V Glam........................36 D7
Ogmore Vale Brdgnd......36 E3
Okeford Fitzpaine
Dorset........................14 F1
Okehampton Devon........10 E5
Oker Side Derbys..........100 F1
Okewood Hill Surrey......31 J4
Old Nhants....................87 L8
Old Aberdeen C Aber.....207 H4
Old Alresford Hants........29 L5
Oldany Highld...............224 D2
Old Auchenbrack
D & G.........................154 D3
Old Basford C Nott.......101 K4
Old Basing Hants............30 A2
Old Beetley Norfk........106 A8
Oldberrow Warwks..........71 K2
Old Bewick Nthumb.......169 G5
Old Bolingbroke
Lincs.........................118 E8
Old Bramhope Leeds....123 J2
Old Brampton
Derbys.......................115 G6
Old Bridge of Urr
D & G.........................146 D2
Old Buckenham
Norfk..........................92 C5
Old Burghclere
Hants..........................41 J8
Oldbury Sandw..............85 H5
Oldbury Shrops..............84 C5
Oldbury Warwks.............86 C5
Oldbury-on-Severn
S Glos.........................38 E2
Oldbury on the Hill
Gloucs........................39 J3
Old Byland N York.........133 H3
Old Cantley Donc..........115 L2
Oldcastle Mons...............53 L3
Old Catton Norfk............92 F2
Old Clee NE Lin............127 G8
Old Cleeve Somset..........25 G3
Old Colwyn Conwy.......110 B6
Oldcotes Notts..............115 L4
Old Dailly S Ayrs...........152 F3
Old Dalby Leics............102 A7
Old Deer Abers.............217 J3
Old Edlington Donc.......115 K3
Old Ellerby E R Yk........126 E3
Old Felixstowe Suffk......79 G7
Oldfield Worcs...............70 E2
Old Fletton C Pete..........89 H4

Oldford Somset...............27 H2
Old Forge Herefs............54 E4
Old Grimsby IoS..............2 a1
Old Hall Green Herts......60 B4
Oldham Oldham............113 L1
Oldhamstocks E Loth...178 F4
Old Harlow Essex...........60 D5
Old Hunstanton
Norfk.........................105 G4
Old Hurst Cambs............89 K7
Old Hutton Cumb.........130 B2
Old Inns Services
N Lans.......................175 K3
Old Kilpatrick
W Duns......................174 E4
Old Knebworth Herts......59 L4
Old Lakenham Norfk......92 F3
Oldland S Glos................38 F6
Old Langho Lancs.........121 K4
Old Leake Lincs............104 C3
Old Malton N York........134 C5
Oldmeldrum Abers........216 F8
Oldmill Cnwll...................6 B2
Old Milverton
Warwks.......................72 C2
Oldmixon N Som............37 M8
Old Newton Suffk...........78 C3
Old Portlethen Abers....207 H6
Old Radford C Nott.......101 K4
Old Radnor Powys..........68 E3
Old Rayne Abers...........216 D8
Old Romney Kent...........21 K2
Old Shoreham
W Susx........................19 G4
Oldshoremore Highld...228 C4
Old Sodbury S Glos........39 H4
Old Somerby Lincs.........102 F5
Oldstead N York...........133 H4
Old Stratford Nhants......73 L6
Old Struan P & K...........194 C4
Old Swinford Dudley......84 F6
Old Thirsk N York.........132 F3
Old Town Cumb.............130 B3
Old Town E Susx............20 C5
Old Town IoS...................2 b2
Old Trafford Traffd.......113 J3
Oldwall Cumb...............148 E3
Oldwalls Swans..............50 F6
Old Warden C Beds........75 G5
Old Weston Cambs.........89 G7
Old Wick Highld...........231 L5
Old Windsor W & M........43 G5
Old Wives Lees Kent......34 E4
Old Woking Surrey..........31 G1
Olgrinmore Highld........231 G5
Olive Green Staffs........100 C8
Oliver's Battery
Hants..........................29 J6
Ollaberry Shet..............235 c3
Ollach Highld................209 H6
Ollerton Ches E.............113 H6
Ollerton Notts..............116 A7
Ollerton Shrops.............98 F7
Olney M Keyn.................74 C4
Olrig House Highld.......231 H3
Olton Solhll....................85 K6
Olveston S Glos..............38 E3
Ombersley Worcs...........70 E2
Ompton Notts...............116 B7
Onchan IoM.................237 d5
Onecote Staffs..............100 B2
Onibury Shrops...............83 J7
Onich Highld................191 K4
Onllwyn Neath...............52 C6
Onneley Staffs...............99 H4
Onslow Green Essex.......61 G4
Onslow Village
Surrey.........................31 G2
Onston Ches W.............112 E6
Opinan Highld..............219 H6
Orbliston Moray...........215 G3
Orbost Highld...............208 D5
Orby Lincs....................119 G7
Orchard Portman
Somset........................25 K6
Orcheston Wilts.............28 B3
Orcop Herefs..................54 C3

Orcop Hill Herefs............54 C3
Ord Abers....................216 C3
Ordhead Abers.............206 C3
Ordie Abers..................205 K5
Ordiequish Moray........215 H3
Ordsall Notts................116 B5
Ore E Susx.....................21 G4
Orford Suffk...................79 J4
Orford Warrtn..............112 E4
Organford Dorset...........15 H4
Orkney Islands Ork.......234 c6
Orkney Neolithic Ork...234 b6
Orlestone Kent...............34 D7
Orleton Herefs................69 J2
Orleton Worcs................70 C2
Orlingbury Nhants.........74 C1
Ormesby R & Cl............142 C4
Ormesby St
Margaret Norfk...........93 K1
Ormesby St Michael
Norfk..........................93 K1
Ormiscaig Highld..........219 K4
Ormiston E Loth...........177 L4
Ormsaigmore Highld...189 L4
Ormsary Ag & B............172 C4
Ormskirk Lancs.............120 F8
Oronsay Ag & B............171 G2
Orphir Ork....................234 b6
Orpington Gt Lon...........45 J4
Orrell Sefton.................111 K3
Orrell Wigan.................112 D2
Orroland D & G.............146 D5
Orsett Essex...................45 M4
Orslow Staffs.................84 E1
Orston Notts................102 C4
Orton Cumb..................138 F5
Orton Nhants.................88 B7
Orton Staffs...................84 F4
Orton Longueville
C Pete.........................89 H4
Orton-on-the-Hill
Leics...........................86 C3
Orton Waterville
C Pete.........................89 H4
Orwell Cambs.................75 L4
Osbaldeston Lancs.......121 J4
Osbaldwick C York.......124 F1
Osbaston Leics...............86 E3
Osbaston Shrops............97 L7
Osborne House IoW.......17 G4
Osbournby Lincs...........103 H5
Oscroft Ches W.............112 D7
Ose Highld...................208 E6
Osgathorpe Leics.........101 H8
Osgodby Lincs..............117 H3
Osgodby N York...........124 F4
Osgodby N York...........135 G3
Oskaig Highld...............209 H6
Oskamull Ag & B..........189 L3
Osmaston Derbys.........100 D4
Osmington Dorset..........14 D5
Osmington Mills
Dorset........................14 E6
Osmondthorpe Leeds...123 L4
Osmotherley N York......141 K7
Osney Oxon...................57 J6
Ospringe Kent...............34 D3
Ossett Wakefd..............123 K6
Ossington Notts...........116 C8
Osterley Gt Lon.............44 D5
Oswaldkirk N York.......133 K4
Oswaldtwistle Lancs....121 L5
Oswestry Shrops............97 L6
Otford Kent....................32 F2
Otham Kent....................33 K3
Othery Somset................26 B5
Otley Leeds...................123 J2
Otley Suffk.....................78 E4
Otterbourne Hants.........29 J6
Otterburn N York..........131 G2
Otterburn Nthumb.......157 M4
Otter Ferry Ag & B........172 F2
Otterham Cnwll...............8 F6
Otterhampton
Somset........................25 K3
Otternish W Isls............232 c5
Ottershaw Surrey............43 G7

Otterswick Shet............ 235 d3
Otterton Devon.................12 E5
Ottery St Mary Devon....12 E4
Ottinge Kent 34 F6
Ottringham E R Yk......127 G5
Oughterside Cumb.......147 K6
Oughtibridge Sheff......114 F3
Oughtrington Warrtn....113 G4
Oulston N York.............133 H5
Oulton Cumb 147 M5
Oulton Norfk 106 D6
Oulton Staffs....................99 K5
Oulton Suffk 93 L5
Oulton Broad Suffk........93 L5
Oulton Street Norfk 106 D6
Oundle Nhants................88 F6
Ounsdale Staffs...............84 F5
Our Dynamic Earth
    C Edin....................177 H4
Ousby Cumb 149 G7
Ousden Suffk 77 G3
Ousefleet E R Yk...........125 K6
Ouston Dur....................151 G4
Outgate Cumb................137 K7
Outhgill Cumb................139 H6
Outhill Warwks 71 K2
Outlane Kirk...................123 G6
Out Rawcliffe Lancs......120 E3
Out Skerries Shet.........235 e4
Outwell Norfk 90 D3
Outwood Surrey...............32 B4
Outwoods Staffs..............99 H8
Ouzlewell Green
    Leeds......................123 L5
Over Cambs 75 L1
Overbury Worcs 71 G6
Overcombe Dorset..........14 D6
Over Compton
    Dorset.......................26 E7
Over Haddon Derbys ...114 D7
Over Kellet Lancs 129 L5
Over Kiddington
    Oxon..........................57 H4
Overleigh Somset............26 C4
Over Norton Oxon 56 F3
Over Peover Ches E......113 H6
Overpool Ches W 111 L6
Overscaig Highld...........225 J4
Overseal Derbys.............86 C1
Over Silton N York........133 G2
Oversland Kent 34 E3
Overstone Nhants............74 B2
Over Stowey Somset.......25 J4
Overstrand Norfk..........106 F4
Over Stratton Somset......26 B7
Overthorpe Nhants..........72 F6
Overton C Aber 207 G3
Overton Hants 29 K2
Overton Lancs................129 J7
Overton N York.............133 H7
Overton Shrops...............69 K1
Overton Swans................50 F7
Overton Wakefd............123 K7
Overtown N Lans..........175 L7
Over Wallop Hants.........28 F4
Over Whitacre
    Warwks.....................86 B5
Over Worton Oxon..........57 H3
Oving Bucks 58 C4
Oving W Susx..................18 B5
Ovingdean Br & H...........19 K5
Ovingham Nthumb.........150 D3
Ovington Dur................140 E4
Ovington Essex................77 H6
Ovington Hants 29 K5
Ovington Norfk...............91 K3
Ovington Nthumb..........150 D3
Ower Hants.....................28 F7
Owermoigne Dorset.......14 E5
Owlerton Sheff.............115 G4
Owlsmoor Br For 42 D7
Owlswick Bucks 58 C6
Owmby Lincs.................117 G4
Owmby Lincs.................117 H1
Owslebury Hants.............29 K6
Owston Donc.................124 E7

Owston Leics....................87 L3
Owston Ferry N Linc 116 D2
Owstwick E R Yk...........127 G4
Owthorne E R Yk..........127 H5
Owthorpe Notts 102 A5
Owton Manor Hartpl 141 L2
Oxborough Norfk............91 G3
Oxcombe Lincs..............118 D6
Oxenholme Cumb.........129 L2
Oxenhope C Brad.........122 F4
Oxen Park Cumb 129 G3
Oxenpill Somset..............26 C3
Oxenton Gloucs 55 L2
Oxenwood Wilts.............40 F8
Oxford Oxon 57 K6
Oxford Airport Oxon.....57 J5
Oxford Services
    Oxon..........................57 L6
Oxhey Herts....................43 J2
Oxhill Dur.....................150 F4
Oxhill Warwks 72 C5
Oxley Wolves 84 F3
Oxley Green Essex 61 L5
Oxlode Cambs.................90 C6
Oxnam Border...............167 L5
Oxnead Norfk................106 F7
Oxshott Surrey.................43 J7
Oxspring Barns 114 F2
Oxted Surrey...................32 D3
Oxton Border.................178 B7
Oxton N York................124 D2
Oxton Notts...................101 M3
Oxton Wirral 111 J4
Oxwich Swans 51 G7
Oxwich Green Swans 50 F7
Oykel Bridge Highld......221 K2
Oyne Abers...................206 D1
Oystermouth Swans 51 H7

P

Pabail W Isls................232 g2
Packington Leics............86 D1
Packmoor C Stke............99 K2
Padanaram Angus......196 C6
Padbury Bucks................58 B2
Paddington Gt Lon.........44 F4
Paddlesworth Kent.........35 G6
Paddlesworth Kent.........46 B7
Paddock Wood Kent.......33 H4
Padiham Lancs..............122 B4
Padside N York..............132 B7
Padstow Cnwll..................4 E2
Padworth W Berk...........41 L7
Pagham W Susx...............18 B6
Paglesham Essex 46 F2
Paignton Torbay 7 K4
Pailton Warwks 86 F6
Painscastle Powys..........68 D5
Painshawfield
    Nthumb..................150 D3
Painsthorpe E R Yk......134 C7
Painswick Gloucs............55 K6
Painter's Forstal
    Kent...........................34 D3
Paisley Rens.................174 E5
Pakefield Suffk................93 L5
Pakenham Suffk..............77 K2
Paley Street W & M........42 E5
Palfrey Wsall..................85 H4
Palgrave Suffk.................92 D7
Pallington Dorset............14 E4
Palmerston E Ayrs........163 L5
Palnackie D & G.............146 E4
Palnure D & G...............145 J3
Palterton Derbys...........115 J7
Pamber End Hants.........41 L8
Pamber Green Hants 41 L8
Pamber Heath Hants.....41 L7
Pamington Gloucs...........55 J2
Pamphill Dorset..............15 J3
Pampisford Cambs..........76 C5
Panbride Angus.............187 J1
Pancrasweek Devon 9 H4
Pandy Mons....................53 M4

Pandy Tudur Conwy......110 B8
Panfield Essex................61 H3
Pangbourne W Berk........41 M5
Pangdean W Susx...........19 J4
Pannal N York...............123 L1
Pannal Ash N York........132 D8
Pant Shrops....................97 L7
Pantasaph Flints 111 G6
Pant-ffrwyth Brdgnd.....36 E4
Pant Glas Gwynd............95 H3
Pantglas Powys...............81 G4
Panton Lincs..................117 K5
Pant-y-dwr Powys..........81 L8
Pant-y-mwyn Flints 111 H8
Panxworth Norfk............93 H2
Papa Stour Shet 235 b5
Papa Stour Airport
    Shet.......................235 b5
Papa Westray Ork.........234 c3
Papa Westray
    Airport Ork...........234 c3
Papcastle Cumb............136 F2
Papigoe Highld..............231 L5
Papple E Loth................178 D4
Papplewick Notts..........101 K3
Papworth Everard
    Cambs.......................75 K3
Papworth St Agnes
    Cambs.......................75 J2
Par Cnwll..........................5 G5
Parbold Lancs................121 G7
Parbrook Somset............26 E4
Parc Gwynd....................96 D5
Parc Seymour Newpt.....38 B3
Pardshaw Cumb............136 F3
Parham Suffk...................79 G3
Park D & G....................154 F4
Park Nthumb.................149 H3
Park Corner Oxon..........42 B3
Parkend Gloucs...............54 E6
Parker's Green Kent 33 G4
Park Farm Kent...............34 D6
Parkgate Ches W...........111 J6
Parkgate D & G 155 H4
Park Gate Hants..............17 G2
Park Gate Leeds............123 J3
Parkgate Surrey..............31 K3
Parkhall W Duns...........174 E4
Parkham Devon...............22 F6
Parkmill Swans................51 G7
Park Royal Gt Lon...........44 D4
Parkside Dur..................151 K5
Parkside N Lans............175 L6
Parkstone BCP................15 J4
Park Street Herts............59 J6
Parracombe Devon 23 L3
Parson Drove Cambs......89 L2
Parson's Heath Essex......62 B3
Partick C Glas...............174 F5
Partington Traffd..........113 G3
Partney Lincs................118 F7
Parton Cumb.................136 D3
Partridge Green
    W Susx.......................19 G2
Parwich Derbys............100 D2
Passenham Nhants.........73 L6
Paston C Pete.................89 H3
Paston Norfk.................107 G5
Patcham Br & H...............19 J4
Patching W Susx.............18 E4
Pathway S Glos..............38 E4
Pateley Bridge
    N York.....................132 B6
Pathhead Fife................186 E8
Pathhead Mdloth..........177 K5
Path of Condie P & K....185 M5
Patna E Ayrs.................163 K7
Patney Wilts....................40 B8
Patrick IoM...................237 b5
Patrick Brompton
    N York.....................132 C2
Patricroft Salfd.............113 H2
Patrington E R Yk.........127 H6
Patrington Haven
    E R Yk.....................127 H6
Patrixbourne Kent..........35 G4
Patterdale Cumb...........137 L4

Pattingham Staffs............84 E4
Pattishall Nhants............73 J4
Pattiswick Green
    Essex.........................61 K3
Paul Cnwll..........................2 E5
Paulerspury Nhants........73 K5
Paull E R Yk..................126 E5
Paulton BaNES................26 F1
Paultons Park Hants......28 F7
Pauperhaugh
    Nthumb..................158 D3
Pavenham Bed...............74 E4
Pawlett Somset...............25 L3
Paxford Gloucs................71 L6
Paxton Border...............179 J7
Payhembury Devon.........12 E3
Paythorne Lancs............122 C1
Peacehaven E Susx.........19 L5
Peak District
    National Park 114 D3
Peak Forest Derbys......114 C5
Peakirk C Pete.................89 H3
Peasedown St John
    BaNES........................39 G8
Peasemore W Berk.........41 J5
Peasenhall Suffk.............79 H2
Pease Pottage
    W Susx.......................31 L5
Pease Pottage
    Services W Susx.......31 L5
Peaslake Surrey..............31 H3
Peasley Cross St Hel.....112 D3
Peasmarsh E Susx..........21 H2
Peathill Abers...............217 H2
Peat Inn Fife..................187 G5
Peatling Magna
    Leics..........................87 H5
Peatling Parva Leics.......87 H5
Pebmarsh Essex..............77 J7
Pebsham E Susx..............20 F4
Pebworth Worcs..............71 K5
Pecket Well Calder........122 E5
Peckforton Ches E...........98 D2
Peckham Gt Lon.............45 G5
Peckleton Leics...............86 F4
Pedlinge Kent..................34 F7
Pedmore Dudley.............85 G6
Pedwell Somset...............26 B4
Peebles Border..............166 C2
Peel IoM........................237 b4
Peene Kent......................35 G6
Pegsdon C Beds...............59 J2
Pegswood Nthumb 159 G5
Pegwell Kent...................35 K2
Peinchorran Highld........209 H7
Peinlich Highld...............208 F3
Peldon Essex...................62 B5
Pelsall Wsall....................85 H3
Pelton Dur.....................151 G4
Pelynt Cnwll......................5 K5
Pemberton Carmth..........51 G5
Pemberton Wigan..........112 D2
Pembrey Carmth..............50 E5
Pembridge Herefs............69 H3
Pembroke Pembks...........49 G7
Pembroke Dock
    Pembks.......................49 G6
Pembrokeshire
    Coast National
    Park Pembks............48 E4
Pembury Kent.................33 G5
Pen-allt Herefs................54 E3
Penallt Mons...................54 D6
Penally Pembks...............49 J7
Penarth V Glam...............37 J6
Pen-bont
    Rhydybeddau
    Cerdgn.......................80 F6
Penbryn Cerdgn..............65 J4
Pencader Carmth...........66 B7
Pencaitland E Loth........177 L5
Pencarnisiog IoA...........108 D6
Pencarreg Carmth...........66 C5
Pencelli Powys.................53 H3
Penclawdd Swans...........51 G6
Pencoed Brdgnd..............36 E4
Pencombe Herefs............69 L4

Pencraig Herefs..............54 E4
Pencraig Powys 97 G6
Pendeen Cnwll.................. 2 C4
Penderyn Rhondd 52 E6
Pendine Carmth 50 B4
Pendlebury Salfd........ 113 H2
Pendleton Lancs........ 121 L3
Pendock Worcs............55 H2
Pendoggett Cnwll............ 8 D8
Pendomer Somset.......13 M1
Pendoylan V Glam 37 G5
Penegoes Powys...........81 G4
Pen-ffordd Pembks......49 J3
Pengam Caerph.............37 J2
Pengam Cardif...............37 K5
Penge Gt Lon..................45 G6
Pengelly Cnwll.................. 8 E7
Penhallow Cnwll............... 3 K2
Penhalvean Cnwll............ 3 J4
Penhill Swindn..............40 D3
Penhow Newpt...............38 B3
Penicuik Mdloth.......... 177 H6
Penifiler Highld 209 G6
Peninver Ag & B.......... 161 J4
Penistone Barns........ 114 E2
Penkill S Ayrs.............. 152 F3
Penkridge Staffs..........85 G2
Penley Wrexhm..............98 B4
Penllyn V Glam 36 F5
Penmachno Conwy 96 C3
Penmaen Caerph 37 J2
Penmaen Swans 51 G7
Penmaenmawr
  Conwy 109 K6
Penmaenpool Gwynd ...95 M8
Penmark V Glam 37 G6
Penmynydd IoA......... 109 G6
Pennal Gwynd.................80 F4
Pennan Abers.............. 216 F2
Pennant Powys...............81 J4
Pennar Pembks.............49 G6
Pennerley Shrops 83 G4
Pennines 122 E4
Pennington Cumb....... 128 F4
Pennorth Powys............53 H3
Penn Street Bucks.........42 F2
Penny Bridge Cumb... 129 G3
Pennycross Ag & B...... 181 G3
Pennyghael Ag & B..... 181 H3
Pennyglen S Ayrs....... 163 H7
Pennymoor Devon........11 K3
Pennywell Sundld 151 J4
Penparc Cerdgn............65 H5
Penperlleni Mons.........53 L6
Penpoll Cnwll.................. 5 J5
Penponds Cnwll.............. 3 H4
Penpont D & G 154 E4
Pen-rhiw Pembks........65 H6
Penrhiwceiber
  Rhondd 37 G2
Pen Rhiwfawr Neath....51 L4
Penrhiwllan Cerdgn 65 K6
Penrhiw-pal Cerdgn 65 K5
Penrhos Gwynd.............94 F5
Penrhos Mons 54 E6
Penrhyn Bay Conwy... 110 A5
Penrhyn-coch
  Cerdgn 80 E6
Penrhyndeudraeth
  Gwynd 95 K5
Penrice Swans..............50 F7
Penrioch N Ayrs......... 161 L1
Penrith Cumb.............. 138 D2
Penrose Cnwll.................. 4 D2
Penruddock Cumb..... 138 B2
Penryn Cnwll.................... 3 K4
Pensarn Conwy.......... 110 C5
Pensax Worcs................70 C2
Penselwood Somset....27 H5
Pensford BaNES...........38 F7
Pensham Worcs............71 G5
Penshaw Sundld........ 151 H4
Penshurst Kent............32 F4
Pensilva Cnwll................. 5 L2
Pensnett Dudley...........85 G5
Pentewan Cnwll.............. 4 F6
Pentir Gwynd 109 H7

Pentire Cnwll 4 C4
Pentlow Essex..............77 J5
Pentney Norfk...............91 G2
Pentonbridge Cumb .. 156 D6
Penton Mewsey
  Hants............................29 G3
Pentraeth IoA............. 109 G5
Pentre Mons...................54 B7
Pentre Rhondd 36 F2
Pentre Shrops 98 A8
Pentrebach Myr Td.......53 G7
Pentre-bach Powys......52 E2
Pentre Berw IoA 108 F6
Pentrecelyn Denbgs.....97 J2
Pentre-celyn Powys 81 J3
Pentre-chwyth
  Swans...........................51 J6
Pentre-cwrt Carmth 65 L6
Pentredwr Denbgs.......97 J3
Pentrefelin Gwynd.......95 J5
Pentrefoelas Conwy......96 D3
Pentregat Cerdgn 65 K4
Pentre-Gwenlais
  Carmth 51 H3
Pentre Hodrey
  Shrops.........................83 G7
Pentre Llanrhaeadr
  Denbgs...................... 110 F8
Pentre Meyrick
  V Glam 36 E5
Pentre-tafarn-y-
  fedw Conwy...............96 C1
Pentrich Derbys......... 101 G3
Pentridge Dorset..........28 B7
Pen-twyn Mons 54 D6
Pentwynmaur Caerph...37 J2
Pentyrch Cardif 37 H4
Penwithick Cnwll............ 5 G5
Penybanc Carmth........51 H2
Penybont Powys 68 C2
Pen-y-bont Powys 97 K7
Penybontfawr Powys ...97 G7
Pen-y-bryn Pembks......65 G6
Pencae Wrexhm 97 L4
Pen-y-clawdd Mons 54 C6
Pen-y-coedcae
  Rhondd 37 G3
Penycwn Pembks 48 E3
Pen-y-felin Flints........ 111 G7
Pen-y-fford Flints..........97 L1
Pen-y-Garnedd
  Powys...........................97 H7
Pen-y-graig Gwynd 94 D5
Penygraig Rhondd 36 F3
Penygroes Carmth........51 H3
Penygroes Gwynd 95 H2
Pen-y-Mynydd
  Carmth 50 F5
Penymynydd Flints........97 L1
Penysarn IoA.............. 108 F4
Pen-y-stryt Denbgs......97 J3
Penywaun Rhondd.......52 F6
Penzance Cnwll.............. 2 E5
Peopleton Worcs...........71 G4
Peplow Shrops 98 F7
Perceton N Ayrs......... 163 J2
Percyhorner Abers..... 217 H2
Perelle Guern.............. 236 b3
Perham Down Wilts....28 E2
Periton Somset..............24 E3
Perivale Gt Lon.............44 D4
Perkins Village
  Devon...........................12 D4
Perlethorpe Notts...... 115 M7
Perranarworthal
  Cnwll............................ 3 K4
Perranporth Cnwll......... 3 K1
Perranuthnoe Cnwll 2 F5
Perranwell Cnwll............ 3 K4
Perranzabuloe Cnwll..... 3 K2
Perry Birm.....................85 J5
Perry Barr Birm 85 J5
Perry Green Wilts.........39 L3
Pershall Staffs...............99 J6
Pershore Worcs.............71 G5
Pertenhall Bed..............74 F2
Perth P & K................. 186 B3

Perthy Shrops 98 A5
Perton Herefs................69 L6
Perton Staffs................84 F4
Peterborough C Pete 89 H4
Peterborough
  Services Cambs........89 G5
Peterchurch Herefs......69 G6
Peterculter C Aber..... 206 F5
Peterhead Abers........ 217 L5
Peterlee Dur................ 151 K6
Petersfield Hants.........30 C6
Peter's Green Herts......59 J4
Petersham Gt Lon.........44 D5
Peters Marland
  Devon...........................10 C3
Peterstone
  Wentlooge Newpt.....37 K4
Peterston-super-
  Ely V Glam 37 G5
Peterstow Herefs..........54 E3
Peter Tavy Devon............ 6 D1
Petham Kent.................34 F4
Petherwin Gate
  Cnwll.............................. 9 H6
Petrockstow Devon......10 D3
Pett E Susx....................21 H3
Pettaugh Suffk.............78 E3
Petterden Angus........ 196 C7
Pettinain S Lans......... 165 J2
Pettistree Suffk............79 G4
Petton Devon.................24 F6
Petts Wood Gt Lon.......45 J6
Pettycur Fife............... 177 H2
Pettymuk Abers......... 207 G1
Petworth W Susx..........31 G6
Pevensey E Susx...........20 D5
Pevensey Bay E Susx...20 D5
Pewsey Wilts.................40 D7
Pewsham Wilts.............39 L6
Phepson Worcs............71 G3
Philham Devon.............22 D6
Philiphaugh Border 166 F4
Phillack Cnwll................. 2 F4
Philleigh Cnwll............... 4 D7
Philpstoun W Loth..... 176 E3
Phoenix Green Hants...30 C1
Pibsbury Somset...........26 C6
Pickburn Donc........... 115 K1
Pickering N York........ 134 C3
Pickford Covtry............86 C6
Pickhill N York........... 132 E3
Picklescott Shrops.......83 J4
Pickmere Ches E......... 113 G6
Pickney Somset............25 J5
Pickwell Leics..............87 L2
Pickworth Lincs......... 103 H5
Pickworth Rutlnd........88 E2
Picton Ches W............ 112 B7
Piddinghoe E Susx......19 L5
Piddington Nhants.......74 B4
Piddington Oxon..........57 M5
Piddlehinton Dorset....14 D3
Piddletrenthide
  Dorset...........................14 D3
Pidley Cambs...............89 K7
Piercebridge Darltn.... 140 F4
Pierowall Ork.............. 234 c3
Pilgrims Hatch Essex...45 L2
Pilham Lincs............... 116 E3
Pillaton Cnwll................. 6 A3
Pillerton Hersey
  Warwks.........................72 C5
Pillerton Priors
  Warwks.........................72 C5
Pilley Barns................ 115 G2
Pilley Hants..................16 D3
Pillgwenlly Newpt........37 L3
Piling Lancs................ 120 E2
Pilning S Glos...............38 D4
Pilsbury Derbys......... 114 C8
Pilsdon Dorset..............13 K3
Pilsley Derbys............ 101 H1
Pilsley Derbys............ 114 E7
Pilson Green Norfk......93 H2
Piltdown E Susx...........19 L2
Pilton Devon.................23 J5

Pilton Nhants................88 E6
Pilton Rutlnd................88 D3
Pilton Somset...............26 E3
Pimlico Herts................59 H6
Pimperne Dorset..........15 G1
Pinchbeck Lincs......... 103 L7
Pin Green Herts............59 L3
Pinhoe Devon................12 C4
Pinley Green Warwks...72 B2
Pinminnoch S Ayrs.... 152 E4
Pinmore S Ayrs.......... 152 E4
Pinn Devon....................12 E5
Pinner Gt Lon...............43 J3
Pinner Green Gt Lon....43 J3
Pinvin Worcs.................71 G5
Pinwherry S Ayrs....... 152 E5
Pinxton Derbys........... 101 J2
Pipe and Lyde Herefs...69 K5
Pipe Aston Herefs........69 J7
Pipe Gate Shrops.........99 G4
Piperdam Angus........ 186 E1
Piperhill Highld.......... 213 K4
Pipewell Nhants...........88 B6
Pirbright Surrey............30 F1
Pirnie Border.............. 167 K4
Pirnmill N Ayrs.......... 161 L1
Pirton Herts..................59 J2
Pishill Oxon..................42 B3
Pistyll Gwynd................94 F4
Pitblae Abers.............. 217 J2
Pitcairngreen P & K.... 185 M3
Pitcalnie Highld......... 223 H6
Pitcaple Abers............ 206 D1
Pitcarity Angus.......... 196 B4
Pitchcombe Gloucs......55 J6
Pitchcott Bucks............58 C4
Pitchford Shrops..........83 K3
Pitch Green Bucks........58 C7
Pitchroy Moray........... 214 E6
Pitcombe Somset.........26 F5
Pitcox E Loth.............. 178 E4
Pitfichie Abers............ 206 D3
Pitglassie Abers......... 216 D5
Pitgrudy Highld.......... 223 H3
Pitlessie Fife.............. 186 E5
Pitlochry P & K........... 194 E5
Pitmachie Abers......... 216 C8
Pitmain Highld........... 203 H5
Pitmedden Abers....... 217 G8
Pitmedden Garden
  Abers......................... 217 G8
Pitminster Somset.......25 K7
Pitmuies Angus......... 196 F6
Pitmunie Abers.......... 206 C3
Pitney Somset..............26 C5
Pitroddie P & K........... 186 C3
Pitscottie Fife............ 187 G5
Pitsea Essex.................46 C3
Pitsford Nhants............73 L2
Pitstone Bucks.............58 F5
Pittarrow Abers......... 197 H2
Pittenweem Fife......... 187 J6
Pitteuchar Fife........... 186 D7
Pittington Dur............ 151 H6
Pittodrie House
  Hotel Abers.............. 206 D1
Pitton Wilts..................28 E5
Pittulie Abers............. 217 H2
Pity Me Dur................ 151 G5
Pixham Surrey..............31 K2
Plains N Lans.............. 175 L5
Plaish Shrops................83 K4
Plaistow Gt Lon............45 H4
Plaistow W Susx...........31 G5
Plaitford Hants.............28 F7
Plawsworth Dur.......... 151 G5
Plaxtol Kent.................33 G3
Playden E Susx.............21 H2
Playford Suffk..............78 F5
Play Hatch Oxon...........42 C5
Playing Place Cnwll....... 4 C7
Playley Green Gloucs...55 L2
Plealey Shrops..............83 H3
Plean Stirlg................. 175 L2
Pleasance Fife............ 186 D5
Pleasington Bl w D..... 121 J5
Pleasley Derbys.......... 115 J8

Pleasurewood Hills
Suffk.............................93 L4
Pleinheaume Guern......236 d2
Plemont Jersey...........236 a5
Plemstall Ches W..........112 C7
Pleshey Essex................61 G5
Plockton Highld............210 C7
Plowden Shrops.............83 H6
Pluckley Kent.................34 B5
Pluckley Thorne Kent.....34 B5
Plumbland Cumb..........147 K6
Plumley Ches E.............113 G6
Plumpton Cumb...........148 E7
Plumpton E Susx............19 K3
Plumpton Nhants...........73 H5
Plumpton Green
  E Susx.........................19 K3
Plumstead Gt Lon.........45 J4
Plumstead Norfk..........106 D5
Plumtree Notts.............101 L6
Plungar Leics...............102 C5
Plurenden Kent..............34 C7
Plush Dorset..................14 D3
Plwmp Cerdgn...............65 K4
Plymouth C Plym.............6 C5
Plympton C Plym.............6 D5
Plymstock C Plym............6 D5
Plymtree Devon..............12 D2
Pockley N York.............133 K3
Pocklington E R Yk........125 J2
Podimore Somset............26 D6
Podington Bed................74 D3
Podmore Staffs...............99 H5
Pointon Lincs...............103 J6
Pokesdown BCP..............15 L4
Polbain Highld..............224 B6
Polbathic Cnwll................6 A4
Polbeth W Loth............176 D5
Poldark Mine Cnwll.........3 H5
Polebrook Nhants...........88 F6
Polegate E Susx..............20 C5
Polesden Lacey
  Surrey........................31 J2
Polesworth Warwks.......86 C3
Polglass Highld............224 C6
Polgooth Cnwll.................4 F5
Polgown D & G.............154 C2
Poling W Susx.................18 E5
Poling Corner
  W Susx........................18 E5
Polkerris Cnwll.................5 H5
Pollington E R Yk..........124 F6
Polloch Highld..............190 F3
Pollokshaws C Glas......175 G6
Pollokshields C Glas......175 G5
Polmassick Cnwll.............4 F6
Polmont Falk................176 C3
Polnish Highld..............200 B8
Polperro Cnwll.................5 K5
Polruan Cnwll..................5 H5
Polstead Suffk................78 B6
Poltalloch Ag & B..........182 B7
Poltimore Devon.............12 C3
Polton Mdloth...............177 J5
Polwarth Border...........178 F7
Polyphant Cnwll................9 H7
Polzeath Cnwll.................4 E1
Pomathorn Mdloth........177 H6
Pondersbridge
  Cambs.........................89 J5
Ponders End Gt Lon......45 G2
Ponsanooth Cnwll............3 K4
Ponsworthy Devon...........7 G2
Pont Abraham
  Services Carmth..........51 H4
Pontac Jersey...............236 e8
Pontantwn Carmth..........50 F3
Pontardawe Neath...........51 K5
Pontarddulais Swans......51 H5
Pont-ar-gothi
  Carmth........................51 G2
Pontarsais Carmth...........66 B8
Pontblyddyn Flints..........97 L1
Pontcysyllte
  Aqueduct Wrexhm......97 L4
Pontefract Wakefd........124 C6
Ponteland Nthumb........158 F7

Ponterwyd Cerdgn..........81 G7
Pontesbury Shrops.........83 H3
Pontesford Shrops.........83 H3
Pontfadog Wrexhm........97 K5
Pontfaen Pembks............64 E7
Pont-faen Powys............67 L7
Pontgarreg Cerdgn.........65 K4
Ponthenri Carmth...........50 F4
Ponthir Torfn.................37 M2
Ponthirwaun Cerdgn......65 J5
Pontllanfraith
  Caerph........................37 J2
Pontlliw Swans...............51 H5
Pontllyfni Gwynd.............95 G3
Pontlottyn Caerph..........53 H6
Pontnêddféchan
  Neath..........................52 D6
Pontnewydd Torfn..........37 L2
Pontrhydfendigaid
  Cerdgn........................67 G2
Pont-rhyd-y-fen
  Neath..........................36 C2
Pontrhydygroes
  Cerdgn........................81 G8
Pontrilas Herefs.............54 B3
Pont Robert Powys..........82 C2
Pontshaen Cerdgn..........66 B5
Pontsticill Myr Td............53 G5
Pontwelly Carmth............65 L6
Pontyates Carmth............50 F4
Pontyberem Carmth........51 G4
Pontybodkin Flints...........97 L2
Pontyclun Rhondd...........37 G4
Pontycymer Brdgnd.........36 D3
Pontymister Caerph.........37 K3
Pont-y-pant Conwy..........96 B2
Pontypool Torfn...............53 L7
Pontypridd Rhondd.........37 G3
Pontywaun Caerph..........37 K2
Pool Cnwll........................3 H3
Poole BCP.......................15 J4
Poole Keynes Gloucs......39 M2
Poolewe Highld..............219 K5
Pooley Bridge Cumb.......138 C3
Poolfold Staffs................99 K1
Poolhill Gloucs................55 G3
Pool in Wharfedale
  Leeds.........................123 J2
Pool of Muckhart
  Clacks........................185 L7
Pool Street Essex............77 H6
Poplar Gt Lon..................45 G4
Porchfield IoW.................16 F4
Poringland Norfk.............92 F3
Porkellis Cnwll...................3 J5
Porlock Somset...............24 D3
Porlock Weir Somset.......24 D2
Portachoillan Ag & B......172 C6
Port-an-Eorna
  Highld.........................210 B7
Port Appin Ag & B..........191 H7
Port Askaig Ag & B.........171 H5
Portavadie Ag & B..........172 F4
Port Bannatyne
  Ag & B.......................173 J5
Portbury N Som...............38 D5
Port Carlisle Cumb.........147 M3
Port Charlotte
  Ag & B.......................170 E6
Portchester Hants..........17 H2
Port Driseach Ag & B......173 G4
Port Ellen Ag & B...........160 C1
Port Elphinstone
  Abers.........................206 E2
Portencalzie D & G........152 B7
Portencross N Ayrs.........173 K8
Port Erin IoM................237 a6
Portesham Dorset...........14 B5
Portessie Moray.............215 K2
Port Eynon Swans...........50 F7
Portfield Gate
  Pembks.......................48 F4
Portgate Devon...............10 B7
Port Gaverne Cnwll...........8 D8
Port Glasgow Inver........174 C4
Portgordon Moray.........215 J2
Portgower Highld...........227 H5

Porth Cnwll.......................4 C4
Porth Rhondd..................36 F3
Porthallow Cnwll...............3 K6
Porthallow Cnwll...............5 K5
Porthcawl Brdgnd............36 C5
Porthcothan Cnwll............4 D2
Porthcurno Cnwll..............2 C6
Port Henderson
  Highld.........................219 H6
Porthgain Pembks...........64 A7
Porthgwarra Cnwll............2 C6
Porthill Staffs..................99 J3
Porthkerry V Glam...........37 G6
Porthleven Cnwll...............3 H6
Porthmadog Gwynd.........95 K5
Porth Navas Cnwll.............3 K5
Porthoustock Cnwll...........3 K6
Porthpean Cnwll...............5 G5
Porthtowan Cnwll.............3 J2
Porthyrhyd Carmth..........51 G3
Portincaple Ag & B........183 J8
Portinfer Jersey.............236 a5
Portington E R Yk...........125 J4
Portinnisherrich
  Ag & B.......................182 D5
Portinscale Cumb..........137 H3
Port Isaac Cnwll................8 D8
Portishead N Som............38 C5
Portknockie Moray.........215 K2
Portland Dorset...............14 D7
Portlethen Abers............207 H6
Portling D & G................146 F4
Portloe Cnwll....................4 E7
Port Logan D & G...........144 D6
Portmahomack
  Highld.........................223 K5
Portmeirion Gwynd.........95 K5
Portmellon Cnwll...............4 F6
Port Mòr Highld..............189 K1
Portnacroish Ag & B......191 H6
Portnaguran W Isls........232 g2
Portnahaven Ag & B......170 D7
Portnalong Highld...........208 E7
Port nan Giuran
  W Isls.........................232 g2
Port nan Long W Isls......232 c5
Port Nis W Isls...............232 g1
Portobello C Edin...........177 J4
Portobello Wolves...........85 G4
Port of Menteith
  Stirlg..........................184 D6
Port of Ness W Isls........232 g1
Porton Wilts....................28 D4
Portpatrick D & G...........144 B4
Port Quin Cnwll.................8 C8
Port Ramsay Ag & B.......191 H7
Portreath Cnwll.................3 H3
Portreath Harbour
  Cnwll............................3 H3
Portree Highld...............209 G5
Port Righ Ag & B............161 K2
Port St Mary IoM............237 b7
Portscatho Cnwll...............4 D8
Portsea C Port.................17 J3
Portskerra Highld...........230 C3
Portskewett Mons...........38 D3
Portslade Br & H.............19 H4
Portslade-by-Sea
  Br & H.........................19 H5
Portslogan D & G...........144 B3
Portsmouth C Port..........17 J3
Portsmouth Calder.........122 D5
Portsmouth
  Dockyard C Port...........17 J3
Port Soderick IoM..........237 c6
Portsonachan Hotel
  Ag & B.......................182 F3
Portsoy Abers................216 B2
Port Sunlight Wirral.......111 K5
Portswood C Sotn............29 H8
Port Talbot Neath...........36 B3
Port Tennant Swans........51 K6
Portuairk Highld.............189 K3
Portway Sandw................85 H6
Portway Worcs................85 J8
Port Wemyss Ag & B......170 D7
Port William D & G.........145 H6

Portwrinkle Cnwll..............6 A5
Portyerrock D & G..........145 K7
Poslingford Suffk............77 H5
Posso Border.................166 B3
Postbridge Devon...........10 F8
Postcombe Oxon.............58 B7
Postling Kent..................34 F6
Postwick Norfk................93 G2
Potarch Abers................206 B6
Potten End Herts............59 G6
Potter Brompton
  N York........................134 F4
Potterhanworth
  Lincs.........................117 H7
Potterhanworth
  Booths Lincs..............117 H7
Potter Heigham
  Norfk.........................107 J8
Potterne Wilts.................39 M8
Potterne Wick Wilts........39 M8
Potters Bar Herts............59 L7
Potters Crouch Herts.......59 J6
Potters Green Covtry......86 D6
Potters Marston
  Leics...........................87 G4
Potterspury Nhants.........73 L6
Potter Street Essex.........60 D6
Potterton Abers..............207 H3
Potto N York..................141 L6
Potton C Beds.................75 J5
Pott Shrigley Ches E......113 L5
Poughill Cnwll...................9 G4
Poughill Devon................11 K3
Poulner Hants.................15 M2
Poulshot Wilts.................39 L7
Poulton Gloucs...............56 C7
Poulton Wirral...............111 J4
Poulton-le-Fylde
  Lancs........................120 D3
Poundbury Dorset...........14 D4
Poundffald Swans...........51 H6
Pound Green E Susx.......20 B2
Pound Green Suffk..........77 G4
Pound Hill W Susx...........32 B5
Poundon Bucks...............57 M3
Poundsgate Devon............7 G2
Poundstock Cnwll.............9 G5
Pouton D & G.................145 K5
Povey Cross Surrey.........31 L3
Powburn Nthumb...........168 F6
Powderham Devon...........12 C5
Powerstock Dorset.........13 M3
Powfoot D & G...............147 K2
Powick Worcs..................70 E4
Powmill P & K................185 L7
Poxwell Dorset................14 E5
Poyle Slough...................43 G5
Poynings W Susx.............19 H4
Poyntington Dorset.........26 F7
Poynton Ches E..............113 L5
Poynton Green
  Wrekin........................98 E8
Praa Sands Cnwll.............3 G5
Praze-an-Beeble
  Cnwll............................3 H4
Prees Shrops..................98 D5
Preesall Lancs...............120 E2
Prees Green Shrops.........98 D6
Prees Heath Shrops.........98 D5
Prees Higher Heath
  Shrops.........................98 E5
Pren-gwyn Cerdgn..........65 L5
Prenteg Gwynd................95 K4
Prescot Knows...............112 C3
Prescott Devon................25 H8
Presnerb Angus..............195 J3
Prestatyn Denbgs..........110 E5
Prestbury Ches E............113 K6
Prestbury Gloucs.............55 L4
Presteigne Powys............69 G2
Prestleigh Somset...........26 F4
Preston Border...............179 G6
Preston Br & H.................19 J4
Preston Devon...................7 K2
Preston Dorset................14 D5
Preston E R Yk...............126 F4
Preston Gloucs................56 B7

Preston Herts 59 K3
Preston Kent....................34 D3
Preston Kent....................35 H3
Preston Lancs 121 H4
Preston Nthumb..............169 H4
Preston Rutlnd.................88 C3
Preston Somset 25 H4
Preston Torbay...................7 K4
Preston Wilts 40 B5
Preston Bagot
   Warwks......................71 L2
Preston Bissett
   Bucks..........................58 A3
Preston Bowyer
   Somset........................25 H6
Preston Brockhurst
   Shrops.........................98 D7
Preston Brook Halton.. 112 E5
Preston Candover
   Hants...........................29 L3
Preston Capes
   Nhants.........................73 H4
Preston Green
   Warwks........................71 L2
Preston Gubbals
   Shrops.........................98 C8
Preston on Stour
   Warwks........................72 B4
Preston on the Hill
   Halton........................112 E5
Preston on Wye
   Herefs..........................69 H6
Prestonpans E Loth.... 177 K4
Preston Patrick
   Cumb..........................129 L3
Preston Plucknett
   Somset........................26 D7
Preston St Mary
   Suffk.............................77 L4
Preston-under-
   Scar N York................131 K2
Preston upon the
   Weald Moors
   Wrekin.........................84 C1
Preston Wynne
   Herefs..........................69 L5
Prestwich Bury 113 J1
Prestwick S Ayrs..........163 J4
Prestwick Airport
   S Ayrs.........................163 J4
Prestwood Bucks..........58 E7
Prickwillow Cambs........90 E6
Priddy Somset................26 D2
Priest Hutton Lancs.. 129 L5
Priestland E Ayrs.........164 B2
Priest Weston Shrops...82 F4
Primrosehill Border 179 G6
Primrose Hill Dudley 85 G6
Primsidemill Border 168 B4
Prince of Wales
   Bridge Mons..............38 D3
Princes Risborough
   Bucks..........................58 D7
Princethorpe Warwks.....72 E1
Princetown Devon............6 E2
Priors Hardwick
   Warwks........................72 F4
Priorslee Wrekin...........84 C2
Priors Marston
   Warwks........................72 F3
Priors Norton Gloucs...55 K3
Priston BaNES 39 G7
Prittlewell Sthend..........46 E3
Privett Hants..................30 B6
Prixford Devon................23 J4
Probus Cnwll....................4 E6
Prora E Loth.................178 C3
Prospect Cumb.............147 K6
Prospidnick Cnwll............3 H5
Protstonhill Abers.......216 F2
Prudhoe Nthumb.........150 D3
Pubil P & K....................193 G2
Publow BaNES................38 F7
Puckeridge Herts...........60 C4
Puckington Somset........26 B7
Pucklechurch S Glos....39 G5
Puddington Ches W....... 111 K6

Puddington Devon 11 J3
Puddletown Dorset......14 E4
Pudsey Leeds................123 J4
Pulborough W Susx......18 E3
Pulford Ches W..............98 A2
Pulham Dorset 14 D2
Pulham Market
   Norfk...........................92 E6
Pulham St Mary
   Norfk...........................92 E6
Pulloxhill C Beds............74 F7
Pulverbatch Shrops......83 H3
Pumpherston W Loth... 176 E4
Pumsaint Carmth..........66 E6
Puncheston Pembks 49 G2
Puncknowle Dorset 14 A5
Punnett's Town
   E Susx..........................20 C2
Purbrook Hants.............17 J2
Purfleet Thurr................45 K4
Puriton Somset..............25 L3
Purleigh Essex..............61 K7
Purley Gt Lon................44 F7
Purley on Thames
   W Berk.........................42 A5
Purse Caundle
   Dorset.........................27 G7
Purtington Somset.......13 K2
Purton Gloucs................54 F6
Purton Gloucs................55 G7
Purton Wilts...................40 C3
Purton Stoke Wilts......40 C3
Pury End Nhants...........73 K5
Pusey Oxon....................41 G2
Putley Herefs.................70 B6
Putley Green Herefs....70 B6
Putney Gt Lon...............44 E5
Puttenham Surrey.........30 F2
Puxley Nhants................73 L6
Puxton N Som................38 B7
Pwll Carmth...................50 F5
Pwll-glâs Denbgs.........97 H2
Pwllgloyw Powys...........68 B7
Pwllheli Gwynd..............94 F5
Pwllmeyric Mons..........38 D2
Pwll-trap Carmth..........50 C3
Pwll-y-glaw Neath........36 C2
Pye Bridge Derbys......101 H3
Pyecombe W Susx.......19 J3
Pyle Brdgnd...................36 C4
Pyleigh Somset..............25 H5
Pylle Somset..................26 E4
Pymoor Cambs..............90 C6
Pymore Dorset..............13 L4
Pyrford Surrey...............43 H8
Pyrton Oxon...................42 B2
Pytchley Nhants............88 C8
Pyworth Devon.................9 J4

Q

Quadring Lincs............. 103 L6
Quadring Eaudike
   Lincs.......................... 103 L5
Quainton Bucks.............58 C4
Quantock Hills
   Somset........................25 J4
Quarff Shet.................. 235 c6
Quarley Hants................28 F3
Quarndon Derbys......... 101 G4
Quarrier's Village
   Inver.......................... 174 C5
Quarrington Lincs....... 103 H4
Quarrington Hill Dur... 151 H7
Quarry Bank Dudley....85 G6
Quarrywood Moray......214 E2
Quarter N Ayrs............ 173 L6
Quarter S Lans........... 175 J7
Quatford Shrops............84 D5
Quatt Shrops..................84 D6
Quebec Dur.................. 150 F6
Quedgeley Gloucs.........55 J5
Queen Adelaide
   Cambs.........................90 E7
Queenborough Kent......46 E5

Queen Camel Somset.....26 E6
Queen Charlton
   BaNES.........................38 F6
Queen Elizabeth
   Forest Park Stirlg... 184 B6
Queenhill Worcs............70 F6
Queen Oak Dorset........27 H5
Queen's Bower IoW......17 H5
Queensbury C Brad.... 123 G4
Queensferry Flints....... 111 K7
Queensferry
   Crossing Fife......... 176 F3
Queenslie C Glas......... 175 H5
Queen's Park Bed........74 F4
Queen's Park Nhants...73 L3
Queenzieburn N Lans.. 175 J3
Quendon Essex..............60 E3
Queniborough Leics.....87 J2
Quenington Gloucs......56 C7
Queslett Birm................85 J4
Quethiock Cnwll.............5 L3
Quidenham Norfk..........92 B6
Quidhampton Wilts......28 C5
Quinton Nhants.............73 L4
Quintrell Downs
   Cnwll.............................4 D4
Quixwood Border....... 179 G5
Quoig P & K................. 185 H3
Quorn Leics...................87 H1
Quothquan S Lans...... 165 J2
Quoyburray Ork........... 234 c6
Quoyloo Ork................. 234 b5

R

Raasay Highld.............. 209 J5
Rachan Mill Border...... 165 L3
Rachub Gwynd.............. 109 J7
Rackenford Devon........24 D7
Rackham W Susx..........18 E3
Rackheath Norfk............93 G1
Racks D & G................ 155 H7
Rackwick Ork............... 234 a7
Radbourne Derbys...... 100 F5
Radcliffe Bury.............. 113 H1
Radcliffe on Trent
   Notts......................... 101 M5
Radclive Bucks..............73 J7
Raddery Highld............ 213 H3
Radernie Fife............... 187 G5
Radford Coventry..........86 D7
Radford Semele
   Warwks........................72 D2
Radlett Herts.................59 K7
Radley Oxon..................57 K7
Radley Green Essex.....60 F6
Radnage Bucks..............42 C2
Radstock BaNES...........27 G1
Radstone Nhants..........73 H6
Radway Warwks............72 D5
Radwell Bed..................74 E3
Radwell Herts................75 J7
Radwinter Essex...........76 E6
Radyr Cardif...................37 H4
Rafford Moray.............. 214 C3
RAF Museum
   Cosford Shrops........84 E3
RAF Museum
   Hendon Gt Lon.......44 E3
Ragdale Leics.............. 102 A8
Raglan Mons..................54 B6
Ragnall Notts............... 116 D6
Raigbeg Highld............ 213 J8
Rainbow Hill Worcs......70 F4
Rainford St Hel............ 112 C2
Rainham Gt Lon............45 K4
Rainham Medway..........46 D6
Rainhill St Hel............. 112 C4
Rainhill Stoops
   St Hel......................... 112 D4
Rainow Ches E............. 113 L6
Rainton N York............ 132 E4
Rainworth Notts.......... 101 L2
Rait P & K.................... 186 D3
Raithby Lincs............... 118 D5

Raithby Lincs............... 118 E7
Rake Hants....................30 D5
Ralia Highld................. 203 H5
Ramasaig Highld......... 208 B5
Rame Cnwll......................3 J4
Rame Cnwll......................6 B6
Rampisham Dorset......14 B3
Rampside Cumb........... 128 F6
Rampton Cambs............76 B2
Rampton Notts............. 116 D5
Ramsbottom Bury........ 122 B6
Ramsbury Wilts.............40 F6
Ramscraigs Highld...... 227 K3
Ramsdean Hants..........30 B6
Ramsdell Hants............41 L8
Ramsden Oxon..............57 G5
Ramsden Bellhouse
   Essex..........................46 B3
Ramsey Cambs..............89 K6
Ramsey Essex...............62 E2
Ramsey IoM................. 237 e3
Ramsey Forty Foot
   Cambs.........................89 K6
Ramsey Heights
   Cambs.........................89 J6
Ramsey Island Essex... 61 M6
Ramsey Island
   Pembks........................48 B3
Ramsey Mereside
   Cambs.........................89 K5
Ramsey St Mary's
   Cambs.........................89 J6
Ramsgate Kent..............35 K2
Ramsgill N York........... 131 L5
Ramshope Nthumb..... 157 J2
Ramshorn Staffs......... 100 B4
Ramsnest Common
   Surrey........................30 F5
Ranby Lincs................. 118 B5
Ranby Notts................. 116 A5
Rand Lincs................... 117 J5
Randwick Gloucs..........55 J6
Ranfurly Rens.............. 174 D5
Rangemore Staffs...... 100 D7
Rangeworthy S Glos.....39 G3
Rankinston E Ayrs...... 163 L6
Rannoch Station
   P & K.......................... 193 G5
Ranscombe Somset......24 E3
Ranskill Notts.............. 116 A4
Ranton Staffs.................99 J7
Ranton Green Staffs.....99 J7
Ranworth Norfk.............93 H1
Raploch Stirlg.............. 185 G7
Rapness Ork................. 234 c4
Rascarrel D & G............ 146 D5
Rashfield Ag & B......... 173 K2
Rashwood Worcs..........71 G2
Raskelf N York............. 133 G5
Rastrick Calder............ 123 H6
Ratagan Highld............ 200 E2
Ratby Leics....................87 G3
Ratcliffe Culey Leics....86 D4
Ratcliffe on Soar
   Notts.......................... 101 J6
Ratcliffe on the
   Wreake Leics.............87 J1
Rathen Abers............... 217 J3
Rathillet Fife............... 186 F3
Rathmell N York.......... 130 F7
Ratho C Edin................ 176 F4
Ratho Station C Edin ... 176 F4
Rathven Moray............. 215 K2
Ratley Warwks...............72 E5
Ratling Kent...................35 H4
Ratlinghope Shrops......83 H4
Rattar Highld............... 231 J2
Rattery Devon...................7 H4
Rattlesden Suffk............77 L3
Ratton Village E Susx....20 C5
Rattray P & K............... 195 J2
Raunds Nhants..............88 E8
Ravenfield Rothm........ 115 J3
Ravenglass Cumb........ 136 F7
Raveningham Norfk......93 H4
Ravenscar N York........ 143 K6
Ravenscraig N Lans.... 175 K6

Ravensden Bed	74	F4
Ravenshead Notts	101	K2
Ravensthorpe Kirk	123	J6
Ravensthorpe Nhants	73	J1
Ravenstone Leics	86	E2
Ravenstone M Keyn	74	B4
Ravenstonedale		
Cumb	139	G6
Ravenstruther S Lans	165	H1
Ravensworth N York	140	E5
Rawcliffe C York	133	J8
Rawcliffe E R Yk	125	G6
Rawdon Leeds	123	J3
Rawling Street Kent	34	B3
Rawmarsh Rothm	115	H3
Rawreth Essex	46	C2
Rawridge Devon	12	F2
Rawtenstall Lancs	122	B6
Raydon Suffk	78	C6
Rayleigh Essex	46	D2
Rayne Essex	61	H4
Raynes Park Gt Lon	44	E6
Reach Cambs	76	E2
Read Lancs	122	B4
Reading Readg	42	B5
Reading Services		
W Berk	42	A6
Reading Street Kent	34	B8
Reading Street Kent	35	K2
Reagill Cumb	138	E4
Realwa Cnwll	3	G4
Rearquhar Highld	223	G3
Rearsby Leics	87	J2
Reay Highld	230	D3
Reculver Kent	47	L6
Red Ball Devon	25	H7
Redberth Pembks	49	J6
Redbourn Herts	59	J5
Redbourne N Linc	116	F2
Redbrook Gloucs	54	D6
Redbrook Wrexhm	98	D4
Redbrook Street		
Kent	34	C7
Redburn Highld	213	L5
Redcar R & Cl	142	D3
Redcastle D & G	146	E2
Redcastle Highld	212	F4
Redding Falk	176	C3
Reddingmuirhead		
Falk	176	C3
Reddish Stockp	113	K3
Redditch Worcs	71	J2
Rede Suffk	77	J4
Redenhall Norfk	92	F6
Redesmouth Nthumb	157	L5
Redford Abers	197	J3
Redford Angus	196	F7
Redford W Susx	30	E6
Redfordgreen Border	166	E6
Redgate Rhondd	36	F3
Redgorton P & K	186	A2
Redgrave Suffk	92	C7
Redhill Abers	206	E4
Red Hill BCP	15	K4
Redhill Herts	59	M2
Redhill N Som	38	D7
Redhill Surrey	32	B3
Redisham Suffk	93	J6
Redland Bristl	38	E5
Redland Ork	234	b5
Redlingfield Suffk	78	E1
Redlingfield Green		
Suffk	78	E1
Red Lodge Suffk	77	G1
Redlynch Somset	27	G5
Redlynch Wilts	28	D7
Redmarley Worcs	70	D2
Redmarley D'Abitot		
Gloucs	55	H2
Redmarshall S on T	141	J3
Redmile Leics	102	D5
Redmire N York	131	K2
Redmyre Abers	197	J2
Rednal Shrops	98	A6
Redpath Border	167	J3
Redpoint Highld	219	H7
Red Roses Carmth	49	L5
Red Row Nthumb	159	G3
Redruth Cnwll	3	J3
Redstone P & K	186	C1
Red Street Staffs	99	J3
Red Wharf Bay IoA	109	G5
Redwick Newpt	38	B4
Redwick S Glos	38	D3
Redworth Darltn	141	G3
Reed Herts	75	L7
Reedham Norfk	93	J3
Reednesss E R Yk	125	J6
Reeds Holme Lancs	122	B5
Reepham Lincs	117	H6
Reepham Norfk	106	D7
Reeth N York	140	C7
Reeves Green Solhll	86	C7
Regil N Som	38	D7
Reiff Highld	224	B5
Reigate Surrey	31	L2
Reighton N York	135	H4
Reinigeadal W Isls	232	e4
Reisque Abers	207	G2
Reiss Highld	231	L5
Relubbus Cnwll	2	F5
Relugas Moray	214	B5
Remenham Wokham	42	C4
Remenham Hill		
Wokham	42	C4
Rempstone Notts	101	L7
Rendcomb Gloucs	56	A6
Rendham Suffk	79	H2
Rendlesham Suffk	79	H4
Renfrew Rens	174	F5
Renhold Bed	74	F4
Renishaw Derbys	115	J6
Rennington Nthumb	169	J3
Renton W Duns	174	D3
Renwick Cumb	149	G6
Repps Norfk	93	J1
Repton Derbys	100	F6
Reraig Highld	210	C8
Resaurie Highld	213	H5
Resipole Burn Highld	190	E4
Reskadinnick Cnwll	3	H3
Resolis Highld	213	G2
Resolven Neath	52	C7
Rest and be		
thankful Ag & B	183	J6
Reston Border	179	H6
Reswallie Angus	196	E6
Retford Notts	116	B5
Rettendon Essex	61	J7
Revesby Lincs	103	M1
Rewe Devon	12	B3
Rew Street IoW	16	F4
Reymerston Norfk	92	B3
Reynalton Pembks	49	J5
Reynoldston Swans	50	F7
Rezare Cnwll	6	A1
Rhandirmwyn		
Carmth	67	H5
Rhayader Powys	67	L2
Rheindown Highld	212	D5
Rhenigidale W Isls	232	e4
Rhes-y-cae Flints	111	G2
Rhewl Denbgs	97	H1
Rhewl Denbgs	97	J4
Rhicarn Highld	224	D4
Rhiconich Highld	228	C5
Rhicullen Highld	222	F6
Rhigos Rhondd	52	E6
Rhives Highld	223	H2
Rhiwbina Cardif	37	J4
Rhiwderyn Newpt	37	K3
Rhiwlas Gwynd	109	H7
Rhoden Green Kent	33	H4
Rhodes Minnis Kent	34	F6
Rhodiad-y-brenin		
Pembks	48	C3
Rhonehouse D & G	146	C3
Rhoose V Glam	37	G6
Rhos Carmth	65	L7
Rhos Neath	51	L5
Rhoscolyn IoA	108	C6
Rhoscrowther		
Pembks	48	F6
Rhosesmor Flints	111	H7
Rhosgoch Powys	68	D5
Rhoshill Pembks	65	H6
Rhoshirwaun Gwynd	94	D6
Rhoslefain Gwynd	80	D3
Rhosllanerchrugog		
Wrexhm	97	L3
Rhosmeirch IoA	108	F6
Rhosneigr IoA	108	D6
Rhosnesni Wrexhm	97	M3
Rhôs-on-Sea Conwy	110	B5
Rhossili Swans	50	E7
Rhostryfan Gwynd	95	H2
Rhostyllen Wrexhm	97	L3
Rhosybol IoA	108	F4
Rhos-y-gwaliau		
Gwynd	96	E5
Rhosymedre Wrexhm	97	L4
Rhu Ag & B	174	B2
Rhualt Denbgs	110	F6
Rhubodach Ag & B	173	H4
Rhuddlan Denbgs	110	E6
Rhunahaorine Ag & B	172	C8
Rhyd Gwynd	95	L4
Rhydargaeau Carmth	50	F1
Rhydcymerau Carmth	66	D6
Rhyd-Ddu Gwynd	95	K3
Rhydlewis Cerdgn	65	K5
Rhydowen Cerdgn	66	B5
Rhyd-uchaf Gwynd	96	D5
Rhyd-y-clafdy		
Gwynd	94	F5
Rhyd-y-foel Conwy	110	C6
Rhydyfro Neath	51	K4
Rhyd-y-groes Gwynd	109	H7
Rhyd-y-pennau		
Cerdgn	80	E6
Rhyl Denbgs	110	D5
Rhymney Caerph	53	H6
Rhynd P & K	186	B4
Rhynie Abers	215	L8
Rhynie Highld	223	J5
Ribbesford Worcs	84	D8
Ribbleton Lancs	121	H4
Ribchester Lancs	121	J4
Riby Lincs	126	F8
Riccall N York	124	F3
Riccarton Border	156	F3
Riccarton E Ayrs	163	K3
Richards Castle		
Herefs	69	J1
Richmond Gt Lon	44	D5
Richmond N York	140	F6
Richmond Sheff	115	H4
Richmond Fort		
Guern	236	b3
Rickerscote Staffs	99	J3
Rickford N Som	38	C8
Rickham Devon	7	H7
Rickinghall Suffk	92	C7
Rickling Green Essex	60	E3
Rickmansworth		
Herts	43	H2
Riddell Border	167	H4
Riddlecombe Devon	10	F3
Riddlesden C Brad	123	G3
Ridge Dorset	15	H5
Ridge Herts	59	K7
Ridge Wilts	27	L5
Ridge Lane Warwks	86	C4
Ridgeway Derbys	115	H5
Ridgewell Essex	77	G6
Ridgewood E Susx	19	M2
Ridgmont C Beds	74	E7
Riding Mill Nthumb	150	C3
Ridlington Norfk	107	H6
Ridlington Rutlnd	88	B3
Ridsdale Nthumb	158	A5
Rievaulx N York	133	J3
Rigg D & G	148	B2
Riggend N Lans	175	K4
Righoul Highld	213	K4
Rigsby Lincs	118	F6
Rigside S Lans	165	G3
Riley Green Lancs	121	J5
Rilla Mill Cnwll	5	L2
Rillington N York	134	D5
Rimington Lancs	122	B2
Rimpton Somset	26	E6
Rimswell E R Yk	127	H5
Rinaston Pembks	49	G3
Rindleford Shrops	84	D4
Ringford D & G	146	C4
Ringland Norfk	92	D2
Ringmer E Susx	19	L3
Ringmore Devon	6	F6
Ringmore Devon	7	L2
Ringorm Moray	215	G5
Ringsfield Suffk	93	J5
Ringsfield Corner		
Suffk	93	J6
Ringshall Herts	59	G5
Ringshall Suffk	78	C4
Ringshall Stocks		
Suffk	78	C4
Ringstead Nhants	88	E7
Ringstead Norfk	105	H4
Ringwood Hants	15	L2
Ringwould Kent	35	K5
Rinmore Abers	205	J3
Ripe E Susx	20	B4
Ripley Derbys	101	H3
Ripley Hants	15	M3
Ripley N York	132	D7
Ripley Surrey	31	H1
Riplington Hants	30	A6
Ripon N York	132	D5
Rippingale Lincs	103	H6
Ripple Kent	35	J5
Ripple Worcs	70	F6
Ripponden Calder	122	F6
Risabus Ag & B	160	B2
Risbury Herefs	69	K4
Risby Suffk	77	H2
Risca Caerph	37	K3
Rise E R Yk	126	E3
Risegate Lincs	103	K6
Riseley Bed	74	F3
Riseley Wokham	42	B7
Rishangles Suffk	78	E2
Rishton Lancs	121	L4
Rishworth Calder	122	F6
Risley Derbys	101	J5
Risley Warrtn	112	F3
Risplith N York	132	C5
River Kent	35	J6
River W Susx	30	F6
Riverford Highld	212	E4
Riverhead Kent	32	F3
Rivington Lancs	121	J7
Rivington Services		
Lancs	121	J7
Roade Nhants	73	L4
Roadmeetings S Lans	176	B7
Roadside E Ayrs	164	B5
Roadside Highld	231	H4
Roadwater Somset	25	G4
Roag Highld	208	D5
Roan of Craigoch		
S Ayrs	153	G2
Roath Cardif	37	J5
Roberton Border	166	F6
Roberton S Lans	165	H4
Robertsbridge E Susx	20	E2
Roberttown Kirk	123	J6
Robeston Wathen		
Pembks	49	J4
Robgill Tower D & G	155	M7
Robin Hood's Bay		
N York	143	K6
Roborough Devon	6	D4
Roborough Devon	10	E2
Robroyston C Glas	175	H5
Roby Knows	112	B4
Rocester Staffs	100	C5
Roch Pembks	48	E3
Rochdale Rochdl	122	D7
Roche Cnwll	4	F4
Rochester Medway	46	C6
Rochester Nthumb	157	L3
Rochford Essex	46	E3
Rochford Worcs	70	B2
Rock Cnwll	4	E2
Rock Nthumb	169	J5
Rock Worcs	70	D1

Rockbeare Devon 12 C4
Rockbourne Hants......28 C7
Rockcliffe Cumb......148 C3
Rockcliffe D & G......146 E4
Rockend Torbay......7 L4
Rock Ferry Wirral......111 K4
Rockfield Highld......223 K5
Rockfield Mons......54 C5
Rockford Devon......24 B2
Rockhampton S Glos......38 F2
Rockhill Shrops......82 F7
Rockingham Nhants......88 C5
Rockland All Saints
  Norfk......92 B4
Rockland St Mary
  Norfk......93 G3
Rockland St Peter
  Norfk......92 B4
Rockley Notts......116 B6
Rockville Ag & B......173 L1
Rockwell End Bucks......42 D3
Rodborough Gloucs......55 J6
Rodbourne Swindn......40 C4
Rodbourne Wilts......39 L4
Rodden Dorset......14 B5
Rode Somset......27 J2
Rode Heath Ches E......99 J2
Rodel W Isls......232 d5
Roden Wrekin......83 L1
Rodhuish Somset......24 F4
Rodington Wrekin......83 L1
Rodington Heath
  Wrekin......83 L1
Rodley Gloucs......55 H5
Rodmarton Gloucs......39 L2
Rodmell E Susx......19 L4
Rodmersham Kent......34 B3
Rodmersham Green
  Kent......34 B3
Rodney Stoke
  Somset......26 C2
Rodsley Derbys......100 D4
Roecliffe N York......132 E6
Roe Green Herts......59 K6
Roe Green Herts......75 K7
Roehampton Gt Lon......44 E5
Roffey W Susx......31 K5
Rogart Highld......226 C7
Rogate W Susx......30 D6
Rogerstone Newpt......37 L3
Roghadal W Isls......232 d5
Rogiet Mons......38 C3
Roke Oxon......41 L2
Roker Sundld......151 J3
Rollesby Norfk......93 J1
Rolleston Leics......87 K4
Rolleston Notts......102 C3
Rolleston on Dove
  Staffs......100 E6
Rolston E R Yk......126 F2
Rolvenden Kent......33 L6
Rolvenden Layne
  Kent......33 L7
Romaldkirk Dur......140 C3
Romanby N York......132 E2
Romanno Bridge
  Border......177 G8
Romansleigh Devon......24 B7
Romesdal Highld......208 F4
Romford Dorset......15 K1
Romford Gt Lon......45 K3
Romiley Stockp......113 L4
Romsey Cambs......76 C3
Romsey Hants......29 G6
Romsley Shrops......84 D6
Romsley Worcs......85 G7
Rona Highld......209 K3
Ronachan Ag & B......172 C7
Rookhope Dur......150 B6
Rookley IoW......17 G5
Rooks Bridge Somset......26 A2
Rooks Nest Somset......25 H5
Rookwith N York......132 C3
Roos E R Yk......127 G4
Roothams Green
  Bed......75 G3
Ropley Hants......29 M5

Ropley Dean Hants......29 L5
Ropsley Lincs......103 G5
Rora Abers......217 K4
Rorrington Shrops......82 F4
Rosarie Moray......215 J4
Rose Cnwll......3 K1
Rose Ash Devon......24 C6
Rosebank S Lans......175 L7
Rosebush Pembks......49 J2
Rosedale Abbey
  N York......142 F7
Rose Green Essex......61 L3
Rose Green Suffk......77 L5
Rose Green Suffk......77 L6
Rose Green W Susx......18 B5
Rosehall Highld......225 K7
Rosehearty Abers......217 H2
Rose Hill Lancs......122 C4
Roseisle Moray......214 E2
Roselands E Susx......20 C5
Rosemarket Pembks......49 G5
Rosemarkie Highld......213 H3
Rosemary Lane
  Devon......25 J7
Rosemount P & K......195 J7
Rosenannon Cnwll......4 E3
Rosewell Mdloth......177 J6
Roseworth S on T......141 K3
Rosgill Cumb......138 D4
Roskhill Highld......208 D5
Rosley Cumb......148 B6
Roslin Mdloth......177 H5
Rosliston Derbys......86 B1
Rosneath Ag & B......174 B2
Ross D & G......146 B6
Rossett Wrexhm......98 A2
Rossett Green N York......132 D8
Rossington Donc......115 L2
Ross-on-Wye Herefs......54 E4
Roster Highld......231 J7
Rostherne Ches E......113 H5
Rosthwaite Cumb......137 H4
Roston Derbys......100 C4
Rosyth Fife......176 F2
Rothbury Nthumb......158 D2
Rotherby Leics......87 J1
Rotherfield E Susx......32 F7
Rotherfield Greys
  Oxon......42 B4
Rotherfield Peppard
  Oxon......42 B4
Rotherham Rothm......115 H3
Rotherthorpe
  Nhants......73 K3
Rotherwick Hants......30 B1
Rothes Moray......215 G4
Rothesay Ag & B......173 J5
Rothiebrisbane
  Abers......216 E6
Rothiemurchus
  Lodge Highld......204 B4
Rothienorman Abers......216 D7
Rothley Leics......87 H2
Rothmaise Abers......216 D7
Rothwell Leeds......123 L5
Rothwell Lincs......117 J2
Rothwell Nhants......88 B7
Rottal Lodge Angus......196 B3
Rottingdean Br & H......19 K5
Rottington Cumb......136 D5
Roucan D & G......155 H6
Rougham Norfk......105 K7
Rougham Suffk......77 K3
Rough Common
  Kent......34 F3
Roughpark Abers......205 H3
Roughton Lincs......118 C8
Roughton Norfk......106 F5
Roughton Shrops......84 D5
Roundbush Green
  Essex......60 F5
Round Green Luton......59 J4
Roundham Somset......13 K1
Roundhay Leeds......123 L3
Rounds Green Sandw......85 H5
Roundswell Devon......23 H5
Roundway Wilts......40 A7

Roundyhill Angus......196 C6
Rousay Ork......234 c4
Rousdon Devon......13 H4
Rousham Oxon......57 J3
Rous Lench Worcs......71 H4
Routenburn N Ayrs......173 L6
Routh E R Yk......126 D3
Row Cumb......129 K2
Rowanburn D & G......156 D6
Rowardennan Stirlg......183 L7
Rowarth Derbys......114 A4
Rowberrow Somset......38 C8
Rowde Wilts......39 L7
Rowen Conwy......109 L6
Rowfoot Nthumb......149 H3
Rowhedge Essex......62 B4
Rowington Warwks......72 B2
Rowland Derbys......114 E6
Rowland's Castle
  Hants......17 K1
Rowlands Gill Gatesd......150 E4
Rowledge Surrey......30 D3
Rowley Dur......150 D5
Rowley Regis Sandw......85 H6
Rowlstone Herefs......54 A3
Rowly Surrey......31 H4
Rowner Hants......17 H3
Rowney Green Worcs......71 J1
Rownhams Hants......29 G7
Rownhams Services
  Hants......29 H7
Rowrah Cumb......136 E4
Rowsham Bucks......58 D4
Rowsley Derbys......114 E7
Rowston Lincs......103 H2
Rowton Ches W......112 C8
Rowton Wrekin......98 E8
Roxburgh Border......167 L4
Roxby N Linc......125 L6
Roxton Bed......75 G4
Roxwell Essex......61 G6
Royal Leamington
  Spa Warwks......72 D2
Royal Sutton
  Coldfield Birm......85 K4
Royal Tunbridge
  Wells Kent......33 G5
Royal Wootton
  Bassett Wilts......40 B4
Royal Yacht
  Britannia C Edin......177 H3
Roy Bridge Highld......192 D1
Roydon Essex......60 C6
Roydon Norfk......92 D7
Roydon Norfk......105 H7
Roydon Hamlet
  Essex......60 C6
Royston Barns......124 B7
Royston Herts......75 L6
Royton Oldham......122 D8
Rozel Jersey......236 e6
Ruabon Wrexhm......97 L4
Ruaig Ag & B......188 D6
Ruan Lanihorne
  Cnwll......4 D7
Ruan Major Cnwll......3 J7
Ruan Minor Cnwll......3 J7
Ruardean Gloucs......54 E5
Ruardean Hill Gloucs......54 F5
Ruardean Woodside
  Gloucs......54 F5
Rubery Birm......85 H7
Rubha Ban W Isls......233 c9
Ruckhall Herefs......69 J6
Ruckinge Kent......34 D7
Ruckley Shrops......83 K4
Rudby N York......141 L6
Rudchester Nthumb......150 E2
Ruddington Notts......101 L6
Rudge Somset......27 J2
Rudgeway S Glos......38 F3
Rudgwick W Susx......31 H5
Rudheath Ches W......112 F6
Rudley Green Essex......61 K7
Rudloe Wilts......39 J6
Rudry Caerph......37 J3
Rudston E R Yk......135 H6

Rudyard Staffs......99 L2
Ruecastle Border......167 J5
Rufford Lancs......120 F7
Rufford Abbey Notts......115 M8
Rufforth C York......124 D1
Rugby Warwks......87 G7
Rugeley Staffs......100 B8
Ruigh'riabhach
  Highld......220 D3
Ruisgarry W Isls......232 c5
Ruishton Somset......25 K6
Ruisigearraidh
  W Isls......232 c5
Ruislip Gt Lon......43 H3
Rùm Highld......198 F5
Rumbach Moray......215 J4
Rumbling Bridge
  P & K......185 L7
Rumburgh Suffk......93 H7
Rumford Cnwll......4 D2
Rumford Falk......176 C3
Rumney Cardif......37 K5
Runcorn Halton......112 D5
Runcton W Susx......18 B5
Runcton Holme
  Norfk......90 E2
Runfold Surrey......30 E3
Runhall Norfk......92 C3
Runham Norfk......93 K2
Runnington Somset......25 H6
Runswick N York......143 G4
Runtaleave Angus......195 L3
Runwell Essex......46 C2
Ruscombe Wokham......42 D5
Rushall Herefs......70 B7
Rushall Norfk......92 E6
Rushall Wilts......28 C1
Rushall Wsall......85 H4
Rushbrooke Suffk......77 K3
Rushbury Shrops......83 K5
Rushden Herts......60 A2
Rushden Nhants......74 D2
Rushenden Kent......46 E5
Rushford Norfk......91 K7
Rush Green Essex......62 E5
Rush Green Gt Lon......45 K3
Rush Green Warrtn......113 G4
Rushlake Green
  E Susx......20 D3
Rushmere Suffk......93 K6
Rushmoor Surrey......30 E4
Rushock Worcs......70 F1
Rusholme Manch......113 J3
Rushton Nhants......88 B6
Rushton Spencer
  Staffs......113 L8
Rushwick Worcs......70 E4
Rushyford Dur......141 G2
Ruskie Stirlg......184 D7
Ruskington Lincs......103 H3
Rusland Cross Cumb......129 H2
Rusper W Susx......31 K4
Ruspidge Gloucs......54 F5
Russell's Water Oxon......42 B3
Russ Hill Surrey......31 L4
Rusthall Kent......32 F5
Rustington W Susx......18 E5
Ruston N York......134 E3
Ruston Parva E R Yk......135 G6
Ruswarp N York......143 H5
Rutherford Border......167 K4
Rutherglen S Lans......175 H6
Ruthernbridge Cnwll......4 F3
Ruthin Denbgs......97 H2
Ruthrieston C Aber......207 H4
Ruthven Abers......215 L5
Ruthven Angus......195 L6
Ruthven Highld......203 H5
Ruthven Highld......213 J2
Ruthvoes Cnwll......4 E4
Ruthwell D & G......147 J2
Ruyton-XI-Towns
  Shrops......98 B7
Ryal Nthumb......158 C7
Ryall Dorset......13 K4
Ryall Worcs......70 F6
Ryarsh Kent......33 H2

Rydal Cumb 137 K6
Ryde IoW 17 H4
Rye E Susx 21 H2
Rye Foreign E Susx 21 H2
Rye Street Worcs 70 D7
Ryhall Rutlnd 88 F2
Ryhill Wakefd 124 B7
Ryhope Sundld 151 K4
Ryland Lincs 117 G5
Rylands Notts 101 K5
Rylstone N York 131 H7
Ryme Intrinseca
  Dorset 14 B1
Ryther N York 124 E3
Ryton Gatesd 150 E3
Ryton Shrops 84 D3
Ryton-on-
  Dunsmore
  Warwks 86 E8
RZSS Edinburgh
  Zoo C Edin 177 G4

S

Sabden Lancs 122 B3
Sacombe Herts 60 B4
Sacriston Dur 151 G5
Sadberge Darltn 141 H4
Saddell Ag & B 161 K3
Saddington Leics 87 J5
Saddlebow Norfk 90 E1
Saddlescombe
  W Susx 19 H4
Saffron Walden
  Essex 76 D6
Sageston Pembks 49 H6
Saham Hills Norfk 91 K3
Saham Toney Norfk 91 K3
Saighton Ches W 98 C1
St Abbs Border 179 J5
St Agnes Border 178 E5
St Agnes Cnwll 3 J2
St Agnes IoS 2 a2
St Agnes Mining
  District Cnwll 3 J2
St Albans Herts 59 J6
St Allen Cnwll 4 C5
St Andrew Guern 236 c3
St Andrews Fife 187 H4
St Andrews Botanic
  Garden Fife 187 H4
St Andrews Major
  V Glam 37 H6
St Andrews Well
  Dorset 13 L4
St Anne's Lancs 120 D5
St Ann's D & G 155 J4
St Ann's Chapel
  Cnwll 6 B2
St Ann's Chapel
  Devon 6 F6
St Anthony-in-
  Meneage Cnwll 3 K6
St Anthony's Hill
  E Susx 20 D5
St Arvans Mons 38 D2
St Asaph Denbgs 110 E6
St Athan V Glam 36 F6
St Aubin Jersey 236 b7
St Austell Cnwll 4 F5
St Bees Cumb 136 D5
St Blazey Cnwll 5 G5
St Boswells Border 167 J3
St Brelade Jersey 236 b7
St Brelade's Bay
  Jersey 236 b7
St Breock Cnwll 4 F2
St Breward Cnwll 5 H1
St Briavels Gloucs 54 E6
St Bride's Major
  V Glam 36 D5
St Brides-super-Ely
  V Glam 37 H5
St Brides
  Wentlooge Newpt 37 L4

St Budeaux C Plym 6 C4
Saintbury Gloucs 71 K6
St Buryan Cnwll 2 D6
St Catherines
  Ag & B 183 G6
St Chloe Gloucs 55 J7
St Clears Carmth 50 C3
St Cleer Cnwll 5 K3
St Clement Cnwll 4 D6
St Clement Jersey 236 e8
St Clether Cnwll 9 G7
St Colmac Ag & B 173 H5
St Columb Major
  Cnwll 4 E3
St Columb Minor
  Cnwll 4 D4
St Columb Road
  Cnwll 4 E4
St Combs Abers 217 K2
St Cross South
  Elmham Suffk 93 G6
St Cyrus Abers 197 J4
St David's P & K 185 K4
St Davids Pembks 48 C3
St Davids Cathedral
  Pembks 48 C3
St Day Cnwll 3 J3
St Dennis Cnwll 4 E4
St Dogmaels Pembks 65 G5
St Dominick Cnwll 6 B3
St Donats V Glam 36 E6
St Endellion Cnwll 4 F1
St Enoder Cnwll 4 D4
St Erme Cnwll 4 D6
St Erney Cnwll 6 B4
St Erth Cnwll 2 F4
St Erth Praze Cnwll 3 G4
St Ervan Cnwll 4 D2
St Eval Cnwll 4 D3
St Ewe Cnwll 4 F6
St Fagans Cardif 37 H5
St Fagans: National
  History Museum
  Cardif 37 H5
St Fergus Abers 217 K4
St Fillans P & K 184 F3
St Florence Pembks 49 J7
St Gennys Cnwll 8 F5
St George Conwy 110 D6
St Georges N Som 38 B7
St George's V Glam 37 H5
St Germans Cnwll 6 A4
St Giles in the
  Wood Devon 23 H7
St Giles-on-the-
  Heath Devon 9 K6
St Harmon Powys 81 L8
St Helen Auckland
  Dur 140 F2
St Helen's E Susx 21 G4
St Helens IoW 17 J5
St Helens St Hel 112 D3
St Helier Gt Lon 44 E6
St Helier Jersey 236 d7
St Hilary Cnwll 2 F5
St Hilary V Glam 36 F5
St Ippolyts Herts 59 K3
St Ishmael's Pembks 48 E6
St Issey Cnwll 4 E2
St Ive Cnwll 5 L3
St Ives Cambs 75 K1
St Ives Cnwll 2 F3
St James's End
  Nhants 73 L3
St James South
  Elmham Suffk 93 G7
St Jidgey Cnwll 4 E3
St John Cnwll 6 B5
St John Jersey 236 c5
St John's E Susx 32 E6
St John's IoM 237 b5
St John's Kent 32 F3
St Johns Surrey 43 G8
St Johns Worcs 70 E4
St John's Chapel
  Devon 23 H5
St John's Chapel Dur .. 149 M7

St John's Fen End
  Norfk 90 D2
St John's Kirk S Lans .. 165 J3
St John's Town of
  Dalry D & G 154 B6
St John's Wood
  Gt Lon 44 F4
St Judes IoM 237 d3
St Just Cnwll 2 C5
St Just-in-Roseland
  Cnwll 4 D8
St Just Mining
  District Cnwll 2 D5
St Katherines Abers 216 E7
St Keverne Cnwll 3 K6
St Kew Cnwll 5 G1
St Kew Highway
  Cnwll 5 G2
St Keyne Cnwll 5 K4
St Lawrence Essex 62 A6
St Lawrence IoW 17 G6
St Lawrence Jersey 236 c6
St Lawrence Kent 35 K2
St Leonards Bucks 58 E6
St Leonards Dorset 15 L2
St Leonards E Susx 20 F4
St Levan Cnwll 2 C6
St Lythans V Glam 37 H6
St Mabyn Cnwll 5 G2
St Madoes P & K 186 C3
St Margarets Herefs 69 G7
St Margarets Herts 60 B5
St Margaret's at
  Cliffe Kent 35 K5
St Margaret's Hope
  Ork 234 c7
St Margaret South
  Elmham Suffk 93 G6
St Marks IoM 237 c6
St Martin Cnwll 3 J6
St Martin Cnwll 5 K5
St Martin Guern 236 d3
St Martin Jersey 236 e6
St Martin's IoS 2 b1
St Martin's P & K 186 B2
St Martin's Shrops 97 L5
St Mary Jersey 236 b6
St Mary Bourne
  Hants 29 H2
St Marychurch
  Torbay 7 L3
St Mary Church
  V Glam 36 F6
St Mary Cray Gt Lon 45 J6
St Mary in the
  Marsh Kent 34 E8
St Mary's IoS 2 b1
St Mary's Ork 234 c6
St Mary's Bay Kent 21 L1
St Mary's Hoo
  Medway 46 D5
St Mary's Platt Kent 33 G2
St Maughans Green
  Mons 54 C5
St Mawes Cnwll 3 L5
St Mawgan Cnwll 4 D3
St Mellion Cnwll 6 B3
St Mellons Cardif 37 K4
St Merryn Cnwll 4 D2
St Michael
  Caerhays Cnwll 4 F7
St Michael Church
  Somset 25 L5
St Michael Penkevil
  Cnwll 4 D7
St Michaels Kent 34 B7
St Michaels Worcs 69 L2
St Michael's Mount
  Cnwll 2 F5
St Michael's on
  Wyre Lancs 120 F3
St Minver Cnwll 4 F1
St Monans Fife 187 H6
St Newlyn East Cnwll 4 C5
St Neot Cnwll 5 J3
St Neots Cambs 75 H3
St Nicholas Pembks 64 C7

St Nicholas V Glam 37 H5
St Nicholas-at-
  Wade Kent 47 L6
St Ninians Stirlg 185 G8
St Olaves Norfk 93 J4
St Osyth Essex 62 D5
St Ouen Jersey 236 b6
St Owen's Cross
  Herefs 54 D3
St Paul's Cray Gt Lon 45 J6
St Paul's Walden
  Herts 59 K4
St Peter Jersey 236 b6
St Peter Port Guern 236 d3
St Peter's Guern 236 b3
St Peter's Kent 35 K2
St Peter's Hill Cambs 89 J8
St Pinnock Cnwll 5 J3
St Quivox S Ayrs 163 J5
St Sampson Guern 236 d2
St Saviour Guern 236 c3
St Saviour Jersey 236 d7
St Stephen Cnwll 4 E5
St Stephens Cnwll 6 B4
St Stephens Cnwll 9 J7
St Teath Cnwll 8 E8
St Thomas Devon 11 K6
St Tudy Cnwll 5 G1
St Twynnells Pembks 48 F7
St Veep Cnwll 5 J5
St Vigeans Angus 197 G7
St Wenn Cnwll 4 F3
St Weonards Herefs 54 D3
Salcombe Devon 7 H7
Salcombe Regis
  Devon 12 F5
Salcott-cum-Virley
  Essex 61 M5
Sale Traffd 113 H3
Saleby Lincs 118 F5
Sale Green Worcs 71 G3
Salehurst E Susx 20 F2
Salem Cerdgn 80 F6
Salen Ag & B 190 C7
Salen Highld 190 D4
Salford C Beds 74 D6
Salford Oxon 56 F3
Salford Salfd 113 J3
Salford Priors
  Warwks 71 J4
Salfords Surrey 32 B4
Salhouse Norfk 93 G1
Saline Fife 185 L8
Salisbury Wilts 28 C5
Salisbury Plain Wilts 28 B3
Salkeld Dykes Cumb 148 F7
Salle Norfk 106 D7
Salmonby Lincs 118 D6
Salperton Gloucs 56 B4
Salsburgh N Lans 175 L5
Salt Staffs 99 L6
Saltaire C Brad 123 H3
Saltaire C Brad 123 H3
Saltash Cnwll 6 B4
Saltburn Highld 223 G7
Saltburn-by-the-
  Sea R & Cl 142 E3
Saltby Leics 102 D7
Saltcoats N Ayrs 163 G2
Saltdean Br & H 19 K5
Salterbeck Cumb 136 D3
Salterforth Lancs 122 D2
Salterton Wilts 28 C4
Saltfleet Lincs 118 F3
Saltfleetby All
  Saints Lincs 118 F4
Saltfleetby St
  Clement Lincs 118 F3
Saltfleetby St Peter
  Lincs 118 F4
Saltford BaNES 39 G6
Salthouse Norfk 106 C4
Saltley Birm 85 K6
Saltmarshe E R Yk 125 J5
Saltney Flints 111 L8
Salton N York 133 L4
Saltrens Devon 23 G6

Saltwood Kent..................34 F7
Salvington W Susx.........18 F5
Salwarpe Worcs.............70 F3
Salway Ash Dorset.........13 L3
Sambourne Warwks......71 J3
Sambrook Wrekin..........99 G7
Sampford Arundel
Somset........................25 H7
Sampford Brett
Somset........................25 H4
Sampford
Courtenay Devon.......10 F5
Sampford Moor
Somset........................25 H7
Sampford Peverell
Devon..........................25 G8
Sampford Spiney
Devon............................6 D2
Samsonlane Ork.........234 d5
Samuelston E Loth 178 B4
Sanaigmore Ag & B....170 E4
Sancreed Cnwll...............2 D5
Sancton E R Yk...........125 L3
Sandaig Highld............199 L5
Sandal Magna
Wakefd........................123 L6
Sanday Ork...................234 d4
Sanday Airport Ork 234 d4
Sandbach Ches E..........99 H1
Sandbach Services
Ches E..........................99 H1
Sandbank Ag & B........173 K3
Sandbanks BCP.............15 K5
Sandend Abers............216 B2
Sanderstead Gt Lon 45 G7
Sandford Cumb...........139 G4
Sandford Devon............11 J4
Sandford Dorset...........15 H5
Sandford Hants............15 M3
Sandford IoW................17 G6
Sandford N Som...........38 B8
Sandford S Lans..........164 E2
Sandford-on-
Thames Oxon.............57 K7
Sandford Orcas
Dorset..........................26 F7
Sandford St Martin
Oxon..............................57 H3
Sandgate Kent.............35 G7
Sandhaven Abers........217 H2
Sandhead D & G..........144 D5
Sand Hills Leeds..........124 B3
Sandhills Oxon..............57 K6
Sandhills Surrey...........30 F4
Sandhoe Nthumb.........150 B2
Sandhole Ag & B.........182 E7
Sand Hole E R Yk.........125 J3
Sandholme E R Yk.......125 J4
Sandhurst Br For...........42 D7
Sandhurst Gloucs.........55 J4
Sandhurst Kent.............33 K7
Sandhutton N York......132 F3
Sand Hutton N York....133 L7
Sandiacre Derbys.......101 J5
Sandilands Lincs.........119 G5
Sandleheath Hants.......28 C7
Sandleigh Oxon.............57 J7
Sandley Dorset.............27 H6
Sandness Shet.............235 b5
Sandon Essex...............61 H6
Sandon Herts................75 K7
Sandon Staffs...............99 L6
Sandon Bank Staffs......99 L6
Sandown IoW.................17 H5
Sandplace Cnwll.............5 K4
Sandridge Herts............59 K6
Sandringham Norfk.....105 H6
Sandsend N York.........143 H5
Sandtoft N Linc...........125 H4
Sandway Kent...............34 B5
Sandwich Kent.............35 J3
Sandwick Shet............235 c7
Sandwick W Isls..........232 g2
Sandwith Cumb...........136 D4
Sandy C Beds................75 H5
Sandyford D & G..........155 L4
Sandygate Devon...........7 K2

Sandygate IoM............237 d3
Sandyhills D & G..........146 F4
Sandylands Lancs........129 J6
Sandy Lane Wilts.........39 L6
Sandy Park Devon.........11 G6
Sangobeg Highld.........228 F3
Sangomore Highld.......228 F3
Sankyn's Green
Worcs............................70 E2
Sanna Highld................189 K3
Sanndabhaig W Isls ...232 g2
Sannox N Ayrs.............162 C1
Sanquhar D & G...........164 F7
Santon Bridge Cumb ..136 F6
Santon Downham
Suffk............................91 J6
Sapcote Leics...............86 F5
Sapey Common
Herefs..........................70 C2
Sapiston Suffk..............91 K7
Sapley Cambs...............89 J8
Sapperton Gloucs.........55 L7
Sapperton Lincs.........103 G5
Saracen's Head Lincs..104 B6
Sarclet Highld.............231 L6
Sarisbury Hants............17 G2
Sarn Powys..................82 E5
Sarnau Cerdgn..............65 K4
Sarnau Powys...............82 E1
Sarn Mellteyrn
Gwynd..........................94 D6
Sarn Park Services
Brdgnd..........................36 D4
Saron Carmth................51 H3
Saron Gwynd..............109 G7
Sarratt Herts.................59 H7
Sarre Kent....................47 L6
Sarsden Oxon................56 F4
Satley Dur....................150 E6
Satterleigh Devon.........23 L6
Satterthwaite Cumb....129 H2
Sauchen Abers............206 D3
Saucher P & K.............186 C2
Sauchieburn Abers.....197 G3
Saul Gloucs..................55 H6
Saundby Notts............116 C4
Saundersfoot
Pembks.........................49 K6
Saunderton Bucks........58 C7
Saunton Devon............23 G4
Sausthorpe Lincs........118 E7
Savile Town Kirk.........123 K6
Sawbridge Warwks.......73 G2
Sawbridgeworth
Herts............................60 D5
Sawdon N York...........134 E3
Sawley Lancs...............122 B2
Sawley N York.............132 C6
Sawston Cambs............76 C5
Sawtry Cambs...............89 H6
Saxby Leics.................102 D8
Saxby Lincs.................117 G4
Saxby All Saints
N Linc..........................126 B7
Saxelbye Leics............102 B7
Saxham Street Suffk....78 C3
Saxilby Lincs...............116 E6
Saxlingham Norfk.......106 B5
Saxlingham Green
Norfk............................92 F4
Saxlingham
Nethergate Norfk.......92 F4
Saxlingham Thorpe
Norfk............................92 E4
Saxmundham Suffk......79 H2
Saxondale Notts.........102 B4
Saxon Street Cambs.....76 F3
Saxtead Suffk................78 F2
Saxtead Green Suffk....78 F2
Saxtead Little Green
Suffk............................78 F2
Saxthorpe Norfk.........106 D6
Saxton N York.............124 D3
Sayers Common
W Susx.........................19 H3
Scackleton N York.....133 K5
Scadabay W Isls.........232 e4

Scadabhagh W Isls.....232 e4
Scafell Pike Cumb......137 H5
Scaftworth Notts........116 A3
Scagglethorpe
N York.........................134 C5
Scalasaig Ag & B........180 E8
Scalby E R Yk..............125 K5
Scalby N York.............134 F2
Scaldwell Nhants.........73 L1
Scaleby Cumb.............148 D3
Scalebyhill Cumb........148 D3
Scales Cumb................129 G5
Scales Cumb................137 K2
Scalford Leics.............102 C7
Scaling N York.............142 F4
Scalloway Shet............235 c6
Scalpay Highld............209 J7
Scalpay W Isls............232 e4
Scamblesby Lincs.......118 C5
Scamodale Highld.......191 G2
Scampston N York......134 D4
Scampton Lincs...........116 F5
Scaniport Highld.........212 F6
Scapegoat Hill Kirk....123 G7
Scarba Ag & B.............181 K6
Scarborough N York...135 G2
Scarcewater Cnwll........4 E5
Scarcliffe Derbys.........115 J7
Scarcroft Leeds...........124 B3
Scarfskerry Highld......231 J2
Scarinish Ag & B.........188 D7
Scarisbrick Lancs........120 E7
Scarning Norfk..............91 L2
Scarrington Notts.......102 B4
Scartho NE Lin............118 C1
Scatsta Airport Shet....235 c4
Scaur D & G.................146 E4
Scawby N Linc............116 F1
Scawsby Donc.............115 K1
Scawthorpe Donc.......115 K1
Scawton N York..........133 H3
Scayne's Hill W Susx...19 K2
Scethrog Powys...........53 H3
Scholar Green
Ches E..........................99 J2
Scholes Kirk...............123 H8
Scholes Leeds.............124 B3
Scholes Rothm...........115 H3
Scholes Wigan...........112 E1
Scissett Kirk...............123 K7
Scleddau Pembks.........64 C7
Scofton Notts.............115 M5
Scole Norfk...................92 D7
Scone P & K................186 B3
Sconser Highld...........209 H7
Scoonie Fife...............186 F6
Scopwick Lincs...........103 H2
Scoraig Highld............220 C3
Scorborough E R Yk...126 C2
Scorrier Cnwll................3 J3
Scorton Lancs.............121 G2
Scorton N York...........141 G7
Scotby Cumb...............148 D4
Scotch Corner N York..140 F6
Scotch Corner Rest
Area N York...............140 F6
Scotforth Lancs...........129 K7
Scothern Lincs............117 G6
Scotlandwell P & K.....186 C6
Scotscalder Station
Highld..........................231 G4
Scot's Gap Nthumb.....158 C5
Scotsmill Abers...........206 D2
Scotstoun C Glas.........174 F5
Scotswood N u Ty......150 F3
Scotter Lincs...............116 E2
Scotterthorpe Lincs....116 E2
Scottish Seabird
Centre E Loth.............178 C2
Scottish Wool
Centre Stirlg..............184 C7
Scotton Lincs..............116 E2
Scotton N York...........132 E7
Scotton N York...........140 F7
Scoulton Norfk.............92 B4
Scourie Highld............228 B6
Scourie More Highld ..228 B6

Scousburgh Shet.........235 c7
Scrabster Highld.........231 G2
Scraesburgh Border 167 K5
Scrane End Lincs........104 C4
Scraptoft Leics..............87 J3
Scratby Norfk................93 K1
Scrayingham N York ...133 L7
Scredington Lincs.......103 H4
Scremby Lincs............118 F7
Scremerston Nthumb..179 L8
Screveton Notts..........102 B4
Scriven N York............132 E7
Scrooby Notts.............115 M4
Scropton Derbys.........100 D6
Scrub Hill Lincs...........103 L2
Scruton N York............132 D2
Scullomie Highld........229 J4
Sculthorpe Norfk........105 L6
Scunthorpe N Linc.....125 K7
Seaborough Dorset......13 K2
Seabridge Staffs...........99 J4
Seabrook Kent..............35 G7
Seaburn Sundld..........151 J3
Seacombe Wirral........111 K4
Seacroft Leeds............123 L4
Seafield W Loth...........176 D5
Seaford E Susx.............20 A6
Seaforth Sefton...........111 K3
Seagrave Leics............101 L8
Seaham Dur.................151 K5
Seahouses Nthumb.....169 J3
Seal Kent.......................32 F2
Sealand Flints............111 K7
Seale Surrey.................30 E2
Seamer N York............134 F3
Seamer N York............142 B5
Seamill N Ayrs............173 L8
Sea Palling Norfk........107 J6
Searby Lincs................117 H1
Seasalter Kent..............47 H6
Seascale Cumb...........136 E6
Seathwaite Cumb.......137 H7
Seatoller Cumb...........137 H4
Seaton Cnwll..................5 L5
Seaton Cumb...............136 E2
Seaton Devon................13 G4
Seaton E R Yk..............126 E2
Seaton Kent..................35 G3
Seaton Nthumb...........159 H6
Seaton Rutlnd...............88 C4
Seaton Carew Hartpl...142 B2
Seaton Delaval
Nthumb........................159 H6
Seaton Ross E R Yk 125 J3
Seaton Sluice
Nthumb........................159 H6
Seatown Dorset............13 K4
Seave Green N York 142 C7
Seaview IoW..................17 J4
Seaville Cumb.............147 K4
Seavington St Mary
Somset........................26 B7
Seavington St
Michael Somset.........26 B7
Sebergham Cumb.......148 C6
Seckington Warwks......86 C3
Second Severn
Crossing Mons..........38 D3
Sedbergh Cumb..........130 C2
Sedbury Gloucs............38 D2
Sedbusk N York..........131 G2
Sedgeberrow Worcs.....71 H6
Sedgebrook Lincs.......102 D5
Sedgefield Dur...........141 J2
Sedgeford Norfk.........105 H5
Sedgehill Wilts.............27 K5
Sedgemoor
Services Somset........26 A2
Sedgley Dudley............85 G5
Sedgley Park Bury.....113 J2
Sedgwick Cumb.........129 L3
Sedlescombe E Susx ...20 F3
Sedrup Bucks................58 D5
Seend Wilts...................39 L7
Seend Cleeve Wilts......39 L7
Seer Green Bucks........42 F3
Seething Norfk..............93 G4

Sefton Sefton..............111 K2
Seighford Staffs.........99 K7
Seion Gwynd..............109 H7
Seisdon Staffs.............84 E4
Selattyn Shrops...........97 K5
Selborne Hants...........30 C5
Selby N York..............124 F4
Selham W Susx...........30 F7
Selhurst Gt Lon..........45 G6
Selkirk Border...........167 G4
Sellack Herefs.............54 E3
Sellafield Station
Cumb....................136 E6
Sellafirth Shet............235 d2
Sellindge Kent............34 E6
Selling Kent...............34 D4
Sells Green Wilts........39 L7
Selly Oak Birm...........85 J6
Selmeston E Susx........20 B4
Selsdon Gt Lon...........45 G7
Selsey W Susx.............18 B6
Selside N York...........130 E4
Selsley Gloucs...........55 J7
Selsted Kent...............35 G5
Selston Notts.............101 J2
Selworthy Somset.......24 E3
Semer Suffk................78 B5
Semington Wilts..........39 K7
Semley Wilts................27 K6
Send Surrey................31 G1
Senghenydd Caerph....37 H3
Sennen Cnwll................2 C6
Sennen Cove Cnwll......2 C6
Sennybridge Powys.....52 E3
Sessay N York............133 G4
Setchey Norfk.............90 F2
Seton Mains E Loth....177 L4
Settle N York.............130 F6
Settrington N York.....134 C5
Sevenhampton
Gloucs....................56 B4
Sevenhampton
Swindn...................40 E3
Seven Kings Gt Lon.....45 J3
Sevenoaks Kent..........32 F3
Sevenoaks Weald
Kent.......................32 F3
Seven Sisters Neath....52 C6
Seven Star Green
Essex.....................61 M3
Severn Beach S Glos...38 D4
Severn Bridge S Glos...38 E3
Severn Stoke Worcs....70 F5
Severn View
Services S Glos........38 E3
Sevington Kent...........34 D6
Sewards End Essex.....76 E6
Sewell C Beds.............59 G4
Sewerby E R Yk.........135 J5
Seworgan Cnwll............3 J5
Sewstern Leics...........102 E7
Sgalpaigh W Isls........232 e4
Sgiogarstaigh W Isls..232 g1
Shabbington Bucks.....58 A6
Shackerstone Leics.....86 D3
Shackleford Surrey......30 F3
Shader W Isls.............232 f1
Shadforth Dur............151 H6
Shadingfield Suffk......93 J6
Shadoxhurst Kent.......34 C6
Shadwell Leeds..........123 L3
Shadwell Norfk...........91 L6
Shaftenhoe End
Herts......................76 B6
Shaftesbury Dorset.....27 K6
Shafton Barns............124 B7
Shakerley Wigan........113 G2
Shalbourne Wilts........40 F7
Shalden Hants.............30 B3
Shaldon Devon.............7 L2
Shalfleet IoW..............16 E5
Shalford Essex............61 H3
Shalford Surrey..........31 G3
Shalford Green
Essex.....................61 H3
Shalmsford Street
Kent.......................34 E4

Shalstone Bucks.........73 J7
Shamley Green
Surrey....................31 G3
Shandford Angus.......196 D4
Shandon Ag & B........174 B2
Shandwick Highld.....223 J6
Shangton Leics...........87 K4
Shanklin IoW..............17 H6
Shantron Ag & B.......174 C2
Shap Cumb................138 E4
Shapinsay Ork...........234 c5
Shapwick Dorset.........15 H3
Shapwick Somset........26 B4
Shard End Birm...........85 L5
Shardlow Derbys.......101 H6
Shareshill Staffs..........85 G3
Sharlston Wakefd.....124 B6
Sharman's Cross
Solhll.......................85 K7
Sharnbrook Bed.........74 E3
Sharnford Leics...........86 F5
Sharoe Green Lancs..121 G4
Sharow N York...........132 E5
Sharpenhoe C Beds.....59 H2
Sharperton Nthumb...158 B2
Sharpness Gloucs........54 F7
Sharrington Norfk.....106 C5
Shatterford Worcs.......84 E7
Shaugh Prior Devon......6 D3
Shavington Ches E......99 G3
Shaw Oldham............122 D8
Shaw Swindn.............40 C4
Shaw W Berk.............41 J6
Shaw Wilts.................39 K7
Shawbirch Wrekin.......84 B2
Shawbost W Isls........232 e2
Shawbury Shrops........98 E7
Shawell Leics..............87 G7
Shawford Hants..........29 J6
Shawhead D & G........154 F6
Shaw Mills N York.....132 C6
Shawsburn S Lans.....175 K7
Shearington D & G....147 H2
Shearsby Leics............87 J5
Shearston Somset......25 L5
Shebbear Devon..........10 C3
Shebdon Staffs............99 H7
Shebster Highld........230 E3
Shedfield Hants...........29 K8
Sheen Staffs..............100 C1
Sheepridge Kirk........123 H6
Sheepscar Leeds........123 L4
Sheepscombe Gloucs..55 K6
Sheepstor Devon...........6 E3
Sheepwash Devon......10 C4
Sheepy Magna Leics...86 D3
Sheepy Parva Leics....86 D3
Sheering Essex............60 E5
Sheerness Kent...........46 F5
Sheerwater Surrey......43 G7
Sheet Hants................30 C6
Sheffield Sheff..........115 G4
Sheffield Park E Susx..19 L2
Shefford C Beds...........75 G6
Sheigra Highld...........228 B4
Sheinton Shrops..........83 L3
Shelderton Shrops......83 H7
Sheldon Birm...............85 L6
Sheldon Derbys.........114 D7
Sheldon Devon............12 E2
Sheldwich Kent...........34 D4
Shelfanger Norfk........92 D6
Shelford Notts...........102 A4
Shelley Kirk..............123 J7
Shelley Suffk...............78 B6
Shellingford Oxon.......40 F2
Shellow Bowells
Essex.....................60 F6
Shelsley
Beauchamp
Worcs....................70 D2
Shelsley Walsh
Worcs....................70 C2
Shelton Bed................74 F2
Shelton Norfk.............92 F5
Shelton Notts............102 C4
Shelton Lock C Derb..101 G6

Shelton Under
Harley Staffs..........99 J5
Shelve Shrops.............83 G4
Shelwick Herefs..........69 K6
Shenfield Essex...........45 L2
Shenington Oxon........72 D6
Shenley Herts.............59 K7
Shenley Brook End
M Keyn..................74 B7
Shenley Church End
M Keyn..................74 B7
Shenmore Herefs........69 H6
Shennanton D & G....145 H3
Shenstone Staffs.........85 K3
Shenstone Worcs........84 F8
Shenton Leics.............86 E4
Shenval Moray..........214 F7
Shephall Herts............59 L4
Shepherd's Bush
Gt Lon....................44 E4
Shepherdswell Kent...35 H5
Shepley Kirk..............123 J8
Shepperton Surrey.....43 H6
Shepreth Cambs..........76 B5
Shepshed Leics..........101 J8
Shepton
Beauchamp
Somset....................26 B7
Shepton Mallet
Somset....................26 F3
Shepton Montague
Somset....................27 G5
Shepway Kent............33 K3
Sheraton Dur.............151 K7
Sherborne Dorset........26 F7
Sherborne Gloucs........56 D5
Sherborne Somset......26 E1
Sherborne St John
Hants......................29 L1
Sherbourne Warwks...72 C3
Sherburn Dur............151 H6
Sherburn N York.......134 E4
Sherburn Hill Dur.....151 H6
Sherburn in Elmet
N York...................124 D4
Shere Surrey...............31 H2
Shereford Norfk........105 L6
Sherfield English
Hants......................28 F6
Sherfield on
Loddon Hants.........42 B8
Sherford Devon............7 H6
Sheriffhales Shrops.....84 D2
Sheriff Hutton N York.133 K6
Sheringham Norfk.....106 E4
Sherington M Keyn....74 C5
Shernborne Norfk.....105 H6
Sherrington Wilts.......27 L4
Sherston Wilts............39 J3
Sherwood C Nott......101 K4
Sherwood Forest
Notts....................101 L1
Shetland Islands
Shet......................235 c5
Shettleston C Glas....175 H5
Shevington Wigan.....121 H8
Sheviock Cnwll.............6 B5
Shibden Head
C Brad...................123 G5
Shide IoW..................16 F5
Shidlaw Nthumb.......168 B2
Shiel Bridge Highld...200 E2
Shieldaig Highld........210 C4
Shieldhill D & G........155 H5
Shieldhill Falk...........176 B3
Shieldhill House
Hotel S Lans..........165 J2
Shields N Lans...........175 K7
Shielfoot Highld........190 D3
Shielhill Angus..........195 C5
Shielhill Inver...........173 L4
Shifnal Shrops............84 D2
Shilbottle Nthumb.....169 J7
Shildon Dur...............141 G3
Shillford E Rens.........174 E6
Shillingford Devon.....24 F6
Shillingford Oxon.......41 L2

Shillingford Abbot
Devon.....................11 K6
Shillingford St
George Devon..........11 K7
Shillingstone Dorset....14 F1
Shillington C Beds......75 G7
Shilton Oxon..............56 E6
Shilton Warwks..........86 E6
Shimpling Norfk.........92 D6
Shimpling Suffk..........77 J4
Shimpling Street
Suffk.......................77 K4
Shincliffe Dur............151 H6
Shiney Row Sundld....151 H4
Shinfield Wokham.......42 B6
Shinness Highld........225 L5
Shipbourne Kent.........33 G3
Shipdham Norfk..........91 L3
Shipham Somset..........38 C8
Shiphay Torbay............7 K3
Shiplake Oxon............42 C5
Shipley C Brad..........123 H3
Shipley W Susx............31 J6
Shipley Bridge
Surrey....................32 B5
Shipmeadow Suffk.....93 H5
Shippon Oxon.............41 J2
Shipston-on-Stour
Warwks....................72 B6
Shipton Gloucs............56 B4
Shipton N York...........133 H7
Shipton Shrops............83 L5
Shipton Bellinger
Hants......................28 E3
Shipton Gorge
Dorset......................13 L4
Shipton Green
W Susx....................17 L3
Shipton Moyne
Gloucs.....................39 K3
Shipton-on-
Cherwell Oxon.........57 J5
Shiptonthorpe E R Yk..125 K2
Shipton-under-
Wychwood Oxon......56 F4
Shirburn Oxon............42 B2
Shirdley Hill Lancs....120 E7
Shirebrook Derbys....115 K7
Shiregreen Sheff.......115 G3
Shirehampton Bristl...38 D5
Shiremoor N Tyne.....159 H7
Shirenewton Mons.....38 C2
Shireoaks Notts........115 K5
Shirland Derbys.........101 H2
Shirley C Sotn............29 H8
Shirley Derbys...........100 E4
Shirley Gt Lon............45 G6
Shirley Solhll..............85 K7
Shirrell Heath Hants..29 L8
Shirwell Devon............23 J4
Shiskine N Ayrs........162 B4
Shobdon Herefs..........69 H3
Shobrooke Devon.......11 K5
Shoby Leics...............102 B7
Shocklach Ches W......98 C3
Shoeburyness Sthend..46 F3
Sholden Kent..............35 K4
Sholing C Sotn............16 F1
Shop Cnwll...................9 G2
Shoreditch Gt Lon......45 G4
Shoreditch Somset.....25 K6
Shoreham Kent...........45 K7
Shoreham-by-Sea
W Susx....................19 H5
Shorley Hants.............29 L6
Shorne Kent................46 B6
Shortgate E Susx........20 A3
Short Heath Birm.......85 K5
Short Heath Wsall......85 H4
Shortlanesend Cnwll....4 C6
Shortlees E Ayrs.......163 K3
Shorwell IoW..............16 F5
Shoscombe BaNES.....27 G1
Shotesham Norfk........92 F4
Shotgate Essex...........46 C2
Shotley Suffk...............78 F7
Shotley Bridge Dur...150 D4

Shotley Gate Suffk 78 F7
Shotley Street Suffk 78 F7
Shottenden Kent 34 D4
Shottery Warwks............71 L4
Shotteswell Warwks 72 E5
Shottisham Suffk............79 G5
Shottlegate Derbys ...100 F3
Shotton Dur 151 K6
Shotton Flints 111 J7
Shotton Colliery Dur...151 J6
Shotts N Lans 176 B6
Shotwick Ches W 111 K6
Shougle Moray 214 F4
Shouldham Norfk 90 F2
Shouldham Thorpe
Norfk 90 F2
Shoulton Worcs.............70 E3
Shrawardine Shrops 83 H1
Shrawley Worcs 70 E2
Shrewley Warwks..........72 B2
Shrewsbury Shrops 83 J2
Shrewton Wilts 28 B3
Shripney W Susx 18 C5
Shrivenham Oxon..........40 E3
Shropham Norfk 92 B5
Shroton Dorset..............27 K8
Shucknall Herefs 69 L6
Shudy Camps Cambs.....76 E5
Shuna Ag & B 181 M5
Shurdington Gloucs 55 L4
Shurlock Row W & M 42 D5
Shurrery Highld 230 F4
Shurrery Lodge
Highld 230 F4
Shurton Somset............25 J3
Shustoke Warwks 86 B5
Shute Devon 11 K5
Shute Devon 13 G3
Shutford Oxon 72 E6
Shut Heath Staffs 99 K7
Shuthonger Gloucs 70 F7
Shutlanger Nhants 73 K4
Shuttington Warwks 86 B3
Shuttlewood Derbys ...115 J6
Shuttleworth Bury 122 B6
Siabost W Isls 232 e2
Siadar W Isls 232 f1
Sibbertoft Nhants 87 K6
Sibford Ferris Oxon.....72 D6
Sibford Gower Oxon....72 D6
Sible Hedingham
Essex 77 H7
Sibley's Green Essex 60 F3
Sibsey Lincs 104 B3
Sibson Cambs 89 G4
Sibson Leics..................86 D4
Sibster Highld 231 K5
Sibthorpe Notts 102 C4
Sibthorpe Notts 116 B6
Sibton Suffk 79 H1
Sicklesmere Suffk 77 K3
Sicklinghall N York 124 B2
Sidbury Devon 12 E4
Sidbury Shrops.............84 C6
Sidcot N Som 38 B8
Sidcup Gt Lon 45 J5
Siddington Ches E 113 J2
Siddington Gloucs 56 B7
Sidestrand Norfk 106 F4
Sidford Devon 12 E4
Sidlesham W Susx 18 B6
Sidley E Susx 20 E4
Sidmouth Devon 12 E5
Sigglesthorne E R Yk ..126 E2
Sigingstone V Glam......36 F6
Silchester Hants 41 L7
Sileby Leics 87 H1
Silecroft Cumb.............128 D3
Silfield Norfk................92 D4
Silkstone Barns 114 F1
Silkstone Common
Barns 114 F1
Silk Willoughby
Lincs 103 H4
Silloth Cumb 147 K4
Silpho N York 134 E2
Silsden C Brad 122 F2

Silsoe C Beds 74 F7
Silton Dorset 27 H5
Silverburn Mdloth........177 G6
Silverdale Lancs 129 K4
Silverdale Staffs 99 J3
Silver End Essex 61 K4
Silverford Abers 216 E2
Silverstone Nhants........73 J5
Silverton Devon.............12 B2
Silvington Shrops..........84 B7
Simonburn Nthumb 157 L7
Simonsbath Somset......24 B4
Simonstone Lancs 122 B4
Simprim Border 168 C1
Simpson M Keyn...........74 C7
Simpson Cross
Pembks 48 F4
Sinclair's Hill Border ...179 G7
Sinclairston E Ayrs.......163 L6
Sinderby N York...........132 E3
Sinderland Green
Traffd 113 G4
Sindlesham Wokham......42 C6
Sinfin C Derb 101 G6
Singleton Kent 34 D6
Singleton Lancs 120 E3
Singleton W Susx...........18 B3
Singlewell Kent 46 A6
Sinnarhard Abers 205 K3
Sinnington N York 134 B3
Sinton Worcs 70 E3
Sinton Worcs 70 F2
Sinton Green Worcs......70 E2
Sissinghurst Kent..........33 K5
Siston S Glos 39 G5
Sithney Cnwll 3 H5
Sittingbourne Kent........34 B3
Six Ashes Shrops 84 E5
Sixhills Lincs 117 K4
Six Mile Bottom
Cambs 76 E3
Sixpenny Handley
Dorset 27 M7
Six Rues Jersey 236 c6
Skaill Ork 234 d6
Skara Brae Ork 234 b5
Skares E Ayrs 164 B6
Skateraw Abers 207 G6
Skateraw E Loth 178 F4
Skeabost Highld 208 F5
Skeeby N York 140 F6
Skeffington Leics..........87 L3
Skeffling E R Yk 127 J6
Skegby Notts 101 J1
Skegby Notts 116 C7
Skegness Lincs 119 H8
Skelbo Highld 223 H3
Skelbo Street Highld....223 H3
Skelbrooke Donc 124 D7
Skeldyke Lincs 104 B5
Skellingthorpe Lincs ..116 F6
Skellow Donc 124 E7
Skelmanthorpe Kirk 123 J7
Skelmersdale Lancs 112 C1
Skelmorlie N Ayrs 173 L5
Skelpick Highld 229 L4
Skelston D & G 154 E5
Skelton C York 133 J7
Skelton Cumb 148 D7
Skelton E R Yk 125 H5
Skelton R & Cl 142 E4
Skelton on Ure
N York 132 E5
Skelwith Bridge
Cumb 137 K6
Skendleby Lincs 118 F7
Skene House Abers 206 E4
Skenfrith Mons.............54 C4
Skerne E R Yk 135 G7
Skerray Highld 229 K3
Skerricha Highld 228 C5
Skerton Lancs 129 K6
Sketchley Leics 86 E5
Sketty Swans 51 J6
Skewsby N York 133 K5
Skiall Highld 230 E3
Skidby E R Yk 126 C4

Skigersta W Isls............232 g1
Skilgate Somset 24 F6
Skillington Lincs..........102 E7
Skinburness Cumb 147 K4
Skinflats Falk 176 B2
Skinidin Highld 208 C5
Skipness Ag & B 172 F6
Skipper's Bridge
D & G 156 C5
Skipsea E R Yk 135 J8
Skipton N York 122 E1
Skipton-on-Swale
N York 132 E4
Skipwith N York 125 G3
Skirlaugh E R Yk..........126 E3
Skirling Border 165 L2
Skirmett Bucks.............42 C3
Skirpenbeck E R Yk 134 B7
Skirwith Cumb 149 G7
Skirza Highld 231 L2
Skokholm Island
Pembks 48 C6
Skomer Island
Pembks 48 C5
Skulamus Highld 199 K2
Skye Green Essex..........61 L4
Skye of Curr Highld.....204 B1
Slack Cumb 122 E5
Slacks of
Cairnbanno Abers...216 F5
Slad Gloucs 55 K6
Slade Devon 23 H3
Slade Green Gt Lon......45 K5
Slade Hooton Rothm ...115 K4
Slaggyford Nthumb.....149 H4
Slaidburn Lancs 130 D8
Slaithwaite Kirk 123 G7
Slaley Nthumb 150 B4
Slamannan Falk 176 B4
Slapton Bucks 58 F4
Slapton Devon 7 J6
Slapton Nhants 73 J5
Slaugham W Susx 31 L5
Slaughterford Wilts 39 J5
Slawston Leics 87 L5
Sleaford Hants 30 D4
Sleaford Lincs 103 H4
Sleagill Cumb 138 E4
Sleapford Wrekin..........84 B1
Sleasdairidh Highld....222 E3
Sledmere E R Yk 134 E6
Sleetbeck Cumb 156 E6
Sleights N York 143 H5
Slickly Highld 231 K3
Sliddery N Ayrs...........162 B5
Sligachan Highld.........209 G7
Sligrachan Ag & B 173 K1
Slimbridge Gloucs 55 H7
Slindon Staffs...............99 J6
Slindon W Susx 18 C4
Slinfold W Susx 31 J5
Slingsby N York 133 L4
Slip End C Beds 59 H4
Slip End Herts...............75 K6
Slipton Nhants.............88 D7
Slitting Mill Staffs......100 B8
Slockavullin Ag & B 182 B7
Sloncombe Devon.........11 H7
Sloothby Lincs 119 G7
Slough Slough 43 G4
Slough Green
Somset 25 L7
Slumbay Highld 210 D6
Slyne Lancs 129 K6
Smailholm Border 167 K3
Smallburgh Norfk 107 G7
Smallburn E Ayrs........164 D4
Small Dole W Susx 19 G3
Smalley Derbys 101 H4
Smallfield Surrey..........32 B5
Small Heath Birm.........85 K6
Small Hythe Kent 34 B8
Smallridge Devon 13 H3
Smallthorne C Stke......99 K3
Smallworth Norfk 92 B7
Smannell Hants 29 G2
Smarden Kent 34 B6

Smarden Bell Kent........34 B6
Smart's Hill Kent..........32 F5
Smeatharpe Devon 12 F1
Smeeth Kent 34 E6
Smeeton Westerby
Leics 87 K5
Smerral Highld 227 L2
Smestow Staffs 84 F5
Smethwick Sandw........85 H6
Smirisary Highld 190 D2
Smisby Derbys 101 G8
Smithfield Cumb 148 D3
Smith's Green Essex.....76 F6
Smithstown Highld 219 J6
Smithton Highld 213 H5
Smoo Highld 228 F3
Smythe's Green
Essex 61 L4
Snade D & G 154 E5
Snailbeach Shrops.......83 G3
Snailwell Cambs 76 F2
Snainton N York 134 E3
Snaith E R Yk 124 F6
Snape N York 132 D3
Snape Suffk 79 H3
Snape Street Suffk........79 H3
Snaresbrook Gt Lon 45 H3
Snarestone Leics 86 D2
Snarford Lincs 117 H5
Snargate Kent 34 D8
Snave Kent 34 D8
Sneaton N York 143 J5
Snelland Lincs 117 H5
Snelston Derbys 100 D4
Snetterton Norfk 92 B5
Snettisham Norfk 105 G5
Snitter Nthumb 158 C2
Snitterby Lincs 117 G3
Snitterfield Warwks.....72 B3
Snitton Shrops.............83 L7
Snodland Kent 46 B7
Snowdon Gwynd 95 K2
Snowdonia National
Park 96 C6
Snow End Herts 60 C3
Snowshill Gloucs.........71 K7
Soake Hants 17 J1
Soay Highld 199 G3
Soberton Hants.............29 L7
Soberton Heath
Hants 29 L8
Sockburn Darltn..........141 J6
Soham Cambs 90 E8
Solas W Isls 232 c5
Soldridge Hants 29 M4
Sole Street Kent 34 E5
Sole Street Kent 46 A6
Solihull Solhll 85 L7
Sollers Dilwyn
Herefs 69 H4
Sollers Hope Herefs 54 E2
Solva Pembks 48 D3
Solwaybank D & G 156 B6
Somerby Leics 87 L2
Somerby Lincs 117 H1
Somercotes Derbys 101 H2
Somerford BCP.............15 M4
Somerford Keynes
Gloucs 40 A2
Somerley W Susx 17 M3
Somerleyton Suffk 93 K4
Somersal Herbert
Derbys 100 C5
Somersby Lincs 118 D6
Somersham Cambs 89 L7
Somersham Suffk.........78 C5
Somerton Oxon.............57 J3
Somerton Somset 26 C5
Somerton Suffk 77 J4
Sompting W Susx 19 G5
Sonning Wokham 42 C5
Sonning Common
Oxon 42 B4
Sopley Hants 15 M3
Sopwell Herts 59 J6
Sopworth Wilts 39 J3
Sorbie D & G 145 J5

Sordale Highld.............. 231 G3
Sorisdale Ag & B.......... 189 H4
Sorn E Ayrs................. 164 B4
Sornhill E Ayrs............. 163 M3
Sortat Highld................ 231 K3
Sotby Lincs................. 117 K5
Sotterley Suffk...............93 J6
Soughton Flints.......... 111 H7
Soulbury Bucks............58 E3
Soulby Cumb............. 139 H5
Souldern Oxon...............57 K2
Souldrop Bed..............74 E3
Sound Ches E...............98 F3
Sound Muir Moray 215 H4
Soundwell S Glos..........38 F5
Sourton Devon...............10 D6
Soutergate Cumb....... 128 F3
South Acre Norfk...........91 J2
South Alkham Kent.....35 H6
Southall Gt Lon.............43 J4
South Allington
    Devon...................... 7 J7
South Alloa Falk....... 185 J8
Southam Gloucs...........55 L3
Southam Warwks..........72 E3
South Ambersham
    W Susx....................30 E7
Southampton C Sotn ... 29 H8
Southampton
    Airport Hants 29 J7
South Anston Rothm ... 115 K5
South Ashford Kent......34 D6
South Baddesley
    Hants......................16 D3
South Ballachulish
    Highld..................... 191 K5
South Bank C York..... 124 F1
South Barrow
    Somset...................26 E5
South Beddington
    Gt Lon.....................44 F7
South Benfleet Essex...46 C3
Southborough Gt Lon....45 H6
Southborough Kent......33 G5
Southbourne BCP 15 L4
Southbourne W Susx...17 L2
South Bramwith
    Donc...................... 124 F7
South Brent Devon.......... 7 G4
South Brewham
    Somset...................27 G4
South Broomhill
    Nthumb 159 G3
Southburgh Norfk 92 B3
South Burlingham
    Norfk.......................93 H3
Southburn E R Yk....... 134 F8
South Cadbury
    Somset...................26 F6
South Carlton Lincs..... 116 F6
South Carlton Notts 115 L5
South Cave E R Yk..... 125 L4
South Cerney Gloucs....40 B2
South Chailey E Susx...19 K3
South Charlton
    Nthumb 169 H5
South Cheriton
    Somset...................27 G6
South Church Dur........ 140 F2
Southchurch Sthend.....46 E3
South Cliffe E R Yk..... 125 K4
South Clifton Notts...... 116 D7
South Cockerington
    Lincs...................... 118 E4
South Cornelly
    Brdgnd...................36 C4
Southcott Cnwll.............. 9 G5
Southcott Devon...........11 H8
Southcourt Bucks........58 D5
South Cove Suffk..........93 K7
South Creake Norfk..... 105 K5
South Croxton Leics.....57 K2
South Dalton E R Yk... 126 B2
South Darenth Kent.....45 K6
South Dell W Isls........ 232 g1
South Downs
    National Park 19 K4

South Duffield N York.. 125 G4
South Earlswood
    Surrey.....................32 B4
Southease E Susx........19 L5
South Elkington
    Lincs...................... 118 D4
South Elmsall
    Wakefd.................. 124 D7
Southend Ag & B........ 161 H7
Southend Airport
    Essex.......................46 E3
Southend-on-Sea
    Sthend.....................46 E3
Southerndown
    V Glam....................36 D5
Southerness D & G..... 147 G4
South Erradale
    Highld.................... 219 H7
Southerton Devon........12 D4
Southery Norfk............90 E5
South Fambridge
    Essex.......................46 E2
South Ferriby N Linc... 126 B6
South Field E R Yk..... 126 C5
Southfield Falk........... 175 L4
Southfleet Kent...........45 L5
Southgate Gt Lon.........44 F2
Southgate Swans........51 G7
South Gorley Hants 15 M1
South Gosforth
    N u Ty.................... 151 G2
South Green Essex 46 B2
South Green Kent........33 L2
South Green Norfk.......92 C2
South Gyle C Edin...... 177 G4
South Hanningfield
    Essex.......................61 H8
South Harting
    W Susx....................30 C7
South Hayling Hants 17 K3
South Heath Bucks......58 E7
South Heighton
    E Susx.....................19 L5
South Hetton Dur 151 J6
South Hiendley
    Wakefd.................. 124 B7
South Hill Cnwll............. 5 M2
South Hinksey Oxon.....57 K7
South Holmwood
    Surrey.....................31 K3
South Hornchurch
    Gt Lon.....................45 K4
South Huish Devon 7 G7
South Hykeham
    Lincs...................... 116 F8
South Hylton Sundld... 151 J4
Southill C Beds.............75 H6
Southington Hants........29 J2
South Kelsey Lincs..... 117 H2
South Kessock
    Highld.................... 213 G5
South Killingholme
    N Linc.................... 126 E7
South Kilvington
    N York................... 132 F3
South Kilworth Leics......87 H6
South Kirkby Wakefd... 124 C7
South Kyme Lincs...... 103 K3
Southleigh Devon.........12 F4
South Leigh Oxon.........57 H6
South Leverton Notts.. 116 C5
South Littleton
    Worcs.....................71 J5
South Lopham Norfk....92 C7
South Luffenham
    Rutlnd.....................88 D3
South Lynn Norfk....... 104 F8
South Malling E Susx...19 L4
South Marston
    Swindn...................40 D3
South Merstham
    Surrey.....................32 B3
South Milford N York.. 124 D4
South Milton Devon....... 7 G7
South Mimms Herts.....59 L7
South Mimms
    Services Herts 59 L7

Southminster Essex 62 A7
South Molton Devon......23 L6
South Moor Dur 150 F5
Southmoor Oxon..........41 H2
South Moreton Oxon.....41 K3
Southmuir Angus........ 196 C5
South Mundham
    W Susx.....................18 B5
South Newbald
    E R Yk.................... 125 L4
South Newington
    Oxon.......................57 H2
South Newton Wilts 28 C4
South Normanton
    Derbys.................... 101 H2
South Norwood
    Gt Lon.....................45 G6
South Ockendon
    Thurr.......................45 L4
Southoe Cambs...........75 H2
Southolt Suffk..............78 E2
South Ormsby Lincs 118 E6
Southorpe C Pete.........88 F3
South Otterington
    N York.................... 132 E3
Southover Dorset.........14 C4
South Owersby Lincs .. 117 H3
Southowram Calder..... 123 G5
South Park Surrey........31 L2
South Perrott Dorset.....13 L2
South Petherton
    Somset...................26 B7
South Petherwin
    Cnwll........................ 9 J8
South Pickenham
    Norfk.......................91 J3
South Pill Cnwll............ 6 B4
South Pool Devon......... 7 H7
South Poorton
    Dorset....................13 M3
Southport Sefton........ 120 D6
South Queensferry
    C Edin.................... 176 F3
South Rauceby Lincs... 103 G4
South Raynham
    Norfk...................... 105 L7
South Reddish
    Stockp.................... 113 K3
Southrepps Norfk........ 106 F5
South Reston Lincs...... 118 E5
Southrey Lincs............ 117 J7
South Ronaldsay Ork... 234 c7
Southrop Gloucs..........56 D7
Southrope Hants..........30 A3
South Runcton Norfk.....90 F2
South Scarle Notts...... 116 D8
Southsea C Port...........17 J3
South Shian Ag & B.... 191 H7
South Shields S Tyne... 151 J2
South Shore Bpool..... 120 D4
Southside Dur............ 140 E2
South Stainley N York.. 132 D6
South Stifford Thurr......45 L4
South Stoke BaNES......39 H7
South Stoke Oxon.........41 L4
South Stoke W Susx......18 D4
South Street Kent.........34 E3
South Street Kent.........47 J6
South Tarbrax S Lans... 176 D7
South Tawton Devon......10 F6
South Tehidy Cnwll........ 3 H3
South Thoresby Lincs.. 118 E6
Southtown Norfk..........93 L3
South Uist W Isls........ 233 c8
Southwaite Cumb...... 148 D6
South Walsham
    Norfk.......................93 H2
Southwark Gt Lon........44 F4
South Warnborough
    Hants......................30 B3
Southwater W Susx......31 J6
Southway C Plym......... 6 C4
South Weald Essex.......45 L2
Southwell Notts.......... 102 B2
South Weston Oxon......42 B2

South Wheatley
    Notts...................... 116 C4
Southwick Hants 17 J2
Southwick Nhants.........88 E5
Southwick Sundld....... 151 J4
Southwick W Susx........19 H5
Southwick Wilts............27 J1
South Widcombe
    BaNES.....................38 E8
South Wigston Leics.....87 H4
South
    Willesborough
    Kent........................34 D6
South Willingham
    Lincs...................... 117 K5
South Wingfield
    Derbys.................... 101 G2
South Witham Lincs 102 F8
Southwold Suffk...........93 K7
South Woodham
    Ferrers Essex...........61 J7
South Wootton Norfk.. 105 G7
South Wraxall Wilts.......39 J7
South Zeal Devon.........10 F6
Sovereign Harbour
    E Susx.....................20 D5
Sowerby Calder......... 122 F6
Sowerby N York......... 132 F4
Sowerby Bridge
    Calder.................... 122 F5
Sowood Calder........... 123 G6
Sowton Devon............... 6 D3
Sowton Devon...............12 C4
Soyland Town Calder .. 122 F6
Spain's End Essex........76 F6
Spalding Lincs............ 103 L7
Spaldington E R Yk..... 125 H4
Spaldwick Cambs.........89 G8
Spalford Notts............ 116 D7
Spanby Lincs............. 103 H5
Sparham Norfk........... 106 C8
Spark Bridge Cumb.... 129 G3
Sparkford Somset........26 E6
Sparkhill Birm.............85 K6
Sparkwell Devon........... 6 E4
Sparrowpit Derbys...... 114 C5
Sparrows Green
    E Susx.....................33 H6
Sparsholt Hants...........29 H5
Sparsholt Oxon...........41 G3
Spaunton N York........ 133 L2
Spaxton Somset...........25 K4
Spean Bridge Highld... 201 K8
Spearywell Hants.........28 F6
Speen Bucks...............58 D7
Speen W Berk.............41 J6
Speeton N York.......... 135 J5
Speke Lpool............... 112 C5
Speldhurst Kent...........32 F5
Spellbrook Herts..........60 D4
Spencers Wood
    Wokham 42 B6
Spen Green Ches E.......99 J1
Spennithorne N York ... 131 L2
Spennymoor Dur........ 151 G7
Spetchley Worcs..........70 F4
Spetisbury Dorset.........15 G3
Spexhall Suffk.............93 H7
Spey Bay Moray......... 215 H2
Speybridge Highld...... 204 C1
Speyview Moray......... 215 G6
Spilsby Lincs.............. 118 E7
Spinkhill Derbys......... 115 J5
Spinningdale Highld.... 222 F4
Spital Wirral.............. 111 K5
Spital Hill Donc.......... 115 L3
Spittal E Loth............ 178 B3
Spittal Highld............. 231 H5
Spittal Nthumb.......... 179 L7
Spittal Pembks.............49 G3
Spittalfield P & K....... 195 H7
Spital of
    Glenmuick Abers ... 205 G7
Spittal of Glenshee
    P & K..................... 195 H3
Spittal-on-Rule
    Border.................... 167 J5

Spixworth Norfk..................92 F1
Splatt Devon.....................10 E4
Splayne's Green
 E Susx 19 L2
Splott Cardif.....................37 J5
Spofforth N York 124 B1
Spondon C Derb...........101 H5
Spooner Row Norfk........92 D4
Sporle Norfk.....................91 J2
Spott E Loth...................178 E4
Spottiswoode Border .. 178 D7
Spratton Nhants...............73 K1
Spreakley Surrey 30 D3
Spreyton Devon...............11 G5
Spriddlestone Devon........6 D5
Spridlington Lincs.........117 G5
Springburn C Glas.........175 G5
Springfield D & G 148 B2
Springfield Essex..............61 H6
Springfield Fife 186 E5
Springholm D & G 154 E7
Springside N Ayrs..........163 J2
Springthorpe Lincs........116 E4
Springwell Sundld.........151 H4
Sproatley E R Yk...........126 F4
Sproston Green
 Ches W 113 G7
Sprotbrough Donc 115 K2
Sproughton Suffk............78 D5
Sprouston Border 168 A3
Sprowston Norfk.............92 F2
Sproxton Leics...............102 D7
Sproxton N York 133 J3
Spurstow Ches E..............98 D2
Spyway Dorset.................14 A4
Stableford Shrops............84 D4
Stacey Bank Sheff 114 F4
Stackhouse N York 130 F6
Stackpole Pembks...........49 G7
Stackpole Elidor
 Pembks 49 G7
Staddiscombe
 C Plym 6 D5
Stadhampton Oxon.........57 L7
Stadhlaigearraidh
 W Isls.............................233 b7
Staffield Cumb................148 F6
Staffin Highld.................218 D7
Stafford Staffs.................99 L7
Stafford Services
 (northbound)
 Staffs..............................99 K6
Stafford Services
 (southbound)
 Staffs..............................99 K6
Stagsden Bed...................74 E5
Stainburn Cumb.............136 E2
Stainby Lincs..................102 E7
Staincross Barns.............123 L7
Staindrop Dur................140 E3
Staines-upon-
 Thames Surrey.............43 G6
Stainforth Donc.............124 F7
Stainforth N York 130 F6
Staining Lancs................120 D4
Stainland Calder............123 G6
Stainsacre N York 143 J5
Stainton Cumb...............129 L3
Stainton Cumb...............138 C2
Stainton Donc................115 K3
Stainton Dur..................140 D4
Stainton Middsb.............141 L4
Stainton by
 Langworth Lincs.....117 H6
Staintondale N York 143 K7
Stainton le Vale
 Lincs.............................117 K3
Stainton with
 Adgarley Cumb 128 F5
Stair E Ayrs...................163 K5
Stairhaven D & G..........144 E4
Staithes N York 143 G4
Stakes Hants....................17 K2
Stalbridge Dorset............27 G7
Stalbridge Weston
 Dorset.............................27 G7
Stalham Norfk................107 H7

Stalisfield Green
 Kent...............................34 C4
Stallen Dorset..................26 E7
Stallingborough
 NE Lin 126 F7
Stalmine Lancs...............120 E2
Stalybridge Tamesd......113 L2
Stambourne Essex...........77 G6
Stambourne Green
 Essex..............................77 G6
Stamford Lincs................88 E3
Stamford Nthumb..........169 J5
Stamford Bridge
 Ches W 112 C7
Stamford Bridge
 E R Yk 133 L7
Stamfordham
 Nthumb.........................158 D7
Stamford Hill Gt Lon......45 G3
Stanbridge C Beds...........58 F3
Stanbury C Brad.............122 F3
Stand N Lans..................175 K5
Standburn Falk...............176 C4
Standeford Staffs.............85 G3
Standen Kent....................33 L5
Standerwick Somset........27 J2
Standford Hants...............30 D4
Standingstone
 Cumb............................147 J7
Standish Wigan..............121 H7
Standlake Oxon................57 H7
Standon Hants..................29 H6
Standon Herts..................60 C4
Standon Staffs..................99 J5
Stane N Lans..................176 B6
Stanfield Norfk...............105 M7
Stanford C Beds...............75 H6
Stanford Kent..................34 F6
Stanford Bishop
 Herefs.............................70 C4
Stanford Bridge
 Worcs..............................70 C2
Stanford Dingley
 W Berk............................41 L6
Stanford in the Vale
 Oxon..............................41 G2
Stanford le Hope
 Thurr..............................46 B4
Stanford on Avon
 Nhants............................87 H7
Stanford on Soar
 Notts.............................101 K7
Stanford on Teme
 Worcs..............................70 C2
Stanfree Derbys..............115 J6
Stanghow R & Cl...........142 E4
Stanground C Pete..........89 H4
Stanhoe Norfk................105 J5
Stanhope Border............165 L4
Stanhope Dur.................150 C6
Stanhope Kent.................34 D6
Stanion Nhants................88 D6
Stanley Derbys...............101 H4
Stanley Dur....................150 F4
Stanley P & K................186 B2
Stanley Staffs...................99 L3
Stanley Crook Dur.........150 E7
Stanley Pontlarge
 Gloucs.............................55 M3
Stanmer Br & H................19 K4
Stanmore Gt Lon.............44 D2
Stanmore Hants...............29 J5
Stannersburn
 Nthumb.........................157 J5
Stanningfield Suffk..........77 K3
Stannington Nthumb......158 F6
Stannington Sheff..........114 F4
Stannington Station
 Nthumb.........................158 F5
Stansbatch Herefs............69 G3
Stansfield Suffk................77 H4
Stanstead Suffk................77 J5
Stanstead Abbotts
 Herts..............................60 C5
Stansted Kent...................45 L7
Stansted Airport
 Essex..............................60 E4

Stansted
 Mountfitchet
 Essex..............................60 E3
Stanton Gloucs.................71 J7
Stanton Nthumb.............158 E4
Stanton Staffs.................100 C4
Stanton Suffk...................91 L8
Stanton by Bridge
 Derbys...........................101 G6
Stanton by Dale
 Derbys...........................101 J5
Stanton Drew BaNES......38 E7
Stanton Fitzwarren
 Swindn...........................40 D3
Stanton Harcourt
 Oxon..............................57 H6
Stanton in Peak
 Derbys...........................114 E8
Stanton Lacy Shrops......83 K7
Stanton Lees Derbys 114 E8
Stanton Long Shrops......83 L5
Stanton-on-the-
 Wolds Notts................101 M6
Stanton Prior BaNES......39 G7
Stanton St Bernard
 Wilts...............................40 C7
Stanton St John
 Oxon..............................57 L6
Stanton St Quintin
 Wilts...............................39 K4
Stanton Street Suffk......77 L2
Stanton under
 Bardon Leics.................86 F2
Stanton upon Hine
 Heath Shrops................98 E7
Stanton Wick BaNES......38 E7
Stanway Essex.................61 M3
Stanway Gloucs................56 B2
Stanwell Surrey................43 H5
Stanwick Nhants.............74 E1
Stanwix Cumb................148 D4
Staoinebrig W Isls..........233 b8
Stape N York...................143 G7
Stapeley Ches E................99 G3
Stapenhill Staffs.............100 E7
Staple Kent......................35 H4
Staple Cross Devon..........25 G7
Staplecross E Susx...........20 F2
Staplefield W Susx...........32 B7
Staple Fitzpaine
 Somset............................25 K7
Stapleford Cambs............76 C4
Stapleford Herts...............60 A5
Stapleford Leics.............102 D8
Stapleford Lincs.............102 E2
Stapleford Notts.............101 J5
Stapleford Wilts................28 B4
Stapleford Abbotts
 Essex..............................45 K2
Staplegrove Somset........25 K6
Staplehay Somset.............25 K6
Staplehurst Kent..............33 K5
Staplers IoW....................17 G4
Staplestreet Kent..............34 E3
Stapleton Herefs..............69 G2
Stapleton Leics.................86 E4
Stapleton N York 141 G5
Stapleton Shrops..............83 J3
Stapleton Somset.............26 C7
Stapley Somset.................25 J8
Staploe Bed......................75 G3
Staplow Herefs.................70 C6
Star Fife..........................186 E6
Star Pembks......................65 H7
Star Somset......................38 C8
Starbeck N York 132 E7
Starbotton N York 131 H5
Starcross Devon...............12 C6
Stareton Warwks..............72 D1
Starlings Green
 Essex..............................60 D2
Starston Norfk..................92 F6
Startforth Dur................140 D4
Startley Wilts....................39 L4
Statenborough Kent.........35 J4
Statham Warrtn..............112 E3
Stathe Somset...................26 A5

Stathern Leics................102 C6
Staughton Green
 Cambs.............................75 G2
Staunton Gloucs...............54 D5
Staunton Gloucs...............55 H3
Staunton on Arrow
 Herefs.............................69 G3
Staunton on Wye
 Herefs.............................69 G5
Staveley Cumb...............138 C7
Staveley Derbys..............115 H6
Staveley N York 132 E6
Staveley-in-
 Cartmel Cumb 129 H3
Staverton Devon................7 J3
Staverton Gloucs..............55 K4
Staverton Nhants.............73 G3
Staverton Wilts.................39 J7
Stawell Somset.................26 A4
Stawley Somset.................25 G6
Staxigoe Highld..............231 L5
Staxton N York 134 F4
Staynall Lancs................120 E2
Stean N York 131 K5
Stearsby N York 133 J5
Steart Somset...................25 L3
Stebbing Essex.................61 G3
Stechford Birm.................85 K6
Stedham W Susx...............30 E6
Steelend Fife..................185 L8
Steele Road Border.........156 F4
Steen's Bridge
 Herefs.............................69 K3
Steep Hants......................30 C6
Steep Lane Calder..........122 F5
Steeple Essex....................61 M7
Steeple Ashton Wilts.......27 K1
Steeple Aston Oxon.........57 J3
Steeple Bumpstead
 Essex..............................76 F6
Steeple Claydon
 Bucks..............................58 B3
Steeple Gidding
 Cambs.............................89 G7
Steeple Langford
 Wilts...............................28 B4
Steeple Morden
 Cambs.............................75 K6
Steeton C Brad 122 F2
Stein Highld....................208 D3
Stelling Minnis Kent........34 F5
Stembridge Somset..........26 B7
Stenalees Cnwll..................4 F4
Stenhouse D & G 154 D4
Stenhousemuir Falk.......176 B2
Stenscholl Highld...........218 D7
Stenson Fields
 Derbys...........................101 G6
Stenton E Loth...............178 D4
Steornabhagh W Isls .. 232 f2
Stepaside Pembks.............49 K6
Stepford D & G 154 E5
Stepney Gt Lon................45 G4
Steppingley C Beds..........74 E7
Stepps N Lans................175 H5
Sternfield Suffk................79 H3
Stert Wilts.........................40 B8
Stetchworth Cambs..........76 F3
Stevenage Herts...............59 L3
Stevenston N Ayrs..........163 H2
Steventon Hants...............29 K2
Steventon Oxon................41 J3
Steventon End Essex.......76 E6
Stevington Bed.................74 E4
Stewartby Bed..................74 E6
Stewartfield S Lans.........175 H7
Stewarton Ag & B...........161 H5
Stewarton E Ayrs...........163 K1
Stewkley Bucks.................58 D3
Stewley Somset.................25 L7
Steyning W Susx...............19 G4
Steynton Pembks..............48 F6
Stibb Cnwll..........................9 G3
Stibbard Norfk................106 B6
Stibb Cross Devon...........10 C2
Stibb Green Wilts.............40 E7
Stibbington Cambs...........88 F4

Stichill Border 167 L2
Sticker Cnwll 4 F5
Stickford Lincs 104 B1
Sticklepath Devon 10 F6
Stickney Lincs 104 B2
Stiffkey Norfk 106 A4
Stifford Clays Thurr 45 L4
Stilligarry W Isls 233 b7
Stillingfleet N York 124 F3
Stillington N York 133 J6
Stillington S on T 141 J3
Stilton Cambs 89 H5
Stinchcombe Gloucs 55 G2
Stinsford Dorset 14 D4
Stiperstones Shrops 83 G4
Stirchley Wrekin 84 C3
Stirling Abers 217 L6
Stirling Stirlg 185 G8
Stirling Castle Stirlg 185 G8
Stirling Services
  Stirlg 175 L2
Stirtloe Cambs 75 H2
Stirton N York 131 H8
Stisted Essex 61 J3
Stithians Cnwll 3 J4
Stivichall Covtry 86 D7
Stixwould Lincs 117 K7
St Michaels Fife 187 G3
Stoak Ches W 112 B6
Stobo Border 166 B2
Stoborough Dorset 15 H5
Stobs Castle Border 167 H7
Stobswood Nthumb 158 F3
Stock Essex 61 H7
Stock N Som 38 C7
Stockbridge Hants 29 G4
Stockbriggs S Lans 164 F3
Stockbury Kent 46 D7
Stockcross W Berk 41 H6
Stockerston Leics 88 B4
Stock Green Worcs 71 H3
Stocking Herefs 54 F2
Stockingford Warwks 86 D5
Stocking Pelham
  Herts 60 D3
Stockland Devon 13 G2
Stockland Bristol
  Somset 25 K3
Stockleigh English
  Devon 11 K4
Stockleigh Pomeroy
  Devon 11 K4
Stockley Wilts 39 M6
Stocklinch Somset 26 B7
Stockport Stockp 113 K4
Stocksbridge Sheff 114 E2
Stocksfield Nthumb 150 D3
Stockton Herefs 69 K3
Stockton Norfk 93 H5
Stockton Shrops 84 C4
Stockton Warwks 72 E2
Stockton Wilts 27 M4
Stockton Wrekin 84 D1
Stockton Brook
  Staffs 99 K3
Stockton Heath
  Warrtn 112 E4
Stockton-on-Tees
  S on T 141 K4
Stockton on Teme
  Worcs 70 C2
Stockton on the
  Forest C York 133 K7
Stockwell End
  Wolves 84 F4
Stockwood Bristl 38 F6
Stockwood Dorset 14 B2
Stock Wood Worcs 71 H3
Stodmarsh Kent 35 G3
Stody Norfk 106 C5
Stoer Highld 224 C3
Stoford Somset 26 E8
Stoford Wilts 28 B4
Stogumber Somset 25 H4
Stogursey Somset 25 J3
Stoke Covtry 86 D7
Stoke Devon 22 C6

Stoke Hants 17 K3
Stoke Hants 29 H2
Stoke Medway 46 D5
Stoke Abbott Dorset 13 L3
Stoke Albany Nhants 88 B5
Stoke Ash Suffk 78 D1
Stoke Bardolph
  Notts 101 M4
Stoke Bliss Worcs 70 B2
Stoke Bruerne
  Nhants 73 L4
Stoke-by-Clare Suffk 77 G5
Stoke-by-Nayland
  Suffk 78 B7
Stoke Canon Devon 12 B3
Stoke Charity Hants 29 J4
Stoke Climsland
  Cnwll 6 A2
Stoke Cross Herefs 70 B4
Stoke D'Abernon
  Surrey 43 J8
Stoke Doyle Nhants 88 E6
Stoke Dry Rutlnd 88 C4
Stoke Edith Herefs 69 L6
Stoke Farthing Wilts 28 B6
Stoke Ferry Norfk 91 G4
Stoke Fleming Devon 7 K6
Stokeford Dorset 15 G5
Stoke Gabriel Devon 7 J4
Stoke Gifford S Glos 38 F4
Stoke Golding Leics 86 E4
Stoke Goldington
  M Keyn 74 B5
Stokeham Notts 116 C6
Stoke Hammond
  Bucks 58 E3
Stoke Holy Cross
  Norfk 92 F3
Stokeinteignhead
  Devon 7 L2
Stoke Lacy Herefs 70 B5
Stoke Lyne Oxon 57 K3
Stoke Mandeville
  Bucks 58 D6
Stokenchurch Bucks 42 C2
Stoke Newington
  Gt Lon 45 G3
Stokenham Devon 7 J7
Stoke-on-Trent
  C Stke 99 K3
Stoke Orchard
  Gloucs 55 K3
Stoke Poges Bucks 42 F4
Stoke Prior Herefs 69 K3
Stoke Prior Worcs 71 G2
Stoke Rivers Devon 23 K4
Stoke Rochford Lincs 102 F6
Stoke Row Oxon 42 B4
Stoke St Gregory
  Somset 25 M6
Stoke St Mary
  Somset 25 K6
Stoke St Michael
  Somset 26 F3
Stoke St
  Milborough
  Shrops 83 L6
Stokesby Norfk 93 J2
Stokesley N York 142 B5
Stoke sub Hamdon
  Somset 26 C7
Stoke Talmage Oxon 58 B7
Stoke Trister Somset 27 H5
Stoke upon Tern
  Shrops 98 F6
Stolford Somset 25 K3
Stondon Massey
  Essex 60 F7
Stone Bucks 58 C5
Stone Gloucs 39 G2
Stone Rothm 115 K4
Stone Staffs 99 K5
Stone Worcs 84 F7
Stone Allerton
  Somset 26 B2
Ston Easton Somset 26 F2
Stonebridge N Som 38 B7

Stonebridge Warwks 86 B6
Stonebroom Derbys 101 H2
Stone Cross Kent 35 J4
Stonecrouch Kent 33 J6
Stoneferry C KuH 126 D4
Stonefield Castle
  Hotel Ag & B 172 E4
Stonegate E Susx 33 H7
Stonegrave N York 133 K4
Stonehaven Abers 207 G7
Stonehenge Wilts 28 C3
Stonehouse C Plym 6 C5
Stonehouse Gloucs 55 J6
Stonehouse S Lans 164 E1
Stone in Oxney Kent 21 J1
Stoneleigh Warwks 86 D8
Stonesby Leics 102 D7
Stonesfield Oxon 57 H4
Stones Green Essex 62 E3
Stone Street Kent 33 G3
Stone Street Suffk 93 H6
Stonewells Moray 215 G2
Stoneybridge W Isls 233 b8
Stoneyburn W Loth 176 D5
Stoneygate C Leic 87 H3
Stoneykirk D & G 144 C4
Stoney Middleton
  Derbys 114 E6
Stoney Stanton Leics 86 F4
Stoney Stoke Somset 27 G5
Stoney Stratton
  Somset 26 F4
Stoneywood C Aber 207 G3
Stoneywood Falk 175 L2
Stonham Aspal Suffk 78 D3
Stonnall Staffs 85 J3
Stonor Oxon 42 B3
Stonton Wyville
  Leics 87 K4
Stony Houghton
  Derbys 115 J7
Stony Stratford
  M Keyn 73 L6
Stoodleigh Devon 23 K5
Stoodleigh Devon 24 E7
Stop 24 Services
  Kent 34 F7
Stopham W Susx 18 D2
Stopsley Luton 59 J3
Stornoway W Isls 232 f2
Stornoway Airport
  W Isls 232 g2
Storrington W Susx 18 E3
Storth Cumb 129 K4
Storwood E R Yk 125 H2
Stotfield Moray 214 F1
Stotfold C Beds 75 J7
Stottesdon Shrops 84 C6
Stoughton Leics 87 J3
Stoughton Surrey 31 G2
Stoughton W Susx 17 L1
Stoulton Worcs 70 F4
Stourbridge Dudley 84 F6
Stourhead Wilts 27 H5
Stourpaine Dorset 15 G1
Stourport-on-
  Severn Worcs 70 E1
Stour Provost Dorset 27 H6
Stour Row Dorset 27 J7
Stourton Staffs 84 F6
Stourton Warwks 72 C6
Stourton Wilts 27 H5
Stourton Caundle
  Dorset 27 G7
Stove Shet 235 c7
Stoven Suffk 93 J6
Stow Border 167 G1
Stow Lincs 116 E5
Stow Bardolph Norfk 90 F3
Stow Bedon Norfk 91 L4
Stowbridge Norfk 90 E3
Stow-cum-Quy
  Cambs 76 D3
Stowe Shrops 82 F8
Stowe by Chartley
  Staffs 100 A6
Stowell Somset 27 G6

Stowey BaNES 38 E7
Stowford Devon 10 C7
Stowlangtoft Suffk 77 L2
Stow Longa Cambs 75 G1
Stow Maries Essex 61 K7
Stowmarket Suffk 78 C3
Stow-on-the-Wold
  Gloucs 56 D3
Stowting Kent 34 F6
Stowupland Suffk 78 C3
Straanruie Highld 204 B3
Strachan Abers 206 D6
Strachur Ag & B 182 F6
Stradbroke Suffk 92 F8
Stradishall Suffk 77 H4
Stradsett Norfk 90 F3
Stragglethorpe Lincs 102 F3
Straiton Mdloth 177 H5
Straiton S Ayrs 153 H2
Straloch Abers 207 G2
Straloch P & K 195 G4
Stramshall Staffs 100 B5
Strang IoM 237 c5
Strangeways Salfd 113 J2
Strangford Herefs 54 E3
Stranraer D & G 144 C3
Stratfield Mortimer
  W Berk 42 A7
Stratfield Saye Hants 42 B7
Stratfield Turgis
  Hants 42 B7
Stratford Gt Lon 45 H3
Stratford St Andrew
  Suffk 79 H3
Stratford St Mary
  Suffk 78 C7
Stratford sub Castle
  Wilts 28 C5
Stratford Tony Wilts 28 C6
Stratford-upon-
  Avon Warwks 72 B4
Strath Highld 219 J5
Strathan Highld 224 D4
Strathan Highld 229 J3
Strathaven S Lans 164 D1
Strathblane Stirlg 175 G3
Strathcanaird Highld 220 F2
Strathcarron Highld 210 E6
Strathcoil Ag & B 181 K2
Strathdon Abers 205 H3
Strathkinness Fife 187 G4
Strathloanhead
  W Loth 176 C4
Strathmashie House
  Highld 202 F6
Strathmiglo Fife 186 C5
Strathpeffer Highld 212 D3
Strathtay P & K 194 E5
Strathwhillan N Ayrs 162 D3
Strathy Highld 230 B3
Strathy Inn Highld 230 B3
Strathyre Stirlg 184 C4
Stratton Cnwll 9 G4
Stratton Dorset 14 C4
Stratton Gloucs 56 A7
Stratton Audley Oxon 57 L3
Stratton-on-the-
  Fosse Somset 26 F2
Stratton St
  Margaret Swindn 40 D3
Stratton St Michael
  Norfk 92 E5
Stratton Strawless
  Norfk 106 F7
Streat E Susx 19 K3
Streatham Gt Lon 44 F5
Streatley C Beds 59 H3
Streatley W Berk 41 L4
Street Devon 12 F5
Street Somset 26 C4
Street Ashton
  Warwks 86 F6
Street Dinas Shrops 97 M5
Street End Kent 34 F4
Street End W Susx 18 A5
Streethay Staffs 85 K2
Streetlam N York 141 H7

Streetly End Cambs........76 E5
Street on the Fosse
Somset......................26 F4
Strelitz P & K..............186 C1
Strelley Notts..............101 K4
Strensall C York........133 K7
Strensham Services
(northbound)
Worcs.......................70 F6
Strensham Services
(southbound)
Worcs.......................70 F6
Stretcholt Somset........25 L3
Strete Devon..................7 J6
Stretford Traffd.........113 H3
Strethall Essex............76 C6
Stretham Cambs..........90 D8
Strettington W Susx.....18 B4
Stretton Derbys........101 H1
Stretton Rutlnd...........88 D1
Stretton Staffs............84 F2
Stretton Staffs..........100 E7
Stretton Warrtn..........112 F5
Stretton Grandison
Herefs.......................70 B5
Stretton-on-
Dunsmore
Warwks....................86 E8
Stretton on Fosse
Warwks....................72 B6
Stretton Sugwas
Herefs.......................69 J6
Stretton under
Fosse Warwks..........86 F7
Stretton Westwood
Shrops......................83 L4
Strichen Abers..........217 H4
Stringston Somset.......25 J3
Strixton Nhants..........74 C3
Stroat Gloucs..............38 E2
Strollamus Highld.....209 J8
Stroma Highld...........231 L1
Stromeferry Highld....210 D7
Stromness Ork..........234 b6
Stronaba Highld........201 J8
Stronachlachar Stirlg..183 L5
Stronafian Ag & B......173 H3
Stronchrubie Highld ..224 F5
Strone Ag & B............173 L3
Strone Highld.............192 B1
Strone Highld.............212 E8
Stronmilchan Ag & B...183 G2
Stronsay Ork.............234 d5
Stronsay Airport
Ork.........................234 d5
Strontian Highld........191 G4
Strood Medway............46 B6
Stroud Gloucs.............55 J6
Stroud Hants...............30 B6
Stroud Green Gloucs ...55 J6
Stroxton Lincs...........102 E6
Struan Highld.............208 E6
Struan P & K..............194 C4
Strumpshaw Norfk.......93 H3
Strutherhill S Lans.....175 K7
Struthers Fife............186 F5
Struy Highld...............212 B6
Stuartfield Abers......217 H5
Stubbington Hants.......17 G2
Stubbins Lancs..........122 B6
Stubton Lincs.............102 E3
Stuckton Hants............28 D8
Studham C Beds...........59 G5
Studland Dorset...........15 J6
Studley Warwks...........71 J2
Studley Wilts................39 L6
Studley Roger N York ..132 D5
Studley Royal N York ...132 D5
Studley Royal Park
& Fountains
Abbey N York...........132 D5
Stuntney Cambs...........90 D7
Sturmer Essex..............77 G5
Sturminster
Common Dorset......27 H8
Sturminster
Marshall Dorset.....15 H3

Sturminster Newton
Dorset......................27 H8
Sturry Kent..................35 G3
Sturton N Linc...........116 F2
Sturton by Stow
Lincs......................116 E5
Sturton le Steeple
Notts......................116 C5
Stuston Suffk..............92 D7
Stutton N York...........124 D3
Stutton Suffk..............78 D7
Styal Ches E...............113 J5
Stynie Moray..............215 H3
Styrrup Notts.............115 L4
Succoth Ag & B...........183 K6
Suckley Worcs..............70 C4
Sudborough Nhants......88 D6
Sudbourne Suffk..........79 J4
Sudbrook Lincs...........102 F4
Sudbrook Mons.............38 D3
Sudbrooke Lincs.........117 G6
Sudbury Derbys.........100 D6
Sudbury Gt Lon............44 D3
Sudbury Suffk..............77 K6
Suffield N York..........134 F2
Suffield Norfk............106 F6
Sugnall Staffs.............99 H6
Sugwas Pool Herefs.....69 J6
Suisnish Highld..........199 J3
Sulby IoM..................237 d3
Sulgrave Nhants..........73 G5
Sulham W Berk............41 M5
Sulhamstead W Berk.....41 M6
Sullom Shet...............235 c4
Sullom Voe Shet........235 c4
Sully V Glam................37 J6
Sumburgh Airport
Shet.......................235 c8
Summerbridge
N York.....................132 C6
Summercourt Cnwll........4 D5
Summerfield Norfk.....105 J5
Summerhill Pembks......49 K6
Summerhouse Darltn...140 F4
Summersdale W Susx....18 B4
Summerseat Bury........122 B7
Summertown Oxon........57 K6
Sunbury-on-
Thames Surrey.......43 J6
Sundaywell D & G.......154 E5
Sunderland Ag & B......170 E5
Sunderland Cumb........147 L7
Sunderland Lancs......129 J7
Sunderland Sundld....151 J4
Sunderland Bridge
Dur........................151 G7
Sundhope Border.......166 E4
Sundon Park Luton......59 H3
Sundridge Kent...........32 E3
Sunningdale W & M......42 F6
Sunninghill W & M......42 F6
Sunningwell Oxon........57 J7
Sunniside Dur............150 E7
Sunniside Gatesd.......150 F3
Sunnyhill C Derb.......101 G6
Sunnyhurst Bl w D.....121 K6
Sunnylaw Stirlg.........185 G7
Sunnymead Oxon..........57 J6
Surbiton Gt Lon...........44 D6
Surfleet Lincs...........103 L6
Surlingham Norfk........93 H3
Surrex Essex................61 L4
Sustead Norfk............106 E5
Susworth Lincs...........116 D2
Sutcombe Devon.............9 J3
Sutcombemill Devon......9 J3
Sutterby Lincs...........118 E6
Sutterton Lincs..........103 M5
Sutton C Beds..............75 J5
Sutton C Pete..............89 G4
Sutton Cambs..............90 C7
Sutton Devon.................7 G7
Sutton E Susx..............20 A5
Sutton Gt Lon...............44 E7
Sutton Kent..................35 J5
Sutton N York.............124 D5
Sutton Norfk..............107 H7

Sutton Notts..............102 C5
Sutton Oxon................57 H6
Sutton Shrops..............83 K2
Sutton Shrops..............84 D6
Sutton Staffs...............99 H7
Sutton Suffk................79 G5
Sutton W Susx.............18 D3
Sutton-at-Hone
Kent........................45 K6
Sutton Bassett
Nhants.....................87 L5
Sutton Benger Wilts....39 L5
Sutton Bonington
Notts......................101 J7
Sutton Bridge Lincs...104 D7
Sutton Cheney Leics....86 E4
Sutton Coldfield
Birm.......................85 K4
Sutton Courtenay
Oxon........................41 J2
Sutton cum Lound
Notts......................116 B5
Sutton Green Surrey....31 G1
Sutton Howgrave
N York.....................132 D4
Sutton-in-Ashfield
Notts......................101 J1
Sutton-in-Craven
N York.....................122 F2
Sutton Maddock
Shrops......................84 C3
Sutton Mallet Somset...26 A4
Sutton Mandeville
Wilts........................27 M5
Sutton Montis
Somset......................26 F6
Sutton-on-Hull
C KuH.....................126 E4
Sutton on Sea Lincs...119 G5
Sutton-on-the-
Forest N York........133 J6
Sutton on the Hill
Derbys....................100 E5
Sutton on Trent
Notts......................116 D7
Sutton St Edmund
Lincs.......................89 L2
Sutton St James
Lincs......................104 C8
Sutton St Nicholas
Herefs......................69 K5
Sutton Scotney
Hants........................29 J4
Sutton-under-
Brailes Warwks......72 C6
Sutton-under-
Whitestonecliffe
N York.....................133 G3
Sutton upon
Derwent E R Yk.....125 G2
Sutton Valence Kent....33 L4
Sutton Veny Wilts........27 K3
Sutton Waldron
Dorset......................27 K7
Sutton Weaver
Ches W....................112 D5
Sutton Wick BaNES......38 E8
Sutton Wick Oxon........41 J2
Swaby Lincs...............118 E6
Swadlincote Derbys....100 F8
Swaffham Norfk...........91 J2
Swaffham Bulbeck
Cambs......................76 D3
Swaffham Prior
Cambs......................76 E2
Swafield Norfk...........107 G6
Swainby N York..........141 L6
Swainsthorpe Norfk.....92 F4
Swainswick BaNES.......39 H6
Swalcliffe Oxon...........72 E6
Swalecliffe Kent...........47 J6
Swallow Lincs............117 K2
Swallow Beck Lincs....116 F7
Swallowcliffe Wilts......27 L6
Swallowfield Wokham...42 B7
Swanage Dorset...........15 J6
Swanbourne Bucks.......58 D3

Swan Green Ches W.....113 G6
Swanland E R Yk........126 B5
Swanley Kent................45 K6
Swanley Village Kent....45 K6
Swanmore Hants...........29 L7
Swannington Leics.......86 E1
Swannington Norfk......106 D8
Swanpool Lincs..........116 F7
Swanscombe Kent..........45 L5
Swansea Swans............51 J6
Swansea Airport
Swans......................51 H7
Swansea West
Services Swans.......51 J5
Swanton Abbot
Norfk......................106 F7
Swanton Morley
Norfk......................106 B8
Swanton Novers
Norfk......................106 B6
Swan Village Sandw.....85 H5
Swanwick Derbys........101 H6
Swanwick Hants...........17 G1
Swarby Lincs.............103 H4
Swardeston Norfk.........92 E3
Swarkestone Derbys....101 G6
Swarland Nthumb........158 F2
Swarraton Hants..........29 K4
Swarthmoor Cumb.......129 G4
Swaton Lincs.............103 J5
Swavesey Cambs...........75 L2
Sway Hants..................16 C3
Swayfield Lincs..........103 G7
Swaythling C Sotn........29 H7
Sweetham Devon...........11 K5
Sweethaws E Susx........32 E7
Sweets Cnwll..................8 F5
Sweetshouse Cnwll........5 H4
Swefling Suffk..............79 H2
Swepstone Leics..........86 D2
Swerford Oxon..............57 G2
Swettenham Ches E.....113 J7
Swilland Suffk..............78 E4
Swillington Leeds......124 B4
Swimbridge Devon........23 K5
Swimbridge
Newland Devon......23 J5
Swinbrook Oxon............56 F5
Swincliffe N York.......132 C7
Swinderby Lincs.........116 E8
Swindon Gloucs............55 L3
Swindon Staffs.............84 F5
Swindon Swindn............40 D4
Swine E R Yk...............126 E4
Swinefleet E R Yk......125 H6
Swineshead Bed............74 F2
Swineshead Lincs.......103 L4
Swiney Highld.............227 M2
Swinford Leics.............87 H7
Swingfield Minnis
Kent........................35 G6
Swingfield Street
Kent........................35 H6
Swingleton Green
Suffk........................77 L5
Swinhoe Nthumb.........169 J4
Swinithwaite N York...131 K2
Swinside Cumb............137 H3
Swinstead Lincs.........103 G7
Swinton Border..........179 H8
Swinton N York..........132 C4
Swinton N York..........134 B5
Swinton Rothm..........115 J2
Swinton Salfd...........113 H2
Swithland Leics...........87 G2
Swordale Highld........212 E2
Swordland Highld.......200 B6
Swordly Highld...........229 M3
Swynnerton Staffs.......99 J5
Swyre Dorset................13 M5
Sychtyn Powys.............81 L3
Syde Gloucs.................55 L5
Sydenham Gt Lon..........45 G5
Sydenham Oxon............58 B7
Sydenham Damerel
Devon........................6 B2
Syderstone Norfk.......105 K6

Sydling St Nicholas
Dorset.................14 C3
Sydmonton Hants.............41 J8
Syerston Notts 102 C3
Sykehouse Donc 124 F6
Symbister Shet 235 d4
Symington S Ayrs 163 J3
Symington S Lans 165 J3
Symondsbury Dorset....13 K4
Symonds Yat (West)
Herefs.................54 E5
Syre Highld............229 L6
Syreford Gloucs.........56 B4
Syresham Nhants........73 J6
Syston Leics............87 J2
Syston Lincs 102 F4
Sytchampton Worcs.....70 E2
Sywell Nhants..........74 B2

T

Tackley Oxon............57 J4
Tacolneston Norfk.......92 D4
Tadcaster N York.......124 D2
Taddington Derbys......114 C7
Tadley Hants............41 L7
Tadlow Cambs...........75 K5
Tadmarton Oxon.........72 E6
Tadworth Surrey.........44 E8
Taff's Well Rhondd......37 H4
Taibach Neath..........36 B3
Tain Highld............223 G5
Tain Highld............231 J3
Tairbeart W Isls........232 e4
Takeley Essex...........60 F4
Takeley Street Essex....60 E4
Talaton Devon...........12 D3
Talbenny Pembks........48 E5
Talbot Village BCP......15 K4
Taleford Devon..........12 E3
Talerddig Powys.........81 K4
Talgarreg Cerdgn........65 L4
Talgarth Powys..........68 D7
Talisker Highld........208 E7
Talke Staffs............99 J2
Talke Pits Staffs.......99 J3
Talkin Cumb............148 F4
Talladale Highld........219 L7
Talla Linnfoots
Border.................165 M5
Tallaminnock S Ayrs... 153 J3
Tallarn Green
Wrexhm.................98 C4
Tallentire Cumb........147 K7
Talley Carmth...........66 E7
Tallington Lincs........88 F2
Talmine Highld.........229 J3
Talog Carmth...........50 D1
Talsarn Cerdgn.........66 D4
Talsarnau Gwynd........95 K5
Talskiddy Cnwll 4 E3
Talwrn IoA.............109 G6
Tal-y-bont Cerdgn......80 E5
Tal-y-bont Conwy......109 L7
Tal-y-bont Gwynd.......95 K7
Tal-y-bont Gwynd......109 J7
Talybont-on-Usk
Powys..................53 H4
Tal-y-Cafn Conwy......109 M7
Tal-y-coed Mons........54 B5
Talysarn Gwynd.........95 H2
Tamar Valley Mining
District Devon......... 6 C3
Tamerton Foliot
C Plym................. 6 C4
Tamworth Staffs........86 B3
Tamworth Services
Warwks.................86 B4
Tandridge Surrey........32 C3
Tanfield Dur...........150 F4
Tanfield Lea Dur.......150 F4
Tangasdale W Isls......233 b9
Tangley Hants..........28 F2
Tangmere W Susx........18 B4
Tankerness Ork.........234 c6

Tankersley Barns 115 G2
Tankerton Kent............47 J6
Tannach Highld.........231 K6
Tannachie Abers........206 E8
Tannadice Angus.......196 D5
Tanner's Green
Worcs...................85 J8
Tannington Suffk........78 F2
Tannochside N Lans....175 J6
Tansley Derbys.........100 F1
Tansor Nhants..........88 F5
Tantobie Dur...........150 F4
Tanworth in Arden
Warwks..................71 K1
Tan-y-groes Cerdgn......65 J5
Taobh Tuath W Isls....232 d5
Taplow Bucks...........42 E4
Tarbert Ag & B........172 B7
Tarbert Ag & B........172 E5
Tarbert W Isls.........232 e4
Tarbet Ag & B.........183 K6
Tarbet Highld..........200 B6
Tarbet Highld..........228 B5
Tarbolton S Ayrs.......163 K4
Tarbrax S Lans.........176 D7
Tardebigge Worcs.......71 H2
Tarfside Angus........196 D1
Tarland Abers..........205 K4
Tarleton Lancs.........120 F6
Tarlton Gloucs..........55 L7
Tarnock Somset.........26 B2
Tarporley Ches W......112 D8
Tarrant Crawford
Dorset..................15 H2
Tarrant Gunville
Dorset..................27 L8
Tarrant Hinton
Dorset..................15 H1
Tarrant Keyneston
Dorset..................15 H2
Tarrant Launceston
Dorset..................15 H1
Tarrant Monkton
Dorset..................15 H2
Tarrant Rawston
Dorset..................15 H2
Tarrant Rushton
Dorset..................15 H2
Tarring Neville
E Susx..................19 L5
Tarrington Herefs.......70 B6
Tarskavaig Highld......199 J4
Tarves Abers..........217 G7
Tarvin Ches W.........112 C7
Tasburgh Norfk.........92 E4
Tatenhill Staffs.......100 D7
Tathwell Lincs.........118 D5
Tatsfield Surrey........32 D2
Tattenhall Ches W.......98 C2
Tatterford Norfk.......105 K6
Tattersett Norfk.......105 K6
Tattershall Lincs......103 K2
Tattershall Thorpe
Lincs..................103 L1
Tattingstone Suffk......78 D6
Tattingstone White
Horse Suffk.............78 D6
Tatton Park Ches E....113 H5
Tatworth Somset........13 J2
Tauchers Moray........215 J4
Taunton Somset.........25 K6
Taunton Deane
Services Somset........25 J7
Taverham Norfk.........92 E2
Tavernspite Pembks......49 K5
Tavistock Devon......... 6 C2
Tavistock Devon......... 6 C2
Taw Green Devon.........10 F5
Tawstock Devon.........23 J5
Taxal Derbys..........114 A5
Tay Bridge C Dund....187 G2
Taychreggan Hotel
Ag & B................182 F3
Tay Forest Park
P & K.................194 C4
Tayinloan Ag & B......161 H1
Taynton Gloucs.........55 G4

Taynton Oxon...........56 E5
Taynuilt Ag & B.......182 E2
Tayport Fife...........187 G2
Tayvallich Ag & B.....172 C2
Tealby Lincs...........117 J4
Tealing Angus.........196 C8
Team Valley Gatesd....151 G3
Teangue Highld........199 K4
Teanord Highld........212 F2
Tebay Cumb............138 E6
Tebay Services Cumb...138 E6
Tebworth C Beds........59 G3
Tedburn St Mary
Devon...................11 J6
Teddington Gloucs......55 L2
Teddington Gt Lon......44 D6
Tedstone Delamere
Herefs..................70 C3
Tedstone Wafer
Herefs..................70 C3
Teeton Nhants..........73 K1
Teffont Evias Wilts.....27 M5
Teffont Magna Wilts....27 M5
Tegryn Pembks..........65 H7
Teigh Rutlnd...........88 C1
Teigngrace Devon........ 7 K2
Teignmouth Devon.......12 B7
Teindside Border......166 F7
Telford Wrekin.........84 C2
Telford Services
Shrops.................84 D2
Tellisford Somset.......27 J1
Telscombe E Susx.......19 L5
Tempar P & K..........193 L5
Templand D & G........155 J5
Temple Cnwll........... 5 J2
Temple Mdloth.........177 J6
Temple Bar Cerdgn......66 C4
Temple Cloud BaNES....38 F8
Templecombe
Somset..................27 G6
Temple Grafton
Warwks..................71 K4
Temple Guiting
Gloucs..................56 C3
Temple Hirst N York...124 F5
Temple Normanton
Derbys.................115 H7
Temple of Fiddes
Abers..................206 F8
Temple Sowerby
Cumb...................138 E2
Templeton Devon........11 K3
Templeton Pembks.......49 J5
Templetown Dur........150 E5
Tempsford C Beds.......75 H4
Tenbury Wells Worcs....69 L2
Tenby Pembks...........49 J7
Tendring Essex.........62 D3
Tendring Green
Essex...................62 D3
Tendring Heath
Essex...................62 D3
Ten Mile Bank Norfk....90 E4
Tenterden Kent.........34 B7
Terling Essex..........61 J5
Ternhill Shrops.........98 F6
Terregles D & G.......155 G6
Terrington N York.....133 K5
Terrington St
Clement Norfk.........104 E7
Terrington St John
Norfk...................90 D7
Teston Kent............33 J3
Testwood Hants.........29 G8
Tetbury Gloucs.........39 K2
Tetchill Shrops........98 B6
Tetcott Devon.......... 9 J5
Tetford Lincs.........118 D6
Tetney Lincs..........118 D2
Tetsworth Oxon.........58 B7
Tettenhall Wolves......84 F4
Tettenhall Wood
Wolves..................84 F4
Teversal Notts........101 J1
Teversham Cambs........76 C3
Teviothead Border.....156 D2

Tewin Herts............59 L5
Tewkesbury Gloucs.......55 K2
Teynham Kent...........34 C3
Thackley C Brad.......123 H3
Thainstone Abers......206 E2
Thakeham W Susx........18 F3
Thame Oxon.............58 B6
Thames Ditton
Surrey..................44 D6
Thamesmead Gt Lon......45 J4
Thamesport Medway.....46 E5
Thanington Kent........34 F4
Thankerton S Lans.....165 J2
Tharston Norfk.........92 E5
Thatcham W Berk........41 K6
Thaxted Essex..........60 F2
Theakston N York......132 D3
Thealby N Linc........125 K6
Theale Somset..........26 C3
Theale W Berk..........41 M6
Thearne E R Yk........126 D3
The Beeches Gloucs......56 B7
Theberton Suffk.........79 J2
The Braes Highld......209 H7
The Broads.............93 K2
The Brunt E Loth......178 E4
The Bungalow IoM......237 d4
The Burf Worcs.........70 E2
The City Bucks.........42 C2
The Common Wilts.......28 E5
Theddingworth Leics....87 J6
Theddlethorpe All
Saints Lincs..........118 F4
Theddlethorpe St
Helen Lincs...........119 G4
The Deep C KuH........126 D5
The Den N Ayrs........174 C7
The Forstal Kent.......34 D6
The Green Cumb........128 E3
The Green Essex........61 J4
The Green N York......143 G6
The Green Wilts........27 K5
The Headland Hartpl...151 M7
The Hill Cumb.........128 E3
The Lee Bucks..........58 E6
The Lhen IoM..........237 d2
Thelnetham Suffk.......92 B7
The Lochs Moray.......215 G2
Thelveton Norfk........92 E7
Thelwall Warrtn.......112 F4
Themelthorpe Norfk....106 C7
The Middles Dur.......150 F5
The Moor Kent..........33 K7
The Mumbles Swans......51 J7
The Murray S Lans.....175 H7
The Neuk Abers........206 D5
Thenford Nhants........73 G5
The Reddings Gloucs....55 K4
Therfield Herts........75 L6
The Ross P & K........185 G3
The Spring Warwks......86 C8
The Stocks Kent........21 H1
The Strand Wilts.......39 L8
Thetford Norfk.........91 K6
Thetford Forest
Park...................91 J5
Theydon Bois Essex......60 D7
Thickwood Wilts........39 J5
Thimbleby Lincs........118 C7
Thimbleby N York......141 K7
Thingwall Wirral......111 J5
Thirkleby N York......133 G4
Thirlby N York.........133 G3
Thirlestane Border....178 C6
Thirn N York..........132 C3
Thirsk N York.........132 F3
Thistleton Lancs......120 E3
Thistleton Rutlnd.....102 E8
Thistley Green Suffk....90 F7
Thixendale N York.....134 C7
Thockrington
Nthumb................158 B6
Tholomas Drove
Cambs...................90 B3
Tholthorpe N York.....133 G6
Thomastown Abers......216 B6
Thompson Norfk.........91 K4

Thongsbridge Kirk...... 123 H8
Thoralby N York............ 131 J3
Thoresway Lincs 117 K3
Thorganby Lincs 117 K3
Thorganby N York 125 G3
Thorgill N York 142 E7
Thorington Suffk 93 J8
Thorington Street
  Suffk...................... 78 B7
Thorlby N York............ 131 H8
Thorley Herts 60 D4
Thorley Street IoW 16 D5
Thormanby N York....... 133 G5
Thornaby-on-Tees
  S on T 141 K4
Thornage Norfk........... 106 C5
Thornborough Bucks 73 L7
Thornborough N York.. 132 D4
Thornbury C Brad 123 J4
Thornbury Devon 9 K3
Thornbury Herefs......... 70 B3
Thornbury S Glos.......... 38 F3
Thornby Nhants............ 87 J7
Thorncliff Staffs........... 100 A2
Thorncombe Dorset 13 J2
Thorndon Suffk............ 78 D1
Thorndon Cross
  Devon..................... 10 D6
Thorne Donc 125 G7
Thorner Leeds 124 B3
Thorne St Margaret
  Somset 25 H7
Thorney C Pete........... 89 K3
Thorney Notts.............. 116 E6
Thorney Somset 26 B6
Thorney Hill Hants........ 16 A3
Thorney Island
  W Susx.................... 17 L2
Thornfalcon Somset 25 L6
Thornford Dorset.......... 26 E8
Thorngrafton
  Nthumb 149 K2
Thorngumbald E R Yk.. 126 F5
Thornham Norfk 105 H4
Thornham Magna
  Suffk...................... 78 D1
Thornham Parva
  Suffk...................... 92 D8
Thornhaugh C Pete...... 88 F4
Thornhill C Soth 29 J8
Thornhill Cumb 136 D5
Thornhill D & G 154 F3
Thornhill Derbys 114 D5
Thornhill Kirk 123 K6
Thornhill Stirlg........... 184 E7
Thornholme E R Yk.... 135 H6
Thornicombe Dorset 15 G2
Thornington Nthumb ... 168 D3
Thornley Dur 150 E7
Thornley Dur 151 J6
Thornliebank E Rens ... 174 F6
Thorns Suffk................ 77 G4
Thornsett Derbys........ 114 A4
Thornthwaite Cumb.... 137 H3
Thornthwaite N York... 132 B7
Thornton Angus 196 C6
Thornton Bucks............ 73 L7
Thornton C Brad 123 G4
Thornton E R Yk 125 H2
Thornton Fife.............. 186 E7
Thornton Lancs 120 D3
Thornton Leics 86 F3
Thornton Middsb 141 L4
Thornton Nthumb....... 179 K8
Thornton Curtis
  N Linc 126 D6
Thorntonhall S Lans 175 G7
Thornton Heath
  Gt Lon 44 F6
Thornton Hough
  Wirral 111 J5
Thornton-in-
  Craven N York........ 122 D2
Thornton in
  Lonsdale N York...... 130 D5
Thornton-le-Beans
  N York.................... 132 F2

Thornton-le-Clay
  N York.................... 133 L6
Thornton-le-Dale
  N York.................... 134 C3
Thornton le Moor
  Lincs...................... 117 H3
Thornton-le-Moor
  N York.................... 132 F2
Thornton-le-Moors
  Ches W................... 112 C6
Thornton-le-Street
  N York.................... 132 F3
Thorntonloch E Loth.... 178 F4
Thornton Rust N York.. 131 H2
Thornton Steward
  N York.................... 132 B3
Thornton Watlass
  N York.................... 132 C3
Thornydykes Border 178 D8
Thornythwaite Cumb... 137 L3
Thoroton Notts........... 102 C4
Thorp Arch Leeds........ 124 C2
Thorpe Derbys 100 D3
Thorpe E R Yk............ 126 B2
Thorpe N York 131 J6
Thorpe Notts.............. 102 C3
Thorpe Surrey............. 43 G6
Thorpe Abbotts
  Norfk 92 E7
Thorpe Arnold Leics.... 102 C7
Thorpe Audlin
  Wakefd................... 124 D7
Thorpe Bassett
  N York.................... 134 D5
Thorpe Bay Sthend..... 46 E3
Thorpe by Water
  Rutlnd 88 C4
Thorpe Constantine
  Staffs..................... 86 C2
Thorpe End Norfk........ 93 G2
Thorpe Green Essex.... 62 E4
Thorpe Green Suffk..... 77 L4
Thorpe Hesley Rothm.. 115 G3
Thorpe in Balne
  Donc 124 F7
Thorpe Langton
  Leics...................... 87 L5
Thorpe Lea Surrey 43 G6
Thorpe-le-Soken
  Essex..................... 62 E4
Thorpe le Street
  E R Yk.................... 125 K2
Thorpe Malsor
  Nhants.................... 88 B7
Thorpe Mandeville
  Nhants.................... 73 G5
Thorpe Market Norfk .. 106 F5
Thorpe Marriot
  Norfk 92 E1
Thorpe Morieux
  Suffk...................... 77 L4
Thorpeness Suffk......... 79 K3
Thorpe on the Hill
  Lincs...................... 116 E7
Thorpe Park Surrey 43 G6
Thorpe St Andrew
  Norfk 92 F2
Thorpe St Peter
  Lincs...................... 104 D1
Thorpe Salvin Rothm... 115 K5
Thorpe Satchville
  Leics...................... 87 K2
Thorpe Thewles
  S on T 141 J3
Thorpe Tilney Lincs...... 103 J2
Thorpe Underwood
  N York.................... 133 G7
Thorpe Waterville
  Nhants.................... 88 E7
Thorpe Willoughby
  N York.................... 124 E4
Thorrington Essex 62 C4
Thorverton Devon 11 L4
Thrandeston Suffk....... 92 D7
Thrapston Nhants........ 88 E7
Threapwood Ches W.... 98 C4
Threapwood Staffs...... 100 B4

Threave S Ayrs............. 163 J7
Three Bridges
  W Susx..................... 32 B5
Three Chimneys
  Kent........................ 33 L5
Three Cocks Powys 68 D6
Three Crosses Swans.... 51 H6
Three Cups Corner
  E Susx..................... 20 D2
Threekingham Lincs..... 103 H5
Three Leg Cross
  E Susx..................... 33 H6
Three Legged Cross
  Dorset...................... 15 K2
Three Mile Cross
  Wokham................... 42 B6
Threemilestone
  Cnwll 3 K3
Threemiletown
  W Loth.................... 176 E3
Three Oaks E Susx........ 21 G3
Threlkeld Cumb........... 137 J3
Threshers Bush
  Essex....................... 60 D6
Threshfield N York....... 131 J6
Thrigby Norfk.............. 93 K2
Thrintoft N York.......... 132 D2
Thriplow Cambs........... 76 B5
Throcking Herts........... 60 B3
Throckley N u Ty......... 150 E2
Throckmorton Worcs.... 71 H4
Throop BCP................ 15 L4
Thropton Nthumb....... 158 C2
Throsk Stirlg............... 176 B1
Throughgate D & G..... 154 F5
Throwleigh Devon 11 G6
Throwley Forstal
  Kent........................ 34 C4
Thrumpton Notts........ 101 J6
Thrumster Highld........ 231 L6
Thruncoe NE Lin 127 H8
Thrupp Gloucs 55 K7
Thrussington Leics....... 87 J1
Thruxton Hants........... 28 F3
Thruxton Herefs.......... 69 J7
Thrybergh Rothm....... 115 J3
Thulston Derbys.......... 101 H6
Tilgate W Susx............. 31 L4
Thundersley Essex....... 46 C3
Thurcaston Leics.......... 87 H2
Thurcroft Rothm........ 115 J4
Thurgarton Norfk....... 106 E5
Thurgarton Notts....... 102 B3
Thurgoland Barns 114 F2
Thurlaston Leics.......... 87 G4
Thurlaston Warwks..... 72 F1
Thurlbear Somset........ 25 K7
Thurlby Lincs.............. 89 G1
Thurlby Lincs............. 102 E1
Thurlby Lincs............. 119 G6
Thurleigh Bed............. 74 F3
Thurlestone Devon........ 7 G7
Thurloxton Somset....... 25 L5
Thurlstone Barns........ 114 E2
Thurlton Norfk............ 93 J4
Thurmaston Leics........ 87 H2
Thurnby Leics.............. 87 J3
Thurne Norfk............... 93 J1
Thurnham Kent........... 33 K2
Thurning Nhants.......... 88 F6
Thurning Norfk.......... 106 C6
Thurnscoe Barns........ 115 J1
Thurrock Services
  Thurr 45 L4
Thursby Cumb............ 148 B5
Thursford Norfk......... 106 B5
Thursley Surrey........... 30 E4
Thurso Highld............ 231 G2
Thurstaston Wirral..... 111 H5
Thurston Suffk............ 77 K2
Thurstonfield Cumb.... 148 B4
Thurstonland Kirk...... 123 H7
Thurton Norfk............ 93 G4
Thurvaston Derbys..... 100 E5
Thuxton Norfk............ 92 B3
Thwaite N York.......... 139 K7
Thwaite Suffk............. 78 D2
Thwaite Head Cumb.... 129 H2

Thwaite St Mary
  Norfk 93 G4
Thwing E R Yk............ 135 G5
Tibbermore P & K 185 L3
Tibbers D & G 154 E3
Tibberton Gloucs......... 55 H4
Tibberton Worcs.......... 70 F3
Tibberton Wrekin......... 99 G7
Tibenham Norfk.......... 92 D5
Tibshelf Derbys 101 H1
Tibshelf Services
  Derbys.................... 101 H1
Tibthorpe E R Yk........ 134 E7
Ticehurst E Susx.......... 33 H7
Tichborne Hants.......... 29 L5
Tickencote Rutlnd........ 88 E2
Tickenham N Som 38 C6
Tickhill Donc.............. 115 L3
Ticklerton Shrops......... 83 J5
Ticknall Derbys 101 G7
Tickton E R Yk............ 126 D3
Tidcombe Wilts............ 40 F8
Tiddington Oxon.......... 57 M6
Tiddington Warwks...... 72 B4
Tidebrook E Susx.......... 33 G7
Tideford Cnwll 6 A4
Tidenham Gloucs......... 38 E2
Tideswell Derbys 114 D6
Tidmarsh W Berk........ 41 M5
Tidmington Warwks..... 72 C6
Tidworth Wilts............. 28 E2
Tiers Cross Pembks...... 48 F5
Tiffield Nhants............. 73 K4
Tigerton Angus.......... 196 E4
Tigh a' Ghearraidh
  W Isls...................... 233 b6
Tigharry W Isls........... 233 b6
Tighnabruaich
  Ag & B.................... 173 G4
Tigley Devon 7 H4
Tilbrook Cambs............ 74 F2
Tilbury Thurr 45 M5
Tile Cross Birm 85 L6
Tile Hill Covtry............ 86 C7
Tilehurst Readg........... 42 A5
Tilford Surrey.............. 30 E3
Tilgate W Susx............. 31 L4
Tilham Street Somset... 26 E4
Tillicoultry Clacks....... 185 J7
Tillietudlem S Lans..... 164 F1
Tillingham Essex.......... 62 B7
Tillington Herefs.......... 69 J5
Tillington W Susx......... 30 F6
Tillington Common
  Herefs..................... 69 J5
Tillybirloch Abers....... 206 D4
Tillyfourie Abers........ 206 C3
Tillygreig Abers.......... 207 G2
Tillyrie P & K............. 186 B6
Tilmanstone Kent........ 35 J4
Tilney All Saints
  Norfk 104 F8
Tilney High End
  Norfk 104 E8
Tilney St Lawrence
  Norfk 90 D2
Tilshead Wilts............. 28 B2
Tilstock Shrops............ 98 D5
Tilston Ches W............. 98 C3
Tilstone Fearnall
  Ches W..................... 98 E1
Tilsworth C Beds.......... 59 G3
Tilton on the Hill
  Leics....................... 87 J3
Tiltups End Gloucs....... 39 J2
Timberland Lincs........ 103 J2
Timbersbrook Ches E.. 113 K8
Timberscombe
  Somset 24 E3
Timble N York............ 132 B8
Timpanheck D & G..... 156 B7
Timperley Traffd........ 113 H4
Timsbury BaNES.......... 38 F8
Timsbury Hants........... 29 G5
Timsgarry W Isls......... 232 d2
Timsgearraidh
  W Isls...................... 232 d2

Timworth Suffk 77 J2
Timworth Green
  Suffk.........................77 J2
Tincleton Dorset............14 E4
Tindale Cumb.................149 G3
Tingewick Bucks...........58 A2
Tingrith C Beds............59 G2
Tingwall Airport
  Shet..........................235 c6
Tingwell Ork...............234 c5
Tinhay Devon 9 K7
Tinsley Sheff 115 H4
Tinsley Green W Susx...32 B5
Tintagel Cnwll 8 E7
Tintern Mons.................54 D7
Tintinhull Somset 26 D7
Tintwistle Derbys.......114 A3
Tinwald D & G 155 H5
Tinwell Rutlnd..............88 E3
Tipton Sandw.................85 G5
Tipton Green Sandw.......85 G5
Tipton St John
  Devon..........................12 E4
Tiptree Essex 61 L5
Tiptree Heath Essex.....61 L5
Tirabad Powys................67 J6
Tiree Ag & B 188 D7
Tiree Airport Ag & B.....188 C7
Tiretigan Ag & B...........172 C6
Tirley Gloucs.................55 J3
Tiroran Ag & B..............181 G2
Tirphil Caerph...............53 H7
Tirril Cumb...................138 D2
Tisbury Wilts...................27 L5
Tissington Derbys.......100 D3
Titchberry Devon..........22 C6
Titchfield Hants............17 G2
Titchmarsh Nhants........88 E7
Titchwell Norfk 105 J4
Tithby Notts 102 B5
Titley Herefs..................69 G3
Titsey Surrey.................32 D3
Titson Cnwll 9 H5
Tittensor Staffs..............99 K5
Tittleshall Norfk...........105 L7
Titton Worcs....................70 E1
Tiverton Ches W..............98 D1
Tiverton Devon...............24 E8
Tivetshall St
  Margaret Norfk........92 E6
Tivetshall St Mary
  Norfk.........................92 E6
Tixall Staffs....................99 L7
Tixover Rutlnd................88 E4
Toab Shet......................235 c8
Tobermory Ag & B 189 L5
Toberonochy
  Ag & B........................181 L5
Tobha Mòr W Isls........233 b7
Tocher Abers................216 D7
Tochieneal Moray.......215 L2
Tockenham Wilts..........40 B4
Tockholes Bl w D 121 K6
Tockington S Glos........38 E3
Tockwith N York 133 G8
Todber Dorset................27 J7
Toddington C Beds........59 G3
Toddington Gloucs......56 B2
Toddington
  Services C Beds........59 G3
Todenham Gloucs........72 B7
Todhills Rest Area
  Cumb.........................148 C3
Todmorden Calder.......122 D5
Todwick Rothm............115 J5
Toft Cambs......................75 L4
Toft Lincs........................88 F1
Toft Shet.......................235 c3
Toft Hill Dur 140 E2
Toft Monks Norfk.........93 J4
Toft next Newton
  Lincs..........................117 H4
Toftrees Norfk.............105 L6
Togston Nthumb 159 G2
Tokavaig Highld...........199 J3
Tokers Green Oxon 42 B5

Tolastadh bho
  Thuath W Isls..........232 g2
Tolland Somset..............25 H5
Tollard Royal Wilts.......27 L7
Toll Bar Donc...............124 E8
Toller Fratrum
  Dorset........................14 B3
Toller Porcorum
  Dorset........................14 B3
Tollerton N York 133 H6
Tollerton Notts............101 L5
Tollesbury Essex...........62 A6
Tolleshunt D'Arcy
  Essex..........................61 L5
Tolleshunt Knights
  Essex..........................61 L5
Tolleshunt Major
  Essex..........................61 L5
Toll of Birness
  Abers........................217 J7
Tolpuddle Dorset 14 E4
Tolworth Gt Lon............44 D6
Tomatin Highld............213 J8
Tomchrasky Highld......201 K3
Tomdoun Highld..........201 H5
Tomich Highld..............211 L8
Tomich Highld..............212 E5
Tomich Highld..............222 F7
Tomich Highld..............226 A7
Tomintoul Moray.........204 E2
Tomnacross Highld......212 D6
Tomnavoulin Moray.....204 F1
Tonbridge Kent.............33 G4
Tondu Brdgnd................36 D4
Tonedale Somset..........25 H6
Tong C Brad.................123 J4
Tong Kent.......................34 C4
Tong Shrops...................84 E3
Tong W Isls...................232 g2
Tonge Leics..................101 H7
Tongham Surrey............30 E2
Tongland D & G 146 C4
Tong Norton Shrops.....84 E2
Tongue Highld..............229 J4
Tongwynlais Cardif.......37 H4
Tonmawr Neath.............36 C2
Tonna Neath...................52 B7
Tonwell Herts.................60 B5
Tonypandy Rhondd.......36 F3
Tonyrefail Rhondd.........36 F3
Toot Baldon Oxon..........57 K7
Toot Hill Essex...............60 E7
Toothill Swindn.............40 C4
Tooting Gt Lon..............44 F5
Tooting Bec Gt Lon........44 F5
Topcliffe N York 132 F4
Topcroft Norfk...............92 F5
Topcroft Street Norfk...92 F5
Toppesfield Essex.........77 G6
Toprow Norfk.................92 E4
Topsham Devon..............12 C5
Torbeg N Ayrs..............162 A4
Torboll Highld..............223 G2
Torbreck Highld...........213 G6
Torbryan Devon...............7 J3
Torcastle Highld..........192 B2
Torcross Devon...............7 J7
Tore Highld...................212 F4
Torinturk Ag & B 172 D5
Torksey Lincs...............116 D5
Torlundy Highld...........192 B2
Tormarton S Glos..........39 H5
Tormore N Ayrs............161 M3
Tornagrain Highld........213 J4
Tornaveen Abers..........206 C4
Torness Highld.............212 E8
Toronto Dur..................140 F2
Torpenhow Cumb 147 L6
Torphichen W Loth.......176 C4
Torphins Abers.............206 C5
Torpoint Cnwll................6 C5
Torquay Torbay................7 L3
Torquhan Border..........177 L8
Torran Highld...............209 J5
Torrance E Duns...........175 H4
Torranyard N Ayrs.........163 J1
Torridon Highld............210 D3

Torridon House
  Highld........................210 D3
Torrin Highld................199 J2
Torrisdale Ag & B..........161 K3
Torrisdale Highld..........229 K3
Torrish Highld...............227 G5
Torrisholme Lancs 129 K6
Torrobull Highld...........226 A7
Torry C Aber.................207 H4
Torryburn Fife..............176 D2
Torteval Guern..............236 b4
Torthorwald D & G 155 H6
Tortington W Susx........18 D5
Torton Worcs..................84 E8
Tortworth S Glos............39 G2
Torvaig Highld..............209 H5
Torver Cumb.................137 J7
Torwood Falk................175 L2
Torwoodlee Border 167 G2
Torworth Notts.............116 A4
Toscaig Highld..............209 L6
Toseland Cambs............75 J3
Tosside Lancs...............130 E7
Tostock Suffk..................77 L2
Totaig Highld................208 C4
Tote Highld...................208 F5
Tote Highld...................209 H3
Totland IoW.....................16 D5
Totley Sheff..................114 F5
Totley Brook Sheff 114 F5
Totnes Devon 7 J4
Toton Notts..................101 J5
Totronald Ag & B..........188 F5
Totscore Highld............208 F2
Tottenham Gt Lon.........45 G3
Tottenhill Norfk.............90 F2
Totteridge Gt Lon..........44 E2
Totternhoe C Beds........59 G4
Tottington Bury...........122 B7
Totton Hants..................29 G8
Toulston Somset............25 J5
Toulvaddie Highld........223 J5
Tovil Kent.......................33 K3
Toward Ag & B..............173 K5
Toward Quay Ag & B.....173 J5
Towcester Nhants.........73 K5
Towednack Cnwll.............2 E4
Tower of London
  Gt Lon.......................45 G4
Towersey Oxon..............58 B6
Towie Abers..................205 K3
Tow Law Dur.................150 E6
Town End Cambs............90 B4
Townend W Duns..........174 D3
Townhead Barns...........114 D2
Townhead D & G............155 H4
Townhead of
  Greenlaw D & G.......146 C3
Townhill Fife................176 F1
Town Littleworth
  E Susx........................19 L3
Townshend Cnwll............3 G5
Town Street Suffk..........91 H6
Town Yetholm Border...168 B4
Towthorpe C York 133 K7
Towton N York 124 D3
Towyn Conwy...............110 D5
Toxteth Lpool...............111 K4
Toynton All Saints
  Lincs..........................118 E8
Toy's Hill Kent...............32 E3
Trabboch E Ayrs...........163 K5
Trabbochburn E Ayrs...163 L5
Tradespark Highld........213 K3
Trafford Park Traffd......113 H3
Trallong Powys...............52 B3
Tranent E Loth.............177 L4
Tranmere Wirral..........111 J4
Trantelbeg Highld........230 C5
Trantlemore Highld......230 C5
Trap Carmth...................51 J2
Traprain E Loth............178 D4
Traquair Border............166 E3
Trawden Lancs.............122 D3
Trawsfynydd Gwynd......96 A5
Trealaw Rhondd.............36 F3
Treales Lancs................120 F4

Trearddur Bay IoA.......108 C5
Trebetherick Cnwll..........4 E1
Treborough Somset.......24 F4
Trebullett Cnwll..............5 M1
Treburley Cnwll...............6 A1
Trecastle Powys.............52 D3
Trecwn Pembks..............64 D7
Trecynon Rhondd...........52 F7
Tredegar Blae G.............53 H6
Tredington Gloucs.........55 K3
Tredington Warwks.......72 C5
Trednnock Mons...........38 B2
Treen Cnwll......................2 D6
Treeton Rothm.............115 H4
Trefasser Pembks..........64 C6
Trefecca Powys..............53 H2
Trefeglwys Powys..........81 L5
Treffgarne Pembks.......49 G3
Treffgarne Owen
  Pembks......................48 E3
Trefilan Cerdgn..............66 D3
Trefin Pembks................64 B7
Trefnant Denbgs..........110 E7
Trefonen Shrops.............97 K6
Trefor Gwynd..................94 F4
Treforest Rhondd...........37 G3
Trefriw Conwy..............109 L8
Tregadillett Cnwll............9 H7
Tregare Mons................54 B6
Tregaron Cerdgn............66 F3
Tregarth Gwynd...........109 H7
Tregeare Cnwll.................9 H7
Tregeiriog Wrexhm........97 J5
Tregele IoA..................108 D3
Treglemais Pembks.......48 D2
Tregonetha Cnwll...........4 E3
Tregonning &
  Gwinear Mining
  District Cnwll...............3 G5
Tregony Cnwll.................4 E6
Tregorrick Cnwll.............4 F5
Tregoyd Powys...............68 E6
Tre-groes Cerdgn...........65 L5
Tregynon Powys............82 C4
Tre-gynwr Carmth.........50 E2
Trehafod Rhondd...........37 G3
Trehan Cnwll....................6 B4
Treharris Myr Td............37 H2
Treherbert Rhondd........52 E7
Trekenner Cnwll..............6 A1
Treknow Cnwll.................8 D7
Trelawnyd Flints..........110 F5
Trelech Carmth..............65 J7
Treleddyd-fawr
  Pembks......................48 C2
Trelewis Myr Td.............37 H2
Trelights Cnwll................8 C8
Trelill Cnwll......................5 G1
Trellech Mons................54 D6
Trelogan Flints.............110 F5
Tremadog Gwynd...........95 K4
Tremail Cnwll..................8 F7
Tremain Cerdgn.............65 H5
Tremaine Cnwll...............9 G6
Tremar Cnwll...................5 K3
Trematon Cnwll...............6 B4
Tremeirchion
  Denbgs.....................110 F6
Trenance Cnwll................4 D3
Trenance Cnwll................4 E2
Trench Wrekin................84 C2
Trenear Cnwll..................3 H5
Treneglos Cnwll..............9 G7
Trent Dorset..................26 E7
Trentham C Stke.............99 K4
Trentishoe Devon..........23 K2
Trent Vale C Stke............99 K4
Treoes V Glam...............36 E5
Treorchy Rhondd...........36 E2
Trequite Cnwll.................5 G1
Trerhyngyll V Glam........36 F5
Trerulefoot Cnwll............5 M4
Tresaith Cerdgn.............65 J4
Tresco IoS.......................2 a1
Trescowe Cnwll...............3 G5
Tresean Cnwll.................4 C4
Tresham Gloucs.............39 H3

Treshnish Isles
Ag & B **189** G7
Tresillian Cnwll.............. **4** D6
Treskinnick Cross
Cnwll....................... **9** G5
Tresmeer Cnwll **9** G7
Tresparrett Cnwll............. **8** F6
Tressait P & K **194** C4
Tresta Shet **235** c5
Tresta Shet **235** e3
Treswell Notts **116** C5
Tre Taliesin Cerdgn........**80** E5
Trethevey Cnwll............. **8** E6
Trethewey Cnwll............. **2** C6
Trethurgy Cnwll............. **5** G5
Tretire Herefs..............**54** D4
Tretower Powys **53** J4
Treuddyn Flints **97** K2
Trevalga Cnwll **8** E6
Trevalyn Wrexhm........**98** B2
Trevarrian Cnwll............. **4** D3
Treveal Cnwll............. **4** C4
Treveighan Cnwll............. **8** E8
Trevellas Downs
Cnwll **3** J2
Trevelmond Cnwll........... **5** K3
Treverva Cnwll............. **3** K5
Trevescan Cnwll............. **2** C6
Treviscoe Cnwll **4** E5
Trevone Cnwll............. **4** D2
Trevor Wrexhm...........**97** L4
Trewalder Cnwll **8** E7
Trewarmett Cnwll............. **8** E7
Trewavas Mining
District Cnwll............... **3** G6
Trewen Cnwll **9** H7
Trewint Cnwll **9** G8
Trewithian Cnwll............. **4** D7
Trewoon Cnwll............. **4** F5
Treyford W Susx...........**30** D7
Trimdon Dur **151** J7
Trimdon Colliery Dur.. **151** J7
Trimdon Grange Dur.. **151** J7
Trimingham Norfk........ **107** G5
Trimley St Martin
Suffk......................**78** F6
Trimley St Mary
Suffk......................**79** G7
Trimsaran Carmth...........**50** F5
Trimstone Devon...........**23** H3
Trinafour P & K........... **194** B4
Tring Herts **58** F5
Trinity Angus **196** F4
Trinity Jersey **236** d6
Trinity Gask P & K.... **185** K4
Triscombe Somset...........**25** J4
Trislaig Highld.............. **191** L2
Trispen Cnwll............. **4** D5
Tritlington Nthumb.. **158** F4
Trochry P & K.............. **194** F7
Troedyraur Cerdgn........**65** K5
Troedyrhiw Myr Td........**53** G7
Trois Bois Jersey **236** c6
Troon Cnwll............. **3** H4
Troon S Ayrs **163** H3
Tropical World
Roundhay Park
Leeds................. **123** L3
Trossachs Stirlg.......... **184** B5
Trossachs Pier Stirlg .. **184** B6
Troston Suffk..............**91** K8
Trotshill Worcs **70** F4
Trottiscliffe Kent...........**33** H2
Trotton W Susx...........**30** D6
Troutbeck Cumb......... **137** L6
Troutbeck Bridge
Cumb................... **137** L7
Troway Derbys **115** H5
Trowbridge Wilts...........**39** J8
Trowell Notts **101** J4
Trowell Services
Notts **101** J4
Trowse Newton
Norfk....................**92** F3
Trudoxhill Somset...........**27** H3
Trull Somset..............**25** K6
Trumpan Highld.......... **208** C3

Trumpet Herefs.................**70** B6
Trumpington Cambs.......**76** C4
Trunch Norfk.................. **107** G5
Truro Cnwll **4** C6
Trusham Devon...........**11** K7
Trusley Derbys **100** E5
Trusthorpe Lincs **119** G5
Trysull Staffs..............**84** F5
Tubney Oxon **57** H7
Tuckenhay Devon............. **7** J5
Tuckhill Shrops.............**84** E6
Tuckingmill Cnwll............. **3** H3
Tuckingmill Wilts...........**27** L5
Tuckton BCP **15** L4
Tuddenham Suffk...........**77** G1
Tuddenham Suffk...........**78** E5
Tudeley Kent.............**33** G4
Tudhoe Dur **151** G7
Tudweiliog Gwynd...........**94** D5
Tuffley Gloucs **55** J5
Tufton Hants **29** J3
Tufton Pembks **49** H2
Tugby Leics..............**87** L4
Tugford Shrops...........**83** L6
Tughall Nthumb.......... **169** J4
Tullibody Clacks **185** H7
Tullich Abers **205** J6
Tullich Highld.............. **212** F8
Tullich Highld.............. **223** J6
Tulliemet P & K.......... **194** F5
Tulloch Abers.............. **216** F7
Tullochgorm Ag & B.. **182** D7
Tulloch Station
Highld.................. **192** F1
Tullymurdoch P & K.... **195** J5
Tullynessle Abers **206** B2
Tulse Hill Gt Lon............**44** F5
Tumble Carmth...........**51** G3
Tumby Lincs **103** L1
Tumby Woodside
Lincs **103** L2
Tummel Bridge
P & K **194** B5
Tunbridge Wells
Kent....................**33** G5
Tundergarth D & G..... **155** L6
Tunga W Isls **232** g2
Tunley BaNES **39** G8
Tunstall E R Yk **127** H4
Tunstall Kent.............**34** B3
Tunstall Lancs **130** B5
Tunstall N York.......... **140** F7
Tunstall Norfk.............**93** J2
Tunstall Staffs..............**99** H6
Tunstall Suffk.............**79** H4
Tunstall Sundld.......... **151** J4
Tunstead Derbys **114** C6
Tunstead Norfk.......... **107** G7
Tunstead Milton
Derbys.................. **114** B4
Tupsley Herefs...........**69** K6
Turgis Green Hants.......**42** B8
Turkdean Gloucs **56** C4
Tur Langton Leics.......**87** K5
Turleigh Wilts...........**39** J7
Turnastone Herefs...........**69** G7
Turnberry S Ayrs **152** E2
Turnditch Derbys **100** F3
Turners Hill W Susx...........**32** C6
Turnhouse C Edin........ **177** G4
Turnworth Dorset...........**14** F2
Turriff Abers.............. **216** D4
Turton Bottoms
Bl w D.................. **121** L7
Turves Cambs...........**89** L4
Turvey Bed **74** D4
Turville Bucks **42** C3
Turweston Bucks...........**73** H6
Tushielaw Inn Border .. **166** D5
Tutbury Staffs.......... **100** E6
Tutshill Gloucs...........**38** D2
Tuttington Norfk........ **106** F6
Tuxford Notts.............. **116** C7
Twatt Ork.............. **234** b5
Twatt Shet.............. **235** c5
Twechar E Duns.......... **175** J3
Tweedbank Border **167** H3

Tweedmouth Nthumb .. **179** K7
Tweedsmuir Border **165** L4
Twelveheads Cnwll............. **3** K3
Twemlow Green
Ches E.................. **113** H7
Twenty Lincs **103** J7
Twerton BaNES...........**39** G7
Twickenham Gt Lon........**44** D5
Twigworth Gloucs........**55** J4
Twineham W Susx...........**19** H2
Twinstead Essex **77** J6
Twitchen Devon...........**24** C5
Two Dales Derbys **114** F8
Two Gates Staffs...........**86** B4
Two Waters Herts...........**59** H6
Twycross Leics...........**86** D3
Twycross Zoo Leics........**86** C3
Twyford Bucks **58** A3
Twyford Hants **29** J6
Twyford Leics...........**87** K2
Twyford Norfk.......... **106** B7
Twyford Wokham...........**42** C5
Twynholm D & G........ **146** B4
Twyning Green
Gloucs..................**70** F6
Twynllanan Carmth........**51** L2
Twywell Nhants **88** D7
Tyberton Herefs...........**69** H6
Tyburn Birm **85** K5
Tycroes Carmth...........**51** H4
Tycrwyn Powys...........**97** H8
Tydd Gote Lincs.......... **104** D8
Tydd St Giles Cambs.......**90** B1
Tydd St Mary Lincs...... **104** C8
Tye Green Essex...........**76** E7
Tyldesley Wigan...........**113** G2
Tyler Hill Kent...........**34** F3
Tylorstown Rhondd...........**36** F2
Ty-nant Conwy...........**96** F4
Tyndrum Stirlg.......... **183** K2
Ty'n-dwr Denbgs...........**97** K4
Tynemouth N Tyne........ **151** J2
Tyne Tunnel S Tyne **151** H2
Tyninghame E Loth...... **178** D3
Tynron D & G.............. **154** E4
Tynygraig Cerdgn...........**66** F1
Ty'n-y-Groes Conwy...... **109** L7
Tyrie Abers.............. **217** H2
Tyringham M Keyn...........**74** C5
Tyseley Birm...........**85** K6
Tythegston Brdgnd...........**36** D5
Tytherington Ches E...... **113** K6
Tytherington S Glos........**38** F3
Tytherington Wilts...........**27** K3
Tytherleigh Devon...........**13** H2
Tytherton Lucas
Wilts.....................**39** L5
Tywardreath Cnwll **5** H5
Tywyn Gwynd...........**80** D4

U

Ubbeston Green
Suffk.....................**79** G1
Ubley BaNES...........**38** D8
Uckfield E Susx...........**19** M2
Uckinghall Worcs...........**70** F6
Uckington Gloucs...........**55** K3
Uddingston S Lans **175** J6
Uddington S Lans **165** G3
Udimore E Susx...........**21** G2
Udny Green Abers...... **207** G1
Udny Station Abers...... **207** G1
Uffculme Devon...........**25** G8
Uffington Lincs...........**88** F3
Uffington Oxon...........**41** K4
Uffington Shrops...........**83** K2
Ufford C Pete...........**89** G3
Ufford Suffk...........**79** G4
Ufton Warwks...........**72** E3
Ufton Nervet W Berk.... **41** M6
Ugadale Ag & B........ **161** K4
Ugborough Devon............. **7** G5
Uggeshall Suffk...........**93** J7
Ugglebarnby N York...... **143** H5

Ughill Sheff **114** E4
Ugley Essex **60** E3
Ugley Green Essex........**60** E3
Ugthorpe N York.......... **143** G5
Uibhist A Deas
W Isls.................. **233** c8
Uibhist A Tuath
W Isls.................. **233** b6
Uig Ag & B.............. **188** F5
Uig Highld.............. **208** C4
Uig Highld.............. **208** F2
Uig W Isls.............. **232** d2
Uigshader Highld........ **209** G5
Uisken Ag & B **180** E4
Ulbster Highld.............. **231** K7
Ulceby Lincs.............. **118** F6
Ulceby N Linc.............. **126** D7
Ulceby Skitter
N Linc.................. **126** E7
Ulcombe Kent...........**33** L4
Uldale Cumb.............. **147** M7
Uley Gloucs...........**55** H7
Ulgham Nthumb.......... **159** G4
Ullapool Highld.......... **220** E3
Ullenhall Warwks...........**71** K2
Ulleskelf N York.......... **124** D3
Ullesthorpe Leics...........**87** G6
Ulley Rothm...........**115** J4
Ullingswick Herefs...........**69** L4
Ullinish Lodge
Hotel Highld.......... **208** E6
Ullock Cumb.............. **136** E3
Ullswater Cumb.............. **138** B3
Ullswater Steamers
Cumb.................. **137** L4
Ulpha Cumb.............. **128** E2
Ulrome E R Yk.......... **135** J7
Ulsta Shet.............. **235** d3
Ulva Ag & B.............. **189** K7
Ulverley Green
Solhll...................**85** K6
Ulverston Cumb.......... **129** G4
Ulwell Dorset...............**15** J6
Ulzieside D & G.......... **164** F7
Umberleigh Devon........**23** K6
Unapool Highld.......... **224** F2
Underbarrow Cumb...... **129** K2
Under Burnmouth
Border.................. **156** E5
Undercliffe C Brad........ **123** J4
Underdale Shrops...........**83** K2
Underriver Kent...........**32** F3
Underwood Notts.......... **101** J3
Undy Mons...........**38** C3
Union Mills IoM.......... **237** c5
Unst Shet.............. **235** d1
Unstone Derbys.......... **115** G6
Upavon Wilts...........**28** C1
Upchurch Kent...........**46** D6
Upcott Devon...........**24** B5
Up Exe Devon...........**12** B2
Upgate Norfk.......... **106** D8
Uphall Dorset...........**14** B2
Uphall W Loth.......... **176** E4
Upham Devon...........**11** K3
Upham Hants...........**29** K7
Uphampton Herefs...........**69** H2
Uphampton Worcs...........**70** E2
Uphill N Som...........**37** L8
Up Holland Lancs........ **112** D1
Uplawmoor E Rens...... **174** E7
Upleadon Gloucs...........**55** H3
Upleatham R & Cl...... **142** D4
Uploders Dorset...........**13** L4
Uplowman Devon...........**24** F7
Uplyme Devon...........**13** H4
Up Marden W Susx........**30** D8
Upminster Gt Lon...........**45** K3
Up Mudford Somset...........**26** E7
Up Nately Hants...........**30** B2
Upottery Devon...........**12** F2
Upper Affcot Shrops...........**83** J6
Upper Arley Worcs...........**84** D7
Upper Badcall
Highld.................. **228** B7
Upper Basildon
W Berk.................**41** L5

Upper Beeding
W Susx 19 G4
Upper Benefield
Nhants.............................88 E5
Upper Bentley Worcs 71 H2
Upper Bighouse
Highld..........................230 C4
Upper Boddington
Nhants.............................72 F4
Upper Brailes
Warwks............................72 C6
Upper Broadheath
Worcs...............................70 E4
Upper Broughton
Notts 102 B7
Upper Bucklebury
W Berk..............................41 K6
Upper Burgate Hants....28 D7
Upperby Cumb 148 D4
Upper Caldecote
C Beds..............................75 H5
Upper Chapel Powys......67 L6
Upper Chicksgrove
Wilts.................................27 L5
Upper Chute Wilts..........28 F2
Upper Clapton
Gt Lon...............................45 G3
Upper Clatford Hants....29 G3
Upper Cound Shrops......83 K3
**Upper
Cumberworth**
Kirk................................123 J8
Upper Dallachy
Moray.............................215 H2
Upper Deal Kent..............35 K4
Upper Dean Bed..............74 F2
Upper Denby Kirk 114 E1
Upper Dicker E Susx......20 B4
Upper Dounreay
Highld............................230 E3
Upper Dovercourt
Essex................................62 F2
Upper Drumbane
Stirlg 184 E6
Upper Dunsforth
N York.............................133 G6
Upper Eashing
Surrey...............................30 F3
Upper Eathie
Highld............................213 J2
Upper Egleton
Herefs...............................70 B5
Upper Elkstone
Staffs.............................100 B2
Upper Ellastone
Staffs.............................100 C4
Upper Farringdon
Hants................................30 B4
Upper Framilode
Gloucs...............................55 H6
Upper Froyle Hants 30 C3
Upperglen Highld.........208 E4
Upper Godney
Somset.............................26 C3
Upper Gravenhurst
C Beds..............................75 G7
Upper Green W Berk......41 G7
**Upper Grove
Common** Herefs 54 E3
Upper Hale Surrey..........30 D2
Upper Halliford
Surrey...............................43 H6
Upper Hambleton
Rutlnd..............................88 C3
Upper Harbledown
Kent..................................34 F3
Upper Hartfield
E Susx...............................32 E6
Upper Hatherley
Gloucs...............................55 L4
Upper Heaton Kirk.......123 H6
Upper Helmsley
N York.............................133 L7
Upper Hergest
Herefs...............................68 F4
Upper Heyford
Nhants..............................73 J3

Upper Heyford Oxon.......57 J3
Upper Hill Herefs 69 J4
Upper Hopton Kirk 123 J6
Upper Hulme Staffs......100 A1
Upper Inglesham
Swindn.............................40 D2
Upper Killay Swans.........51 H6
Upper Kinchrackine
Ag & B...........................183 G2
Upper Knockando
Moray.............................214 E5
Upper Lambourn
W Berk..............................40 F4
Upper Landywood
Staffs................................85 H3
Upper Langford
N Som...............................38 C7
Upper Langwith
Derbys............................115 K7
Upper Largo Fife...........187 G6
Upper Leigh Staffs........100 A5
Upper Lochton
Abers..............................206 D6
Upper Longdon
Staffs................................85 J2
Upper Lybster Highld ..231 J7
Upper Lydbrook
Gloucs...............................54 E5
Upper Lye Herefs...........69 H2
Uppermill Oldham........113 M1
Upper Milton Worcs......84 E8
Upper Minety Wilts........40 A3
Upper Mulben
Moray.............................215 H4
Upper Netchwood
Shrops..............................83 L5
Upper Nobut Staffs......100 B5
Upper Norwood
W Susx..............................18 C3
Upper Poppleton
C York.............................133 H8
Upper Ratley Hants 28 F6
Upper Rissington
Gloucs...............................56 D4
Upper Rochford
Worcs...............................70 B2
Upper Ruscoe
D & G.............................145 L3
Upper Sapey Herefs......70 C2
Upper Seagry Wilts........39 L4
Upper Shelton
C Beds..............................74 E5
Upper Sheringham
Norfk..............................106 D4
Upper Skelmorlie
N Ayrs.............................173 L5
Upper Slaughter
Gloucs...............................56 D4
Upper Soudley
Gloucs...............................54 F6
Upper Standen Kent......35 H6
Upper Stoke Norfk..........92 F3
Upper Stondon
C Beds..............................75 H7
Upper Stowe Nhants......73 J3
Upper Street Hants........28 D7
Upper Street Norfk..........93 H1
Upper Street Norfk.......107 G8
Upper Street Suffk..........77 H4
Upper Street Suffk..........78 D4
Upper Sundon
C Beds..............................59 H3
Upper Swell Gloucs.........56 D3
Upper Tean Staffs.........100 A5
Upperthong Kirk...........123 H8
Upperton W Susx............30 F6
Upper Town Herefs........69 L5
Upper Town Highld 231 L1
Upper Town N Som.........38 D7
Upper Town Suffk..........77 K2
Upper Tumble
Carmth.............................51 G3
Upper Tysoe Warwks......72 D5
Upper Victoria
Angus.............................187 J1
Upper Wardington
Oxon.................................72 F5

Upper Welland
Worcs...............................70 D6
Upper Wellingham
E Susx...............................19 L3
Upper Weybread
Suffk.................................92 F7
Upper Wield Hants.........29 L4
Upper Winchendon
Bucks................................58 C5
Upper Woodford
Wilts.................................28 C4
Upper Wraxall Wilts.......39 J5
Uppingham Rutlnd.........88 C4
Uppington Shrops...........83 L2
Upsall N York.................133 G3
Upsettlington Border ..168 C1
Upshire Essex.................60 C7
Up Somborne Hants......29 H5
Upstreet Kent.................35 G3
Upton Bucks..................58 C5
Upton C Pete..................89 G4
Upton Cambs..................89 H7
Upton Ches W 112 B7
Upton Cnwll.....................5 L2
Upton Devon.....................7 G7
Upton Devon....................12 E2
Upton Dorset...................14 E5
Upton Dorset...................15 J4
Upton Halton..................112 C4
Upton Hants....................29 G1
Upton Hants....................29 G7
Upton Leics......................86 D4
Upton Lincs....................116 E4
Upton Norfk.....................93 H2
Upton Notts....................102 B2
Upton Notts....................116 C6
Upton Oxon......................41 K3
Upton Slough...................43 G5
Upton Somset...................24 F5
Upton Somset...................26 C6
Upton Wakefd.................124 D7
Upton Wirral....................111 J4
Upton Bishop
Herefs...............................54 F3
Upton Cheyney
S Glos................................39 G6
Upton Cressett
Shrops..............................84 B5
Upton Grey Hants...........30 B2
Upton Hellions
Devon................................11 J4
Upton Lovell Wilts..........27 L4
Upton Magna Shrops......83 K2
Upton Noble Somset.......27 G4
Upton Pyne Devon..........11 L5
Upton St Leonards
Gloucs...............................55 K5
Upton Scudamore
Wilts.................................27 K2
Upton Snodsbury
Worcs...............................71 G4
Upton-upon-Severn
Worcs...............................70 F6
Upton Warren Worcs......71 G2
Upwaltham W Susx.........18 C3
Upwell Norfk....................90 C3
Upwood Cambs................89 J6
Urchfont Wilts.................40 B8
Urmston Traffd..............113 H3
Urquhart Moray.............215 G2
Urquhart Castle
Highld............................212 E8
Urra N York...................142 C6
Urray Highld..................212 D4
Usan Angus....................197 H5
Ushaw Moor Dur............151 G6
Usk Mons........................54 B7
Usselby Lincs.................117 H3
Usworth Sundld..............151 H4
Utkinton Ches W 112 D7
Utley C Brad...................122 F3
Uton Devon......................11 J5
Utterby Lincs.................118 D3
Uttoxeter Staffs.............100 C5
Uxbridge Gt Lon.............43 H4
Uyeasound Shet.............235 d2
Uzmaston Pembks..........49 G5

V

Vale Guern....................236 d2
Valley IoA.....................108 C5
Valtos Highld..................209 H2
Valtos W Isls..................232 d2
Vange Essex....................46 B3
Vatsetter Shet...............235 d3
Vatten Highld.................208 D5
Vaynor Myr Td.................53 G6
Veensgarth Shet............235 c6
Velindre Powys................68 D7
Venngreen Devon..............9 K3
Venn Ottery Devon..........12 D1
Ventnor IoW.....................17 G6
Venton Devon.....................6 E4
Vernham Dean Hants......29 G1
Vernham Street
Hants................................41 G8
Verwood Dorset...............15 K2
Veryan Cnwll.....................4 E7
Vickerstown Cumb........128 E5
Victoria Cnwll...................4 F4
Vidlin Shet....................235 d4
Viewfield Moray.............215 G2
Viewpark N Lans............175 J6
Vigo Kent........................45 M7
Village de Putron
Guern..............................236 d3
Ville la Bas Jersey.........236 a5
Villiaze Guern.................236 c3
Vines Cross E Susx.........20 C3
Virginia Water Surrey.....43 G6
Virginstow Devon..............9 K6
Vobster Somset...............27 G2
Voe Shet........................235 c4
Vowchurch Herefs...........69 G7

W

Waberthwaite Cumb....128 D2
Wackerfield Dur.............140 E3
Wacton Norfk...................92 E5
Wadborough Worcs.........70 F5
Waddesdon Bucks............58 C5
Waddesdon Manor
Bucks................................58 B5
Waddeton Devon................7 K4
Waddingham Lincs.........117 G3
Waddington Lancs.........121 L2
Waddington Lincs..........116 F8
Waddon Gt Lon................44 F7
Wadebridge Cnwll.............4 F2
Wadeford Somset............13 H1
Wadenhoe Nhants...........88 E6
Wadesmill Herts..............60 B4
Wadhurst E Susx.............33 H6
Wadshelf Derbys............114 F7
Wadworth Donc..............115 K3
Wainfleet All Saints
Lincs..............................104 D2
Wainfleet St Mary
Lincs..............................104 D2
Wainhouse Corner
Cnwll..................................9 G5
Wainscott Medway...........46 C6
Wainstalls Calder...........122 F5
Waitby Cumb..................139 H5
Waithe Lincs...................118 C2
Wakefield Wakefd............123 L6
Wake Green Birm............85 K6
Wakehurst Place
W Susx..............................32 C6
Wakerley Nhants..............88 D4
Wakes Colne Essex...........61 L3
Walberswick Suffk...........93 K8
Walberton W Susx...........18 C4
Walbutt D & G................146 D2
Walcombe Somset...........26 D3
Walcot Lincs...................103 H5
Walcot Shrops.................83 L2
Walcot Swindn.................40 D4
Walcote Leics...................87 H6
Walcot Green Norfk..........92 D7

Walcott Lincs 103 J2
Walcott Norfk 107 H6
Walden Stubbs
  N York 124 E6
Walderslade Medway 46 C7
Walderton W Susx 17 L1
Walditch Dorset 13 L4
Waldridge Dur 151 G5
Waldringfield Suffk 79 G5
Waldron E Susx 20 B2
Wales Rothm 115 J5
Wales Somset 26 E6
Walesby Lincs 117 J3
Walesby Notts 116 B7
Walford Herefs 54 E4
Walford Herefs 83 H8
Walford Heath
  Shrops 98 C8
Walgherton Ches E 99 G3
Walgrave Nhants 74 B1
Walkden Salfd 113 G2
Walker N u Ty 151 H3
Walkerburn Border 166 E3
Walkeringham Notts 116 C3
Walkerith Lincs 116 C3
Walkern Herts 59 M3
Walker's Bank Birm........ 85 J7
Walkerton Fife 186 D6
Walkford BCP 16 B4
Walkhampton Devon 6 D2
Walkington E R Yk 126 B3
Walkley Sheff 115 G4
Walk Mill Lancs 122 C5
Walkwood Worcs 71 J2
Wall Nthumb 150 A2
Wall Staffs 85 K3
Wallacetown S Ayrs 153 G2
Wallacetown S Ayrs 163 J5
Wallands Park
  E Susx 19 L4
Wallasey Wirral 111 J3
Wallasey
  (Kingsway)
  Tunnel Wirral.......... 111 K4
Wall Heath Dudley 84 F5
Wallingford Oxon 41 L3
Wallington Gt Lon 44 F6
Wallington Hants............ 17 H2
Wallington Herts 75 K7
Wallisdown BCP 15 K4
Walliswood Surrey 31 J4
Walls Shet. 235 b5
Wallsend N Tyne 151 H2
Wallyford E Loth 177 K4
Walmer Kent 35 K5
Walmer Bridge Lancs.. 121 G5
Walmley Birm 85 K5
Walmley Ash Birm.......... 85 K5
Walpole Suffk 93 H8
Walpole Cross Keys
  Norfk 104 E8
Walpole Highway
  Norfk 90 D2
Walpole St Andrew
  Norfk 104 D8
Walpole St Peter
  Norfk 90 C1
Walsall Wsall 85 H4
Walsden Calder 122 D6
Walsgrave on Sowe
  Covtry. 86 E7
Walsham le Willows
  Suffk. 78 B1
Walshford N York 132 F8
Walsoken Norfk.............. 90 C2
Walston S Lans 165 K1
Walsworth Herts............. 59 K3
Walter's Ash Bucks........ 42 D2
Waltham Kent................. 34 E5
Waltham NE Lin 118 C2
Waltham Abbey
  Essex 60 C7
Waltham Chase
  Hants............................ 29 K7
Waltham Cross Herts.... 60 B7
Waltham on the
  Wolds Leics............... 102 H2

Waltham St
  Lawrence W & M......... 42 D5
Walthamstow Gt Lon 45 G3
Walton C Pete 89 H3
Walton Cumb 148 F3
Walton Derbys 115 G7
Walton Leeds 124 C2
Walton Leics 87 H6
Walton M Keyn............... 74 C7
Walton Powys 68 F3
Walton Somset 26 C4
Walton Suffk 79 G7
Walton W Susx 17 M2
Walton Wakefd.............. 123 L6
Walton Wrekin 98 E8
Walton Cardiff
  Gloucs 55 K2
Walton East Pembks 49 H3
Walton Highway
  Norfk 90 C2
Walton-in-Gordano
  N Som 38 B5
Walton-le-Dale
  Lancs......................... 121 H5
Walton-on-Thames
  Surrey 43 J6
Walton-on-the-Hill
  Staffs............................. 99 L7
Walton-on-the-Hill
  Surrey 31 L1
Walton-on-the-
  Naze Essex 62 F4
Walton on the
  Wolds Leics................ 101 L8
Walton-on-Trent
  Derbys 100 E8
Walton Park N Som......... 38 B6
Walton West Pembks 48 E5
Walworth Darltn........... 141 G4
Walworth Gt Lon 45 G4
Walwyn's Castle
  Pembks 48 E5
Wambrook Somset........ 13 H2
Wanborough Surrey 30 F2
Wanborough Swindn 40 E4
Wandsworth Gt Lon 44 E5
Wangford Suffk.............. 93 K7
Wanlip Leics 87 H2
Wanlockhead D & G 165 G6
Wannock E Susx............ 20 C5
Wansford C Pete 88 F4
Wansford E R Yk 135 G7
Wanshurst Green
  Kent............................. 33 K4
Wanstead Gt Lon........... 45 H3
Wanstrow Somset........... 27 G3
Wanswell Gloucs............ 55 G7
Wantage Oxon 41 H3
Wappenbury Warwks..... 72 E2
Wappenham Nhants 73 J5
Warbleton E Susx 20 C3
Warborough Oxon......... 41 L2
Warboys Cambs.............. 89 K7
Warbreck Bpool 120 D3
Warbstow Cnwll.............. 9 G6
Warburton Traffd 113 G4
Warcop Cumb 139 H4
Warden Nthumb........... 150 A2
Ward End Birm............... 85 K5
Wardington Oxon 72 F5
Wardle Ches E 98 E2
Wardle Rochdl.............. 122 D6
Wardley Gatesd........... 151 H3
Wardley Rutlnd.............. 88 B4
Wardlow Derbys........... 114 D6
Wardy Hill Cambs.......... 90 C6
Ware Herts 60 B5
Wareham Dorset........... 15 H5
Warehorne Kent............. 34 D7
Warenford Nthumb 169 H4
Wareside Herts............... 60 C5
Waresley Cambs........... 75 J4
Warfield Br For............... 42 E6
Warfleet Devon................ 7 K6
Wargrave Wokham........ 42 C5
Warham Norfk 105 M4
Wark Nthumb 157 L6

Wark Nthumb.............. 168 C2
Warkleigh Devon 23 K6
Warkton Nhants............ 88 C7
Warkworth Nhants 72 F6
Warkworth Nthumb 159 G2
Warlaby N York 132 E2
Warleggan Cnwll 5 J3
Warley Town Calder 122 F5
Warlingham Surrey........ 32 C2
Warmfield Wakefd........ 124 B6
Warmingham Ches E...... 99 G1
Warmington Nhants....... 88 F5
Warmington Warwks..... 72 E5
Warminster Wilts 27 K3
Warmley S Glos 38 F5
Warmsworth Donc 115 K2
Warmwell Dorset............ 14 E5
Warner Bros. Studio
  Tour Herts.................. 59 H7
Warnford Hants.............. 29 L6
Warnham W Susx........... 31 J5
Warningcamp
  W Susx........................ 18 D4
Warninglid W Susx 31 L6
Warren Ches E 113 K7
Warren Pembks 48 F7
Warrenhill S Lans 165 J2
Warren Row W & M 42 D4
Warren Street Kent........ 34 C4
Warrington M Keyn....... 74 C4
Warrington Warrtn....... 112 E4
Warriston C Edin 177 H4
Warsash Hants 16 F2
Warslow Staffs 100 C2
Warter E R Yk 125 K1
Warthermaske N York.. 132 C4
Warthill N York............. 133 K7
Wartling E Susx 20 D4
Wartnaby Leics............. 102 B7
Warton Lancs 120 E5
Warton Lancs 129 K5
Warton Warwks............. 86 C3
Warwick Warwks............ 72 C2
Warwick Bridge
  Cumb 148 E4
Warwick Castle
  Warwks...................... 72 C2
Warwick Services
  Warwks...................... 72 D3
Wasbister Ork 234 c4
Wasdale Head Cumb ... 137 G5
Washaway Cnwll 5 G2
Washbourne Devon.......... 7 J5
Washbrook Suffk............ 78 D6
Washfield Devon 11 L2
Washford Somset............ 25 G3
Washford Pyne
  Devon 11 J3
Washingborough
  Lincs 117 G7
Washington Sundld..... 151 H4
Washington W Susx 18 F3
Washington
  Services Gatesd...... 151 G4
Washwood Heath
  Birm............................. 85 K5
Wasperton Warwks........ 72 C3
Wass N York 133 H4
Wast Water Cumb.......... 137 G6
Watchet Somset.............. 25 G3
Watchfield Oxon 40 E3
Watchgate Cumb 138 D7
Water Devon................... 11 H8
Waterbeach Cambs........ 76 C2
Waterbeach W Susx....... 18 B4
Waterbeck D & G 155 M6
Water End E R Yk 125 J3
Waterfall Staffs............ 100 B3
Waterfoot Ag & B......... 161 K3
Waterfoot E Rens......... 175 G7
Waterford Herts............. 60 A5
Waterheads Border...... 177 H7
Waterhouses Staffs....... 100 B3
Wateringbury Kent........ 33 H3
Waterloo Highld 199 K2
Waterloo N Lans 175 L7
Waterloo P & K............ 195 G8

Waterloo Pembks............ 49 G6
Waterloo Sefton 111 K2
Waterlooville Hants........ 17 J1
Watermead Bucks.......... 58 D5
Watermillock Cumb 138 C3
Water Newton
  Cambs 89 G4
Water Orton Warwks 85 L5
Waterperry Oxon 57 L6
Waterrow Somset 25 G6
Watersfield W Susx 18 D3
Waterside Bl w D 121 K5
Waterside E Ayrs.......... 163 K7
Waterside E Ayrs.......... 163 L2
Waterside E Duns 175 J4
Waterstein Highld........ 208 B5
Waterstock Oxon 57 M6
Waterston Pembks 48 F6
Water Stratford
  Bucks 73 J7
Waters Upton Wrekin..... 98 F8
Watford Herts................ 43 J2
Watford Nhants 73 H2
Watford Gap
  Services Nhants........ 73 H2
Wath N York 132 B6
Wath N York 132 E4
Wath upon Dearne
  Rothm........................ 115 H2
Watlington Norfk............ 90 E2
Watlington Oxon............ 42 B2
Watten Highld.............. 231 J5
Wattisfield Suffk............ 92 B8
Wattisham Suffk............ 78 B4
Watton Dorset................ 13 L4
Watton E R Yk.............. 126 C1
Watton Norfk 91 K4
Watton-at-Stone
  Herts 60 A4
Wattston N Lans 175 K4
Wattsville Caerph............ 37 J3
Waulkmill Abers 206 C6
Waunarlwydd Swans...... 51 H6
Waunfawr Cerdgn.......... 80 E6
Waunfawr Gwynd........... 95 J2
Wavendon M Keyn........ 74 C6
Waverbridge Cumb 147 L5
Waverton Ches W 112 C8
Waverton Cumb............ 147 L5
Wawne E R Yk 126 D3
Waxham Norfk............. 107 J7
Wayford Somset............. 13 K2
Waytown Dorset............. 13 L3
Way Village Devon......... 11 K3
Weacombe Somset......... 25 H4
Weald Oxon.................... 56 F7
Wealdstone Gt Lon........ 44 D3
Weardley Leeds............ 123 K2
Weare Somset................ 26 B2
Weare Giffard Devon..... 23 G6
Wearhead Dur............. 149 L6
Wearne Somset.............. 26 B5
Weasenham All
  Saints Norfk............. 105 K7
Weasenham St
  Peter Norfk.............. 105 K7
Weaste Salfd 113 J2
Weaverham Ches W..... 112 E6
Weaverthorpe N York .. 134 E5
Webheath Worcs........... 71 H2
Wedderlairs Abers 216 F7
Weddington Warwks...... 86 D5
Wedhampton Wilts 40 B8
Wedmore Somset........... 26 C2
Wednesbury Sandw....... 85 H4
Wednesfield Wolves...... 85 G4
Weedon Bucks................ 58 D4
Weedon Bec Nhants 73 J3
Weedon Lois Nhants...... 73 H5
Weeford Staffs.............. 85 K3
Weeke Hants.................. 29 J5
Weekley Nhants............. 88 C7
Week St Mary Cnwll 9 H5
Weel E R Yk 126 D3
Weeley Essex................. 62 D4
Weeley Heath Essex...... 62 D4
Weem P & K 194 D6

Weethley Warwks 71 J4
Weeting Norfk..................91 H5
Weeton E R Yk...............127 H6
Weeton Lancs 120 E4
Weeton N York................123 K2
Weetwood Leeds 123 K3
Weir Lancs 122 C5
Weir Quay Devon 6 C3
Weisdale Shet 235 c5
Welborne Norfk.................92 C2
Welbourn Lincs 102 F2
Welburn N York.............133 L6
Welbury N York.............141 J6
Welby Lincs 102 F5
Welcombe Devon............22 C7
Weldon Nhants 88 D5
Welford Nhants..............87 J7
Welford W Berk 41 H5
Welford-on-Avon
    Warwks...........................71 K4
Welham Leics 87 L5
Welham Notts 116 B5
Welham Green Herts 59 L6
Well Hants 30 C3
Well Lincs 118 F6
Well N York...................132 D3
Welland Worcs................70 E6
Wellbank Angus 196 D8
Wellesbourne
    Warwks...........................72 C4
Well Head Herts 59 K3
Welling Gt Lon 45 J5
Wellingborough
    Nhants............................74 C2
Wellingham Norfk 105 L7
Wellingore Lincs 103 G2
Wellington Cumb 136 F6
Wellington Herefs..........69 K5
Wellington Somset........25 H7
Wellington Wrekin.........84 B2
Wellington Heath
    Herefs.............................70 C6
Wellow BaNES 39 H8
Wellow IoW 16 E5
Wellow Notts 116 A7
Wells Somset.................26 D3
Wells-next-the-Sea
    Norfk............................ 105 L4
Wellstye Green Essex....61 G4
Welltree P & K 185 K3
Wellwood Fife 176 E2
Welney Norfk..................90 D5
Welshampton Shrops 98 C5
Welsh Frankton
    Shrops............................98 A6
Welsh Newton
    Herefs.............................54 D4
Welshpool Powys 82 E3
Welsh St Donats
    V Glam.............................36 F5
Welton Cumb 148 C6
Welton E R Yk 126 B5
Welton Lincs 117 G5
Welton Nhants 73 H2
Welton le Marsh
    Lincs 119 G7
Welton le Wold Lincs .. 118 C4
Welwick E R Yk 127 H6
Welwyn Herts 59 L5
Welwyn Garden City
    Herts...............................59 L5
Wem Shrops 98 D6
Wembdon Somset..........25 L4
Wembley Gt Lon 44 D3
Wembury Devon...............6 D6
Wemworthy Devon 10 F3
Wemyss Bay Inver......173 L4
Wendens Ambo
    Essex.............................76 D7
Wendlebury Oxon...........57 K4
Wendling Norfk...............91 L2
Wendover Bucks 58 E6
Wendron Cnwll.................3 H5
Wendron Mining
    District Cnwll..................3 L2
Wendy Cambs 75 K5
Wenhaston Suffk............93 J7

Wennington Cambs.........89 J7
Wennington Gt Lon.........45 K4
Wennington Lancs 130 C5
Wensley Derbys 100 E1
Wensley N York..............131 K2
Wentbridge Wakefd 124 D6
Wentnor Shrops 83 H5
Wentworth Cambs..........90 C7
Wentworth Rothm 115 G2
Wenvoe V Glam 37 H6
Weobley Herefs..............69 H4
Wepham W Susx.............18 E4
Wereham Norfk................90 F3
Werrington C Pete..........89 H3
Werrington Cnwll..............9 J7
Wervin Ches W.............. 112 B6
Wesham Lancs.............. 120 F4
Wessington Derbys 101 G2
West Acre Norfk..............91 H1
West Alvington
    Devon...............................7 G6
West Anstey Devon.......24 D6
West Ashby Lincs......... 118 C6
West Ashling W Susx 17 M2
West Ashton Wilts..........27 K1
West Auckland Dur 140 F3
West Ayton N York 134 F3
West Bagborough
    Somset...........................25 J5
West Bank Halton 112 D5
West Barkwith Lincs.....117 K5
West Barnby N York 143 G5
West Barns E Loth 178 E3
West Barsham Norfk 105 L5
West Bay Dorset.............13 L4
West Beckham Norfk .. 106 D5
West Bedfont Surrey.....43 H5
Westbere Kent................35 G3
West Bergholt Essex 62 A3
West Bexington
    Dorset............................13 M5
West Bilney Norfk...........91 G1
West Blatchington
    Br & H 19 J4
West Boldon S Tyne 151 J3
Westborough Lincs 102 D4
Westbourne BCP............15 K4
Westbourne W Susx 17 L2
West Bowling C Brad...123 H4
West Bradenham
    Norfk..............................91 K2
West Bradford Lancs ... 121 L2
West Bradley Somset 26 E4
West Bretton Wakefd ...123 K7
West Bridgford
    Notts 101 L5
West Bromwich
    Sandw............................85 H5
Westbrook Kent...............35 J2
Westbrook W Berk..........41 H6
West Buckland
    Devon.............................23 K5
West Buckland
    Somset...........................25 J7
West Burrafirth Shet... 235 b5
West Burton N York......131 J3
Westbury Bucks...............73 J7
Westbury Shrops 83 G2
Westbury Wilts................27 K2
Westbury Leigh Wilts....27 K2
Westbury-on-
    Severn Gloucs 55 G5
Westbury-on-Trym
    Bristl..............................38 E5
Westbury-sub-
    Mendip Somset...........26 D2
West Butterwick
    N Linc........................... 116 D1
Westby Lancs 120 E4
West Byfleet Surrey.......43 H7
West Cairngaan
    D & G............................144 D8
West Caister Norfk..........93 K2
West Calder W Loth.....176 D5
West Camel Somset........26 E6
West Chaldon Dorset.....14 E5
West Challow Oxon.........41 G3

West Charleton
    Devon...............................7 H7
West Chiltington
    W Susx............................18 E3
West Chinnock
    Somset...........................26 C8
West Clandon Surrey.....31 H2
West Cliffe Kent...............35 J5
Westcliff-on-Sea
    Sthend............................46 E3
West Coker Somset........26 D8
Westcombe Somset........27 G4
West Compton
    Somset...........................26 E3
West Compton
    Abbas Dorset...............14 B4
Westcote Gloucs 56 E4
Westcote Barton
    Oxon...............................57 H3
Westcott Bucks...............58 B5
Westcott Devon...............12 C2
Westcott Surrey...............31 J2
West Cottingwith
    N York.......................... 125 G3
Westcourt Wilts...............40 E7
West Cowick E R Yk 124 F6
West Cross Swans 51 H7
West Curthwaite
    Cumb............................ 148 B5
Westdean E Susx............20 B5
West Dean W Susx.........18 B3
West Dean Wilts..............28 E6
West Deeping Lincs.......89 G2
West Derby Lpool 111 L3
West Dereham Norfk......90 F4
West Down Devon..........23 H3
Westdowns Cnwll.............8 E7
West Drayton Gt Lon......43 H4
West Drayton Notts 116 B6
West Dunnet Highld.....231 J2
West Ella E R Yk........... 126 C5
West End Bed..................74 E4
West End Hants...............29 J8
West End N Som..............38 C6
West End Norfk................93 K2
West End Surrey.............42 F7
West End Surrey.............43 J7
West End Wilts................27 M6
West End Green
    Hants..............................42 A7
Wester Aberchalder
    Highld...........................202 E2
Westerdale Highld 231 G5
Westerdale N York 142 E6
Westerfield Suffk............78 E5
Westergate W Susx 18 C5
Westerham Kent..............32 D3
Westerhope N u Ty 150 F2
Westerland Devon............7 K4
Westerleigh S Glos.........39 G4
Western Isles W Isls....232 d5
Wester Ochiltree
    W Loth.......................... 176 D4
Wester Pitkierie Fife.....187 J6
Wester Ross Highld.....220 C5
Westerton of Rossie
    Angus............................197 G5
Westerwick Shet 235 c6
West Farleigh Kent.........33 J3
West Farndon Nhants.....73 G4
West Felton Shrops........97 M7
Westfield BaNES 26 F2
Westfield Cumb 136 D2
Westfield E Susx.............21 G3
Westfield Highld 230 F3
Westfield N Lans 175 J4
Westfield Norfk................92 B2
Westfield W Loth 176 C4
Westfields Herefs...........69 K6
Westfields of
    Rattray P & K 195 J6
Westgate Dur 150 A7
Westgate N Linc 116 C2
Westgate-on-Sea
    Kent...............................35 J2
West Grafton Wilts.........40 E7
West Green Hants 30 C1

West Grimstead
    Wilts...............................28 E6
West Grinstead
    W Susx............................31 K6
West Haddlesey
    N York.......................... 124 E5
West Haddon Nhants.....73 J1
West Hagbourne
    Oxon...............................41 K3
West Hagley Worcs........84 F7
Westhall Suffk.................93 J7
West Hallam Derbys 101 H4
West Halton N Linc...... 125 L6
Westham Dorset.............14 C6
Westham E Susx.............20 D5
West Ham Gt Lon 45 H4
Westham Somset............26 B3
Westhampnett
    W Susx............................18 B4
West Handley Derbys... 115 H6
West Hanney Oxon..........41 H2
West Hanningfield
    Essex.............................61 H7
West Harnham Wilts......28 C5
West Harptree
    BaNES............................38 E8
West Harting W Susx.....30 C7
West Hatch Somset........25 L7
West Hatch Wilts.............27 L5
West Haven Angus 187 J1
Westhay Somset.............26 C3
West Heath Birm 85 J7
West Helmsdale
    Highld...........................227 H5
West Hendred Oxon........41 H3
West Heslerton
    N York.......................... 134 E4
West Hewish N Som.......38 B7
Westhide Herefs..............69 L5
Westhill Abers 206 F4
West Hill Devon...............12 D4
Westhill Highld 213 H5
West Hoathly W Susx....32 C6
West Holme Dorset.........15 G5
Westhope Herefs.............69 J4
Westhope Shrops............83 J6
West Horndon Essex......45 M3
Westhorpe Lincs 103 L6
Westhorpe Suffk.............78 C2
West Horrington
    Somset...........................26 E3
West Horsley Surrey......31 H2
West Hougham Kent 35 H6
Westhoughton
    Bolton........................... 112 F1
Westhouse N York........ 130 D5
Westhouses Derbys..... 101 H2
West Howe BCP..............15 K4
Westhumble Surrey........31 K2
West Huntingtower
    P & K 185 M3
West Huntspill
    Somset...........................25 L3
West Hythe Kent..............34 F7
West Ilsley W Berk..........41 J4
West Itchenor
    W Susx............................17 L3
West Kennett Wilts.........40 C6
West Kilbride N Ayrs....173 L8
West Kingsdown
    Kent...............................45 L7
West Kington Wilts.........39 J5
West Kirby Wirral 111 H4
West Knapton N York... 134 D4
West Knighton
    Dorset............................14 D5
West Knoyle Wilts...........27 K5
Westlake Devon.................6 F5
West Lambrook
    Somset...........................26 B7
West Langdon Kent 35 J5
West Lavington
    W Susx............................30 E7
West Lavington Wilts......28 A2
West Layton N York 140 E5
West Leake Notts 101 K7
Westleigh Devon.............23 G5

Westleigh Devon..............25 G7
West Leigh Somset.........25 H5
Westleton Suffk.............79 J2
West Lexham Norfk 91 J1
Westley Suffk..................77 J2
Westley Waterless
  Cambs.........................76 E3
West Lilling N York 133 K6
Westlington Bucks 58 C6
West Linton Border 176 F7
Westlinton Cumb 148 D3
West Littleton S Glos.....39 H5
West Lockinge Oxon 41 H3
West Lulworth
  Dorset..........................14 F6
West Lutton N York...... 134 E5
West Lydford Somset.....26 E5
West Lyng Somset 25 L5
West Lynn Norfk 104 F7
West Malling Kent..........33 H2
West Malvern Worcs......70 D5
West Marden W Susx.....30 C8
West Markham Notts .. 116 B6
Westmarsh Kent.............35 H3
West Marsh NE Lin 127 G8
West Marton N York 122 D1
West Melbury Dorset 27 K7
West Meon Hants 29 M6
West Mersea Essex.........62 B5
Westmeston E Susx.......19 K3
West Midland Safari
  Park Worcs.................84 E7
Westmill Herts 60 B3
West Milton Dorset........13 L3
Westminster Gt Lon 44 F4
Westminster Abbey
  & Palace Gt Lon 44 F4
West Molesey Surrey.....43 J6
West Monkton
  Somset.........................25 K5
West Moors Dorset 15 K2
West Morden Dorset 15 G4
West Morriston
  Border....................... 167 J2
West Mudford
  Somset.........................26 E7
Westmuir Angus............ 196 B5
Westnewton Cumb 147 K6
West Newton E R Yk.... 126 F3
West Newton Norfk 105 H6
West Newton Somset 25 L5
West Norwood
  Gt Lon..........................44 F5
Westoe S Tyne............. 151 J2
West Ogwell Devon.........7 J2
Weston BaNES...............39 G6
Weston Ches E...............99 G3
Weston Devon................12 E3
Weston Devon................12 F5
Weston Hants 30 B6
Weston Herts 59 L3
Weston Lincs................ 103 M7
Weston N York.............. 123 H2
Weston Nhants...............73 H5
Weston Notts 116 C7
Weston Shrops...............83 L5
Weston Shrops...............97 L6
Weston Staffs.................99 L6
Weston W Berk...............41 H5
Weston Beggard
  Herefs..........................69 L6
Westonbirt Gloucs.........39 J3
Weston by Welland
  Nhants..........................87 L5
Weston Colville
  Cambs.........................76 E4
Weston Corbett
  Hants............................30 B3
Weston Coyney
  C Stke...........................99 L4
Weston Favell Nhants...73 L3
Weston Green Cambs....76 F4
Weston Heath Shrops....84 D2
Westoning C Beds 59 G2
Weston-in-Gordano
  N Som...........................38 C5

Weston Jones Staffs 99 H7
Weston Longville
  Norfk............................92 D1
Weston Lullingfields
  Shrops..........................98 B7
Weston-on-the-
  Green Oxon 57 K4
Weston Park Staffs.......84 E2
Weston Patrick
  Hants............................30 B3
Weston Rhyn Shrops 97 L5
Weston-sub-Edge
  Gloucs..........................71 K6
Weston-super-
  Mare N Som 37 L7
Weston Turville
  Bucks............................58 D6
Weston-under-
  Lizard Staffs...............84 E2
Weston under
  Penyard Herefs...........54 F4
Weston-under-
  Redcastle Shrops 98 E6
Weston under
  Wetherley
  Warwks.........................72 D1
Weston Underwood
  Derbys........................ 100 F4
Weston Underwood
  M Keyn..........................74 C4
Weston-upon-Trent
  Derbys........................ 101 H6
Westonzoyland
  Somset.........................25 M4
West Orchard Dorset.....27 J7
West Overton Wilts........40 C6
Westow N York............. 134 B6
West Park Abers 206 E5
West Parley Dorset........15 K3
West Peckham Kent.......33 H3
West Pelton Dur........... 151 G4
West Pennard
  Somset.........................26 D4
West Pentire Cnwll 4 B4
West Perry Cambs.........75 G2
West Porlock Somset 24 D3
Westport Somset...........26 B7
West Putford Devon........9 K2
West Quantoxhead
  Somset.........................25 H3
Westquarter Falk........ 176 B3
West Rainton Dur........ 151 H5
West Rasen Lincs........ 117 H4
Westray Ork................. 234 c2
Westray Airport Ork.... 234 c2
West Raynham Norfk .. 105 L2
Westrigg W Loth.......... 176 B5
Westrop Swindn 40 D2
West Rounton N York.. 141 K6
West Row Suffk.............90 F7
West Rudham Norfk .. 105 K6
West Runton Norfk 106 E4
Westruther Border 178 D7
Westry Cambs 90 B4
West Saltoun E Loth... 178 B5
West Sandford Devon...11 J4
West Sandwick Shet .. 235 d3
West Scrafton N York .. 131 K3
West Stafford Dorset ...14 D4
West Stockwith
  Notts......................... 116 C3
West Stoke W Susx.......17 M2
West Stour Dorset.........27 H6
West Stourmouth
  Kent.............................35 H3
West Stow Suffk............77 J1
West Stowell Wilts........40 C7
West Street Suffk..........78 B1
West Tanfield N York .. 132 D4
West Taphouse Cnwll......5 J3
West Tarbert Ag & B... 172 E5
West Tarring W Susx ...18 F5
West Thirston
  Nthumb...................... 158 F3
West Thorney W Susx ..17 L3
West Thorpe Notts 101 L7
West Thurrock Thurr....45 L4

West Tilbury Thurr......... 46 A4
West Tisted Hants..........29 M5
West Torrington
  Lincs......................... 117 J5
West Town Hants...........17 K3
West Town N Som..........38 C6
West Tytherley Hants....28 F5
West Walton Norfk........90 C2
Westward Cumb 148 B6
Westward Ho! Devon.....23 G5
Westwell Kent................34 D5
Westwell Oxon...............56 E6
Westwell Leacon
  Kent.............................34 C5
West Wellow Hants........28 F7
West Wembury
  Devon.............................6 D6
West Wemyss Fife........ 186 E7
Westwick Cambs............76 B2
West Wickham
  Cambs.........................76 E5
West Wickham
  Gt Lon..........................45 G6
West Williamston
  Pembks 49 H6
West Winch Norfk 90 F1
West Winterslow
  Wilts............................28 E5
West Wittering
  W Susx..........................17 L3
West Witton N York 131 K2
Westwood Devon...........12 C3
Westwood Kent..............35 K2
Westwood Wilts.............39 J8
West Woodburn
  Nthumb...................... 157 M5
West Woodhay
  W Berk..........................41 H7
Westwoodside N Linc.. 116 C2
West Worldham
  Hants............................30 C4
West Worthing
  W Susx..........................18 F5
West Wratting
  Cambs.........................76 E4
West Wylam
  Nthumb...................... 150 E3
Wetheral Cumb 148 E4
Wetherby Leeds 124 B2
Wetherby Services
  N York........................ 124 C1
Wetherden Suffk............78 B3
Wetheringsett Suffk 78 D2
Wethersfield Essex........61 H2
Wetherup Street
  Suffk............................78 D2
Wetley Rocks Staffs......99 L3
Wettenhall Ches E.........98 F1
Wetton Staffs............... 100 C2
Wetwang E R Yk.......... 134 E7
Wetwood Staffs.............99 H5
Wexcombe Wilts............40 F8
Weybourne Norfk 106 D4
Weybourne Surrey........30 D2
Weybread Suffk..............92 F7
Weybread Street
  Suffk............................92 F7
Weybridge Surrey..........43 H7
Weycroft Devon.............13 H3
Weydale Highld............ 231 H3
Weyhill Hants.................28 F3
Weymouth Dorset..........14 D6
Whaddon Bucks.............74 B7
Whaddon Cambs............75 L5
Whaddon Gloucs...........55 J5
Whaddon Wilts...............28 D6
Whaddon Wilts...............39 K7
Whaley Derbys............. 115 K7
Whaley Bridge
  Derbys........................ 113 M5
Whaley Thorns
  Derbys........................ 115 K7
Whaligoe Highld.......... 231 K7
Whalley Lancs.............. 121 L4
Whalsay Shet............... 235 d4
Whalton Nthumb......... 158 E6
Whaplode Lincs........... 104 A7

Whaplode Drove
  Lincs............................89 K2
Wharf Warwks................72 E2
Wharfe N York.............. 130 E5
Wharles Lancs.............. 120 F4
Wharley End C Beds......74 D5
Wharncliffe Side
  Sheff.......................... 114 F3
Wharram-le-Street
  N York........................ 134 D6
Wharton Herefs.............69 K4
Whashton N York 140 E6
Whasset Cumb............. 129 L4
Whatcote Warwks.........72 C5
Whateley Warwks.........86 B4
Whatfield Suffk.............78 B5
Whatley Somset.............13 J2
Whatley Somset.............27 G3
Whatlington E Susx.......20 F3
Whatton-in-the-
  Vale Notts................. 102 C5
Whauphill D & G.......... 145 J3
Wheal Peevor Cnwll........3 J3
Wheatacre Norfk 93 K5
Wheathampstead
  Herts...........................59 K5
Wheatley Hants.............30 C4
Wheatley Oxon...............57 L6
Wheatley Hill Dur........ 151 J6
Wheatley Hills Donc... 115 L1
Wheaton Aston
  Staffs..........................84 F2
Wheddon Cross
  Somset.........................24 E4
Wheeler's Green
  Wokham........................42 C6
Wheelock Ches E...........99 H2
Wheelton Lancs............ 121 J6
Wheldrake C York 125 G2
Whelford Gloucs............56 D7
Whelpley Hill Bucks......59 G6
Whempstead Herts........60 A4
Whenby N York............ 133 K5
Whepstead Suffk............77 J3
Wherstead Suffk............78 E6
Wherwell Hants.............29 H3
Wheston Derbys........... 114 C6
Whetsted Kent...............33 H4
Whetstone Leics............87 G4
Whicham Cumb............ 128 D3
Whichford Warwks.........72 C7
Whickham Gatesd....... 150 F3
Whiddon Down
  Devon...........................11 G6
Whigstreet Angus........ 196 D7
Whilton Nhants..............73 J2
Whimple Devon..............12 D3
Whimpwell Green
  Norfk.......................... 107 H2
Whinburgh Norfk..........92 B2
Whinnieliggate
  D & G.......................... 146 C4
Whinnyfold Abers....... 217 K7
Whippingham IoW........16 F4
Whipsnade C Beds 59 G4
Whipsnade Zoo ZSL
  C Beds..........................59 G4
Whipton Devon...............12 B4
Whisby Lincs................ 116 E7
Whissendine Rutlnd......88 B2
Whissonsett Norfk 105 L7
Whistlefield Ag & B.... 183 J8
Whistlefield Inn
  Ag & B........................ 183 G8
Whistley Green
  Wokham........................42 C6
Whiston Knows............ 112 C3
Whiston Nhants.............74 B3
Whiston Rothm............ 115 H4
Whiston Staffs...............84 F2
Whiston Staffs............. 100 B3
Whitbeck Cumb........... 128 D3
Whitbourne Herefs..... 170 D3
Whitburn S Tyne.......... 151 J3
Whitburn W Loth........ 176 C5
Whitby N York............. 143 J5
Whitchester Border ... 178 F6

Whitchurch BaNES 38 F6
Whitchurch Bucks 58 D4
Whitchurch Cardif 37 J4
Whitchurch Devon 6 D2
Whitchurch Hants 29 J2
Whitchurch Herefs 54 D4
Whitchurch Oxon 41 M5
Whitchurch Pembks 48 D3
Whitchurch Shrops 98 D4
Whitchurch
Canonicorum
Dorset 13 K4
Whitchurch Hill
Oxon 41 M5
Whitcombe Dorset 14 D5
Whitcot Shrops 83 H5
Whitcott Keysett
Shrops 82 F6
Whiteacre Heath
Warwks 86 B5
White Ball Somset 25 H7
Whitebridge Highld 202 D3
Whitebrook Mons 54 D6
Whitebushes Surrey 32 B4
Whitecairns Abers 207 H2
Whitechapel Gt Lon 45 G4
White Chapel Lancs 121 H3
White Colne Essex 61 L3
Whitecraig E Loth 177 K4
Whitecrook D & G 144 E4
White Cross Cnwll 3 H6
Whitecross Falk 176 C3
Whiteface Highld 222 F4
Whitefarland N Ayrs 161 L2
Whitefaulds S Ayrs 163 H7
Whitefield Bury 113 J1
Whitefield Somset 25 G5
Whiteford Abers 206 D1
Whitegate Ches W 112 F7
Whitehall Ork 234 d5
Whitehaven Cumb 136 D4
Whitehill and
Bordon Hants 30 C5
Whitehills Abers 216 C2
Whitehouse Abers 206 C3
Whitehouse Ag & B 172 D6
Whitehouse
Common Birm 85 K4
Whitekirk E Loth 178 D3
White Lackington
Dorset 14 D3
Whitelackington
Somset 26 B7
White Ladies Aston
Worcs 71 G4
Whiteleaf Bucks 58 D6
Whiteley Hants 17 G1
Whiteley Bank IoW 17 G6
Whitemire Moray 214 B4
Whitemoor C Nott 101 K4
Whitemoor Cnwll 4 F4
Whiteness Shet 235 c6
White Notley Essex 61 J4
Whiteparish Wilts 28 E6
White Pit Lincs 118 E6
Whiterashes Abers 206 F2
White Roding Essex 60 E5
Whiterow Highld 231 L5
Whiterow Moray 214 C3
Whiteshill Gloucs 55 J6
Whitesmith E Susx 20 B3
Whitestaunton
Somset 13 H1
Whitestone Cross
Devon 11 K6
White Waltham
W & M 42 D5
Whitewell Lancs 121 K2
Whitfield C Dund 187 G2
Whitfield Kent 35 J5
Whitfield Nhants 73 H6
Whitfield Nthumb 149 K4
Whitfield S Glos 38 F3
Whitford Devon 13 G4
Whitford Flints 111 G5
Whitgift E R Yk 125 J6
Whitgreave Staffs 99 K6

Whithorn D & G 145 J6
Whiting Bay N Ayrs 162 D4
Whitkirk Leeds 124 B4
Whitland Carmth 49 L4
Whitlaw Border 167 G6
Whitletts S Ayrs 163 J5
Whitley N York 124 E6
Whitley Readg 42 B6
Whitley Sheff 115 G3
Whitley Wilts 39 K6
Whitley Bay N Tyne 159 J7
Whitley Chapel
Nthumb 150 B4
Whitley Lower Kirk 123 J6
Whitminster Gloucs 55 H6
Whitmore Staffs 99 J4
Whitnage Devon 25 G7
Whitnash Warwks 72 D2
Whitney-on-Wye
Herefs 68 F5
Whitsbury Hants 28 C7
Whitsome Border 179 H7
Whitson Newpt 38 B4
Whitstable Kent 47 J6
Whitstone Cnwll 9 H5
Whittingham Nthumb .. 168 F6
Whittingslow Shrops 83 H5
Whittington Derbys 115 G6
Whittington Gloucs 55 M4
Whittington Lancs 130 B4
Whittington Norfk 91 G4
Whittington Shrops 97 L6
Whittington Staffs 84 F6
Whittington Staffs 85 L2
Whittington Warwks 86 C4
Whittington Worcs 70 F4
Whittlebury Nhants 73 K5
Whittle-le-Woods
Lancs 121 H6
Whittlesey Cambs 89 J4
Whittlesford Cambs 76 C5
Whitton N Linc 125 L5
Whitton Nthumb 158 D3
Whitton Powys 68 F2
Whitton S on T 141 J3
Whitton Shrops 83 L8
Whittonstall Nthumb ... 150 D4
Whitway Hants 41 J8
Whitwell Derbys 115 K6
Whitwell Herts 59 K4
Whitwell IoW 17 G6
Whitwell N York 141 G7
Whitwell Rutlnd 88 D2
Whitwell-on-the-
Hill N York 133 L6
Whitwell Street
Norfk 106 D7
Whitwick Leics 86 E1
Whitworth Lancs 122 D6
Whixall Shrops 98 D5
Whixley N York 133 G2
Whorlton Dur 140 E4
Whyle Herefs 69 L3
Whyteleafe Surrey 32 C2
Wibsey C Brad 123 H4
Wibtoft Warwks 86 F6
Wichenford Worcs 70 D3
Wichling Kent 34 B4
Wick BCP 15 L4
Wick Highld 231 L5
Wick S Glos 39 G5
Wick V Glam 36 E6
Wick W Susx 18 D5
Wick Worcs 71 G5
Wicken Cambs 76 E1
Wicken Nhants 73 L6
Wicken Bonhunt
Essex 60 D2
Wickenby Lincs 117 H5
Wicken Green
Village Norfk 105 K6
Wickersley Rothm 115 J3
Wicker Street Green
Suffk 77 L6
Wickford Essex 46 C2
Wickham Hants 17 H1
Wickham W Berk 41 H6

Wickham Bishops
Essex 61 K5
Wickhambreaux
Kent 35 G3
Wickhambrook Suffk 77 H4
Wickhamford Worcs 71 J6
Wickham Green
Suffk 78 D2
Wickham Market
Suffk 79 G4
Wickhampton Norfk 93 J3
Wickham St Paul
Essex 77 J7
Wickham Skeith
Suffk 78 C2
Wickham Street
Suffk 78 C1
Wick John o' Groats
Airport Highld 231 L5
Wicklewood Norfk 92 C3
Wickmere Norfk 106 E5
Wick St Lawrence
N Som 38 A7
Wicksteed Park
Nhants 88 C7
Wickwar S Glos 39 G3
Widdington Essex 60 E2
Widdrington Nthumb .. 159 G3
Widdrington Station
Nthumb 159 G4
Widecombe in the
Moor Devon 7 G1
Widegates Cnwll 5 L4
Widemouth Bay
Cnwll 9 G4
Wide Open N Tyne 159 G7
Widford Essex 61 H6
Widford Herts 60 C5
Widmer End Bucks 42 E2
Widmerpool Notts 101 M6
Widmore Gt Lon 45 H6
Widnes Halton 112 D4
Widworthy Devon 13 G3
Wigan Wigan 112 E1
Wigborough Somset 26 C7
Wiggaton Devon 12 E4
Wiggenhall St
Germans Norfk 90 E2
Wiggenhall St Mary
Magdalen Norfk 90 E2
Wiggenhall St Mary
the Virgin Norfk 90 E2
Wigginton C York 133 J7
Wigginton Herts 58 F6
Wigginton Oxon 57 H2
Wigginton Staffs 86 B3
Wigglesworth
N York 130 F7
Wiggonby Cumb 148 B4
Wighill N York 124 D2
Wighton Norfk 105 M4
Wightwick Wolves 84 F4
Wigley Hants 29 G7
Wigmore Herefs 69 H2
Wigmore Medway 46 D6
Wigsley Notts 116 E7
Wigsthorpe Nhants 88 F6
Wigston Leics 87 H4
Wigston Fields Leics 87 H4
Wigston Parva Leics 86 F5
Wigthorpe Notts 115 L5
Wigtoft Lincs 103 L5
Wigton Cumb 148 A5
Wigtown D & G 145 J4
Wike Leeds 123 L3
Wilbarston Nhants 88 B5
Wilberfoss E R Yk 125 H1
Wilburton Cambs 90 C7
Wilby Nhants 74 C2
Wilby Norfk 92 B5
Wilby Suffk 78 F1
Wilcot Wilts 40 C7
Wildboarclough
Ches E 113 M7
Wilden Bed 75 G4
Wilden Worcs 84 E8

Wildmanbridge
S Lans 175 L7
Wildmill Brdgnd 36 D4
Wildmoor Worcs 85 G7
Wildsworth Lincs 116 D3
Wilford C Nott 101 K5
Wilkesley Ches E 98 F4
Wilkhaven Highld 223 K4
Wilkieston W Loth 176 F5
Willand Devon 12 D1
Willaston Ches E 99 G3
Willaston Ches W 111 K6
Willen M Keyn 74 C6
Willenhall Covtry 86 D7
Willenhall Wsall 85 H4
Willerby E R Yk 126 C4
Willerby N York 134 F4
Willersey Gloucs 71 K6
Willersley Herefs 68 F5
Willesborough Kent 34 D6
Willesborough Lees
Kent 34 D6
Willesden Gt Lon 44 E3
Willesley Wilts 39 J3
Willett Somset 25 H5
Willey Shrops 84 C4
Willey Warwks 86 F6
Willey Green Surrey 30 F2
Williamscot Oxon 72 F5
Willian Herts 59 L2
Willingale Essex 60 F6
Willingdon E Susx 20 C5
Willingham Cambs 76 B1
Willingham by Stow
Lincs 116 E5
Willingham St Mary
Suffk 93 J6
Willington Bed 75 G4
Willington Derbys 100 F6
Willington Dur 150 F7
Willington Kent 33 K3
Willington N Tyne 151 H2
Willington Warwks 72 C6
Willitoft E R Yk 125 H4
Williton Somset 25 G3
Willoughby Lincs 119 G6
Willoughby Warwks 73 G2
Willoughby-on-
the-Wolds Notts 101 M7
Willoughby
Waterleys Leics 87 H5
Willoughton Lincs 116 F3
Willows Green Essex 61 H4
Willtown Somset 26 B6
Wilmcote Warwks 71 L3
Wilmington Devon 13 G3
Wilmington E Susx 20 B5
Wilmington Kent 45 K5
Wilmslow Ches E 113 J5
Wilpshire Lancs 121 K4
Wilsden C Brad 123 G3
Wilsford Lincs 103 G4
Wilsford Wilts 28 C4
Wilsford Wilts 40 C8
Wilshaw Kirk 123 G8
Wilsill N York 132 B6
Wilson Leics 101 H7
Wilsontown S Lans 176 C7
Wilstead Bed 74 F5
Wilsthorpe Lincs 88 F2
Wilstone Herts 58 E5
Wilton Herefs 54 E3
Wilton N York 134 D3
Wilton R & Cl 142 C4
Wilton Wilts 28 C5
Wilton Wilts 40 E7
Wilton Dean Border 167 G6
Wimbish Green
Essex 76 E7
Wimbledon Gt Lon 44 E6
Wimblington Cambs 90 B5
Wimboldsley Ches W ... 113 G8
Wimborne Minster
Dorset 15 J3
Wimborne St Giles
Dorset 28 B8
Wimbotsham Norfk 90 E3

Wimpole Cambs............75 L4
Wimpstone Warwks 72 B5
Wincanton Somset.........27 G5
Winchburgh W Loth 176 E4
Winchcombe Gloucs....56 A3
Winchelsea E Susx 21 H3
Winchester Hants..........29 J5
Winchester
  Services Hants........29 K4
Winchet Hill Kent........33 J5
Winchfield Hants............30 C1
Winchmore Hill
  Bucks.......................42 F2
Winchmore Hill
  Gt Lon......................44 F2
Wincle Ches E................ 113 L7
Wincobank Sheff....... 115 G3
Windermere Cumb..... 137 L7
Windermere Jetty
  Cumb........................ 137 L7
Winderton Warwks....72 D6
Windhill Highld........... 212 E5
Windlesham Surrey......42 F7
Windmill Cnwll............... 4 D2
Windmill Hill E Susx 20 D4
Windmill Hill Somset....25 L7
Windrush Gloucs....56 D5
Windsole Abers........... 216 B3
Windsor W & M.............42 F5
Windsor Castle
  W & M......................42 F5
Windsoredge Gloucs....55 J7
Windsor Green
  Suffk.......................77 K4
Windygates Fife 186 E7
Wineham W Susx..........31 L7
Winestead E R Yk....... 127 G5
Winfarthing Norfk.......92 D6
Winford IoW..................17 G5
Winford N Som..............38 D7
Winforton Herefs.........68 F5
Winfrith Newburgh
  Dorset.....................14 F5
Wing Bucks..................58 E4
Wing Rutlnd..................88 C3
Wingate Dur................ 151 J7
Wingerworth Derbys .. 115 G7
Wingfield C Beds 59 G3
Wingfield Suffk 92 F7
Wingfield Wilts............27 J1
Wingham Kent 35 H3
Wingrave Bucks............58 E4
Winkburn Notts........ 102 B2
Winkfield Br For............42 E6
Winkfield Row Br For 42 E6
Winkhill Staffs........... 100 B3
Winkleigh Devon..........10 F4
Winksley N York........ 132 C5
Winlaton Gatesd....... 150 F3
Winless Highld........... 231 K5
Winmarleigh Lancs..... 120 F2
Winnall Hants...............29 J5
Winnersh Wokham.......42 C6
Winnington Ches W..... 112 F6
Winscombe N Som........38 B8
Winsford Ches W....... 112 F7
Winsford Somset..........24 E4
Winsham Somset..........13 J2
Winshill Staffs........... 100 F7
Winshwen Swans...........51 K6
Winskill Cumb............ 149 G7
Winsley Wilts 39 J7
Winslow Bucks..............58 C3
Winson Gloucs....56 C6
Winsor Hants................28 F8
Winster Cumb............ 129 J2
Winster Derbys........... 100 E1
Winston Dur............... 140 E4
Winston Suffk 78 E3
Winstone Gloucs....55 L6
Winswell Devon..........10 D3
Winterborne Came
  Dorset.....................14 D5
Winterborne
  Clenston Dorset......14 F2
Winterborne
  Houghton Dorset.....14 F2

Winterborne
  Kingston Dorset........15 G3
Winterborne
  Monkton Dorset 14 D5
Winterborne
  Stickland Dorset.....14 F2
Winterborne
  Whitechurch
  Dorset.....................14 F3
Winterborne
  Zelston Dorset........15 G3
Winterbourne S Glos....38 F4
Winterbourne
  W Berk......................41 J6
Winterbourne
  Abbas Dorset...........14 C4
Winterbourne
  Bassett Wilts............40 C5
Winterbourne
  Dauntsey Wilts.........28 D4
Winterbourne Earls
  Wilts........................28 D5
Winterbourne
  Gunner Wilts............28 D4
Winterbourne
  Monkton Wilts.........40 C6
Winterbourne
  Steepleton Dorset....14 C4
Winterbourne Stoke
  Wilts........................28 B3
Winterburn N York.... 131 H7
Winteringham N Linc .. 125 L6
Winterley Ches E............99 H2
Winterslow Wilts..........28 E5
Winterton N Linc....... 125 L6
Winterton-on-Sea
  Norfk...................... 107 K8
Winthorpe Notts........ 102 D2
Winton BCP...................15 K4
Winton Cumb............. 139 H5
Wintringham
  N York..................... 134 D5
Winwick Cambs............89 G7
Winwick Nhants............87 J8
Winwick Warrtn 112 E3
Wirksworth Derbys 100 F2
Wirral 111 J4
Wirswall Ches E............98 D4
Wisbech Cambs............90 C2
Wisbech St Mary
  Cambs......................90 B2
Wisborough Green
  W Susx......................31 H6
Wiseman's Bridge
  Pembks.....................49 K6
Wiseton Notts........... 116 B4
Wishaw N Lans........... 175 L7
Wishaw Warwks............85 L5
Wisley Garden RHS
  Surrey 43 H8
Wispington Lincs....... 117 K6
Wissett Suffk................93 H7
Wissington Suffk..........61 M2
Wistanstow Shrops 83 H6
Wistanswick Shrops......98 F6
Wistaston Ches E............99 G2
Wistaston Green
  Ches E......................99 G2
Wiston Pembks............49 H4
Wiston S Lans........... 165 J3
Wiston W Susx.............18 F3
Wistow Cambs............89 K7
Wistow N York........... 124 F4
Wiswell Lancs........... 121 L3
Witcham Cambs............90 C7
Witchampton Dorset....15 J2
Witchford Cambs..........90 C7
Witcombe Somset........26 C6
Witham Essex................61 K5
Witham Friary
  Somset.....................27 H3
Witham on the Hill
  Lincs...................... 103 H8
Witham St Hughs
  Lincs...................... 102 E1
Withcall Lincs............. 118 C5
Withdean Br & H...........19 J4

Witherenden Hill
  E Susx.......................33 H7
Witheridge Devon........11 J3
Witherley Leics............86 D4
Withern Lincs.............. 118 F5
Withernsea E R Yk....... 127 H5
Withernwick E R Yk..... 126 F3
Withersdale Street
  Suffk.......................92 F7
Withersfield Suffk........76 F5
Witherslack Cumb....... 129 J3
Withiel Cnwll................. 4 F3
Withiel Florey
  Somset.....................24 F5
Withington Gloucs....56 B5
Withington Herefs........69 L5
Withington Manch....... 113 J3
Withington Shrops........83 L2
Withington Staffs....... 100 B5
Withleigh Devon..........11 K3
Withnell Lancs........... 121 J6
Withybed Green
  Worcs.......................85 H8
Withybrook Warwks....86 E6
Withycombe Somset....24 F3
Withyham E Susx..........32 E6
Withypool Somset........24 D4
Withywood Bristl.........38 E6
Witley Surrey................30 F4
Witnesham Suffk..........78 E4
Witney Oxon................57 G6
Wittering C Pete..........88 F3
Wittersham Kent..........21 H1
Witton Birm..................85 J5
Witton Norfk................93 G2
Witton Norfk.............. 107 H6
Witton Gilbert Dur..... 151 G5
Witton le Wear Dur 140 E2
Witton Park Dur......... 140 F2
Wiveliscombe
  Somset.....................25 G5
Wivelrod Hants............30 A4
Wivelsfield E Susx........19 K2
Wivelsfield Green
  E Susx.......................19 K2
Wivenhoe Essex............62 C4
Wiveton Norfk........... 106 C4
Wix Essex......................62 E3
Wixams Bed..................74 F5
Wixford Warwks............71 K4
Wixoe Suffk...................77 G6
Woburn C Beds.............58 F2
Woburn Safari Park
  C Beds......................74 D7
Woburn Sands
  M Keyn.....................74 D7
Woking Surrey..............43 G8
Wokingham Wokham 42 D6
Woldingham Surrey.......32 C3
Wold Newton E R Yk.... 135 G5
Wold Newton NE Lin.... 118 C3
Wolfclyde S Lans....... 165 K3
Wolferton Norfk......... 105 G6
Wolfhill P & K............ 186 B2
Wolf's Castle Pembks 49 G3
Wolfsdale Pembks.......48 F3
Wollaston Dudley.........84 F6
Wollaston Nhants.........74 C2
Wollaston Shrops.........83 G2
Wollaton C Nott......... 101 K4
Wollaton Hall &
  Park C Nott............. 101 K5
Wollerton Shrops.........98 F6
Wollescote Dudley.......85 G6
Wolseley Bridge
  Staffs..................... 100 A7
Wolsingham Dur........ 150 D7
Wolstanton Staffs........99 J3
Wolston Warwks............86 E7
Wolvercote Oxon........57 J6
Wolverhampton
  Wolves.....................85 G4
Wolverhampton
  Halfpenny Green
  Airport Staffs..........84 E5
Wolverley Worcs..........84 E7
Wolverton Hants..........41 K8

Wolverton M Keyn........74 B6
Wolverton Warwks......72 B3
Wolverton Wilts............27 H5
Wolvesnewton Mons....54 C7
Wolvey Warwks............86 E6
Wolvey Heath
  Warwks....................86 E5
Wolviston S on T........ 141 K3
Wombleton N York..... 133 K3
Wombourne Staffs.......84 F5
Wombwell Barns....... 115 H2
Womenswold Kent.......35 G5
Womersley N York..... 124 E6
Wonersh Surrey............31 G3
Wonford Devon............12 B4
Wonston Dorset............14 E2
Wonston Hants............29 J4
Wooburn Bucks............42 E3
Wooburn Green
  Bucks.......................42 E3
Woodacott Devon......... 9 K4
Woodall Rothm........... 115 J5
Woodall Services
  Rothm..................... 115 J5
Woodbastwick Norfk....93 G1
Wood Bevington
  Warwks....................71 J4
Woodborough Notts... 101 M3
Woodborough Wilts.....40 C7
Woodbridge Suffk.......78 F5
Woodbury Devon........12 C5
Woodbury Salterton
  Devon......................12 C5
Woodchester Gloucs....55 J7
Woodchurch Kent........34 C7
Woodcombe Somset....24 E3
Woodcote Gt Lon........44 F7
Woodcote Oxon............41 M4
Woodcote Wrekin........84 D1
Woodcroft Gloucs....38 D2
Wood Dalling Norfk.... 106 C6
Woodditton Cambs......76 F3
Woodeaton Oxon.........57 K5
Wood End Gt Lon.........43 J4
Wood End Herts............60 B3
Woodend Highld........ 190 F4
Woodend Nhants.........73 H5
Woodend W Loth....... 176 C4
Woodend W Susx.........17 M2
Wood End Warwks.......71 K1
Wood End Wolves.......85 G4
Wood Enderby
  Lincs...................... 118 C8
Woodfalls Wilts............28 D7
Woodford Cnwll............. 9 G3
Woodford Gloucs....39 G2
Woodford Gt Lon.........45 H2
Woodford Nhants.........88 D7
Woodford Stockp 113 K5
Woodford Bridge
  Gt Lon......................45 H2
Woodford Green
  Gt Lon......................45 H2
Woodford Halse
  Nhants.....................73 G4
Woodford Wells
  Gt Lon......................45 H2
Woodgate Birm............85 H5
Woodgate Devon.........25 H7
Woodgate W Susx.......18 C5
Woodgate Worcs.........71 H2
Wood Green Gt Lon......44 F2
Woodgreen Hants........28 D7
Woodhall N York........ 131 J2
Woodhall Spa Lincs.... 117 K8
Woodham Bucks...........58 B4
Woodham Surrey.........43 H7
Woodham Ferrers
  Essex.......................61 J7
Woodham Mortimer
  Essex.......................61 K6
Woodham Walter
  Essex.......................61 K6
Wood Hayes Wolves....85 G3
Woodhead Abers....... 216 E6
Woodhill Shrops...........84 D6
Woodhill Somset..........26 A6

Woodhorn Nthumb 159 H4
Woodhouse Leeds........ 123 K4
Woodhouse Leics........87 G1
Woodhouse Sheff........ 115 H4
Woodhouse Wakefd 124 B6
Woodhouse Eaves
  Leics........................87 G2
Woodhouselee
  Mdloth........................ 177 H5
Woodhouselees
  D & G............................ 156 D6
Woodhouses
  Oldham........................ 113 K2
Woodhouses Staffs..... 100 D8
Woodhurst Cambs........89 K7
Woodingdean
  Br & H............................19 K5
Woodkirk Leeds........ 123 K5
Woodland Abers........ 207 G2
Woodland Devon............. 6 F5
Woodland Devon............. 7 J3
Woodland Dur.......... 140 D2
Woodland S Ayrs........ 152 E3
Woodlands Abers........ 206 E6
Woodlands Donc........ 124 E8
Woodlands Dorset.........15 K2
Woodlands Hants..........16 C1
Woodlands N York........ 132 E8
Woodlands Park
  W & M............................42 E5
Woodleigh Devon........... 7 H6
Woodley Wokham..........42 C5
Woodmancote
  Gloucs........................39 H2
Woodmancote
  Gloucs........................55 L3
Woodmancote
  Gloucs........................56 A6
Woodmancote
  W Susx........................17 L2
Woodmancote
  W Susx........................19 H3
Woodmancott Hants......29 K3
Woodmansey E R Yk 126 C3
Woodmansgreen
  W Susx........................30 E6
Woodmansterne
  Surrey........................32 B2
Woodmanton Devon......12 C5
Woodnesborough
  Kent............................35 J4
Woodnewton
  Nhants........................88 F5
Wood Norton Norfk 106 B6
Woodplumpton
  Lancs........................ 121 G4
Woodrising Norfk..........92 B3
Wood's Corner
  E Susx........................20 D2
Woodseaves Staffs........99 H7
Woodsetts Rothm........ 115 K5
Woodsford Dorset..........14 E4
Wood's Green E Susx.....33 H6
Woodside Br For..........42 F6
Woodside Fife........ 187 G5
Woodside Gt Lon..........45 G6
Woodside P & K........ 195 K8
Woodstock Oxon..........57 H5
Woodston C Pete..........89 H4
Wood Street Norfk 107 H7
Wood Street Village
  Surrey........................30 F2
Woodton Norfk..........93 G5
Woodtown Devon..........22 F6
Woodville Derbys........ 100 F8
Wood Walton Cambs......89 J7
Woofferton Shrops........69 K2
Wookey Somset..........26 D3
Wookey Hole Somset.....26 D2
Wool Dorset..............14 F5
Woolacombe Devon........23 G3
Woolage Green Kent......35 H5
Woolaston Gloucs..........54 E7
Woolaston Common
  Gloucs........................54 E7
Woolavington
  Somset........................25 M3

Woolbeding W Susx.........30 E6
Woolbrook Devon..........12 E5
Wooler Nthumb.......... 168 E4
Woolfardisworthy
  Devon............................11 J3
Woolfardisworthy
  Devon............................22 E7
Woolfords S Lans.... 176 D6
Woolhampton
  W Berk........................41 L6
Woolhope Herefs..........69 L7
Woolland Dorset..........14 E2
Woolley BaNES............39 H6
Woolley Cambs............89 G8
Woolley Wakefd........ 123 L7
Woolley Edge
  Services Wakefd 123 K7
Woolmere Green
  Worcs........................71 G2
Woolmer Green
  Herts............................59 L4
Woolminstone
  Somset........................13 K2
Woolpit Suffk..............77 L3
Woolstaston Shrops........83 J4
Woolsthorpe by
  Belvoir Lincs.......... 102 D5
Woolsthorpe-by-
  Colsterworth
  Lincs........................ 102 F7
Woolston C Sotn 16 E1
Woolston Shrops..........97 L7
Woolston Somset..........25 H4
Woolston Somset..........26 F5
Woolston Warrtn........ 112 F4
Woolstone Gloucs..........55 L3
Woolstone M Keyn..........74 C6
Woolstone Oxon..........40 F3
Woolston Green
  Devon............................. 7 H3
Woolton Lpool........ 112 B4
Woolton Hill Hants......41 H7
Woolverstone Suffk........78 E6
Woolverton Somset..........27 H2
Woolwich Gt Lon..........45 H4
Woonton Herefs..........69 G4
Woore Shrops............99 G4
Wootten Green Suffk 92 F8
Wootton Bed..............74 E5
Wootton Kent..............35 G5
Wootton N Linc........ 126 D7
Wootton Nhants..........73 L3
Wootton Oxon............57 H4
Wootton Oxon............57 J7
Wootton Staffs.......... 100 C4
Wootton Bassett
  Wilts........................40 B4
Wootton Bridge IoW......17 G4
Wootton Courtenay
  Somset........................24 E3
Wootton Fitzpaine
  Dorset........................13 J4
Wootton Rivers Wilts 40 D7
Wootton St
  Lawrence Hants..........29 L2
Wootton Wawen
  Warwks........................71 L2
Worcester Worcs..........70 F4
Worcester Park
  Gt Lon........................44 E6
Wordsley Dudley 84 F6
Worfield Shrops..........84 D4
Workington Cumb 136 D2
Worksop Notts........ 115 L5
Worlaby N Linc........ 126 C7
Worlds End Hants..........29 M8
Worlds End W Susx........19 J2
Worle N Som..............38 A7
Worleston Ches E..........98 F2
Worlingham Suffk..........93 J5
Worlington Devon..........11 H3
Worlington Suffk..........91 G8
Worlingworth Suffk........78 F2
Wormbridge Herefs........54 B2
Wormegay Norfk..........90 F2
Wormelow Tump
  Herefs........................54 C3

Wormhill Derbys........ 114 C6
Wormingford Essex......61 M2
Worminghall Bucks......57 M6
Wormington
  Gloucs........................71 J7
Wormit Fife.......... 186 F3
Wormleighton
  Warwks........................72 F4
Wormley Herts............60 B6
Wormley Surrey............30 F4
Wormshill Kent............34 B3
Wormsley Herefs..........69 H5
Worplesdon Surrey........30 F2
Worrall Sheff.......... 114 F3
Worsbrough Barns........ 115 G2
Worsbrough Bridge
  Barns........................ 115 G2
Worsbrough Dale
  Barns........................ 115 G2
Worsley Salfd.......... 113 H2
Worstead Norfk........ 107 G7
Worsthorne Lancs........ 122 C4
Worston Devon............. 6 E5
Worston Lancs........ 122 B3
Worth Kent..............35 J4
Wortham Suffk............92 C7
Worthen Shrops..........83 G3
Worthenbury
  Wrexhm........................98 B4
Worthing Norfk........ 106 B8
Worthing W Susx..........18 F5
Worthington Leics 101 H7
Worth Matravers
  Dorset........................15 H6
Wortley Barns........ 114 F2
Wortley Leeds........ 123 K4
Worton N York.......... 131 H2
Worton Wilts............39 L8
Wortwell Norfk..........92 F6
Wotton-under-
  Edge Gloucs..........39 H2
Wotton Underwood
  Bucks........................58 B5
Woughton on the
  Green M Keyn..........74 C6
Wouldham Kent............46 B7
Wrabness Essex..........62 E2
Wrafton Devon............23 H4
Wragby Lincs........ 117 J6
Wragby Wakefd........ 124 C6
Wrangaton Devon............ 7 G4
Wrangle Lincs.......... 104 C3
Wrangway Somset..........25 H7
Wrantage Somset..........25 L6
Wrawby N Linc........ 126 C8
Wraxall N Som............38 C6
Wraxall Somset..........26 E4
Wray Lancs.......... 130 B6
Wraysbury W & M..........43 G5
Wrayton Lancs........ 130 C5
Wrea Green Lancs........ 120 E4
Wreay Cumb.......... 148 D5
Wrecclesham
  Surrey........................30 D3
Wrekenton Gatesd 151 G3
Wrelton N York........ 134 B3
Wrenbury Ches E..........98 E3
Wreningham Norfk........92 E4
Wrentham Suffk..........93 K6
Wrentnall Shrops........83 H3
Wressle E R Yk........ 125 G4
Wressle N Linc........ 126 B8
Wrestlingworth
  C Beds........................75 J5
Wretton Norfk..........91 G4
Wrexham Wrexhm........97 M3
Wrexham Industrial
  Estate Wrexhm..........98 B3
Wribbenhall Worcs........84 E7
Wrinehill Staffs..........99 H3
Wrington N Som..........38 C7
Writhlington BaNES......27 G1
Writtle Essex............61 G2
Wrockwardine
  Wrekin........................84 B2
Wroot N Linc.......... 116 B2
Wrose C Brad........ 123 H3

Wrotham Kent............33 G2
Wroughton Swindn......40 C4
Wroxall IoW..............17 G6
Wroxall Warwks............72 B1
Wroxeter Shrops........83 L2
Wroxham Norfk........ 107 G8
Wroxton Oxon............72 E6
Wyaston Derbys........ 100 D4
Wyberton Lincs........ 104 A4
Wyboston Bed............75 H3
Wybunbury Ches E........99 G3
Wychbold Worcs..........71 G2
Wychnor Staffs............85 L1
Wyck Rissington
  Gloucs........................56 D4
Wycliffe Dur.......... 140 E4
Wycoller Lancs........ 122 D3
Wycomb Leics.......... 102 C7
Wycombe Marsh
  Bucks........................42 E3
Wyddial Herts............60 B2
Wye Kent..............34 E5
Wyke C Brad........ 123 H5
Wyke Dorset..............27 H6
Wyke Champflower
  Somset........................26 F4
Wykeham N York........ 134 E3
Wyken Covtry............86 D7
Wyken Shrops............84 D4
Wyke Regis Dorset........14 C6
Wykey Shrops............98 B7
Wylam Nthumb........ 150 E3
Wylde Green Birm........85 K5
Wylye Wilts............28 A4
Wymeswold Leics...... 101 L7
Wymington Bed............74 D2
Wymondham Leics...... 102 D8
Wymondham Norfk........92 D3
Wynford Eagle
  Dorset........................14 B3
Wyre Piddle Worcs........71 G5
Wysall Notts.......... 101 L6
Wythall Worcs............85 J7
Wytham Oxon............57 J6
Wythenshawe
  Manch........................ 113 J4
Wyton Cambs............89 K8
Wyton E R Yk........ 126 E4
Wyverstone Suffk........78 C2
Wyverstone Street
  Suffk........................78 B2

Y

Yaddlethorpe N Linc 116 E1
Yafforth N York.......... 141 H7
Yalberton Torbay........... 7 K4
Yalding Kent..............33 J3
Yanwath Cumb.......... 138 D2
Yanworth Gloucs..........56 B5
Yapham E R Yk........ 125 J1
Yapton W Susx............18 D5
Yarborough N Som........38 B8
Yarburgh Lincs........ 118 E3
Yarcombe Devon............13 G2
Yard Devon..............24 B6
Yardley Birm............85 K6
Yardley Gobion
  Nhants........................73 L5
Yardley Hastings
  Nhants........................74 C3
Yardley Wood Birm........85 K7
Yarkhill Herefs..........69 L6
Yarley Somset..........26 D3
Yarlington Somset........26 F5
Yarm S on T.......... 141 K5
Yarmouth IoW............16 D4
Yarnbrook Wilts..........27 K1
Yarnfield Staffs..........99 K6
Yarnscombe Devon........23 J6
Yarnton Oxon............57 J5
Yarpole Herefs..........69 J2
Yarrow Border........ 166 E4
Yarrow Feus
  Border........................ 166 E4

Yarrowford Border........ 166 F4
Yarwell Nhants.............88 F4
Yate S Glos........................39 G4
Yateley Hants....................42 D7
Yatesbury Wilts 40 B6
Yattendon W Berk...........41 K5
Yatton Herefs..................69 H2
Yatton N Som...................38 B7
Yatton Keynell Wilts 39 K5
Yaverland IoW 17 H5
Yaxham Norfk...................92 B2
Yaxley Cambs 89 H5
Yaxley Suffk.....................92 D8
Yazor Herefs.....................69 H5
Yeading Gt Lon 43 J4
Yeadon Leeds.................123 J3
Yealand Conyers
   Lancs...........................129 K5
Yealand Redmayne
   Lancs...........................129 K4
Yealmpton Devon 6 E5
Yearsley N York.............133 J5
Yeaton Shrops.................98 B8
Yeaveley Derbys.............100 D4
Yeavering Nthumb 168 D4
Yedingham N York 134 D4

Yelford Oxon 57 G6
Yell Shet.......................... 235 d3
Yelling Cambs 75 J3
Yelvertoft Nhants.............87 H7
Yelverton Devon..............6 D3
Yelverton Norfk...............93 G3
Yenston Somset...............27 G7
Yeoford Devon 11 D3
Yeolmbridge Cnwll............9 J7
Yeovil Somset..................26 D7
Yeovil Marsh Somset 26 D7
Yeovilton Somset 26 D6
Yesnaby Ork.................. 234 b5
Yetminster Dorset 14 B1
Yettington Devon...........12 D5
Yetts o'Muckhart
   Clacks........................ 185 L6
Yew Tree Sandw 85 H4
Y Felinheli Gwynd 109 G7
Y Ferwig Cerdgn 65 G5
Y Ffôr Gwynd 95 G5
Yielden Bed......................74 E2
Yieldshields S Lans 176 B7
Yiewsley Gt Lon 43 H4
Ynysboeth Rhondd...........37 G2
Ynysddu Caerph 37 J2

Ynyshir Rhondd................36 F3
Ynystawe Swans 51 K5
Ynysybwl Rhondd............37 G2
Yockleton Shrops.............83 H2
Yokefleet E R Yk 125 J5
Yoker C Glas 174 F5
York C York..................... 124 F1
Yorkletts Kent..................34 E3
Yorkley Gloucs 54 F6
Yorkshire Dales
   National Park 131 G4
York Town Surrey............42 E7
Youlgreave Derbys 114 E8
Youlthorpe E R Yk 134 B7
Youlton N York 133 G6
Yoxall Staffs 100 C8
Yoxford Suffk 79 H2
Y Rhiw Gwynd..................94 D6
Ysbyty Ifan Conwy 96 C3
Ysbyty Ystwyth
   Cerdgn 67 G1
Ysceifiog Flints 111 G7
Ystalyfera Neath 52 B6
Ystrad Rhondd..................36 F2
Ystrad Aeron Cerdgn......66 C4
Ystradfellte Powys.........52 E5

Ystradgynlais Powys 52 C6
Ystrad Meurig
   Cerdgn 66 F2
Ystrad Mynach
   Caerph 37 H2
Ystradowen V Glam........36 F5
Ythanbank Abers........ 217 G7
Ythanwells Abers 216 C6
Ythsie Abers.................. 217 G7

Z

Zeal Monachorum
   Devon............................11 G4
Zeals Wilts......................27 H5
Zelah Cnwll........................ 4 C5
Zennor Cnwll...................... 2 E4
Zouch Notts 101 J7
ZSL London Zoo
   Gt Lon...........................44 F4
ZSL Whipsnade Zoo
   C Beds...........................59 G4

Ireland

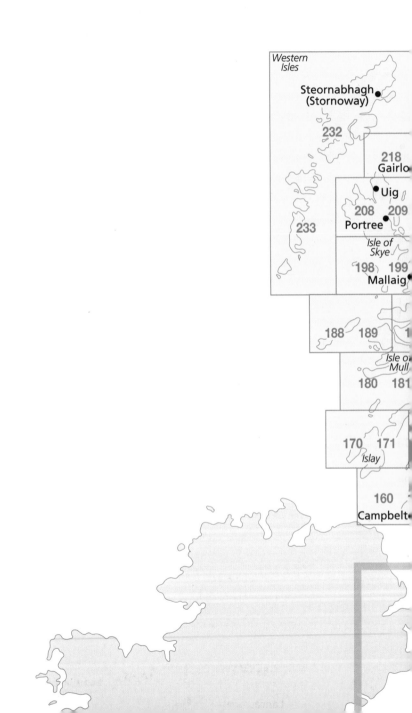

Western
Isles

Steornabhagh•
(Stornoway)

232

218
Gairlo

•Uig
208 209
233 Portree•

Isle of
Skye

198 199
Mallaig•

188 189 1

Isle o
Mull
180 181

170 171
Islay

160
Campbelt